Investment Analysis

4th Edition

For Real Estate Decisions

GAYLON E. GREER

Morris S. Fogelman
Chair of Excellence in Real Estate,
Professor of Finance
University of Memphis

Dearborn
Financial Publishing, Inc.®

Publisher: Carol L. Luitjens
Senior Acquisitions Editor: Tim Vertovec
Associate Development Editor: Nikki Loosemore
Art and Design Manager: Lucy Jenkins
Cover Designer: Elizandro Carrington
Cover Photo: The Pyramid, Memphis, Tennessee.
© 1993 by Jeffrey Jacobs/Architectural Photography, Inc.
Author Photo: © 1996 by Frank Braden Photography, Memphis, Tennessee.

© 1981, 1988, 1993, 1997 by Dearborn Financial Publishing, Inc.®
Published by Dearborn Financial Publishing, Inc.®
155 North Wacker Drive
Chicago, IL 60606-1719
(312) 836-4400
http://www.real-estate-ed.com

Printed in the United States of America.

97 98 99 10 9 8 7 6 5 4 3 2

Library of Congress Cataloging-in-Publication Data

Greer, Gaylon E.
    Investment analysis for real estate decisions/Gaylon E. Greer.—4th ed.
       p. cm.
    Includes bibliographical references and index.
    ISBN 0-7931-2226-0
    1. Real estate investment—Decision making. 2. Investment analysis. I. Title.
HD1382.5.G74   1997
  332.63'24—dc20   96-28207
                                                               CIP

DEDICATION

This Fourth Edition of *Investment Analysis for Real Estate Decisions* is dedicated to the memory of Michael Farrell, my co-author on this and another real estate text. Michael fell ill during the preparation of an earlier edition and died before it went to press. He devoted a significant portion of his all-too-brief life to students who aspired to careers in real estate. A host of DePaul University real estate graduates fondly remember him as their inspiration as well as their mentor. Chicago abounds with eminently successful practitioners who owe an overwhelming debt to Michael's efforts. It is my hope that his memory will be sustained by future readers of this book as well as in the hearts of the students he so well prepared for career tribulations and opportunities. We all miss you, Michael.

Contents

Preface to the Fourth Edition   xvii

PART ONE   Basic Issues in Real Estate Investment
            Analysis   1

1. The Real Estate Investment Decision   3
    State of the Investment Analysis Art   3
    Real Estate as an Investment   4
        Passive and Active Investors   4
        Investment in Equity and Debt   5
    Who Are the Investors?   6
        Institutional Investors   6
        Foreign Participation in U.S. Real Estate Markets   7
    Real Estate Investment Performance   8
    Concepts and Definitions   9
    Estimating Investment Value: An Overview   12
        Steps in the Investment Decision Model   12
        Valuing the Benefit Stream   13
        Investor Objectives and Risk   15
    Summary   17
    Notes   18
    Recommended Readings   19
    Review Questions   19
    Discussion Questions   20

2. Investment Strategy and the Concept of Market Efficiency   21
    Supply, Demand and the Price of Real Estate Assets   22
        Demand for Real Estate Assets   22
        The Supply Element   26
        The Market for Real Estate Assets   27
    Market Efficiency and Profit Opportunities   29
        Defining the Market   31
        Market Structures   32
        Price Searchers and Market Efficiency   33
        Sources of Inefficiency   34
    Strategy Implications   35
    Summary   38

Notes   39
Recommended Readings   39
Review Questions   39
Discussion Questions   40

3. Land Utilization and the Rental Value of Real Estate   **41**
Economic Factors in Land Use Decisions   42
   Systematic Development Patterns   43
   Business Location Decisions   44
Bid-Rent Curves and "Natural" Zoning   44
   Linkages and Transfer Costs   44
   Linkages and Location of Industry   46
   Commercial Location Decisions   48
The Market for Rental Space   48
   Market Adjustments   49
Market Structure and the Need for Market Research   50
Summary   51
Notes   51
Recommended Readings   51
Review Questions   52
Discussion Questions   52

PART ONE: Case Problems   **54**

PART TWO   Market Research and Cash-Flow Forecasting   **57**

4. Market Research Tools and Techniques   **58**
The Need for Market Research   58
   Market Research for Portfolio Decisions   58
   Market Research for Better Property Management   59
How Much Market Research?   59
   The Role of Prevailing Market Conditions   60
   The Role of Complexity   60
   The Cost-Benefit Trade-off   61
   Avoiding Analysis Paralysis   62
A Design for Market Research   62
   Problem Formulation   62
   Data Collection and Analysis   62
   A Four-Quadrant Forecasting Matrix   64
Preparing the Research Report   65
Data Sources   67
   Secondary Data   67
   Primary Data   68

Descriptive Research   69
  Planning for Descriptive Research   69
  Cross-Sectional and Time Series Data   70
  Inferential Analysis   70
Geographic Information Systems   71
Summary   75
Notes   76
Recommended Readings   76
Review Questions   76
Discussion Questions   77

Appendix 4.A   Data Sources   **78**

5. **Reconstructing the Operating History**   **81**
Overview of the Operating Statement   81
Estimating Ability To Command Rent   82
  Collect Data from the Subject Property   82
  Compare with Peer-Group Properties   83
  Identifying Peer Properties within the Market Area 86
Estimating Operating Expenses   87
An Apartment Building Example   88
  Reconstructing Effective Gross Income   88
  Reconstructing Current Operating Expenses   90
  Revised Operating Statement   91
From Reconstruction to Forecast   92
Summary   92
Notes   93
Recommended Readings   93
Review Questions   93
Discussion Questions   94

6. **Forecasting Income and Property Value**   **95**
Forecasting Gross Income   95
  The Influence of Physical Characteristics   96
  The Influence of Locational Characteristics   96
  Analyzing Linkages and Transfer Costs   97
  Analyzing Neighborhood Environmental Factors   98
  The Supply Factor   98
Forecasting Operating Expenses   99
The Net Operating Income Forecast   100
Estimating Future Market Value   103
Additional Information Needed   105
Summary   105
Notes   106
Recommended Readings   106

Review Questions 107
Discussion Questions 107

PART TWO: *Case Problem* **108**

PART THREE   Using Borrowed Money **111**

7. **Financial Leverage and Investment Analysis** **112**
   Why Leverage Is So Popular 112
   Working the Spread 113
   Amplifying the Tax Shelter 114
   Amplifying the Gain on Disposal 114
   Measuring Financial Leverage 116
   How Much Is Enough Financial Leverage? 117
   Debt Coverage Ratios and Available Financing 117
   Loan-to-Value Ratios and Available Financing 118
   Financial Leverage and Risk 118
   Financial Leverage and the Cost of Borrowing 120
   Who Are the Lenders? 121
   Commercial Banks 121
   Insurance Companies and Pension Funds 122
   Conduit Sources 123
   Summary 123
   Notes 124
   Recommended Readings 124
   Review Questions 124
   Discussion Questions 125
   Problems 125

8. **Credit Instruments and Borrowing Arrangements** **127**
   Credit and Security Instruments 127
   Promissory Notes 127
   Mortgages 128
   Deeds of Trust 129
   Credit Terms 130
   Amortization Alternatives 130
   Alternative Interest Rate Provisions 131
   Alternative Financing Arrangements 132
   Installment Sales Contracts 132
   Sales and Leasebacks 133
   Junior Mortgages 133
   Wraparound Mortgages 134
   Government-Sponsored Credit Arrangements 136
   Department of Housing and Urban Development 136

Private Activity Bonds	136
Redevelopment Bonds	137
Summary	137
Notes	138
Recommended Readings	138
Review Questions	138
Discussion Questions	139
Problems	139
9. The Cost of Borrowed Money	**140**
The Many Faces of Interest Expense	140
Nominal and Effective Rates	140
Before-Tax and After-Tax Borrowing Cost	144
Nominal and Real Rates	145
Comparing Financing Alternatives	146
Comparing Effective Interest Rates	147
What Nominal Rate Applies	148
Incorporating Borrowing into the Operating Projection	149
Debt Coverage Ratio Constraint	150
Loan-to-Value Ratio Constraint	150
Anticipated Loan Amount	150
Before-Tax Cash Flow from Maegen's Magic Manor	151
Debt Amortization Schedule for Maegen's Magic Manor	151
Summary	152
Recommended Readings	153
Review Questions	153
Discussion Questions	153
Problems	153
PART THREE: Case Problem	**156**
PART FOUR Income Tax Considerations	**157**
10. Basic Income Tax Issues	**159**
The Nature and Significance of the Tax Basis	159
The Initial Tax Basis	159
Allocating the Initial Tax Basis	160
Adjusting the Basis for Cost Recovery	162
Allowable Cost Recovery Periods	162
Computing the Allowance	162
A Depreciation Schedule for Maegen's Magic Manor	164
Other Adjustments to the Tax Basis	166
Forecasting After-Tax Cash Flows	166
Tax Consequences of Ownership Form	167

Title May Vest in Owners as Individuals   168
Title May Vest in a Corporation   169
Tax Option Corporations   170
Investors May Form a General Partnership   170
A Limited Partnership May Hold Title   170
Limited Liability Companies   176
Tax Consequences of Property Sales   176
Summary   176
Recommended Readings   177
Review Questions   177
Discussion Questions   178
Problems   178

11. Tax Consequences of Property Disposal   180
Computing the Realized Gain or Loss   180
Tax Treatment of Realized Gains or Losses   181
Gains Treated as Ordinary Income   181
When Capital Gain or Loss Rules Apply   182
Why the Difference Is Important   182
Computing Net Capital Gains or Losses   182
Estimating Cash Flow from Selling Maegen's Magic Manor   183
When Realized Gains or Losses Are Recognized   184
Using the Installment Sales Method   185
Advantages of Installment Sales Reporting   185
What Gain Qualifies   186
The Contract Price   186
The Recognized Gain   187
The Imputed Interest Problem   188
The Outstanding Indebtedness Problem   188
Like-Kind Exchanges   188
Exchange Versus Sale and Purchase   189
Purpose for Which Property Is Held   190
What Is Like-Kind Property   190
Tax Consequence of Like-Kind Exchanges   190
Tax Basis of Acquired Property   194
Effect of Losses in Section 1031 Exchanges   197
Allocating the Substitute Basis   199
Nonsimultaneous Exchanges   200
Exchanges Between Related Parties   200
Giving Property Away   201
The Unified Gift and Estate Tax   201
Effect of Giving Property Subject to a Mortgage   201
The Tax Basis of Property Received as a Gift   202
A Gifting Strategy for Highly Appreciated Property   202
Alternatives May Be Less Taxing   203
Summary   203

Notes 204
Recommended Readings 204
Review Questions 204
Discussion Questions 205
Problems 205

12. Other Taxing Issues **207**
Tax Consequences of Financial Leverage 207
Prepaid Interest Must Be Amortized 207
Construction-Period Interest Must Be Capitalized 208
Limits on the Deductibility of Interest 208
Investment Strategy Implications 208
Income Tax Credits for Property Rehabilitation 208
How Tax Credits Work 209
Credits for Rehabilitating Old Buildings 209
Tax Credits for Rehabilitating Historic Structures 210
Low-Income Housing Tax Credits 210
The Amount of the Credit 211
Qualifying for the Credits 212
Special Rules Apply to Acquisition Credit 213
Minimum Compliance Period 213
Annual Limit on Tax Credits 213
Limitation Imposed by the Passive Asset Loss Rules 214
Limitation Imposed by the Alternative Minimum Tax 214
Limitations on the Deductibility of Losses 214
Limited Partners' Income and Expense Is Always Passive 214
Real Estate Rental Income and Expense Is Sometimes Passive 215
An Exception for Small-Scale Operators 215
Taxation of Foreign Investors 216
The Alternative Minimum Tax 217
Summary 217
Recommended Readings 218
Review Questions 219
Discussion Questions 219
Problems 219

PART FOUR: Case Problems **220**

PART FIVE   Measuring Investment Performance **223**

13. Traditional Measures of Investment Worth **224**
Ratio Analysis 224
Income Multipliers 225
Financial Ratios 226

Traditional Profitability Measures   227
    Overall Capitalization Rate   227
    Equity Dividend Rate   227
    Broker's Rate of Return   229
    Payback Period   230
Toward More Rational Analysis   231
    Time-Adjusted Return Measures   231
Summary   232
Recommended Readings   232
Review Questions   232
Discussion Questions   233

14. Discounted Cash-Flow Analysis   **234**
Present Value   234
Net Present Value   235
Internal Rate of Return   236
    Problems with the Internal Rate of Return   237
Comparison of Net Present Value and Internal Rate of Return   241
Shoring Up the Internal Rate of Return   242
    Modified Internal Rate of Return   242
    Adjusted Rate of Return   243
    Financial Management Rate of Return   244
Summary   244
Notes   245
Recommended Readings   245
Review Questions   245
Discussion Questions   246

15. Investment Goals and Decision Criteria   **247**
Choosing a Discount Rate   247
    Summation Technique   248
    Risk-Adjusted Discount Rate   248
    Marginal Cost of Capital   249
    Opportunity Cost of Capital   249
Investment Decisions and Decision Rules   250
    Comparing Projects of Different Size   250
    Choosing among Mutually Exclusive Opportunities   251
    Mutually Dependent Investment Decisions   252
Investment Value and Investment Strategy   252
Applying the Discounted Cash-Flow Technique   254
    Estimating Investment Value   258
Summary   259
Notes   260
Recommended Readings   260
Review Questions   260
Discussion Questions   261

PART FIVE: Case Problem   **262**

PART SIX   The Risk Element   **265**

16.   Risk in Real Estate Investment   **266**
   Major Risk Elements   266
     Financial Risk   267
     Insurable Risk   270
     Business Risk   271
   Controlling Risk   272
     Reducing Risk through Judicious Investment Selection 272
     Diversification as a Risk Management Tool   274
     Market Research as a Risk Control Tool   274
     Property Management To Control Risk   275
     Shifting Risk to Tenants   275
     Hedging to Control Risk   275
   Risk Preferences and Profit Expectations   275
     Degrees of Risk Aversion   277
     Rational Risk Taking   277
   Measuring Risk   278
   Summary   278
   Recommended Readings   279
   Review Questions   279
   Discussion Questions   279

17.   Traditional Risk-Adjustment Methods   **280**
   The Payback-Period Approach   280
   Risk-Adjusted Discount Rate   281
     The Risk-Free Discount Rate   281
     The Risk Premium   282
     Practical and Theoretical Problems   282
   The Certainty-Equivalent Technique   283
     Deriving Certainty-Equivalent Factors   284
     Problems with the Certainty-Equivalent Approach   285
   Partitioning Present Values   286
   Sensitivity Analysis   289
   Summary   292
   Notes   293
   Recommended Readings   293
   Review Questions   294
   Discussion Questions   294

18.   Contemporary Risk Measures   **295**
   Probability as a Risk Measure   296
     Risk Differs from Uncertainty   296

Estimating Probabilities	297
Conventional Probability Rules	299
Application of Joint Probabilities	299
Interpreting Risk Measures	301
Probability Distributions	301
Expected Value	302
Measuring Dispersion	303
Standard Deviation and the Discounted Cash-Flow Model	307
Mean/Standard Deviation Approach	307
Establishing Acceptable Risk Profiles	309
Dealing with More Complex Cash-Flow Patterns	312
Perfectly Correlated Cash Flows	313
Uncorrelated Cash Flows	315
Partially Correlated Cash Flows	315
Summary	317
Notes	317
Recommended Readings	318
Review Questions	318
Discussion Questions	318

19. Risk Management in a Portfolio Context — **319**

Modern Portfolio Theory and Risk Management	319
Systematic and Unsystematic Risk	320
The Efficient Frontier	321
Real Estate's Role in the Efficient Portfolio	323
Real Estate Diversification Strategies	324
Geographic Diversification	324
Summary	325
Notes	326
Recommended Readings	326
Review Questions	326
Discussion Questions	327

PART SIX: Case Problem — **328**

PART SEVEN   The Investment Analysis Process Illustrated — **329**

20. Investment Feasibility Analysis — **330**

The Nature of the Feasibility Question	331
Relationship to Investment Analysis	331
Feasibility Analysis and Valuation Analysis	331
Dimensions of the Feasibility Question	331
The Primacy of the Objective	332
The Significance of Limitations	333

Steps in the Feasibility Analysis Process 333
Preliminary Financial Feasibility 334
  Regulatory Authorities 334
  Lender Objectives 334
  Equity Investors' Objectives 335
  Front-Door Approach 335
  Back-Door Approach 338
Format for a Feasibility Report 341
  Summary 343
  Notes 343
  Recommended Readings 343
  Review Questions 344
  Discussion Questions 344

21. Analyzing Subdivision Proposals 345
Overview of the Subdivision Process 345
  Significance of Location Decisions 346
  Coping with Regulatory Requirements 346
  Creating the Subdivision Plan 346
  Financing the Project 347
Industrial Subdivision: A Case Study 347
  Site Characteristics 348
  Market Research 348
  Investment Analysis 350
Summary 355
Recommended Readings 356
Review Questions 356
Discussion Questions 356

22. Development and Rehabilitation 357
Overview of Development 357
  Feasibility Analysis 358
  Financing Real Estate Development 359
  The Construction Phase 359
A Development Case Study 360
  Financing Arrangements 362
  Project Cost Estimates 362
  Estimated Net Operating Income 362
  Sales Price 363
  Developer's Profit 364
Rehabilitation 365
  Incentives for Rehabilitation 365
  Judging Feasibility of Rehabilitation Proposals 366
Commercial Rehabilitation: A Case Study 367
  Financing 367
  Cost Recovery (Depreciation) Allowances 367

Calculating Annual After-Tax Cash Flows   368
Estimating the Selling Price   369
Estimating Income Tax and Cash Proceeds From Sale   369
Evaluating Expected After-Tax Cash Flows   370
Summary   371
Recommended Readings   371
Review Questions   372
Discussion Questions   372

23. Industrial Property, Office Building and Shopping Center Analysis   **373**
Investing in Industrial Buildings   373
Demand for Industrial Space   373
Locational Factors   374
Types of Industrial Buildings   375
An Industrial Building Case Study   375
Forecasting Income and Expenses   376
Financing   376
Annual Income Tax Consequences   377
Forecasting Sales Proceeds   377
Evaluating After-Tax Cash Flows   379
Investing in Office Buildings   380
An Office Building Case Study   381
Reconstructing the Income and Expense Statement   381
Financing   381
Depreciation Allowance   382
Forecasting Annual After-Cash Flows   383
Forecasting After-Tax Cash Flow from Disposal   384
Analyzing After-Tax Cash-Flow Forecasts   385
Investing in Shopping Centers   386
Neighborhood Shopping Centers   387
Community Shopping Centers   387
Regional Shopping Centers   387
Superregional Malls   387
A Shopping Center Case Study   388
Financing   388
Depreciation Schedule   388
Forecasting Income   389
Forecasting Annual Cash Flows and Taxable Income   390
Estimating Taxable Income and Cash Proceeds From Sale   391
Evaluating After-Tax Cash Flows   392
Summary   394
Notes   394
Recommended Readings   395
Review Questions   395
Discussion Questions   395

PART SEVEN: Case Problem   **396**

PART EIGHT   Real Estate as a Security   **399**

24. Real Estate Syndication   **400**
    Characteristics of Limited Partnerships   400
        Investor Benefits   401
        Disadvantages of Participating as Limited Partners   402
    Regulation   403
        The Uniform Limited Partnership Act   403
        Limited Partnership Syndications and the Internal Revenue
            Service   404
        Limited Partnerships and the Securities and Exchange
            Commission   404
        State Securities Regulation   405
        Documentation   406
    Approaches to Limited Partnership Formation   407
        Blind Pool Syndications   407
    Rewards of Sponsorship   407
    Master Limited Partnerships   409
    Summary   409
    Recommended Reading   410
    Review Questions   410
    Discussion Questions   410

25. Real Estate Investment Trusts   **411**
    REIT Regulation   411
        Tax-Exempt Status   411
        Shareholder Rights   412
        Trustees and Directors   412
    REIT Management   412
        Advisor Responsibilities   413
        Advisor Compensation   413
    REIT Assets   413
    REITS as Investment Vehicles   414
        Income Tax Consequences   415
        Diversification and Liquidity   416
        Professional Guidance   416
        Investment Risk   416
        An Additional Layer of Risk   417
    REIT Mutual Funds   418
    Sources of REIT Information   419
    Summary   419
    Notes   420
    Recommended Readings   420

Review Questions   420
Discussion Questions   421

PART EIGHT: *Case Problem*   **422**

*Appendix A: **Mathematics of Compounding and Discounting***   **425**
Conceptual Basis for Compounding and Discounting   425
How Money Placed on Deposit Will Grow   427
Present Value of a Future Amount   429
How a Series of Deposits Will Grow   431
Present Value of an Annuity   432
Present Value of a Perpetual Annuity   435
Payments to Amortize a Loan   436
Extending the Usefulness of Financial Tables   438
   Finding Values Not in the Tables   438
   Remaining Balance of a Note   440
   Present Value of a Deferred Annuity   441
     Solution Alternative A   441
     Solution Alternative B   442
   Annuities in Advance   443

*Appendix B: **Compounding and Discounting with Financial
     Calculators***   **445**
Future Value of a Dollar   445
Compound Value of an Annuity   447
Present Value of a Dollar   448
Present Value of a Level Annuity   449
Amount to Amortize $1 (Mortgage Constant)   451

*Appendix C: **Financial Tables***   **453**

*Appendix D: **Normal Distribution Table***   **465**

*Appendix E: **Key Formulas and Frequently Used Symbols***   **467**
Summary of Key Formulas   467
   Compound Interest and Discount   467
   Investment Analysis Relationships   467
   Standard Deviation of the Present Value Distribution   468
Frequently Used Symbols   468

Glossary   **469**

Index   **497**

Preface

Reflecting the prolific changes that characterize our industry, *Investment Analysis for Real Estate Decisions* has been revised with increasing frequency over its history. An impressive roster of academicians and practitioners has been enlisted to help with each edition. In a concrete sense, therefore, the book is the creation not just of the author, but of a coalition of real estate professionals. As a consequence, the book has been widely adopted for both graduate and undergraduate use.

Mindful of warnings not to fix things that aren't broken, we were careful in this fourth edition to avoid change for its own sake. Yet, revision has been substantial. The earlier organizational style remains invariant: the material is divided into eight parts, and each part is followed by one or more case problems designed to show the operation of the principles as they occur in the real world. Case problems are coordinated so that they can be treated as a continuing case throughout the text, or can be used in isolation from each other.

KEY CHANGES TO THE FOURTH EDITION

With the collaboration of professional wordsmiths, this fourth edition's prose has been tightened and smoothed to make it even more reader-friendly. Much of the prior edition's material has been compressed; some has been expanded. Several old chapters have been combined, and new chapters have been added. These alterations are designed to pull students more quickly and smoothly into the subject matter, to give them a broader exposure and to ascertain that all material is relevant and current.

A Quicker, Broader Immersion

To more rapidly pull students into the subject, the introductory material in Part One is more compressed than it was in prior editions. Because of growing interest in international and institutional investing, these topics have been added to the introductory section. Material on urban economics that was previously in Part Two is now in the concluding chapter of Part One.

Consolidation To Eliminate Overlap

Combining Parts Two and Three from the third edition into a single, three-chapter presentation has yielded a more readable description of market research tools and techniques. Tightening the prose has created space for a more extensive demonstration of cash flow forecasting.

Outdated Material Revised or Omitted

Changes in laws—particularly in income tax and securities law—had rendered some to the information in the third edition obsolete. That material has been revised to reflect the most recent legislation. An old chapter on the use of computers, rendered superfluous by the accelerating march of computer literacy, has been replaced by references to computer-aided research and analysis where applicable in other chapters.

Extensive New Material

Expanded treatment of mortgage finance, income taxes and risk analysis required adding substantial new information:

- A section on geographic information systems has been added to the market research material in Part Two.
- The third edition had a single chapter on mortgage finance. Users asked for expanded treatment; Part Three of this fourth edition supplies it. Chapter 7 explains the nature and consequences of financial leverage. Common mortgage instruments and borrowing arrangements are described in Chapter 8. The final chapter of Part Three explains how to compute the effective cost of borrowing and shows how to compare alternative financing arrangements.
- Part Four ends with a new chapter that explores income-tax and estate-tax planning strategies.
- Institutional investors' interest in real estate assets has burgeoned in recent years, and a proliferation of equity REITs has altered the institutional investment landscape. In response, Part Six of this fourth edition includes a new chapter on risk analysis in a portfolio context.

Student Spreadsheet Software

To facilitate the use of computerized spreadsheets in solving the end-of-part case problems, a spreadsheet template disk is available to all schools using this text. A computer disk icon appears in the margin next to those case problems with which the Student Spreadsheet Software can be used.

RATIONAL ORGANIZATION

To guide students through the material, each of the text's eight parts begins with a brief explanation of purpose. Each part covers a subject that is fundamental to informed investment decision making:

- Part One sets the stage by explaining fundamental terms and concepts used throughout the text. It describes a widely accepted analytical framework and introduces relevant basic economic ideas.
- Part Two emphasizes the essential nature of market research, introduces key marketing concepts and shows how market research is used to estimate future benefits from ownership.
- Part Three introduces the environment of mortgage lending, demonstrates the likely consequences of using borrowed money and discusses commonly used credit instruments.
- Part Four explains relevant income tax provisions.
- Part Five covers ratio analysis and discounted cash flow analysis, and shows how to apply modern decision criteria to investment analysis.
- Part Six introduces traditional and modern risk analysis. The chapters provide for choice in one's degree of immersion in this complex yet essential subject.
- Part Seven illustrates the use of discounted cash flow analysis to make investment decisions regarding several major categories of real estate.
- Part Eight addresses the growing dimension of real estate as a security.

A BOOK OF MANY TEACHING PATHS

One professor's textual irrelevancy is another's necessity: some emphasize theory, others stress institutions; some like case analysis, others abhor it. Instructional preferences are often conditioned by the academic department that houses the subject: market research is important here, capital budgeting there; one department accentuates real estate economics, another the federal income tax. *Investment Analysis for Real Estate Decisions* resolves this dilemma by combining a wide range of material into a comprehensive analytical framework. It offers an appropriate assignment path for every instructional preference. For example:

- For a theoretical emphasis, omit Parts Six and Seven.
- To stress application, omit Chapters 2, 3, 15, 18 and 19.
- Chapter 10 provides sufficient income tax information for most courses; yet, covering all of Part Four will instill a deeper insight into tax law.

Additional suggestions for using this book can be found in the Instructor's Manual, which includes:

- chapter outlines;
- answers to review questions, discussion questions and problems;
- complete test bank;
- solutions to case problems; and
- overhead transparency masters.

ACKNOWLEDGMENTS

Previous editions of *Investment Analysis for Real Estate Decisions* were reviewed by Joseph Albert, James Madison University; Jaime R. Alvayay, California State University; Roger Cannaday, University of Illinois; Charles P. Edmonds III, Auburn University; Charles Floyd, University of Georgia; William Goolsby, Washington State University; Hans R. Isakson, University of Northern Iowa; Robert Mendelson, then of Southern Illinois University; Wade Ragas, University of New Orleans; James Vernor, Georgia State University; Leonard Zumpano, University of Alabama; Wayne Archer, University of Florida; Jerome Dasso, University of Oregon; Edwin E. Morgan, Baldwin-Wallace College; R. Keith Preddy, University of Tulsa; and Linda Simms, then of DePaul University.

This fourth edition has been reviewed by Andy Do, San Diego State University; Paul R. Goebel, Texas Tech University; Samuel Goldman, New Mexico State University; Joseph J. Virostek, Duquesne University. Additional consultation was provided by Victor Abraham, University of California at Los Angeles; Fred A. Forgey, The University of Texas at Austin; Jonathan C. Keefe, Boston University; Michael J. Murray, Winona State University; Ronald C. Rogers, University of South Carolina; and William C. Goolsby, Washington State University.

PART ONE

Basic Issues in Real Estate Investment Analysis

Investors who consider including real estate assets in their portfolios face a bewildering array of alternatives. They must select from among myriad combinations of opportunities that differ not only in the amount and timing of expected investment benefits but also in the degree of confidence with which investors hold their expectations.

Rational decision making under such circumstances taxes even the most educated and experienced investment analysts. Approaches range from snap judgments based on little more than hunches or "hot tips" to carefully calculated decisions backed by research and sophisticated analysis. These first three chapters lay the groundwork for the latter approach. The nature of the investment decision, the market environment in which decisions must be made and basic considerations incorporated into rational investment analysis are all addressed in Part One.

CHAPTER 1

The Real Estate Investment Decision

A lawyer buys a $100,000 interest in a limited partnership formed to develop shopping centers; a college professor puts $10,000 into a real estate investment trust; a real estate broker buys a $500,000 apartment building; a manufacturing firm invests millions in a new plant; the U.S. government spends billions to create a dam and reservoir system; all have made real estate investment decisions. As diverse as they appear, all these decisions have a common element: each requires giving up something now in anticipation of future benefits. The sacrifice is immediate and certain; rewards will be received in the future, if at all.

The problem is compounded because investors generally have more opportunities than they have resources. They have to choose, and they always have incomplete information. The only way to avoid getting lost in a maddening maze of alternatives is to rank them by their likely contribution to investment objectives, subject to constraints imposed by liquidity needs and ability to tolerate risk.

STATE OF THE INVESTMENT ANALYSIS ART

Real estate investment analysis has consistently lagged behind mainstream finance and investment thought. It wasn't until the late 1960s and early 1970s, for example, that analytical tools and techniques pioneered by economists and corporate financial analysts in the 1950s began to appear in real estate literature. Writing for the *Appraisal Journal* in 1970, Richard Ratcliff and Bernhard Schwab decried the virtual absence from real estate appraisal and investment literature of terms such as *probability, utility function* and *time value of money,* which were used routinely by investment decision theorists.[1]

More recently, modern decision theory has been grafted onto traditional real estate analysis, and the equity valuation technique explained in later chapters has been widely adopted. Computerized modeling to forecast after-tax cash flows and explore the impact of variance from expected operating results or changes in the operating environment (such as altered tax law, new government regulations or shifts in the economic climate) are now commonplace.

State-of-the-art investment analysis treats real estate as a capital asset desired for the stream of benefits it generates. In this context, real estate becomes a special case of modern capital budgeting. Its analysis utilizes discounted cash flow techniques and incorporates risk adjustments.

REAL ESTATE AS AN INVESTMENT

Real estate investors, either directly or indirectly, purchase rights to a stream of future cash flows that are expected to be generated by the real estate. The cash flow might come from rental income, from using the property as loan collateral, from cash savings through offsetting otherwise taxable income with tax-deductible losses from the real property interest, or from net profits upon resale of the property interest.

The price an investor is prepared to pay for a defined property interest depends in part upon the amount and the timing of these anticipated cash flows; how much will be received, and when? It depends also upon the degree of confidence with which expectations are held, and the investor's tolerance for bearing risk. The final variable is the attractiveness of alternative investment opportunities.

Virtually any investment goal can be accommodated with a position in real estate. Speculators can deal in real estate futures (by buying and selling purchase options); developers can reduce risk exposure by using standby loan commitments or taking a position in interest rate futures; investors can buy fixed-income assets such as mortgage loans or net leased properties. Real estate may be even more attractive when approached, not as a simple investment, but as a business opportunity.

In short, the possibilities are constrained primarily by limits on investors' abilities to conceive of alternatives. In Figure 1.1, investors are categorized in four ways: by the nature of their claims *(debt* or *equity),* and according to their degree of involvement in operations *(passive* or *active).*

Passive and Active Investors

Many investors acquire direct title to real estate in which they invest, and either oversee its operation themselves or hire professional property management firms to handle day-to-day supervisory chores. In Figure 1.1, they are charac-

Figure 1.1	Variety in Real Estate Investments

	Debt	Equity

Active	Loan origination:
	    Construction lending
	    Permanent loans
	
	Loan purchases on secondary
	    mortgage market
		Direct ownership of rental
		    property: purchase or
		    development

Passive	Pass-through certificates Mortgage real estate investment trust	Shares in real estate corporation Limited partnership shares Equity real estate investment trust

terized as *active investors*. Their key distinguishing characteristic is that they make decisions—selecting on-site management personnel, negotiating mainte-nance contracts, making rental rate decisions, approving leases and so forth—that directly affect operating results.

In contrast, *passive investors* make no operating decisions. They turn their wealth over to professional asset managers, who in turn acquire interests in real estate, or they acquire shares in corporations, partnerships or trusts that hold extensive real property interests. In any event, their decisions have little direct impact on the outcome of real estate operations.

Investment in Equity and Debt

Also in Figure 1.1, distinctions are made between investment in real assets such as land and buildings, and in real estate-related financial assets such as mortgage-backed promissory notes. Both involve exchanges of certain and immediate assets for uncertain expectations of future gain, but expectations regarding yield and risk may differ radically.

Consider a development such as an office building or an apartment complex. The institution or individual that buys the real property interest is an *equity in-vestor*. Usually though, most of the purchase money comes from a mortgage lender: a *debt investor*. Lenders often sell their mortgage-secured promissory notes to still other investors who prefer debt to equity positions.

Benefits to equity investors are less predictable than those to holders of debt, because an equity investor gets no cash until the debt holder's periodic claims to payment on the promissory note are satisfied. Equity investors also reap the consequences of increases or decreases in property value.

WHO ARE THE INVESTORS?

We are conditioned by how-to books and personal success stories to think of real estate investment as the province of individual investors. Yet real estate has become a major asset in the portfolios of many institutions, and foreign investors have found U.S. real estate equities to be increasingly attractive.

Institutional Investors

With some false starts, real estate investment trusts and pension funds have become major investors in real estate equities. This is due in large part to changes in federal law: a 1961 Internal Revenue Code revision exempted distributed real estate investment trust (REIT) earnings from taxation at the corporate level. Subsequent tax law changes liberalized REIT operating rules: the Employee Retirement Income Security Act of 1974 (ERISA) directed pension fund managers to diversify their portfolios, and thus encouraged them to move more aggressively into real estate equities.

Real Estate Investment Trusts. In 1996, the National Association of Real Estate Investment Trusts reported that 175 member REITs who invest primarily in real estate equities had a market capitalization (aggregate market value of all shares) of approximately $50 billion.[2] Many specialize in certain types of real estate, such as apartments, shopping centers or office or industrial buildings. Others prefer to hold diversified portfolios. Figure 1.2 shows the distribution of real estate equity investments by REITs in 1995, by type of property acquired.

Figure 1.2	REIT Property Acquisitions in 1995 by Property Type (amount invested = $7.55 billion)

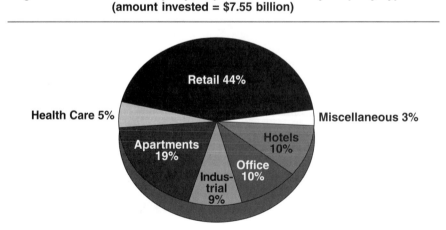

SOURCE: Based on data from National Association of Real Estate Investment Trusts.

Pension Funds.   With their steady and predictable streams of cash flow, Pension funds are ideal real estate investors. Yet their investment in real estate was slight until the 1970s. They moved in aggressively, however, when ERISA mandated more portfolio diversification. After retreating somewhat following market reverses of the late 1980s, they were back in force by the mid-1990s. According to the Roulac Group, aggregate pension fund capital in real estate equities was almost $98 billion at the start of 1995.[3]

Foreign Participation in U.S. Real Estate Markets

Foreigners own a very small percentage of U.S. real estate—about one percent of its dollar value in 1986, according to one estimate.[4] Their impact is distorted by disproportionate representation in certain parts of the country and in specific types of property. For example, Coldwell Banker reports that in 1987 foreigners owned 46 percent of downtown office space in Los Angeles, 39 percent in Houston and 32 percent in Minneapolis.[5]

Government studies, though inconclusive, indicate that foreign direct investment surged during the early 1980s, then stabilized by the middle of that decade but—at least through 1987—remained high by historical standards.[6] Real estate equities fell into widespread disfavor among foreign investors in the late 1980s, but the market heated up again in the early 1990s. The Roulac Group reported that aggregate foreign investment in U.S. in real estate equities exceeded $29 billion by the end of 1994.[7]

Foreign interest in U.S. real estate seems heavily affected by two key factors: foreign exchange rates and relative interest rates between countries. These factors sometimes push demand in the same direction; at other times they work at cross-purposes.

The Influence of Exchange Rates.   When shifts in foreign exchange rates make dollars relatively less expensive to holders of a foreign currency, U.S. real estate also becomes less costly to acquire. Suppose, for example, the British pound sterling sells for $1.75 on the foreign exchange market; a $10 million office building in Chicago will cost 5.7 million pounds sterling. If this and a comparable building in London generate the same operating income and have the same appreciation potential, investors might be indifferent between them. But suppose the pound sterling climbs in value so that it trades at $1.85. Now the $10 million Chicago property costs only 5.4 million pounds sterling, while the comparable building in London still costs 5.7 million pounds; holders of British currency will be inclined to invest in the United States.

A country's currency tends to appreciate on foreign exchange markets when that country's economic and political prospects appear particularly sound. Thus prosperity and political stability create a lure for foreign investors.

The Relevance of Relative Interest Rates.   When interest rates in a country are higher than they are in those with whom the country trades, the higher rates tend to depress real estate prices, while lower rates elsewhere tend to inflate

CLEVER PEOPLE, THOSE FOREIGN INVESTORS

It makes great headlines when foreign investors accelerate the pace of their acquisition of U.S. real estate. But investors, foreign and domestic, tend to become excited about an asset at exactly the wrong time. Whether it is real estate or stocks, transaction volume heats up near cyclical price peaks—the worst of all times to buy—and drops near market bottoms.

True to form, as property prices were reaching for the stratosphere in the mid-1980s, foreign investors' interest in U.S. realty was raising a hue and cry about "the selling of America."

Nowhere did such concerns manifest themselves more ferociously than in the Japanese acquisitions of some of America's most prominent buildings, so-called trophy properties. As the Japanese dickered for landmarks such as Rockefeller Center in New York and the fabulous Pebble Beach Golf Club in California, pundits proclaimed that their domestic owners' inability to hold on to these assets was stark evidence of American economic decline.

A study conducted at the Center for Strategic and International Studies in Washington suggests an entirely different set of factors at work. It seems the owners were merely doing what savvy investors always do: selling when uninformed buyers offer outrageously high prices.

The evidence? Paul Craig Roberts, who conducted the study, reports that Pebble Beach was resold after 17 months by its Japanese investors for $341 million less than they paid. Japanese investors, he notes, paid $762,000 *per room* for a Hawaiian hotel and "from Nevada to Hawaii . . . lost mega-millions in high-class resort projects that have since been abandoned or are operating at below break-even occupancy rates."

SOURCE: Paul Craig Roberts, William E. Simon Professor of Political Economy, Center for Strategic and International Studies. Reported by Scripps Howard News Service, February 29, 1992.

property prices there. The disparity makes real estate in the high-interest-rate country relatively more attractive.

REAL ESTATE INVESTMENT PERFORMANCE

Comparisons between returns on real estate investments and on stocks, bonds or other assets are unreliable, because real estate yield data are sparse and contradictory. Unlike stock and bond markets, where minute-by-minute trading data generate enough information to crash a computer, real estate yield indices typically are computed using quarterly appraisal estimates. This causes a smoothing of trend indicators and makes real estate yields seem less volatile than they might with more frequent and more reliable information about value fluctuations. Yet comparisons, flawed as they are, are essential for rational portfolio decisions.

Surging interest in real estate ownership by institutional investors and the phenomenal growth in public offerings by REITs, described earlier, has contributed immensely to our knowledge about comparative yields. Research results, however, are heavily influenced by the period from which data are drawn.

Real estate became a darling of pension funds during the 1970s. An offspring of this relationship, the commingled real estate fund (CREF), acquires real estate and monitors its operation on behalf of institutional investors. CREFs have become treasure troves of information about real estate investment performance.

Brueggeman, Chen and Thibodeau analyzed asset performance data from two CREFs from 1972 through 1983. They broke the data, which at the time accounted for about 25 percent of all CREF assets, into various subperiods to see whether comparative results varied significantly through time. They found that on a risk-adjusted basis, real estate outperformed the Standard & Poor's index of 500 stocks and the Ibbotson Associates bond index for the entire period and for each subperiod. The real estate portfolio's superior performance differed considerably, however, among sub-periods.[8]

For the entire period, and for the subperiod from 1972 through 1977, the researchers concluded that the CREF portfolio had higher yields than the Standard & Poor's 500 stock index, before and after adjusting for risk. For 1978 through 1983, average yields on the Standard & Poor's index exceeded the CREF yields by a narrow margin before adjusting for risk. The real estate portfolios were less risky, however, and after adjusting for relative risk the advantage shifted back to the CREF portfolio.

Other studies show conflicting results. Michael Giliberto compared total returns to an index of more than 1,200 large REITs with Standard & Poor's 500 stock index for 1978 through 1989 and found that the advantage had shifted decisively to common stocks.[9] In a 1984 analysis of 17 previous comparative yield studies, Zerbst and Cambon concluded that real estate assets have shown returns roughly similar to common stocks since 1950, but that real estate tends to outperform stocks during periods of inflation.[10]

CONCEPTS AND DEFINITIONS

The investment perspective requires a slightly different view of real estate from that to which many are accustomed. An investor must develop a perception of the property's worth as a portfolio asset and compare this with an estimate of the probable price at which the real estate can be acquired. Neither of these values can be determined with certainty. Investors must work with ranges within which they expect the values to lie. This brings us to three key definitions: most probable selling price, investment value and transaction range.

Most Probable Selling Price.   The most likely price at which a property will sell, given the market conditions then prevailing and the financing arrangements available, is commonly called *most probable selling price.* This is not to be confused with market value, which is defined by appraisers as the most probable price when a property is exposed to the market under specific, rigidly prescribed conditions that often do not prevail in the marketplace.

Investment Value.   A property's *investment value* is its worth to a present or specific prospective owner. Investment value is unique to the individual and need not be closely related to most probable selling price. It is the value today, to the specific investor, of anticipated future benefits of ownership. It reflects the investor's assumptions about the asset's future ability to produce revenue, about the likely holding period, selling price, tax consequences, available financing and all other factors that affect net benefits of ownership. Because there will not be precise agreement on all these factors or on the appropriate adjustment for waiting and for uncertainty, each individual's investment value is necessarily unique.

Transaction Range.   The price range within which a transaction can occur and leave both the buyer and the seller better off than before is the *transaction range.* The present owner's investment value sets the lower end of the range; the prospective buyer's sets the upper end. The actual transaction price will fall somewhere between these extremes.

The current owner (prospective seller) establishes a minimum acceptable price based on assumptions about future benefits of continued ownership. This is shown as V_s in Figure 1.3. To be motivated to sell, the owner must conclude that the most probable selling price (shown as V_p in Figure 1.3) is greater than investment value.

As we have observed, the property also has an investment value from the prospective buyer's point of view. That value too, is based on assumptions about future benefits of ownership. It is the maximum amount the prospective buyer is justified in paying for the property. This relationship is illustrated in Figure 1.4. To be motivated to buy, the prospective buyer must conclude that investment value (V_b in Figure 1.4) is greater than the most probable selling price, V_p.

Within the range of possible prices set by the owner's and the prospective buyer's investment values (net of transaction costs), both will gain by getting together. Owners will not take less than a property's investment value to them, and buyers will not pay more than their investment value. This creates a transaction range, as shown in Figure 1.5. The exact price within this range will depend upon the parties' relative bargaining skills.

In Figures 1.3–1.5, it is assumed that buyer and seller agree on most probable price, but that need not be the case. For a transaction to be possible, all that

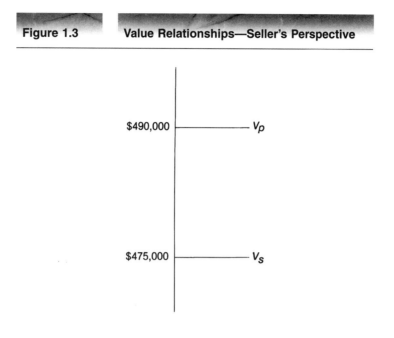

Figure 1.3   **Value Relationships—Seller's Perspective**

$490,000 ——————— V_p

$475,000 ——————— V_s

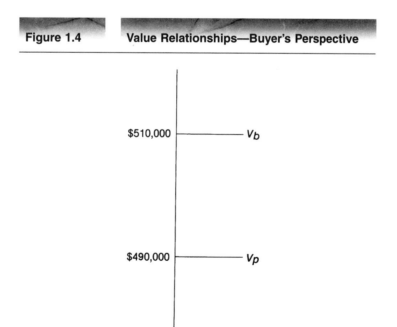

Figure 1.4   **Value Relationships—Buyer's Perspective**

$510,000 ——————— V_b

$490,000 ——————— V_p

is needed is a transaction range—a difference between buyer's and seller's investment values—sufficient to absorb transaction costs.

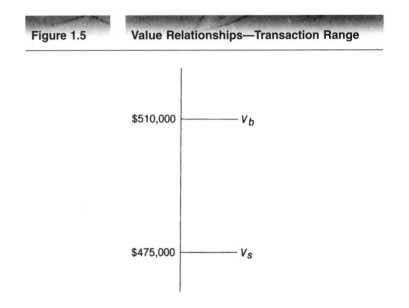

Figure 1.5   Value Relationships—Transaction Range

$510,000 ——————— V_b

$475,000 ——————— V_s

ESTIMATING INVESTMENT VALUE: AN OVERVIEW

Estimating investment value, the most a would-be seller is justified in taking for a property, or the maximum a prospective buyer is justified in paying, is at best a difficult task, requiring analysis of a wide range of disparate yet interwoven elements. The chore is greatly simplified when reduced to a system. This book presents such a system, sometimes called a *decision model,* which is widely used for evaluating real estate investment proposals.

The model is not unique to real estate. In spite of its complexity, real estate investment analysis is not fundamentally different from other investment decision making. Whatever the exact nature of the investment vehicle, for those schooled in modern financial analysis the decision process does not vary.

Steps in the Investment Decision Model

1. *Estimate the stream of expected benefits.* Investment assets are desired only for the benefits that ownership is expected to bestow. Investors in effect purchase a set of assumptions about the property's ability to produce income over the proposed ownership period.
2. *Adjust for timing differences among expected streams of benefits flowing from investment alternatives.* As a general rule, the sooner benefits are expected to be received, the more highly prized they are by investors.
3. *Adjust for differences in perceived risk associated with the alternatives.* Just as investors are not indifferent to the timing of expected benefits, neither are they indifferent to the degree of certainty with which expectations are held.

4. *Rank alternatives according to the relative desirability of perceived risk-return combinations they embody.* Attitudes toward risk differ, but rational investors seek financial return as a reward for bearing the risk.

The investment analysis system explained in this book represents an application of this four-step process. It is an adaptation of capital-budgeting techniques long employed among corporate financial analysts. Three concerns—amount of benefit, and the timing and certainty of their receipt—determine the relative value of all investment alternatives.

Valuing the Benefit Stream

Benefits expected to be received in the far distant future add less to a property's investment value than do those whose anticipated receipt is more imminent. In general, the further in the future expected receipts lie, the less is their value today. The exact nature of the trade-off will differ among investors, depending upon each individual's time preference for money.

Financial analysts have long recognized that the value of a business enterprise is the sum of the value of the outstanding debt plus the value of the equity. Real estate valuation theory also recognizes value of an investment property as the sum of the debt and equity positions. This is evidenced in appraisal techniques in which market value is estimated by capitalizing the property's expected net operating income by the weighted average cost of debt and equity capital.

Investment value can, therefore, be expressed as the present value of the equity position plus the present value of the debt position. This is illustrated in Figure 1.6, which starts with the property's net operating income: operating revenue minus operating expenses (these terms are defined and illustrated in Part Two). Holders of mortgage-secured debt have a senior claim on the property's net operating income; their portion—annual debt service—flows down the left-hand side of Figure 1.6. The remainder accrues to equity investors, but part of this will be siphoned off as income taxes. The residual is the after-tax cash flow to the equity investors, as shown on the right-hand side of Figure 1.6. The bottom of the diagram illustrates the transformation of these expected cash flows into lump-sum equivalents: the investment value of each position.

Present value of the debt position is the amount of available mortgage financing or (in the case of present owners' investment values) the outstanding mortgage loan balance. Present value of the equity position is the value today of the anticipated after-tax cash flow during a prospective ownership period and of the anticipated proceeds from disposal. Investment value can be expressed algebraically as follows:

$$P_e = CF_1/(1 + r) + CF_2/(1 + r)^2 + \ldots + CF_n/(1 + r)^n + CF_d/(1 + r)^n$$
$$P_i = P_d + P_e$$

where:

P_e = Present value of the equity position

P_d = Present value of the debt position

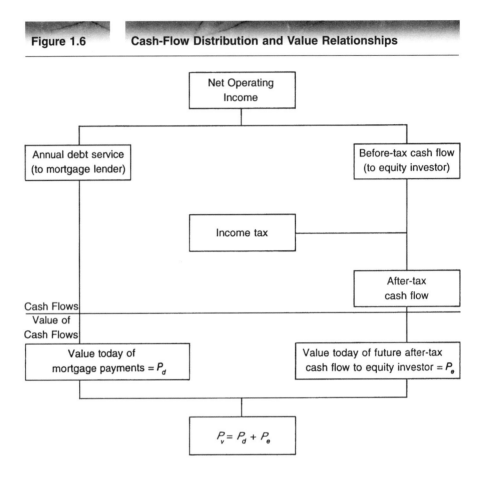

Figure 1.6   Cash-Flow Distribution and Value Relationships

P_i = Present value of total investment position

CF = After-tax cash flows to the equity investor occurring in year t (t = 1, 2, 3 . . . n)

CF_d = After-tax cash flow to the equity investor from property disposal at the end of year n

r = Discount rate

Estimating present value of the equity position requires assumptions about income, operating expenses, amount and terms of financing, sales price and income tax. It also depends upon the investor's opportunity cost of capital (the yield available on equally risky alternative opportunities).

If a prospective purchaser places a higher investment value on a property than the acquisition cost, buying it will increase the buyer's net worth. In like manner, selling a property that has a higher market value than its investment value enhances the seller's total wealth position.

Alternative investment strategies regarding a specific property can also be evaluated using the investment value model. Holding financing constant, the investor varies other investment criteria (such as alternative income tax treatments as discussed in Part Four, or proposed remodeling or rehabilitation) and notes the impact on investment value. Financing or refinancing alternatives can be evaluated by holding all other factors constant and determining the effect of each financing plan on the value of the equity position. The investor accepts the alternative that produces the highest value of equity per dollar of required equity investment, provided each alternative is perceived as entailing equal risk.

We all interpret information according to our own frames of reference, which result from our unique sets of past experiences. For this reason, individuals reviewing the same information will usually draw different conclusions. There will likely be disagreement about the future stream of rental revenue and operating expenses associated with a property. Individuals will also differ in the degree of certainty with which they hold their expectations; they will perceive differing levels of risk associated with expected outcomes. For these reasons, there will seldom be general agreement about investment value.

Income tax situations are seldom exactly comparable. Consequently, most investors will anticipate different after-tax cash-flow streams even when they are in general agreement about the before-tax cash flow.

People also differ in their willingness to defer immediate consumption in the interests of even greater benefits in future years. Those with a high preference for present consumption will require a greater incentive to defer after-tax cash flows. Investment value for such investors will be relatively high for investments with a short-term payoff and relatively low for those requiring greater patience. This subject is pursued at length in Part Three.

We do not all have the same tolerance for risk. Those who are less bothered by the possibility of variance between expected and actual investment outcomes will be inclined to place a greater investment value on risky ventures than will those who prefer to face a more precisely determinable future. Other things being equal, almost all investors will prefer less risk to more risk; they differ greatly regarding the risk premium they attach to proposed investment ventures (that is, the reduction in investment value due to possible variations between expected and actual after-tax cash flows).

Investor Objectives and Risk

Any attempt to discuss investor objectives quickly runs afoul of the nebulous term, *investor.* Like Humpty-Dumpty, we choose to let the expression mean just what we choose it to mean, and we mean it to include any person or entity that takes a debt or an equity position in real estate. This definition could mean something entirely different—it frequently does when used elsewhere.

Given the diverse entities—corporations, partnerships, trusts, pension funds and so forth—that fit our definition of the term, there can be no doubt that investors will have varied objectives. Some (for example, real estate investment trusts, pension funds and commercial banks) are constrained by law and regu-

Study: risk & attitudes toward risk

latory agencies. Others, because of their relatively high income tax obligations, seek tax-shelter situations. Others seek fixed incomes. Some take speculative positions in search of spectacular capital appreciation. Others consider real estate as their inventory in a basic merchandising sense.

There are, however, certain basic traits most investors hold in common, regardless of their motivations or personal objectives. All rational investors seek financial return as a reward for committing resources and as compensation for bearing risk. The amount of expected compensation and the acceptable degree of risk depend on specific investor objectives and individual attitudes toward risk.

Emotional temperament plays a large role in an investor's attitude toward risk. Some people are risk takers by nature; they not only accept it but go out of their way to incur it. These are people who gamble even when they know the game favors the house. They seem to revel in defying the odds. For them, the long shot is worth courting failure.

Other people avoid risk at almost any price. They sacrifice expected returns to hedge their bets, even where the cost of hedging is disproportionate to the relatively small associated risk. As investors, these people favor fixed-income securities that carry a high degree of safety of principal, such as government bonds or insured certificates of deposit at commercial banks.

Most investors probably fall somewhere in between these extremes. They tend to minimize risk exposure, preferring the relatively low-return certainty to the higher-return long shot. Moreover, they tend to become progressively more risk-averse as their total wealth increases. These propositions about investor behavior have been explored at length in the economic and financial literature and are not generally a matter of serious dispute.

Authorities generally agree that, to the extent they are motivated by rational financial considerations, most investors have the attitude toward risk and expected return depicted in Figure 1.7. They prefer a higher return for a given perceived risk, they prefer less risk for a given expected return, and they accept additional perceived risk only if accompanied by additional expected return.

An additional investor characteristic demonstrated in Figure 1.7 is the tendency to become increasingly averse to additional risk as total perceived risk increases. Thus the investor whose attitude is depicted can be induced to accept the additional risk indicated by the distance r_1 to r_2 by the promise of an increase in total reward indicated by the distance p_1 to p_2. But to be induced to accept an identical additional risk increment (from r_2 to r_3), the investor must be able to anticipate a substantially greater reward increment (from p_2 to p_3). In addition, as indicated in the illustration, there is some level of perceived risk (r_4) beyond which the investor cannot be induced to venture, regardless of the possible benefits.

Of course, the exact shape and location of the curve depicted in Figure 1.7 depend on an investor's personal attitude toward risk. A more risk-averse attitude would be depicted by a much more steeply inclined curve, while a less risk-averse attitude would be depicted by a shallower curve. Someone who loves risk would actually trade expected return for additional risk. These various attitudes are shown in Figure 1.8.

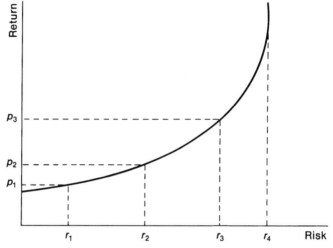

| Figure 1.7 | Relationship Between Perceived Risk and Expected Return for a Risk-Averse Investor |

| Figure 1.8 | Diverse Attitudes Toward Risk |

SUMMARY

Real estate investors make an immediate and certain sacrifice of current purchasing power in expectation of future economic benefit. Investment proposals are evaluated by comparing the magnitude of the sacrifice with the quantity and timing of expected benefits and by considering the level of certainty with which expectations are held. Adjusting for time and uncertainty permits comparison among competing alternatives.

Attempts to measure and compare real estate investment returns with those on other investments have been inconclusive. Outcomes are heavily influenced by the dates over which performance is measured. The preponderance of evidence seems to suggest that real estate and common stocks offer roughly equal long-term yield prospects, but that real estate performs better during periods of inflation. Research suggests that real estate prices are less volatile, but this may be an illusion due to real estate market inefficiencies.

Institutions as well as individuals find real estate an attractive investment medium. Changes in federal laws and regulatory attitudes have in recent years enhanced its appeal to pension funds. Equity REITs have multiplied in the more benign income tax environment of recent years.

Foreign direct investment in U.S. realty became a major public issue when its volume grew dramatically during the early 1980s; concern abated when the net flow of foreign equity capital ebbed at the end of the decade. Foreign investors' interest in U.S. realty is heavily influenced by comparative interest rates, and by foreign exchange rates.

Investment analysis follows a consistent pattern regardless of the investment vehicle or investor entity: The streams of benefits from alternative proposals are forecast and are adjusted for timing and risk differences. Alternatives are then ranked according to their desirability, in terms of the trade-off between perceived risk and anticipated return. Rankings will differ according to the discount rate used for timing adjustments and with varying investor attitudes toward risk.

Investment value is the highest price a prospective buyer is justified in paying for a property or the lowest price a prospective seller is justified in accepting. It is a function of available financing, the investor's income tax position, the yield available on alternative investments and the timing and amount of anticipated benefits flowing from the investment under consideration. The investment decision is subjective, and investment value will be different for each investor.

Investment value can be estimated by summing the present value of the equity position and the debt position associated with a proposed venture. Present value of the equity position is the discounted value of all anticipated future cash flows to the equity position. Present value of the debt position is the available loan or the remaining balance on an existing loan.

Investors differ in both their perceptions of and their attitudes toward risk. The difference among attitudes is sometimes expressed as degrees of risk aversion. The more risk-averse the investor, the greater the expected reward will have to be to induce investment in a given project.

NOTES

1. Richard U. Ratcliff and Bernhard Schwab, "Contemporary Decision Theory and Real Estate Investment," *Appraisal Journal* (April 1970). Reprinted in *Readings in Real Estate Investment Analysis,* vol. 1 (Cambridge, MA: Ballinger Pub. Co., 1977.)

2. Institutional Real Estate, Inc., *Real Estate Capital Markets Report,* vol. 5, no. 3 (Winter 1996) (Walnut Creek, CA, Institutional Real Estate, Inc.) p.18.

3. *Ibid,* vol. 4, no. 2, Spring 1995, p. 11.

4. U.S. Department of Commerce, Bureau of Economic Analysis, *Foreign Direct Investment in the United States: Operations of U.S. Affiliates of Foreign Companies* (Washington, DC: U.S. Department of Commerce, Bureau of Economic Analysis; 1987).

5. National Realty Committee. *America's Real Estate,* (Washington, DC: National Realty Committee, Inc., 1989) p. 54.

6. U.S. Department of Commerce, *op. cit.,* various issues.

7. Institutional Real Estate, Inc., *op. cit.,* p. 14.

8. William Brueggeman, A. H. Chen, and T. G. Thibodeau, "Real Estate Funds: Performance and Portfolio Considerations," *AREUEA Journal* vol. 12, no. 3 (Fall 1994) pp. 333–354.

9. S. Michael Giliberto, "Equity Real Estate Investment Trusts and Real Estate Returns," *The Journal of Real Estate Research,* vol. 5, no. 2 (Summer 1990) pp. 259–263.

10. Robert H. Zerbst and Barbara Cambon, "Real Estate: Historical Returns and Risk," *The Journal of Portfolio Management* (Spring 1984) pp. 4–20.

RECOMMENDED READINGS

Bacow, Lawrence S. "Foreign Investment, Vertical Integration and the Structure of the U.S. Real Estate Industry." *Real Estate Issues,* vol. 15, no. 2 (Fall-Winter 1990) pp. 1–9.

Barrett, G. Vincent, and John P. Blair. *How To Conduct and Analyze Real Estate Market and Feasibility Studies,* 2nd ed. New York: Van Nostrand Reinhold Company, 1988, pp.71–82.

Kolbe, Phillip T., and Gaylon Greer. "Recent Changes in Individual Investors' Attitudes Toward Real Estate." *Real Estate Issues,* vol. 16. no. 1 (Spring-Summer 1991) pp. 6–10.

McMahan, John. "Foreign Investment in U.S. Real Estate." *Real Estate Issues,* vol, 15, no. 2 (Fall-Winter 1990) pp. 48–50.

Swanson, Peggy E. "An Economic Rationale/ Empirical Tests of Foreign Investment in United States Real Estate." *Real Estate Issues,* vol. 13, no. I (Spring-Summer 1988) pp. 40–46.

REVIEW QUESTIONS

1. What are investors really looking for when they invest in real estate?
2. Describe the differences between passive and active investors.
3. What are some major determinants of foreign investment in U.S. real estate?
4. What are the major steps in modern investment decision analysis?
5. Distinguish between the most probable selling price and market value.
6. Explain how the transaction range for a given property is set. What is the role of investment value in arriving at the transaction range?
7. When estimating investment value, what factors are of concern to the investor?
8. What effect does the timing of cash flows have on investment value?
9. List basic traits that most investors have in common.
10. What is the relationship between the amount of risk to which an investor feels exposed, and the investor's attitude toward additional risk?

DISCUSSION QUESTIONS

1. What difficulties might a researcher face when trying to compare the long-term investment performance of real estate and securities portfolios? Discuss problems in measuring yield and in comparing risk.
2. Real estate equity and debt markets are closely intertwined: Most new properties are financed in part with mortgage-secured notes, and there is an active secondary market for both mortgage notes and real estate equity interests. Under what circumstances would prices in these markets most likely move in opposite directions?
3. Under what circumstances would the most probable selling price of a property and its market value be essentially the same? Under what circumstances might they differ significantly?
4. To better determine just what a property is worth in the marketplace, would it make sense to ask an exorbitant price and wait for a series of offers, then accept the first subsequent offer that is higher than any received during the trial, or information-gathering, period? What problems do you see with such a procedure?
5. Gambling is risk-seeking behavior and buying insurance is a risk avoidance measure. Yet many people who gamble also buy insurance. How can these contradictory actions be reconciled?

CHAPTER 2

Investment Strategy and the Concept of Market Efficiency

Chapter 1 explains that investment value (the value of an asset to a specific individual) depends upon the extent of future benefits prospective investors expect, the anticipated timing of the benefits, the degree of confidence with which expectations are held, attitudes toward risk and expected yields from available alternatives. If any of these key factors change, so do investment values.

Most probable price (the midpoint of a probability distribution of possible prices) is also discussed in Chapter 1. Buying opportunities occur when most probable price drops below investment value; seller motivation is sparked when most probable price rises above investment value.

The wider the gap between most probable price and an individual's investment value, the greater is the profit potential from buying or selling. However, the factors that affect investment value (rental rates, operating expenses, income tax rates, the cost of capital) also affect most probable price. Expressed differently, when market participants' investment values go up or down, their market activities—buying or selling—move prices in general and thus each property's most probable price in the same direction. When factors that affect investment value cause immediate changes in market price, opportunities for extraordinary profits are rare and fleeting. If most probable price moves only with a lag, the opportunities will be more frequent and more lasting. The speed with which market prices react to altered circumstances, new information or revised attitudes, is a measure of the market's *efficiency*, and efficiency often differs radically between markets.

SUPPLY, DEMAND AND THE PRICE OF REAL ESTATE ASSETS

To understand the nature and role of market efficiency in investment strategy, we need first to master the concepts of supply and demand, and to understand how their interrelation determines market prices. It then becomes clear how changes in supply or demand alter market prices.

Demand for Real Estate Assets

Economists use *demand* to refer to the relationship between market price and the quantity of a good or service that will be bought per time period, over the entire range of possible prices. The relationship is illustrated in Table 2.1 as a *demand schedule* for prime downtown office space.

A *demand curve* presents the same information in graphic form. Figure 2.1 illustrates the demand schedule from Table 2.1 as a demand curve. Quantity of office space is on the horizontal axis, price per square foot is on the vertical. The first line on Table 2.1 indicates that at $120 per square foot investors will buy 2.3 million square feet per annum. The same information is plotted as point A on Figure 2.1 at $120 along the vertical axis and at 2.3 million units along the horizontal. In like manner, the second entry in Table 2.1 is plotted as point B in Figure 2.1, the third is plotted as point C and so on.

The downward slope of the demand curve in Figure 2.1 (sometimes called a *demand function,* denoting that quantity demanded is a function of price) is representative of the usual relationship between price and quantity demanded; when prices increase, the quantity demanded falls. As prices rise, some potential purchasers opt for less expensive substitutes (suburban office space, perhaps, in our example) or drop out of the market altogether. As prices fall, buyers switch from relatively more expensive substitutes, and quantity demanded increases.

Shifts in Demand.   A specific demand schedule applies only so long as factors other than price that influence buyer behavior remain constant. As time passes, however, other things change. For our office space illustration, variation in the general level of business activity will affect rental rates, vacancy levels and oper-

Table 2.1	Hypothetical Demand Schedule for Downtown Office Space
Price (per sq. ft.)	*Square Feet Demanded (millions)*
$120	2.3
115	2.5
110	2.8
105	3.2
100	3.7
95	4.3

Figure 2.1	**Hypothetical Demand Curve for Downtown Office Space**

ating expenses. The rate of return on property purchased at a given price will change, and investors will revise their responses to posted prices. This represents a shift of the entire demand curve, as illustrated in Figure 2.2.

Movement along a demand curve—buyer responses to price changes, all else remaining constant—represents a change in *quantity demanded;* a shift in the curve's location or slope—a change in causal factors other than price—is a change in *demand.* If the altered relationships in Figure 2.2 make real estate investment less attractive, the depicted shift in demand will be inward to the left, resulting in less space demanded at each possible price. Were the relationships altered in the opposite direction, the shift would be outward to the right, representing greater quantities demanded at every possible price.

Determinants of Demand.   Among the more significant determinants of the location and shape of demand curves for real estate assets are variation in the number of prospective tenants, changes in operating expenses, yields available on other assets, technology and tastes. A change in any of these may cause a shift in the demand curve.

- *Variation in the Number of Prospective Tenants.* If population growth or economic expansion increases the number of businesses or professionals desiring to rent, competition for available office space will drive rental rates up and push vacancies down. Buildings' net operating incomes increase, and at prevailing prices real estate becomes relatively more attractive. Investors shift out of other assets and into real estate, increasing the quantity demanded at every

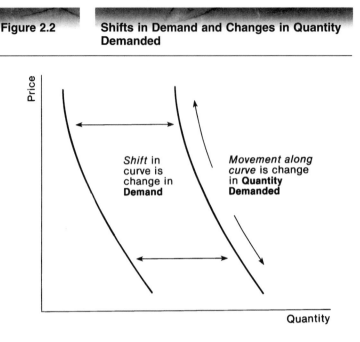

Figure 2.2 | **Shifts in Demand and Changes in Quantity Demanded**

Shift in curve is change in **Demand**

Movement along curve is change in **Quantity Demanded**

possible price. Conversely, a decline in the need for office space will push vacancies up and drive down the general level of rents; real estate investment becomes relatively less desirable, and resources are shifted elsewhere.

- *Changes in Operating Expense Levels.* When the general level of building operating expenses increases or decreases relative to rental revenue, net profits are altered accordingly. This variation in profitability changes the desirability of real estate relative to other investments, and the demand schedule shifts.
- *Yields Available on Other Assets.* Altered yield expectations on investments considered to be acceptable substitutes for real estate will change their relative desirability and cause a transfer of resources. This moving into or out of real estate investment shifts the demand schedule.
- *Technology.* Changes in technology can alter the need for rental space and thereby the derived demand for land and buildings, even with no change in the level of business activity. Computerized data processing, for example, has greatly reduced the time and cost of generating business information and has whetted management's thirst for reports. Many businesses have taken additional office space to accommodate equipment that generates a veritable flood of data.
- *Tastes.* A change in consumer tastes will alter the demand for goods and services produced by tenants and thereby shift the demand curve for productive space. As vacancy and rental rates adjust to new social and business conditions, the profitability of real estate (at prevailing prices) makes ownership more or less desirable than before. Taste in residential rental space affects demand for apartment building ownership in the same manner and even more directly.

Demand Shifters at Work: An Illustration.   To see how demand shifters actually affect demand, consider the demand schedule for rental space in downtown offices, as illustrated in Figure 2.3. Note carefully that this is *not* demand for building and land ownership. For the moment, we are looking at tenants' demand for rentable space. We will return later to the demand for ownership interests.

The curve labeled *D* in Figure 2.3 indicates the quantity of space tenants will want to rent per time period, at every relevant rental rate. The vertical line labeled supply in Figure 2.3 indicates the total amount of office space that exists in the downtown area. It is vertical because no matter what rental rate prevails, over the short term the physical quantity of rental space will be invariant.

At Price *p* (read off the vertical axis) the total supply of rental space (read as *q* on the horizontal axis) will be taken by tenants. Remember that the graph assumes everything except price (in this case, rent—the price of the right to occupy space) remains constant.

But suppose the level of downtown business activity declines, due perhaps to a general economic downturn, or a movement of business to the suburbs. As a consequence, less space will be purchased by tenants at each possible price per square foot. This is illustrated in Figure 2.3 as a shift from demand curve *D* to curve *D′*.

At the previously prevailing rental rate, *p,* there will be temporarily vacant space as indicated by the distance on the quantity (horizontal) axis from *q* to *q′*.

Figure 2.3   **Rental Rate Consequences of a Shift in Demand for Office Space**

Rental concessions will drive the prevailing rate from p to p', a price at which all available space will be taken. This represents a movement along the new demand curve D' from point a to point b.

The Supply Element

Relative scarcity is also a factor in the power of a product or service to command value in exchange. Many items from which we derive great satisfaction have little or no exchange value, while others with little practical utility are precious.

Obvious examples are water and diamonds. Water, a basic requirement of life, has as much want-satisfying power as can be imagined; diamonds bear no relation to survival needs. Why doesn't water cost more than diamonds?

Relative scarcity is the missing element. No matter how useful an item is, it will command little value in exchange if it is relatively abundant. In desert regions or during periods of drought, water may well become more precious than diamonds.

This can be seen by revisiting Figure 2.3. The vertical supply function indicates the total quantity of office rental space that exists in the market area during a specified time period. As demand shifts, price moves to allocate the fixed quantity among prospective tenants. But suppose a large new block of office space comes into existence (a new development, perhaps, or space vacated by an owner-occupant). This will reposition the supply function on Figure 2.3, farther out on the horizontal axis. The new, greater quantity of space will be allocated to prospective tenants at a lower rental rate; the consequence of a reduction in scarcity is a decline in value, manifested as lower rates.

A key phrase in this definition is *during a specified time period.* The supply function differs rather drastically as the time period under consideration is lengthened or shortened.

Price as a Consensus.   Individual efforts to adjust to the market will result in an *equilibrium price* (rent) for space of a particular type within a specific market. Equilibrium denotes a stable, balanced or unchanging system. Equilibrium price, therefore, is the price at which there will be sufficient quantity of a product to satisfy desires of all consumers at that price, but with no surplus remaining on the market. It represents a consensus of value. In the context of our example, it is the rental rate that results in zero vacancies.

With no prospective tenants desiring to rent additional space at the prevailing rate, there will be no competitive bidding to drive the rate still higher. With no significant amount of vacant space on hand, landlords have no incentive to offer rental concessions. At lower rates, however, prospective tenants will put upward pressure on rental rates. At higher rates, tenants' efforts to economize on space use or to shift to a lower-rent market will place downward pressure on rates.

The Time Element in Supply Analysis.   Our illustration of market adjustments to allocate rental space when demand shifts (Figure 2.3) presupposes a fixed quantity of space available for rent. This is a reasonable assumption so long as the time period being considered is too short for additional space to be built. Over a longer term though, more space can be developed and offered for rent. Then supply, like demand, will be responsive to changes in price.

Panel A in Figure 2.4 illustrates the distinction. Supply, the entire range of relationships between price and quantity supplied, is indicated by the curve labeled *S*. Because the time period is long enough for additional quantities to be developed, the curve slopes upward to the right, indicating that at higher rental rates more space will be developed and offered for rent.

Quantity supplied, the amount of space that will be available per time period at a specified rental rate, is measured at the intersection of the supply curve *S* and the demand curve *D*, and is read off the horizontal axis. Price, the rental rate at which all available space will be taken, is also measured at the intersection of the supply and demand curves, and is read off the vertical axis. Thus, for supply curve *S* and the demand curve *D*, the equilibrium rental rate is *p* and the equilibrium quantity is *q*. A shift in demand from *D* to *D'* in panel A of Figure 2.4 changes the quantity supplied as indicated by movement along the supply curve from point *a* to point *b*.

A shift in supply, illustrated on panel B of Figure 2.4 as a jump from curve *S* to *S'*, alters the entire relationship and prompts movement along the demand curve to the new equilibrium price *p'* and new equilibrium quantity *q'*. This might be caused, in our office rental space example, by a change in the cost of construction or by altered levels of optimism among real estate developers.

The Market for Real Estate Assets

The role of time in supply analysis was illustrated using the market for rental space. Even over the short run, however, the supply of real estate assets (owner-

Figure 2.4	**Movement Along a Supply Curve and Shift in Supply Curve**

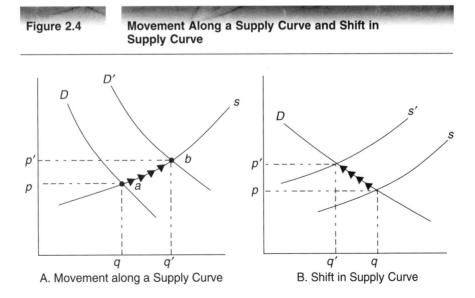

A. Movement along a Supply Curve   B. Shift in Supply Curve ship interests in real estate) is responsive to price variations. That is so because current owners of ownership interests will enter the market as sellers or as buyers, depending on their perceptions of the relationship between market prices and investment value.

To see this, consider a market for ownership interests in which only six people participate (we limit the number of participants to keep the illustration manageable—it could be expanded to any size). Assume that all rental units are completely substitutable (that is, interchangeable) and that each participant's desire to own units is as indicated in Table 2.2. Suppose only 16 rental units exist in this market and that two are held by A, four by B, four by C, three by D, three by E and none by F. These ownership quantities are shown at the bottom of Table 2.2.

At various possible prices, participants will enter the market as buyers or sellers to adjust their portfolios to reflect the new market realities. In Table 2.3, desired adjustments by all parties are shown at various possible prices. The difference between the amount each participant currently owns (shown at the bottom of Table 2.2) and the amount each prefers at different prices are the aggregate quantities demanded (desired for purchase) or supplied (offered for sale) at each price.

The schedule in Table 2.2 shows that at a price of $70 participant B wants to own four units, which is the number in that investor's current portfolio. Participant B therefore will not enter the market at that price. This is shown on Table 2.3: quantity demanded by participant B at a price of $70 is zero. At a higher price, say $90, Table 2.2 shows that B wants to own only one unit. But we see at the bottom of Table 2.2 that B's portfolio contains four units; Table 2.3 shows that at this price B will offer to sell three excess units. At a lower price, say $65, the desired portfolio of five units (shown on Table 2.2) will lead B to enter the market as a purchaser of one unit, as shown on Table 2.3. In like

Table 2.2	**Desired Portfolio of Rental Units**						
Price (per sq. ft.)	*Desired Ownership Quantities (units per market participant)*						
	A	*B*	*C*	*D*	*E*	*F*	*Total*
$95	3	0	2	0	0	0	5
90	4	1	3	0	1	0	9
85	5	2	4	0	1	0	12
80	5	3	4	0	1	1	14
75	5	3	4	1	1	2	16
70	6	4	5	1	1	2	19
65	6	5	5	1	2	3	22
60	6	6	6	2	2	4	26
	Current Ownership Quantities						
	A	*B*	*C*	*D*	*E*	*F*	*Total*
	2	4	4	3	3	0	16

| Table 2.3 | **Quantity of Rental Units Demanded of Supplied at Various Market Prices** |

Price	Market Participants						Aggregate Quantity	
(per sq. ft.)	*A*	*B*	*C*	*D*	*E*	*F*	*Demanded*	*Supplied*
$95	+1	−4	−2	−3	−3	0	1	12
90	+2	−3	−1	−3	−2	0	2	9
85	+3	−2	0	−3	−2	0	3	7
80	+3	−1	0	−3	−2	+1	4	6
75	+3	−1	0	−2	−2	+2	5	5
70	+4	0	+1	−2	−2	+2	7	4
65	+4	+1	+1	−2	−1	+3	9	3
60	+4	+2	+2	−1	−1	+4	12	2

manner, Table 2.3 shows purchases or sales for all participants to adjust their portfolios to the amounts Table 2.2 shows they desire at various market prices.

If at each price we add together all the negative amounts in Table 2.3, we obtain the aggregate quantity supplied at that price. Adding the positive amounts yields the aggregate quantity demanded at each price. These amounts are shown in the last two columns of Table 2.3. The price at which aggregate demand and aggregate supply are equal ($75 per unit) is the price that will permit all mutually advantageous exchanges to occur. At that price, Table 2.2 shows the total desired ownership quantity is 16, exactly the number that exists. This represents the short-term equilibrium price of rental units in this particular market. Figure 2.5 shows these relationships in graphic form.

Over longer periods, supply curves of ownership interests, like those for rental space, are influenced by the cost of construction. When prices of existing improved property move above the cost of new construction, real estate developers have an incentive to build. The higher the market price, the greater the incentive and—other things remaining constant—the rate of construction. As a consequence, long-term supply is considerably more responsive to changes in price.

The longer the time period under consideration, the more responsive the supply function will be. Over the very long term, not only can additional structures be built on available land, but additional land can be cleared or converted from alternative uses. This relationship between the length of the time period involved and the responsiveness of supply to price changes is depicted in Figure 2.6.

MARKET EFFICIENCY AND PROFIT OPPORTUNITIES

We have just seen that in a market economy scarce resources go to those willing and able to pay the most for them. If the market works efficiently (if all relevant information is immediately available at little or no cost, and if there is little cost associated with buying and selling), the highest bidders will be those who reap

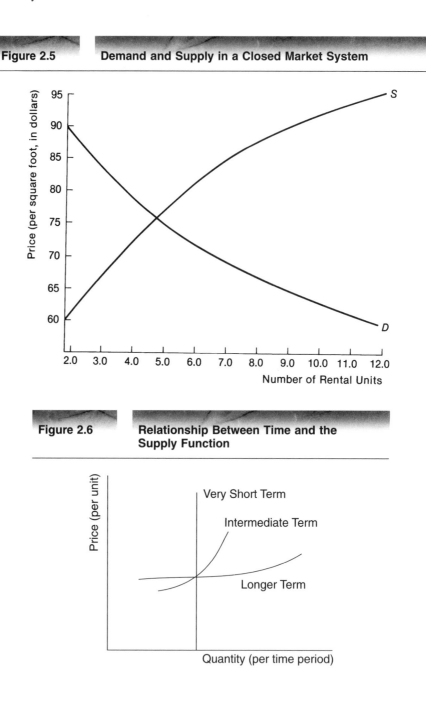

Figure 2.5   **Demand and Supply in a Closed Market System**

Figure 2.6   **Relationship Between Time and the Supply Function**

the greatest utility from consumption. But markets don't always work well, and all are not equally efficient. Before investigating the causes and implications of market imperfections though, we need to more carefully define our terms.

Defining the Market

In general, *markets* are institutional arrangements or mechanisms that enable buyers and sellers to get together. They are not necessarily physical entities or geographic locations. There is, for example, a market for national currencies that is comprised of an informal worldwide network of dealers connected by telephone and computer modem.

A market might be defined in terms of commonality of product. This leads to a description of a real estate market for industrial property, another for farmland, another for commercial sites, and so on. With notable exceptions for large industrial and commercial sites, the market in each of these segments is fragmented geographically, because of the tendency of participants to concentrate in the locale with which they are most familiar. As a consequence, there is no truly national market for most real estate.

Within a geographically localized area, for example, one might find the following distinct markets for residential real estate:

- The single-family, owner-occupant market
- The single-family, renter-occupant market
- The multifamily rental market

Within each of these broad categories, it is necessary to define submarkets within which determinable market forces work more or less uniformly. William Kinnard has described these submarkets as *neighborhoods.*[1] A neighborhood, he explained, is a geographical area within which change has a "direct and immediate effect" on the property under analysis. Delineating neighborhoods this way permits direct investigation of market forces affecting prices of real estate services and real estate assets.

Of course, the "neighborhood" for some types of property might be national in scope. Furthermore, the distinction between market segments gets fuzzy at its edges. Though a mammoth industrial site might clearly appeal to a national or international market and a little welding shop only to local buyers, at some point between, an industrial plant will appeal to some potential buyers both locally and regionally or perhaps nationally and internationally. Whatever framework one chooses, some properties will refuse to fit neatly into the boxes. The relationship between broader and more localized markets is illustrated in Figure 2.7.

Consider the market area from which regional shopping centers draw customers. Such centers are generally widely separated, and each tends to capture almost all customers from its immediate vicinity. Even though a center's attractive power declines geometrically with required travel time, it occasionally pulls in some customers who frequent other relatively nearby centers. Consequently, two or more regional centers may draw substantial clientele from one large geographic area.

Even so, defining the market as best one can is an early step in market analysis, an issue pursued more fully in the next section of the book. Frustration with indistinct categories should be tempered by reassurance that this makes the analyst's intellect a more essential ingredient in the investment selection process.

Figure 2.7	Markets Within Markets

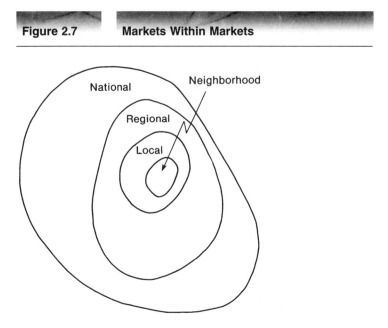

Market Structures

Perhaps nowhere has economic modeling been more useful than in studying the structure of markets. Having propounded a market where all relevant information is instantly reflected in prices and another where prices are set by the seller, economists classify all other market structures in terms of where they fall on the spectrum between these extremes.

Atomistic Markets.   Atomistic markets are so large and diverse that individual participants, regardless of the scale of buying and selling, have no perceptible effect on price. Buyers can purchase as much as they desire, and sellers can sell as much as they wish. There are never shortages or market gluts; there is no need for special "discount" prices to clear away unwanted inventory or for any government-mandated rationing schemes. Sellers do not need to advertise or to maintain an inventory to meet future needs.

Economic literature more frequently uses the term *pure competition* or *perfect competition* to describe atomistic markets, because these names are meaningful to economists. However, they are misleading to everyone else, since competition in atomistic markets is neither more nor less intense than in other markets.

Reducing the quantity offered for sale in an atomistic market does not enable a seller to command higher prices, because no buyer will respond to above-market price quotes. Buyers are in a similar position of not being able to bargain for better prices. All are simply price takers, in that their only choice is to accept prevailing prices or not participate.

Perhaps most nearly atomistic are markets for unprocessed agricultural commodities or for ownership shares in large publicly held corporations. In each case, the units of product are completely undifferentiated and a host of market participants act with roughly equal knowledge of market conditions. These products are sold in auction markets, where each bidder instantly knows the bids of competitors.

Absolute Monopoly.   In markets characterized by *absolute monopoly,* there is only one supplier of a good or service for which there is no reasonably acceptable substitute. The lower the price per unit, the greater will be the sales volume per time period: the monopolist selects the price and buyers decide how much of the good they are willing to take off the market at the posted price.

Markets most nearly characterized by absolute monopoly are those so designated by government fiat. Even here there are substitutes, however flawed. What if a country has only one telephone company? If telephone rates are set too high, hiring messengers, sending telegrams or writing letters becomes economical. Some state governments operate a monopoly in the sale of packaged alcoholic beverages, but their freedom to set prices is circumscribed by actual or potential bootleg or black market competition. Even in the printing of money, government hasn't been able to maintain an absolute monopoly. Entrepreneurs have created a number of financial instruments that are such good substitutes that they are popularly known as "near money" and are included in the supply equations economists use to measure monetary aggregates.

Price Searcher Markets.   Buyers and sellers in atomistic markets were earlier characterized as *price takers.* In contrast, sellers in pure monopoly markets are *price makers.* Between lies a host of markets where participants recognize that they cannot completely control prices but also understand that they do affect them. Each seller must be constantly aware of the impact pricing decisions will have on the decisions of competitors, and every buyer searches for the best deal. Participants in such markets might best be described as *price searchers.*

In an effort to make finer distinctions, economists have classified price searchers' markets into subcategories. *Monopolistic competition* exists when any number of competitors produce goods or services that are sufficiently differentiated that consumers will not be entirely indifferent about which they choose. *Oligopoly* implies that there are only a few sellers, and that market conditions render entry by new purveyors extremely difficult. Economic policy makers consider these to be important distinctions. We need only note that real estate markets fall within the range characterized as either monopolistic competition or oligopoly and that in both categories buyers and sellers exhibit price-searching behavior.[2] Figure 2.8 illustrates the relationships.

Price Searchers and Market Efficiency

If a price searcher had full knowledge of asset supply and demand (that is, of competitors' plans and consumers' desires) and knew the costs of all alterna-

Figure 2.8   **Participants' Reactions to Market Structure**

tives, profit-maximizing behavior would be simple. In fact, however, decisions have to be made without perfect foresight and with incomplete knowledge about current market conditions.

An important economic function of markets is to transmit information so that participants can make rational, informed buying and selling decisions. A market in which information is transmitted quickly and at low cost, and in which the information is immediately reflected in market prices, is said to be efficient. The time required for new information to be reflected in market prices is a measure of market efficiency. Information takes longer to be disseminated in less efficient markets and some information might never be reflected in market prices.

The less efficient the market, the greater will be the degree of price searching behavior. Participants can obtain intelligent perceptions of market clearing prices in inefficient markets only by expending time and effort on research.

The market for real estate equities is characterized by significant inefficiencies. Many real estate transactions occur at prices that reflect little more information than past prices of similar properties. Moreover, because transactions are infrequent and information is difficult and costly to generate, there typically is a considerable lag between the time comparable transactions occur and the time when the informational content of those transactions is fully reflected in market prices.

Sources of Inefficiency

The concept of a market clearing price is unambiguous when applied to a public auction where bids are immediately revealed to all participants. Everyone is immediately aware of all offers so that currently available information is almost certain to be reflected in prices. Real estate transactions, in contrast, are typically a matter of personal negotiation between buyer and seller. The prospective buyer does not know who else might be bidding on the property or what offers they are prepared to make. The seller must accept or reject offers without knowing whether others are forthcoming.

As a consequence, real estate markets may never "clear" in the sense of all parties being able to adjust their portfolios at a stated price. Numerous factors inhibit market adjustments from fully reflecting actual supply and demand conditions:

Information Is Costly and Difficult To Obtain. Information that is too costly to be purchased (that is, the benefits are exceeded by the cost of obtaining the information) will not be reflected in market prices. Real estate market information is relatively costly and difficult to obtain, due to the fragmented character of the market, the difficulty in making meaningful price comparisons among properties and the virtual absence of disclosure requirements.

Transaction Costs Are High. Transaction costs associated with real property markets are considerably greater than those encountered in securities markets, for example. This inhibits real estate portfolio adjustments and thereby increases the time required for new information to be reflected in market prices.

The Product Is Differentiated. Product substitutability contributes to the efficiency of markets. We have noted that every real estate parcel is unique in at least one respect: its location. Even when reasonably acceptable substitutes exist, buyers have specific preferences; in many instances there are no good substitutes. This gives prospective sellers a degree of monopolistic control, and the traditional model of a market-clearing price does not fit.

STRATEGY IMPLICATIONS

Earlier we observed that the supply curve for new property improvements (that is, the production of new buildings) depends on the relationship between production cost and rental rates. In every undergraduate course in microeconomic theory, economists demonstrate that the supply curve (the schedule of quantities that will be produced at various prices) is the same as the schedule of marginal cost of production (the cost of producing one more unit of a good or service).

So long as marginal revenue (the revenue from selling one more unit of good or service) is equal to or greater than marginal cost (the cost of producing the unit), producers in search of profit will expand. If the cost of producing another unit (marginal cost) exceeds marginal revenue (the selling price), it makes no sense to expand production. When the market is in equilibrium (that is, when the product is selling at its market-clearing price) in an atomistic market, the average cost per unit will be the same as the marginal cost. Since marginal revenue is the same as the average revenue (the price is not affected by one individual's production decisions), the average cost of producing units is the same as the market price. This concept is illustrated in Figure 2.9.

Cost, it is important to remember, includes sufficient profit to induce businesses to operate. Management or entrepreneurship is a factor of production,

Figure 2.9   **Equilibrium Revenue-Cost Relationship in Atomistic Market**

and its cost is called profit. Thus in Figure 2.9 the firm is earning a sufficient return to induce it to keep producing at this level but not enough to cause it to expand. Similarly, there is enough profit to keep competitors producing at current levels but not enough to make them expand or to lure additional competitors into the market.

For a real estate firm operating in an atomistic market, marginal revenue will remain constant over the relevant range of production and will be the same as average revenue; it is simply the product's price. This is shown in Figure 2.9 by the flat marginal revenue function.

Costs behave differently from revenue. Beyond some relatively modest level of production, the cost per additional unit produced grows as the rate of production is increased. Economists refer to this as *diseconomies of scale,* by which they mean per-unit cost grows when the number of units per time period increases. As the firm gets larger, for example, overhead grows disproportionately. Speeding up production means hiring more people and accepting some who are less competent than those hired earlier.

As marginal cost escalates it pulls average cost—more slowly, but inexorably—upward. If the firm in Figure 2.9 expands output further, average cost will exceed average revenue. There is no profit potential to encourage expansion.

When firms earn more profit than is needed to keep them in business, the excess is called economic rent. In real estate that term means something entirely different; so let's just think of the phenomenon as extra profit, by which we mean more than is necessary to sustain current levels of output. In an efficiently functioning atomistic market, extra profit is short-lived.

Figure 2.10 illustrates the adjustment process. Panel A shows a situation where average cost (including, remember, enough profit to induce businesses to operate) is less than average revenue. The result is extra profit. This might happen in the market for rental space, for example, because the firm's market research revealed a special amenity that induces tenants to pay more rent per square foot.

In an efficient market, competitors will quickly follow suit. The extra amenity will become standard, and the increased quantity supplied will drive market rent down (remember the impact of an outward shift in aggregate supply—it results in a lower equilibrium price) until the extra profit disappears.

The less efficient the market, the longer the adjustment will take and the more lasting is the reward for innovating. By seeking out pockets of market inefficiency, market niches where there are some monopoly elements or where entry is difficult for other reasons, the extra profit can be reaped even longer. To keep reaping higher-than-average profits in a fairly efficient market, firms have to innovate constantly.

Investors who have differential access to information—they get the information sooner, or at less cost than do most investors—or whose transaction costs are atypically low need not innovate to prosper. Those who get information sooner can exploit market inefficiencies by acting on the information before its impact is fully reflected in prices. If they are able to reduce their average information search costs—perhaps due to the volume of their transactions—or

Figure 2.10   How Markets Adjust

their transaction costs, they can act on information that does not move the market far enough to justify portfolio adjustments for most participants.

To demonstrate key concepts, economists often illustrate the outcome assuming that nothing changes except the variables under analysis. People who must contend with the less tractable behavior of real-world variables often find this frustrating. In a dynamic market environment, everything is in constant flux. Shifts can occur with lightning-like rapidity and in unexpected directions.

The economist's calm assumptions of order and predictability are useful though, because they let us peer through the fog of commercial intercourse and see the underlying cause-and-effect relationships. Real estate investment analysts need to understand the economic concepts of supply and demand because these forces determine the outcomes of multiple-year investment ventures such as those we will be investigating. The balance of Part One of the text investigates the determinents of vacancy and rental rates, and explores relevant dimensions of market research. These are nothing more than the application in a real-world environment of the dry concepts of supply and demand.

SUMMARY

Real estate is one of a wide range of assets available for inclusion in investors' portfolios. The lower the price at which an asset can be acquired relative to the price of competing assets of the same income and risk category, the greater the relative yield on the asset in question. Therefore, the lower-priced asset will be relatively more desirable, other things being equal. Translated into traditional supply and demand language, this means the lower the price the greater the quantity of an asset or service buyers stand ready to take off the market.

For a given level of demand for real estate space (that is, at existing rent levels), each real estate investor develops a perception of appropriate prices for real estate assets. When market prices are below this perceived value, they will be inclined to add to their portfolio. Conversely, they will be inclined to sell when market prices move above the perceived value. Thus, while the supply of space available for rent is relatively fixed over the short term, the supply of property interests is highly responsive to price even over the short term.

Markets are institutional arrangements or mechanisms that bring buyers and sellers into contact. Markets are often defined in terms of commonality of product, such as the residential real estate market or the market for industrial buildings. They are also frequently defined in geographic terms. In this respect, *neighborhood* is a term sometimes used to describe an area in which specific phenomena have a direct and immediate influence on all real estate. Market boundaries are difficult to define, because submarkets tend to overlap.

Economists classify market structures according to the extent to which individual buyers and sellers can influence prices and according to the degree to which relevant market information is readily reflected in prices. Markets in which there is only one supplier of a good or service are called monopolies.

Those having so many participants that no one person or firm has any discernible impact on price are called atomistic. Most markets fall between these extremes.

In efficient markets all relevant information is quickly reflected in market prices. Participants in less efficient markets can benefit by searching for the best available price. Because information in inefficient markets is scarce and expensive, participants with monopolistic access to information may be able to consistently outperform the market.

NOTES

1. William N. Kinnard, Jr., *Income Property Valuation* Lexington, MA: Lexington Books, 1971 p. 302.

2. For an excellent discussion of markets characterized in this fashion, see Armen A. Alchian and William R. Allen, *Exchange and Production Theory in Use,* Belmont, CA: Wadsworth, 1969.

RECOMMENDED READINGS

Alchian, Armen A., and William R. Allen. *Exchange and Production Theory in Use.* Belmont, CA: Wadsworth Publishing Company, Inc., 1969, pp. 62–97.

DePasquale, Denise, and William C. Wheaton. *Urban Economics and Real Estate Markets.* Englewood Cliffs, NJ: Prentice-Hall, 1996, Chapter 2.

Fanning, Stephen F., Terry V. Grissom, and Thomas D. Pearson. *Market Analysis for Real Estate Appraisals.* Chicago: Appraisal Institute, 1994, Chapters 8 and 9.

REVIEW QUESTIONS

1. How are the price and demand for an economic good related?
2. What conditions might cause a shift in demand for office space in a downtown area?
3. What is the relationship between price and the quantity supplied of an economic good?
4. Compare short-term and long-term supply functions in real estate markets.
5. How are real estate markets categorized and how are they defined?
6. Explain the difference between atomistic and monopolistic markets.
7. What are some of the factors inhibiting market adjustments from readily reflecting supply and demand conditions in real estate markets?
8. Look at Table 2.2. Suppose there are 16 units in the market and the market has reached the equilibrium position where the price is $75 per square foot: A holds five units, B holds three units, and so on. Now, suppose that an additional three rental units are added to the supply (due to development activity). With everything else remaining as before, who will acquire the additional units, and what will be the new equilibrium price?

9. What is the relationship between demand for rentable space and demand for land and buildings?
10. Why do supply curves generally become less nearly vertical as the time period under consideration grows longer?

DISCUSSION QUESTIONS

1. Are price and quantity demanded always inversely related? Can you think of circumstances under which increasing the price of a good or service might cause the quantity demanded to increase? Can you think of circumstances under which decreasing the price might cause quantity demanded to decrease?
2. In a dynamic, constantly changing economy, would you expect most markets ever to reach an equilibrium price? What about markets for various classes of real estate?
3. In highly concentrated markets, competition is likely to be just as furious as in atomistic markets, but it is often in arenas other than price. What are some prominent examples of non-price competition?
4. How might modern technology and modern management techniques be used to reduce real estate brokerage costs? What barriers might inhibit introduction of such cost-saving measures?

CHAPTER 3

Land Utilization and the Rental Value of Real Estate

Recall from Chapter 1 that real estate investors in effect buy a set of assumptions about a property's ability to generate a stream of benefits. For investment property, a substantial portion of the benefit stems from net operating income generated by tenants. The balance is in the form of cash flow when the property is sold, and this depends heavily on the property's ability to generate rental income after the sale. The property's rent-generating ability, then, is a key factor in its investment value.

This chapter investigates factors affecting a location's desirability, and thus the rental value of real estate at that location. It demonstrates how competitive bidding allocates the most desirable locations to tenants who benefit sufficiently to be able to pay the most rent. Those who are unable to secure the most desirable locations settle for the best affordable alternative. A hierarchy of choices trailing off from the ideal, or "100 percent," location results. This hierarchy is characterized by a descending order of density of land use and of declining rents as one moves farther from the 100 percent location.

As society's characteristic way of carrying on social and economic activities changes, so does the relative desirability of various locations. However, the cityscape does not readily adapt to altered needs. Its structure yields only grudgingly to changes resulting from individual economic decisions. As a consequence, cities reflect a mélange of development patterns, some created to meet contemporary needs and some that are simply artifacts of a bygone era. In every city, however, individual location decisions have resulted in logical, systematic development patterns whose orderliness may be hidden from untrained eyes.

ECONOMIC FACTORS IN LAND USE DECISIONS

Though it is constrained by collective values expressed in zoning and building codes, choosing a location is primarily an economic decision. For this reason, the pattern of urban development, through an overlay of politically imposed restrictions, reflects basic economic forces. One such force that becomes increasingly evident as cities grow and mature is *specialization of function.* As hamlets become towns and towns evolve into cities, real estate uses of like character tend increasingly to be concentrated in specific functional zones.

This tendency is evident not only among broad categories of use such as residential, industrial and commercial, but within these categories as well. Residential users tend to segregate themselves by social and economic class, resulting in distinct neighborhoods with highly stratified levels of housing size and quality. Within commercial districts there is also notable clustering of like uses.

Market-directed specialization and segregation of uses is, however, never absolute. Decisions about location are often a matter of trial and error, and mistakes are difficult to correct, due to the high cost of altering prior choices. Moreover, variations in the level of economic activity, combined with perpetual change in technology and lifestyles, constantly give birth to new economic motivations, rendering old choices suboptimal and creating maladjustments that lead to reassessment of previous decisions.

Subject to inconsistencies and anomalies induced by the prohibitive cost of making small adjustments, by errors in judgment and by the irrational element in human nature, land utilization in a market system is determined by efforts to extract economic returns. Space is leased to those who can pay the highest rent, and more-productive users can outbid their rivals. The ultimate consequence is an orderly pattern of land use that generates the greatest aggregate economic benefit for the community.

Of course, not all potential users compete directly for the same land. For example, although railroads and freeways detract from the desirability of adjacent locations as residential neighborhoods, factories and warehouses benefit from proximity to these transportation facilities. Low-priced homes are preferably built on a flat plain to minimize construction costs, but buyers of higher priced houses might pay a premium for the excellent view from a hillside location.

However, within broad ranges of potential uses, direct competition does take place. Where the competition is based primarily on economic considerations, the use that results in the greatest rent-paying capacity is that which wrings the most economic benefit from a site.

Although concentration is a natural adaptation to the need and desire to overcome the "friction" of space, decentralization is a normal and continuing counterforce necessitated by market forces. Low-intensity land users are forced out of central locations by those who benefit most from proximity to the center and can therefore afford to pay higher rental rates. Land use density thus tends to be highest at the center of development activity, the spot we characterize here as the "100 percent location." Progressively lower densities are encountered toward the development fringe.

Systematic Development Patterns

Economists are fond of creating abstract models to isolate key elements in economic relationships. These simplified representations of a complex world permit uncluttered concentration on issues chosen for closer examination. A classic example is Johann Heinrich Von Thunen's analysis, more than 170 years ago, of the effects of location on land utilization. In his book *The Isolated State,* he demonstrated how transportation costs affect land use, by assuming an isolated economic area comprised of an urban core surrounded by a flat rural plain. By assuming that climate, soil fertility and transportation facilities are uniform, Von Thunen freed his model from complications such as competing urban areas, aesthetic considerations and differential transportation costs per unit of distance traveled. His analysis held constant all factors except choice of market and land use. Under these circumstances, he demonstrated that land use choices are directly attributable to variations in transportation costs. He showed that the closer land lies to the central market, other things remaining constant, the more intensively it will be employed.[1]

Reasoning similar to Von Thunen's led early urban economists to describe idealized urban development in terms of concentric rings of relatively homogeneous uses, with progressively less intensive land use in the outer rings. Ernest W. Burgess attempted to fit this concentric ring model to the pattern of development existing in Chicago in the early 1920s.[2] Based upon intensity of land use, he argued that the central area will be dominated by financial firms and major retail stores. Outside the central zone will be found wholesaling and light manufacturing businesses, somewhat overlapping a third zone containing the homes of low-income residents. Beyond this will be a zone occupied by heavy manufacturing, which needs ready access to transportation routes to the outside world. Outer rings, he said, will be reserved for residential use, serving progressively wealthier users as distance from the center increases.

Burgess's version of the concentric ring model is designed to explain urban development as it existed in the 1920s, and readers will be hard-pressed to find the patterns today that Burgess detected. His fourth ring, the "zone of transition," in cities such as Chicago no longer contains a significant number of factories, being comprised instead of a mixture of abandoned buildings and redevelopment into middle-class residential structures. Much of industry has moved into what he categorized as the commuter's zone, leaping over residential areas that blocked the expansion of previous manufacturing facilities.

Limitations of the concentric ring model are obvious. Topography and specialized transportation corridors distort the circular pattern. Technology and lifestyle changes alter the relative intensity of land uses among various categories, thereby varying competitors' ability to bid for highly valued sites. Inner-circle users find their expansion needs frustrated by users in the next zone, and are forced to leapfrog to areas beyond.

Business Location Decisions

Market imperfections create substantial deviation from the pattern of land uses dictated by the need for efficiency in human affairs. But a systematic pattern suggestive of Von Thunen's and Burgess's models is nonetheless discernible in every urban area, reflecting the history of rational use decisions over a period of years.

As the single most convenient spot for the greatest number of people, the central business district is the logical place for firms drawing customers from throughout an area. Financial offices are sufficiently land-intensive to justify this area of highest land rents.

Outside the central business district, retail locations create divergent patterns of city structure. Many profit from locating along major traffic arteries, and create business thoroughfares at various locations throughout the city. Others benefit from mutual proximity; they cluster and thus create multiple nuclei or miniature downtowns throughout metropolitan areas.[3]

Businesses locating along major arterial streets create what has been described as a radial or axial development pattern, as illustrated in Figure 3.1. Thus, towns expand first along their major transportation arteries and then "flesh out" with residential and further commercial development in the interstices between these ribbons of growth.

Many businesses benefit from mutual proximity. Convenience shops seek locations adjacent to stores featuring shopping goods, to capture business from customers drawn by their neighbors. Stores carrying similar lines of merchandise frequently benefit from clustering because they collectively draw a larger crowd of shoppers than could any one of them in isolation. Since the early 1950s, real estate entrepreneurs have catered to these special needs of merchants by developing shopping centers that take on the dimensions of modest central business districts.

Why clusters of stores form multiple nuclei at particular locations depends upon such diverse factors as prevailing transportation patterns, the socioeconomic status of potential customers and even the availability of sufficient space. Once formed, the nuclei create peaks in local land values and frequently spawn axial developments of their own.

BID-RENT CURVES AND "NATURAL" ZONING

In the absence of rental charges, every business firm will seek a location that minimizes the costs of overcoming the friction of space. The need to move people and things between sites creates costs that tend to reduce a location's desirability. Ideally, closely linked activities would take place at the same site, thus reducing transfer costs to zero. This, of course, is seldom possible.

Linkages and Transfer Costs

In the course of their daily lives, people must constantly travel between various locations. Children travel from home to school, to the playground and enter-

Figure 3.1 | **Radial and Nodal Development Extends Outward from Central Area**

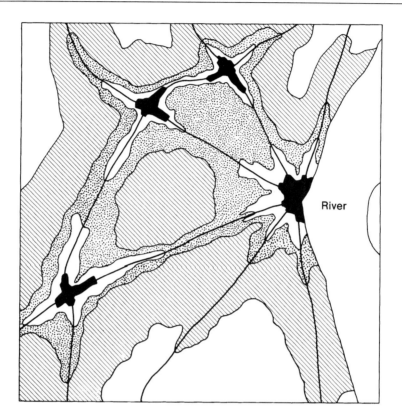

River

tainment facilities and so on. Adults travel between home and work. For many people, work itself takes place at a multitude of different sites. Entire families must travel for medical, dental and legal services, for shopping and entertainment and for a host of other activities.

Similarly, *things* must constantly be shuffled between various locations. Food moves from farms to processing plants to storage, thence to retail outlets and finally to homes or restaurants. Manufacturing processes start at farms or mines, from which raw materials might undergo processing at a variety of different locations before a finished product is moved to a retail location and finally to the site of consumption.

Relationships that require such movement are called *linkages,* and the locations between which people or things move are *linked sites.* Costs of transportation between linked sites are sometimes referred to as *transfer costs,* and may be either explicit or implicit.

Explicit transfer costs get the most attention, perhaps because they are easier to determine. These are costs measurable in dollars: cost per mile of the chosen transportation medium plus the dollar value of time spent en route.

Analysts sometimes err by ignoring or underestimating the importance of *implicit* transfer costs. Although more subtle and difficult to identify, they are no less significant than their explicit counterparts. They include the disutility of moving between linked sites, a cost that is not reflected on accounting statements. Examples include the fear of traveling through areas considered dangerous, and the aggravation and discomfort of coping with congested highways or public transportation facilities.

Linkages and Location of Industry

In addition to affecting the level of transfer costs, a firm's location decision might also affect processing costs. This occurs when a site has natural advantages due to soil fertility, a benign climate or some other natural endowment. Where processing costs are a major consideration, firms might accept considerable additional transfer costs to reduce their processing costs. Where processing costs are relatively minor or are not greatly affected by location, transfer costs become the prime factor in industrial location decisions. The key issue is that a wisely chosen location will minimize the sum of processing and transfer costs.

Figure 3.2 illustrates a "100 percent" location in the absence of differential rents, and the effect on operating costs other than rent as a business moves farther from the 100 percent location. Earlier, we observed that the 100 percent

| Figure 3.2 | Industrial Location Decisions with Constant Rent or No Rent |

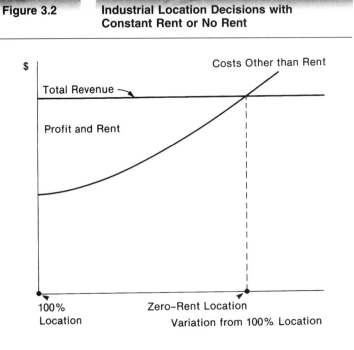

location is usually the center of development activity, where land is most intensely utilized. More precisely, we define it for any activity as the location where the net benefit would be greatest in the absence of rent (in the case of owner-occupants, in the absence of occupancy costs).

If revenue was unaffected by location, a convenient fiction we have incorporated into Figure 3.2, then the best location would be the one that minimizes all costs. Were no rental charges levied, the best location would be at the 100 percent location, the intersection of the axes on Figure 3.2. At that point, the excess of revenue over costs other than rent would be maximized.

Continuing the assumption that revenues are not affected by location, but dropping the assumption that all locations are either free or equally costly, location decisions hinge upon determining what variation from the 100 percent location will minimize the sum of rental charges and all other costs. Rent differentials are created by competition for space at or as close as possible to the 100 percent location. Firms that can benefit the most from the 100 percent location are able to outbid all others, forcing their competitors out into the area of Figure 3.2 between the 100 percent location and the zero-rent location.

An industrial location decision for a given rent gradient is illustrated in Figure 3.3. The firm's total cost at each location is the sum of costs other than rent, plus the rent charged at that site. The sum of these charges is illustrated by the total cost curve at the top of the figure. The optimum location for the firm depicted in Figure 3.3 is the one that minimizes total costs, including rent.

Figure 3.3   **Industrial Location Decisions with Rent Differentials**

Commercial Location Decisions

Firms whose sales are greatly affected by location decisions have more variables to consider. They must factor in transfer costs borne by their customers, shoppers who consider travel time and inconvenience when deciding which stores to visit. Even so, total transfer costs (regardless of who incurs them) determine the relative desirability of various sites. As with industrial firms, in the absence of rent (or the cost of property ownership), commercial firms will want the 100 percent location. But competition for that location drives up the rent there, and that results in a declining rent schedule as one moves farther from the location that would be most desirable in the absence of rent (the 100 percent location). This is illustrated in Figure 3.4, which shows rent and profit before rent declining with distance from the 100 percent location. The optimum location is the one that maximizes net profit: profit before rent, minus rent.

THE MARKET FOR RENTAL SPACE

We saw in Chapter 2 that markets perform the basic function of allocating resources among various users. Thus the interaction of supply-and-demand forces in the market for real estate assets channels property rights to the highest bidders. And, to the extent bid prices are based upon accurate appraisal of the

| Figure 3.4 | Retail Location Decisions |

stream of future benefits flowing from ownership, assets are acquired by users who can wring the greatest net benefit from their use.

Just as there is a market that allocates available ownership interests among various would-be users, so too is there a market that allocates real estate services (shelter and location benefits from occupancy). Competitive bids create the highest rents at what would otherwise be the most desirable location (the 100 percent location), and rents tend to decline as distance from the 100 percent location increases.

Market Adjustments

Reconsider Figure 3.4. The curve labeled "Profit Before Rent" represents the absolute maximum rent a firm with such a profile can pay and still find it worthwhile to remain in business. Where profit before rent drops below the rent gradient, commercial users are priced out of the market by others who can wring greater profit from the locations. Therefore, only the segment of the profit-before-rent curve that is above the rent gradient represents viable commercial locations. This segment is reproduced in Figure 3.5 and is labeled "Commercial Bid-Rent Curve." Were there no other bidders, commercial firms whose profit profiles are represented by this curve would occupy locations ranging from the 100 percent location outward to the point where the commercial bid-rent curve intersects the horizontal axis.

But, of course, there are other contenders for available sites. Firms whose revenues are less dependent upon being near the 100 percent location will not be able to outbid commercial endeavors for nearby locations. But the other firms' bid-rent curves will decline less abruptly with distance, so they will place win-

Figure 3.5   **Bid-Rent Curves and Natural Zoning**

ning bids for more distant sites. Figure 3.5 depicts the bid-rent curve for such an industry, labeled "Industrial Bid-Rent Curve." A third economic group might have a profit profile that generates bid-rent curves such as the one labeled "Agricultural Bid-Rent Curve."

Figure 3.5 reveals that commercial firms will outbid alternative users for space between the 100 percent location and point *a,* whereas industrial users will submit winning bids for the area between point *a* and point *b.* Beyond point *b,* other pursuits can afford to pay higher rents than either commercial or industrial firms. Thus, economic considerations will tend to segregate activities even without the formal zoning regulations adopted by most municipalities.

Because the market is not a perfect allocator of resources, there will be some overlapping of uses, particularly near points *a* and *b* in Figure 3.5. These points represent the locus of zones of transition between predominant uses. This is the economic rationale underlying the concentric ring and the multiple nuclei patterns of urban development discussed earlier.

MARKET STRUCTURE AND THE NEED FOR MARKET RESEARCH

If the real estate market were atomistic (if buyers and sellers, landlords and tenants, were all price takers), there would be little need for market research. Energy would be expended primarily on cost control.

In at least one aspect, though, all real estate is a differentiated product; each site is unique with respect to its exact location. The significance of this distinction differs from situation to situation. Parcels that are somehow unique might command a considerable rent premium. The difference may lie in architectural aesthetics, construction quality, luxurious appointments or any other element that creates a compelling image for tenants.

Distinctions that exist only in the perception of tenants may be far more valuable than actual physical differences. Styling, quality of construction and functional features can be duplicated by competitors, but reputation is unique to individual properties and often is generated consciously to appeal to a specific class of tenant. Depending on the image associated with the address, a property may command premium rents or sell at a discount from prevailing rates for similarly located and outfitted space.

Price searchers who have access to better market intelligence than that available to their competitors may benefit substantially. If they can discern what locations will afford competitive advantages to tenants in the near future, they can acquire title to appropriate parcels before such information is reflected in prices. If they are able to forecast changes in location advantage accurately over the years, they can more precisely estimate a new property's investment value. Comparing investment value with market values that do not yet reflect all pertinent information will enable astute researchers and analysts to consistently outperform the market. It is for this reason that Part Two of the book is devoted to market research.

SUMMARY

Property owners who rent their space to users are in effect selling a service that is comprised of shelter and location. In many cases, the rental rate a property commands is substantially determined by its location; the more desirable the location, the greater the rent per square foot. At progressively more remote locations, both density of use and rental rates tend to decline. This pattern is distorted by the fact that, once a building has been constructed, the most economically advantageous use of the site might be entirely different than if it was still vacant.

Relationships requiring movement of people or things between sites are called linkages. Sites between which movement occurs are said to be linked, and the cost of movement is called *transfer costs.* Space users strive to locate so as to minimize the total cost of rent plus aggregate transfer costs.

Because the market for real estate rental space is relatively inefficient, property owners or managers who are more adept at market research frequently are able to consistently differentiate their product and thereby command premium rents. They are thus able to reap above-average profits. The advantage tends to disappear as competitors become aware and rush to produce close substitutes for the space noted to be in high demand. Constant market research is needed, therefore, to find new sources of product differentiation in order to perpetuate high yields.

NOTES

1. Johann Heinrich Von Thunen, *Der Isolierte Staat,* 1826. For an English translation, see Peter Hall, ed., *Von Thunen's Isolated State* (London: Pergamon Press, 1966).

2. Ernest W. Burgess, "The Growth of the City," in Robert Park et al., *The City* (Chicago: University of Chicago Press, 1994).

3. Richard U. Ratcliff describes these patterns as string street developments and nucleation. See Richard U. Ratcliff, *Real Estate Analysis* (New York: McGraw-Hill, 1961).

RECOMMENDED READINGS

Bradley, David M. "The Laws of Real Estate Dynamics." *The Appraisal Journal,* vol. 54, no. 3 (July 1990) pp. 314–323.

DePasquale, Denise, and William C. Wheaton. *Urban Economics and Real Estate Markets.* Englewood Cliffs, NJ: Prentice-Hall, 1996, Chapters 2 through 65.

Pittman, Robert H., and Maury Seldin. "Real Estate Analysis Using Geographic Data." *Real Estate Issues,* vol. 15, no. 1 (Spring-Summer 1990) pp. 32–38.

Ratcliff, Richard U. *Real Estate Analysis.* New York: McGraw-Hill, 1961, pp. 13–41.

Ratcliff, Richard U. *Valuation for Real Estate Decisions.* Santa Cruz, CA: Democrat Press, 1972, pp. 15–48.

Weber, Bruce R. "Application of Geographic Information Systems to Real Estate Market Analysis and Appraisal." *The Appraisal Journal,* vol. 58, no. 1 (January 1990) pp. 127–132.

REVIEW QUESTIONS

1. What are the limitations of the concentric ring hypothesis as developed by Von Thunen and Burgess?
2. Explain the concept of linkages.
3. How is land utilization determined in a market system?
4. Explain the axial development pattern of cities and the multiple nuclei pattern.
5. What are explicit and implicit transfer costs?
6. What should an industry consider in selecting a location?
7. How do transfer costs affect commercial location decisions?
8. What is the effect on the quantity of rental space in a market area and prevailing market rents, over the short run and the long run, of shifts in demand for rentable space?

DISCUSSION QUESTIONS

1. If you were designing a city to be built on virgin land, to what extent might you copy the pattern suggested by Von Thunen and Burgess? Why might you choose a different pattern and what would your alternate pattern be?
2. Think of a regional or super-regional shopping mall in your city as a central business district, and try to apply what you have read to explain the pattern of adjacent development since the mall was created.
3. Since, by their influence on land values, market forces tend to create "zones" of specialized land uses, what purpose is served by legal zoning? What are some reasons citizens might prefer regulated rather than market-determined land use patterns?

4. A land acquisition specialist for a discount store chain said that when his firm decides to enter a new market, it buys or leases the three best store locations in the area, uses the best one for its new store and makes certain that the other two sites are used only for noncompeting purposes. Discuss this in terms of the text's explanation of bid-rent curves and natural zoning.

PART ONE: Case Problems

1. Suppose the demand curve for "class A" office space in the metropolitan area were as follows.

Rental rate (per square foot)	Quantity demanded (millions of square feet)
$20	3.0
21	2.9
22	2.8
23	2.7
24	2.6
25	2.5
26	2.4

   a. Suppose also the quantity of "class A" office space in the area is 2.9 million square feet. If no market participant is in a Position to affect the market price, and all relevant information is readily available to all market participants, what will be the generally prevailing rental rate per square foot for office space of this class over the short term?

   b. Suppose a new investor enters the market, buys several office buildings and announces that rent will be $23 per square foot for all new tenants and for all lease renewals. What will be the short-term impact on his gross rental income:

   1. If he controls three percent of the office space in this market area?

   2. If he controls 50 percent of the office space in this market?

2. Sterling Silverspoon purchased a parking lot ten years ago for $100,000. He has earned an average annual net operating income of $14,000 and is now considering selling the parking lot. Millicent Mum likes the

parking lot's location and initiates negotiation for its purchase. Silverspoon points out that the city has recently increased parking fees at municipal lots and observes that fees can now be raised on this lot sufficiently to move the net operating income to about $20,000 annually. He notes that the $14,000 per year he has been earning represents a 14 percent per annum return on his investment. He thinks this is a good yield and states that Mum can do equally well, based on the anticipated $20,000 per annum net operating income, by paying about $144,000 for the lot. Mum retorts that Silverspoon will have an assured rate of return once the lot is sold but that Mum will be taking a risk that the anticipated cash flow will not materialize. Therefore, says Mum, she should earn a premium. She suggests an 18 percent yield and offers a price of about $111,000. Both parties earnestly state their desire to be fair and equitable in establishing a price for this property, but they are at odds as to how a price might best be determined. What do you suggest?

3. An office park manager experiments with rental rates and finds that every one percent change in per-square-foot rental rates induces a 1.05 percent change (in the opposite direction) in the amount of rented space. Rents are currently $8 per square foot and occupancy is at 90 percent. Fixed operating expenses (those that do not vary with occupancy level) are $3 per square foot; variable operating expenses (assume they vary directly with occupancy level) are $1 per square foot of occupied space. Total space available is 100,000 square feet.

Assuming the relationship between rental rates and occupancy levels remains invariant at all levels, what rental rate will maximize net operating income (revenue minus operating expenses)?

PART TWO

Market Research and Cash-Flow Forecasting

Real estate investment is an expression of belief in a property's income-generating potential. Cash from operations and from eventual resale are the investor's only material benefits; both are dependent upon the property's ability to command rent. If rental income proves short-lived, market value will plummet and there will be no cash from either source. Thus, in a very real sense investors buy a set of assumptions about a property's ability to produce income.

For that reason, consistently successful investment decisions require an accurate perception of the property's ability to command rent, and reliable analysis incorporates a healthy dose of market research. Part One laid the foundation for such research by explaining how economic forces determine supply-and-demand relationships, the interaction of which sets market-clearing rental rates and property values. Part Two relates these concepts to discrete real estate parcels and the expectations of specific real estate investors.

Chapter 4 introduces tools and techniques for market research, and gives examples of supply and demand analysis. Chapter 5 explains the typical format for reconstructing a property's operating history and extending the analysis into an operating forecast. The payoff, presented in Chapter 6, is a multiple-year forecast of net operating income and an estimate of market value at the end of the forecast period.

CHAPTER 4

Market Research Tools and Techniques

Real estate investment decision-making is essentially a matter of interpreting information about the real estate market in general and the subject parcel in particular, and about the investor who must make a decision. First, however, the information must be collected and organized in a coherent manner. G. Vincent Barrett and John P. Blair have called market research the most difficult and the most consequential part of the real estate development planning process.[1] Their observation is equally true for the real estate investment decision-making process.

THE NEED FOR MARKET RESEARCH

Investors and portfolio managers need market information at every stage in their decision making. They must, for example, estimate the most likely cash flow from each investment alternative and each potential deal structure. They need to know yields available in the marketplace so that cash-flow estimates can be adjusted intelligently for differences in the timing and certainty of expected receipt.

Market Research for Portfolio Decisions

Periodically, every portfolio should be reevaluated and adjusted based on market information. Managers must decide whether to keep the properties that are now in the portfolio, or to adjust the mix. If their decision is to adjust, they must decide how to divest themselves of existing assets (for example, an outright sale, a sale and leaseback, or an exchange). If no divestiture is indicated, they must nevertheless judge whether to refinance, to refurbish or to convert property to a different use. All these decisions depend on the same variables as acquisition decisions, and all require market information.

Market Research for Better Property Management

Market research is also needed to facilitate operating management decisions. Gilbert A. Churchill, Jr., notes that research information is used by operating management for planning, problem solving and control purposes.[2]

As a planning tool, market research can identify opportunities and budding problems. Property managers need to know basic trends in the economic environment within which they must lease and administer rental space, so they can estimate how the trends will affect their operations. Research might reveal, for example, that changing income levels, consumption patterns and work practices will radically alter space needs. This information, in tandem with data on competitive rents, will aid them in setting appropriate rent schedules and advertising budgets.

Market research helps in identifying alterations that will enhance a property's rentability. Information about present and potential tenants' needs and preferences might reveal that some amenities should be phased out because they do not generate enough additional rent to cover their operating and maintenance costs, while others should be added to make the building more competitive. Research helps in deciding whether to lease space on a long-term or a short-term basis, and which lease clauses are likely to meet with least tenant resistance. It indicates what tenant mix will maximize a property's ability to command rents. Should an office building cater to tenants in a specific profession such as law or medicine, for example, or will a more diverse tenant mix lead to lower vacancy rates and greater operating income?

Control-oriented market research permits early identification of existing and potential management trouble spots. Good research helps management assess the quality of current building operations and evaluate proposed changes. By comparing building rental and vacancy rates with those of comparable properties, for example, management can evaluate its marketing program; comparing tenant turnover rates will highlight the degree of tenant satisfaction. Comparative operating expense ratios (expenses as a percent of gross rents) helps management spot operating inefficiencies and permits early corrective action.

HOW MUCH MARKET RESEARCH?

Three basic factors determine the extent to which market research will be worthwhile for investment decision-making: the stability of market conditions, the complexity of the property involved and investors' tolerance for risk. The more stable the market, the less will be the need for data collection and analysis; the larger and more complex the property, the greater will be the need. The exact trade-off between spending time and money to refine the analysis, or economizing by accepting greater uncertainty, depends upon the investors' risk tolerance.

The Role of Prevailing Market Conditions

In a market where supply and demand are in stable equilibrium, very little market research would be warranted; perhaps nothing more than reference to current rental and vacancy rates, and some analysis of the relationship between net operating income and market values would be needed. All these factors can be expected to change over time, but if the changes proceed smoothly and thus predictably, the refinement that additional research permits may not be worth the cost.

But suppose the neighborhood is undergoing change, perhaps a transition from predominately residential to mixed residential and commercial use. The pace of the change and its likely impact on ability to command rent must be analyzed. The likelihood of a successful transition for the subject property, and its most appropriate commercial use, must be investigated.

If vacancy rates are near historically high or low levels, a trend reversal may be sudden and sharp; investors need market information to gauge its likelihood and probable severity. When construction activity is proceeding at a frenetic pace, national or local politics are in a state of flux, or internal migratory patterns are changing noticeably, it may be necessary to collect a substantial amount of data, and to analyze those data extensively, in order to estimate impacts on local real estate markets.

The Role of Complexity

For a fairly simple investment proposition such as a small and smoothly operating apartment building in a stable community, the need for market analysis may be minimal. The property's operating history might be an adequate guide to its future, and prevailing relationships between operating income and market values might be all that one needs to estimate market value at the end of the proposed investment period.

But suppose the investor must choose between buying or trading. Or that the seller is offering a property that has more than one prospective use, and the most profitable use is uncertain. A seller might offer a mortgage loan where the credit terms will affect the transaction price. In all these instances, market data and extensive analysis will be needed. The general rule is, the more complex the proposed arrangement, the greater is the need for market research.

Complexity is often correlated with property size. Investment in a small strip shopping center that has been fully developed and is 100 percent leased, warrants less attention to data collection and analysis than does investment in a regional shopping center that is still in the proposal stage and is to be developed in an untested market.

The Cost-Benefit Trade-off

Carefully planned and appropriately executed market research will always push back the curtain of uncertainty. Its value depends to a large extent on the investor's attitude toward risk. Investors who are more comfortable with ambiguity will make decisions with less information. Those who find uncertainty disquieting will expend more resources in search of predictability, even though the cost of the effort might reduce their portfolio's ultimate profitability. Either strategy is reasonable, providing investors understand the relationship between incremental research costs and benefits.

This issue is illustrated in Figure 4.1. Expected total costs of research and its expected total value are measured on the vertical axis, the vertical distance between the cost and benefit functions represents net benefit derived (benefit minus cost). Maximum net benefit results from the amount of research and analysis represented by point m on the horizontal axis. Additional data gathering and analysis beyond this point costs more than its incremental benefit, and reduces the net benefit from market research.

Figure 4.1   Cost, Benefit and Optimum Level of Research Effort

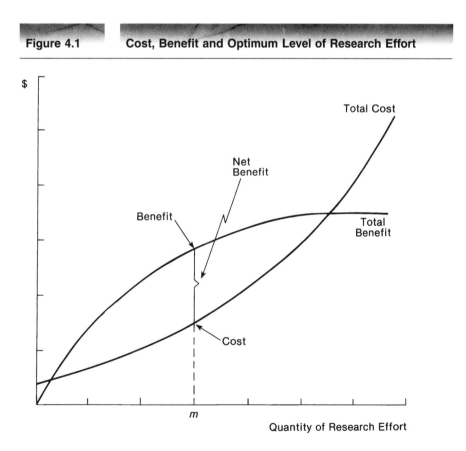

Avoiding Analysis Paralysis

Since the payoff from research is not objectively measurable, decision makers will be sorely challenged to identify the optimum level. James D. Vernor has observed that research proceeds in successive iterations with each round becoming increasingly more complex and costly.[3] Beginning with readily available information incorporated into crude financial synthesis such as first-year ratio analysis, the investigation progresses to successively more detailed data collection and elaborate financial analysis.

However the dilemma is faced, some market intelligence must be gathered before substantial resources are committed to an uncertain venture. But there is some point beyond which research and analysis must cease and a "go or no-go" decision must be made. The problem is phrased succinctly by George Bernard Shaw: "When we have done our utmost to arrive at a reasonable conclusion, we . . . must close our minds for the moment with a snap, and act dogmatically on our own conclusion. The man who waits to make an entirely reasonable will dies intestate."

A DESIGN FOR MARKET RESEARCH

Because investment dilemmas are not uniform, research procedures must be custom-tailored. Yet, even though each project has its own special emphasis, all share a common sequence of steps. The problem to be solved or the question to be answered should be carefully formulated before any data are gathered, because the nature of the problem will largely determine the information to be assembled. Data collection and analysis then proceeds from a broad macro level to an increasingly specific or micro level.

Problem Formulation

As with most of life's dilemmas, carefully defining the investment problem takes one a long way toward its solution. Gilbert Churchill summarized the importance of problem formulation this way.[4]

> One of the more valuable roles marketing research can perform is helping to define the problem to be solved. Only when the problem is carefully and precisely defined can research be designed to provide pertinent information. Part of the process of problem definition includes specifying the objectives of the specific research project or projects that might be undertaken. Each project should have one or more objectives, and the next step in the process should not be taken until these can be explicitly stated.

Data Collection and Analysis

The generally recommended research approach is to work from the general to the specific, starting with an analysis of national and international economic trends (to the extent their consideration is relevant) and working down through metropolitan and neighborhood trends to an analysis of the prospects for the specific property that is the subject of the effort. This sequence is illustrated in Table 4.1.

The first level involves collecting and analyzing relevant national and international economic trends. This involves assessing the impact of economic aggregates such as Federal Reserve monetary policy and government fiscal policy. These should be related to regional and metropolitan economic indicators, to see how local and metropolitan trends might deviate from national trends over the forecast period.

At the regional and metropolitan level, in addition to economic indicators the analyst should collect demographic trend data: information on such factors as population, employment, household size and purchasing power, that will impact on the demand for real estate. Political data that have an impact on real estate supply and demand (examples include local officials' attitudes toward economic growth, business location incentives, local tax policy, and the threat of rent controls) become important at this level.

The objective is to recognize patterns and to spot clues as to how these patterns might change, to relate the patterns to likely future trends. For this, real estate market analysts will generally rely on forecasts produced by individuals and firms that specialize in broad market analysis. Such forecasts are widely available at modest cost; often they are free.

As the focus shifts from overall macro-level analysis to an increasingly specific micro level, reliable information becomes progressively scarce. At this point, the analyst works with the observed relationships between available trends and projections for wider market areas, in order to derive estimates for the neighborhood, trade or market area within which the specific property will compete for tenants.

Table 4.1	Sequential Components of Market Analysis

1. Analyze national and international economic trends (especially inflation, interest rates and the rate of economic growth) that influence local real estate investment conditions.
2. Consider regional and metropolitan economic, demographic and political trends that are relevant to the investment opportunity.
3. Delineate specific geographic boundaries of the neighborhood, trade or market area within which the subject property will directly compete with peer-group properties.
4. Analyze potential tenant demand within the neighborhood, trade or market area, for the specific type of rental property under consideration. Project demand over the forecast period.
5. Identify and analyze competitive (peer group) properties in the neighborhood, trade or market area.
6. Estimate potential additions to the supply of competing properties in the neighborhood, trade or market area over the forecast period. Estimate the subject property's *fair share* of projected demand (projected submarket supply divided by projected submarket demand).
7. Compare the subject property's characteristics with tenant needs and with the characteristics of present and projected competing properties, to estimate probable changes in market share over the forecast period (this is an estimate of the *capture rate,* the percentage of total submarket demand the subject property is likely to secure).

Research objectives at the submarket level are to determine supply-and-demand relationships as they currently exist for the type of rental property under analysis, and to forecast them over the period of the proposed investment. Relationships for the wider regional or metropolitan market are of little direct use, because a specific property will compete with only a limited portion of the wider market. Strip shopping centers, for example, do not compete with large regional malls, and a small suburban office building will seldom compete with office high-rises in the central business district. Submarkets exist because tenants and investors perceive differences in property location, rental rates, property size, building age, condition or design, or other characteristics that make one property more or less desirable than others, and decide which are reasonable substitutes for each other.

A Four-Quadrant Forecasting Matrix

The dilemma is that a wealth of data are available regarding current conditions and for forecasting future conditions in the wider (macro) market, but the goal is to estimate future conditions as they affect a specific property, which may be influenced by only a limited portion of the wider market. We need a technique for proceeding from available regional and metropolitan market data to a forecast regarding that limited portion of the market in which the subject property directly competes.

A four-quadrant matrix such as that illustrated in Figure 4.2 is often used to illustrate the problem. Information about present and historical market conditions in the region or the metropolitan area will generally be available, it fills in the upper-left quadrant. More often than not, similar data have been incorporated into forecasts, and this goes in the upper-right quadrant. Data for the lower-left quadrant, the subject property's share in market rental revenue, its physical characteristics and those of peer-group properties, as well as demographic and

Figure 4.2	Four-Quadrant Forecasting Model

	Present	Future
Regional or City-Wide	C Current and Historical Economic and Demographic Vacancies, Rent	A/D Forecast Economic and Demographic Vacancies, Rent
Specific Property and Immediate Market Area	B Physical Characteristics Demand Characteristics Rent and Vacancies Market Share Estimate	E Property Performance Forecast

socioeconomic characteristics of tenants, is less readily available but can be collected. The challenge is to use the data that relate directly to the property and its market area, which are directly applicable but incomplete, and the data from the region or metropolitan area, which are more extensive but not directly applicable, to develop a micro-level forecast in the lower-right quadrant. Dowel Myers and Kenneth Beck have suggested a detailed approach for navigating the matrix to generate a usable forecast of relevant supply and demand variables in the lower-right quadrant.[5] A synopsis of their strategy is presented here, and is related to Figure 4.2 by using alphabetical indicators for each step.

A. Macro-forecasts of economic aggregates such as regional or metropolitan employment, income, growth rates and demographic composition, have often been generated by other researchers, and the investment analyst will seldom have the resources to prepare a more reliable forecast. These provide the initial market forecast for the upper-right quadrant.
B. Collect physical, economic and demographic information relating to the subject property and peer-group properties (data for the lower-left quadrant) and organize it in a fashion that relates it directly to the available macro-level forecast. Vacancy rates and the rate of change in rental rates, for example, are likely to be functionally related to construction activity and population change.
C. Link the reorganized data for the subject and peer-group properties (the lower-left quadrant data) to similar data for the region or metropolitan area (the upper-left quadrant). For example, relate metropolitan rental and vacancy rates to rental and vacancy rates for the subject and the peer-group properties: When market-wide vacancy or average rental rates change, do the same measures for the subject and its peers change by a lesser or a greater amount? Quantify the observed relationship.
D. Forecast relevant regional or metropolitan variables such as rental and vacancy rates by using observed past relationships between these and other regional or metropolitan variables (such as construction activity, and demographic and economic trends) that have been included in available macro-forecasts. This pushes the relevant variables from the upper-left into the upper-right quadrant.
E. Relate the forecast of relevant regional or metropolitan variables such as vacancies and rental rates that have been pushed into the upper-right quadrant to the same variables for the subject and its peer-group properties, by using the observed past relationship and incorporating any observed trend in the relationships. This pulls the relevant property-specific variables into the lower-right quadrant.

PREPARING THE RESEARCH REPORT

The research report summarizes procedures and reports conclusions. It must be clear, complete, accurate and precise. The report will be only as good as the underlying data and analysis, but no matter how thorough the research or insightful the analysis, it will not be successful unless effectively communicated.

There is a temptation to concentrate on regional or metropolitan data, which are likely to be plentiful, and to skimp on project-specific analysis, where data are generally lacking. One result is reports that bulge with national, regional and metropolitan data, with little or no explanation of how the data relate to the impending investment decision.

At the broadest level, most reports should be limited to bare-bones reporting of trends that will have an impact on supply or demand variables for the subject property (those incorporated into the four-quadrant analysis illustrated on Figure 4.2). As the analysis proceeds to progressively disaggregated levels (from national to submarket and property-specific considerations) it should become progressively more detailed. At every level, all data included in the report should be directly related to the problem the analysis is designed to solve or the question it is designed to answer.

There is no such thing as *the* correct report format. Appropriate organization and presentation depends upon the nature of the problem and the user's needs. Many variations are possible; Table 4.2 presents a general outline of what a complete market analysis report might contain.

Table 4.2   **Outline for a Market Analysis Report**

I. *Executive Summary.* Succinctly state the objectives of the analysis and the analytical methods, data sources, assumptions and conclusions. The executive summary will be the only part of a report that many decision-makers will read. It should be sufficiently specific to alert readers to the key issues and explain how findings were derived.

II. *Overview.* Present an analysis of relevant economic and demographic trends at the national, regional and metropolitan levels, and explain how they relate to demand and supply in the submarket area.

III. *Submarket Delineation and Site Analysis.* Define submarket boundaries and summarize site-specific data (a physical description of site attributes such as the desirability of the location relative to competing properties, the site's geographic orientation and physical features, and the nature, age and condition of the improvements) that bear on the property's competitive position.

IV. *Analysis of Demand.* Project overall demand in the submarket area for property such as the subject. Draw conclusions about absorption rates—the rate at which new and existing vacant space will be taken by tenants.

V. *Analysis of Supply.* Survey the existing stock of competing space and analyze past trends, the current environment and likely future changes, to derive a forecast of the future supply.

VI. *Competitive Analysis.* Compare the subject property's features and advantages with those of existing and projected future competitive properties.

VII. *Forecast Rental Revenue.* Draw conclusions about competitive strengths and weaknesses over the forecast period, and estimate changes in rental rates and market share. Present final estimates of rental rates, vacancy factors and gross rental revenue. If the project is new or is to be rehabilitated, estimate the total marketing time required to achieve stable occupancy levels.

DATA SOURCES

Once the problem is properly defined and clearly specified, researchers logically turn their attention to data collection. At this point, a decision must be made to rely on primary or secondary sources. Primary data are gathered by the researcher precisely for the problem at hand. Secondary data, in contrast, have been previously gathered for some other purpose. A good operating rule is to rely on primary sources only if secondary data are not available.

Secondary Data

Where available, secondary data are almost certain to be less costly and less time-consuming to collect than are primary data. Information that is readily available free of charge in nearby libraries or at modest cost from research firms might cost thousands of dollars and require weeks of effort for a primary researcher to gather. Because this information can be used an infinite number of times until it becomes dated, firms that collect and sell it can reap a tidy profit while charging a small fraction of what it would cost their customers to do their own primary research.

One disadvantage of secondary sources, and a major cause of users' frustration, is that the data are seldom available in precisely the desired form. Units of measure may be inappropriate for the intended purpose, class definitions seldom exactly fit analysts' needs, and the information is seldom as current as one would like. None of these shortcomings are necessarily fatal; reorganizing and updating the information is usually less costly and less time consuming than starting from scratch.

Secondary data are frequently available in raw form from sources that gather them. These include government agencies, universities and private firms (real estate appraisers, brokers and counselors, market research firms, architects, accounting firms and so forth) whose data needs lead them to investigate phenomena of interest to real estate investment analysts. Their data files can save many days of tedious work and costly hours of field investigation. Large commercial data banks (companies that specialize in collecting and reselling information) often have computerized storage and retrieval facilities that permit them to provide information in almost any format and in a variety of classifications, at modest cost.

At the national, regional and metropolitan levels, data constipation is more likely than information starvation. An inundation of data makes it difficult to decide what is appropriate and what is mere window dressing. The sheer volume of statistical information from government and private sources is intimidating. One's best ally is likely to be a research librarian on the staff of a metropolitan or university library. Having made a career of navigating the data thicket, librarians can aim researchers at the right sources. Because the librarian might be a veritable Niagara of general information yet know nothing about real estate, the researcher must be prepared to clearly outline the search parameters. A mismatch between the analyst's needs and what a librarian thinks is needed can initiate a frustrating trip through a madhouse of useless information, a data inundation in which one might metaphorically drown.

The U.S. Bureau of the Census, under the Department of Commerce, is the largest data-gathering agency in the nation. Census data are generally of high quality and are available in a variety of formats, permitting researchers to create their own formats and classifications. Census data tapes or compact disks (CD-ROM) can be purchased from the Bureau of the Census. They are available for use free of charge at most larger metropolitan and state university libraries.

While less prolific than the Census Bureau, other federal agencies are also hooked on data generation. The Department of Labor, the Department of Housing and Urban Development, the various Federal Reserve Banks and a host of other taxpayer-supported institutions are data-generating engines.

State and metropolitan governments' data collection brooms have a narrower sweep, but they are no less thorough. School enrollments, sales tax collections, building permits, highway traffic volume—these are representative data series that have tremendous research value in real estate and are readily available from government agencies. Much of this is stored in public and university libraries, often on microfilm. All data will be cataloged and made available for fingertip retrieval under the guidance of a competent research librarian.

Private information storehouses rival those of government agencies, and are often in a more useful format for real estate market analysis. Once again, it helps to know exactly what one wants before contacting a prospective source. Unlike the government, private sources are under no obligation to make their data public. They are likely to do so only as a professional accommodation, or for a fee.

A host of data storage and retrieval firms earn a living off the mountain of data generated by government and private sources. They do this by reorganizing the information and offering it in a more usable form, often coupled with a forecast generated by extending observed trends. Computerized data storage, processing and retrieval efficiencies, and their large volume of business, enable many of the firms to sell custom-ordered reports at relatively modest prices. The reliability of their small-area forecasts varies widely, however.

Offering to share data with firms active in the submarket area of interest might shake loose information from initially reluctant sources. While raw data might be confidential, and sharing it a violation of confidence from the various sources, researchers can offer to provide a summary of their findings. The key is to know where the information is likely to be, and to have the interpersonal skills and investigative persistence to ferret it out.

Primary Data

Secondary sources sometimes prove inadequate. The data may be hopelessly outdated, unreliable or inappropriately classified. It then becomes necessary to resort to primary data sources to update, supplement, validate or supplant the secondary sources.

Primary data may be gathered by communication or by observation, with the choice usually dictated by the nature of the intelligence desired. Communication involves asking questions. These may be oral or written and can elicit responses in either form. They may be short and to the point, or they might involve in-depth interviews. Observation means checking and recording relevant facts or behavior. For example, a researcher might estimate the boundaries of a store's trade area by checking customers' license plates and noting their counties of origin.

Communication is a more versatile technique than is observation. Whatever it is the researchers want to know, all they have to do is ask. This makes communication faster and more cost-effective for most purposes. Researchers are not forced to wait for events to occur so that they can be observed.

There is, of course, a constant concern about the accuracy of responses. Respondents may be inclined to say what they believe their interrogators want to hear. Responses are also influenced by how questions are structured, and sometimes by the interviewer's demeanor.

Data collected by observation are more likely to be objective and factual. The subject's perceptions play less of a role, and conclusions are likely to be more reliable. Observation tends to be more time-consuming, however, and therefore more expensive.

DESCRIPTIVE RESEARCH

Much of the primary research data needed by real estate investment analysts is descriptive in nature. Examples include:

- *Tenant Profile.* Based on information gathered from tenants in similar buildings, one might attempt to describe the profile of a most likely tenant for a proposed structure, characterizing the tenant with respect to amenities desired, amount of space taken and special facilities required.
- *Consumer/Resident Profile.* One may wish to estimate the proportion of people in a specific population who behave in a particular manner. To illustrate, it might be necessary to estimate the percentage of residents within a certain radius of a proposed shopping center who would shop at the complex.
- *Estimated Reactions to Proposed Alterations in Rental Terms.* This could include changes in the length of leases or the relative degree to which rent depends upon a flat fee versus a percentage-lease clause. One might also wish to estimate typical reactions to separating rental rates for basic facilities and rates for special amenities, such as swimming pools and health club facilities.

Planning for Descriptive Research

Before starting the collection process, clearly specify who is to contribute information, what information is to be collected, and when it is to be solicited. Decide in advance where and how interviews will be conducted. Also in advance, work out an efficient cataloging system.

Doing all this work in advance often unearths analytical problems that might otherwise surface during data collection or after all the interviews have been conducted. A dummy table of cataloged variables (or a computer data storage and retrieval program), fully worked out in advance leaves only the task of actually collecting the information and recording it in the catalog space or the computer data bank provided. With this precaution, for example, researchers are less likely to overlook a crucial variable that should have been included in the data program; they are even less likely to fall into the common trap of gathering information that may be interesting in its own right but does not prove useful for solving the research problem.

Cross-Sectional and Time Series Data

Descriptive surveys may be *cross-sectional* or *time series.* Cross-sectional surveys, which involve a one-time sampling from a population of research interest, are by far the most frequently encountered type of data collection assignment. All elements are measured at a single point in time. The cross-sectional survey thus provides a snapshot of the variables under observation at the time of the survey.

Time series, in contrast, measure changes over time. Sometimes called *longitudinal studies,* they involve repeated measures of the same phenomena, recording any variation through time. Time series analysis in no way implies that time itself is a causal factor in observed change. Rather, the analyst observes changes in the phenomena of interest and other factors presumed to bear a causal relationship.

Inferential Analysis

Modern statistical techniques are a powerful addition to the analyst's repertoire of analytical tools. They permit rapid and inexpensive analysis and synthesis of masses of data. They also permit reliable generalizations to be drawn from a limited sample.

Statistics have received an undeserved reputation for requiring high-order mathematical skills. Deriving or proving fundamental rules (mathematicians call them *theorems*) may require daunting degrees of knowledge; applying generally accepted techniques is an entirely different matter. The most commonly employed statistical tools require no more knowledge of arithmetic than might be acquired in a typical high school. What is needed is an understanding of the statistical relationships themselves: their strengths and weaknesses, their uses and potential misuses.

This makes statistical analysis particularly valuable for market research, where conclusions about consumer preferences must be drawn from questionnaires distributed to only a small proportion of the total market or where predictions about the future must be based on past trends.

Statistical applications divide conveniently into two broad categories. *Descriptive statistics* involve measuring characteristics that are important to a problem and bringing them together in summary form. Descriptive statistics employ quantitative expressions to describe characteristics of a sample or an underlying population. Knowledgeable and busy analysts appreciate the inexpensive and timely reduction of large masses of data to essentials.

Inferential statistics involve drawing conclusions from evidence contained in the data. Real estate analysts frequently use such techniques to draw inferences about a general class of phenomena from a small sample or to estimate future occurrences by studying data from the recent past.

GEOGRAPHIC INFORMATION SYSTEMS

Much of the data employed in real estate investment analysis is *spatially related:* analysts are concerned not simply with *how much* or *what kind,* but also with *where.* Examples of spatially related data of particular interest include topological features such as streets, zoning, traffic density, population density, income levels, spending patterns, population age distribution, household size and so forth.

The traditional way of presenting spatially related information has been with transparent overlays that are layered one after another on a map of the market area. This cumbersome but effective technique lets analysts see how each key variable relates spatially to the property under analysis, and permits limited "what-if" speculation by using overlays with various trend projections. In recent years, the technique has been rendered more versatile and more effective by the advent of powerful and relatively inexpensive computers.

Computerization has also given this technique a new name: *geographic information systems,* or GIS. The computerized technique, called *spatial modeling,* permits layered data to be retrieved from a data storage system and directly displayed on a computer screen or a printed map. An example is illustrated in Figure 4.3.

A spatially related model might, for example, display all geographic areas where residents live more than ten minutes' driving time from a shopping center, and show population densities in each area. Or all vacant commercial-zoned parcels of more than 12,000 square feet that face on a major traffic artery might be displayed if they are within one mile of population concentrations that contain at least, for example, 1,000 households.

These same data could be displayed on a map with population growth and the growth in traffic density projected forward for a number of years. This would highlight sites with potential for significant market improvement, in many cases before the potential is reflected in market prices.

Until very recently, the technology for GIS required expensive computer systems, and operators who were highly trained specialists. Moreover, accumu-

Figure 4.3   **GIS: Map Overlays, Referenced to an Underlying Grid**

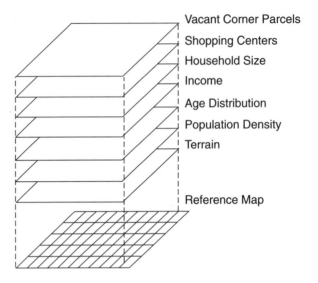

Vacant Corner Parcels
Shopping Centers
Household Size
Income
Age Distribution
Population Density
Terrain

Reference Map

lating relevant data and loading it into computer memory was expensive and time consuming. Simpler programs, coupled with expanded computer speed and capacity, now permit GIS to be run on personal computers. Many of the programs written for personal computers can import data files from the Census Bureau's TIGER (Topologically Integrated Geographically Encoded Reference) System, which contains spatially related information on income, age, race, sex, households, and so forth. TIGER System data are available on CD-ROM disks and can be purchased from the Bureau of the Census. They are also available at most major libraries.

Many commercial vendors sell related information sets that are decomposed to the level of census tracts and blocks or post office ZIP codes. For larger metropolitan areas the data are often further available for ZIP code plus an additional four-digits that further decompose the geographic area. These data sets are compatible with most widely-available GIS software packages.

Beyond specific site analysis, area markets can be analyzed by integrating TIGER file data with other information to identify economic and social characteristics and key linkages within a market area. The systems are particularly valuable for analyzing linkages where distances must be measured along road networks rather than in straight lines, and where traffic congestion and bottlenecks must be factored in.

Data for different time periods can be overlaid on a market-area or metropolitan map to create a graphic representation of change through time. In this manner analysts can identify neighborhoods by stages of growth and determine which are in an early growth phase, which are at or near maturity, and which are in decline.

Know abt GIS

GIS AT WORK

An investment enterprise interested in constructing a large shopping mall within the perimeter of the town of Anysville has decided that the potential location should meet the following requirements:

a. Must be within a half-mile zone outside the urban area.
b. Should be located no more than 200 yards from existing high-traffic roads or no more than 100 yards from medium- or light-duty roads.
c. Should be located in an area that does not infringe on existing forested lands.
d. Selected parcels must be at least 12 acres in size.

From map layers of Anysville, a half-mile buffer zone surrounding the town is identified (A); 200-yard and 100-yard buffer zones are generated along existing heavy-duty and medium/light-duty roads (B). By overlaying these two map layers, the desired areas are identified (C). The forested areas are introduced and "removed" from the selected areas (D). Areas below the required size of 12 acres are eliminated to provide the potential mall sites (E).

SOURCE: Devlin Fung, "Managing by the Map." In *Business Perspectives,* Bureau of Business and Economic Research, University of Memphis, 8(2):15–17.

GIS AT WORK

A real estate company wants to investigate the average cost of houses sold in Shelby County in 1980 and 1990, and the change within that period. Data needed includes houses sold during the two periods, the street/road map, and the housing zones based on the Multiple Listing Service (MLS). The location of each house can be identified on the street map, using the address-matching function of the GIS software (A). The average prices of houses for the two respective years are summarized, based on the MLS zones (B and C). Finally, by overlaying the two maps, the changes in price for each zone can be computed and displayed (D). The resulting map helps identify the spatial distribution and the magnitude of changes in average home prices within the period in Shelby County.

SOURCE: Devlin Fung, "Managing by the Map." In *Business Perspectives*, Bureau of Business and Economic Research, University of Memphis, 8(2):15–17.

SUMMARY

Market research is an essential element in rational investment decision making. Reliable revenue and expense forecasts and estimates of future market values require market research and analysis. Market data permits evaluation of management performance and identification of potential areas of performance improvement. Research should be pursued to the point where incremental research and analysis costs equal incremental benefits anticipated.

To a significant extent, market research programs are dictated by the nature of the research problems. Generally, however, the program will start with a definition of the problem and proceed to selection of data collection methods and research design. Data are collected, analyzed and interpreted, and the research report is prepared.

Usually, the most useful approach is to proceed from the general to the particular, from wide-area market and demographic forecasts to projections about a specific property. Because wide-area data are generally more readily available and more amenable to reliable forecasting, analysts depend heavily upon identifying consistent relationships between regional and neighborhood phenomena. They exploit observed relationships to generate useful estimates of a property's prospects, based on the relationship and an aggregate forecast.

Data sources are designated as primary or secondary, depending upon whether data are collected specifically for a current research problem or for some other purpose. Secondary data (collected for other uses) are generally more convenient and less costly to collect but are likely to be in a format or in units other than those needed. Primary data should be collected only after exhausting all available sources of secondary data.

Primary data are gathered by communicating with research subjects or by observing and reporting upon their actions. Communication is more versatile and, where practical, tends to be faster and more cost-effective. Subjectivity is sometimes introduced, however, by the tendency of respondents to give answers they believe researchers expect.

Most market research is descriptive in nature. Descriptive studies may involve a one-time sampling from a population of research interest (cross-sectional data) or repeated measures of the same phenomena to detect changes over time (time series data).

Inferential statistics permit conclusions to be drawn about an entire class of phenomena from observing a sample of the population. Where possible, samples from which inferences are to be drawn are collected on a random basis. Generally, however, real estate data represent judgment samples in which observations are judged to be representative of the underlying population of interest.

Computerized geographic information systems permit data to be displayed in an endless variety of combinations, all spatially related. Maps can display the data as it exists currently or, based on forecasts, as it is likely to exist at specified future dates.

NOTES

1. G. Vincent Barrett and John P. Blair, *How To Conduct and Analyze Real Estate Market and Feasibility Studies,* 2nd ed. (New York: Van Nostrand Reinhold, 1988) p. 10.

2. Gilbert A. Churchill, Jr., *Marketing Research: Methodological Foundations,* 5th ed. (Ft. Worth, TX: The Dryden Press, 1994).

3. James D. Vernor of Georgia State University, in private correspondence.

4. Churchill, *op. cit.,* pp. 21–24.

5. Dowell Myers and Kenneth Beck, "A Four-Square Design for Relating the Two Essential Dimensions of Real Estate Market Studies." Included in James R. DeLisle and J. Sa-Aadu, Ed., *Appraisal, Market Analysis, and Public Policy in Real Estate* (Boston: Kluwer Academic Publishers, 1994) pp. 259–288.

RECOMMENDED READINGS

Antenucci, J. C., K. Brown, P. L. Croswell, M. J. Kevany, and H. Archer. *Geographic Information Systems: A Guide to the Technology.* New York: Van Nostrand Reinhold, 1991.

Cam, Neil, Joseph Rabianski, Ronald Racster and Maury Seldin. *Real Estate Market Analysis: Techniques and Applications.* Englewood Cliffs, NJ: Prentice-Hall, Inc., 1988.

Clapp, John M. *Handbook for Real Estate Market Analysis,* Englewood Cliffs, NJ: Prentice Hall, Inc., 1987.

Fanning, Stephen F., Terry V. Grissom and Thomas D. Pearson. *Market Analysis for Valuation Appraisals.* Chicago: Appraisal Institute, 1994, chapters 1–11.

Graaskamp, James A. "Identification and Delineation of Real Estate Market Research." *Real Estate Issues,* vol. 10, no. 1 (Spring-Summer 1985) pp. 6–12.

Madizia, Emil E. "A Note on Real Estate Marketing Research." *The Journal of Real Estate Research,* vol. 5, no. 3 (Fall 1990) pp. 393–402.

Marks, A. P., C. Stanley and G. I. Thrall. "Evaluation of GIS Software For Real Estate Analysis." *Journal of Real Estate Literature,* vol. 2, no. 2, 1994, pp. 227–241.

McIntosh, Willard. "Forecasting Cash Flows: Evidence from the Financial Literature." *The Appraisal Journal,* vol. 58, no. 2 (April 1990) pp. 221–229.

Miles, Mike E., Richard L. Haney, Jr., and Gayle Berens. *Real Estate Development: Principles and Process,* 2nd Ed. Washington, DC: The Urban Land Institute, 1995, pp. 205–218.

Pittman, Robert H. and Maury Seldin. "Real Estate Analysis Using Geographic Data." *Real Estate Issues,* vol. 15, no. 1 (Spring/Summer 1990) pp. 32–38.

Rodriguez, Mauricio, C. F. Sirmans, and Allen P. Marks. "Using Geographic Information Systems to Improve Real Estate Analysis." *The Journal of Real Estate Research,* vol. 10, no. 2, 1995, pp. 163–74.

Star, J., and J. Estes. *Geographic Information Systems: An Introduction.* Englewood Cliffs, NJ: Prentice-Hall, 1990.

Weber, Bruce R. "Application of Geographic Information Systems to Real Estate Market Analysis and Appraisal." *The Appraisal Journal,* vol. 12, no. 1 (January 1990) pp. 128–132.

REVIEW QUESTIONS

1. Why is there a need for market research in real estate investment decisions?
2. How much market research should be done?

3. What steps are customarily employed in research procedures?
4. Which are preferable, primary or secondary data sources?
5. Describe some methods of collecting primary data.
6. Describe the four-quadrant research model for deriving a property-specific market forecast.

DISCUSSION QUESTIONS

1. One of your investment clients intends to put virtually all of her capital into a large apartment complex. Another client is acquiring a portfolio that will eventually include more than 100 duplex apartments, which he says will be scattered more or less randomly over the cityscape. In what ways might your recommended market analysis for these two clients differ?
2. What are some local sources of secondary market data that might prove useful for real estate investment analysis, and how might one go about gaining access to these data?

Appendix 4.A: Data Sources

There are in fact ten different censuses, all of interest to real estate analysts to greater or lesser extent.

1. *Population.* Every ten years, the entire population is counted. The result is a detailed breakdown of population statistics by characteristics such as age, sex, marital status, race, education, family size, occupation, income and so forth. Data are provided on a regional basis within each category. Annual Current Population Reports update the census data by incorporating the latest information on changes in population characteristics.

2. *Housing.* Since 1940, the Decennial Census has reported detailed data on housing, including the size, condition and type of structures; number of occupants per household; average market value; average rents and facilities such as plumbing and major kitchen appliances. Current Housing Reports are issued annually to update this data.

3. *Retail Trade.* The Census of Retail Trade, conducted every five years, reports detailed data on the number of stores of various types, total sales and number of employees. Data are reported by relatively small geographic areas such as counties, cities and standard metropolitan statistical areas. Monthly Retail Trade Reports provide the current data.

4. *Service Industries.* Taken every five years, the Census of Service Industries provides data on receipts, number of firms, employment and types of business within the service industries. Current data are published in monthly Selected Services Reports.

5. *Wholesale Trade.* Wholesalers are classified into more than 150 separate business groups in the Census of Wholesale Trade. The census reports are published every five years and contain statistics on sales volume, warehouse space, expenditures, employment and so forth. Current data are reported in monthly Wholesale Trade Reports.

6. *Manufacturers.* Every five years, the Census of Manufacturers is authorized to report manufacturing data in about 450 different classifications of manufacturing activity. Detailed data are generated on the number of firms, their output, employment, wages, sales and value added and a number of additional measures. Supplementary data are found in the Annual Survey of Manufacturers and in Current Industrial Reports, published monthly.

7. *Mineral Industries.* Also intended to be generated every five years, the Census of Mineral Industries provides information similar to the Census of Manufacturers but reports on mineral industries in approximately 50 separate categories. Annual data similar (but not directly comparable) to those

contained in the Census of Mineral Industries are reported annually in the Minerals Yearbook (Bureau of Mines, Department of the Interior).

8. *Transportation.* Also published at five-year intervals, the Census of Transportation provides statistics on passenger travel, truck and bus use and commodities shipped by various categories of carriers.

9. *Agriculture.* The Census of Agriculture offers detailed information on land uses, employment, quantity and value of products and land-use practices every five years. Data are presented by county within each state. Annual publications, Agriculture Statistics and Commodity Yearbook, provide current information.

10. *Government.* General characteristics of state and local governments (employment, payroll, indebtedness, revenues and operating expenses and so forth) are reported every five years in the Census of Government.

Many private publishers provide information of special interest to real estate analysts. Here are eight that are particularly useful:

1. *Dollars and Cents of Shopping Centers.* Published every two or three years by the Urban Land Institute, 1200 Eighteenth St. N.W., Washington, DC 20036. Contains statistical data on operation of super-regional, community and neighborhood shopping centers. Presents operating results by geographic location and shopping center age. Also contains tenant information and characteristics. Some information is provided for Canadian centers.

2. *Downtown and Suburban Office Building Experience Exchange Report.* Published annually by the Building Owners and Managers Association, 1221 Massachusetts Ave. N.W., Washington, DC 20005. Provides statistical data about income and expenses for office building operations. Data are divided into downtown and suburban categories. Information is further subdivided according to building age, geographic location, size and height. The publication includes some time series data.

3. *Expense Analysis: Condominiums, Cooperatives and PUDs.* Published annually by the Institute of Real Estate Management, 430 N. Michigan Ave., Chicago, IL 60611. Provides expense data for condominiums, cooperatives and Planned Unit Developments. Data are classified by building age, geographic location and price range. Includes statistical series on interior and exterior common area maintenance costs, utilities expense breakdown and a summary of building amenities.

4. *Income-Expense Analysis: Conventional Apartments.* Published annually by the Institute of Real Estate Management, 430 N. Michigan Ave., Chicago, IL 60611. Provides income and expense data for apartment buildings in each of the following categories:

    • Garden-type, unfurnished
    • Furnished elevator buildings
    • Low-rise, 12 to 24 units, unfurnished
    • Low-rise, 25 or more units, unfurnished
    • Furnished units

Data are presented by region, location and building age. Separate series are provided for major metropolitan areas. Includes vacancy losses, tenant turn-over, bad-debt losses and parking revenue. Some trend data are provided.

5. *Income-Expense Analysis: Office Buildings.* Published annually by the Institute of Real Estate Management, 430 N. Michigan Ave., Chicago, IL 60611. Income and expense data for suburban office buildings are provided on national, regional and major metropolitan area bases. Data are divided according to building size, age, rental range and building type. Utility cost analysis and trend data are included.

6. *Income-Expense Analysis: Shopping Centers.* Published annually by the Institute of Real Estate Management, 430 N. Michigan Ave., Chicago, IL 60611. Income and expense data for shopping centers are provided on national, regional and major metropolitan area bases, and are provided separately for open and enclosed malls. Data are divided according to building size and age group. Analysis and trend data on expansion and renovation activity, property taxes, sales, marketing, leasing, food courts and ownership interests are included.

7. *Trends in the Hotel Industry.* Published annually by Pannell, Kerr and Forster, 4201 Lexington Ave., New York, NY 10170. Provides revenue and expense data separately for hotels and motels, transient hotels, resort hotels, motels with restaurants and motels without restaurants. Includes data on occupancy rates, room rental rates, total revenues and expenses, energy costs and property taxes.

8. *U.S. Lodging Industry.* Published annually by Laventhol and Horwath, Certified Public Accountants, 1845 Walnut St., Philadelphia, PA 14103. Contains descriptive information about the lodging industry around the nation. Also provides income and expense data. Facilities are listed according to location as center city, airport, suburban or highway and resort. Buildings are classified into four different size categories. Includes occupancy rate data, food and beverage sales data and ratios of sales per room.

CHAPTER 5

Reconstructing the Operating History

Most important chapter

Astute real estate investors are interested in the physical aspects of their property only because of the economic benefits ownership bestows. (This is not to argue that nonfinancial aspects of ownership are unimportant. Aesthetics may well be valued as an end in themselves, apart from the question of economic worth. Such issues, however, transcend the investment decision.). As an investment medium, real estate is only a means to the ultimate end of financial gain; its desirability is strictly a function of the amount, timing and certainly of economic benefits, net of federal, state and local income taxes.

The starting point for forecasting benefits from a proposed venture is the property's immediate past operating history and the recent history of comparable properties. This experience is incorporated into a forecast by considering how anticipated changes in the economic, social and political environment will influence the property's ability to generate rents and how they will affect the cost of maintaining and operating the property. Rational analysis must also include a forecast of the likely change in a property's market value over the anticipated holding period.

OVERVIEW OF THE OPERATING STATEMENT

Unlike traditional income statements, which show revenues and expenses when earned or incurred whether or not payments have been made, real estate operating statements report cash receipts and disbursements. The cash flows might stem from rental operations, or from nonoperating transactions such as borrowing and repaying debt, interest payments on outstanding indebtedness, income taxes, or capital expenditures. All are reported on the operating statement. A typical income-property operating statement is illustrated in Table 5.1.

Potential gross rent is the amount of rental revenue a property would generate with no vacancies and no uncollectible accounts. Adjusting potential gross rent to reflect losses from vacancies and uncollectible accounts and to include income from sources other than rents results in *effective gross income.* On a historical basis, this is the gross revenue a building has actually produced.

Operating expenses, shown in the next section of the operating statement in Table 5.1, include all cash expenditures required to maintain and operate the property so as to generate the gross rent. *Net operating income* is simply the difference between effective gross income and operating expenses. Were there no income taxes or other nonoperating transactions, this would also be the net cash flow to the equity investors.

ESTIMATING ABILITY TO COMMAND RENT

The usual starting point for estimating effective gross income is the property's operating records. But unless they are prepared by a reliable and disinterested party using information from original source documents, these records are suspect. Analysts seek to verify them, and test their reasonableness by comparing them with rents from comparable properties.

Collect Data from the Subject Property

To estimate recent gross income, inspect the property's rent roll. If properly maintained, it will show actual rental collections, delinquent rents and vacant

Table 5.1	Rental Property Annual Net Operating Income		
Potential Gross Rent			$1,500,000
Less: Allowance for Vacancies and Rent Loss			45,000
			$1,455,000
Plus: Other Income (Parking)			9,000
Effective Gross Income			$1,464,000
Less: Operating Expenses			
Management Fee		$ 72,750	
Salary Expense		133,900	
Utilities		157,700	
Insurance		74,400	
Supplies		19,000	
Advertising		9,000	
Maintenance and Repairs		116,000	
Property Tax		183,000	765,750
Net Operating Income			$ 698,250

rental space. Review individual leases to determine contract rental rates (the rates tenants were contractually obligated to pay) and *concessions* (agreements between landlords and tenants that make effective rents less than contract rates). Verify the information, if possible, by conversing with the building's manager and tenants.

Compare with Peer-Group Properties

Comparable properties are frequently the most valuable source of data for estimating a property's recent operating history. The challenge is to find properties that are truly comparable. For estimating ability to command rents, a comparable property must function as a close substitute for the property under analysis. This means it must appeal to the same subset of prospective tenants (the market segment) and must be considered equally desirable by them. Its location must be equally appealing, and it must offer approximately the same amenities. First, define the market area. Then identify property in the area that competes directly with the subject.

Establishing the Market Area.   The geographic area from which tenants will be drawn is a property's *market area.* Properties that are close substitutes in the minds of prospective tenants will involve roughly similar linkages and transfer costs. They will have equally desirable environments, or environmental effects will offset differences in transfer costs.

- *Linkages Will Be Similar.* Economic specialization creates interdependence among sites and requires movement of people or things between them. Relationships that create such movement are called *linkages,* as explained in Chapter 3, and properties between which the movement occurs are said to be linked. Examples include travel between places of residence and work, school or shopping; movement of raw material from place of origin to manufacturing locations; transport of semi-finished and finished goods from manufacturer or processor to wholesalers and through retail outlets to points of consumption.
- *Transfer Costs Will Be Comparable.* The costs of moving people and things between linked sites are called *transfer costs.* We learned in Chapter 3 that these may be implicit (accounting costs per trip, multiplied by the number of trips) or explicit (frustration and worry from moving along congested transportation arteries or across dangerous terrain). Sites that offer greater transfer cost economies, perhaps because of shorter distances or more convenient transport links (freeway interchanges, airport or river terminals, for example), have a competitive advantage that enhances their ability to command rent. Peer-group properties will have roughly equal transfer costs, or the property with higher costs will offer offsetting advantages such as more desirable neighborhood influences.
- *Neighborhood Influences May Offset Higher Transfer Costs.* Other things being equal, sites with lower transfer costs will be more desirable. Some tenants, however, choose locations that increase transfer costs, because they like the neighborhood. Desirable neighborhood factors—environmental influ-

ences that increase a site's value due to their attractiveness—include aesthetic or prestige considerations, a perception of safety or neighbors whose activities somehow complement one's own.

Defining a Residential Market Area.   The market area for housing has been defined as the area "within which all dwelling units are linked together in a chain of substitution."[1] Within such an area, housing that is physically comparable and similarly priced will be mutually substitutable by prospective renters.

Precise market area boundaries are impossible to define, but they can be approximated. One need only establish the most probable linkages with respect to a particular category of tenants. A major linkage, for example, is place of employment, and the range of possible employment from any given residential site is determined by the time, expense and difficulty of the journey to work. Whether this is measured in terms of automobile driving time and distance or of accessibility and cost of public transportation depends upon the characteristic transportation mode of the market segment most likely to find the housing affordable and otherwise desirable.

To determine commuting patterns, one might distribute brief questionnaires at nearby employment centers. Responses will reveal tolerable commuting time and expense, and a map can be drawn to show the geographic area of employment from which an apartment building's tenants are likely to be drawn. Major employment centers within these boundaries constitute the employment base for prospective tenants. Other residential areas that are equally accessible to these employment centers form the competitive market area; apartment buildings within this area that offer similar amenities and are of equal quality will be peer-group properties. Figure 5.1 shows maps of a market area and areas of competing rental units.

Determining Retail Trade Area Boundaries.   A retail store's trade area is the geographic area from which the major portion of patronage is drawn. Within the trade area, the strongest drawing power is felt close to the site itself; drawing power diminishes as travel time increases.

Several techniques have been recommended for estimating trade area boundaries for various types of retail or service establishments, and analysts will need specialized study to appreciate the strengths and weaknesses of each. John McMahan advises estimating trade area boundaries by the time required for potential customers to reach the facility. He further suggests the following rough rules of thumb:[2]

• Neighborhood shopping centers: 5 to 10 minutes
• Community shopping centers: 10 to 15 minutes
• Regional malls: 15 to 30 minutes

McMahan's rules of thumb correspond closely to counsel from the Urban Land Institute, which characterizes trade areas as primary, secondary and tertiary. The primary trade area is viewed as that requiring not more than about five minutes of travel to reach stores offering convenience items and ten minutes of

Figure 5.1   **Estimating the Market Area**

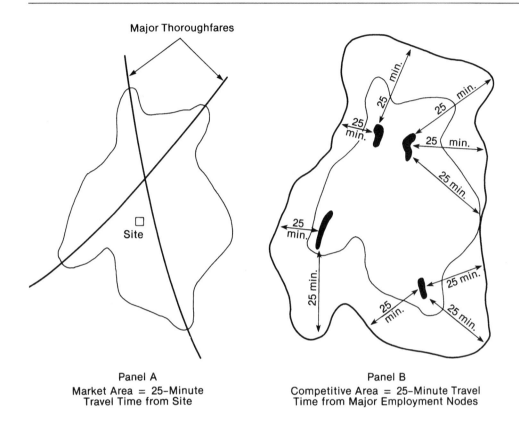

Major Thoroughfares

Site

Panel A
Market Area = 25–Minute
Travel Time from Site

Panel B
Competitive Area = 25–Minute Travel
Time from Major Employment Nodes

travel time to those offering big-ticket items for which consumers will do comparative shopping. The Urban Land Institute estimates that about 60 to 70 percent of ultimate sales volume will come from populations within this area. The balance will be drawn from the secondary and tertiary areas, which are farther away and for which the store or shopping center is less accessible. The institute characterizes the tertiary trade area as the farthest from which even major regional shopping centers can expect to draw customers. They set the outer distance in travel time at about 25 to 30 minutes.[3] *Outlet malls* do not fit into the traditional three-category classification used by McMahan. They draw customers from much greater distances.

Estimating Office Market Boundaries.   The size and nature of a proposed office project determine the extent of the competitive survey. Office buildings tend to be developed in clusters or local nodes within a metropolitan area.[4] Figure 5.2 illustrates a typical nodal development pattern. Small to medium-sized office buildings intended as general office space compete primarily with

| Figure 5.2 | Nodal Pattern of Office Building Development |

other buildings in the same node. Larger buildings or those catering to specialized users may compete with buildings throughout an entire metropolitan area. In each instance the survey will encompass the area within which major competitive buildings are located.

Identifying Peer Properties within the Market Area

Comparable properties within the market area will be physically similar to the property under analysis, to the extent physical structure affects the ability to command rent. Analysis is facilitated by classifying buildings and other property improvements in terms of their functional efficiency and physical durability.

Determining Functional Efficiency. How well a property is designed to do the job it is intended to perform is the measure of its *functional efficiency*. Even though properties are intended for the same use and are located in the same market area, they are unlikely to be directly competitive if their functional efficiency differs significantly.

Functional efficiency is related to specific property uses and can be evaluated only in that context: houses are compared with design needs for modern family lifestyles, warehouse design is evaluated in terms of compatibility with modern storage and transportation technology, office buildings are judged according to modern business needs.

Well-designed structures may be very functionally efficient when first put into service but may be rendered less appropriate for their tasks as lifestyles, taste and technology alter use patterns. Less well-designed buildings may be functionally inefficient from the outset. Older warehouses, for example, may have load-bearing columns that are too close together to facilitate the use of modern forklift vehicles. Three-bedroom apartments will be functionally less efficient if the average family size in the market area contracts. Loss of efficiency due to defective or dated design *(functional obsolescence)* diminishes a building's competitive position and may eventually lead to abandonment or to an alternative use.

Determining Physical Durability.   A structure's remaining physical life and the extent of deferred maintenance is the measure of its *physical durability.* This is a function of soundness of design plus the extent to which routine maintenance has forestalled structural deterioration. Buildings that differ radically in physical durability are not likely to appeal to the same market segment, even when their intended use is the same.

Some clues to life-shortening defects can be noted by comparing the building's physical appearance with others of similar age. Past abuse leaves physical traces (foundation cracks, dry rot, termite infestation and so on) that suggest whether future deterioration is likely to proceed more or less rapidly compared with competing buildings.

ESTIMATING OPERATING EXPENSES

As with gross income, the starting point for estimating operating expenses is the property's operating history. The experience of peer-group properties are often more reliable indicators, however, because the influence of above or below-standard management tends to offset when the experience of several properties are being compared.

Published sources that give average operating expenses for various types and sizes of properties are readily available. These data are drawn from samples reported by members of trade groups, and they give little or no information about the dispersion around the mean of the sample. For this reason, while they comprise informative benchmarks against which to compare tentative conclusions for reasonableness, they are a poor substitute for detailed information drawn from the subject or from peer-group properties. The most frequently used sources are listed in Appendix 4.A.

AN APARTMENT BUILDING EXAMPLE

Maegen's Magic Manor is a 280-unit apartment complex consisting of 50 two-bedroom units, each having 1,000 square feet of living area; 150 one-bedroom units, each containing 700 square feet of living area; and 80 studio-type units, each with 500 square feet of living space. The owner provides a statement of the property's most recent operating results, which is presented in Table 5.2.

Reconstructing Effective Gross Income

Inspecting the rent roll, analysts discover that some tenants are on 24-month leases, some are on 12-month leases and some are renting on a month-to-month basis. While talking with tenants and reading leases, they note that several tenants received special inducements (concessions), such as special decorating allowances or discounts on parking fees at a nearby garage operated by the same management company. The concessions seem to be related to periods when vacancies were particularly high, but this is impossible to verify because both the owner and the management firm refuse to confirm concessions reported by tenants but not included in leases.

Fortunately, a number of apartment buildings in the immediate neighborhood offer similar accommodations. Services provided by these other properties are essentially the same as those of the property being analyzed. All the units chosen as sources of comparable market data offer single baths and kitchen–dining room combinations, which conforms to the profile of units in the property under analysis. The data on comparable properties are as follows:

Table 5.2 **Maegen's Magic Manor Prior Owner's Operating Statement for Year Ended December 31, 19XX**

Gross Revenue		
Rent Receipts		$1,512,000
Parking Fees		97,000
Total		$1,609,000
Expenses		
Management Fees (5% of gross)	$ 80,000	
Salaries	133,900	
Utilities	157,700	
Insurance	74,400	
Supplies	19,000	
Advertising	9,000	
Maintenance and Repairs	142,000	
Property Taxes	90,000	706,000
Net Income for the Year		$ 903,000

- Property A contains a total of 250 units: 175 two-bedroom units with 890 square feet of living area rent for $540 per month, 50 single-bedroom units with 625 square feet rent for $405 per month and 25 studios with 500 square feet rent for $325 per month. Currently, five two-bedroom units and seven studios are vacant. All the one-bedroom units are under lease.
- Property B is a 185-unit building with 75 two-bedroom, 75 one-bedroom and 35 studio units. The two-bedroom units have 925 square feet of living area and rent for $575 per month. The single-bedroom apartments have 650 square feet of living area and rent for $415. The studios contain 510 square feet and command rents of $330. Currently, ten one-bedroom and five studio units are vacant. All the two-bedroom units are occupied.
- Property C has 360 units, of which 225 are two-bedroom and 75 are one bedroom apartments. The remaining 60 units are all studios. Two-bedroom units contain 870 square feet of living area and rent for $535. One-bedroom units have 630 square feet of living area and rent for $405. Studios, which have 495 square feet of living area, rent for $315. This complex currently has two vacant two-bedroom units and 15 vacant studios. All one-bedroom units are rented.
- Property D is a 300-unit building containing 100 two-bedroom, 125 one bedroom and 75 studio apartments. Two-bedroom units each have 895 square feet of living area and rent for $545. The one-bedroom units have 655 square feet of living area and rent for $412. Studios rent for $350 and have 550 square feet of living area. There are ten vacant one-bedroom and ten vacant studio apartments.

Gross rental data from the comparable rental units are consolidated in Table 5.3. Expressing gross rents on a per-square-foot basis by type of rental unit

Table 5.3 **Derivation of Market Rental Rates on Properties Deemed Comparable to Maegen's Magic Manor**

	Comparable Property			
	A	*B*	*C*	*D*
Two-Bedroom Units				
Monthly Rental	$540	$575	$535	$545
Square Feet	890	925	870	895
Rent per Square Foot	$ .61	$ .62	$ .61	$ .61
One-Bedroom Units				
Monthly Rental	$405	$415	$405	$412
Square Feet	625	650	630	655
Rent per Square Foot	$ .65	$ .64	$ .64	$ .63
Studio Units				
Monthly Rental	$325	$330	$315	$350
Square Feet	500	510	495	550
Rent per Square Foot	$ .65	$ .65	$ .64	$ .64

eliminates differences due to variation in the unit size or type. The data suggest that if the building's two-bedroom units were vacant and available, they would rent for about 61 cents per square foot. Sixty-four cents per square foot appears the best estimate for one-bedroom units and studios. Studio apartments renting for no more per square foot than one-bedroom units is cause for reflection, but the conclusion is reinforced by the higher vacancy rate for studios.

Vacancy data for the comparable apartments are consolidated and arrayed on Table 5.4. Comparable property B has an unusually high vacancy rate in its one-bedroom units, and this has a disproportionate impact on the average for the group. An uncharacteristically high rate in one property might be attributable to a transient difficulty (a malfunctioning heating or cooling system perhaps, or a disruptive tenant that has since been evicted), or by incompetent management. For Maegen's Magic Manor apartments, the analysts conclude that market estimates in fact reflect most likely experience under typically competent management.

Data concerning market rental rates and most probable vacancy experience, drawn from the comparable properties and exhibited in Tables 5.3 and 5.4, are employed to arrive at estimates of potential gross rent and allowance for vacancy losses for Maegen's Magic Manor. Final conclusions are computed in Table 5.5 and are incorporated into the reconstructed operating report, which is shown in Table 5.6.

 ## Reconstructing Current Operating Expenses

Recall that operating expenses are cash expenditures required to maintain properties in sufficient condition to generate the effective gross revenue. A first

Table 5.4	**Derivation of Market Vacancy Factors Applicable to Maegen's Magic Manor**				
	Comparable Property				
	A	*B*	*C*	*D*	*Total (Weighted Average)*
Two-Bedroom Units					
Number of Units	175	75	225	100	575
Vacancies	5	0	2	0	7
Percent Vacant	2.9	0	0.9	0	(1.2)
One-Bedroom Units					
Number of Units	50	75	75	125	325
Vacancies	0	10	0	10	20
Percent Vacant	0	13.3	0	8.0	(6.2)
Studios					
Number of Units	25	35	60	75	195
Vacancies	7	5	15	10	37
Percent Vacant	28.0	14.3	25.0	13.3	(19.0)

Table 5.5	Estimated Gross Revenue and Vacancy Rates for Maegen's Magic Manor		
	Two-Bedroom	*One-Bedroom*	*Studio*
Estimated Potential Gross			
Monthly			
Market Value per Square Foot	$ .61	.64	.64
Square Feet per Unit	×1000	×700	×500
Rent per Unit	$ 610	448	320
Number of Units	×50	×150	×80
Total Potential Monthly Rent	$ 30,500	67,200	25,600
Annual (Monthly × 12)	$366,000	806,400	307,200
Estimated Vacancy Factor			
Annual Potential Gross	$366,000	$806,400	$307,200
Vacancy Factor (from Table 5.4)	×.012	×.062	×.190
Vacancy Loss Estimate	$ 4,392	49,997	58,368

Total Annual Potential Gross Revenue (rounded to nearest $1,000) = $1,480,000
Total Annual Vacancy Loss Estimate (rounded to nearest $1,000) = $113,000

[handwritten margin note: remember: use current taxes]

step toward estimating a property's current operating expenses is to convert the current owner's statement to a more useful format. The present owner's reported operating results for Maegen's Magic Manor are shown in Table 5.2.

Questioning the owner about reported maintenance and repair charges, the analysts learn that the owner and her sons held other expenses down by doing much of the maintenance work themselves. Comparison with similar buildings in the area reveals that a proper maintenance and repair program would have consumed between 11.5 and 12.0 percent of effective gross income.

The owner's operating statement also shows property taxes that are too low. A check with the County Assessor's office reveals that last year's taxes were $210,000 and that they are unlikely to change prior to the next reassessment, which is scheduled in two years.

All other reported maintenance items appear reasonable for a building of this size and age, based upon the analyst's experience with comparable properties and upon reference to published standards. Therefore, no other adjustments are indicated.

Revised Operating Statement

Effective gross income for the preceding year, after including revised estimates of vacancy losses and parking income, is $1,464,000. Revised operating expenses total $723,600. These adjustments yield reconstructed net operating income of $740,400. The reconstructed operating statement is shown on Table 5.6.

Table 5.6	Reconstructed Prior-Year Operating Statement for Maegan's Magic Manor	
Potential Gross Rent		$1,480,000
Less: Allowances for Vacancies		113,000
		$1,367,000
Plus: Other Income		97,000
Effective Gross Income		$1,464,000
Less: Operating Expenses		
Management Fee	$ 73,200	
Salary Expense	133,900	
Utilities	61,100	
Insurance	43,500	
Supplies	19,000	
Advertising	9,000	
Maintenance and Repairs	173,900	
Property Taxes	210,000	723,600
Net Operating Income (Annual)		$ 740,400

FROM RECONSTRUCTION TO FORECAST

The sole purpose of reconstructing the property's operating history is in the anticipation that the history will serve as a guide to the immediate future. In the absence of any changes in the property itself or in its operating environment, there is no reason to expect that the operating results will change through time.

But of course changes do occur. Change is a constant factor that must always be incorporated into the analysis. Forecasting, therefore, represents an attempt to estimate the nature of change in the factors that affect operating results, and to determine the impact those changes will have on the property's future operations. Estimating the changes and their impact is the subject of Chapter 6.

SUMMARY

The starting point for forecasting the stream of benefits that will flow from a rental property is to reconstruct the operating history. Past trends are projected into the future, with revisions to reflect perceived changes in the economic, political and social environment that are likely to affect the property's ability to generate future benefits.

All benefits are expressed on an after-tax cash-flow basis. A typical operating statement starts with an expression of the gross rent the property would generate if fully rented. This is adjusted for vacancies and rent losses, plus revenue from sources other than rent, to arrive at effective gross revenue. Subtracting operating expenses from the effective gross revenue yields net operating income. Further adjustments, for financing costs, income taxes and other non-operating cash flows, yields an estimate of net cash flow to the equity investor.

Sources of information regarding rental revenue and operating expenses include the past operating history of the property itself, the operating records of comparable properties, and data from published sources. The last source provides benchmarks against which to gauge the reasonableness of conclusions.

NOTES

1. The Institute for Urban Land Use and Housing Studies, Columbia University, *Housing Market Analysis: A Study Of Theory And Methods.* (Washington, DC: Housing and Home Finance Agency, 1953).

2. John McMahan, *Property Development: Effective Decision Making in Uncertain Times* (New York: McGraw-Hill, 1976) p. 161.

3. The Urban Land Institute, *Shopping Center Development Handbook,* 2nd ed. (Washington, DC: The Urban Land Institute, 1985) pp. 22–23.

4. McMahan, *op. cit.,* 182.

RECOMMENDED READINGS

Jaffe, Austin J., and C. F. Sirmans. *Fundamentals of Real Estate Investment.* 3rd ed. (Englewood Cliffs, NJ: Prentice-Hall, 1995).

REVIEW QUESTIONS

1. How do income and expense statements prepared by accountants differ from operating statements used by real estate investment analysts?
2. What items should be considered when forecasting income and expenses over an investor's anticipated holding period?
3. Carefully inspect the prior owner's operating statement for Maegen's Magic Manor apartments (Table 5.2). Do you see any problems with the owner's presentation of income and expenses?
4. Describe the process used to estimate rentals for Maegen's Magic Manor.
5. List some of the considerations inherent in the expense items as presented by the current owner of Maegen's Magic Manor.
6. What is the value of published data in developing an estimate of the operating history of a property?
7. What are some of the forces affecting the ability of a property to generate rents?

DISCUSSION QUESTIONS

1. Offering brochures for rental property frequently state that current rental rates can be raised. Comment on such claims.
2. How does our concept of gross income and operating expenses differ from those you studied in accounting? Which is the correct definition?
3. You are analyzing a new apartment complex (the only one of its kind) recently constructed on the fringe of an urban area. Because of its access to open areas and freedom from congestion, noise and so forth, the units are in great demand. In fact, net operating income per rental unit is almost 50 percent above that of slightly older but otherwise comparable units that are clustered in an area closer to the central city. Because of the high rents and virtual zero vacancies that yield a 50 percent premium in net operating income, the owner argues that his property is worth 50 percent more than the other units. Comment on this assertion.

CHAPTER 6

Very important

Forecasting Income and Property Value

Reconstructing a property's operating history and estimating the results of current operations as they would have been with typically competent management, as explained and illustrated in Chapter 5, is the starting point for estimating cash flows over the investment period. Rational investment decisions require such an estimate, and to get there one first has to forecast operating results and future market value. Those forecasts are the objective of this chapter.

In order to develop an operating forecast, one must first project changes in key variables that determine gross income, and then estimate related operating expenses to derive a net operating forecast. With the operating forecast in hand, projecting future market value is a matter of measuring the relationship between net operating income and value, then projecting changes in that relationship over the forecasting period. This chapter addresses each of these steps in the indicated sequence.

FORECASTING GROSS INCOME

A property's income-generating potential depends upon (1) the interaction of supply and demand in its market area, which determines market-clearing rental rates and the amount of rental space that will be occupied, and (2) its desirability relative to competing properties in the market area, which determines its share of the market. Forecasting gross rental income therefore requires estimating future changes in supply and demand relationships and changes in a property's market share.

Supply and demand, and their role in setting market-clearing prices, are introduced in Chapter 2; Chapter 4 explains a technique for translating theory into a gross income forecast for a specific property. If the property's proportional share of market rent remains stable, the technique works beautifully. The missing link is how to accumulate evidence and exercise judgment to determine likely changes in market share.

Competitive weapons in the battle for market share are location and a specific set of physical amenities. The final step in forecasting future rent-generating capacity is to anticipate changes in these variables and in their desirability to prospective tenants.

The Influence of Physical Characteristics

A property's physical characteristics—buildings and other site improvements—by their very nature have limited useful lives. As their usefulness wanes, the facility becomes less desirable relative to competing properties that are newer or have been better maintained. Estimating the extent of this inexorable decline in competitive posture is a crucial element in accurately projecting market share. The task is simplified by considering the functional efficiency and physical durability of the physical characteristics.

Declining Functional Efficiency.   The appropriateness of a facility's design or engineering for its intended use is the measure of its functional efficiency, as explained in Chapter 5. Diminished usefulness due to declining conformity with current standards leads inevitably to a decreasing share of market-wide rental revenue. This loss of competitive position due to defective or dated design or engineering is called *functional obsolescence*. In many cases, it leads to abandonment or recycling into alternative uses.

Changes in manufacturing, transportation and storage technology, for example, inject obsolescence into factories and warehouses and cause them to be abandoned, demolished or converted. Modern industrial techniques that favor single-story manufacturing plants render older, multi-storied facilities obsolete. Warehouses lose competitive position because of ceilings with insufficient clearance, floors with inadequate load-bearing capacity, and load-bearing columns with bay widths that hamper the movement of materials-handling machinery.

Declining Physical Durability.   Chapter 5 defines *physical durability* as the measure of how long a structure will continue to be productive. In-depth evaluation of this factor is usually beyond a real estate analyst's technical capabilities, and requires the services of a building design or construction engineering consultant.

The Influence of Locational Characteristics

A property's location relative to prospective tenants' needs and to the locations of competing sites is a primary determinant of its market share. Some elements of locational desirability are property-specific, a function of the relationship between the site and locations with which it is linked. Others are environment-related, dependent upon the relationship between the site and surrounding geography. Unlike physical features, which can be altered more or less at will, locational elements are generally not amenable to manipulation and control.

Locational analysis is always important. It becomes more so when investment success hinges on anticipated changes in locational factors. Examples include acquiring vacant land in the path of expected urban expansion or rehabilitating property in older neighborhoods with the expectation of imminent urban economic revival.

Analyzing Linkages and Transfer Costs

Identifying linkages—relationships that require movement of people or things between linked sites—that result from existing or intended land use is the first step in locational analysis. This involves studying present or planned economic activity at the site to determine major geographic points to or from which there will be movement of people or products.

The analyst then judges the relative importance of each linkage and estimates transfer costs—the costs of movement between the linked sites. Comparing these costs with those incurred by people engaged in the same activity at competing locations yields an estimate of the location's contribution to a property's ability to command rent.

Linkages and transfer costs are discussed at length in Chapter 3. Recall that transfer costs might be explicit or implicit, and that total transfer cost is the product of the cost per trip, both implicit and explicit, and the number of trips made per period of time. A significant change in the relative importance of linkages or in the relative dimensions of transfer costs will alter a site's competitive position.

Linkages May Change. Altered lifestyles, emerging business patterns or shifts in technology can sever existing linkages and create new ones. The transition from urban to suburban living, for example, created linkages between communities and regional shopping centers while reducing the significance of old linkages between residential neighborhoods and the central business district. Concomitantly, increasing congestion in urban areas has added value to industrial sites that are outside yet convenient to major urban concentrations.

Relative Transfer Costs May Be Altered. Modifying or supplanting existing transportation networks can drastically alter relative transfer costs. Contemporary examples include the rerouting of major highways, the closing of railway spurs, and alterations in the cost and availability of parking facilities. Such changes may sever ready access to linked sites and thereby destroy the locational value of proximity to places of work or shopping. A bridge over a previously impassable river or a new limited-access highway can diminish a site's locational advantage by providing ready access to competing sites. Freeway construction in many areas has altered traffic patterns and shifted the relative advantages of locations that share common linkages.

Analyzing Neighborhood Environmental Factors

A site's desirability relative to competing properties is influenced by the economic and social status of the immediate neighborhood. These are subject to change, so analysts should assess the neighborhood's ability to retain its attractiveness over the projection period and adjust revenue forecasts to reflect the consequences of expected changes.

Closing or relocating support facilities such as schools, churches, playgrounds or police substations may significantly impact a residential neighborhood's desirability. Demolishing physical barriers such as a railroad embankment or a large public building, or creating new ones, can have the same effect. Altering barriers that are more psychological than physical, such as a small park or an architecturally distinctive building that has become a symbol of neighborhood solidarity or uniqueness, for example, can have the same outcome.

Changes in zoning laws can accelerate a locale's incipient transition from one predominant use to another. The process might enhance or diminish the desirability of existing rental space, even while pushing land value in the opposite direction. Rezoning from residential to commercial use, for example, might make an area less desirable to residential tenants and thereby reduce the competitive strength of existing residential rental properties, while making the land more valuable because it can be developed with strip shopping centers, fast-food outlets and so forth.

The Supply Factor

As explained in Chapter 2, a site's desirability interacts with the relative scarcity and price of close substitutes to determine its value. A forecast of changes in the supply of comparable rental space is therefore an essential element in the analysis of a property's ability to command rent over the projection period.

Land Availability and Supply Analysis.   The four-quadrant matrix analysis investigated in Chapter 4 indirectly takes into account demographic and economic factors that affect supply; it does not directly address the question of whether land is available to expand the quantity of rental space in a market area. The inventory of developable land includes previously developed sites whose buildings are nearing the end of their useful economic lives, and thus are candidates for razing and redevelopment, as well as vacant sites that are properly zoned and currently available. It also includes advantageously located sites that are not appropriately zoned, if there is a decent likelihood of their being rezoned during the forecast period.

Product Differentiation and Supply Analysis.   Real estate that has unique features can command premium rents. In marketing terms, the differences—

whether real or spurious—desensitize tenants to price differentials. The distinction may lie in unique architecture, high-quality construction, luxurious appointments or other elements that create a compelling image for potential tenants.

Physical differences may be less significant than those that exist only in the perception of tenants. Styling, quality and functional features can be duplicated by competitors. Image, in contrast, is unique to individual properties and is often generated consciously to appeal to a specific market segment. Due solely to its reputation, a property may consistently command a premium price or sell at a discount from prevailing rates for similarly located and outfitted competitors. By successfully cultivating and protecting a uniquely desirable property image, one can capture some of the monopoly advantages associated with unique location. Such a property is far less vulnerable to competition from otherwise comparable rental space.

FORECASTING OPERATING EXPENSES

In at least one respect, projecting operating expenses is a simpler task than projecting gross revenue: expenses are less sensitive to minor variations in a property's location. Operating costs for a particular class of property will of course vary from one part of the country to another, because of the influence of such factors as climate and prevailing wage scales. Snow removal, for example, is a major item for properties in some parts of the country, while air-conditioning looms large in others. Within a single metropolitan area though, the cost of operating similar properties and maintaining them at reasonably similar levels of repair should be closely related.

This means analysts can look farther afield in search of peer-group properties to derive operating expense estimates. Buildings of similar age and construction quality, housing tenants of roughly similar socioeconomic class, should cost about the same to operate and maintain anywhere in the city.

If buildings' age or construction quality differ significantly, operating costs may vary widely. Other things being equal, older buildings will be more expensive to operate, and operating expense will consume a larger portion of the gross income. Poorly constructed buildings of any age generally require more extensive maintenance than better quality buildings, and those with less insulation will cost more to heat and cool.

The main impact tenants will have on operating costs is the extent to which they exercise responsibility in using the facility. Some residential neighborhoods, for example, might be characterized by apartment tenants who are less responsible, and who include vandals among their families or friends. Some office and retail complexes will be occupied by tenants whose clients or customers create higher-than-average wear and tear on facilities.

For that reason, published averages are likely to be poor indicators of an individual property's operating expenses. The trade groups who collect and report such data (the most widely distributed publications are listed in Appendix 4.A) make only a limited effort to discriminate their samples by quality of construction or by socioeconomic characteristics of tenants or users.

Several years' operating expense data are useful in establishing a trend. Based on the trend, analysts can estimate future expenses by noting indicated political, economic or social changes that might alter the trend during the forecasting period. These changes might occur at the national, state or metropolitan level. A shift in federal reserve monetary policy will affect future inflation rates, and thus the cost of operating and maintaining a rental property. A shift in federal fiscal policy might have similar implications because of its impact on employment and wage levels. Impending changes in federal minimum wage laws might have a measurable effect on operating expenses, and these are also frequently signaled by earlier shifts in national political alignments.

Other examples of regional or metropolitan economic phenomena that signal a change in operating costs include shifts in the labor market, a trend to or away from unionization or changes in supply and demand relationships for key materials or supplies. If a booming local economy threatens labor shortages, analysts might project labor costs to rise faster than the overall operating expense trend; if the regional or metropolitan economy is softening, the estimated growth in labor cost might be lower than the overall operating expense trend line.

THE NET OPERATING INCOME FORECAST

To see how a reconstructed operating statement might be transmuted into a multiple-year forecast, please study Table 5.6, which presents the prior year's reconstructed operating results for an apartment complex, Maegen's Magic Manor, to show what the results would have been with typically competent management. The analyst notes that, as a consequence of abnormally high vacancies and stagnant rents, there has for the past three years been no significant new construction in the market area. Further investigation reveals a steady drop in vacancy rates, from a high of 14 percent three years back to about 7.6 percent last year. Coincident with the decline in vacancies to a rate close to the long-term average, our analyst notes that market rents began moving up about six months ago. The tightening rental market will be increasingly reflected in the rent roll of Maegen's Magic Manor as leases expire and are renewed or new tenants are signed. After including revised estimates of vacancy losses and parking income, the analyst anticipates that potential gross rent during the first year of the forecast period will be about $1,517,000, representing an increase of 2.5 percent above last year's reconstructed amount. Vacancies are expected to decline to an average of 7.5 percent. Based on past experience of this and comparable other properties, operating expenses other than management fees and property taxes are expected to grow at about 3.5 percent per annum. Management fees are expected to be 5 percent of the effective gross income. Property taxes should remain at the current $210,000 until the next scheduled reappraisal by the county tax assessor. The estimated first-year net operating income, therefore, is $759,200. These revenue and expense estimates are shown on the operating forecast in Table 6.1.

The 2.5 percent increase in potential gross rents forecasted for the first year reflects growth that has occurred almost exclusively during the past six months, representing an annual rate of 5.0 percent. With local employment booming, vacancy rates declining precipitously, and no new construction pending, a shortage of apartment space seems to be looming.

Maegen's Magic Manor apartments are advantageously located near the periphery of a major office-zoned district that has been heavily developed. The analyst concludes that with competent management Maegen's Magic Manor should experience an occupancy level and command rents at least equal to the average for the market area: occupancy should hit 96 percent (a 4.0 percent vacancy rate) by the second year of the forecast, and rents should grow at about five percent per annum until new apartments become available.

When vacancies drop below their historical average (about 6.0 percent in this market area), developers become interested. The analyst notes that several local developers have recently bought apartment-zoned land, indicating plans for imminent development. By the fourth year of the forecast, additions to supply should drive vacancy rates back to their historical average of about six percent. Rental increases will moderate and are expected to grow at the projected 3.5 percent inflation rate after the third year. Other income (primarily parking fees) is expected to hold fairly constant at about 7.0 percent of rental collections.

Stagnant rental rates and high vacancies have not hindered the growth in operating expenses, most of which are not radically affected by occupancy levels. In recent years, operating expenses for peer-group apartment complexes have grown at about 3.5 percent per annum, approximately at the general rate of inflation. Except for management and property taxes, Maegen's Magic Manor's

Table 6.1	First-Year Operating Forecast for Maegen's Magic Manor	
Potential Gross Rent		$1,517,000
Less: Allowances for Vacancies [7.5 %, rounded]		114,000
		$1,403,000
Plus: Other Income		97,000
Effective Gross Income		$1,500,000
Less: Operating Expenses		
Management Fee [5% of EGI]	$ 75,000	
Salary Expense	138,600	
Utilities	63,200	
Insurance	45,000	
Supplies	19,700	
Advertising	9,300	
Maintenance and Repairs	180,000	
Property Taxes	210,000	740,800
Net Operating Income (Annual)		$ 759,200

expenses are expected to keep pace with inflation, which is expected to remain stable at around 3.5 percent per annum over the forecast period. Management fees will remain at 5 percent of effective gross income. Property taxes are scheduled for reassessment in two years (the increased rate will apply in the third year of the forecast). Based on the anticipated changes in revenue and expenses, the tax assessment will probably increase by about 7.0 percent.

Incorporating these expectations into the analysis, and starting with the one-year forecast from Table 6.1, the analyst constructs a six-year operating forecast for Maegen's Magic Manor apartments. The forecast is shown on Table 6.2.

As a check on the forecast's reasonableness, our analyst computes the ratio between forecasted operating expenses and effective gross income (this is the *operating expense ratio,* and is explained further in Chapter 13). The ratio, shown on Table 6.3 for each year of the forecasting period, is derived by dividing line 15 of Table 6.2 by line 5.

Consulting the most recent annual edition of *Income/Expenses Analysis, Conventional Apartments* (Chicago: Institute of Real Estate Management), the analyst compares the forecast operating ratios shown in Table 6.3 with the average for low-rise apartments built since 1978 and containing more than 25 units—the reported category that fits Maegen's Magic Manor—in the metropolitan area. The reported ratios have grown gradually during recent years, approximately in tandem with increasing vacancy rates, so our analyst considers it reasonable to expect them to drop back to their historical level of about 45 percent as average vacancies drop and rents escalate. Since that is the pattern reflected by the forecast on Table 6.3, it tends to validate the forecast.

Table 6.2	Six-Year Operating Forecast Maegen's Magic Manor Apartments					
		Year 1	*Year 2*	*Year 3*	*Year 4*	*Year 5*	*Year 6*
1.	Potential Gross Rent	$1,517,000	$1,592,900	$1,672,500	$1,731,000	$1,791,600	$1,854,300
2.	*Less:* Vacancy Allowance	114,000	63,700	66,900	103,900	107,500	111,300
3.		$1,403,000	$1,529,200	$1,605,600	$1,627,100	$1,684,100	$1,743,000
4.	*Add:* Other Income	97,000	107,000	112,400	113,900	117,900	122,000
5.	Effective Gross Income	$1,500,000	$1,636,200	$1,718,000	$1,741,000	$1,802,000	$1,865,000
6.	*Less:* Operating Expenses						
7.	Management Fee	$ 75,000	$ 81,800	$ 85,900	$ 87,000	$ 90,100	$ 93,300
8.	Salary Expense	138,600	143,400	148,500	153,700	159,000	164,600
9.	Utilities	63,200	65,400	67,700	70,100	72,500	75,100
10.	Insurance	45,000	46,600	48,200	49,900	51,600	53,400
11.	Supplies	19,700	20,100	21,100	21,100	21,800	22,600
12.	Advertising	9,300	9,600	10,000	10,300	10,700	11,100
13.	Maintenance and Repairs	180,000	186,300	192,800	200,000	206,600	213,800
14.	Property Taxes	210,000	210,000	210,000	220,500	220,500	220,500
15.	Total Expenses	$ 740,800	$ 763,200	$ 784,200	$ 812,600	$ 832,800	$ 854,400
16.	Net Operating Income	$ 759,200	$ 873,000	$ 933,800	$ 928,400	$ 969,200	$1,010,600

Rounding: All forecast items are rounded to the nearest $100.

Table 6.3	Forecasted Operating Expense Ratios for Maegen's Magic Manot Apartments

Forecast Year	Operating Expense Ratio
1	49.4
2	46.6
3	45.6
4	46.7
5	46.2
6	45.8

ESTIMATING FUTURE MARKET VALUE

Our investor will probably plan on selling the property at some future time, and the value of the expected after-tax proceeds from selling may comprise a substantial portion of the property's investment value. Income tax consequences of selling or exchanging are addressed in Chapter 11. First though, it is necessary to estimate the eventual selling price. A convenient way to approach this is to forecast the relationship between net operating income and market value, and to apply the forecasted relationship to the net operating income projected for the final year in the forecasting period.

The ratio of a property's net operating income to its market value is called a *capitalization rate.* The relationship is:

$$R = \frac{NOI}{Value}$$

where *R* is the capitalization rate and *NOI* is the net operating income (this can be the most recent income or the projected income).

Capitalization rates change with the cost of capital and with investors' perceptions of future cash flows from investment. At best, therefore, we can only estimate what the rate will be at the end of the expected holding period. Fortunately for our purposes, these changes tend to be modest and to occur gradually.

To illustrate, Table 6.4 charts nationwide average capitalization rates for apartment properties on a semiannual basis from the last quarter of 1985 through the last quarter of 1994. They range from a high of 9.7 percent to a low of 8.6 percent over a nine-year period that encompasses a major speculative boom and a recession of wrenching proportions. The arithmetic mean for the period (based on semiannual observations) is just under nine percent, and the semiannual rate varied from the mean by more than five percentage points only during a brief period when the economy was emerging from recession. For that brief period, the variation from the average hit a high of 7.5 percentage points. It regressed toward the mean when market values followed the upward trajectory of rental

Table 6.4	Apartment Building Capitalization Rates from Survey of 53 Apartment Markets 1985–1994

Year/Quarter	Capitalization Rate
1985/4	8.8%
1986/2	8.7%
1986/4	8.8%
1987/2	8.8%
1987/4	8.7%
1988/2	8.7%
1988/4	8.6%
1989/2	8.6%
1989/4	8.7%
1990/2	8.7%
1990/4	8.9%
1991/2	9.1%
1991/4	9.2%
1992/2	9.5%
1992/4	9.7%
1993/2	9.6%
1993/4	9.6%
1994/2	9.4%
1994/4	9.3%

SOURCE: National Real Estate Index, Market History Report, July, 1995

income with an 18-month lag. Similar patterns are reported for other categories of rental property.

One can legitimately object that these national averages can mask a multitude of variations in specific markets. Investigation reveals, however, that rates in most metropolitan areas exhibited similar stability. Apartment capitalization rates for Chicago during that same period, for example, ranged from 8.4 percent to 9.4, a variation from the mean (the mean was 8.9 percent) that never exceeded 5.7 percentage points.

Anticipating similar stability in the relationship between net operating income and market value in the market area that includes Maegen's Magic Manor, our analyst estimates what the market value will be after six years by applying the average capitalization rate for similar properties in this market area. The long-term average rate has been 9.0 percent, so the forecasted market value at the end of the anticipated six-year holding period is the expected sixth year's income divided by .09. This is $11,228,889 or, rounded, $11,230,000:

$$\$1,010,600 \ / \ .09 = \$11,228,889$$

It should be noted that even where an investor's plan does not include eventual property disposal, the income capitalization technique is useful. It enables one to place a value, at any point in time, on an infinite series of future cash flows. This topic is explained in Appendix A.

ADDITIONAL INFORMATION NEEDED

We have come a long way since page one, but rational investment analysis requires still more information. To move from the operating forecast developed on Table 6.2 to a rational investment decision, we must use our estimate of future net operating income and future market value to derive a forecast of after-tax cash flow to the equity investor. Recall from Chapter 1 that the value placed on those after-tax cash flows comprises the value of the equity position. Adding the estimated mortgage loan gives us an estimate of investment value, as described in Chapter 1 and illustrated on Figure 1.6.

To derive a forecast of after-tax cash flows from the operating forecast, we must incorporate the following:

• *Consequences of using borrowed money.* Using borrowed money wisely gives investors more mileage from their personal (equity) funds. This topic is addressed in Section Three.
• *Income tax consequences.* Tax collectors have first dibs on investment income. Relevant aspects of the Internal Revenue Code are discussed in Section Four.

SUMMARY

Revenue forecasting is essentially a marketing research problem. Demand for rental space at a specific location depends upon the level of demand in the market area, and upon the desirability of amenities and locational factors the site confers. It depends also upon the price and availability of competing sites, which offer about the same level of want-satisfying power. Thus, both physical and locational characteristics affect a property's ability to command rents. Physical characteristics include geological features and improvements such as landscaping and buildings; locational characteristics relate to how well a location is suited for its intended use.

The contribution that physical characteristics make to a property's competitive position changes over time. These changes are attributable both to physical deterioration and to altered needs or tastes on the part of prospective tenants. Improvements become less suitable with age, as a result of decline in their attractiveness and due to increased maintenance costs. Technological innovation or variation in style and tastes may render existing physical structures less desirable than before, even without the factor of physical deterioration.

Linkages, neighborhood influences and institutional factors all contribute to relative locational desirability. Linkages require movement of goods or people between properties and give rise to transfer costs. The importance of locations that minimize transfer costs increases with the relative importance of these costs to the total cost of a tenant's use of the site. Both explicit and implicit transfer costs must be factored into location decisions.

Linkages are almost certain to change over time. Altered lifestyles, new technology, shifts in consumer tastes—these and a host of other phenomena may promote the emergence of important new linkages as well as a decline in the significance of old ones. Because linkages play such a dominant role in determining a property's ability to command rent, accurate perception of emerging trends is a major factor in reliable income forecasting.

Even if linkage relationships remained virtually constant, their impact on a property's income-generating capacity might shift due to changes in relative transfer costs. As the cost of moving people or goods between linked sites is increased or decreased by modification of transportation facilities or other economic shifts, the linkage's impact on a site's ability to command rent may be altered.

Sites are subject to both desirable and undesirable neighborhood influences. Such influences are particularly important in real estate decisions because site immobility prohibits moving to escape the influence of neighborhood factors. Building and zoning ordinances, fire codes and federal, state and local land use laws are frequently designed to protect against the encroachment of neighborhood factors deemed to be undesirable. Private agreements are often designed with the same objective.

Demand and supply considerations must be factored into revenue forecasts. This involves estimating probable changes in site linkages, in neighborhood influences and in institutional factors that may influence demand or supply. Supply is a less troublesome consideration when significant monopoly elements are present. Monopoly elements may result from unique physical or locational factors, or they may exist only in the perception of potential tenants. Regardless of their origin, they reduce the property's vulnerability to competitive inroads from comparable property.

NOTES

1. National Real Estate Index, *Market History Reports, 1985–1994* (Emeryville, CA: Koll, July 1995).

2. *Ibid.*

RECOMMENDED READINGS

American Institute of Real Estate Appraisers. *The Appraisal of Real Estate.* 10th ed. Chicago: Appraisal Institute, 1992, pp. 428–465.

Barrett, G. Vincent, and John P. Blair. *How To Conduct and Analyze Real Estate Market and Feasibility Studies.* 2nd ed. New York: Van Nostrand Reinhold Company, 1988.

Miles, Mike E., Richard L. Haney Jr., and Gayle Berens. *Real Estate Development: Principles and Process.* Washington, DC: The Urban Land Institute, 1995, Chapters 11 and 12.

Fanning, Stephen F., Terry V. Grissom, and Thomas D. Pearson. *Market Analysis for Valuation Appraisals.* Chicago: Appraisal Institute, 1994.

REVIEW QUESTIONS

1. List some of the key physical characteristics that influence a property's income-producing capability.
2. List some of the locational factors that will influence a property's ability to command rents.
3. What future trends must be considered in forecasting the rent-generating ability of a property?
4. How does supply affect the rent-generating capability of property?
5. List the relationship between price and supply of rental property.
6. The text distinguishes between the responsiveness of short-run and long-run supply curves to changes in rental rates. What determines the length of time that comprises the "long" rather than the "short" run?
7. What is functional obsolescence and how does it affect a property's ability to command rent?
8. What are linkages and how do they influence tenants' location decisions?
9. How do explicit and implicit transfer costs differ? Give some examples of both.
10. Give at least two examples of institutional arrangements that can either enhance or detract from a property's ability to command rent.

DISCUSSION QUESTIONS

1. In an inflationary environment, cash flows in future years will have less purchasing power than those in earlier years. Thus, a multiple-year cash flow forecast is not a consistent measure of a property's performance. How might this difficulty be addressed?
2. Operating expenses cannot be estimated based on past experience and are totally unrelated to revenue projections. Do you agree? Discuss.
3. What examples (other than those in the text) can you think of where significant new linkages have emerged or the importance of existing linkages has shifted significantly to alter the relative value of properties that are imperfect substitutes?
4. Give some examples from your community where relative transfer costs have been altered enough to shift the competitive positions of properties in the area.
5. Give examples from your community where a site has been differentiated from the competition through imaginative marketing or by controlling a unique location.

PART TWO: Case Problem

Arnold Benedict is thinking of buying an apartment complex that is offered for sale by the firm of Getabinder and Flee. The price, $2.25 million, equals the property's market value. The following statement of income and expense is presented for Benedict's consideration:

The Sated Satyr Apartments Prior Year's Operating Results Presented by Getabinder and Flee, Brokers		
30 units, all two-bedroom apartments, $975 per month		$351,000
Laundry room and soda machines		20,000
Gross annual income		$371,000
Less Operating Expenses:		
Manager's salary	$10,000	
Maintenance staff (one person, part-time)	11,700	
Seedy landscapers	1,950	
Property taxes	13,500	37,150
Net Operating Income		$333,850

By checking the electric meters during an inspection tour of the property, Benedict determines the occupancy rate to be about 80 percent. He learns by talking to tenants that most have been offered inducements such as a month's free rent or special decorating allowances. A check with competing apartment houses reveals that similar apartment units rent for about $895 per month and that vacancies average about five percent, Moreover, these other apartments have pools and recreation areas that make their units worth about $20 per month more than those of the Sated Satyr, which has neither.

The tax assessor states that the apartments were reassessed 12 months ago, and that the current taxes are $71,400.

Benedict learns that the resident manager at Sated Satyr, in addition to a $10,000 salary, gets a free apartment for her services. He also discovers other expenses: insurance will cost $6.50 per $1,000 of coverage, based on estimated replacement cost of about $1.8 million; workers' compensation ($140 per annum) must be paid to the state; utilities, incurred to light hallways and other common areas, cost about $95 per month for similar properties; supplies and miscellaneous expenses typically run about 0.25 percent of effective gross rental income. Professional property management fees in the market area typically are about 5 percent of effective gross income.

Assignment

1. Develop a prior-year's reconstructed operating statement, assuming typically competent, professional management. Based on the reconstructed net operating income and the current market value, determine the capitalization rate.

2. Develop a seven-year forecast of net operating income for the Sated Satyr Apartments, incorporating the following assumptions:
   a. Potential gross rent and miscellaneous other income will grow at 2.5 percent per annum over the forecast period.
   b. Vacancies in the market area will remain constant over the forecast period.
   c. Operating expenses other than management fees and property taxes will grow at 2.5 percent per annum over the forecast period.
   d. Management fees as a percent of effective gross income will remain constant over the forecast period.
   e. Property taxes will be adjusted every fourth year. The assessment rate (property taxes as a percent of market value) will be the same at each quadrennial reassessment, so the revised property tax at each adjustment point will represent a fixed percentage of the property's market value at that time (*Note:* for this calculation, assume that the capitalization rate will remain constant over the forecasting period).

3. Assuming that the capitalization rate will remain constant, develop an estimate of the property's market value at the end of the projected holding period.

4. Suggest some reasons why the capitalization rate might not remain constant. Why might it become larger or smaller that the currently prevailing rate?

PART THREE

Using Borrowed Money

A veritable cornucopia of real estate folklore tells of fortunes made using other people's money. Stories of investors and developers building real estate empires on financial shoestrings are fascinating and inspirational, but can bewilder and discourage those who have just been denied credit at a local lending institution. It all sounds so easy in the wheeler-dealer biographies and popular get-rich-quick books. Yet it can become so very complicated in practice.

Books intended for popular consumption may overstate the benefits of borrowing and short-change the risk, but the fact is that few real estate deals are consummated without at least some borrowed money. If no third-party lender is involved, it is usually because the seller agrees to take back a promissory note for a substantial part of the consideration. Financing arrangements are often a more critical issue than price, and languishing projects can sometimes be resuscitated by restructuring the financing. Real estate-related borrowing is an intricate—frequently arcane—craft. Its masters are eagerly sought by investors who appreciate the value of favorable financial leverage.

Sophisticated investors understand the importance of an unusually keen grasp of financial markets, arrangements and procedures. These markets, arrangements and procedures are the topic of Part Three. We begin with Chapter 7, which introduces the concept and the consequences of borrowing. Chapter 8 describes common credit instruments and borrowing arrangements. Part Three concludes with Chapter 9, which explains the cost of borrowing and describes ways to compare alternative financing arrangements.

CHAPTER 7

Financial Leverage and Investment Analysis

Most real estate transactions involve debt financing, and borrowing is usually the major source of funds. Sometimes this is the only way to gain control of a project. But even where it is not necessary for control, investors borrow to enhance the expected yield on equity resources.

This chapter explains the popularity of borrowing in connection with real estate investments, by exploring the concept of financial leverage. The chapter then addresses the question of determining how much borrowing is appropriate. It concludes with a survey of the most common sources of borrowed funds.

WHY LEVERAGE IS SO POPULAR

Mixing borrowed funds with equity creates *financial leverage.* The higher the ratio of borrowing to equity, the greater the degree of leverage. When the rate of return on assets exceeds borrowing costs, leverage is said to be favorable. If the cost of borrowing is greater than the return on assets, leverage is unfavorable.

A bevy of best-selling books preach the gospel of "leveraging out," buying entirely with borrowed funds. The popularity of mortgage borrowing stems from its potentially positive impact on equity investment: favorable leverage magnifies the yield on equity funds, multiplies the tax deduction for depreciation expense (by permitting the purchase of a more expensive property with available equity funds) and amplifies the benefit from favorable tax rates applicable to capital gains.

Working the Spread

The difference between the rate of return on assets and the cost of borrowing is often called the *spread.* In a highly leveraged investment, even a small favorable spread greatly magnifies return on equity. Leverage cuts both ways, though; a small negative spread (unfavorable leverage) on a high-leverage deal will devastate the yield to equity investors, and can make what would otherwise have been a modestly successful investment venture a total disaster.

Example 7.1

A property that has a market value of $1.5 million is expected to generate annual net operating income of $210,000. A $1 million mortgage loan that will be repaid in equal monthly installments over 20 years, with interest at 9 percent per annum, is available. The monthly payments of approximately $8,997 include accrued interest and sufficient principal to retire the loan over its 20-year term. Annual debt service is simply 12 times this amount, or approximately $107,964.

Example 7.1 can be used to illustrate the potential impact of financial leverage. In the example, net operating income is 14 percent of the property's market value. If the equity investors decide against financial leverage, their equity investment will be $1.5 million and they will expect to receive the full $210,000 per annum net operating income; a current yield of 14 percent (*total yield,* the current yield plus the benefits of appreciation, will be even greater if the property's value increases. It will be lower if value declines). This information is summarized in the first column of Table 7.1.

Should the investors elect to borrow the $1 million, approximately $107,964 of the net operating income will be siphoned off as debt service (principal and interest payments on the mortgage loan). Only the remaining $102,036 will flow to the equity investors. The impact on before-tax cash flow and current yield on the equity investment is shown in the second column of Table 7.1.

Now see what happens when even greater financial leverage is employed. Assume that an 80 percent loan ($1,200,000) is also available on the investment in Example 7.1. This loan will be for the same period (20 years) and at the same interest rate (9.0 percent) as the lesser loan set forth in the example. The larger loan reduces both the required equity investment and the cash flow to the equity position: the monthly payment required by the alternative loan will be approximately $10,797 and the annual debt service will be 12 times this amount, or approximately $129,564. Expected cash flow to the equity investors drops to $210,000 minus $129,564, or $80,436, while the equity investment is reduced to $300,000. The impact on cash flow to the equity position, expressed as a percentage of the initial equity investment, is summarized in the third column of Table 7.1.

Table 7.1	Cash Flow Consequences of Financing Alternatives In Example 7.1		

	No Loan	$1,000,000 Loan	$1,200,000 Loan
Net Operating Income	$ 210,000	$ 210,000	$ 210,000
Less: Annual Debt Service	0	107,964	129,564
Before-Tax Cash Flow	$ 210,000	$ 102,036	$ 80,436
Purchase Price	$1,500,000	$1,500,000	$1,500,000
Less: Loan Amount	0	1,000,000	1,200,000
Equity Invested	$1,500,000	$ 500,000	$ 300,000
Ratios			
Debt Service / Loan Amount	n.a.	.108	.108
Net Operating Income / Cost	.140	.140	.140
Before-Tax Cash Flow / Equity	.140	.204	.268

The fundamental principle illustrated by Table 7.1 is that, so long as the debt service constant (the annual debt service expressed as a percentage of the amount borrowed) is less than the rate of return on total assets, additional financial leverage increases cash flow to the equity position as a percentage of the equity investment. In Table 7.1, the current yield on assets (net operating income divided by market value) is seen to be 14 percent; the annual debt service constant is only 10.8 percent.

Amplifying the Tax Shelter

Income tax law creates a major incentive to financial leverage. Interest payments are generally deductible from taxable income on a dollar-for-dollar basis (Part Four of this text explores exceptions and special limitations on the deductibility of interest expense). Yet, investors are also allowed an annual tax deduction (called an allowance for depreciation or cost recovery) even when they are purchased with borrowed money. Thus, buying with borrowed funds greatly amplifies the amount of tax deductible expenses an investor can claim with the same level of equity investment.

Amplifying the Gain on Disposal

When market values are increasing, favorable financial leverage will multiply the gain from appreciation. This is illustrated in Example 7.2 by assuming a current yield of zero; no benefits accrue other than from appreciation. Because the interest rate on the purchase-money mortgage in the example is less than the expected rate of increase in the market value of the property, financial leverage amplifies the expected yield impressively. The expected annual rate of return on equity (total return, the current yield—zero in this case—plus appreciation), calculated on a before-tax basis under both of the available financing alternatives, is presented in Table 7.2.

Example 7.2

A parcel of land that is well situated to benefit from rapid urban growth can be acquired for $600,000. A prospective investor expects that the land will double in value during the next five years, after which she plans to sell. During the interim, the land can be leased to a turnip farmer for an annual rental that just covers the property tax liability, so there will be zero annual cash flow before debt service and income taxes (because there are no improvements on or to the land—just raw farm land—there is no cost recovery allowance to consider).

The land can be purchased for $600,000 cash, or the present owner will agree to accept a $150,000 down payment accompanied by a note and purchase-money mortgage for $450,000. Both the principal and the accumulated interest on the note will be due and payable at the end of the fifth year, with interest accumulating at a compound annual rate of 9.0 percent.

The $692,381 balance due on the purchase-money note in the *"with leverage"* calculation represents the value, after five years, of a $450,000 deposit (the face amount of the note) drawing interest at a compound rate of 9 percent per annum. The annual rates of return (27.6 percent and 14.9 percent) represent compound annual growth rates that will make the initial equity cash outlays under each alternative approximately equal to the net equity proceeds on sale after five years. Compound interest and discount calculations are explained in detail in Appendix A.

Because interest expense is deductible and the gain on disposal is taxable, both at the same incremental rate in our example, the after-tax rate of return on the equity investment is simply the before-tax rate times one, minus the incremental income tax rate. The positive consequences are further amplified when

Table 7.2	**Cash Flow Consequences of Financing Alternatives in Example 7.2.**	
	With Leverage	*Without Leverage*
Proceeds from sale after 5 years	$1,200,000	$1,200,000
Less: Balance due on loan	692,381	0
Net sales proceeds, before tax	$ 507,619	$1,200,000
Initial cash outlay	$ 150,000	$ 600,000
Approximate annual pre-tax rate of return	27.6%	14.9%

carrying costs (that is, the interest on borrowed money) are tax deductible at the investor's incremental income tax rate, yet the gain on sale is taxed at a lower rate applicable to long-term capital gains. These issues are addressed in Part Four, which explains federal income tax rules.

MEASURING FINANCIAL LEVERAGE

Financial leverage can be measured as the relationship between an equity investment and the total market value of assets acquired. Corporate financial analysts frequently express this relationship as a *debt-to-equity ratio,* the ratio between borrowed funds and equity funds. For reasons having to do more with its origin than with its usefulness, the ratio between borrowed funds and the market value of the asset being financed (a *loan-to-value ratio*) is more commonly employed in real estate circles.

The loan-to-value ratio is a measure of the mortgage lender's margin of safety in the event of default, and it is for this purpose that the measure was initially devised. The ultimate cure for default is public sale of the mortgaged property, and the lender expects to recoup the loan balance from the sales proceeds. Should the sale bring less than the loan balance (plus costs incident to the sale), the lender is almost certain to suffer financial loss. The loan-to-value ratio as an expression of the risk of such a loss. The ratio for the property in Example 7.1 ($1.0 million/$1.5 million = .67, or 67 percent) expresses the fact that, in the event of immediate default, the property could sell for as much as one-third (1 – .67) below its current value before the lender would suffer a significant loss.

Loan-to-value ratios serve an entirely different function for investment analysts. They provide a measure of the dollar amount of real estate that can be controlled with a given amount of equity funds. If, for example, the available loan-to-value ratio is 0.67, then an investor can control [$1 / (1 – 0.67)], or $3 of real estate for every $1 of equity funds invested. This is the case in Example 7.1, where $500,000 of equity investment confers control of a $1.5 million asset. The loan-to-value ratio, therefore, serves as a measure of possible financial leverage.

The debt-to-equity ratio expresses the same relationship in a slightly different fashion. In Example 7.1 the debt-to-equity ratio is $1.0 million to $500,000, or two to one. This indicates that the investor can borrow $2 for every $1 of equity funds employed.

Another ratio designed to express the risk associated with financial leverage is the *debt coverage ratio,* the ratio between net operating income and the annual debt service obligation. It is a measure of the extent to which net operating income can fall below expectations before it becomes insufficient to service the debt. In equation form, it is as follows:

$$\text{Debt coverage ratio} = \frac{\text{Annual net operating income}}{\text{Annual debt service}}$$

The debt coverage ratio in Example 7.1 is 1.95, calculated by dividing the $210,000 net operating income by the $107,967 annual debt service requirement. This expresses an expectation that annual cash flow before debt service will be approximately 1.95 times the amount required to service the debt. It indicates a substantial cushion for underestimated expenses or overestimated revenues before actual net operating income falls below that required to service the mortgage indebtedness.

HOW MUCH IS ENOUGH FINANCIAL LEVERAGE?

Recall from Example 7.1 that the greater the amount of favorable leverage employed, the greater is the return on equity capital. This suggests that one can't have too much favorable financial leverage. Yet there does seem to be an optimal capital structure, and there are definite limits on the amount of debt financing lenders are willing to supply. Someone has suggested that financial leverage is like flavoring in a cake: too little or too much is disastrous; just the right amount creates a delicious concoction.

Debt Coverage Ratios and Available Financing

Choosing the right amount of financial leverage presupposes lenders' willingness to advance funds. The first question to be addressed, therefore, is how much leverage is available. Only then is it meaningful to ask how much of the available leverage should be used.

On all except very small investment properties, lenders can be confident that borrowers will honor their debt service obligations only if the properties generate sufficient cash flow for this purpose. Moreover, since a property's value depends upon its ability to generate income, the value of mortgaged property will decline if the anticipated income does not materialize. An important measure of the lender's security, therefore, is the relationship between annual net operating income from a property and the debt service obligation associated with a mortgage loan.

We have seen that this relationship is expressed as a debt coverage ratio. Mortgage lenders often specify minimum acceptable debt coverage ratios as a constraint on the amount they are willing to lend. Dividing the estimated annual net operating income by the minimum acceptable debt coverage ratio yields the maximum amount of annual debt service a property will support. Dividing this by the annual loan constant for the most likely loan terms results in an estimate of the loan that the property will support. Example 7.3 illustrates.

The expected $400,000 income from the property in Example 7.3 must be at least 1.2 times as great as the annual debt service obligation. The debt service obligation, therefore, cannot exceed $400,000/1.2, or $333,333. The amortization table in Appendix C at the end of the text (Appendix A explains how to use

DCR: $\dfrac{400K}{333,333} = 1.20$

loan amt = $3,687,356$

loan const = $\dfrac{3,087,356}{333,333}$

Example 7.3

Conversation with lenders results in an estimation that they will insist on a debt coverage ratio of not less than 1.20 and will lend at 9 percent per annum, to be repaid in equal monthly installments of principal and interest over 20 years. The property is expected to yield first-year net operating income of $400,000.

the table) reveals that a 9 percent, 20-year, fully amortizing loan requires monthly payments of $.0089973 per dollar borrowed. The annual debt service per dollar borrowed is simply 12 times this amount, or $.10797. Since the maximum debt service the net operating income will support is $333,333, the property will support a maximum loan of $333,333/.10797 = $3,087,274.

Loan-to-Value Ratios and Available Financing

In addition to specifying minimum acceptable debt coverage ratios, lenders usually specify maximum acceptable loan-to-value ratios. The actual loan they will make is the one that satisfies the most restrictive of these constraints.

For example, if the property whose income is given in Example 7.3 has a value of $4 million and the lender cites a maximum loan-to-value ratio of 70 percent, the maximum amount that could be borrowed is 0.7 times $4 million, or $2.8 million. This is true even though the debt coverage constraint would permit a loan of slightly more than $3 million. Conversely, if the property was worth $5 million, the loan-to-value ratio would permit a loan of $3.5 million, yet the debt coverage ratio constraint would limit the loan to just over $3 million.

Financial Leverage and Risk

The popular image of lenders is of tight-fisted money-mongers who will make a loan only when borrowers are so prosperous and wealthy they don't need the funds. Yet, toward the peak of each real estate investment cycle, when the competition to place loans is greater than borrowers' problems in qualifying, lenders sometimes engage in a veritable lending frenzy. Moreover, even in normal times lenders' restrictions can often be circumvented by convincing the seller to provide supplementary financing.

Just because the money is available does not mean it should be borrowed, though. Two negative consequences can result from increasing dependence on borrowed funds: the venture becomes increasingly risky, and the cost of borrowing escalates.

Even if borrowing costs do not increase, the net benefit of borrowing will eventually be whittled down by offsetting increases in financial risk. We saw earlier that the benefits are predicated on an assumption that leverage will be favorable. But this assumption is based on a forecast that is fraught with un-certainty. If the operating forecast proves overly optimistic and the total return on assets falls below the cost of borrowed money, the negative consequences of the flawed investment strategy grow directly with the degree of financial leverage employed.

Look at Example 7.1 again. Remember that the $210,000 net operating income is only an expectation. The actual operating income might be considerably less. Suppose it proved to be only $150,000. The actual current yield on assets drops to 10.0 percent, which is less than the debt service constant. Using financial leverage drops rather than increases the actual current yield on equity, and the greater the degree of financial leverage, the smaller is the current equity yield. (Whether leverage is ultimately favorable or unfavorable depends on the *total return* on assets: current yield plus-or-minus the rate of change in asset value. It depends also upon the income tax consequences.) The impact on current yield to the equity investor when leverage is used and net operating income falls below expectations is illustrated in Table 7.3.

Look again at the investment described in Example 7.2. Table 7.2 illustrates how financial leverage increases the expected yield on the investment, from 14.9 percent without financial leverage to 27.6 percent with financial leverage. But the example and the table assume that the property doubles in value over five years, a compound rate of appreciation of about 14.9 percent per annum. What if the property appreciates at a rate of less than 9.0 percent per annum (the cost of borrowed money)? Then financial leverage will be negative rather than positive; it will *reduce* the rate of return on equity funds. Note also that the balance due on the $450,000 loan (principal plus cumulative interest) will be $692,381. If the land sale nets less than that amount, there will not be sufficient cash flow to pay off the loan.

Table 7.3   **Cash Flow Consequences of Financing Alternatives in Example 7.1 with Less-Than-Expected Net Operating Income**

	No Loan	*$1,000,000 Loan*	*$1,200,000 Loan*
Net Operating Income	$ 150,000	$ 150,000	$ 150,000
Less: Annual Debt Service	0	107,964	129,564
Before-Tax Cash Flow	$ 150,000	$ 42,036	$ 20,436
Purchase Price	$1,500,000	$1,500,000	$1,500,000
Less: Loan Amount	0	1,000,000	1,200,000
Equity Invested	$1,500,000	$ 500,000	$ 300,000
Ratios			
Debt Service / Loan Amount	n.a.*	.108	.108
Net Operating Income / Cost	.100	.100	.100
Before-Tax Cash Flow / Equity	.100	.084	.068

*Not applicable

Financial Leverage and the Cost of Borrowing

Besides increasing the range of possible outcomes to equity investors though, increasing financial leverage also drives up the cost of borrowing. As leverage increases, lenders insist on additional effective interest as compensation for their additional risk exposure. The increase may take the form of larger front-end fees or higher contract interest rates, or both. The result is greater incremental borrowing costs, as illustrated in Figure 7.1.

Figure 7.1 depicts only the explicit costs: those charged by the lender. There is a second layer of cost, however, that borrowers must factor into their leverage decisions. This is the implicit cost expressed as greater risk exposure. Earlier, we saw that the greater the amount of borrowed money relative to equity funds, the greater is the range of possible outcomes for the equity investors, and dispersion of possible outcomes around the expected outcome is a common way of measuring risk. As discussed in Chapter 1, investors typically prefer less risk and expect to be compensated for assuming more. Risk-bearing, therefore, can be thought as an implicit cost of using borrowed money.

Figure 7.2 replicates Figure 7.1 but adds two additional elements. The flat, horizontal line depicts the expected rate of return on assets. Since the source of investment funds does not affect the return on assets, the marginal rate is the same at all levels of financial leverage.

Before considering risk, the optimal amount of financial leverage is L_1, where the incremental cost of borrowing exactly equals the incremental return on assets. Additional leverage would cost more than the expected rate of return on assets, and so would pull down the expected rate of return to the equity investors.

When the implicit cost of additional risk attendant to financial leverage is factored into the analysis, the incremental cost of borrowing is more appropriately depicted by the heavy, upward-sloping line in Figure 7.2. This is the explicit cost as depicted by the stair-step cost line, plus the implicit cost of added

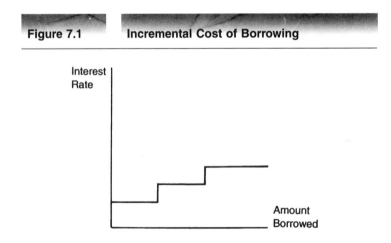

| Figure 7.1 | Incremental Cost of Borrowing |

Figure 7.2	Optimum Amount of Financial Leverage

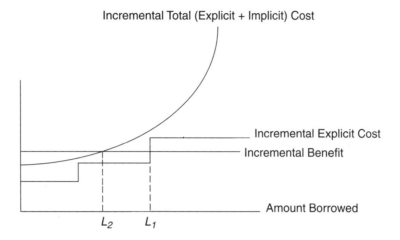

Incremental Total (Explicit + Implicit) Cost

Incremental Explicit Cost

Incremental Benefit

Amount Borrowed

L_2 L_1

uncertainty. With consideration of risk, the optimal amount of financial leverage is reduced to L_2, where the marginal return on assets equals the risk-adjusted marginal cost of borrowing.

WHO ARE THE LENDERS?

Real estate investors depend on a different set of mortgage lenders than do home buyers. The cast of players changes through time, and there has been a major realignment over the past decade. Today's most frequent sources are commercial banks, insurance companies, pension funds and an odd mixture referred to as conduits.

Commercial Banks

Because a substantial portion of their funds are from demand deposits, commercial banks have greater liquidity needs than do most other commercial mortgage lenders, and commit only a modest portion of their portfolio to mortgage lending. Yet, the tremendous volume of deposits available to them make them a major source of mortgage loan funds. They typically originate several times the dollar volume of commercial mortgage loans as does the life insurance industry, the second most significant source.

Banks face federally imposed limits on the amount they can loan relative to the dollar value of collateral. With certain specified exceptions, they cannot lend more than 85 percent of the market value of improved property other than one-to-four family residences. They are limited to 80 percent of the market value with respect to loans to finance nonresidential construction, 75 percent for land development loans, and 65 percent of value when financing acquisition of raw land.

Because of banks' liquidity needs, real estate loans of short duration are more suitable for their portfolios than are traditional, long-term, fully amortizing mortgage loans. As a consequence, they favor loans to finance construction (due dates typically are one to three years), short-term loans (typically six to 12 months) to mortgage companies to finance the companies' mortgage loan portfolio until it can be sold. Also, they often make medium-term (ten- to 15-year) mortgage loans to favored commercial customers. They are a major player in the home loan origination business, but these loans are usually sold to investors in the secondary market.

Insurance Companies and Pension Funds

Insurance companies have long been a mainstay of mortgage funds for investment property. Their predictable inflow of investable funds and the long term nature of most of their obligations make mortgage loans a particularly appropriate investment. Figure 7.3 shows the volume and composition of the insurance industry's commercial mortgage loan portfolio in mid-1995.

Life insurance companies' lending practices are regulated by state insurance agencies, which vary from state to state. The regulators typically set limits on the types of investments insurance companies can make and the percentage of their investment portfolios that can be devoted to each category. Within the constraints set by regulators, the big insurance companies exhibit a preference for loans on very large ventures. They often acquire an equity participation interest

| Figure 7.3 | Composition of Life Insurance Industry's Mortgage Loan Portfolios |

Total = $172.9 billion

SOURCE: American Council of Life Insurance

(that is, part ownership). Smaller insurers are inclined to reach further down the mortgage loan feeding chain; some make individual home loans in their locale.

Pension funds' cash flows are very similar to life insurance companies in terms of predictability and term structure, yet they have not been a major player in commercial real estate mortgage lending until recently. They moved aggressively into the market during the mid-1990s, and their growing presence prompted *Real Estate Capital Markets Report* to began showing them as a commercial mortgage source for the first time in 1995.

Conduit Sources

A major source of real estate debt financing (approximately $10 billion was borrowed this way during the first six months of 1994, according to one source) [1] is funded with commercial mortgage-backed securities—CMBS. These are securities that represent shares in a pool of mortgages. Holders of the securities get the scheduled cash flow from the mortgage pool, minus the servicing fee. Commercial mortgage-based securities are attractive investments for regulated institutions because, as securities, the instruments typically require a substantially smaller liquid reserve than do real estate or mortgage investments.

In the past, most CMBS were issued by lenders who originated the loans or by entities that acquired ownership of the originating institutions. In recent years, however, numerous lenders and investment bankers have formed partnerships that enable mortgage borrowers to tap the CMBS market by using conduits.

According to the publisher of *Commercial Mortgage Alert,* 25 commercial mortgage conduits were in operation in mid-1994.[2] The reported volume of conduit loans during the first half of 1994 was approximately $853 million, about 8.5 percent of all CMBS volume.[3]

SUMMARY

Financial leverage, the use of borrowed money, enables investors to acquire a much more expensive property than would otherwise be possible. It also permits acquiring more separate properties and thus may reduce overall risk.

Risk that cash flow from an investment will be insufficient to meet associated mortgage-debt payments is called financial risk. Increasing financial leverage also increases financial risk. The borrowing decision involves weighing offsetting elements of enhanced earnings potential and increased financial risk.

Interest expense may be deducted from taxable income, thereby decreasing the after-tax cost of borrowing. Borrowing enables investors to control a much larger financial investment, with the consequent possibility of claiming greatly increased income tax deductions for cost recovery allowances. An increased probability of ultimately realizing a substantial gain on disposal of the property also results.

NOTES

1. *Real Estate Capital Markets Report* (Walnut Creek, CA: Institutional Real Estate, Inc.) 4(2):36 (Fall 1994), p. 36.

2. Andrew Albert, "Mortgage Conduits Prepare for Market Invasion," *Real Estate Capital Markets Report* (Walnut Creek, CA: Institutional Real Estate, Inc.) vol. 3, no. 4 (Spring 1994), pp. 22–23.

3. Terry Fleming, "Conduits Struggle To Gain Market Foothold," *Real Estate Capital Markets Report* (Walnut Creek, CA: Institutional Real Estate, Inc.) vol. 4, no. 2 (Fall 1994), pp. 36–37.

RECOMMENDED READINGS

Boykin, James H., and Richard L. Haney, Jr. *Financing Real Estate.* 2nd ed. (Englewood Cliffs, N.J.: Prentice-Hall, 1993).

Downs, Anthony. *The Revolution in Real Estate Finance.* Washington, D.C.: The Brookings Institution, 1985.

Fascitelli, Michael D., Frank J. Walter and Christopher C. Andrysiak. "The Role of the Investment Banker in Real Estate Development." Chapter 15 of Alenick, Jerome B. *Real Estate Development Manual.* Boston: Warren, Gorham and Lamont, 1990.

Marron, Edward W. Jr., and Robert S. Blumenthal. "Real Estate Merchant Banking: The Next Wave in Finance for the Real Estate Developer." Chapter 16 of Alenick, Jerome B. *Real Estate Development Manual.* Boston: Warren, Gorham and Lamont, 1990.

Miles, Mike E., Richard L. Haney, Jr., and Gayle Berens. *Real Estate Development Principles and Process.* 2nd ed. Washington, D.C.: Urban Land Institute, 1996. Part II pp. 51–101.

Stein, Joshua. "Mortgage Loan Structures for the 1990s," *Real Estate Review,* 24(1):15–20 (Spring, 1994).

REVIEW QUESTIONS

1. How do income tax laws create an incentive to borrow money?
2. When financial leverage is used, what is the potential impact on before-tax cash flow and the current before-tax yield to the equity position?
3. Explain the meaning of the loan-to-value ratio from a mortgage lender's perspective and from the viewpoint of an investor.
4. Describe financial risk in real estate investment and explain a useful method of measuring financial risk.
5. How can the debt coverage ratio be used to determine the amount of available financing for a project?
6. Financial leverage can amplify the gain realized on the disposal of a property. Explain how this occurs.

DISCUSSION QUESTIONS

1. The initial interest rate charged on variable-rate mortgage loans is usually lower than that charged on fixed-rate loans of equal length.
   a. Why is this so?
   b. As a borrower, what are some factors you should consider in deciding whether to accept a variable-rate or a fixed-rate loan, when the variable rate is somewhat lower than the fixed-rate?
2. William Zeckendorf, a legendary real estate developer and promoter, is said to have commented during a real estate negotiation, "You can name the price if I can name the terms." What was the logic (if any) of Zeckendorf's position?
3. Two loans are negotiated for the same amount of money, at the same annual interest rate. They require equal periodic payments to fully amortize the loans over 20 years. One loan calls for level monthly payments, the other for level annual payments.
   a. Will the annual payment loan require a payment of exactly 12 times the monthly payment on the other loan? Explain.
   b. Over the full 20-year repayment period, will the cumulative total interest paid on the two loans be the same? Explain.

PROBLEMS

1. A property is expected to generate $300,000 of net operating income over the next 12 months. Discussion with lenders leads to the conclusion that the minimum acceptable debt coverage ratio will be 1.20 and that loan terms will be 8 percent per annum, with 20-year amortization (monthly payments).
   a. What is the maximum supportable annual debt service?
   b. What size loan does this imply?
2. Discussion with lenders indicates that a loan can be obtained for 75 percent of a property's market value. Loan terms will probably be 8 percent interest, 20-year amortization (monthly payments), with the rate renegotiable after seven years. The property is estimated to be worth $200,000.
   a. How much can be borrowed?
   b. What will be the annual debt service?
   c. What is the expected annual loan constant?
3. A property that can be purchased for $1.7 million has an expected first-year net operating income of $190,000. An investor is considering two loan alternatives:
   Loan A: A 70 percent loan-to-value ratio, with interest at 7.5 percent per annum. The loan will require level monthly payments to amortize the principal over 20 years.

Loan B: An 80 percent loan-to-value ratio, with interest at 8.0 percent per annum. This loan will require level monthly payments to amortize the principal over 25 years.

Required: For each loan, determine:

a. The *expected* before-tax cash flow (net operating income minus annual debt service) as a percent of the equity investment.

b. The *actual* before-tax cash flow as a percentage of the equity investment, if the actual net operating income falls ten percent below expectations.

c. The percentage by which actual net operating income can fall below expectations before it is just sufficient to provide for annual debt service.

CHAPTER 8

Credit Instruments and Borrowing Arrangements

Most real estate loans are evidenced with promissory notes and secured by mortgages that pledge the realty as collateral. Standard interest and repayment provisions are sometimes modified, however, to give lenders more attractive yields, to shift risk from lenders to borrowers, or to make loans more attainable. Alternative security instruments have evolved; the best choice depends upon the character of pledged property and on borrowers' and lenders' objectives.

CREDIT AND SECURITY INSTRUMENTS

Precedent and state statutes have established strict procedures and extensive documentation requirements for real estate loans. These documents and procedures, evolved from ceaseless contention between borrowers and lenders, each vying for advantage, are designed to safeguard security interests and to assert claims against pledged property in the event an underlying debt obligation is not honored. Some reflect legislation aimed at protecting borrowers against rapacious money lenders; others comply with laws that give lenders greater recourse against deadbeat borrowers.

Promissory Notes

A promissory note is a written promise by the *obligor* to pay a specified sum of money to another person, called the *payee* or *obligee,* under terms and conditions agreed upon by the parties. Notes used in real estate finance are generally referred to as *mortgage notes.* They differ from other promissory notes only in their reference to the real estate that serves as security for the promise to pay.

Since it documents a private agreement between contracting parties, a promissory note may contain any legal provision upon which the parties agree. As a practical matter, most include basically the same provisions. The note must show the following:

- The amount of the debt
- The promise to pay
- The interest rate charged
- Payment terms (amount and timing of payments)
- A reference to the real estate pledged as collateral

Other provisions that are frequently incorporated, although they are not essential to create a legally binding obligation and security interest, include the following:

- An *acceleration clause,* which permits the lender to demand immediate repayment of the entire loan balance if the borrower defaults on any provision
- Default provisions, which usually include a waiver of certain legal rights that might exist in the absence of specific wording to the contrary
- Terms under which prepayment may be made, including prepayment penalties if applicable

It is not at all uncommon for a promissory note's terms to be repeated in the accompanying security instrument, a mortgage or deed of trust. The note and security instrument together comprise the contract between borrower and lender, and in fact are often combined. Should provisions of the two documents (when they are not combined) conflict, those of the note prevail.

Mortgages

Notes and mortgages work together: the note acknowledges the debt and is a promise to pay; the mortgage pledges specific assets as security for the promise. Mortgages also specify the lender's rights in a borrower's estate in the event of default. If there is no default, a mortgage creates no interest in the pledged property.

Because laws vary, mortgage provisions differ from state to state. Mortgages are contracts, and are subject to the same limitations as other contracts: they must involve competent parties, and there must be an offer and acceptance, consideration, and legality of purpose. Because they are subject to the *statute of frauds,* mortgages must be in writing, and signed by all parties, to be enforceable.

Basic mortgage provisions are determined by statute in the state where the mortgaged property is located, regardless of where the loan is originated. Since they are contracts between borrowers and lenders, mortgages may be adapted to suit any legal purpose. Beyond the basics, their provisions are governed by intent of the parties.

Several widespread mortgage innovations have evolved to suit special types of real property pledges. Of particular interest to real estate investors are purchase-money mortgages, blanket mortgages and open-ended mortgages.

Purchase-Money Mortgages. Any mortgage given by a buyer to a seller to secure a note in partial payment of the purchase price is called a *purchase-money mortgage* (also known as a *take-back mortgage*). The major distinction between a purchase-money mortgage and a mortgage securing a third-party loan lies in the order of priority of the underlying lien. If a purchase-money mortgage is executed and recorded simultaneously with the deed, it takes precedence over all the mortgagor's subsequent debts.

To protect the priority of a purchase-money mortgage, it must be recorded at the same time as the deed conveying the associated property.

Blanket Mortgages. A borrower may at times pledge two or more parcels of property as security for a single loan. The mortgage thereby created is known as a *blanket mortgage* and may contain special clauses to meet specific borrower needs. A blanket mortgage might be used to finance a building that is to be converted to condominiums, for example. As each unit is sold, it must be released from the mortgage so that the buyer can pledge the property as security for a loan to finance the transaction. This requires a provision for partial release in the blanket mortgage. A *partial release clause* typically provides for segments of a mortgaged property to be released after specified lump-sum payments on the mortgage note.

Open-Ended Mortgages. A mortgage can be written so that it will secure future as well as current loans. Even when the exact amount of the subsequent advances cannot be precisely forecast, a properly drawn open-ended mortgage enables the lender to make subsequent payout and have the lien securing these additional funds be senior to other liens that may have been created during the interval between payouts. Such mortgages are called *open-ended* or, more simply, *open* mortgages. They are often used to finance purchases and subsequent renovation or additional construction.

Deeds of Trust

Whereas a mortgage is a straightforward contract between two parties (borrower and lender), a *deed of trust* or *trust deed* involves a third party designated to act as a trustee in the transaction. The borrower conveys the property to the trustee, who holds title for the lender's benefit. In several states, this procedure has largely supplanted mortgage arrangements.[1] In others, both mortgages and trust deeds are used.[2]

A trustee takes title via a deed accompanied by a *trust agreement* (sometimes incorporated into the deed itself), which sets forth terms of the security arrangement and instructs the trustee in the event of default. Trust agreements usually instruct the trustee to conduct a public sale of the property in the event of default (in some states, foreclosure on a deed of trust requires essentially the same proceeding as with a mortgage). Proceeds of the sale are distributed in accordance with the trust agreement, the terms of which are generally prescribed by statute. Funds generally are employed first to cover the trustee's expenses, then to satisfy the balance of indebtedness plus accrued interest, with any remaining money going to the defaulting debtor.

Deeds of trust embody some advantages for lenders, even in states that require foreclosure to proceed in the same fashion as with a defaulted mortgage. Selling a note secured by a deed of trust, for example, involves less legal expense and bother than one secured by a conventional mortgage. Moreover, a note secured by a deed of trust can be held without ownership becoming a matter of public record, since the owner of record is the trustee rather than the lender. This is impossible with a mortgage note, because the assignment of a mortgage needs to be recorded to protect the assignee.

CREDIT TERMS

Until the 1970s, real estate lending practices had evolved only modestly from their roots in the post-depression restructuring of the 1930s. The pace of change accelerated gradually but inexorably during the 1970s until, late in that decade, it reached a level that can safely be called revolutionary. Wildly fluctuating interest rates, lowered yields to equity capital, intensified competition among lenders, partial deregulation of financial markets, and frequent changes in federal income tax law dislocated the mortgage lending industry and caused restructuring on a scale unprecedented since the economic turmoil of the 1930s.

Amortization Alternatives

From the late 1930s to the 1970s, real estate mortgage loans (other than those for construction and development) made by institutional lenders called for equal monthly payments of combined principal and interest sufficient to retire the loan over 25 to 30 years or longer. Such loans are said to be *fully amortizing,* and are still the norm in home finance. In mortgage lending on investment properties, however, the fully amortizing long-term loan has been substantially supplanted.

Partially Amortizing Loans. Probably the most common arrangement today, the partially amortizing mortgage might require equal periodic payments to retire the principal over 20 or 25 years. Instead of running full term though, the balance becomes due and payable in a much shorter time—perhaps five to ten years. The final payment, which includes the remaining principal amount, is called a *balloon payment.*

Nonamortizing Loans. Also called *straight-term* or *interest-only* loans, the nonamortizing loan requires periodic payments of accrued interest but no principal payments until the note matures. The entire principal amount then becomes due and payable. A special variant of the nonamortizing loan, called a *bullet loan* or *gap financing,* is often used when a construction loan expires and long-term financing has not yet been procured. Typically, an interest-only loan is negotiated to run from two to ten years, with interest but no principal payments during the term, and no provision for early payment or loan renewal.

Deferred Interest Loans.   All, or some portion, of the interest on a mortgage-secured loan might be unpaid until late in a loan term or until maturity. Examples include *graduated payment mortgages* and *reverse annuity mortgages,* both used primarily in connection with single-family residential mortgage loans. Graduated payment mortgages require early payments that cover only a portion of the interest and none of the principal, then later—and larger—payments to amortize the principal and the accrued interest over the remaining loan term. Reverse annuity mortgages involve periodic payments by the lender to the borrower over the term of the loan, with each disbursement and the accruing interest added to the balance of the loan. The cumulative amount becomes due and payable in a lump sum when the mortgage note matures.

Alternative Interest Rate Provisions

Persistent price inflation and rising interest rates combined during the decade of the 1970s to ravage mortgage lenders' profitability and threaten their long-term survival. When interest rates escalated, lenders holding a portfolio of long-term, fixed-rate loans found the spread—the difference between interest rates earned on mortgage loans and rates paid to depositors—shrinking alarmingly. They responded with a spate of innovative financing arrangements designed to transfer interest-rate risk to borrowers.

Adjustable Rate Loans.   Loans with interest rates that vary with some market index such as the average yield on Treasury securities, the average cost of funds to insured lenders or average mortgage rates, are called *adjustable rate mortgages* (ARMS). In some places, ARMs are called by other names, including *variable rate mortgages* (VRMs), which actually include all types of mortgages with varying rates or payments to counteract the effect of inflation. Whatever the local name, the purpose is to shift from lender to borrower a portion of the risk of unanticipated changes in interest rates.

Renegotiable Rates.   *Renegotiable rate mortgages* (RRMs) are fixed-rate, level-payment instruments with payments designed to amortize the loan over 20 to 30 years. After a relatively short period, however (typically, three to five years), the principal balance is due and payable. The balance is then refinanced by the lender over the remaining years at currently prevailing interest rates, with the remaining principal balance falling due once again in three to five years. In this manner, the interest rate is adjusted to the market periodically over the entire amortization term. This type of mortgage is sometimes called a *rollover loan,* and is used extensively in Canada. In some circles it is referred to as *Canadian rollover* loan.

Equity Participation. Financial institutions, having observed developers and investors reaping the benefits of sustained inflation while lenders bore the brunt of risk associated with new projects, began experimenting with ways to share the largess from successful projects while continuing to insulate themselves from the consequences of poor performance. Their experiments have spawned a covey of contract clauses that permit lenders to receive a portion of the economic benefit that previously accrued solely to borrowers; this is in addition to the lender's interest charges. The provisions are collectively referred to as *equity kickers.*

One common form of equity participation involves a share in gross property revenue above some specified base figure, plus a share in capital appreciation upon ultimate sale of a project (or, if the project isn't sold, when the mortgage is retired). The instrument used to accomplish this is often called a *shared equity participation* (SEP) mortgage. The other common arrangement is for the lender to share only in the increase in market value during the loan term. This is accomplished with a *shared appreciation mortgage* (SAM). These arrangements do not involve actual ownership interests, but are merely contingent interests.

ALTERNATIVE FINANCING ARRANGEMENTS

Third-party loans secured by mortgages or deeds of trust are by far the most common vehicles for generating financial leverage. However, they are not the only strategies available. Many investors further amplify financial leverage with installment sales contracts, through sale and leaseback arrangements, or by recourse to junior financing.

Installment Sales Contracts

When sellers fund a portion of the transaction price, an *installment sales contract* may be employed instead of a note and mortgage. Sometimes called *land contracts, contracts for deed* or *articles of agreement,* installment sales contracts spell out terms and conditions under which sellers *(vendors)* are obligated to render deeds of conveyance to buyers *(vendees)* at some future date. During the interim, vendors retain title in their own names, and continue as owners of record. The contracts remain *executory* (incomplete) until all preconditions have been met and the deeds are delivered.

Since the seller retains legal title under an installment sales contract, a buyer has only those rights granted by contract terms or by specific provisions of state statutes. Typical arrangements give buyers the right of possession during the term of their contracts, and require them to pay all property taxes and assessments, to acquire and maintain hazard insurance, and to maintain the property in good repair. Sellers often are not required to have good title during the term of the contract, but must acquire title in order to convey as the contract prescribes.

Installment sales contracts frequently stipulate that default extinguishes all of a vendee's rights in the property. Where such provisions are enforceable, defaulting vendees lose not only their rights to possession and collection of rents, but also forfeit any equity accumulated due to debt retirement or increases in property value.

Buyers sometimes strengthen their positions in installment sales transactions by insisting that the seller provide title insurance and by recording the transaction. Title insurance assures that the vendor has good title, or reveals exceptions as listed on the insurance document; recordation gives constructive notice to the world of the vendee's claim against the property.

Sales and Leasebacks

Although no credit is involved, sale and leaseback arrangements serve as a alternative means of financing, and have become a popular strategy for generating development capital. By selling a site and leasing it back with a provision that the new landowner's interest will be subordinated to a mortgage taken out by the lessee, a developer can radically reduce the need for equity capital.

Builders and developers also use sale and leaseback arrangements to generate funds to retire construction loans. This might involve only the land under the project, or it might involve selling and leasing back the entire project on a long term *net lease* (the lessee pays all operating expenses and remits a net amount to the owner). This gives investors an assured periodic cash flow with freedom from management responsibility, and an income tax deduction for depreciation expense.

Junior Mortgages

Mortgage loans are characterized as senior or junior, according to the order of priority for repayment in the event of default. Should a foreclosure sale occur, the proceeds go first to satisfy claims secured by a first mortgage, then to those secured by a second mortgage, then to a third mortgage and so on until all secured loans are honored or until funds are exhausted. Generally, the order of priority is determined by the time documents are submitted to the county recorder or registrar of deeds. The mortgage loans that represent claims subordinate to the first mortgage are called *junior liens* or *junior mortgages.*

Junior mortgage loans are often extended by sellers in lieu of all or a part of the gap between the transaction price and a first mortgage loan available from an institutional lender. In addition to their primary goal of expediting the transaction, sellers may get a higher price for their property when they provide financing. Moreover, the interest rate on the junior mortgage might be higher than the rate of return on alternative investment opportunities. Sellers might also reap income tax advantages by reporting such sales using the installment sales method, as described in Chapter 10.

Other sources of junior mortgage loans include real estate investment trusts (see Chapter 26), finance companies and private individuals that make such loans as a regular line of business. Some financial institutions make a limited number of long-term second mortgage loans, though their ability to do so is constrained by regulatory provisions.

✳ Wraparound Mortgages

A special category of junior mortgage, called a *wraparound* or *all-inclusive mortgage* has become popular in recent years. The face amount of the wraparound note includes the balance due on an existing note in addition to any amount to be disbursed on the new note. The wraparound lender assumes responsibility for meeting debt-service obligations on the old mortgage note that has been "wrapped."

Wraparound loans—sometimes called *wraps* or *WAMs*—are frequently used to stretch out payments on an existing loan, thus reducing a borrower's periodic debt-service obligation. Or, they might be used to raise additional money. Sometimes a wraparound loan does both.

Example 8.1

A property owner still has ten years to pay on a $250,000, seven percent, 30-year first mortgage note. Monthly payments, including both principal and interest, are $1,663, and the remaining principal balance is approximately $143,228.

To see how a stretched-out payment wrap might work, consider Example 8.1. The borrower might reduce the monthly payments by negotiating a new, long-term wraparound mortgage loan for exactly the remaining balance of the existing note; $143,228.

If the wraparound note is payable in monthly payments over 25 years with interest at 9.5 percent, monthly payments will be only $1,251. No funds are actually disbursed as a consequence of the new note. Instead, the wraparound lender makes all further payments on the underlying first mortgage note. The borrower will thereby have reduced the monthly payment obligation by $412 (the old payment of $1,663 minus the new payment of $1,251), at the cost of extending the payment period from the ten years remaining on the old mortgage to the 25-year term of the new.

Remaining payments on the old loan ($1,663 monthly for 10 years) will become an obligation of the wraparound lender, who will incur a monthly net cash outflow of $412:

Monthly payment on "wrapped" loan	$1,663.00
Monthly receipt from wraparound note	1,251.00
Monthly net outlay for remaining life of "wrapped" note	$ 412.00

After ten years, the old note is retired and the lender's monthly payment obligation ceases. Monthly receipts, however, will continue for another 15 years. The lender's cash flow expectation at the time the wraparound note is negotiated is as follows:

Years	Monthly Cash Flow		
	Inflow	*Outflow*	*Net*
1–10	$1,251	$1,663	($412)
11–25	1,251	-0-	1,251

Assuming, for simplicity, that the lender receives no loan origination fee and charges no discount points, the average annual yield on funds actually extended will be the discount rate that makes the present value of the forecast cash flow exactly zero. This higher yield for the lender explains why lenders offer the wraparound at a lower rate than a standard mortgage and especially lower than a risky second mortgage. Briefly, the yield rate is determined by solving for r in the following equation, and multiplying by 12:

$$0 = \sum_{t=0}^{n} CF_t / (1 + r)^t$$

$$\therefore \text{Yield} = 12.85\%$$

where:

CF = the monthly net cash flow

n = the number of months in the repayment period

r = the discount rate that satisfied the equality by making the present value of the negative flows exactly equal to that of the positive flows (Appendix A explains how to do the calculation.)

If, in addition to stretching out payments on existing indebtedness, the borrower in Example 8.1 wanted to raise additional funds, this could be accomplished with the same wraparound mortgage note. If an additional $75,000 were needed, then the amount of the wraparound note would include the $143,228 balance of the old mortgage plus $75,000. Monthly payments on a 9.5 percent, 25-year wraparound mortgage note for this amount would be $1,907, compared with $1,663 payments on the underlying first mortgage. The lender's monthly cash flow would then be:

Years	Monthly Cash Flow		
	Inflow	*Outflow*	*Net*
Zero	-0-	$75,000	($75,000)
1–10	$1,907	$1,663	244
11–25	$1,907	-0-	$1,907

The yield rate to the mortgage lender would then be 12 times the rate, r, that satisfies the equality in the following equation:

$$0 = \sum_{t=1}^{n} [CF_t / (1 + r)^t] - \$75,000$$

$$\therefore \text{Yield} = 10.8\% \text{ (rounded)}$$

where the factors n and CF_t have the same meanings as before, and yield is 12 times the monthly rate that satisfies the equality.

The wraparound mortgage may be an attractive alternative for a borrower who is considering a second mortgage loan, because the interest rate on the wraparound is usually lower than that for a conventional second mortgage. If the borrower in this example had obtained a new second mortgage for the $75,000, the lender would charge a higher interest rate to compensate for the additional risk. If that rate was at, say, 12 percent, the combined payment on the first and the second mortgage notes ($1,663 plus $790; for a total of $2,453) would be substantially higher than the $1,907 payment on the wrap.

GOVERNMENT-SPONSORED CREDIT ARRANGEMENTS

The federal government has experimented extensively over the years with special incentives to encourage investment in rental housing for low-to-moderate income tenants. Many of the experiments are defunct, but some tax-exempt financing remains for low-income rental housing.

Department of Housing and Urban Development

Over the years, the Department of Housing and Urban Development (HUD) has sponsored long-term, low-interest loans as an incentive for investing in low-income housing. HUD programs change with sufficient regularity to provide full-time employment for a host of researchers trying to track the red tape.

Private Activity Bonds

For many years, state and local governments were empowered to issue bonds whose interest was exempt from federal (and, in some locales, state) income taxes. Local governments used the bonds, whose tax exempt status permitted them to carry a much lower interest rate than conventional private-source bonds, to finance private business development.

Beginning in 1986, the Internal Revenue Code (in Section 142) restricted the use of tax exempt bonds issued to finance private commercial activities. Code Section 142 exempts from these restrictions only qualifying bonds to finance specifically enumerated projects:

- Airports, docks and wharves, mass communication facilities and high-speed intercity rail facilities owned by government units, though they may be leased to private companies under strictly limited conditions
- Water, sewage, and solid or hazardous waste disposal facilities, as well as local or district utilities, that will provide services available to the general public
- Qualified residential projects. Bonds to finance residential rental projects will qualify for tax exemption only if, during a "qualified project period" which may last for 15 years or longer, a prescribed portion of the tenants are sufficiently impoverished. At least 40 percent of the units must by occupied by tenants whose income does not exceed 60 percent of the area median, or at least 20 percent must be occupied by tenants whose income does not exceed 50 percent of the area median.

Redevelopment Bonds

Tax exempt redevelopment bonds may be issued to finance land acquisition and preparation (razing existing structures and so forth), for relocating tenants out of the redevelopment area and for rehabilitating buildings in areas designated as "blighted" by local government. The debt service on redevelopment bonds must be underwritten to a significant degree by local government, either by pledging general tax revenue or the incremental property tax revenue that will result from enhanced property values in the redeveloped area.[3]

SUMMARY

Promissory notes represent a promise to pay a debt, and specify the terms and conditions. The promise may be secured or unsecured. If real estate is pledged as security for the promise, this is usually accomplished by a mortgage or a deed of trust. These appear to be actual transfers of ownership, but contain a defeasance clause that renders the transfer inoperative if the promissory note is honored by the borrower.

Common variations of security instruments include purchase money mortgages, blanket mortgages, open-ended mortgages, equity participation mortgages and wraparound mortgages. Purchase money mortgages secure notes given in part payment for property, while blanket mortgages pledge two or more parcels of property as security for a single loan. Open-ended mortgages are written so that additional funds can be advanced under the security of the same mortgage. Equity participation loans permit lenders to share in earnings or appreciation without relinquishing their positions as creditors. Wraparound mortgages are junior financing devices that enable junior lienholders to control payments to the senior lienholders.

Installment sales contracts are an alternative financing arrangement wherein the seller agrees to deliver a deed only after the buyer satisfies contractual arrangements—usually payment of the purchase price plus interest. Sale and leaseback arrangements also substitute for conventional mortgage financing. In this arrangement the financier buys the property and leases it back to the user.

State and local governments issued a spate of tax-exempt bonds as a real estate financing device. Income tax law revisions in the 1980s drastically curtailed the uses to which such bond financing can be put.

NOTES

1. California, Colorado, Connecticut, Mississippi, Missouri, Oregon, Tennessee, Texas, Virginia, West Virginia.

2. Alaska, Delaware, Idaho, Kansas, Kentucky, Nevada, South Carolina.

3. Internal Revenue Code Section 144(c).

RECOMMENDED READINGS

Brougham, Sharen, K. "Reminder: The Wrap Is Back." *Commercial Investment Real Estate Journal,* vol. 9, no. 1 (Winter 1990) pp. 10–14.

Clauretie, Terrance M., and G. Stacy Sirmans. *Real Estate Finance, Theory and Practice,* 2nd ed. (Upper Saddle River, NJ: Prentice Hall, 1996).

Downs, Anthony. *The Revolution in Real Estate Finance.* Washington, DC: The Brookings Institution, 1985.

Greenberg, Alan. "Back to Basics: Negotiating Financing in the 1990s." *Real Estate Finance Journal,* vol. 7, no. 3 (Winter 1992) pp. 33–37.

Pollack, Bruce. "Real Estate Loan Underwriting Revisited." *Real Estate Finance Journal,* vol. 7, no. 2 (Winter 1992) pp. 63–68.

Hudsick, Clifford A. "A Tax-Exempt, Credit-Enhanced Bond Financing." *Real Estate Review,* vol. 25, no. 3 (Fall 1995) pp.32–37.

Stein, Joshua. "Cures for the (Sometimes) Needless Complexity of Real Estate Documents." *Real Estate Review,* vol. 25, no. 3 (Fall 1995) pp. 63–67.

REVIEW QUESTIONS

1. How do mortgage notes differ from other promissory notes?
2. List five provisions that must be included in mortgage notes.
3. What functions do mortgages serve?
4. How do purchase money mortgages differ from other mortgages?
5. What is an open-ended mortgage?
6. Describe the role of the trustee in a trust deed arrangement.

7. For what real estate uses can tax exempt bond financing be used under current income tax regulations?
8. What are some representative uses of wraparound mortgage loans?
9. What is the attraction of adjustable rate loans to borrowers? To lenders?

DISCUSSION QUESTIONS

1. Why is there so much variety in loan documentation among the various states? Would a uniform national system be useful?
2. It has been argued that the wording on loan documents favors lenders over borrowers, while courts' interpretations favor borrowers over lenders. Discuss.
3. If mortgaged property is in one state and the mortgage lender is in another, which state's laws should govern the mortgage loan transaction?
4. What is to keep an unscrupulous seller under an installment contract from mortgaging the property after the installment contract has been negotiated, so that the buyer discovers a first mortgage lien on the property when the deed is eventually delivered?
5. Why might a business elect to dispose of its buildings in a sale and leaseback arrangement, even though it will continue to need the premises for an indefinite period? Why not keep ownership of the property as an additional investment, and thereby avoid having to pay rent?
6. There were very few successful mortgage loan innovations in this country during the decades of the 1950s and 1960s. Then, the following two decades witnessed a spate of innovations. What might have caused this abrupt shift in the rate of innovation?

PROBLEMS

1. A $750,000 mortgage loan that is being fully amortized with level monthly payments over 20 years has five years remaining. The contract interest rate is 7.0 percent. The borrower refinances with a 15-year, fully amortizing wraparound loan that carries a contract interest rate of 8.25 percent. In order to keep the monthly payment below $3,000, over how many years must the wraparound be amortized? Round your answer to the nearest whole year.
2. If the borrower negotiates the wraparound loan described in problem 1, what will be the annual net cash flow to the wraparound lender (a) for the first five years of the new loan, and (b) in subsequent years?

CHAPTER 9

The Cost of Borrowed Money

Chapter 8 explores borrowing options but does not explain how cost is computed. Explicit cost comparisons are the focus of this chapter. We first address the mechanics of computing payments and the annual debt service, then consider a way to compare the incremental costs and benefits of alternative debt structures.

THE MANY FACES OF INTEREST EXPENSE

The cost of using borrowed money is, of course, interest expense. Like so many costs and benefits, however, interest expense is not always what it seems. An early step in mastering mortgage finance issues is to understand the difference between nominal or contract interest, effective interest and real interest.

Nominal and Effective Rates

Of all the aspects of interest, the easiest to understand is the *nominal rate* or *contract rate*. This is simply the rate of interest stipulated in the promissory note. It is usually stated as an annual rate, even though payments are most often made monthly.

A step further removed from simplicity is the *effective interest rate*. This is the rate actually paid for the use of borrowed funds, and it often differs strikingly from the contract rate. Effective rates are a function of the amount borrowed and the amount and timing of the required repayment.

Common instances of differences between nominal and effective rates on term loans occur when the borrower pays a *loan origination fee* or *discount points.* The borrower has the use of only a fraction of the funds stipulated in the promissory note (the face amount of the note, minus the origination fee or discount points). Interest and principal payments, however, are based on the full face amount of the note. Interest expense computed on the funds that the borrower actually has available as a consequence of the loan—effective interest—is then higher than the nominal or contract rate.

Example 9.1

A borrower signs a $100,000 mortgage note payable in equal monthly installments over 25 years, with interest at 9 percent per annum on the unpaid balance. The lender charges a loan origination fee equal to 2 percent of the face amount of the loan.

To see this, consider Example 9.1. Monthly payments on the $100,000 mortgage note are $839.20. This can be determined using a financial calculator or by reference to Table C.4 in Appendix C. However, the borrower has the use of only $98,000. This amount, called the *loan proceeds,* is determined by subtracting the loan origination fee from the face amount of the loan:

$$
\begin{aligned}
\text{Loan proceeds} &= \text{(Face amount of note)} - \text{(Origination fee)} \\
&= \$100,000 - (.02 \times \$100,000) \\
&= \$100,000 - \$2,000 \\
&= \$98,000
\end{aligned}
$$

Since the borrower must pay $839.20 per month but only has the use of $98,000, the effective interest rate is that which makes the monthly payments to amortize a $98,000 loan equal $839.20 for 25 years. To determine the effective rate, view the problem as a monthly annuity of $839.20 and solve for the internal rate of return: the discount rate that makes the present value of the annuity stream equal to the $98,000 loan proceeds. This rate is 9.25 percent, determined as follows:

$$
V_0 = \text{payment} \; \sum \left(\frac{1}{I + \frac{e}{12}} \right)^{12t}
$$

$$
= \$839.20 \; \sum \left(\frac{1}{1 + \frac{e}{12}} \right)^{12t}
$$

$$
= \$98,000
$$

where

V_0 = amount of the loan proceeds

t = ranges over the amortization period (in months)

e = effective monthly interest rate

The annual rate is simply 12 times the monthly rate, *e*. Solving for *e* in the equation is somewhat involved; it requires a logarithmic transformation. Alternatively, the solution can be found by successive approximations; using various possible values for *e* that are slightly in excess of the contract interest rate until the equation yields a present value of $98,000. The easiest approach, of course, is to use a financial calculator.

The problem can also be solved using loan amortization factors such as those in Table C.4. An excerpt is presented here as Table 9.1. Recall that when payments are unknown they are determined from the table by the following equation:

$$\text{Payment} = \text{Note amount} \times \text{Amortization factor}$$

where the amortization factor is for the contract rate of interest. With known payments, the effective interest rate can be determined by restructuring the equation as follows:

$$\text{Payments} = \text{Loan proceeds} \times \text{Amortization factor}$$

Table 9.1   **Monthly Payment To Amortize a One-Dollar Debt**

Number of Years	Annual Interest Rate						
	6.0%	7.0%	8.0%	9.0%	10.0%	12.0%	14.0%
1	.086066	.086527	.086988	.087451	.087916	.088849	.089787
2	.044321	.044773	.045227	.045685	.046145	.047073	.048013
3	.030422	.030877	.031336	.031800	.032267	.033214	.034178
4	.023485	.023946	.024413	.024885	.025363	.026334	.027326
5	.019333	.019801	.020276	.020758	.021247	.022244	.023268
6	.016573	.017049	.017533	.018026	.018526	.019550	.020606
7	.014609	.015093	.015586	.016089	.016601	.017653	.018740
8	.023141	.013634	.014137	.014650	.015174	.016253	.017372
9	.012006	.012506	.013019	.013543	.014079	.015184	.016334
10	.011102	.011611	.012133	.012668	.013215	.014347	.015527
11	.010367	.010884	.011415	.011961	.012520	.013678	.014887
12	.009759	.010284	.010825	.011380	.011951	.013134	.014371
13	.009247	.009781	.010331	.010897	.011478	.012687	.013951
14	.008812	.009354	.009913	.010489	.011082	.012314	.013605
15	.008439	.008988	.009557	.010143	.010746	.012002	.013317
16	.008114	.008672	.009249	.009845	.010459	.011737	.013077
17	.007831	.008397	.008983	.009588	.010212	.011512	.012875
18	.007582	.008155	.008750	.009364	.009998	.011320	.012704
19	.007361	.007942	.008545	.009169	.009813	.011154	.012559
20	.007164	.007753	.008364	.008997	.009650	.011011	.012435
25	.006443	.007068	.007718	.008392	.009087	.010532	.012038
30	.005996	.006653	.007338	.008046	.008776	.010286	.011849

where the amortization factor is for the effective interest rate rather than the contract rate. Substituting numbers from Example 9.2 into the above equation gives the following:

$$\$839.20 = \$98,000 \times \text{Amortization factor}$$

Therefore:

$$\text{Amortization factor} = \frac{\$839.20}{\$98,000} = .008563$$

Reference to the 25-year row of Table 9.1 reveals that this amortization factor lies between 9 percent and 10 percent. Interpolation in the manner described in Appendix A reveals that the effective rate is approximately 9.25 percent.

Our computation presupposes that the note remains in effect until fully amortized. Thus if a borrower anticipates no early payment she will reasonably expect the effective interest rate, on a pre-tax basis, to be approximately 9.25 percent. She will compare this loan with alternative proposals, based on the 9.25 percent rate.

But suppose our investor expects to refinance in, say, five years. Such an anticipation might be reasonable in a market where values are growing rapidly, so that she anticipates borrowing a substantially greater sum in the future, or where interest rates are expected to decline. The prospective borrower will want to determine the effective interest rate based on amortizing the front-end fee over the abbreviated five-year borrowing period.

The proceeds from borrowing, and the annual debt service, will be unaffected by the altered time perspective. But after five years there will be a lump-sum payoff equal to the outstanding balance of the loan.

As explained in Appendix A, the remaining balance is the value of the remaining payments, when discounted at the contract rate. The contract rate in Example 9.1 is 9.0 percent per annum (9/12, or 0.75 per cent per month) and, after five years, there remain 20 years (12 × 20, or 240 months) of payments at $839.20 per month.

Using a financial calculator, one can determine that the present value of $839.20 per period for 240 periods (25 years times 12 months), discounting at 0.75 percent (9.0 percent per annum divided by 12), is $93,272.85. Alternatively, the solution can be pulled from the amortization table (Table C.4 in Appendix C) by using the factor for a 9.0 percent per annum, 20-year loan, and solving for the loan amount that results in a monthly payment of $839.20 (there will be a rounding error of approximately $2.69 in the final answer):

$$\text{Payment} = \text{Loan} \times \text{Amortization factor}$$

Therefore:

$$\text{Loan} = \text{Payment} \times \frac{1}{\text{Amortization factor}} = \$839.20 \times \frac{1}{.008997} = \$93,275.54$$

The effective interest rate with a five-year holding period is the discount rate that makes the present value of $839.20 per month for 59 months plus the present value of a $94,112.05 after 60 months (this is the 60th monthly payment of $839.20, plus the remaining loan balance of $93,272.85) have a present value equal to the $98,000 loan proceeds (note the cumulative rounding error of $0.08):

Months	Monthly Payments	Present Value When Discounting at The Effective Rate*
1–59	$839.20	$39,418.42
60	$839.20 + $93,272.85 = $94,112.05	58,581.50
		$97,999.92

*Effective rate is 9.5189% per annum.

The problem is easily and quickly solved with a financial calculator. With tables the problem is often complicated by the absence of a precisely correct interest rate column in the table (the most nearly correct column in Table 9.1 is 9 percent) and by not knowing what column to use. The solution is to use successive approximations, starting with the first rate in the table that is higher than the contract rate (since amortizing a front-end fee will always make the effective rate higher). When two trial rates have been found to closely bracket the target present value (one yielding a present value slightly higher than the loan proceeds, the other slightly lower), the answer can be approximated by interpolation, as explained in Appendix A.

Before-Tax and After-Tax Borrowing Cost

Because interest payments are usually a tax-deductible expense in the year paid (see Chapter 10 for details and important exceptions), federal and state governments in effect pay part of the cost of borrowing. The only cost relevant to the borrower is the after-tax cost.

If interest expense is fully deductible in the year paid, the after-tax cost of borrowing is $[i \times (1 - t)]$, where i is the before-tax rate and t is the incremental income tax rate. Applying this formula to Example 9.1 and assuming that the borrower is in the 40 percent (combined state and federal) income-tax bracket, the after-tax rate is $[9.0 \times (1 - .40)]$, or 5.4 percent per annum. If the loan is a straight term loan (that is, only the interest is paid currently), the annual after-tax debt service is $5,400 per annum:

Face Amount of Note	$100,000
Times: Contract Interest Rate	.09
Annual Interest Payments	9,000
Less: Tax Savings (.40 × $9,000)	3,600
After-Tax Cost of Borrowing	$5,400

Paying discount points or loan origination fees complicates the arithmetic, but the basic rule remains unchanged: The after-tax cost is the before-tax cost minus the income tax saving. The complication stems from the way tax law requires prepaid interest to be handled. As explained in Chapter 10, the prepaid amount (discount points or loan origination fees) on a loan to finance business or investment property must be deducted ratably over the term of the loan.

Nominal and Real Rates

The real rate of interest is the effective rate, adjusted for inflation. The nominal rate is a real rate plus a premium for expected inflation. Inflation has a major impact on interest rates because the money that mortgage lenders receive back from borrowers (interest and principal payments) will buy less than the money they lend. If, for example, a $1,000 loan is to be repaid in one year with cumulative interest at 8.0 percent, the borrower receives the $1,000 loan proceeds and repays $1,080 in 12 months. The nominal rate is 8 percent (to keep the example simple, the nominal and the effective rates are the same) but the real rate depends on price level changes during the interim.

Suppose during the year the average level of prices increases by 4 percent. Using the time the loan proceeds were disbursed as the base year, the purchasing power of the principal and accumulated interest paid a year later is $1,080/1.04, or $1,038.46. The real interest (that is, the amount of purchasing power paid for the use of money) has been only $38.46, and the real rate of interest (on a before-tax basis) has been [$38.46/$1,000 × 100], or 3.85 percent.

Expressed generically, for any single compounding period the real rate of interest (I_r) is as follows:

$$I_r = \frac{1 + I_n}{1 + P} - 1$$

where:

I_r = real rate of interest

I_n = nominal rate of interest

P = percentage change in the general price level

Applying the generalized formula to our example, we have

$$I_r = \frac{1 + .08}{1 + .04} - 1 = \frac{1.08}{1.04} - 1 = .03846, \text{ or } 3.85\%$$

So far we have applied price-level adjustments on a before-tax basis. On an after-tax basis, the reduction in real interest rates as a consequence of inflation is even more dramatic. This is because the interest expense deduction is based on the nominal rather than the real interest. If the borrower in our continuing example (a $1,000, 8 percent loan for one year, with interest and principal due at year-end) is in the 40 percent combined federal and state income tax brackets, and if the interest expense is fully deductible in the year incurred and paid, the after-tax real rate of interest is approximately 0.77 percent:

$$\text{Nominal After-Tax Rate} = (\text{Before-Tax Rate}) \times (1 - \text{Tax Rate})$$
$$= .08 \times .60$$
$$= .048, \text{ or } 4.8 \text{ percent}$$

$$\text{Real After-Tax Rate} = \frac{1 + I_n}{1 + P} - 1 = \frac{1.048}{1.04} - 1 = .00769, \text{ or } .77\%$$

At first blush it seems from these computations that inflation is uniquely kind to borrowers. But lenders understand the impact of inflation and demand an interest rate premium for expected inflation. If the consensus about future price level changes is an accurate reflection of what actually happens, the real interest rate will be unaffected by price level changes, because the actual changes will have been reflected in the nominal interest rate. If lender consensus overestimates inflation, the inflation premium embedded in nominal rates will cause the real rate to be higher than it otherwise would have been; if the consensus inflation forecast errs on the low side, the real rate will be lower than otherwise.

COMPARING FINANCING ALTERNATIVES

Everyone who has ever shopped for a loan knows that borrowers face a bewildering array of alternatives. Various lenders quote different combinations of interest rates and front-end fees, and offer alternative rates coupled with different amortization periods. This is illustrated in Table 9.2, which summarizes the results of inquiries at seven life insurance firms. Required occupancy levels that had to be achieved before the loan proceeds would be disbursed ranged from a low of 60 percent to a high of 90 percent. Four of the lenders were willing to commit

Table 9.2 **Loan Quotes for a New Apartment Complex, from Seven Insurance Companies, Mid-1995**

Company	A	B	C	D	E	F	G
Required Occupancy	60%[†]	84%[‡]	90%	80%	90%	80%	n.a .*
Interest Rate Lock-In:							
At Application		X	X[§]	X[§]	X[§]	X	
On Acceptance	X						
At Commitment							X
Amortization	25 years	30 years	20/25 years	25 years	25/30 years	30 years	25 years
Term	12 years	10 years	10/20 years	10 years	10/25 years	10 years	10/15 years

*Not applicable
[†]Additional security via a letter of credit until occupancy reaches 93 percent.
[‡]Loan can be funded before 84 percent occupancy, if letter of credit is provided.
[§]Interest rate can be locked in at this point, for a fee.

themselves to a specific interest rate at time of application, two would commit at the time of loan approval, and one only when a commitment letter was issued. Loan terms ranged from ten to 12 years, with amortization over 20 to 30 years. No simple rule of thumb serves as a reliable guide through the loan alternative wilderness, but the concepts we have investigated in this chapter provide the needed analytical tools.

Comparing Effective Interest Rates

A particularly confusing issue is the range of interest rates offered, where they are coupled with different front-end fees. To estimate the effective interest rate coupled with loan alternatives, first estimate the amount and timing of debt service payments for each. Then find the related effective rates. Next, array the effective rates and compare each with the related risk (however risk is measured) to determine which expected rate and related risk of higher rates seems most appealing, given the borrower's attitude toward risk.

Example 9.2 presents three alternatives. The first step in analyzing them is to compare the loan proceeds. This, you should recall, is the face amount of the note minus the front-end charges. The net loan proceeds are shown on the third line of Table 9.3.

Example 9.2

An investor is offered three alternative $1 million loan proposals. All the loans are fully amortizing and require monthly payments.

a. There is a 2.5 percent origination fee for Loan A. The interest rate is 7.5 percent per annum. The amortization period is 20 years, and there is no prepayment penalty.

b. Loan B requires a one-half percent loan origination fee. The contract interest rate is 8.0 percent and the amortization period is 25 years. There is no prepayment penalty.

c. Loan C requires no loan origination fee. The interest rate is 8 percent and the amortization period is 25 years. There is a prepayment penalty of 2.0 percent of the prepaid amount.

In each case the effective interest rate is that which makes the present value of the monthly payments equal to the loan proceeds. If the loan remains outstanding for its entire term, the best alternative is loan A. As shown on Table 9.3, loan C is marginally less expensive than B, since their contract interest rates are the same and C entails no front-end fee.

If the expected period of the loan is only five years, however, the relative costs shift. The effective interest rate is the discount rate that makes the present value of the monthly payments plus the present value of the final, balloon payment (discounting on a monthly basis) exactly equal to the loan proceeds. The

Table 9.3	Effective Interest Rate with Three Borrowing Alternatives, When Loans Run Full-Term		

	Loan Proposal		
	A	*B*	*C*
Face Amount of Note	$1,000,000	$1,000,000	$1,000,000
Less: Front-End Charges	25,000	5,000	0
Loan Proceeds	$975,000	$995,000	$1,000,000
Monthly Payment	$8,055.93	$7,718.16	$7,718.16
Effective Pre-tax Rate	7.84	8.06	8.0

first step toward a solution is to determine the amount of that final payment. The remaining balances after five years are shown in the first column of Table 9.4 (the calculations are shown in Appendix A; the easy way is to use the amortization function on a financial calculator).

Table 9.4 also shows effective rates when the loans are paid off early. Amortizing Loan A's hefty origination fee over just 5 years drives its effective rate above that for Loan B, which has a smaller front-end fee to be amortized. Because of its prepayment penalty, however, loan C is most radically affected. After five years the remaining balance on that loan is still $922,739, and this amount is subject to the two percent prepayment penalty.

What Nominal Rate Applies

In a dynamic interest rate environment, lenders are loath to quote a definite contract interest rate. Instead, many prefer to express rates in terms of a benchmark. By way of illustration, note the typical rates quoted by various categories of lending agents in mid-1995, presented on Table 9.5. Most of the lenders were quoting rates ranging from 130 to 200 basis points (that is, 1.3 to 2.0 percentage

Table 9.4	Effective Interest Rates for Three Loan Alternatives, with Prepayment after Five Years.		

	Loan Proposal		
	A	*B*	*C*
Remaining Balance after Five Years	$869,021	$922,739	$922,739
Add: Prepayment penalty	0	0	18,455
Payoff amount	$869,021	$922,739	$941,194
Effective Pre-tax Rate	8.15	8.13	8.31

Table 9.5	Commercial Mortgage Loan Interest Rates and Terms Prevailing During the Second Quarter of 1995		

	Insurance Companies and Pension Funds*	*Commercial Banks**	*Conduits*†
Interest Rates:			
Fixed	7.25%–7.75%	7.5%–8.25%	8.25%–8.75%
(Spread)‡	125–175 points	150–225 points	225–275 points
Floating		7.4%–8.0%	
(Spread)§		125–200 points	
Loan/Value Ratios	75%	75%	75%
Debt Coverage Ratio	1.20	1.15–1.2	1.2
Term	7–10 years	1–10 years	5–10 years

*A quality real estate only.
†*B* and *C* quality real estate. This includes older properties and properties in less than top-notch locations.
‡Spread on fixed-rate loans is expressed as basis points (100 basis points equals one percentage point) above the rate on U.S. Treasury securities of comparable maturity.
§Spread on floating-rate loans is expressed as basis points above LIBOR (London Interbank Offered Rate) rate.
SOURCE: National Real Estate Index, Summer 1995.

points) above the rate on U.S. Treasury notes of corresponding term. Thus, if a mortgage loan was to run for 10 years and 10-year U.S. Treasury notes were earning 7.0 percent, one might have been able to borrow at nominal rates ranging from 8.3 percent to 9.0 percent.

INCORPORATING BORROWING INTO THE OPERATING PROJECTION

In Chapter 6, we developed a six-year operating forecast for a 280-unit apartment complex called Maegen's Magic Manor. We are now equipped to incorporate a projection of the consequences of using financial leverage, and derive an estimate of the before-tax cash flow to the equity investor.

After checking with several lenders that are the most likely source of a mortgage loan, we conclude that the likely borrowing terms include interest at 8.0 percent, and level monthly payments to amortize the loan over 25 years. At this rate we can avoid paying a loan origination fee. The lender will probably require the rate to be renegotiated after seven years, but this is beyond our six-year projected holding period. We also conclude that the loan-to-value ratio cannot exceed 70 percent and the debt coverage ratio cannot be less than 1.2.

The loan requirements regarding the loan-to-value ratio and the debt coverage ratio constitute constraints on the amount we can borrow. The more severe restraint is the debt coverage ratio.

Debt Coverage Ratio Constraint

The permissible debt coverage ratio is based on the first-year operating projection. We expect the net operating income to be $759,200, and it must comprise at least 1.2 times the annual debt service. This implies debt service of no more than $632,666.67:

$$\text{Debt Coverage Ratio} = 1.20 = \frac{\text{NOI}}{\text{Debt Service}} = \frac{\$759,200}{\text{Debt Service}}$$

Therefore:

$$\text{Maximum Debt Service} = \frac{\$759,200}{1.20} = \$632,666.67$$

Since this constraint limits the annual debt service to $632,666.67, the monthly mortgage loan payment cannot exceed 1/12 of $632,666.67, or $52,722.22. Using a financial calculator and incorporating the expected 8.0 percent interest rate and 20-year amortization period, we determine this to imply a loan of no more than $6,303,167.67. Using financial tables, the solution will differ modestly due to rounding error. The permissible loan amount will in any event be rounded by the lender, probably to $6,300,000.

Loan-to-Value Ratio Constraint

To estimate the maximum loan that will satisfy the expected 70 percent loan-to-value ratio constraint, we must first estimate the market value of the property. We note that similar apartment buildings in the same market area have recently sold at around five times their potential gross rent. Using the reconstructed prior-year potential gross rent from Table 5.6, this implies a market value of 5 × $1,400,000, or $7,400,000. The lender will probably lend no more than 70 percent of this amount: .70 × $7,400,000 = $5,180,000.

Anticipated Loan Amount

Prevailing lending policies place constraints on the debt coverage ratio and the loan-to-value ratio. The more severe constraint will govern the amount that can be borrowed. We have estimated the amounts to be as follows:

Based on permissible debt coverage ratio: $6,300,000.

Based on permissible loan-to-value ratio: $5,180,000.

Since the more severe constraint governs, we estimate the most we can borrow on the strength of a first mortgage pledged as security is $5,180,000. Additional funds might be available by pledging additional collateral or, if the borrower assumes personal liability for the loan, based on a personal credit rating.

Before-Tax Cash Flow from Maegen's Magic Manor

Since the investor can expect to borrow $5,180,000 at 8.0 percent, to be amortized by monthly payments over 20 years, a financial calculator can quickly reveal that the monthly payment will be $43,327.60. The same solution (with a small rounding error) will result from using the Amortization Table in Appendix C or the excerpt shown in Table 9.1. The annual debt service is simply 12 times this amount, or (rounded to the nearest whole dollar) $519,931.

If the only nonoperating cash flows are debt service and income taxes, the before-tax cash flow for each year will be the net operating income minus the annual debt service. Table 9.6 extends the forecast from Table 6.2 to derive a six-year before-tax cash flow projection.

Debt Amortization Schedule for Maegen's Magic Manor

The annual debt service will be comprised in part of interest payments and in part principal payments. Initially, virtually the entire annual debt service will be consumed by the interest expense. Gradually, as the principal amount is whittled down, more and more of the debt service will be applied to reduce the loan balance. To extend the forecast to after-tax cash flow, we will have to divide the payments into principal and interest, because the interest payments are tax-deductible but the principal payments are not.

Table 9.6		**Six-Year Before-Tax Cash Flow Projection** **Maegen's Magic Manor Apartments**				
	Year 1	*Year 2*	*Year 3*	*Year 4*	*Year 5*	*Year 6*
1. Potential Gross Rent	$1,517,000	$1,592,900	$1,672,500	$1,731,000	$1,791,600	$1,854,300
2. *Less:* Vacancy Allowance	114,000	63,700	66,900	103,900	107,500	111,300
3.	$1,403,000	$1,529,200	$1,605,600	$ 1,627,100	$1,684,100	$1,743,000
4. *Add:* Other Income	97,000	107,000	112,400	113,900	117,900	122,000
5. Effective Gross Income	$1,500,000	$1,636,200	$1,718,000	$1,741,000	$1,802,000	$1,865,000
6. *Less:* Operating Expenses						
7. Management Fee	$ 75,000	$ 81,800	$ 85,900	$ 87,000	$ 90,100	$ 93,300
8. Salary Expense	138,600	143,400	148,500	153,700	159,000	164,600
9. Utilities	63,200	65,400	67,700	70,100	72,500	75,100
10. Insurance	45,000	46,600	48,200	49,900	51,600	53,400
11. Supplies	19,700	20,100	21,100	21,100	21,800	22,600
12. Advertising	9,300	9,600	10,000	10,300	10,700	11,100
13. Maintenance and Repairs	180,000	186,300	192,800	200,000	206,600	213,800
14. Property Taxes	210,000	210,000	210,000	220,500	220,500	220,500
15. Total Expenses	$ 740,800	$ 763,200	$ 784,200	$ 812,600	$ 832,800	$ 854,400
16. Net Operating Income	$ 759,200	$ 873,000	$ 933,800	$ 928,400	$ 969,200	$1,010,600
17. *Less:* Debt Service	519,900	519,900	519,900	519,900	519,900	519,900
18. Before-Tax Cash Flow	$ 239,300	$ 353,100	$ 413,900	$ 408,500	$ 449,300	$ 490,700

Rounding: All forecast items are rounded to the nearest $100.

Table 9.7	Loan Amortization Schedule for Maegen's Magic Manor Apartments[1]			
Year	*Debt Service*	*Interest*	*Principal*	*Loan Balance*
1	$519,931	$410,443	$109,488	$5,070,512
2	519,931	401,356	118,575	4,951,937
3	519,931	391,514	128,417	4,823,520
4	519,931	380,856	139,076	4,684,446
5	519,931	369,312	150,619	4,533,826
6	519,931	356,811	163,120	4,370,706
7	519,931	343,272	176,659	4,194,047

[1] All numbers rounded to nearest $1.

A table that divides the payments into interest and principal components is called an *amortization schedule.* Most financial calculators are programmed to develop such a schedule; their use is explained in Appendix B. Electronic spreadsheets on personal computers will also produce amortization schedules. A more involved method, using the amortization table in Appendix C, is described in Appendix A. However it is derived, the results (with minor differences due to rounding error if one uses the amortization table in Appendix C) will be as shown on Table 9.7.

SUMMARY

Interest, the cost of borrowed money, is usually specified in the promissory note. This contract rate (called the nominal rate) will differ from the effective rate when borrowers pay a fee in connection with the loan, or when the amount of money actually disbursed by the lender is less than the face amount of the loan. To determine the effective rate, find the discount rate that makes the present value of all payments to be made by the borrower exactly equal to the loan funds disbursed.

Because interest expense incurred to acquire or carry income-generating assets is tax-deductible, the after-tax cost of borrowing is reduced. The higher the borrower's marginal income tax rate, the lower becomes the after-tax cost of borrowing.

A distinction must be made between the nominal rate and the real interest rate. The real rate is the nominal rate, adjusted for price inflation over the period between borrowing and paying the interest.

Borrowing decisions are complicated by variety in the loan terms offered. A key variable in the choice between alternatives is the comparative effective interest rates, the discount that makes the future payment obligation equal to the net loan proceeds.

RECOMMENDED READINGS

Downs, Anthony. *The Revolution in Real Estate Finance.* Washington, DC: The Brookings Institution, 1985.

Roulac, Stephen E., and Neil F. Dimick. "Real Estate Capital Markets Undergo Fundamental Changes." *Real Estate Finance Journal,* vol 6, no. 3 (Winter 1991) p. 717.

REVIEW QUESTIONS

1. Describe the difference between nominal and effective interest rates.
2. Under what circumstances might the nominal and effective rates be the same? What makes them differ?
3. Under what circumstances will paying off a loan balance before maturity cause the effective interest rate to be higher?
4. If financial leverage is favorable, why would an investor want to repay a loan before its due date?
5. Distinguish between nominal and real interest rates.

DISCUSSION QUESTIONS

1. Why would a lender charge a lower contract interest rate coupled with a front-end fee? Why not simply incorporate the effective rate into the contract rate?
2. Since inflation causes real interest rates to be lower, won't lenders simply factor inflation into their contract rates so that the real rate remains constant? With rational borrowers and lenders, shouldn't adjustments for anticipated inflation cancel out inflation's impact?
3. The deductibility of interest expense for federal income tax purposes radically alters the consequences of borrowing. Should interest expense be deductible? Why make interest expense (payment to the debt position) deductible when dividends or partnership payouts, for example, (payment to the equity position) are not?

PROBLEMS

1. Compute the effective interest rate on each of the following loans. Each is for $100,000, fully amortizing over 20 years, and the contract interest rate is 9.0 percent:

    a. A 6.0 percent front-end fee, with no prepayment anticipated.

    b. A 5.0 percent front-end fee, with prepayment planned after five years (there is no prepayment penalty).

    c. A 4.0 percent front-end fee and prepayment planned after ten years (there will be a prepayment penalty equal to 2.0 percent of the unpaid balance).

2. A prospective borrower is offered a $500,000 first mortgage loan with interest at 8 percent per annum. Monthly payments will be required to amortize the loan over 25 years. Two alternatives are offered:

    a. A five-year loan with a 1.0 percent front-end fee or

    b. A seven-year loan with a 1.5 percent front-end fee.

    Required

    (1) Which loan alternative carries the lower pre-tax effective interest rate, assuming they run full term?

    (2) Which loan alternative carries the lower pre-tax effective rate if they are to be retired through refinancing after three years (assume there is no prepayment penalty)?

    (3) If the borrower intends to let the loan run full-term, then refinance with another mortgage loan equal to the remaining balance, what consideration should be factored into the loan choice, other than the effective interest rate?

3. An investor seeks to borrow funds for a long-term investment. The investment is virtually certain to generate profits of 10 percent per annum, but has no prospects for a higher yield or for appreciation. It is a one-time opportunity that will accommodate all the funds the investor can raise, and it can be liquidated at any time with no transaction costs. The investor has no cash available but can borrow on the following terms:

    a. A 25-year, 8.5 percent loan with a 2.5 percent origination fee and no prepayment permitted. The loan will be fully amortized over the 25 year term. Loan proceeds (net of the front-end fee) will be $50,000.

    b. A 25-year, 8.0 percent loan, fully amortizing, with no loan origination fee and no prepayment permitted. Loan proceeds will be $40,000.

    Required Given that there is no other source of funds available for investment and that this is the only investment opportunity available, and assuming the investor is not a taxable entity (for computational convenience, ignore income taxes), if all other factors remain equal, which loan should the investor take?

4. You are considering three loan proposals to finance the purchase of investment property. The purchase price is $500,000 and the expected net operating income is $60,000. The alternatives are:

    a. Loan-to-value ratio is 90 percent, interest rate is 9 percent, terms are 25 years level amortizing with monthly payments.

    b. Loan-to-value ratio is 80 percent, interest is 8 percent, terms are 25 years level amortizing with monthly payments.

    c. Loan-to-value ratio is 80 percent, interest is 7.5 percent + three points, terms are 25 years, fully amortizing with monthly payments.

Determine

(1) The effective interest rate for each loan, assuming the loan is outstanding for the full 25-year amortization term;

(2) The incremental rate of interest paid for the additional funds provided in Loan a over Loan b.

PART THREE: Case Problem

Please refer to the case problem for Part Two. Assignment number two of that problem called for a seven-year forecast of net operating income for the Sated Satyr apartments. If you have not yet completed that assignment, please do so now.

Assignment

1. Based on net operating income projection for the first year, estimate the mortgage loan that will be available if the lender requires a debt coverage ratio of not less than 1.20. Anticipated loan terms are interest at 8.5 percent per annum, and level monthly payments to amortize the loan over 20 years. No discount points or loan origination fee is anticipated.

2. Round your mortgage loan estimate from assignment 1 above, to the nearest $100,000. Modify the Sated Satyr Apartments projection to derive a seven-year projection of before-tax cash flow, based on this loan.

3. Using the mortgage loan from assignment 2 above, develop a seven-year amortization schedule for the Sated Satyr Apartments. Include an anticipated remaining mortgage balance at the end of seven years.

4. Using the forecasted future market value developed in Assignment 3 of the Case Problem for Part Two (rounded to the nearest $100,000), estimate before-tax cash flow from disposal, assuming the following:
   a. The property is sold at the end of the seventh year (that is, before the first debt service payment falls due for the eighth year).
   b. Transaction costs (brokerage, legal and accounting fees, and so forth) equal 8 percent of the selling price.

Save your work. It will be needed to solve case problem one for Part Four.

PART FOUR

Income Tax Considerations

Income taxes constitute a claim superior to that of equity investors, whose interest is a mere residual. The relevant measure of investment outcomes, therefore, is the value of after-tax cash flows, and expected income tax consequences are a vital part of the analysis. Moreover, a multitude of income tax savings opportunities become available when one joins the property-owning class. But with these opportunities comes a host of potential problems. This section outlines major tax opportunities and tax traps associated with real estate investing.

Our perspective is that of the individual (noncorporate) taxpayer who holds real estate for use in a trade or business or for production of income. Tax rules affecting real estate held for personal use differ radically, and tax law applicable to corporations varies significantly from noncorporate tax law.

Federal income tax law is found in a bulky document known as the *Internal Revenue Code,* frequently referred to merely as *the Code.* Approximately 18 pages of the Code are devoted to explaining what income is taxable. This is followed by more than 3,000 pages of exceptions, amplifications and attempts at clarification. The Treasury Department has supplemented the Code with more than 5,000 pages of regulations to make its provisions more nearly comprehensible, and the Internal Revenue Service publishes voluminous material devoted to clarifying Treasury Department regulations. All this is overshadowed by a massive library of court decisions in settlement of disputes between tax collector and taxpayers.

In the next three chapters, we will cover only a minute portion of the tax issues addressed by this massive outpouring of mind-numbing material. Our concern is with the segments of the Code and implementing regulations that directly influence income tax consequences of real estate investment. Even so, we must limit ourselves to an overview of most issues in order to discuss in greater detail matters of overriding importance.

The economics of textbook publishing prohibit issuing a new edition every time the Congress convenes, yet lawmakers have become notorious for almost constant tinkering with the Internal Revenue Code. Since it takes about a year for a book to get from the writer's word processor to a reader's hands, some of these tax rules will probably have been superseded by the time you read about them. Inexpensive annual tax guides that do give up-to-the-minute changes in the Code are readily available. One such guide is included in the recommended readings at the end of each tax chapter.

CHAPTER 10

Basic Income Tax Issues

This chapter outlines basic income tax issues that are of vital concern to real estate investors. Because the investor's tax basis in a property is so significant to investment outcomes, that is the first issue addressed. The chapter then considers the tax consequences of ownership forms. It concludes with an introduction to the income tax consequences of property disposal.

THE NATURE AND SIGNIFICANCE OF THE TAX BASIS

From the time a property is acquired, owners have a *tax basis* in all their property. During the ownership period, the basis may be adjusted to reflect disinvestment or additional capital investment. This tax basis is a primary determinant of tax consequences during the holding period. Selling or exchanging a property generates a gain or loss equal to the difference between the sales price and the adjusted basis of the property at the time of disposal.

THE INITIAL TAX BASIS

One's initial tax basis in a newly acquired property depends in part on how it is acquired. If the property is received as a gift, its initial tax basis will be the same as the adjusted tax basis of the donor, unless the donor incurs gift tax liability. In that case, the initial tax basis will include the portion of the donor's gift tax liability that was incurred because the property increased in value while it was owned by the donor. The initial tax basis in inherited property is its market value as determined for estate tax purposes (gift and estate taxes are explained in Chapter 11).

The initial basis in property acquired by purchase is its cost of acquisition. This includes everything of value given in exchange. It also includes all costs incurred in obtaining and defending title. Thus, cost includes purchase commissions (if any), legal fees, title insurance and other items that are incurred in connection with acquisition and are not deductible as current operating expenses. Example 10.1 illustrates.

Example 10.1

An apartment building is purchased on the following terms: $50,000 in cash at closing, with the purchaser taking title subject to an existing mortgage note, which has a remaining balance of $400,000, and signing a note and second mortgage for $50,000. The buyer also pays $2,000 into a property-tax and insurance escrow account (escrow involves the holding by a third party, an escrow agent, of something of value that is the subject of a contract between two other parties, until that contract has been consummated), $240 for the seller's prepaid water bill, $250 for heating oil remaining in the building's tanks, $25 for document recording and $90 for state documentary stamps. Other expenditures include $1,500 for legal representation, $210 for an owner's title insurance policy, $450 for a lender's title insurance policy and $180 for a credit report.

The purchaser's initial tax basis is $501,825, determined as follows:

Purchase Price		
Cash Down Payments	$ 50,000	
Second Mortgage Note	50,000	
First Mortgage Note	400,000	$500,000
Attorney's Fee		1,500
Owner's Title Policy		210
Recording Fee		25
Documentary Stamps		90
Initial Tax Basis		$501,825

All other outlays represent costs of obtaining financing or are incidental to the purchase and therefore are not properly includable in the initial basis.

ALLOCATING THE INITIAL TAX BASIS

If two or more assets (land and buildings, for example) are acquired as a single transaction, the initial tax basis must be allocated among them in accordance with their relative market values. This implies that relative values are known; in fact they generally have to be estimated. The following techniques, if properly applied, will survive IRS scrutiny:

- Specify the price of each asset in the original purchase contract. If the purchase is an arm's-length transaction, such contractual determination forms a defensible cost allocation basis.
- Use the ratio of land value to building value estimated by the tax assessor, who usually assesses land and improvements separately. Although the assessor's estimate of total value might differ considerably from the investor's initial tax basis, the relative estimates nevertheless provide a generally acceptable way of allocating the basis.
- Have an independent appraiser estimate the asset's relative values. If a third-party lender finances the transaction, an appraisal will usually be required. In addition to its intended purpose, the appraisal can be used to allocate the tax basis.

Example 10.2

The cost of a property, including all transactions that are properly includable in the initial tax basis, totals $800,000. The property includes land and two buildings. The values, based on the tax assessor's appraisal and an independent appraiser, are as follows:

	Assessor	Appraiser
Land	$100,000	$150,000
Building A	250,000	400,000
Building B	150,000	300,000
Total	$500,000	$850,000

Consider the property in Example 10.2. Neither the tax assessor's or the independent appraiser's value estimate correspond to the actual purchase price. Yet they can be used to allocate the initial tax basis between the three assets that the taxpayer has acquired in a single purchase. If the assessor's estimates are used the initial tax basis will be allocated as follows:

	Assessor's Estimate	Percent of Total	Purchaser's Allocation
Land	$100,000	20	$160,000
Building A	250,000	50	400,000
Building B	150,000	30	240,000
Total	$500,000	100	$800,000

If the taxpayer elects to allocate based on the independent appraiser's value estimate, the allocation will be as follows:

	Appraiser's Estimate	Percent of Total	Purchaser's Allocation
Land	$150,000	17.65	$141,200
Building A	400,000	47.06	376,480
Building B	300,000	35.29	282,320
Total	$850,000	100.00	$800,000

ADJUSTING THE BASIS FOR COST RECOVERY

Taxpayers are entitled to deduct from otherwise taxable revenue an allowance for recovery of invested capital. The allowance, called a *depreciation allowance,* is sufficient to recover the cost of buildings and land improvements such as roads and walkways, over periods specified in the Internal Revenue Code.

Only assets held for business or income purposes qualify for the depreciation allowance. Note that the determining factor is *intent* to produce income, rather than actual success in doing so. Thus an owner of rental property may claim a depreciation allowance regardless of whether a tenant actually occupies the premises. But the Internal Revenue Service may insist upon evidence of intent. For example, a house previously occupied by the owner will not qualify for a deduction when vacated and offered for sale. It will be considered income property and therefore qualify for a depreciation allowance only if the owner actively seeks to rent it after moving out.

Allowable Cost Recovery Periods

Lawmakers adjust allowable recovery periods from time to time with no apparent regard to actual useful lives of assets. The decision appears to be primarily conditioned upon a need to enhance tax receipts (when recovery periods are lengthened) or encourage investment (when the periods are shortened). Currently, the tax basis of qualifying residential structures—buildings from which at least 80 percent of gross rents stem from residential tenants—is recovered over 27.5 years; that of nonresidential structures (if put into service after May 12, 1993) is 39 years. The tax basis of land improvements such as walks, roads, sewers, gutters and fences is recoverable over 15 years.

✳ Computing the Allowance

The tax basis of buildings are recovered in equal annual increments over the recovery period. If a property is owned for less than 12 months during a particular taxable year, the allowance during that year is permitted only for the number of months that it is owned. Half a month's allowance is permitted during the month in which a taxpayer first puts a property into service, regardless of how many days during that month the property is actually in service. Another half month's allowance is claimed in the month of disposition, again without regard to the actual number of days the property is owned that month.

Example 10.3

During March 1996, a taxpayer who files tax returns on a calendar-year basis acquires a residential income property that she operates until November 1998, the month in which she sells. The portion of the purchase price (including applicable transactions costs) properly attributable to the building is $2,400,000.

To see how the allowance is computed, consider Example 10.3. Since the property is residential in nature, the $2,400,000 initial tax basis of the building will be recovered over 27.5 years. The monthly allowance, therefore, will be $7,272.73:

$$\frac{\text{Recoverable Amount}}{12 \times \text{Recovery Period}} = \frac{\$2,400,000}{330} = \$7,272.73$$

During the year of acquisition, the depreciation allowance is $7,272.73 times the number of months held, including a half month's allowance for March. Hence our investor's first-year allowance, rounded to the nearest whole dollar, is $69,091:

$$\text{Months in Use} \times \text{Monthly Allowance} = 9.5 \times \$7,272.73 = \$69,091$$

During each whole year of this investor's ownership, the allowance will be 12 times $7,272.73, or $87,273. During the year of disposal the taxpayer will claim the allowance for only 10.5 months. Thus, the final year's allowance will be 10.5 times $7,272.73, or $76,364.

Had the property in Example 10.3 been nonresidential—perhaps an office or a store building—the allowance would have been smaller. Since the recovery period for nonresidential properties is 39 years, the monthly allowance for this property would have been $5,128.21:

$$\frac{\text{Recoverable Amount}}{12 \times \text{Recovery Period}} = \frac{\$2,400,000}{468} = \$5,128.21$$

Under the revised assumption that the property in Example 10.3 is nonresidential, therefore, the first year's allowance will be 9.5 times $5,128.21, or $48,718. The annual allowance during each full year of ownership will be 12 times $5,128.21, or $61,539. In the year of disposal the taxpayer will claim an allowance of 10.5 times $5,128.21, or $53,846.

Improvements on and to the land, as previously noted, are recovered over 15 years. Taxpayers are permitted to use an accelerated technique, called the *150 percent declining balance method*, that permits larger allowances during earlier years offset by smaller allowances later. They may shift to the straight line method for the remainder of the 15-year period when doing so will generate a higher annual allowance. Example 10.4 illustrates.

Example 10.4

Assuming a $60,000 cost attributable to land improvements that qualify for the cost recovery allowance, the annual allowance for the first five years, using the 150 percent declining balance method over 15 years, is:*

(1.5 × 1/15) × ($60,000, minus cumulative allowances)

During the first five full years, the annual allowance will be:

Year	Declining Balance	×	Rate	=	Allowance
1	$60,000 – $ 0 = $60,000		1.5 × 1/15 = .10		$6,000
2	$60,000 – $6,000 = $54,000		.10		$5,400
3	$54,000 – $5,400 = $48,600		.10		$4,860
4	$48,600 – $4,860 = $43,740		.10		$4,374
5	$43,740 – $4,374 = $39,366		.10		$3,937

*After five years the taxpayer will shift to the straight line method and will take 1/10, or 10 percent of the remaining balance [($39,366 – $3,937) / 10] every year.

A Depreciation Schedule for Maegen's Magic Manor

In Chapter 5, we developed a reconstructed operating statement for a 250-unit apartment complex called Maegen's Magic Manor. The reconstructed statement is presented in Table 5.6. Starting with that statement, we developed (in Chapter 6) a six-year operating forecast. The forecast is presented in Table 6.2. Then, in Chapter 9, we extended the forecast to include before-tax cash flows. That projection is presented in Table 9.6.

We can also develop a schedule of expected depreciation allowances for Maegen's Magic Manor, but first we must have an estimate of the purchase price and the relative value of land and improvements. In Chapter 9, to estimate the size of the mortgage loan, we derived a market value estimate of $7.4 million. If our investor acquires the property at this price and incurs $150,000 of transaction costs that must be capitalized, the initial tax basis will be $7.55 million. Assuming the land value to be $1.75 million, the amount allocable to the improvements and therefore recoverable via annual depreciation allowances is $5.8 million:

Initial tax basis if land and improvements	
Purchase price	$7,400,000
Add: Transaction costs	150,000
Total initial tax basis	$7,550,000
Less: Tax basis of land	1,750,000
Amount to be recovered	$5,800,000

The monthly depreciation allowance is an amount that will enable the investor to recover the $5.8 million over 27.5 years:

$$\text{Monthly allowance} = \frac{\$5,800,000}{12 \times 27.5} = \$17,575.76$$

The annual allowance (other than in the year of acquisition and the year of disposal) will be 12 times the monthly amount. During the year of purchase and the year of disposal, the allowance will be computed based on the number of months of ownership, including half a month's allowance during the initial month and the final month (without regard to the actual day of the month on which transactions occur). The computations are shown in Table 10.1.

Table 10.1	Projected Annual Depreciation Allowances for Maegen's Magic Manor Apartments

Year	Allowance
1*	$202,121.24
2	$210,909.12
3	$210,909.12
4	$210,909.12
5	$210,909.12
6*	$202,121.24

Depreciable Amount:	
Estimated purchase price	$7,400,000
Add: Estimated transaction costs	150,000
Initial tax basis, land and improvements	$7,550,000
Less: Amount allocable to land	1,750,000
Depreciable amount	$5,800,000

Recover period: 27.5 years

Monthly allowance: $\dfrac{\$5,800,000}{12 \times 27.5} = \$17,575.76$

*Incorporates the half-month convention. Assumes purchase during first month of taxable year and sale during final month of taxable year.

OTHER ADJUSTMENTS TO THE TAX BASIS

A number of factors other than depreciation allowances result in adjustments to the tax basis. Some of these decrease the basis, others increase it.

The tax basis is reduced when a portion of an asset is sold or destroyed by casualties such as fire, flood or storm. A partial sale requires the tax basis to be reduced by the portion of the basis properly attributable to the part sold. In the case of casualty losses, the basis must be reduced to reflect allowable loss deductions in the year of the casualty, plus any loss for which compensation is received.

Expenditures that materially increase the value or useful life of an asset must be added to the tax basis. Generally this includes any expenditure that is not deductible as a current expense. Examples include items such as a new central heating or cooling system, a new roof or new wall-to-wall carpeting. Treasury Regulation 1.162-4 distinguishes between capital expenditures and currently deductible repairs and maintenance.

The cost of improvements, alterations or additions that must be capitalized (that is, added to the tax basis) will be written off via depreciation allowances in the same manner as the initial recoverable cost. But the deductions must be based on an entirely separate recovery schedule that begins with the month that the improvements, alterations or additions are first placed in service.

Transaction costs associated with acquiring or disposing of property are also added to the adjusted basis. We saw earlier how transaction costs incurred to acquire property, but not those to get it financed, are added to the basis. In the same manner, transactions costs at disposal are added.

FORECASTING AFTER-TAX CASH FLOWS

We now have enough information to extend the cash flow forecast from Chapter 9 to include income tax consequences. Table 9.6 presents a six-year forecast of before-tax cash flows, Table 9.7 presents an amortization schedule for the mortgage loan that is incorporated in the analysis, and Table 10.1 shows the projected schedule of depreciation allowances. The only additional information we need to extend the analysis to after-tax cash flow is the investor's marginal income tax bracket. Table 10.2 shows after-tax cash flow projection, assuming the appropriate (combined federal and state) income tax bracket is estimated to be 40 percent.

Lines 1 through 16 of Table 10.2 are taken directly from Table 9.6. Starting with line 17, we derive an estimate of taxable income by subtracting tax-deductible items that are not considered operating expenses and therefore do not reduce net operating income. The items are interest expense (line 17 on Table 10.2, taken from Table 9.7) and the deprecitation allowance (line 18 on Table 10.2, taken from Table 10.1). The result, on line 19, is taxable income.

Multiplying taxable income by the 40 percent marginal income tax rate (line 20) results in the expected income tax obligation, shown on line 21. Line 22 is

Table 10.2	**Projected After-Tax Cash Flow from Operations** **Maegen's Magic Manor Apartments**					
	Year 1	*Year 2*	*Year 3*	*Year 4*	*Year 5*	*Year 6*
1. Potential Gross Rent	$1,517,000	$1,592,900	$1,672,500	$1,731,000	$1,791,600	$1,854,300
2. *Less:* Vacancy Allowance	114,000	63,700	66,900	103,900	107,500	111,300
3.	$1,403,000	$1,529,200	$1,605,600	$1,627,100	$1,684,100	$1,743,000
4. *Add:* Other Income	97,000	107,000	112,400	113,900	117,900	122,000
5. Effective Gross Income	$1,500,000	$1,636,200	$1,718,000	$1,741,000	$1,802,000	$1,865,000
6. *Less:* Operating Expenses						
7. Management Fee	$ 75,000	$ 81,800	$ 85,900	$ 87,000	$ 90,100	$ 93,300
8. Salary Expense	138,600	143,400	148,500	153,700	159,000	164,600
9. Utilities	63,200	65,400	67,700	70,100	72,500	75,100
10. Insurance	45,000	46,600	48,200	49,900	51,600	53,400
11. Supplies	19,700	20,100	21,100	21,100	21,800	22,600
12. Advertising	9,300	9,600	10,000	10,300	10,700	11,100
13. Maintenance and Repairs	180,000	186,300	192,800	200,000	206,600	213,800
14. Property Taxes	210,000	210,000	210,000	220,500	220,500	220,500
15. Total Expenses	$ 740,800	$ 763,200	$ 784,200	$ 812,600	$ 832,800	$ 854,400
16. Net Operating Income	$ 759,200	$ 873,000	$ 933,800	$ 928,400	$ 969,200	$1,010,600
17. *Less:* Interest Expense	410,400	401,400	391,500	380,900	369,300	356,800
18. Depreciation Allowance	202,100	210,900	210,900	210,900	210,900	202,100
19. Taxable Income (Loss)	$ 146,700	$ 260,700	$ 331,400	$ 336,600	$ 389,000	$ 451,700
20. *Times:* Marginal Tax Rate	40	40	40	40	40	40
21. Income Tax (Tax Savings)	$ 58,680	$ 104,300	$ 132,600	134,600	155,600	180,700
22. Net Operating Income	$ 759,200	$ 873,000	$ 933,800	$ 928,400	$ 969,200	$1,010,600
23. *Less:* Debt Service	519,900	519,900	519,900	519,900	519,900	519,900
24. Before-Tax Cash Flow	$ 239,300	$ 353,100	$ 413,900	$ 408,500	$ 449,300	$ 490,700
25. *Less:* Income Taxes	58,680	104,300	132,600	134,600	155,600	180,700
26. After-Tax Cash Flow	$ 180,620	$ 248,800	$ 281,300	$ 273,900	$ 293,700	$ 310,000

Rounding: All forecast items are rounded to the nearest $100.

simply a restatement of net operating income, brought down from line 16. Line 23 adjusts for debt service to arrive at before-tax cash flow (line 24), which is the same as shown on Table 9.6. Subtracting estimated income tax liability (or adding back expected income tax savings) due to the investment, as show on line 23, yields line 24, the estimated after-tax cash flow from the investment.

TAX CONSEQUENCES OF OWNERSHIP FORM

Investors face a bewildering array of ownership entity choices. Legal and financial distinctions among the alternatives may appear inconsequential; the reality is that the choice of title-holding entity is often crucial to a venture's outcome.

A decision to involve other investors in some form of pooling-of-equity arrangement vests the entity question with particular urgency. Outside investors generally insist upon an arrangement that limits their personal financial liability.

Asset liquidity is interrelated with the issue of financial liability and is significantly affected by choice of ownership entity. The ability to liquidate a position at the investor's own volition is often a powerful determinant of willingness to enter into cooperative ventures. To enhance liquidity, cooperative ventures generally employ an entity that enables investment shares to be transferred in relatively small increments.

A continuous thread running through all deliberations concerning the entity question is the importance of maintaining decision-making control over operational matters. Sacrificing control to induce associates to contribute additional funds is self-defeating if the associates prove to be inept managers. The entity decision should be made only after careful consideration of its impact on operational control.

Title May Vest in Owners as Individuals

Having title vest directly in an investor as an individual is the least involved alternative. Where more than one investor is to take an equity position, a possible alternative to individual ownership is a *co-tenancy arrangement.*

Co-tenancies are not tax-paying entities. All profits and losses accrue to the co-tenants as individual taxpayers and are reported on their personal tax returns. Profits and losses are divided among the co-tenants in accordance with their relative ownership interests in the property. With respect to a personal interest in the property, therefore, the investors are in the same tax position as if they held title to a part of the property as sole owners.

The cotenancy arrangements most commonly encountered are *tenancy in common* and *joint tenancy.* The exact wording in a deed of conveyance to create joint tenancy as opposed to tenancy in common differs among the states. In either case, agreement among co-tenants regarding operational matters can be arranged as they please but should be in writing and signed by all parties to avoid misunderstanding and to serve as a guide for settling possible disputes. To ensure enforceability and access to legal remedies, any such agreement should be made under the guidance of legal counsel.

Tenants in Common.   When property is held as a tenancy in common, each investor's name appears on the deed, and each holds an undivided interest in the whole property. The interests need not be equal (for example, one party might hold a 10 percent interest, another a 25 percent interest and yet another a 65 percent interest), but they are necessarily undivided; unless there is a specific agreement to the contrary, each tenant in common has the use of the whole property. Substantial alterations or improvements require agreement among the owners, thereby effectively reducing the operational control of any one owner. The usual arrangement is to provide that one owner operates the property under a limited power of attorney from the others.

Joint Tenancy. Joint tenancy has essentially the same characteristics as tenancy in common, with two important exceptions: (1) the joint tenants' property interests are always equal, and (2) in the event of a joint tenant's death, the deceased person's interest in the property goes to the other joint tenant or tenants rather than to the deceased tenant's heirs. Because of the right of survivorship, joint tenancy is obviously inappropriate unless the joint tenant is someone to whom you intend to bequeath your property interest in any case. Observations made earlier about control and special operating agreements among tenants in common apply also to joint tenants.

Title May Vest in a Corporation

Corporations are legal entities with an identity separate and distinct from that of their owners (shareholders). Corporations can buy or sell property and otherwise enter into contracts, sue and be sued, and transact all manner of business in the same manner as individuals.

Corporations are also taxable entities. They must file corporate income tax returns and pay taxes on their net earnings. For this reason, flow-through accounting treatment (as discussed later with respect to limited partnerships) is not available to corporate shareholders.

Any distribution of corporate earnings in the form of cash dividends is taxable to corporate stockholders as regular income (there is a special exception for corporations that qualify under Subchapter S of the Internal Revenue Code. These corporations, also called tax option corporations, are discussed in the next section). This, in effect, results in double taxation of distributed earnings. Moreover, refusal to declare a cash dividend may result in an even higher tax on accumulated earnings that exceed the corporation's legitimate needs. This *excess accumulated earnings tax,* when added to the regular tax, is essentially confiscatory.

In spite of its obvious disadvantages, the corporate entity should not be casually dismissed. It does offer several offsetting advantages. Chief among these are:

- *Limited shareholder liability.* Unless they voluntarily enter into a contrary arrangement, stockholders are not liable for debts contracted by the corporation. Thus they are personally exposed to risk only to the extent of their investments in the corporation.
- *Liquidity.* Fractional interests in the form of one or more shares of stock can be issued as a means of transferring small portions of ownership—a procedure that might be awkward or impossible if the real property were held in the names of corporal investors.
- *Simplified transactions.* Corporate ownership shares are personalty rather than realty. Procedures for transferring ownership are different for personalty and, in most cases, less involved than for realty.
- *Simplified estate settlement procedures.* When the estate of a decedent owns realty in more than one state, there is the possibility that both states will try to collect death taxes based on the property's value. Since corporate shares are personalty rather than realty, using a corporate ownership entity avoids this complication.

Tax Option Corporations

Owners of certain corporations may elect to have income from the corporation (other than certain specified capital gains) taxable directly to shareholders rather than to the corporation. Losses are also passed through to shareholders, but only to the extent of the shareholders' adjusted tax bases in the stock. Additional losses must be carried forward until the stockholder makes further contributions to the corporation. Unlike real estate partnership interests, the basis of stock is not increased by a pro rata share of mortgage debt. Corporations that qualify for and make this election are called *S corporations* (reflecting the location of the rules, in Subchapter S of the Code), or *tax option corporations.*

Qualifying for the special treatment afforded under Subchapter S can be quite complex. Success requires an intimate knowledge of the statute and implementing regulations.

Investors May Form a General Partnership

Unlike corporations, partnerships are not taxable entities. income and losses are taxed directly to the individual partners, and the nature of the income and loss items (e.g., ordinary income or capital gains) is not affected by the partnership's existence. Partnerships must file tax returns, but these are purely informational. The return must show the amount and nature of income, expenses and deductions and indicate how each item is allocated among the partners. Partners must in turn report these individual items on their personal income tax returns.

In the absence of specific contrary agreements, general partners share profits and losses equally and have equal authority over the partnership business. They are jointly and severally liable for all partnership obligations, even if the obligation is created as a consequence of one partner having exceeded the authority granted under the partnership agreement.

Shared management authority, combined with unlimited joint and several liability, places severe limitations upon the usefulness of general partnerships as real estate ownership entities. As a practical matter, general partnerships tend to be limited to a few business associates who are well acquainted and share a high degree of mutual confidence.

A Limited Partnership May Hold Title

Real estate investors who contribute capital but do not participate in day-to-day management may object to being personally liable for financial obligations arising from the venture. A limited partnership gives them freedom from personal liability without the double taxation that results from the corporate ownership entity.

Limited partnerships have one or more general partners, who conduct partnership business and who have unlimited personal liability for partnership obligations. There will also be one or more limited partners, who have no personal liability but who share in partnership profits and losses in the same way partners do in a general partnership.

At-Risk Rule. Generally, a partner's tax basis does not include any portion of partnership property financed by partnership borrowing unless that partner is personally liable for the indebtedness. Code Section 465 makes a specific exception for partnerships whose principal business is real estate ownership. The exception applies if the partnership incurs mortgage indebtedness for which no partner has personal liability, providing the debt stems from an arm's-length third-party loan secured solely by a mortgage on the real estate. "Commercially reasonable" loans that are not arm's-length may be treated as arm's-length in applying the at-risk rule if loan terms are substantially the same as those available from arms-length sources. If the loan qualifies for the special exception, the partners' interests are determined by their ratios for sharing profits under the partnership agreement.

Example 10.5

Three investors form a limited partnership and buy an apartment complex. Partner Able is the general partner and assumes general liability for the debts of the partnership. For her role as general partner, Able receives a 20 percent interest in all profits and asset distributions and bears 20 percent of all partnership losses. Partners Baker and Charles contribute cash but assume the role of limited partners. The partners agree that Baker and Charles, each of whom contributes $200,000, will each receive 40 percent of all profits or assets distributed and bear 40 percent of all losses up to the amount of their interests in the partnership. It is agreed that Baker and Charles assume no personal liability beyond their initial $200,000 investments. The partnership buys an apartment complex having a total market price of $1,500,000, paying $400,000 down and signing a note and mortgage for the balance of $1,100,000.

Consider the facts in Example 10.5. Unless the general partner is specifically exculpated from personal liability for the mortgage loan or the limited partners specifically assume personal liability, the limited partners' initial tax basis is only $200,000 each (the amount invested in the partnership). Their cumulative losses from the partnership to be reported on their personal tax returns cannot exceed their tax bases, no matter how large their actual losses might be. Losses in excess of their bases may be carried forward indefinitely, however, and charged off in future years when partnership profits result in an increase in their total bases equal to the charges so deferred, or when they dispose of their partnership interest.

But consequences are altered dramatically if the mortgage-secured loan in Example 10.5 contains a clause relieving the general partner of personal liability for the balance on the note (even though she remains liable for all other partnership obligations). If no partner has personal liability for the mortgage debt and if it stems from arm's-length financing, the partners' bases are increased in the same proportion as their shares in the profits. The limited partners, therefore, each have their basis increased by 40 percent of the mortgage debt, or $440,000 each. The adjusted basis of each limited partner's interest is now $640,000: the initial $200,000 of cash contributions and the $440,000 increase due to assumption by the partnership of debt for which no partner has personal liability. Each limited partner may now claim cumulative basis reductions of $640,000 before losses must be carried over.

Adjustments to the Partner's Basis.   A partner's tax basis in a partnership is adjusted to reflect subsequent transactions. Additional capital contributions increase the basis, as does the partner's share of undistributed partnership income. A partner's basis may also be increased to reflect a pro rata share of newly acquired partnership liabilities. This would be the case, however, only if the partner assumes personal liability for a portion of the debt or if no partner has personal liability.

The tax basis of partnership interests are decreased by the partners' distributive shares of partnership losses (without regard to whether the losses can be currently offset against other income), by their shares of partnership expenditures that are not chargeable either to expenses or to capital (for example, charitable contributions) and by the amount of cash or the adjusted basis of non-cash assets distributed to them. Example 10.6 illustrates the impact of a series of partnership transactions.

Example 10.6

At the end of the prior year's operations, a limited partner's investment, representing a ten percent interest in the partnership, had an adjusted basis of $110,000. During the current year, the partnership earns taxable income of $100,000 before accounting for cost recovery and makes a charitable contribution of $1,000. Cost recovery allowances for the year are $140,000. The partnership distributes a total of $10,000 in cash to the partners.

At the end of the taxable year the partner's adjusted basis is $104,900, determined as follows:

Adjusted Basis at Beginning of Year		$110,000
Less: Distributive Share of Net Loss		
Cost Recovery Allowance		$140,000
Minus Income Before Recovery Allowance		100,000
Net Loss for Year		$40,000
Times: Partner's Distributive Interest		.10
Partner's Distributive Share of Loss		$4,000
Less:		
Distributive Share of Contributions (10% of $1,000)	100	
Cash Distributed to Partner (10% of $10,000)	1,000	
Total Deductions		5,100
Adjusted Basis at End of Year		$104,900

Partnership Tax Pitfalls. Tax conduit treatment—the provision that partnership revenue and expense items are reported on the individual partners' income tax returns—is an essential element in the desirability of many partnerships. Yet this desirable—sometimes crucial—characteristic can be lost due to the partnership being deemed a "partnership to be taxed as a corporation," or due to the Internal Revenue Code's passive loss limitation rules.

An organization is treated as a partnership for tax purposes if it does not have more corporate than partnership characteristics. Treasury regulations spell out six characteristics, two of which—the existence of associates and the objective to carry on a business and divide the profits—are common to both partnerships and corporations. The remaining four determine whether the entity is treated as an association or a partnership. The four critical corporate characteristics are:

1. Continuity of life
2. Centralized management
3. Limited liability for all partners
4. Free transferability of interests

Treasury Regulation 301.7701-2 contains rules for determining whether these corporate characteristics exist. It states that continuity of life does not exist if an organization is not continued in the event of death, insanity, bankruptcy, retirement, resignation or expulsion of any member, without the express agreement of all remaining members. Since such a provision is included in the Uniform Limited Partnership Act, continuity of life does not exist for limited partnerships in states having statutes that correspond to the uniform act. In other states, an article in the partnership agreement to the effect that unanimous agreement is required to continue the partnership under these circumstances should assure that the partnership lacks continuity of life.

Centralized management is deemed to exist under Regulation 301.7701-2 when a general partner resembles "in powers and functions the directors of a statutory corporation." This implies that management is empowered to make independent business decisions on behalf of the organization without need for ratification. The regulation goes on to state that limited partnerships generally do not have centralized management unless ". . . substantially all the interests in the partnership are owned by the limited partners."

The corporate characteristic of limited liability exists if partnership creditors may look only to the assets of the organization for satisfaction. In a limited partnership, of course, debtors may look to the general partner or partners for satisfaction when debts exceed the assets of the partnership. If general partners are not possessed of "substantial assets" from which to satisfy such claims, however, their personal liability may be ruled a sham by the Internal Revenue Service. The partnership would then be considered to provide limited liability for all partners. Just what constitutes substantial assets is not specified by the Internal Revenue Service. The IRS has, however, specified net worth requirements for general partners before it provides an advance ruling on the question.

Free transferability of interests is the final corporate characteristic not always present in partnerships. If a member's interest can be transferred to an outsider without the consent of other members, conferring on the outsider all rights and privileges of the transferor, then free transferability exists. A mere assignment of rights to share in profits does not constitute free transferability as contemplated by the regulation. It is generally relatively simple to avoid the free transferability of interests characterization by making the transfer to outsiders subject to a consent requirement, though the consent requirement may be ruled a sham if it is routinely given.

Remember that to be treated as a taxable association, the partnership must have more corporate than partnership characteristics. This means that three of the four characteristics must be present. A carefully drawn agreement should circumvent this eventuality without sacrificing the flexibility needed by general partners to assure successful pursuit of investment goals. Treasury Regulation 301.7701-3(b)(2) contains two examples of real estate organizations that qualify for treatment as partnerships. These examples are reproduced here as Examples 10.7 and 10.8.

Example 10.7

Three individuals form an organization that qualifies as a limited partnership under the laws of the state in which the organization was formed. The purpose of the organization is to acquire and operate various pieces of commercial and other investment property for profit. Each of the three individuals who are general partners invests $100,000 in the enterprise. Five million dollars of additional capital is raised through contributions of $100,000 or more by each of 30 limited partners. The three general partners are personally capable of assuming a substantial part of the obligations to be incurred by the organization. While a limited partner may assign his right to receive a share of the profits and a return of his contribution, his assignee does not become a substituted limited partner except with the unanimous consent of the general partners. The life of the organization as stated in the certificate is 20 years, but the death, insanity or retirement of a general partner prior to the expiration of the 20-year period will dissolve the organization. The general partners have exclusive authority to manage the affairs of the organization but can act only upon the unanimous consent of all of them. The organization has associates and an objective to carry on business and divide the gains therefrom, which characterize both partnerships and corporations. While the organization has the corporate characteristic of centralized management since substantially all of the interests in the organization are owned by the limited partners, it does not have the characteristics of continuity of life, free transferability of interests or limited liability. The organization will be classified as a partnership for all purposes of the Internal Revenue Code.

Example 10.8

Three individuals form an organization that qualifies as a limited partnership under the laws of the state in which the organization was formed. The purpose of the organization is to acquire and operate various pieces of commercial and other investment property for profit. The certificate provides that the life of the organization is to be 40 years, unless a general partner dies, becomes insane or retires during such period. On the occurrence of such death, insanity or retirement, the remaining general partners may continue the business of the partnership for the balance of the 40-year period under a right so to do stated in the certificate. Each of the three individuals who is a general partner invests $50,000 in the enterprise and has means to satisfy the business obligations of the organization to a substantial extent. Five million dollars of additional capital is raised through the sale of freely transferable interests in amounts of $10,000 or less to limited partners. Nine hundred such interests are sold. The interests of the 900 limited partners are fully transferable; that is, a transferee acquires all the attributes of the transferor's interest in the organization. The general partners have exclusive control over management of the business, their interests are not transferable and their liability for debts of the organization is not limited to their capital contributions. The organization has associates and an objective to carry on business and divide the gains therefrom. It does not have the corporate characteristics of limited liability and continuity of life. It has centralized management, however, since the three general partners exercise exclusive control over the management of the business and since substantially all of the interests in the organization are owned by the limited partners. While the interests of the general partners are not transferable, the transferability test of an association is met since substantially all of the interests in the organization are represented by transferable interests. The organization will be classified as a partnership for all purposes of the Internal Revenue Code.

Even though a partnership has been carefully structured to assure conduit treatment, limited partners may find the deductibility of their partnership operating losses is limited to the amount of offsetting partnership profits. This is a consequence of the *passive activity rules* of Code Section 469. Income and losses from activities characterized as passive must be segregated from income generated by portfolio-type investments such as stocks and bonds and from general income sources such as wages, salary and profit from a trade or business. Net losses from these passive activities cannot be offset against income from other sources (there are several exceptions, but none of them apply to net losses incurred by limited partners).

Instead, the net losses must be carried over and offset against passive income in future years. Any passive losses carried over and not yet offset against passive income become deductible when the related asset is sold or otherwise disposed of in a taxable transaction.

Passive activities include all trade or business activity in which a taxpayer has an ownership interest but does not materially participate. Limited partnership interests are specifically included by the wording of Code Section 469(h)(2), which says, "Except as provided in regulations, no interest in a limited partnership as a limited partner shall be treated as an interest with respect to which a taxpayer materially participates."

Limited Liability Companies

To gain the income tax advantages of a partnership entity and the limited liability benefits of the corporate form, investors may consider a limited liability company (LLC). This ownership entity is relatively new, but is now authorized in most states. Instead of shareholders (as in corporations) or partners (as in partnerships), the LLC has members. The company is operated in accordance with an operating agreement that resembles corporate by-laws and is managed by designated parties who need not be members.

Limited Liability for All Members.   Neither the members nor the managing parties of a LLC have personal liability. In this respect, the LLC is more like a corporation than a partnership.

Tax Conduit Treatment.   If structured in compliance with Internal Revenue Service rulings, LLCs will be treated as pass-through entities in essentially the same manner as partnerships. As a consequence, members are taxed in the same way as are partners in a partnership or shareholders in a subchapter S corporation.

TAX CONSEQUENCES OF PROPERTY SALES

Recall that an investor's adjusted tax basis in a property is the initial tax basis adjusted for cost recovery allowances and property improvements, plus certain other adjustments that may sometimes apply. The gain or loss on disposal is simply the difference between the amount realized from sale or exchange and the adjusted basis at the time of the transaction. The tax consequences depend in part on how the transaction is structured. Chapter 11 addresses this issue in more detail.

SUMMARY

Investors have an initial tax basis in all newly acquired property. If two or more assets are acquired in a single transaction, the initial basis must be allocated between assets in accordance with their relative market values. Periodically the basis is adjusted, sometimes upward and sometimes downward, but it can never fall below zero. When the property is sold, the gain on disposal is computed by deducting the adjusted tax basis from the selling price.

Owners of real property held for use in a trade or business or for production of income are allowed to deduct a depreciation allowance to provide for recovery of their investment in buildings and other improvements. All depreciation allowances represent downward adjustments to the tax basis.

Taking title to property in one's own name or jointly with another investor has the attraction of legal simplicity—the deed merely conveys property to the investors by name. If title is to be held jointly by two or more people, the wording in the deed of conveyance is a major determinant of the exact nature of the cotenancy.

Corporations are legal entities and thus may hold title to property in their own names. Corporations are also taxable entities and must file income tax returns in much the same fashion as individuals. Income is first taxable to the corporation, and then any earnings distributed as dividends are taxable to the shareholders. Moreover, any tax-deductible losses on corporate-owned real estate accrue to the corporation rather than to the corporate shareholders; corporations (other than those qualifying for and electing S corporation status) are not tax conduits.

Partnership entities offer indirect ownership without the double taxation problem associated with corporations. Title is recorded in the partnership name, but individual partners report income and losses from partnership operations on their personal income tax returns. If properly documented and reported, income is not taxable to the partnership. Each item of partnership income and expense retains its character when reported on the tax returns of the individual partners. For this reason partnerships are said to be tax conduits.

RECOMMENDED READINGS

Commerce Clearing House. *U.S. Master Tax Guide.* Chicago: Commerce Clearing House. Published annually.

Journal of Real Estate Taxation. A quarterly periodical published by Warren, Gorham & Lamont, 210 South St., Boston, MA 02111.

REVIEW QUESTIONS

1. How is a taxpayer's initial tax basis in a property determined?
2. Describe three common methods of allocating the tax basis between land and other assets.
3. List the basic conditions under which depreciation allowances are permitted.

4. List several adjustments that decrease the basis of a property and several that increase the basis.
5. Describe the differences between joint tenancy and tenancy in common.
6. List the major advantages and disadvantages of the corporation as an ownership form.
7. List the major characteristics of a limited partnership.
8. What are the major functions of the general partners in a limited partnership?
9. Under what conditions might a partnership be treated for tax purposes as an association to be taxed as a corporation?
10. Describe the major advantages of an S corporation.

DISCUSSION QUESTIONS

1. In view of the increasing frequency of income tax legislation, discuss the wisdom of relying on favored income tax treatment as a major element in the flow of benefits from property ownership.
2. Explain why a corporation whose shares are traded publicly might wish to show one measure of depreciation or cost recovery when reporting taxable income to the Internal Revenue Service and an entirely different measure when reporting operating results to shareholders.
3. Why do you suppose Congress has provided shorter cost recovery periods for residential than for nonresidential property?
4. Can you suggest reasons why the Internal Revenue Service might resist setting forth precise rules for determining whether an expenditure will be treated as a repair or an improvement?
5. Should government policy be designed to influence the choice between partnership and corporate ownership forms? Explain your reasoning.

PROBLEMS

1. An investor buys a property for $1 million, with 40 percent of the purchase price attributable to the land and the balance to a single structure. The purchaser incurs transaction costs equal to five percent of the purchase price (these must be capitalized). The investor then spends $400,000 to rehabilitate the structure (she is entitled to no tax credits). Subsequently she claims $110,000 of cost recovery allowances. She then sells the land but retains title to the building and a long-term leasehold interest in the land. The sale price is $600,000, including transaction costs, which equaled ten percent of the selling price.

    What is the investor's adjusted tax basis in the remaining asset after accounting for all of these transactions?

2. A residential rental property is acquired during the first month of the taxable year, at a total cost (including transaction costs) of $1,200,000. Of this amount, $200,000 is properly attributable to the land. Determine the annual depreciation allowance for the first year and for each of the ensuing nine years.

3. Assume that, during the last month of the tenth year of ownership, the property in Problem 2 is sold for $1,500,000. Assume also that the seller incurs transaction costs equaling six percent of the sales price. What is the amount of the gain or loss on the sale?

4. A 50,000-square-foot parcel of land (which has equal value per square foot) is purchased by a developer who pays $10,000 in cash, takes title subject to an existing $70,000 first mortgage note that she assumes and agrees to pay and signs a note and purchase-money mortgage for an additional $20,000 (transaction costs are zero). The developer constructs a building on the easternmost 25,000 square feet at a total construction cost of $75,000. The westernmost 25,000 square feet are improved with sewers, grading and parking facilities at a total cost of $18,000. The developer then borrows $100,000 from a mortgage lender and uses the loan proceeds to retire the existing first mortgage loan, the purchase-money mortgage note that was created when the land was purchased, and a short-term personal loan that was used to help finance construction. This new $100,000 loan is secured by a new first mortgage on the easternmost 25,000 square feet of property, leaving the westernmost 25,000 square feet clear of all liens (all promissory notes call for interest at current market rates). At this point the developer sells the westernmost 25,000 square feet of property for $80,000, net of transaction costs. The developer also claims an $8,333 cost recovery (depreciation) allowance on the building that she has constructed on the easternmost 25,000 square feet of property. What is the developer's adjusted tax basis in this property after accounting for all of this activity?

CHAPTER 11

Tax Consequences of Property Disposal

The tax consequences of property disposal depend in part on the amount and nature of the gain or loss (if any), and in part on how the transaction is structured. This chapter demonstrates how to compute gains and losses, and explains what determines the nature of the gain or loss. It then considers the tax consequences of special deal structures.

COMPUTING THE REALIZED GAIN OR LOSS

Everything of economic value received in exchange for a property comprises the *consideration*. This includes the balance due on any mortgage to which a property remains subject, whether or not the purchaser assumes personal liability. If the seller receives other property or services as a part of the deal, these must be included at their fair market value. The principle is illustrated in Example 11.1.

> ### Example 11.1
>
> A taxpayer transfers title to a vacant commercial lot (which is owned free and clear) in exchange for $50,000 in cash at the time of the transaction and a note for $100,000 due in 12 months. The purchaser also transfers title to a vacant lot (market value $70,000) and a pickup truck (market value $8,000). In addition, the purchaser, who is an attorney, agrees to represent the seller without cost in divorce proceedings that are

scheduled in the near future. The value of this legal service is $12,000. The buyer takes title subject to an existing mortgage-secured note, which has a remaining balance of $300,000. Total consideration involved in the transaction is $540,000.

The realized gain or loss on a transaction is the difference between the consideration received and the adjusted tax basis at the time of the transaction. Example 11.2 illustrates.

Example 11.2

Suppose the seller in Example 11.1 incurred transaction costs of $3,000 and had an adjusted basis (just prior to the sale) of $42,000. The gain on disposal is $495,000, computed as follows:

Sales Price		$540,000
Less Adjusted Tax Basis:		
Basis Prior to Sale	$42,000	
Add: Selling Costs	3,000	45,000
Realized Gain on Disposal		$495,000

TAX TREATMENT OF REALIZED GAINS OR LOSSES

Realized gains may be treated as ordinary income or as capital gains. If they are capital in nature, they are accorded special tax treatment. Likewise, losses may comprise reductions in ordinary taxable income for the year, or may be treated as capital losses and only offset ordinary taxable income to a limited extent.

Gains Treated as Ordinary Income

Gains are ordinary income when they result from recapture of depreciation or cost recovery allowances. They are also ordinary income when they result from selling assets that are held for resale in the ordinary course of business.

Recapturing Depreciation or Cost Recovery Allowances.   Investors who put their properties into use before the effective date of 1986 tax law changes had the option of computing depreciation or cost recovery allowances using an accelerated method. Gains on disposal of property written off on an accelerated schedule will often be characterized as recapture. To the extent they are so characterized, they will be recognized as ordinary income rather than capital gains.

Property Held Primarily for Resale.   People who hold real estate for resale in the ordinary course of business are called dealers, and property held primarily for that purpose is called *dealer property*. The sale of dealer property results in ordinary income rather than capital gains. The only exception to this rule involves large-block sales of inventory for liquidation purposes—such sales may give rise to capital gains or losses.

When Capital Gain or Loss Rules Apply

Gains realized from the sale or taxable exchange of long-lived assets held for use in a trade or business or for production of income (not intended primarily for resale in the ordinary course of business) are treated as capital gains unless characterized as recapture of depreciation or cost recovery allowances. The capital gain is long term if the asset was held for more than 12 months. Otherwise, it is short term.

Long-lived assets (that is, those that ordinarily last more than one year) intended for personal use (a personal residence, household furnishings, autos and so forth) are also considered capital items when there is a gain on disposal. Losses on the sale of personal assets, however, have no income tax consequences whatsoever.

A special rule applies to assets used in a trade or business, as apposed to those held for investment purposes or for personal use. Reflecting the applicable section of the Internal Revenue Code, these are called *Section 1231 assets*. Gains on the sale of Section 1231 assets are treated as capital gains, to the extent they exceed losses on the sale of other Section 1231 assets during the same taxable year; losses (net of offsetting gains) are treated as reductions in ordinary income for the year. Rental real estate with respect to which the owner is actively engaged in management and which has been owned more than 12 months is considered a Section 1231 asset.

Why the Difference Is Important

The Code places an upper limit on the rate at which long-term capital gains will be taxed. If the taxpayer's incremental tax rate applicable to ordinary income is less than 28 percent, then the applicable rate on ordinary income applies. If the incremental rate applicable to ordinary income is greater than 28 percent, then net long-term capital gains are taxed at 28 percent. Moreover, there is a limit to the amount of capital losses that can be deducted from ordinary income during any one taxable year.

Computing Net Capital Gains or Losses

Transactions involving capital assets or Section 1231 assets are cataloged according to whether they result in gains or losses. Capital gains and losses are further subdivided according to whether they are long term or short term (A long term capital gain or loss is incurred from the sale or exchange of a capital asset that has been held for more than one year; a short-term capital gain or loss is from an asset that is held for one year or less).

Gains and losses are offset against each other within each category: Section 1231 gains and losses are offset against other, short-term gains and losses are offset against each other, and long-term gains and losses are offset against each other. The ultimate tax consequences of each depends upon whether gains or losses are greater.

Net Section 1231 Gains or Losses. If there is a net Section 1231 loss, it is offset against ordinary income. If there is a net Section 1231 gain, it is treated as ordinary income to the extent that net Section 1231 losses have been used to offset ordinary income during the previous 5 years. Any remaining net Section 1231 gains are treated as long-term capital gains.

Net Capital Gains or Losses. When there are net capital losses in one category (long term or short term) and net capital gains in the other, the two are offset against each other.

- If what remains is a net capital loss, it is offset against ordinary income, but only to the extent of $3,000. Any remaining net capital loss must be carried forward to the next taxable year. The carried-forward losses retain their identity as short term or long term in the next taxable year.
- If what remains is a net short-term capital gain, it is taxed as ordinary income for the year.
- If the net long-term capital gains (including net Section 1231 gains) exceed offsetting short-term capital losses, the remainder is defined by Code Section 1222(11) as *Net Capital Gains.* They are subjected to a maximum tax rate of 28 percent.

ESTIMATING CASH FLOW FROM SELLING MAEGEN'S MAGIC MANOR

In Chapter 6 we estimated the future value of a 280-unit apartment complex called Maegen's Magic Manor. By capitalizing the projected sixth-year income, we estimated that the property would have a market value of $11.23 million at the end of an anticipated six-year holding period. In Chapter 9 we developed a loan amortization schedule, which is presented on Table 9.7. Then, in Chapter 10, we projected annual depreciation allowances which are presented in Table 10.1. Using this information and incorporating an estimate of transaction costs incurred in selling, we can project after-tax cash flow from disposing of Maegen's Magic Manor at the end of an anticipated six-year holding period.

The realized gain on disposal is simply the selling price minus the adjusted tax basis at the time of sale. The tax basis prior to the sale is the initial tax basis (computed in Table 10.1) minus cumulative depreciation allowances (also shown

Table 11.1	Estimate of Investor's Adjusted Tax Basis in Maegen's Magic Manor at Time of Disposal	
Purchase Price		$7,400,000
Add: Transaction Costs		150,000
Initial Tax Basis		$7,550,000
Less: Cumulative Depreciation Allowances (from Table 10.2, rounded)		1,247,800
Adjusted Basis Prior to Sale		$6,302,200
Add: Selling Costs (0.05 × $11,230,000)		561,500
Adjusted Tax Basis at Time of Disposal		$6,863,700

Rounding: All values rounded to nearest $100.

in Table 10.1). Transaction costs incurred on disposal (assumed here to be 5.0 percent) are added to derive the adjusted tax basis at the time of sale. The calculations are shown in Table 11.1.

The taxable gain on disposal is the selling price minus the adjusted tax basis at the time of sale. Multiplying this amount by the applicable tax rate (assumed in this case to be 28 percent) yields the expected income tax consequences of the sale. This is shown in Table 11.2. The anticipated after-tax cash flow is the sales receipts minus all disbursements associated with the sale. These are shown in Table 11.3.

WHEN REALIZED GAINS OR LOSSES ARE RECOGNIZED

A distinction has been made between *realized* and *recognized* gains or losses. Recall that a gain or loss is realized at the time of asset disposition. Whether the gain or loss is recognized for income tax purposes, and tax consequences thereby incurred in the taxable year of the transaction, depends on how the transaction is structured.

Table 11.2	Estimated Income Tax Consequences of Selling Maegen's Magic Manor Apartments	
Selling Price		$11,230,000
Less: Adjusted Tax Basis (from Table 11.1)		6,863,700
Taxable gain		$ 4,366,300
Times: Long-term Capital Gains Tax Rate		.28
Tax Consequences of Disposal		$ 1,222,564

Rounding: All values rounded to nearest $100.

Table 11.3	Estimate of After-Tax Cash Flow from Disposal of Maegen's Magic Manor Apartments		
Selling Price			$11,230,000
Less: Selling Costs (from Table 11.1)		$ 561,500	
Income Taxes (from Table 11.2)		1,222,564	
Mortgage Balance (from Table 9.7)		4,194,000	5,978,064
After-Tax Cash Flow			$ 5,251,936

Rounding: All values rounded to nearest $100.

If a transaction is a cash sale (regardless of how the buyer arranges financing) and the seller realizes a gain, the gain will be recognized in the year of the transaction. If the seller realizes a loss, we have seen that a portion may have to be carried forward and recognized in future taxable years.

When a seller takes back a promissory note in part payment, or receives assets of like kind (i.e., real estate traded for real estate), all or a portion of a gain or loss might be deferred. The deferral is sometimes mandatory, sometimes optional, as explained later in this chapter.

USING THE INSTALLMENT SALES METHOD

When a seller receives only partial payment for real property during the year of sale, reporting the transaction under the *installment sales method* permits a portion of the income tax liability to be deferred until the balance of the cash is collected. Tax liability is incurred only on a pro rata basis with each year's collection of sales proceeds.

Advantages of Installment Sales Reporting

When third-party mortgage loans are expensive or difficult to obtain, sellers who provide a substantial portion of the necessary financing can greatly facilitate property disposal. Installment sales provisions in the Internal Revenue Code are intended to make this possible without the unfortunate side effect of having income tax liability exceed cash collections in the year of the transaction.

A possible by-product of the installment sales method, of great potential benefit, is that taxes on the gain may be deferred until the seller is in a lower tax bracket. A sale might be arranged during peak income-earning years, for example, with payments spread over the seller's retirement years. The amount of taxable gain and the nature of the gain (ordinary income and/or capital gain) are determined at the time of the transaction. But the applicable tax rate is that in effect when taxes become due.

What Gain Qualifies

Owners who have used an accelerated method to compute depreciation or cost recovery allowances may find a portion—sometimes all—of their gain characterized as ordinary income due to recapture of these allowances. The portion of a gain that represents recapture does not qualify for reporting under the installment method. The *installment method gain,* therefore, is the total gain on a transaction, minus the portion that represents recapture. This is illustrated in Example 11.3.

Example 11.3

Residential income property that has an adjusted tax basis of $1,600,000 is sold for $2,000,000. The buyer takes title subject to the $1,500,000 balance of an existing mortgage-secured promissory note, pays $50,000 in cash at the closing and agrees to pay the $450,000 balance of the purchase price in ten equal annual installments payable at the end of each succeeding year, with interest at 8 percent on the unpaid balance. The seller pays a broker's commission of $60,000. Other closing costs incurred by the seller total $25,000. As a consequence of his having used an accelerated cost recovery method, $100,000 of the seller's gain on disposal is characterized as ordinary income due to recapture. The gain on the sale is $315,000, of which only $215,000 qualifies for reporting under the installment method:

Selling Price		$2,000,000
Less:		
Adjusted Basis Prior to Sale	$1,600,000	
Broker's Commission	60,000	
Other Transaction Costs	25,000	1,685,000
Gain on Sale		$ 315,000
Less: Recapture		100,000
Installment Method Gain		$ 215,000

The Contract Price

The *contract price* is the total selling price (that is, the market value of all consideration tendered by the buyer), less the balance of any mortgage note payable by the purchaser to a third party. Note, however, that if the property is sold subject to such a mortgage (whether or not the buyer assumes personal liability for the balance to which the transfer is subject), then the contract price is reduced by only that portion of the mortgage note that does not exceed the seller's adjusted tax basis in the property. The contract price for the transaction in Example 11.3 is $500,000:

Selling Price	$2,000,000
Less: Balance of Old Note, To Be Paid by Buyer	1,500,000
Contract Price	$ 500,000

If the existing mortgage note had exceeded $1,685,000 (the seller's adjusted tax basis after adjusting for transaction costs incurred on the sale), then the excess would have to be included in the contract price.

The Recognized Gain

The relationship between installment method gain and the contract price determines the portion of each year's collections on the contract that must be recognized as a taxable gain. Divide the installment method gain by the contract price to derive this percentage figure. Then multiply the year's collections on the principal amount of the contract by this ratio. The product is the currently taxable installment method gain. The balance of the year's collections (other than the interest, which is taxable as ordinary income in the year received) represents recovery of capital and has no tax consequences.

These instructions can be reduced to a six-step procedure:

1. Compute the realized gain just as if the installment sales method were not to be used.
2. Divide the realized gain into two portions: recapture and installment method gain.
3. Compute the contract price by subtracting from the total selling price the balance of any mortgage note that calls for payments by the purchaser to a third party and adding back any amount by which any preexisting note (to which the property remains subject) exceeds adjusted tax basis of the seller.
4. Divide the installment method gain (from step 2) by the contract price (from step 3) to determine the portion of annual collections on the principal amount of the contract that represents collection of the installment method gain.
5. Determine the amount of the principal collected during the year. Be careful to exclude from this calculation any amount collected that represents payment by the purchaser of interest on the indebtedness. Only the principal portion is included.
6. Multiply the principal collected (from step 5) by the percentage that represents the gain (from step 4). This is the amount of receipts that is to be recognized as installment method gain for the year. The balance of the principal collected represents a return of the taxpayer's investment and is not taxable.

Recall from Example 11.3 that payments on the new note are to be made annually. It follows that no payments will be collected in the taxable year of the transaction. The recognized gain that year will be based on the collections at the time of the transaction itself. The gain to be recognized is $121,500:

Initial Payments	
Down Payment	$ 50,000
Additional Principal Payments during Year	0
Amount of Mortgage Assumed by Buyer in Excess of Seller's	
Adjusted Tax Basis	0
Total Initial Payments	$ 50,000
Gross Profit Ratio	
Installment Method Gain (Computed Earlier)	$215,000
Total Contract Price (Computed Earlier)	500,000
Ratio ($215,000/$500,000)	.43
Recognized Gain in the Year of the Transaction:	
Installment Method Gain To Be Recognized ($50,000 × 0.43) =	$ 21,500
Plus: Recapture (Computed Earlier)	100,000
Recognized Gain in Year of Transaction	$121,500

The Imputed Interest Problem

A buyer usually signs a note as evidence of obligation for the unpaid portion of the purchase price. Credit terms ordinarily provide for periodic payments to retire the note, plus interest payments on the unpaid balance. The principal portion of these payments is considered a part of the purchase price. The interest payments, in contrast, are simply additional income taxable to the seller and generally have no impact on recognition of the gain on sale.

The Internal Revenue Service insists that any installment sales contract or mortgage note include a provision for a reasonable rate of interest. If no such provision exists, the IRS imputes interest by reducing the total selling price to an amount representing the value of the down payment plus the present value of the obligation to make future payments, when the future payments are discounted at a minimum rate of interest as stipulated by the Commissioner of the Internal Revenue Service.

The Outstanding Indebtedness Problem

Sellers who employ the installment method of reporting gains but who themselves owe substantial sums will find the benefits of the installment method greatly reduced. The Internal Revenue Code incorporates complex rules requiring a seller to recognize progressively greater portions of an installment method gain as the total amounts of the taxpayer's own indebtedness grows.

LIKE-KIND EXCHANGES

Otherwise taxable gains or tax-deductible losses realized on an exchange of like-kind assets are not recognized in the year of the transaction. Rather, they are deferred until a future, taxable transaction occurs with respect to the substitute property. When gains are involved, a series of such exchanges can pyramid one's real estate holdings by retaining wealth that would otherwise be chipped away in tax liability with each transaction. The government in effect extends an interest-free loan in the amount of taxes so deferred.

Enabling legislation for like-kind exchanges, sometimes (erroneously) called tax-free exchanges, is contained in Section 1031 of the Internal Revenue Code. Reflecting this, they are sometimes referred to simply as Section 1031 exchanges.

Example 11.4

An investor has been investing all available savings in small parcels of real estate such as single-family dwellings, duplexes and small stores. Over the years a substantial equity in those properties has accrued, so the investor is considering moving into a large property that can be managed professionally and will yield economies of scale.

The properties have an aggregate market value of $1.5 million and are subject to mortgages totaling $1 million. The investor, who is in the 40 percent (combined federal and state) income tax bracket, has an adjusted tax basis of $700,000. Cash available for reinvestment if the investor sells these properties (and assuming, for simplicity, that transaction costs are zero) will be $180,000, calculated as follows:

Taxable Gain on Transaction:		
Selling Price		$1,500,000
Less: Adjusted Tax Basis		700,000
Taxable Gain		$ 800,000
Income Tax Liability at 40%		$ 320,000
Cash Flow Available for Reinvestment:		
Selling Price		$1,500,000
Less:		
Income Tax (.4 × $800,000)	$ 320,000	
Mortgage Balance	1,000,000	1,320,000
Net Cash Flow		$ 180,000

In Example 11.4, the investor pays a heavy price for moving into an alternative investment opportunity: His $500,000 equity is reduced to $180,000 due to the income tax. If, instead of selling and reinvesting the after-tax net proceeds, the investor negotiates a tax-deferred exchange, the entire $500,000 equity will transfer to the new property.

Exchange Versus Sale and Purchase

To qualify under Section 1031, there must have been a bona fide exchange of the assets involved. It appears that the question of whether a transaction is treated as an exchange or as a sale and purchase is more a matter of form than of intent. Investors must ascertain that proper steps are taken by all parties to document transactions as bona fide exchanges. The other parties might not be in a position to have their tax liability deferred under Section 1031, regardless of the form of the transaction. They may therefore be considerably less motivated to structure the transaction appropriately.

Purpose for Which Property Is Held

To qualify as a like-kind exchange, property conveyed must have been held for productive use in a trade or business or as an investment and must be exchanged for like-kind property that is also to be used in a trade or business or held as an investment. Properties may qualify if they fall into either of these categories: property held for use in a trade or business may be exchanged for investment property and vice versa.

Certain types of property, however, are specifically excluded by statute. These include securities or evidence of indebtedness (stocks, bonds, notes and so forth), beneficial interests in trusts, and inventory. For real estate investors the latter category is likely to prove the most troublesome, since inventory includes one's stock in trade or other property (including real estate) held primarily for resale.

What Is Like-Kind Property?

Only like-kind property qualifies for tax-deferred exchange treatment. The like-kind concept relates to the nature of the property, but not to its quality or grade. The implication for real estate investors is that real estate may be exchanged for other real estate without regard for the type of realty involved, so long as it is held as an investment or for use in a trade or business. Examples issued by the Treasury to amplify this point include:[1]

1. Property held for use in trade or business, together with cash, for other property intended for use in a trade or business
2. Urban real estate for a farm or ranch
3. Improved for unimproved real estate held for investment purposes
4. A leasehold (with not less than 30 years to run) for a freehold
5. Mineral interest in land (not merely an assignment of payments) for a fee title in real estate.

An additional exception to the general rule has been more recently written into the Internal Revenue Code: real estate in the United States and real estate in foreign countries are not like-kind under Code Section 1031.

Tax Consequence of Like-Kind Exchanges

If all property involved in an exchange qualifies as like-kind and all parties qualify, then no party to the exchange may recognize any gain or loss on the transaction. Note that this is mandatory, not elective. Any gain or loss realized in an exchange but not recognized for income tax purposes is reflected in the tax basis of the newly acquired property.

Should some of the property involved in an exchange fail the like-kind test, then some portion of a gain (but not of a loss) must be recognized in the year of the transaction. The balance of the realized gain is deferred as before and is reflected in the adjusted basis of acquired property.

Not All Parties Need Qualify.   The test of whether a transaction qualifies as a tax-deferred exchange is applied separately to each party to the trade. To qualify, individuals must not have been holding their property for resale or for personal use. A property must have been held either as an investment or for use in a trade or business (but not as inventory). If one party's motive for ownership was inappropriate under Section 1031, the other party to the transaction may nevertheless qualify.

Example 11.5

Alice Accumulator wants to acquire Larry D. Liquidator's property in an exchange. Liquidator is willing to sell outright but has no interest in Accumulator's property. The broker finds a third party who is willing to buy Accumulator's property. The deal is completed by an exchange of property interests between Accumulator and Liquidator and a purchase by the third party of the property acquired by Liquidator from Accumulator. Accumulator has a tax-deferred exchange; Liquidator does not.

In Example 11.5, Accumulator may defer any gain on the transaction because she acquired like-kind property to be held as an investment. Liquidator, however, does not qualify and so must recognize any realized gain. Liquidator is disqualified because the property acquired from Accumulator is held for resale. The flow of assets between the parties is illustrated in Figure 11.1.

Even if Liquidator had not found an immediate buyer for property acquired from Accumulator in Example 11.5, it is possible that recognition of gains could not be deferred under Section 1031. Had the property traded to Accumulator been listed for sale for a period of time immediately before the exchange, this would have established that it also was held primarily for sale. The important point here is that the tax consequences to Accumulator are independent of those to Liquidator.

Effect of Receiving Unlike Property.   Receipt of property that does not meet the like-kind definition has the effect of partially disqualifying a gain from deferral under Section 1031. The person receiving unlike property, or boot, must recognize any gain realized on the transaction to the extent of the boot received.

Figure 11.1   A Two-Way Exchange with a Third-Party Buyer

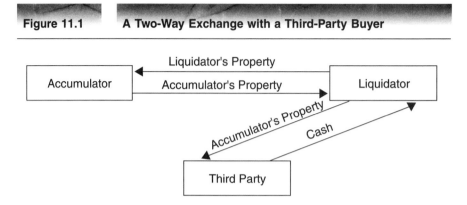

Boot includes anything of economic value other than like-kind assets involved in the transaction. Examples include cash, services rendered or an obligation to render services, debt forgiveness and a promise to convey something of value in the future.

A special rule applies to one category of unlike property: the transfer of like-kind property subject to mortgage indebtedness. The amount of debt relief involved in such a transfer is treated as receipt of unlike property, whether or not the other party assumes and agrees to pay the indebtedness. However, when each party takes title subject to an outstanding mortgage, only the party that receives net debt relief is considered to have received boot, and the amount is the difference between the two mortgages. Example 11.6 illustrates.

Example 11.6

Smith and Jones agree that their respective equities are equal in value. They agree to trade equities, each party taking title subject to the mortgage note on the property received. Their positions before the exchange were as follows:

	Smith	*Jones*
Market Value of Property	$750,000	$1,400,000
Less: Balance of Mortgage	250,000	900,000
Value of Equity	$500,000	$ 500,000

Jones has received boot of $650,000 in the form of net debt relief (the old debt of $900,000 minus the new debt of $250,000). Therefore, Jones incurs an income tax liability for any gain realized on the transaction, to the extent of the $650,000 of net debt relief.

An investor may receive net debt relief and yet have to pay cash to balance the market value of assets exchanged. In that case, only the difference between net debt relief and the cash paid is treated as boot received. However, receipt of cash or other unlike assets is not offset against net mortgage liability assumed. Example 11.7 illustrates.

Example 11.7

Freddy Front and Betty Back agree to exchange properties. Each party is to assume the balance of the outstanding mortgage note on realty received in the exchange, and Back agrees to pay cash to Front to "balance the equities." Their positions before the exchange were as follows:

	Front	Back
Market Value of Realty	$1,100,000	$1,100,000
Less: Balance of Mortgage	600,000	700,000
Market Value of Equity	$ 500,000	$ 400,000

Based on this analysis, Back agrees to pay Front $100,000. Even though she receives net debt relief in the exchange, Back has not received boot as defined in Section 1031 and need not report a taxable gain. This is because the net debt relief is offset by payment of cash boot. The effect is the same as if the $100,000 cash had been applied instead to reduce the mortgage balance prior to the trade. Offsetting the $100,000 of net debt relief against the $100,000 cash paid by Back results in an even trade from Back's point of view.

When cash is received, however, it is not offset by mortgage liability assumed. Front, therefore, has received $100,000 boot in the form of cash, notwithstanding the fact that he has assumed $100,000 of additional mortgage liability.

A party who receives unlike property in an exchange must recognize any gain to the extent of the value of boot received. Note that this applies only to gains. Losses realized in a transaction may not be recognized if the exchange qualifies even partly as like-kind.

Treatment of Transaction Costs.   Transaction costs include such items as brokerage commissions, recording fees, transfer taxes and Attorneys' fees. Transaction costs may be thought of as a reduction in proceeds from the old property or an addition to the purchase price of the new. In either case, they reduce the realized gain and thereby become a part of the tax basis of newly acquired property. Transaction costs may also be offset against any unlike property (boot) received and thereby reduce the portion of the realized gain that must be recognized.[2]

Tax Basis of Acquired Property

Property acquired in a like-kind exchange has a substitute tax basis that reflects the deferred gain or loss. It consists of the adjusted basis of the property conveyed, with further adjustments reflecting the circumstances of the exchange.

Example 11.8

Ronald Chump exchanges property that has an adjusted tax basis of $900,000 for like-kind property with a market value of $1.5 million. He pays transaction costs of $1,500 but neither receives nor pays any boot. Both properties are exchanged on a free and clear basis.

To see how this rule works, consider Example 11.8. Chump has a realized gain of $598,500 and a substitute tax basis of $901,500. His realized gain is computed as follows:

Market Value of Property Received		$1,500,000
Less:		
Transaction Costs	$ 1,500	
Adjusted Basis of Old Property	900,000	901,500
Realized Gain on Transaction		$ 598,500

Chump's substitute tax basis is determined by adding to his old adjusted tax basis his transaction costs and any additional consideration he paid, then subtracting any additional consideration received and any recognized gain:

Basis of Old Property		$900,000
Plus:		
Additional Consideration Paid	0	
Transaction Costs Incurred	$1,500	1,500
		$901,500
Less: Additional Consideration Received		0
Tax Basis of Substitute Property		$901,500

The same result can be reached by subtracting from the fair market value of the property Chump received the amount of any gain he realized but not recognize:

Market Value of Substitute Property		$1,500,000
Less: Deferred Gain		
Realized Gain	$598,500	
Minus Recognized Gain	0	
Amount Deferred		598,500
Tax Basis of Substitute Property		$ 901,500

When Chump sells the substitute property acquired in Example 11.8, his taxable gain is computed on the difference between the net proceeds and adjusted basis at that time. And since the basis of the substitute property reflects the deferred gain, selling the substitute property triggers recognition of the gain.

We have deliberately kept examples simple to better illustrate how the basis of a newly acquired property is computed. Example 11.9 is a more complex exercise designed to demonstrate how the same rules can carry an analyst through the computational thicket.

Example 11.9

Ima Gottsome owns income property with a market value of $2 million and a mortgage of $750,000. Her adjusted basis before the transaction is $1.2 million. She exchanges this for another income property with a market value of $3.5 million that is subject to a mortgage of $1.5 million. Gottsome pays $750,000 cash for the difference in equities, and each party takes title subject to existing mortgages. Gottsome pays transaction costs of $20,000.

Gottsome's realized gain is the difference between the market value and the adjusted tax basis of her original property, minus transaction costs:

Market Value of Assets Received		$3,500,000
Less Tax Basis of Assets Tendered:		
Real Estate (Basis before Exchange)	$1,200,000	
Transaction Costs	20,000	
Cash	750,000	
Net Debt Assumed	750,000	2,720,000
Realized Gain		$ 780,000

Having received only like-kind property in the exchange, however, Gottsome defers recognition of the entire gain. The initial basis of the new property is determined as follows:

Adjusted Basis before the Exchange		$1,200,000
Add:		
Transaction Costs	$ 20,000	
Mortgage Assumed	1,500,000	
Cash Paid	750,000	2,270,000
		$3,470,000
Less: Old Mortgage (Debt Relief)		750,000
Tax Basis of Substitute Property		$2,720,000

Note that the basis of the substitute property in Example 11.9 is simply its fair market value less any unrecognized gain: $3,500,000 minus $780,000, or $2,720,000.

If, due to receiving unlike property, some portion of a realized gain must be recognized, the basis of substitute property is increased by the amount of the recognized gain. This is illustrated in Example 11.10.

Example 11.10

Dr. Dudly Dullbit exchanges his dental office building (market value of $1,528,000) for another office and a used cabin cruiser (market value estimated to be $28,000). Dr. Dullbit owes a mortgage balance of $800,000 on his building, and his adjusted tax basis is $1,000,000. Each party agrees to assume the existing mortgage on property received in the exchange. The building received by Dr. Dullbit has an outstanding mortgage balance of $700,000 and a fair market value of $1,400,000. Transaction costs to Dr. Dullbit are $50,000.

Dr. Dullbit has a realized gain, part of which must be recognized since he receives unlike property in exchange. The realized gain is $478,000, computed as follows:

Market Value of Assets Received		
Real Estate		$1,400,000
Personalty		28,000
Net Debt Relief		100,000
Total		$1,528,000
Less: Basis of Assets Tendered		
Real Estate (Basis before exchange)	$1,000,000	
Transaction Costs	50,000	1,050,000
Realized Gain on Exchange		$ 478,000

The realized gain generates tax liability to the extent of any unlike property received in the exchange, net of transaction costs. Dr. Dullbit must therefore recognize $78,000 of the realized gain as currently taxable.

Mortgage on Old Property	$800,000
Less: Mortgage Assumed	700,000
Net Debt Relief	$100,000
Value of Other Unlike Property Received	28,000
Total Value of Unlike Property Received	$128,000
Less: Transaction Costs	50,000
Net Boot Received	$ 78,000

The tax basis of the new property received by Dr. Dullbit is the adjusted basis of his old property, increased by any additional payments made and any recognized gain and reduced by any other value received:

Adjusted Basis of Old Property		$1,000,000
Plus:		
Transaction Costs	$ 50,000	
Debt Assumed	700,000	
Recognized Gain	78,000	828,000
		$1,828,000
Less:		
Old Mortgage	$800,000	
Personalty Received	28,000	828,000
Basis of New Property		$1,000,000

The substitute tax basis computed in Example 11.10 can be proved by reducing the market value of the new property by the amount of the unrecognized gain. The results should be the same as in the example. The calculations are as follows:

Market Value of Property Received		$1,400,000
Less: Unrecognized Gain		
Realized Gain (Example 11.9)	$478,000	
Minus: Recognized Gain	78,000	
Unrecognized Portion of Gain		400,000
Basis of New Property		$1,000,000

Effect of Losses in Section 1031 Exchanges

So far, all examples have assumed a gain on the exchange, with the discussion centering on whether a portion of the gain must be recognized and on the resulting tax basis of substitute property. But what happens if there is a loss on an exchange? If a transaction qualifies fully under Section 1031 as like-kind, then neither a gain nor a loss may be recognized. We have seen, however, that if an investor realizes a gain and receives any unlike property, then a portion of the gain must be recognized. This partial recognition relates only to gains; receipt of some unlike property in an otherwise like-kind exchange never triggers partial recognition of a loss.

Example 11.11

Sovery Smart trades income-producing real estate for like-kind property. The property received by Smart has a fair market value of $80,000 and is subject to a mortgage of $55,000. Smart's old property has an adjusted basis of $95,000 and is subject to a mortgage of $60,000. The parties exchange equities, each assuming the mortgage on the property received. Transaction costs are zero.

The transaction in Example 11.11 qualifies under Section 1031 as a like kind exchange, but Ms. Smart has received unlike property in the form of net debt relief. Had there been a gain, it would be recognized to the extent of Smart's net debt relief ($5,000). In this example, though, Smart has experienced a loss rather than a gain:

Market Value of Property Received	$80,000	
Mortgage Assumed by Other Party	60,000	$140,000
Less:		
Mortgage Assumed by Smart	55,000	
Adjusted Basis of Old Property	95,000	150,000
Gain (Loss) on the Exchange		(10,000)

Although Smart may not recognize her loss in the year of the transaction, it is reflected in her tax basis for the new property. Thus, its recognition is merely deferred until the new property is sold. Smart's basis for the new property is her old basis, adjusted for the other property involved in the transaction. The illustration assumes there are no transaction costs. Were such costs incurred, they would be added to the new basis. Smart's new basis is:

Basis of Old Property	$ 95,000
Plus: Mortgage Assumed	55,000
	$150,000
Less: Mortgage Assumed by Other Party	60,000
Basis of New Property	$ 90,000

Note that the basis of Smart's new property is simply its market value adjusted by adding any additional value given by Smart and subtracting any value received plus any unrecognized loss or less any unrecognized gain:

Market Value of Property Received	$80,000
Plus: Unrecognized Loss	10,000
Basis of New Property	$90,000

Note also that the substitute basis of Smart's new property exceeds its fair market value by the amount of the unrecognized loss. It would also include any transaction costs incurred by Smart. If she subsequently sells the property, her recognized loss on the sale will reflect this substitute basis in excess of fair market value. The deferred loss will be recognized at that time.

Allocating the Substitute Basis

Just as the initial basis of purchased property must be allocated between land and improvements to determine cost recovery allowances, so must the substitute basis of property acquired in a Section 1031 exchange be allocated. The basic rule remains invariant: allocate on the basis of relative market values.

Example 11.12

Geltloss and Smith trade like-kind properties. Both parties own their properties on a free and clear basis. Relative values before the exchange are agreed to be as follows:

	Adjusted Basis	*Market Value*	
		Dollar Amount	*Percentage of Total*
Geltloss			
Land	$200,000	$200,000	40%
Improvements	100,000	300,000	60
Total	$300,000	$500,000	100
Smith			
Land	$ 50,000	$ 50,000	10%
Improvements	200,000	450,000	90
Total	$250,000	$500,000	100

Consider Example 11.12. To keep the illustration simple, assume there are no transaction costs. Since no boot is involved, Geltloss will have a substitute basis equaling the adjusted basis of his old property: $300,000. This basis is allocated to the acquired land and improvements in the ratio of their relative market values: ten percent to the land and 90 percent to the improvements. Geltloss's basis after the exchange is as follows:

Land (10%)	$ 30,000
Improvements (90%)	270,000
Total Basis (100%)	$300,000

Our illustration assumes that relative market values are known. In a real situation, these values must be determined. This may be accomplished by agreement between the parties in an arm's-length transaction, by an independent appraisal or by using relative values as determined by the property-tax assessor.

These do not exhaust the potential means of arriving at an estimate of relative market values, but they are all approaches that have been accepted in the past.

If more than one property is received in an exchange, the substitute basis is allocated among acquired properties in the ratio of their relative market values as of the date of the exchange. The allocated substitute basis of each property is in turn allocated between land and improvements on the basis of relative values. To illustrate, assume the property received from Smith in Example 11.12 consists of a store building on one small plot of land and an adjoining vacant lot. Assume further that each of the lots is worth $25,000 if unimproved, and the store building alone is worth $450,000 before considering the value of the site. Geltloss's $300,000 substitute basis is first allocated to the two separate properties in the ratio of their relative values: 5 percent to the vacant lot and 95 percent to the store and site. The substitute basis of the store and site (.95 × $300,000 = $285,000) is then allocated to site and improvements based on their relative values. The resulting substitute basis is as follows:

	Market Value	Percentage of Total Value	Substitute Basis
Vacant Lot	$ 25,000	5%	$ 15,000
Store			
Site	25,000	5	15,000
Improvements	450,000	90	270,000
Total	$500,000	100%	$300,000

Nonsimultaneous Exchanges

When exchanges do not involve simultaneous transfers of ownership, there are strict time requirements within which the entire transaction must be completed. To qualify for tax deferral the substitute property must be identified within 44 days following the day of the initial property transfer, and the final transfer must be completed by the earlier of (a) 179 days following the day of the initial property transfer or (b) the due date for the taxes that would be imposed if the transaction did not qualify for tax deferral.

When titles are not transferred simultaneously, the usual arrangement is to use a qualified intermediary, an escrow account or a trust that receives the taxpayer's relinquished property, acquires the like-kind substitute, then transfers the replacement property to the taxpayer. The IRS has issued a regulation [Reg. 1.1031(k)-1(g)(4)] that sets forth rules governing the responsibilities of an intermediary.

Exchanges Between Related Parties

If a like-kind exchange is between related parties, then both parties must hold their substitute properties for at least two years after the date of the exchange. If either party disposes of their substitute property early, then the party who qualified for and claimed a deferred gain under the like-kind exchange rules must recognize the deferred gain in the year that the disposition occurs. Exceptions to this general rule are provided in the following cases:

- The death of either party
- Involuntary disposal due to the property's destruction, seizure, condemnation or imminent threat of condemnation

GIVING PROPERTY AWAY

If property is owned free and clear and is given to someone else, no consideration is involved in the transaction and there is no realized gain or loss. Since no gain or loss has been realized, of course none is recognized. There may, however, be gift tax consequences.

The Unified Gift and Estate Tax

All bona fide gifts and all property passed as a legacy at death is subject to a unified and graduated gift and estate tax. The tax is imposed on the giver or, in the case of a legacy, on the estate of the deceased. There are several exemptions and exclusions:

- Taxpayers may give up to $10,000 per person per year to as many individuals as they wish, with no gift tax implications. The gifts must be present interests (that is, the recipient must have immediate access to the gift), unless the recipient is a minor. If the recipient is a minor, the gift can be placed in trust until the recipient becomes an adult. If husband and wife jointly make gifts, they may give up to $20,000 per recipient per year without incurring gift tax liability, but they must file an information gift tax return in the year of the gift.
- There is an unlimited exemption for gifts or legacies to one's spouse, providing the spouse is a U.S. citizen at the time of the gift. For spouses who are not U.S. citizens, tax-exempt gifts are limited to $100,000 per annum.
- There is an unlimited exemption for payment of tuition and medical expenses for others, providing payment is made directly to the education or health care provider.

All other gifts are subject to the unified, graduated tax shown in Table 11.4. Gift taxes are due in the taxable year of the gift, but lifetime gifts are cumulated to determine the rate at which the tax is levied.

In addition to the exclusions and exemptions previously listed, every taxpayer has a $192,800 lifetime credit against the unified gift and estate tax. The credit offsets the tax on the first $600,000 of taxable gifts or legacies.

Effect of Giving Property Subject to a Mortgage

If a property is transferred subject to a mortgage, there will be both sale and gift elements to the transfer. This is because relief from indebtedness is valuable

Table 11.4		Estate and Gift Taxes, Unified Tax Rate Schedule		
If the Taxable Amount Is:		*Tentative Tax Is:*		
From	*To*	*Tax on Amount in First Column*	*+%*	*On Excess over*
$ —	$ 10,000	$ —	18	$ —
10,000	20,000	1,800	20	10,000
20,000	40,000	3,800	22	20,000
40,000	60,000	8,200	24	40,000
60,000	80,000	13,000	26	60,000
80,000	100,000	18,200	28	80,000
100,000	150,000	23,800	30	100,000
150,000	250,000	38,800	32	150,000
250,000	500,000	70,800	34	250,000
500,000	750,000	155,800	37	500,000
750,000	1,000,000	248,300	39	750,000
1,000,000	1,250,000	345,800	41	1,000,000
1,250,000	1,500,000	448,300	43	1,250,000
1,500,000	2,000,000	555,800	45	1,500,000
2,000,000	2,500,000	780,800	49	2,000,000
2,500,000	3,000,000	1,025,800	53	2,500,000
3,000,000	and over	1,290,800	55	3,000,000

consideration (even though the giver may be liable for the debt, the recipient must pay it to retain control of the mortgaged property). If the mortgage balance exceeds the giver's adjusted tax basis, the difference will be a realized gain. The difference between the property's market value and the mortgage balance is a gift and is potentially subject to the gift tax.

The Tax Basis of Property Received as a Gift

The tax basis of a gift recipient's interest in a property will be the same as the giver's, unless the giver incurred a gift tax liability. In that case, the recipient's tax basis will be increased by the portion of the gift tax that results from the property's value having grown during the giver's period of ownership.

A Gifting Strategy for Highly Appreciated Property

If the sale of a property will result in a substantial realized gain, considerable tax savings may be realized by utilizing a gifting strategy. Where two individuals who consider themselves an integral economic unit (so that it doesn't really matter who holds title) are in different income tax brackets, consider transferring property to the party in the lower bracket, and letting that party sell. The gain on disposal will then be taxed at their lower marginal bracket and the after-tax proceeds will be greater.

This strategy is defeated, of course, if the transfer results in gift tax liability. The gift tax may be avoided by exploiting the unified credit, which offsets the gift tax on $600,000 of taxable transfers. Otherwise, consider transferring title in $10,000 annual increments.

Alternatives May Be Less Taxing

Alternatives to an outright gift may be advisable even where two parties who consider themselves an integral economic unit are in substantially different income tax brackets. If, instead of being transferred as a gift, a highly appreciated property is transferred as a legacy, the recipient gets a stepped-up tax basis equal to the value on which estate taxes are based. This means that all appreciation during the lifetime of the deceased owner escapes income taxes altogether. It is wise, therefore, to consider holding highly appreciated real estate so that it will benefit from the stepped-up basis rule. If a portion of the equity needs to be liquidated during the interim, this can be accomplished by additional borrowing against the property. We have seen that borrowing is not a taxable event, yet it liquidates equity as surely as does an outright sale.

Should property owners desire to defer recognition of taxable gains during their lifetimes but nonetheless wish to adjust their portfolios, they should consider like-kind exchanges as previously discussed. There is no limit to the number of substitute properties that can be acquired in a series of such exchanges, with all gains being deferred. When the property owners die, their heirs take title with stepped-up tax basis, and all the deferred gains are permanently avoided.

SUMMARY

When sellers take back promissory notes in part payment for property, they may defer recognition of taxable gains until they collect proceeds from the notes. The gain is recognized on a pro rata basis as the principal portion of the note is collected. Deferral does not affect the recognized gain's status as ordinary income or a capital gain.

Taxes due to gains on disposal of real estate are deferred if the property is exchanged for other property in a qualifying like-kind exchange. The tax liability is deferred until the property received in the trade is itself disposed of in a transaction that does not qualify as like-kind. To qualify as a like-kind exchange, both old and the substitute property must be held for use in a trade or business or for production of income. Certain types of property are specifically excluded from like-kind exchange treatment. These include securities and evidence of indebtedness, beneficial interests in trusts, and inventory.

If some unlike property (boot) is received in an otherwise qualifying like-kind exchange, then any realized gain must be recognized for tax purposes, to the extent of the value of the unlike property received. The balance of the gain is deferred until the substitute property is sold. No part of a realized loss may be recognized, however, if the transaction qualifies even in part as a like-kind exchange.

When property is given away, the tax basis in the hands of a new owner is the same as it was in the hands of the previous owners. The only exception is when the previous owners incurred some gift tax liability due to increases in property value during their ownership period. If property is transferred subject to mortgage indebtedness, the amount of the debt is considered to be consideration for the transaction. Only the remaining value is a gift.

NOTES

1. Treasury Regulation 1.1031(a)–1.1031(b).
2. Revenue Ruling 72–456.

RECOMMENDED READINGS

Commerce Clearing House. *U.S. Master Tax Guide.* Chicago: Commerce Clearing House. Published annually.
Journal of Real Estate Taxation. A quarterly periodical published by Warren, Gorham & Lamont, 210 South St., Boston, MA 02111.

REVIEW QUESTIONS

1. What is the principal advantage of using the installment sales method of reporting property sales?
2. List the qualifications necessary for an exchange of property to be considered a like-kind exchange for tax purposes.
3. How are gains and losses in a like-kind exchange treated?
4. How is the tax basis of property acquired in a like-kind exchange determined?
5. Describe the allocation of the basis of property acquired in a like-kind exchange.
6. How is the tax basis of property received as a gift determined?
7. Under what circumstances will giving away property be considered in part a sale or exchange?
8. What is the relationship between federal gift taxes and federal estate taxes?
9. How large a gift can be made to an individual other than one's spouse during a single calendar year, without the gift being subject to gift taxes?

DISCUSSION QUESTIONS

1. Why do you suppose the taxes on installment sales are permitted to be deferred? Does this provision seem to represent good public policy? Why or why not?
2. From a public policy perspective, is there any reason to accord like-kind exchanges different income tax treatment from that associated with selling the old property and buying the substitute? In either instance, are there compelling public policy reasons to permit income taxes to be deferred?

PROBLEMS

1. Mr. Bawl N. Bicker, partner in Bicker, Barter and Steel, owns rental property worth $1 million and subject to a mortgage of $250,000. His adjusted tax basis in the property is $400,000. He trades for a like-kind property worth $1,500,000, which is subject to a mortgage balance of $600,000. Bicker pays $150,000 cash to balance the equities, and each party takes title subject to existing mortgages. Bicker pays transaction costs of $45,000. What is Bicker's substitute tax basis?
2. Dr. Dullbit Drillum, partner in the dental firm of Drillum, Fillum and Billum, exchanges an office building (market value = $1,528,000) for an apartment building (market value = $1,400,000). Dr. Drillum owes $800,000 on a note secured by a mortgage on his office building, which has an adjusted tax basis of $1,000,000. The building he will receive in the exchange is encumbered with a mortgage that has a balance of $700,000. Dr. Drillum incurs transaction costs of $50,000. Each party agrees to take title subject to the existing mortgage on the substitute building; cash will be tendered to balance the equities. What will be Dr. Drillum's substitute tax basis after the exchange?
3. Mr. Vicker owns income property with a market value of $1,000,000 that is subject to a mortgage of $250,000. The adjusted basis is $400,000. He exchanges the property for another that has a market value of $1,500,000 (land value is $250,000; the rest is the value of the improvements) and is subject to a mortgage of $600,000. Vicker pays $150,000 cash for the difference in equities, and each party takes title subject to existing mortgages. Vicker pays transaction costs of $6,500. What is the substitute tax basis of Vicker's new building and other improvements (excluding the basis of the land)?
4. I.0. Bigbucks is considering selling an apartment building that he bought several years ago for $820,000, including transaction costs. He has claimed total (cumulative) depreciation (cost recovery allowances) of $255,000. He has made no capital improvements during his holding period.

   Bigbucks has been offered $900,000 for this property ($300,000 over the existing $600,000 mortgage note, to which the property will remain subject when sold). Terms of the offer are: $90,000 in cash at the closing. Buyer assumes the $600,000 balance on the existing first mortgage note and signs a note and purchase-money mortgage for the remaining $210,000 of the purchase price. The $210,000 note provides for three equal annual payments including principal and interest, with interest at 12 percent.

Required: If Bigbucks accepts this offer and incurs $45,000 of sales costs, what will be the resultant increase in his taxable income in the year of the transaction and in each of the three succeeding years, assuming he uses the installment method of reporting the sale? Bigbucks has no imputed interest problem, and the property would generate zero taxable income each year if it were not sold. Bigbucks has no other outstanding debts.

CHAPTER 12

Other Taxing Issues

Framers of the Internal Revenue Code deliberately incorporated a number of special tax-saving opportunities either as breaks for special interest groups or as encouragement for certain types of economic activity considered to be in the public interest. A good portion of these special opportunities involves real estate investment. But failure to fully understand the tax implications can result in tax liability—in many cases, long after the intended income tax benefit has been fully dissipated. This chapter alerts readers to provisions that represent special opportunities or particularly pernicious tax traps.

TAX CONSEQUENCES OF FINANCIAL LEVERAGE

Borrowing or repaying money is not a taxable event—it neither increases nor decreases tax liability. Interest on borrowed money secured by a mortgage on rental real estate, in contrast, is usually deductible in the taxable year that it is paid. The most significant exceptions to this general rule involve special treatment of prepaid interest and construction-period interest, and deduction limitations incorporated into passive activity loss rules, discussed later in the chapter.

Prepaid Interest Must Be Amortized

Prepaid interest is generally not deductible by the borrower until the interest is actually earned by the lender. Consequently, discount points and loan origination fees, both of which are explored in Chapter 9, must be deducted ratably (amortized) over the term of the loan on which they are incurred. Loans to purchase or to finance improvements to a personal residence are exempted from this rule, providing the discount points are representative of those charged in the market area.

Construction-Period Interest Must Be Capitalized

Interest incurred during construction of real estate improvements is considered a part of the construction cost. Thus, it is a part of the initial tax basis of the improvements and figures into the cost recovery allowance.

Limits on the Deductibility of Interest

Deductions for interest incurred to acquire or carry portfolio assets such as stocks and bonds are limited to the amount of income earned by the portfolio. Any investment interest in excess of portfolio income is carried forward and claimed as offsets against portfolio income in subsequent years.

There are also overall limits on the amount of net losses from real estate that can be offset against income from other sources, if the real estate is deemed to be a passive investment (the passive asset limitation rules are explored later in this chapter).

These limitations may prevent some interest expense from being deducted in the year incurred. Should that occur, the interest expense is carried forward and treated as interest expense incurred in the following year. There are no limits on the number of years that interest expense can be carried forward in this manner.

Investment Strategy Implications

Because selling a property may result in income tax liability, while borrowing against it does not, investors will often benefit from borrowing rather than selling. One's equity in a property is the difference between market value and the balance of mortgage indebtedness. Selling a property is often referred to as *liquidating the equity,* because it results in the equity interest being converted to cash. Borrowing does the same thing, by reducing the difference between market value and mortgage indebtedness, but—unlike selling—the borrowing is not a taxable event.

INCOME TAX CREDITS FOR PROPERTY REHABILITATION

Tax shelter benefits, though extensively curtailed by legislation since 1986, are still available to investors involved in real estate renovation and rehabilitation. But not all opportunities are created equal. If they conform to rigorously detailed criteria, expenditures to renovate low-income housing or selected nonresidential properties generate special benefits in the form of tax credits. Tax credits for rehabilitating certified historic structures are even more generous.

How Tax Credits Work

Tax credits, dollar-for-dollar reductions in tax liability, are not to be confused with tax deductions. A credit is subtracted after the amount of income taxes is computed, then is subtracted from tax liability. Taxpayers in the 35 percent marginal income tax bracket, for example, would find their income taxes reduced by one dollar for every dollar of tax credits, but only 35 cents for every dollar of tax deductions.

Credits for Rehabilitating Old Buildings

Provided they meet carefully specified criteria, expenditures to rehabilitate buildings that were placed in service before 1936 qualify for a rehabilitation tax credit equal to 10 percent of the rehabilitation expenditure. Credits for rehabilitating historically significant structures or low-income rental housing—explained later—are even more generous.

To qualify for the 10 percent rehabilitation credit, a rehabilitation project must leave at least 50 percent of the building's existing external walls intact and functioning as external walls. Moreover, at least 75 percent of existing external walls must be retained as either internal or external walls, and at least 75 percent of the building's internal structural framework must be retained in place. Rehabilitation expenditures must have totaled more than $5,000, and they must have exceeded the taxpayer's adjusted basis in the property before rehabilitation.

There are special rules for claiming a rehabilitation tax credit in connection with work on certified historic structures. These rules, and the associated tax credit, are discussed in the next section. Expenditures on a certified historic structure, if they do not meet the criteria for the special credit associated with such rehabilitations, will not qualify for any tax credit. Taxpayers seeking the credit for rehabilitating structures that are not certified as historic, therefore, must carefully ascertain that the buildings are not certified. If a building is located in a registered historic district, the Secretary of the Interior must certify that the building is not of historical significance to the district, in order to qualify for the general rehabilitation tax credit.

If a taxpayer claims the tax credit and then sells property within five years, a portion of the credit will be subject to recapture and will become a tax liability in the year of sale. The portion that is subject to recapture depends upon how long the property is held after rehabilitation:

Number of Years Held after Rehabilitation	Percent of Tax Credit Subject to Recapture
Less than 1	100%
Less than 2	80
Less than 3	60
Less than 4	40
Less than 5	20
5 or more	0

An investor's tax basis in the rehabilitated property must be reduced to reflect the amount of the tax credit, and will be increased by the amount of any credit recaptured. A gain or loss on disposal is then computed based on the adjusted basis.

Tax Credits for Rehabilitating Historic Structures

Rehabilitation of properties that federal functionaries deem of historical significance is more heavily subsidized via tax credits. Whereas the maximum allowable tax credit for other older buildings (other than qualifying low-income rental housing, explained later) is 10 percent of the rehabilitation outlay, qualifying historic property rehabilitations earn a credit equal to 20 percent of the amount expended.

A *certified historic structure* is any structure that is either listed in the National Registry of Historic Places or located in a registered historic district. In the case of a structure in a registered historic district but not certified as being of historical significance, however, the Secretary of the Interior must certify that the structure is of historic significance to the district.

A *registered historic district* is any district listed as such in the National Registry of Historic Places. The designation also includes any district so identified by appropriate state or local statute, provided that the Secretary of the Interior certifies that the statute will substantially achieve its purpose of preservation and rehabilitation and that the district meets substantially all the requirements for listing in the National Registry.

The recapture rules that apply to other rehabilitation credits (discussed earlier) apply also to credits for rehabilitating certified historic structures. If the property is held for at least five years after rehabilitation, no recapture occurs.

LOW-INCOME HOUSING TAX CREDITS

As part of the 1986 Tax Reform Act that decimated most existing tax-sheltered investment programs, Congress enacted a new tax credit program designed as an incentive to build, rehabilitate or make substantial repairs to low-income rental housing. Like the credits discussed above, this one is a fixed percentage of specified acquisition and development costs. Unlike the previously discussed credits, however, the low-income housing credit is received on an annual basis over ten years.

The program requires that the housing be targeted to tenants whose incomes fall substantially below the area median. The criteria are that, based on a four-person household, either (a) at least 20 percent of the project's units be occupied by tenants whose income does not exceed 50 percent of the area median, as determined by HUD, or (b) at least 40 percent of the units be occupied by tenants whose income does not exceed 60 percent of the area median. Property owners must make an irrevocable choice between these alternatives at the time the project is placed in service.

The household income limit is adjusted to reflect variations in household size above or below four persons, using a HUD-devised formula. HUD is empowered to make additional adjustments in areas of unusually high or unusually low income levels. HUD also specifies the maximum rental charge. The qualifying tenant income levels and maximum rental rates are recomputed annually.

The downside of the low-income housing tax credit program is its mind-boggling complexity. The following general rules (stripped of their agonizing detail, and thus oversimplified) begin to communicate this.

The Amount of the Credit

The amount of the tax credit is computed using a formula that is intended to provide an aggregate tax credit, spread over ten years, that has a present value equal to a specified percentage of the qualified costs: 70 percent of the acquisition cost of new construction and of the cost to "substantially" rehabilitate existing units, 30 percent of acquisition cost for existing housing units that qualify for the rehabilitation credit, and 30 percent of the total cost—acquisition and rehabilitation—of most projects that benefit from federally subsidized mortgage loans.

The rate employed in the discounting to compute the present value of the credits is intended to be the prevailing after-tax interest rate. Table 12.1 shows the annual credit as a percent of cost, when the prevailing rate is 4.85 percent or 6.0 percent. Credits for new construction or for rehabilitation of existing buildings (but *not* for acquisition of the existing buildings) may be increased by 30 percent if the property is located in a specially designated low-income census tract or an area deemed to have high housing costs relative to income levels. The designation is made by the Secretary of Housing and Urban Development.

Table 12.1   **Tax Credit as a Percent of Qualifying Acquisition and Rehabilitation Costs, When Applicable Discount Rate Is 4.85% and 6.0%**

		Approximate Annual Credit (As % of Cost) When Prevailing Rate Is	
	Allowable Present Value of Credit*	*4.85%*	*6.0%*
New Construction	70	9%	9.5%
Rehabilitation	70	9%	9.5%
Building Acquisition and Minor Rehabilitation	30	4%	4.1%
Federally Subsidized Acquisition or Rehabilitation Costs	30	4%	4.1%

*Present value of credits, which are spread over ten years.

Qualifying for the Credits

To qualify for low-income housing credits, rehabilitation cost must be at least $3,000 per dwelling unit, and cannot be less than 10 percent of the taxpayer's unadjusted tax basis in the building. There are no exceptions with regard to qualifying for the *rehabilitation* credit, and no exceptions to the minimum rehabilitation expenditure of $3,000 per unit with respect to qualifying for the *acquisition* credit. But with respect to *acquisition credits only* (not rehabilitation credits), there are two exceptions to the 10 percent-of-basis rule:

1. For buildings acquired from a governmental agency, the *acquisition* credit requires rehabilitation expenditures of no more than $3,000 per unit, without reference to the tax basis.
2. The IRS can issue a waiver in order to avoid the loss of rental units from the low-income housing stock. The minimum rehabilitation cost to qualify for the *acquisition* credit is then reduced to $2,000 per unit instead of the usual $3,000.

If some of the rental units are occupied by tenants who do not meet the low-income definition, only the cost of rehabilitating the low-income units and the common areas that benefit low-income units qualifies for the credit. To determine the qualifying expenditures, total costs to rehabilitate the low-income units and related common areas are allocated equally to all low-income units: all the low-income units must qualify if any of them are to qualify.

DOING GOOD WHILE DOING WELL

Though largely unheralded and little understood even by most of the real estate development community, the tax credit for developing or rehabilitating low-income rental housing is having major impact on the lives it touches. Since its enactment in 1987, the tax credit program has attracted more than $12 billion in private equity investment to low-income housing and has been a factor—in most cases, the deciding factor—in developing or rehabilitating approximately 800,000 dwelling units.*

The program has spawned a covey of nonprofit neighborhood housing development corporations across the country. It is credited with sparking spin-off development activity and encouraging homeowners to undertake major renovation that is pumping new life into what were previously urban wastelands. The development corporations earn the tax credits and sell them to corporate investors who use them to offset business and investment income. The list of tax credit buyers includes financial heavyweights such as BankAmerica Corp. and Berkshire Hathaway, Inc., as well as large manufacturers and regional and nationwide retail chains.

*Reported in *The Wall Street Journal,* November 29, 1995, page B8.

Special Rules Apply to Acquisition Credit

Credits will be disallowed for acquisition of an existing building (though they may still qualify for rehabilitation tax credits) in the following instances:

- Building ownership has changed during the previous ten years, or
- Rehabilitation work costing more than 25 percent of the building's adjusted tax basis has been performed within the previous ten years, or
- The building has previously received a low-income housing tax credit for which the 15-year compliance period (explained later) is still in effect, or
- The building has been acquired from a related party (except that the seller can hold up to a 10 percent interest in an acquiring partnership).

There are of course exceptions to these general rules. The Treasury can waive the requirement that a building must not have changed hands during the previous ten years, if any of the following circumstances exist:

- The building is a distressed property where a federally insured mortgage is at risk due to impending default.
- The property is federally assisted low-income housing that is eligible for mortgage prepayment, and there is danger that the mortgage will be prepaid and the units removed from the low-income housing pool.
- The building is to be acquired from a federally insured depository institution that is in default, or from a conservator or receiver for such an institution.
- The building is a single-family house and the prior purchaser was an owner-occupant who used it solely as a principal residence.
- The previous transfer was a tax deferred exchange under Code Section 1031 or a nontaxable contribution of property to a partnership in exchange for a partnership interest.
- Transfers within the ten-year period were due to the owner's death, due to acquisition by a government agency or a nonprofit organization or due to mortgage foreclosure. If due to foreclosure, the property must have been reconveyed within 12 months after the foreclosure transfer.

Minimum Compliance Period

Once a project qualifies and a tax credit is claimed, the project must continue to satisfy the qualifying criteria regarding the minimum number of units occupied by low-income tenants and the maximum gross rents, for a period of at least 15 years, even though the credits are available for only ten years. If the 15-year compliance period is not satisfied (with special exceptions) a portion of the tax credits plus interest are subject to recapture.

ANNUAL LIMIT ON TAX CREDITS

There is no limit on the dollar amount of tax credits a taxpayer can earn, but the maximum amount of earned credit that can be used to offset income tax liability in any one year is limited by several Code provisions. The details are too extensive to be included here, but an overview is included to alert you to possible limitations on benefits from tax credits.

Limitation Imposed by the Passive Asset Loss Rules

Passive asset loss rules, discussed in the next section, were aimed primarily at depreciation deductions on rental real estate. The rules cast a wide net, however, and apply to real estate tax credits as well. Unless an investor meets one of the exceptions that are explained in the section on "Limitation on the Deductibility of Losses," real estate tax credits that exceed the tax on passive activity income must be carried forward and used to offset passive activity income in future years.

Limitation Imposed by the Alternative Minimum Tax

After computing their income tax liability the regular way, net of all allowable tax credits, taxpayers are required to complete a second computation to determine their minimum tax liability. In this second computation, called the *alternative minimum tax,* most itemized deductions, the standard deduction and many adjustments to gross income that are a part of the regular computation, are not permitted. Taxpayers with modest gross income are permitted a deduction from this amount, and the alternative minimum tax is imposed at a flat rate on the balance. The larger of the regular tax or the alternative minimum tax must be paid.

In the alternative minimum tax computation, tax credits for rental real estate activities, including low-income housing, are not permitted. Tax credits, therefore, cannot reduce tax liability below the alternative minimum tax.

LIMITATIONS ON THE DEDUCTIBILITY OF LOSSES

The Internal Revenue Code, in Section 469, requires taxpayers to report separately their income and losses from activities characterized as *passive.* With limited exceptions, net losses from passive activities cannot be offset against income from other sources. Instead, the net losses must be carried forward and offset against passive income in future years. Any remaining passive loss carryovers become deductible when the passive activity asset to which they apply is sold or otherwise disposed of in a taxable transaction.

Passive activities include ownership interests in most rental property and in any trade or business in which the taxpayer does not materially participate in management. *Material participation* is said to be lacking if the owner is not actively involved, year-round, on a "regular, continuous and substantial basis."

Limited Partners' Income and Expense Is Always Passive

Limited partnership interests are specifically included in the passive activities category by the statute. Code Section 469(h)(2) says, "Except as provided in regulations, no interest in a limited partnership as a limited partner shall be treated as an interest with respect to which a taxpayer materially participates." Section 469(i)(6)(C) says, "No interest as a limited partner in a limited partnership shall be treated as an interest with respect to which the taxpayer actively participates." Taken together, these two provisions effectively foreclose any possibility that limited partnership interests might escape being characterized as passive activities.

Real Estate Rental Income and Expense Is Sometimes Passive

Real estate held for rental purposes is defined as a passive activity by the wording of Code Section 469(c)(2), which states, "The term 'passive activity' includes any rental activity." Additional wording excludes the following:

- Rental income that is incidental to the primary business activity or where substantial personal service is involved (hotels, motels and resorts, for example). Elsewhere, the Code contains special provisions that exempt real estate under certain circumstances.
- Rental income when the taxpayer is actively engaged in a real property trade or business such as brokerage, development, or management. To be considered *actively engaged*, the taxpayer (or the taxpayer's spouse if they file a joint return) must have at least a 5 percent ownership interest in the business, and more than 50 percent of their working hours must be devoted to the activity, which must occupy more than 750 hours annually.

AN EXCEPTION FOR SMALL-SCALE OPERATORS

A specific provision that applies only to real estate permits up to $25,000 annually of passive activity losses (and loss-equivalent tax credits) from operating rental real estate to be offset against otherwise taxable income from such activities as wages and profits from business activities. But this exception is phased out ratably as adjusted gross income (computed *before* adjusting for net passive losses and loss-equivalent credits, and with some other modifications from the way taxpayers report their adjusted gross income on their annual tax returns) moves from $100,000 to $150,000. There are two exceptions to this phase-out rule:

- With respect to passive activity tax credits that are attributable to the rehabilitation tax credit described earlier, the exception is phased out ratably only as adjusted gross income (before adjusting for net passive losses and loss-equivalent credits) moves from $200,000 to $250,000.
- With respect to credits attributable to the low-income housing credit, there is no adjusted gross income limitation.

To qualify for the exception, a taxpayer must have at least a 10 percent ownership interest in the property and (other than for the pass-through of low-

Figure 12.1   **Determining the Character of Real Estate Rental Income**

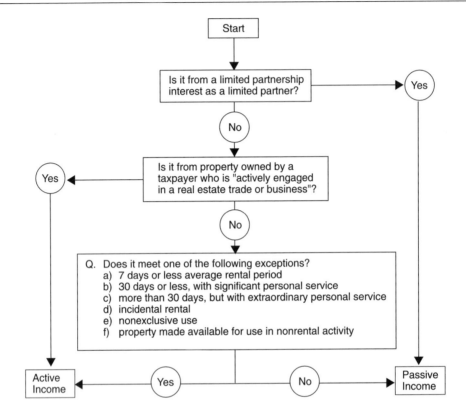

income housing or rehabilitation credits) must be an active participant in the real estate rental operation. The requirement of active participation is less strenuous than the material participation requirement described earlier. The Senate Finance Committee, in reporting on the enabling legislation, described *active participation* as making management decisions or arranging for others to provide services such as repairs and maintenance. Moreover, services performed by a taxpayer's spouse are attributed to the taxpayer in determining whether the active participation test is met.

TAXATION OF FOREIGN INVESTORS

The intensified interest of foreign investors in United States real estate, discussed in Chapter 1, prompted concern in the Treasury Department that some foreign investors might be escaping taxation on their gains. The U.S. Congress responded with the Foreign Investment Real Property Tax Act of 1980 (FIRPTA).

The Act, as amended, requires any person acquiring a U.S. real property interest from a seller who is not a U.S. citizen to withhold and remit to the Internal Revenue Service 10 percent of the gross purchase price.

A buyer who fails to withhold the correct amount may be liable for the amount in question, plus interest and penalties. There are certain other, rather esoteric exceptions, but the withholding is generally required unless any of the following conditions exist:

- The property is worth no more than $300,000 and is for the purchaser's use as a personal residence.
- The transaction is protected from taxation pursuant to a U.S. tax treaty with another country, and the buyer and seller are unrelated.
- The seller or buyer obtains a "withholding certificate" from the Internal Revenue Service, which reduces the amount to be withheld.

Reporting and withholding requirements are extensive and complex, and their specifics are beyond the scope of this text. They are designed to ascertain that taxes are paid before assets are moved beyond the reach of the United States Treasury.

THE ALTERNATIVE MINIMUM TAX

The alternative minimum tax was mentioned earlier as a limitation on the use of real estate tax credits. After determining their taxable income and income tax obligation using the regular computational procedure, taxpayers must compute an alternative minimum taxable income and alternative minimum tax. As the name *alternative minimum tax* implies, taxpayers must pay the larger of the alternative or the regular tax.

A host of taxable and tax deductible items are treated less leniently under the alternative minimum computation than under the regular tax computation. Among these are cost recovery allowances; the cost must be recovered over a greater number of years. Moreover, certain gains on disposal which can be deferred or are treated preferentially under the regular tax computation method are treated as regular taxable income under the alternative method. As a consequence, some of the anticipated tax advantages associated with real estate investment might be jerked away due to the alternative minimum tax. Though it is beyond the scope of this text, prudent investors will always consider the alternative minimum tax consequences of their investment initiatives.

SUMMARY

Numerous incentives are incorporated into the Internal Revenue Code to induce taxpayer actions that are considered socially desirable. Investors who exploit these provisions may be able to significantly reduce their income tax liability. Real estate-related opportunities include tax-oriented use of financial leverage, earning tax credits by acquiring and rehabilitating older or historically significant structures, or structures that house low-income tenants.

Borrowing is not a taxable event, and interest expense incurred on loans that encumber real estate is generally deductible when incurred and paid. By re-leveraging their position when they desire to liquidate a portion of their equity, investors can avoid the tax liability that would result from selling.

Tax credits, direct offsets against income tax liability, are available for qualifying expenditures to rehabilitate certified historic structures. These are structures listed in the National Registry of Historic Places or located in a registered historic district and certified by the Secretary of the Interior as being of significance to the district. Tax credits for rehabilitating qualifying historic structures equal 20 percent of the qualifying rehabilitation expenditures.

Rehabilitating structures that are not considered historically significant may nevertheless qualify an investor for rehabilitation tax credits, albeit at a reduced rate. Qualifying expenditures to rehabilitate such structures may earn the investor a tax credit equal to ten percent of the expenditure.

A more recent, and more involved, tax credit program relates specifically to the cost of acquiring or rehabilitating rental housing for low-income tenants. Tax credits are spread over ten years and are designed to have a present value equal to 30 or 70 percent of qualifying expenditures, depending upon the nature of the expenditure.

With significant exceptions, operating losses on rental real estate cannot be used to offset otherwise taxable income from salaries, wages or profit from business or portfolio operations. Key exceptions are for modest losses reported by individuals with limited adjusted gross income, losses on certain low-income rental housing, and losses incurred by persons actively engaged in a real property trade or business.

The extent of foreign investment in U.S. real estate has prompted tax code provisions designed to assure payment of income tax liability on foreign-company transactions. To a substantial extent, the burden of enforcement has been imposed on taxpayers who buy real estate from foreign owners.

RECOMMENDED READINGS

Commerce Clearing House. *U.S. Master Tax Guide.* Chicago: Commerce Clearing House. Published annually.

Guggenheim, Joseph. *Tax Credits for Low Income Housing.* 6th ed. (Glen Echo, MA: Simon Publications, 1991).

Journal of Real Estate Taxation. A quarterly periodical published by Warren, Gorham & Lamont, 210 South St., Boston, MA 02111.

REVIEW QUESTIONS

1. How does the tax treatment of expenditures for interest on borrowed money differ from that on expenditures to repay the loan?
2. When is prepaid interest deductible?
3. Explain the tax treatment of construction-period interest expense.
4. How do tax credits differ from tax deductions?
5. How does the tax credit for rehabilitating historically significant structures differ from that for other older buildings?
6. How long must a rehabilitated structure (other than low-income housing) be held to avoid recapture of the rehabilitation tax credit?
7. How does the timing of tax credits for low-income housing differ from that of credits for rehabilitating other structures?
8. Generally, how long must property meet the minimum qualifying criteria, to avoid recapture of the low-income housing tax credit?
9. Describe the annual limit on the amount of tax credits a taxpayer can use to offset income tax liability.
10. Describe the general criteria for exemption from the passive activity loss rules for persons engaged in a real property trade or business.

DISCUSSION QUESTIONS

1. Are tax credits for property rehabilitation the best way to subsidize these activities?
2. Should property rehabilitation be subsidized at all, either through investment tax credits as is now done or in any other way?
3. Discuss the public policy implications of imposing on buyers the responsibility of assuring collection of taxes due from foreign sellers of domestic real estate.

PROBLEMS

1. B. A. Planner has an option on an historically significant apartment building that is badly in need of rehabilitation. Acquisition cost will be $250,000, and 40 percent of this is properly attributable to the land. Rehabilitation costs are estimated to be approximately $300,000. The units will be completely rehabilitated and available for residential tenants within 12 months. Planner will borrow 70 percent of acquisition and rehabilitation costs.
   a. Net of investment tax credits, how much of his own money (that is, equity funds) will Planner have to commit to this project?
   b. When the project is completed and put into service, what will be Planner's annual depreciation allowance?

PART FOUR: Case Problems

1. Please refer to the case problem for Part Three. Assignment number 2 of that case required you to develop a seven-year projection of before-tax cash flows from The Sated Satyr apartments. If you have not yet completed that assignment, please do so now. Using the format illustrated in Table 10.2 (or an alternative format prescribed by your instructor), incorporate income tax consequences and extend the forecast to include after-tax cash flow from operation. In developing your projection, make the following assumptions:

   a. Our taxpayer expects to be in the 40 percent marginal income tax bracket during each year of the forecast.
   b. Because she is engaged full time as a real estate practitioner, she is not subject to the passive activity rules.
   c. She will incur no liability for the alternative minimum tax during the projection period.

2. Assignment number 4 of the case problem for Part Three asks you to estimate before-tax cash flow from disposal of The Sated Satyr after seven years. If you have not yet done so, please complete that assignment now. Using the format illustrated in Tables 11.1, 11.2 and 11.3 (or the format recommended by your instructor), extend the forecast to include after-tax cash flow from disposal, assuming that the gain on disposal will be taxed at a 28 percent rate.

Save your work from case problems one and two. It will be needed to solve subsequent cases.

3. Shurly I. Cheetum, a founding partner in the firm of Dewey, Cheetum and Howe, has a prospering professional practice. Ms. Cheetum has decided to investigate real estate as an estate-building mechanism and has asked you for advice concerning the property described

below. You promptly arrange a consultation, at which time you obtain a retainer and determine the following facts:

a. Cheetum's earnings from her professional practice are sufficient to place her firmly in the 35 percent marginal income tax bracket (combined federal and state). She expects this situation to continue into the indefinite future.
b. Long-term capital gains are expected to be taxed at a 28 percent marginal tax rate.
c. Cheetum has other investments but is in no danger of incurring liability for the alternative minimum tax.

You investigate several properties that seem to fit Cheetum's needs and conclude that one seems particularly well suited to her investment picture. Information on the property, an apartment building, is as follows:

- Market value (and asking price) = $2,150,000
- Next year's expected gross income = $425,000
- Next year's expected operating expenses = $210,000
- Building value/total property value = .80
- Available mortgage = $1,600,000
- Mortgage terms: 9 percent interest, 25-year, fully amortizing note with monthly payments and a seven-year call provision. There is no penalty for prepayment and no loan origination fee.
- Operating forecast: Operating income and operating expenses alike are expected to increase at a compound annual rate of three percent for an indefinite period.
- Holding period: If Cheetum acquires the property, she will most likely sell after six years and pay off the balance of the mortgage note out of the sales proceeds.
- The gross income multiplier is expected to remain constant over the holding period.
- Transaction costs associated with disposal after six years (at the end of her sixth year of ownership) are expected to be about six percent of the sales price.

Required: Develop a comprehensive six-year after-tax cash-flow forecast for this property, including estimated after-tax cash from disposal.

PART FIVE

Measuring Investment Performance

Forecasting after-tax cash flows from investment proposals, as discussed in Part One through Part Four, is a necessary step in rational investment decision making. In itself, however, forecasting is not sufficient. Investors must apply decision criteria to the forecasts.

Chapter 13 surveys traditional approaches to the task. It explains the virtues and weaknesses of traditional techniques, which range from simple ratios between price and expected first-year revenue to more complex attempts that incorporate considerations such as income tax consequences and equity buildup.

Contemporary techniques require a basic understanding of the mathematics of compound interest and discount. Readers who lack this background should study Appendix A before venturing farther into Part Five. Chapters 14 and 15 use the mathematical techniques from Appendix A to present a state-of-the-art investment decision model. Chapter 16 shows how computer-assisted analysis can reduce the model's arithmetical tediousness.

CHAPTER 13

Traditional Measures of Investment Worth

Investment analysts must sift through a veritable mountain of informational chaff to glean intelligence for rational decision making. Approaches range from snap judgments based on little more than hot tips to careful and time-consuming analysis of reams of financial and economic data. Investors often compromise by using rules of thumb based on past experience or benchmark measures of profitability based on market observation.

This chapter introduces the most commonly encountered traditional techniques. It proceeds from popular ratios measuring profit/price relationships and operating results to more complex tools employed extensively by those educated in traditional real estate investment analysis. It then introduces more advanced techniques that are explored at length in subsequent chapters.

RATIO ANALYSIS

Ratios are widely used to gauge the reasonableness of relationships between various measures of value and performance: income multipliers express the relationship between market value and operating income; operating ratios highlight the relationship between gross income and operating expenses; break-even ratios show the percent of gross income required to meet cash expenditure requirements; debt coverage ratios show the relationship between net operating income and debt service obligations.

Income Multipliers

Income multiplier analysis is a simple technique whose contemporary usefulness belies its antiquity. It highlights the relationship between price and either gross or net income. For single-family rental properties, monthly income is often used in the analysis; for all other properties the convention is to use annual income.

Multipliers do not serve as sufficient tools of analysis in isolation, but they enable analysts to swiftly and inexpensively weed out obviously unacceptable proposals. More extensive (and more costly) analysis can then be concentrated on properties that show greater promise. To use multiplier analysis as a filter, first determine the relationship prevailing in the market area. Then automatically reject all opportunities whose multipliers exceed this benchmark figure. Subject to further analysis only those opportunities that pass the preliminary screening test.

Example 13.1

An investment opportunity that costs $100,000 and requires a 25 percent down payment is expected to yield the following operating results during the first year:

Potential Gross Rent	$27,000
Less: Allowance for Vacancies and Rent Loss	2,000
Effective Gross Income	$25,000
Less: Operating Expenses	13,000
Net Operating Income	$12,000
debt serv.	7553

Other relevant information includes the following: B-TCF 4447

1. There is available a $75,000, 25-year mortgage loan that requires equal monthly payments with interest at 9 percent per annum (monthly payments are $692.40; annual debt service is $7,552.77). 2,668 (A-TCF)
2. Best estimates indicate that the property will increase in market value at a compound rate of about 5 percent per annum.
3. The investor is subject to a marginal income tax rate of 40 percent.

Gross Income Multipliers.   Also referred to as gross rent multipliers, *gross income multipliers* highlight the relationship between a property's price and its gross income. The effective gross income multiplier in Example 13.1 is 4.0:

$$\text{Gross Income Multiplier} = \frac{\text{Market Price}}{\text{Effective Gross Income}} = \frac{\$100,000}{\$25,000} = 4.0$$

Analysts who use gross income multipliers must decide whether to focus on potential gross rent or effective gross income. The determining factor is likely to be data availability. When information on vacancy rates and credit losses is unreliable and difficult to verify, the most appropriate measure might be potential gross rent. Using potential gross rent, the gross multiplier in Example 13.1 is approximately 3.7:

$$\text{Gross Income Multiplier} = \frac{\text{Market Price}}{\text{Potential Gross Income}} = \frac{\$100,000}{\$27,000} = 3.7$$

Net Income Multipliers.   Calculated the same way as gross multipliers, *net income multipliers* express the relationship between value and net operating income. They differ from gross multipliers only in their use of net instead of gross income. For Example 13.1, the net income multiplier is 8.33:

$$\text{Net Income Multiplier} = \frac{\text{Market Price}}{\text{Net Operating Income}} = \frac{\$100,000}{\$12,000} = 8.33$$

Financial Ratios

Ratio analysis is frequently employed to facilitate interproperty comparisons. Commonly encountered examples include the operating ratio, the break-even ratio and the debt coverage ratio.

Operating Ratio.   The percentage of effective gross income consumed by operating expenses is expressed as an *operating ratio*. However, the operating ratio can be misleading because it reflects in part the efficiency of management as well as of the property itself. Some investors, in fact, look for properties with high operating ratios, intending to reduce the ratios through efficient management and thereby increase indicated property values. The operating ratio for Example 13.1 is 52 percent:

$$\text{Operating Ratio} = \frac{\text{Operating Expenses}}{\text{Effective Gross Income}} = \frac{\$13,000}{\$25,000} = .52, \text{ or } 52\%$$

Break-Even Ratio.   Sometimes called default ratios, *break-even ratios* are most useful when employed on a before-tax cash-flow basis. They indicate the relationship between cash inflows and outflows from all sources. The lower the break-even ratio, the greater the decline in gross revenue (or the increase in operating expenses) can be before investors experience negative cash flow from a project. Applying the formula to the project in Example 13.1, the ratio is 82.2 percent:

$$\text{Break-Even Ratio} = \frac{\text{Operating Expenses} + \text{Debt Service}}{\text{Effective Gross Income}}$$

$$= \frac{\$13,000 + \$7,553}{\$25,000} = .822, \text{ or } 82.2\%$$

Debt-Coverage Ratio.   The *debt coverage ratio* expresses the extent to which net operating income can decline before it becomes insufficient to meet the debt service obligation. This gives an indication of safety associated with the use of borrowed funds. The debt coverage ratio in Example 13.1 is 1.59:

$$\text{Debt Coverage Ratio} = \frac{\text{Net Operating Income}}{\text{Annual Debt Service}} = \frac{\$12,000}{\$7,553} = 1.59$$

TRADITIONAL PROFITABILITY MEASURES

A shared characteristic of all traditional profitability measures is an attempt to relate cash investment to expected cash returns in some systematic fashion. The techniques differ in the degree to which they incorporate available data. They differ also in that some ignore the issue of risk and others make rudimentary attempts to adjust for risk differentials.

Overall Capitalization Rate

Also known as the *free-and-clear rate of return,* the *overall capitalization rate* expresses the first year's expected net operating income as a percentage of market price. The rate in Example 13.1 is 12 percent:

$$\text{Overall Capitalization Rate} = \frac{\text{Net Operating Income}}{\text{Market Price}} = \frac{\$12,000}{\$100,000} = .12, \text{ or } 12\%$$

Recall that the net income multiplier is price divided by net operating income. The overall capitalization rate, therefore, is simply the reciprocal of the net income multiplier. The reciprocal of 0.12 is 8.33, which we saw earlier is the net income multiplier for Example 13.1.

In a typical negotiating session there is an acknowledged trade-off between price and financing terms. Since this trade-off is not reflected in the overall capitalization rate, comparison of rates between properties with significantly different financing arrangements can be misleading. This limits the usefulness of overall capitalization rates as an investment analysis tool.

Equity Dividend Rate

A measure that does to some extent incorporate the effect of using borrowed money is the *equity dividend rate.* It compares equity cash flow with the amount of the equity investment. As generally calculated, the equity dividend rate expresses before-tax cash flow (net operating income minus debt service) as a percentage of the required initial equity cash outlay (purchase price minus borrowed funds). The equation is:

$$\text{Equity Dividend Rate} = \frac{\text{Before-Tax Cash Flow}}{\text{Initial Cash Outlay}}$$

Calculating the equity dividend rate for the property in Example 13.1 requires prior determination of the *equity dividend* (net operating income minus debt service) and the initial equity investment (purchase price minus mortgage loans). These calculations are as follows:

Equity Dividend (Before-Tax Cash Flow):	
Net Operating Income	$ 12,000
Less: Debt Service	7,553
Equity Dividend	$ 4,447
Initial Cash Outlay:	
Purchase Price	$100,000
Less: Available Mortgage	75,000
Initial Equity	$ 25,000

Using these values, the equity dividend rate applicable to Example 13.1 can be determined. It is 17.8 percent:

$$\text{Equity Dividend Rate} = \frac{\$4,447}{\$25,000} = .1779, \text{ or } 17.8\%$$

The equity dividend rate's usefulness is limited because the analysis does not incorporate income tax considerations. Cash flow measured on a before-tax basis will be helpful in discriminating between investment opportunities only if the alternatives have reasonably similar income tax consequences.

To render it more useful the measure, also called the *cash-on-cash rate of return,* can be calculated on an after-tax basis. The modified equation expresses the first year's expected net spendable cash (after all financing costs and income taxes) as a percentage of the initial cash investment.

If the property in Example 13.1 is acquired on the first day of the year, interest expense for the first year will be $6,713 (the procedure for determining this is explained in Chapter 8). As explained in Chapter 10, the depreciation or cost recovery allowance depends on several factors not given in the current example. For this illustration, simply assume the allowance to be $2,700. Combining these two bits of information with the projected net operating income from Example 13.1 permits an estimate of the first year's income tax obligation:

Net Operating Income		$12,000
Less:		
Interest Expense	$6,713	
Cost Recovery Allowance	2,700	9,413
Taxable Income		$ 2,587
Times: Marginal Tax Rate		.28
Income Tax Obligation		$ 724

After-tax cash flow to the equity position is the net operating income minus debt service and income tax payments:

Net Operating Income	$12,000
Less: Debt Service Obligation	7,553
Before-Tax Cash Flow	$ 4,447
Less: Income Tax (computed above)	724
After-Tax Cash Flow	$ 3,723

With this information, the cash-on-cash rate of return for Example 13.1 can be calculated on an after-tax basis. The computation is:

$$\text{Cash-on-Cash} = \frac{\text{After-Tax Cash Flow}}{\text{Equity Investment}} = \frac{\$3,723}{\$25,000} = .149, \text{ or } 14.9\%$$

Even with the inclusion of income tax consequences, this measure's usefulness is limited, because it fails to incorporate the impact on investment performance of changes in the property's value and of changes in after-tax cash flow through time. Rational analysis demands that all consequences for the projected holding period be included in the analysis.

Broker's Rate of Return

Seeking to cast the best possible image of a property they are trying to sell, brokers sometimes argue that the cash-on-cash rate of return should be modified to reflect the buildup of an investor's equity. The *broker's rate of return* adjusts the equity dividend or cash-on-cash rate to include both income tax consequences and equity buildup resulting from amortization of mortgage debt. This increases the indicated return to the equity position and thereby makes the property appear more attractive.

For the property in Example 13.1, the broker's indicated rate of return is 18.3 percent, determined as follows:

$$\text{Broker's Return} = \frac{\text{After-Tax Cash Flow} + \text{Equity Buildup}}{\text{Initial Equity}}$$

$$= \frac{\$3,723 + \$840}{\$25,000} = .183, \text{ or } 18.3\%$$

To after-tax cash flow plus equity buildup, some brokers add the anticipated rate of increase in property value. By making the broker's rate of return even higher, this further enhances the apparent attractiveness of the investment proposition.

Though widely used, the broker's rate of return is misleading. The important measure of potential cash flow from disposal is the difference between market value and remaining balance on mortgage indebtedness, less estimated brokerage commission and other transaction costs. Since this cash flow is not realized on an annual basis, but only upon property sale, it is inconsistent to include equity buildup in the measure of annual cash flow.

Payback Period

One of the simplest and perhaps most common rules of thumb is to estimate the number of years required to recoup one's initial cash investment in a project. In *payback period* analysis, alternative opportunities are ranked according to the time required for the anticipated cash proceeds to equal the initial cash investment.

When anticipated cash flow from a project is the same amount each year, the payback period can be calculated simply: divide initial cash outlay by the expected annual cash flow. Thus, for a project that requires an initial cash outlay of $10,000 and is expected to yield an annual cash flow of $2,500, the payback period is four years:

$$\text{Payback Period} = \frac{\text{Cash Outlay}}{\text{Annual Cash Flow}} = \frac{\$10,000}{\$2,500} = 4 \text{ years}$$

Of course, expected cash flow from real estate is seldom the same from year to year. Consequently, payback period calculations are not as straightforward as the example suggests. In most instances, the period must be determined by summing expected proceeds from year to year until the total equals initial outlay.

Example 13.2 illustrates the procedure. The third column is simply the summation of all after-tax cash-flow estimates from the second column. With required equity investment of $48,330, the initial equity expenditure is expected to have been fully recovered at some point during the sixth year. Therefore, the payback period (expressed in whole years) is six years.

Example 13.2

A property can be acquired with an initial equity expenditure (that is, a down payment) of $48,330. Annual after-tax cash flows are expected to be as indicated in the second column below. Anticipated cumulative cash flows are indicated in the third column.

Year	After-Tax Cash Flow	
	Current Year	Cumulative
1	$ 7,145	$ 7,145
2	8,185	15,330
3	9,222	24,552
4	10,171	34,723
5	11,115	45,838
6	12,054	57,892
7	12,895	70,787

The appeal of payback period analysis is its apparent simplicity and its adaptability as a policy tool. Investors can specify a maximum payback period for real estate of a specific type or in a given location, based on their perceptions of associated risks.

The major shortcoming of this method is that it ignores all cash flows beyond the payback period. This failure will cause assets with poor appreciation prospects to look more promising than those with potential for growth in value over the holding period. A second problem is that the method fails to discriminate among cash flows with different timing, even during the payback period. A project with most of the benefits in the early years would look no better than one offering the same total benefit spread evenly over the entire payback period, or with the bulk of its cash flow in later years. The time value of money is thus ignored, and the project with the greatest potential return may not be chosen.

TOWARD MORE RATIONAL ANALYSIS

To understand the shortcomings of traditional investment performance measures, we need first to review the major components of expected return. There is of course an initial equity cash commitment, for which the investor expects to receive cash flow from operations during the holding period and cash from disposal upon termination of the investment position. Five major factors interact to govern the relative attractiveness of investment proposals:

1. The amount and timing of the initial cash commitment
2. The amount and timing of expected net cash inflows
3. The certainty with which expectations are held
4. Yields available from other investments
5. The investor's attitude toward risk

Regardless of particular investor predispositions, anticipated investment benefits must be adjusted for quantity, quality and timing. *Quantity* refers to the amount of expected net cash flows, after incorporating all income tax consequences and adjusting for debt service obligations arising from financial leverage. *Timing* refers to when the forecasted net cash flows are expected to be received. *Quality* refers to the certainty with which these expectations are held. These factors must be evaluated in terms of risk-adjusted yields available from other investments (the opportunity cost of capital) and the investor's attitude toward bearing risk.

An ideal measure of profitability will incorporate all these elements. A common weakness of traditional profitability measures is that they ignore the question of timing of net cash inflows. For this reason they have become mere adjuncts to time-adjusted measures.

Time-Adjusted Return Measures

Time-adjusted techniques discount expected future cash flows to make them more nearly comparable to those receivable in the present. Some techniques adjust purely for the time value of money, while others include an adjustment for risk. One popular version takes the adjustment factor as a variable that equates future and present cash flows. All these measures are considered in Chapter 14.

SUMMARY

Traditional techniques for evaluating investments include ratios for comparing income to market price, and ratios for evaluating profitability and financial risk. They also include several measures of profitability designed to compare anticipated cash flows with required initial cash expenditures. These traditional techniques are useful as filters, but none of them properly account for the time value of money. This is a serious failing because the timing of cash inflows and outflows is a major element in the comparative desirability of investment alternatives. Time-adjusted measures of return are an essential tool of rational investment analysis.

RECOMMENDED READINGS

American Institute of Real Estate Appraisers. *The Appraisal of Real Estate.* 10th ed. Chicago: Appraisal Institute, 1992, pp. 414–424, 467–480.

REVIEW QUESTIONS

1. How are income multipliers used in measuring investment worth?
2. Why might some investors search out properties with high operating ratios?
3. What is a characteristic common to all traditional profitability measures? What are the weaknesses in these forms of measurement?
4. Compare the concept of the overall capitalization rate with the equity dividend rate.
5. How is the broker's rate of return calculated? What is its major drawback?
6. List major factors governing the relative attractiveness of a real estate investment.
7. List the advantages and disadvantages of using the payback period as a measure of investment worth.
8. Slumland East, a 28-unit apartment building, is offered for sale at $325,000. If it is purchased for the asking price, subject to its existing $204,500 mortgage loan balance, an investor in the 28 percent marginal income tax bracket can expect the following outcome during the first full year of ownership:

Potential Gross Rent	$74,760
Plus: Miscellaneous Income	420
	$75,180
Less: Vacancy Allowance	3,759
Effective Gross Income	$71,421
Less: Operating Expenses	40,060
Net Operating Income	$31,361
Less: Debt Service	25,334
Before-Tax Cash Flow	$ 6,027
Plus: Principal Paid	837
Less: Cost Recovery Allowance	9,060
Taxable Income (Loss)	($ 2,196)
Times: Marginal Tax Rate	.28
Income Tax (Tax Savings)	($ 615)
Before-Tax Cash Flow	$ 6,027
Plus: Tax Savings	615
After-Tax Cash Flow	$ 6,642

Required: Based on the first-year forecast and assuming the property is purchased for the asking price, compute:

a. The potential gross income multiplier   4.3 *or* 4.5$_{EGI}$
   $_{PGI}$
b. The operating ratio   0.56
c. The debt coverage ratio   1.24
d. The overall capitalization rate   0.096
e. The cash-on-cash rate of return   0.055

DISCUSSION QUESTIONS

1. What traditional ratios employed in real estate analysis are most closely related to the following concepts employed in stock market analysis?
   a. Dividend yield
   b. Price earnings ratio
2. What impact might the inflation rate have on the usefulness of traditional
   profitability measures such as the cash-on-cash return, payback period and
   equity dividend rate?

CHAPTER 14

Discounted Cash-Flow Analysis

Modern investment analysis is a practical application of the economic theory of the firm, which states that one should operate at the point where marginal revenue equals marginal cost. Translated into the language of investment analysis, this means ventures are acceptable as long as the rate of return on investment at least equals the cost of investable funds.

This chapter considers at length two common applications of the basic decision criterion: present value and internal rate of return. Both have merit as investment analysis techniques, both can be supported with compelling logical arguments and several variations of each have been developed in the literature.

PRESENT VALUE

Present value, discussed in detail in Appendix A, is the value today of benefits that are expected to accrue in the future. It is derived by adjusting all anticipated future cash flows at a predetermined rate per time period. A present value in excess of the required initial equity cash outlay means a project is expected to yield a rate of return in excess of the discount rate employed. If the discount rate is the minimum acceptable rate of return, this implies that the project is worthy of further consideration. A present value that is less than the required initial equity expenditure results in automatic rejection.

To use this approach, discount all anticipated future cash flows at the minimum acceptable rate of return. The result is the present value of expected cash flows:

$$PV = CF_1/(1 + i) + CF_2/(1 + i)^2 + CF_3/(1 + i)^3 + \ldots + CF_n/(1 + i)^n$$

where i is the minimum acceptable rate of return, n is the number of years in the projection period, CF_1 is the cash flow expected in the first year, CF_2 that for the second year and so on through the cash-flow expectation for year n. As explained in Appendix A, a more succinct mathematical shorthand for expressing the relationship is

$$PV = \sum_{t=1}^{n} CF_t / (1 + i)^t$$

where Σ simply means add together the value of $[CF_t / (1 + i)^t]$, where the values of t range from one through n. In Example 14.1 the present value is approximately $98,684:

Year	Expected Cash Flow	Present Value Factor (Rounded)	Present Value at 10% (Rounded)
1	$15,000	.909091	$13,636
2	15,000	.826446	12,397
3	15,000	.751315	11,270
4	15,000	.683013	10,245
5	15,000	.620921	9,314
6	15,000	.564474	8,467
7	15,000	.513158	7,697
8	55,000	.466507	25,658
		TOTAL	$98,684

Example 14.1

An investment proposal is expected to generate $15,000 of after-tax cash flow each year for eight years and $40,000 of after-tax cash flow from disposal at the end of the eighth year. The required equity cash outlay to acquire the asset is $90,000. The minimum acceptable rate of return is 10 percent.

NET PRESENT VALUE

Subtracting the required initial equity expenditure from the present value of projected cash flows yields net present value. A positive net present value means a project is expected to yield a rate of return in excess of the discount rate and therefore merits further consideration. A net present value of less than zero means the project is expected to yield a rate of return less than the minimum acceptable rate and therefore should be rejected.

Discounting at the minimum acceptable rate of 10 percent, the net present value of anticipated cash flows from the investment opportunity described in Example 14.1 is approximately $8,684:

Present value of future cash flows (rounded)	$98,684
Less: Initial cash outlay	90,000
Net Present Value	$ 8,684

Since this is greater than zero, the expected rate of return exceeds the 10 percent minimum acceptable rate, and the project merits further consideration.

INTERNAL RATE OF RETURN

Since—as explained in Appendix A—there is an inverse relationship between discount rates and present value, there must be some rate that will exactly equate the present value of a projected stream of cash flows with any positive initial cash investment. This rate is known as the *internal rate of return*. The equation for the internal rate of return is:

$$0 = \sum_{t=1}^{n} [CF_t / (1 + k)^t] - \text{Initial Cash Outlay}$$

where CF_t is the cash flow projected for year t and k is the discount rate that satisfies the equality condition. All the terms in the equation are taken as known except k, for which the appropriate value is determined.

Consider a project expected to yield a cash-flow stream, CF_1, CF_2, . . ., CF_n over n future periods. The internal rate of return is simply a rate k such that if the initial cash outlay were deposited at an interest rate equaling that rate for each period, withdrawing the amount CF_1 at the end of period 1, CF_2 at the end of period 2, and so on through CF_n at the end of period n, would exactly exhaust the fund at the end of the nth period.

If the internal rate of return is equal to or greater than an investor's required rate of return, a project is considered further. If the internal rate of return is less than the minimum acceptable rate of return, the project is rejected.

In Example 14.1, the internal rate of return is approximately 12.2 percent. This is determined by trial and error, using successive approximations of the appropriate discount rate. Cash flows are discounted using a financial calculator or factors from Appendix C. Tables are considerably more awkward to use than calculators, because the calculator program of successive approximations must be replicated manually by table users.

Since annual cash flow from operations in Example 14.1 represents a level annuity, the annuity table (Table C.3) would be employed if a financial calculator were not available. Table C.1 would be used to calculate the present value of the final sum expected in year eight. Discounting at 13 percent, the present value of all expected cash flows equals approximately $87,029. This is somewhat less than the initial cash outlay required, so the internal rate of return must be slightly less than 13 percent. Discounting again at the next lower rate for which the table provides factors, the present value at 12 percent is seen to be approximately $90,670, slightly more than the initial cash outlay. Interpolating between 12 and 13 percent, as described in Appendix A, reveals the rate that equates the present value of expected future cash flows with the required initial outlay, approximately 12.2 percent (some error is introduced in the interpolation process).

Having calculated the internal rate of return based on expected cash flows in Example 14.1, the investor compares the result with the required rate of return. Since the internal rate of return exceeds the required rate (12.2 versus 10.0 percent), the project is considered further. Ultimate acceptance or rejection depends on estimates of relative riskiness and on the relative attractiveness of alternative investment opportunities.

The major distinction between the internal rate of return approach and the present value approach is that the latter requires a predetermined discount rate to be introduced early in the analysis. This difference, however, is more illusory than substantive as an argument for one method over the other. Those who use the internal rate of return technique must specify some minimal threshold rate against which the internal rate of return is measured, to determine its acceptability. Internal rate of return users, therefore, delay but do not escape the necessity of estimating an investor's required rate of return.

Decision criteria based on internal rate of return analysis can easily be expressed in present value or net present value terms. Internal rate of return thus appears to have little to recommend it over alternative techniques based on the same discounting concept.

Problems with the Internal Rate of Return

While the internal rate of return has no substantive advantage over alternative methods of applying discount rates to projected cash flows, it does have serious weaknesses not found in the alternatives. Persistent support of a flawed technique might be admirable were there no substitutes that possess equal power to discriminate between acceptable and unacceptable opportunities. Such is not the case, however, with the internal rate of return approach. Its continued advocacy is therefore somewhat curious. Austin Jaffe has suggested a possible explanation. He notes that research and debate in the real estate literature tend to lag behind general financial analysis literature by a number of years. Real estate analysts are perhaps now debating an issue that has long been resolved by those in the financial and economics mainstream.[1]

Problems associated with the internal rate of return can result in conflicting decision signals from this and other discounted cash-flow approaches. Generally, such a conflict arises because the internal rate of return signal is distorted. If heeded, it might result in serious investment error. Potential dissonance stems from peculiarities of the internal rate of return equation, which can yield more than one solution, and from problems associated with the reinvestment assumption inherent in choices among alternative investments that exhibit different patterns of anticipated after-tax cash flows.

The Reinvestment Rate Problem.   Interproject comparisons using internal rate of return analysis involves an implicit assumption that funds are reinvested at the internal rate of return. The internal rate of return method reliably discriminates among alternatives only if other acceptable opportunities expected to yield an equally high rate are available. This, of course, is an unlikely prospect when the internal rate of return is considerably above the opportunity cost of capital.

Example 14.2

An investor must select from two alternatives that require equal initial cash outlays and have identical time horizons. Expected cash flows from the alternatives are as follows:

	Investment Alternative	
	A	*B*
Initial Equity Expenditure	$10,694	$10,694
Net Cash Inflow, Year 1	7,000	0
Net Cash Inflow, Year 2	7,000	14,890

Consider the investment alternatives in Example 14.2. Internal rate of return analysis makes alternative A seem more desirable than B. This is because alternative A has an internal rate of return of approximately 20 percent, whereas B's internal rate of return approximates only 18 percent. To satisfy yourself that this is so, discount the cash flows from each project at these rates and note that the present value of anticipated future cash flows in each case approximates the required $10,694 initial equity expenditure.

If cash flows during the holding period can be reinvested at 20 percent, then alternative A will indeed result in a total return of 20 percent per annum over the two-year period. To see this, consider the cumulative cash that results if the first year's $7,000 cash flow is in fact reinvested at 20 percent. It will grow to $8,400 in one year. When this is added to the $7,000 to be received at the end of the second year, the cumulative total is $15,400. Discounting this amount over a two-year period at 20 percent yields a present value equal to the $10,694 initial equity expenditure. Here are the computations (terminal value is the future value of all intermediate cash flows when compounded forward, at a designated rate, to the end of the investment holding period):

Terminal Value of Cash Inflow with 20% Reinvestment Rate:	
Year 1 (Cash Inflow $7,000)	$ 8,400
Year 2 (Cash Inflow $7,000)	7,000
Cumulative Terminal Value at 20%	$15,400
Times: Present Value Factor at 20%	.6944
Present Value of $15,400 Due in Two Years	$10,694
Less: Initial Cash Outlay	10,694
Net Present Value at 20%	$ 0

If the first year's net cash flow from alternative A is reinvested at any rate less than 12.7 percent, the yield on invested funds over the two-year period will be less than the internal rate of return on alternative B. Suppose, for example, that the best return available on funds reinvested at the end of the first year is ten percent. The total return on alternative A for the two-year period will then be only 17.24 percent. Here is the arithmetic:

Terminal Value of Net Cash Flow with 10% Reinvestment Rate:	
Year 1 (Net Cash Flow $7,000)	$ 7,700
Year 2 (Net Cash Flow $7,000)	7,000
Cumulative Terminal Value at 10%	$14,700
Times: Present Value Factor at 17.24%	.7275
Present Value of $14,700 Due in Two Years	$10,694
Less: Initial Equity Outlay	10,694
Net Present Value at 17.24%	0

The reinvestment rate problem also limits the usefulness of the internal rate of return technique when choosing between alternatives that have different useful lives or different holding periods. If the indicated internal rate of return is unrealistically high, reinvestment at that rate is not a reasonable assumption and the internal rate of return will give an ambiguous decision signal.

Example 14.3

An investor must select from alternatives having the following cash-flow characteristics:

	Investment Alternative	
	A	B
Required Initial Cash Outlay	$22,832	$33,522
Annual Cash Inflow First Three Years	10,000	10,000
Annual Cash Inflow Years 4 and 5	0	10,000

Example 14.3 demonstrates this problem. Both investment alternatives have an expected 15 percent internal rate of return, but they are equally desirable only if the reinvestment rate is also 15 percent. In that case the yield over the five year investment horizon will be exactly 15 percent with either alternative, as the following computations indicate:

	A	B
Terminal Value of Cash Flow with		
15% Reinvestment Rate		
Year 1 (Reinvested for 4 Years)	$17,490	$17,490
2 (Reinvested for 3 Years)	15,209	15,209
3 (Reinvested for 2 Years)	13,225	13,225
4 (Reinvested for 1 Year)	0	11,500
5 (Reinvested for 0 Years)	0	10,000
Totals	$45,924	$67,424
Times: Present Value Factor at 15%	.49718	.49718
Present Value of Terminal Value at 15%	$22,832	$33,522
Less: Initial Cash Outlay	22,832	33,522
Net Present Value at 15%	$ 0	$ 0

But if the reinvestment rate is less than 15 percent, then alternative A will not offer an equally high total return over the five-year investment horizon. At a reinvestment rate of ten percent per annum, for example, total return over the entire five-year period will be approximately 11.9 percent per annum for alternative A and approximately 12.7 percent for B. These computations are shown below:

	A	B
Terminal Value of Cash Flow with		
10% Reinvestment Rate		
Year 1 (Reinvested for 4 Years)	$14,641	$14,641
2 (Reinvested for 3 Years)	13,310	13,310
3 (Reinvested for 2 Years)	12,100	12,100
4 (Reinvested for 1 Year)	0	11,000
5 (Reinvested for 0 Years)	0	10,000
Terminal Value of All Cash Flows	$40,051	$61,051
Approximate Discount Rate To Equate		
Terminal Value with Initial Cash Outlay	11.9%	12.7%

The Multiple-Solutions Problem.   Generally, a project's net present value is a decreasing function of the discount rate employed. With successively higher discount rates, a point is reached where the net present value becomes zero. This rate is the internal rate of return, and any higher discount rate will result in a negative net present value. When the discounting equation is well behaved in this fashion, there is but one internal rate of return, one discount rate that equates all cash inflows with all cash outflows.

Unfortunately, not all cash flow forecasts are this accommodating. Investment proposals may have any number of internal rates of return, depending on the pattern of anticipated cash flows. It is possible to have as many internal rates of return as the number of reversals in sign (positive to negative or vice versa) of the cash flow stream. Yet sign reversals are a common characteristic of cash flow streams from real estate projects. There is often junior mortgage financing that requires a balloon payment (that is, a final payment—substantially larger than the regular debt service—that retires the remaining balance). Net cash flow will usually be negative in the year the junior mortgage note matures. For each sign reversal there is an additional solution to the internal rate of return equation. Most of these alternative solutions will be outside the realm of real numbers, and there is but one internal rate of return solution. It is possible, however, for multiple solutions to fall within the realm of real numbers.

Eugene F. Brigham presents a simple illustration by citing a coal-mining firm's analysis of an open-pit mining operation that requires an initial cash outlay of $4.4 million and is expected to generate positive cash flow of $27.7 million during the first year of operations. During the second year, in accordance with state and federal regulations, land will be returned to its "natural" state at an estimated cost of $25 million. This cash-flow pattern generates two internal rate of return solutions: 9.2 percent and 420 percent.[2]

COMPARISON OF NET PRESENT VALUE AND INTERNAL RATE OF RETURN

Under most circumstances, the internal rate of return and net present value approaches will give the same decision signals. When this occurs, there is little significance in the choice of one over the other. The rules are as follows:

- When using internal rate of return, reject all projects whose internal rate of return is less than the minimum required rate. Projects with an internal rate of return equal to or greater than the minimum acceptable rate (the *hurdle rate*) are considered further.
- When using net present value, discount at the minimum acceptable rate of return and reject all projects with a net present value of less than zero. Projects with a net present value of zero or greater are considered further.

The essential similarity of these decision criteria is reflected in their mathematical formulation. The only structural difference is the discount rate. Remember that the discount rate employed in the internal rate of return is the effective yield; the net present value will be exactly zero when the internal rate of return equals the minimum required rate of return.

There are, however, some conditions under which contradictory signals emerge. We have seen that the two techniques may rank alternatives in different order. Since investors must often choose among alternatives rather than make a simple choice to accept or reject one investment, this can be a serious problem. Limited equity funds frequently dictate choice from among several opportunities, all of which may meet minimum acceptance criteria. Inconsistent rank-ordering can occur where projects differ in the size of the initial investment or in the timing of cash receipts and disbursements.

Where internal rate of return and net present value analysis give different decision signals, results of net present value analysis are usually preferred. This follows from most financial analysts having accepted the idea that investors should strive to maximize their wealth. Doubters are referred to an extensive discussion of the relative merits of these approaches by authors generally acknowledged as eminent authorities as well as pioneers in the theoretical aspects of capital budgeting methodology.[3]

SHORING UP THE INTERNAL RATE OF RETURN

Numerous attempts have been made to modify the internal rate of return to eradicate the multiple solutions and reinvestment-rate dilemmas. Three approaches are particularly worth noting for their ingenuity, if not for their usefulness. None eliminates the serious problem of failure to consistently give solutions consonant with the objective of maximizing investor wealth.

Modified Internal Rate of Return

One approach, called a *modified internal rate of return,* solves the multiple root problem by discounting all negative cash flows back to the time at which the investment is acquired and compounding all positive cash flows forward to the end of the final year of the holding period. This eliminates all sign changes and allows a unique solution.

Example 14.4

An investment proposition requires an initial cash expenditure of $1,600 and is expected to generate a net cash flow of $10,000 at the end of one year. Due to income tax and mortgage financing factors, the venture is expected to yield a negative $10,000 when terminated at the end of the second year.

Example 14.4 incorporates a numerical illustration developed by James H. Lorie and Leonard J. Savage to demonstrate the problem.[4] Discounting future cash flows at either 25 or 400 percent yields a net present value of exactly zero;

both are indicated internal rates of return. Since there is no unique solution, there is no "correct" internal rate of return.

Proponents of the modified internal rate of return would eliminate the double solution problem by discounting negative cash flows back to year zero and compounding positive cash flows forward to the end of the investment holding period. For Example 14.4, if we assume an opportunity cost of capital (the presumed appropriate rate for the discounting and compounding operating) of 20 percent, there results an 18.51 percent discount rate, which equates the positive terminal value with the negative initial amount. First, discount the second year's anticipated negative cash flow back to the time of the initial cash outlay and sum its (negative) present value with the $1,600 expenditure actually encountered at that time:

Cash Expected in Year 2	($10,000)
Times: Present Value Factor for Two Years at 20%	.69444
Present Value of Second Year's Cash Flow	($ 6,944)
Plus: Initial Cash Flow	(1,600)
Initial Value	$ (8,544)

Now compound the first year's anticipated positive cash flow forward to the end of year two, again at the presumed 20 percent opportunity cost of capital. This yields a terminal value of $12,000:

Cash Flow Expected in Year 1	$10,000
Times: Compound Value Factor for One Year at 20%	1.200
Terminal Value	$12,000

There remains only to find a discount rate that will make $12,000 due in two years have a present value of $8,544. A quick calculator computation (or reference to tables such as those in Appendix C) yields a modified internal rate of return of approximately 18.5 percent.

In addition to its intimidating complexity, this technique is extremely sensitive to variations in the rate chosen for preliminary discounting and compounding. To see this for yourself, repeat the exercise related to Example 14.4, using 10 percent as the appropriate rate. Now try 15 percent. You will find the modified internal rates of return to be approximately 5.6 percent and 12 percent, respectively.

Adjusted Rate of Return

Adjusted rates of return are particularly well explained by Donald Valachi.[5] Assuming cash flows as described in Example 14.4, Valachi suggests that an investor has in essence "borrowed" $10,000 from the project at the end of year one and repaid the "loan" at the end of year two. Assuming a reinvestment rate of 20 percent, the first year's $10,000 cash flow will have grown to $12,000 by the end of the second year. Offsetting this against the $10,000 net outflow at the end of the second year yields a net terminal value of $2,000. The discount rate that gives this $2,000 terminal value a present value equal to the $1,600 initial cash expenditure is approximately 11.8 percent (there are actually two roots; the other is a negative 2.1 percent).

This technique works well for the cash flows illustrated in Example 14.4, but consider the following series:[6]

Initital Cash Outlay	$ 1,000
Cash Flow in Year 1	6,000
Cash Flow in Year 2	(11,000)
Cash Flow in Year 3	6,000

This cash-flow pattern produces internal rate of return solutions of zero percent, 100 percent and 200 percent. Since it is unlikely that year one's cash flow will be compounded at a rate high enough to allow it to cover year two's negative cash flow, some other course of action is necessary. One might "borrow" from year three by discounting part of that cash flow back to year two. Or one might discount all of year three's cash flow back to year two and compound only part of year one's cash flow forward. The results of these alternatives are two drastically different adjusted internal rates of return. As variable rate mortgages become increasingly commonplace, cash flows more frequently alternate between negative and positive, and rules needed to apply the adjusted rate of return become devilishly complex.

Financial Management Rate of Return

M. Chapman Findley and Stephen D. Messner have developed a widely publicized variation on the internal rate of return, called the *financial management rate of return*. Their version incorporates two intermediate rates, one a cost of capital rate employed to discount negative cash flows back to year zero and the other a specified reinvestment rate for compounding positive cash flows to the end of the projection period. Interested readers will do well to start their research with a study of articles by Michael Young and H. S. Kerr, both of whom provide definitive critiques of the model.[7]

SUMMARY

Modern investment evaluation techniques generally involve some variation of a discounted cash-flow model expressing the present value of all anticipated future cash flows. Most common are the internal rate of return and the present value/net present value models. The internal rate of return model is conceptually appealing to many, but it contains flaws that make it less desirable than the present value/net present value approach.

NOTES

1. Austin Jaffe, "Is There a 'New' Internal Rate of Return Literature?" *AREUEA Journal,* vol. 4 (Winter 1977) p. 483.

2. Eugene F. Brigham, *Financial Management: Theory and Practice,* 8th ed. (Ft. Worth, TX: The Dryden Press, 1996).

3. See, for example, Harold Bierman, Jr., and Seymour Smidt, *The Capital Budgeting Decision* (New York: Macmillan, 1971) pp. 38–54.

4. James H. Lorie and Leonard J. Savage, "Three Problems in Rationing Capital," *Journal of Business,* October 1955, pp. 229–39.

5. Donald J. Valachi, "More on the Arithmetic of Multiple and Imaginary Rates of Return," *Real Estate Appraiser and Analyst,* September–October 1980, pp. 19–20.

6. These numbers are taken from an example propounded by James C. Van Hone in *Financial Management and Policy,* 4th ed. (Englewood Cliffs, NJ: Prentice-Hall, 1977), p. 105.

7. Michael Young, "FMRR: A Clever Hoax?" *Appraisal Journal,* vol. 47 (July 1979) pp. 359–69; H. S. Keff, "A Final Word on FMRR," *Appraisal Journal,* vol. 48 (January 1980) pp. 95–103.

RECOMMENDED READINGS

Bierman, Harold Jr., and Seymour Smidt. *The Capital Budgeting Decision.* 8th ed. (Upper Saddle River, NJ: Prentice Hall, 1996).

Brigham, Eugene F. *Essentials of Managerial Finance.* 11th ed. (Ft. Worth, TX: The Dryden Press, 1996).

REVIEW QUESTIONS

1. Under what conditions will a project be rejected when using present value in investment decision making?
2. Describe the internal rate of return.
3. What assumption is made about reinvestment of cash flows in net present value calculations? In internal rate of return calculations?
4. What is the major difference between the internal rate of return approach and the present value approach?
5. Under what conditions might the internal rate of return yield multiple solutions?
6. List some conditions under which the present value and the internal rate of return might yield conflicting decision signals. When this occurs, which should be selected?
7. What are the advantages and disadvantages of the modified internal rate of return, the adjusted rate of return and the financial management rate of return?
8. What is the difference between present value and net present value?

DISCUSSION QUESTIONS

1. What is the relationship among present value, net present value and internal rate of return? Is there a consistent relationship at all possible values for these measures?
2. If you were judging the extent to which a financial consultant exercised due diligence in evaluating an investment proposal, would you be influenced by the consultant's choice between internal rate of return and present value as an evaluation methodology?
3. Since cash-flow projections and cost of capital estimates are, at best, inexact in most cases, does it really make a practical difference whether an analyst uses present value or internal rate of return as a decision criterion?

CHAPTER 15

Investment Goals and Decision Criteria

This chapter explains methods for selecting a discount rate. It then explores how the discounted cash-flow technique might be applied to various categories of investment decisions, and to develop an investment negotiating strategy that uses the investment value concept introduced in Chapter One.

CHOOSING A DISCOUNT RATE

Choice of discount rate is critical when selecting among alternative opportunities as well as when deciding what opportunities merit additional consideration. Analysts who use the internal rate of return approach need not select a discount rate, but do not avoid the problem. They still must decide on a minimum acceptable rate of return as a yardstick against which to measure the internal rate of return.

Minor adjustments in the selected rate can result in rather dramatic changes in net present value. The further into the future cash-flow projections are made, the greater the influence of discount rate variations. Moreover, relative rankings of opportunities can be changed by altering the discount rate when opportunities differ in the timing of anticipated cash flows.

Example 15.1 illustrates how relative rankings can be altered when a different discount rate is used. At a rate of 15 percent, respective net present values are $25,469 and $23,592 and project A appears preferable to project B. But at a rate of 14 percent the relative rankings are switched, with project B's revised net present value of $34,872 being preferable to project A's new net present value of $30,403. Thus with a discount rate of 14 percent or less, project B appears more desirable, while project A is more desirable with discount rates of 15 percent or more.

Example 15.1

An investor must choose between two projects, both of which require an initial equity expenditure of $100,000. Project A is expected to generate $25,000 of after-tax cash flow each year for ten years, after which the assets will be worthless. Project B offers a projected $500,000 of after-tax cash flow, all of which is expected to be received at the end of the tenth year of ownership.

 Summation Technique

One of the earliest methods proposed for developing discount rates, the *summation technique* is based upon the proposition that investors seek compensation for deferring consumption, for bearing risk, for sacrificing liquidity and for portfolio management. The sum of the compensation rates for each of these items is held to comprise the appropriate discount rate.

Table 15.1 illustrates how the summation technique might be used to derive an estimate of a discount rate, if one knew the appropriate values for the various factors. The difficulty of estimating appropriate values is the major weakness of this technique. The greater the number of factors employed, the greater is the opportunity for error.

Risk-Adjusted Discount Rate

Practical problems associated with estimating appropriate compensation for various components renders the summation technique impractical. A frequently advocated alternative lumps compensation for all elements other than waiting (the safe, or risk-free, rate) into one "reduced form" rate, called a *risk premium*. The sum of the risk-free rate and the risk premium is held to be the appropriate discount rate.

Table 15.1	The Summation Technique
Safe Rate	0.120
Compensation for Risk	0.020
Compensation for Illiquidity	0.015
Compensation for Burden of Management	0.001
Discount Rate (Summation of Above)	0.156

The Risk-Free Rate. The risk-free rate is compensation solely for waiting, with no premium for risk. The yield on extremely short term Treasury Bills issued by the federal government is frequently taken as a reasonable approximation of the risk-free rate. The risk of default is virtually zero, and the risk of loss in purchasing power due to inflation or loss of interest income due to illiquidity are small because of the short maturities.

The Risk Premium. The risk premium, an additional rate of return increment required to compensate for bearing risk, differs according to the investor's conception of a project's riskiness. The greater the perceived risk, the higher the discount rate employed. The acceptable trade-off between risk and return is a function of the individual investor's attitude toward risk.

Marginal Cost of Capital

Textbooks in corporate finance generally advocate using *marginal cost of capital* as the appropriate discount rate.[1] The marginal cost of anything is the cost of one additional unit of the item. The marginal cost of capital, therefore, is the cost of an additional dollar of new funds. A problem arises in trying to apply this concept when funds are raised from several sources, because marginal cost from each source differs. Under such circumstances, some authorities recommend using several different discount rates, depending on the circumstances surrounding the decision.[2] Perhaps the most common solution is to apply a weighted average rate that incorporates the marginal cost of all sources, with the cost of each weighted in accordance with the percent of total new capital to be generated from that source.

For most real estate projects, the cost of debt is easily identifiable, and this cost (expressed as annual debt service) is subtracted from gross income to arrive at an estimate of after-tax cash flow to equity investors. When treated in this manner, the cost of borrowed capital must not also be incorporated into the discount rate. The marginal cost of equity capital then becomes the appropriate determinant of the discount rate.

Marginal cost of equity for corporations whose shares are actively traded is estimated by comparing earnings per share with the market price of the shares. For privately held corporations or noncorporate investors no such market index is available, and marginal cost of capital is a difficult concept to apply. Under those circumstances the opportunity cost of equity capital is a more meaningful basis for determining the appropriate discount rate.

Opportunity Cost of Capital

The question facing an analyst is: What rate of return can be earned on the best available alternative use of funds that does not appreciably increase an investor's exposure to risk? This is the investor's *opportunity cost of capital.* It serves admirably as a minimum acceptable rate of return, or *hurdle rate,* since investors are unlikely to accept any project promising a rate of return below that available elsewhere with the same degree of risk.

Using opportunity cost as a discount rate permits direct comparison among projects of the same general risk category. This eliminates difficulties that might otherwise arise when cash-flow projections from alternative proposals differ drastically in amount or timing.

Finally, a uniform discount rate for all competing projects greatly facilitates risk analysis of the type discussed in Part Six. It permits risk analysis to be incorporated into policy guidelines, and enables subordinates or analysts to screen investment proposals in much greater detail than is otherwise possible.

INVESTMENT DECISIONS AND DECISION RULES

Precise rules for making investment decisions necessarily depend upon the nature of the problem. While general principles are universally applicable, their specific application depends upon situational factors. This section examines a number of situations and the appropriate application of general principles for each.

Comparing Projects of Different Size

Net present value does not give an unambiguous decision signal when projects require different levels of initial cash outlay. But the measure can be converted to a cost/benefit ratio, which does this task admirably. The ratio, called a *profitability index* (PI), is calculated by dividing the present value of expected future cash flows by the amount of the initial cash outlay. The quotient represents present value per dollar of initial cash expenditure. The general decision rule, then, is to accept the project with the greatest profitability index (assuming, of course, that there is no difference in the risk profile of competing opportunities).

Example 15.2

The present value of expected cash flows from an investment is $74,340, when discounted at the opportunity cost of capital. The required equity cash outlay to acquire the asset is $60,000.

Applying the profitability index technique to Example 15.2 results in a tentative decision to accept the project, since there is $1.24 of present value for every $1 of initial cash investment. The calculation is as follows:

$$PI = \frac{\text{Present Value}}{\text{Cost}} = \frac{\$74,340}{\$60,000} = 1.24$$

When using the profitability index as an initial screening device, reject all projects with an index of less than one. This is, of course, a simple variant of the rule of rejecting any project whose net present value is less than zero. Only projects with a profitability index equal to or greater than one are subjected to additional analysis.

The profitability index is simply an alternate way of expressing net present value data, since instead of subtracting initial cash outlay from present value, we divide by that amount. Therefore, when present value minus initial cash outlay equals zero, the profitability index will equal one. It follows that when net present value is less than zero, the profitability index will be less than one; and when net present value is more than zero, the profitability index will be more than one.

Choosing among Mutually Exclusive Opportunities

Investors often must select from among nominally desirable investment alternatives. They must, for example, decide among alternative allowable capital recovery methods (depreciation). Financing alternatives, lease or buy choices, decisions to accept or reject offers to buy or sell, selection from among alternate lease terms or tenants and alternate forms of ownership all constitute examples of mutually exclusive choices. Investors deciding among mutually exclusive alternatives should accept the one producing greater (positive) net present value.

We have seen that the profitability index expresses the relative profitability and thus is useful for comparing projects that require differing amounts of cash outlay. For choosing among mutually exclusive projects, however, the net present value approach is preferred, because it expresses in absolute terms the project's expected economic contribution.

Example 15.3

An investor owns a site that is worth $60,000. Using her equity in the land (which she owns on a free-and-clear basis) as collateral, she can secure a mortgage loan to cover the cost of constructing a strip shopping center. Alternatively, she can construct a small multiple-story office building. The office project, however, will require that she invest an additional $15,000 of equity funds to bridge the gap between construction cost and available mortgage funds. The present value of after-tax cash flows from the strip shopping center is estimated to be $90,000; from the office building, $108,000.

To illustrate, consider the mutually exclusive uses of a building site described in Example 15.3. Using the profitability index, the shopping center alternative appears preferable, but the net present value approach shows the office building to be preferable. Because the net present value criterion shows the net economic contribution of the project, we would prefer the office building on the site. Table 15.2 summarizes the computations.

Table 15.2	Summary of Investor's Development Alternatives	
	Shopping Center	*Office Building*
Present Value of Net Cash Flows	$90,000	$108,000
Less: Initial Equity Outlay	60,000	75,000
Net Present Value	$30,000	$ 33,000
Profitability Index	1.50	1.44

Mutually Dependent Investment Decisions

Investment proposals are mutually dependent if acceptance of one forces the investor to accept the other. If investment decisions are related in this fashion, group the mutually dependent ventures into consolidated units and treat each unit as a single investment venture. Accept the mutually dependent combination having the highest net present value, provided it is greater than zero. If the consolidated units differ in the amount of initial equity commitment, compare the combinations' profitability indexes.

INVESTMENT VALUE AND INVESTMENT STRATEGY

Investment value was defined in Chapter One as the value of an income-producing property to a particular investor. Prospective investors will be motivated to buy if they believe investment value is greater than market price. Owners will be motivated to sell if they believe they will receive more than their properties are worth to them as elements in their personal investment portfolios.

Example 15.4

An investor estimates that a property has a present value of anticipated future equity cash flows of $250,000. He suspects he can acquire the property for about $725,000, paying $225,000 in cash and financing the balance via a first mortgage loan. The present owner believes she can sell for about $725,000 and that the present value of future after-tax cash flows if she continues to hold the property in her portfolio is about $400,000. An existing mortgage loan on the property has a remaining balance of $200,000. If the owner in fact sells for $725,000, she estimates that her taxes and transaction costs will total about $100,000.

Consider the position of the prospective buyer in Example 15.4. Summing the $250,000 present value of anticipated after-tax cash flows (the value of the expected equity cash expenditure) and the expected $500,000 mortgage loan (the cost of which is incorporated into the present value computations) yields an investment value of $750,000 to the prospective purchaser. If, as the investor suspects, the property can be acquired for $725,000, only $225,000 of equity cash will be required. Present value of future cash receipts less required equity (the cost to acquire the future cash flows) yields a net present value of $25,000. Buying this property is expected to increase the investor's net worth by $25,000. These relationships are summarized in Table 15.3.

Now consider the current owner's position. Summing the $400,000 present value of anticipated future after-tax cash flows and the $200,000 remaining balance of the existing mortgage produces an investment value of $600,000 if she continues her ownership. She can sell for $725,000 and net $625,000 after taxes and transaction costs. Therefore, she can improve her position by selling.

Selling the property for the expected $725,000 will net her $425,000 of after-tax cash flow (sales price minus loan balance, transaction costs and income taxes). She in effect exchanges the $400,000 present value of future cash flows for $425,000 in net cash proceeds from selling. The net present value of a decision to sell is therefore estimated to be $25,000. These relationships are summarized in Table 15.4.

Marked differences in investment value, like those for the prospective buyer and seller in Example 15.4, occur because investors differ in their access to debt capital and the opportunity cost of equity. They occur also because of different perceptions of a property's potential and due to differences in income tax positions.

The relationship between subjective investment values in Example 15.4 is diagramed in Figure 15.1. The greater the spread between investment value and transaction price for both buyer and seller, the greater the possible increase in both investors' net wealth. Keep in mind that neither party will know the other's investment value. Since the buyer does not know the minimum amount the seller will accept and the seller does not know the maximum amount the buyer will pay, both parties bargain with incomplete information. This uncertainty increases the importance of good bargaining strategy.

Table 15.3	Summary of Buyer's Position
Present Value of Equity	$250,000
Add: Available Financing	500,000
Buyer's Investment Value	$750,000
Expected Purchase Price	$725,000
Less: Available Debt Financing	500,000
Expected Equity Investment	$225,000
Present Value of Equity Position	$250,000
Less: Expected Equity Investment	225,000
Net Present Value	$ 25,000

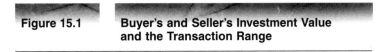

Table 15.4   Summary of Seller's Position

Investment Value

Present Value of Equity Position	$400,000
Add: Mortgage Loan Balance	200,000
Seller's Investment value	$600,000

Net Present Value

Expected Sales Price		$725,000
Less: Mortgage Loan Balance	$200,000	
Taxes and Transaction Costs	100,000	300,000
Expected After-Tax Cash Flow from Sale		$425,000
Less: Present Value of Equity Position		400,000
Net Present Value of Seller's Position		$ 25,000

**Figure 15.1   Buyer's and Seller's Investment Value
and the Transaction Range**

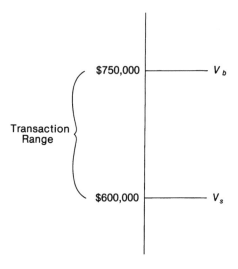

APPLYING THE DISCOUNTED CASH-FLOW TECHNIQUE

This final section applies previously discussed procedures for developing after-tax cash-flow projections and discounts them at the minimum acceptable rate of return. Space limitations require that several assumptions be made about key variables that, in a realistic situation, would be subject to debate and judgmental variation. Now examine Example 15.5.

> ## *Example 15.5*
>
> A wife-and-husband investment team is considering a 48-unit apartment complex, expected to be available for $1.3 million. The couple expect to be able to arrange an $840,000, 8 percent, 25-year, fully amortizing first mortgage loan, which will require monthly payments. Whether or not they make this commitment, they will be in the 40 percent (combined federal and state) marginal income tax bracket throughout the contemplated investment period (they file a joint tax return). Long-term capital gains taxes are expected to be levied at 28 percent. If the couple invests, they expect to hold the property for approximately six years and then to sell for cash to finance their retirement plan. The investors' minimum acceptable rate of return on investments of this type is 12 percent per annum.
>
> The investors note that the area is fully developed, with no land available for significant new, competing buildings, and they detect no discernible trend of either rapid growth or decline. They conclude that both rents and expenses over the next few years are likely to move approximately in concert with the general change in consumer prices. They expect the consumer price index to increase at about 4 percent per annum (compounded) over the next few years, and they take this as the expected rate of increase in both rents and operating expenses.

The first step in analyzing the opportunity in Example 15.5 is to forecast revenue and expenses for the property over the expected holding period. Starting with the previous owner's operating statement, adjusting as explained in Part Three, the investment team generates the forecast of first-year operating figures shown in Table 15.5.

Having determined that operating results are most likely to increase at an average rate of 4 percent per annum over the holding period, forecasting becomes a mechanical projection at that rate. The forecast must be made on an after-tax cash-flow basis, however. This requires that taxable income or tax-deductible losses also be forecast for each year of the prospective holding period. To calculate interest expense for this purpose, an amortization table for available financing must be developed. This information is shown in Table 15.6.

The investors' expected taxable income from the investment for each year consists of the expected net operating income minus interest expense and depreciation allowances. Since the investors expect to be in the 40 percent marginal income tax bracket with or without this investment, the tax (or tax savings) for each year will be computed at the 40 percent rate. These calculations are presented in the upper half of Table 15.7.

Depreciation allowances reduce taxable income, but they do not affect before-tax cash flow from an investment. Conversely, reduction of the principal amount of mortgage indebtedness reduces cash flow without affecting taxable

Table 15.5 **First-Year Operating Forecast**

Potential Gross Rent		$262,000
Less: Allowance for Vacancies		17,500
		$244,500
Plus: Other Income (Parking)		1,600
Effective Gross Income		$246,100
Less: Operating Expenses		
Management Fee	$12,300	
Salary Expense	22,500	
Utilities	26,500	
Insurance	12,500	
Supplies	3,200	
Advertising	1,500	
Maintenance and Repairs	20,000	
Property Tax	30,700	
Total Operating Expenses		$129,200
Net Operating Income (Annual)		$116,900

Table 15.6 **Mortgage Amortization Schedule***

Year	Interest	Principal	Total Debt Service	Ending Balance
1	$66,803	$10,996	$77,799	$829,004
2	65,890	11,909	77,799	817,095
3	64,901	12,898	77,799	804,197
4	63,831	13,968	77,799	790,229
5	62,672	15,127	77,799	775,102
6	61,415	16,384	77,799	758,718

*Computed with a financial calculator. Computations using tables will differ slightly due to rounding. Computations assume a mortgage loan of $840,000, to be repaid in equal monthly installments over 25 years, with interest at 8 percent per annum.
Monthly payment = $6,483.26
Annual debt service = 12 × $6,483.26 = $77,799

income. The lower half of Table 15.7 contains after-tax cash-flow forecasts, which start with net operating income and are adjusted for debt service and income tax effects.

If the current gross rent multiplier continues to apply, this property will have a market value of approximately $1,650,000 when sold at the end of the sixth year of ownership. Subtracting estimated transaction costs (5 percent of the sales price) and the owners' adjusted basis before the sale (cost minus accumulated depreciation allowances) yields the anticipated gain on disposal. Multiplying this by the anticipated 28 percent long-term capital gains tax rate results in an anticipated income tax liability of $137,552. Table 15.8 summarizes these calculations.

Table 15.7   **After-Tax Cash-Flow Forecast**

	Year 1	Year 2	Year 3	Year 4	Year 5	Year 6
Effective Gross Income	$246,000	$256,000	$266,000	$277,000	$288,000	$299,000
Less: Operating Expenses	129,000	134,000	140,000	145,000	151,000	157,000
Net Operating Income	$117,000	$122,000	$126,000	$132,000	$137,000	$142,000
Less: Interest Expense	66,803	65,890	64,901	63,831	62,672	61,416
Depreciation Allowance*	36,242	37,818	37,818	37,818	37,818	36,242
Taxable Income	$ 13,955	$ 18,292	$ 23,281	$ 30,351	$ 36,510	$ 44,342
Times: Marginal Tax Rate	.40	.40	.40	.40	.40	.40
Income Tax	$ 5,582	$ 7,317	$ 9,312	$ 12,140	$ 14,604	$ 17,737
Net Operating Income	$117,000	$122,000	$126,000	$132,000	$137,000	$142,000
Less: Debt Service	77,799	77,799	77,799	77,799	77,799	77,799
Before-Tax Cash Flow	$ 39,201	$ 44,201	$ 48,201	$ 54,201	$ 59,201	$ 64,201
Less: Income Tax	5,582	7,317	9,312	12,140	14,604	17,737
After-Tax Cash Flow	$ 33,619	$ 36,884	$ 38,889	$ 42,061	$ 44,597	$ 46,464

Rounding: Rounded to nearest $1,000
*Assumes that 80 percent of the $1,300,000 purchase price is properly attributable to the building, and that purchase closes during the first month and sale closes during the last month of the respective taxable years. See Chapter 10 for details.

Table 15.8   **Income Tax Consequences from Disposal**

Sales Price		$1,650,000
Less:		
Transaction Costs (at 5%)	$ 82,500	
Adjusted Basis (Cost Minus Depreciation)	1,076,244	1,158,744
Gain on Sale		$ 491,256
Tax on Sale, at 28%		$ 137,552

Table 15.9 converts the expected selling price and income tax consequences into a forecast of after-tax cash flow from disposal. This involves subtracting the estimated transaction costs, income tax liability and mortgage balance from the forecasted selling price of the property.

Table 15.9   **Forecast of After-Tax Cash Flow from Disposal**

Sales Price		$1,650,000
Less:		
Transaction Costs (from Table 15.8)	$ 82,500	
Income Tax (from Table 15.8)	137,552	
Mortgage Balance (from Table 15.6)	758,718	978,770
Net Cash Flow		$ 671,230

Anticipated after-tax cash flows are discounted in Table 15.10, to adjust for differences in timing of the expected receipts. Since the present value of all anticipated future cash flows exceeds the required initial equity investment ($502,744 present value compared to an investment of only $460,000), we conclude that the venture is expected to generate a yield in excess of the investors' 10 percent minimum acceptable rate.

Estimating Investment Value

An alternative presentation of the data from Example 15.5 involves estimating the maximum purchase price to yield the lowest acceptable rate of return. This approach is a particularly valuable source of intelligence for improved negotiating. With the mortgage financing assumed to be available for the property in Example 15.5, the investors can pay the present value of cash flow to the equity position plus the amount of the available mortgage and still expect to receive a 10 percent return on equity funds. Investment value for this couple is therefore equal to the $502,744 present value plus the $840,000 mortgage, which gives a total of $1,342,744. This computation is shown at the bottom of Table 15.10.

The effect of mortgage-financing assumptions on investment value serves to emphasize the most valuable use of this computation—its contribution to negotiating position. Since present value differs with the amount and cost of available financing, investment value will also vary. There is, therefore, a different investment value for every possible set of financing arrangements. When a seller finds a prospective purchaser's investment value unacceptably low, there is the possibility of a trade-off between price and credit terms.

Preparatory to negotiating price and terms, an investor should compute investment value under a variety of potential prices with attendant terms for partial seller financing. These alternatives give the investor a basis for counteroffers, as well as a means to quickly evaluate the other side's proposals.

Table 15.10   Present Value of Anticipated After-Tax Cash Flows

Year	After-Tax Cash Flow	Present Value Factor at 12%	Present Value (Rounded)
1	$ 33,619	.892857	$ 30,017
2	36,884	.797194	29,404
3	38,889	.711780	27,680
4	42,061	.635518	26,731
5	44,597	.567427	25,306
6	46,464	.506631	23,540
6 (from Disposal)	671,230	.506631	340,066
Present Value of All Anticipated Cash Flows			$ 502,744
Plus: Available Mortgage Loan			840,000
Investment Value			$1,342,744

Note that computing the investment value requires a presumption of a purchase price. This is because the depreciation allowance, an integral element in the cash-flow forecast, depends on the price. If investment value proves to be less than the presumed purchase price, do the calculations again using the initial calculation as the revised purchase price. This will yield a closer approximation between presumed price and tentative investment value. A third calculation will yield an even closer approximation. Successive approximations quickly generate an investment value so close to the presumed price that the difference will be inconsequential. Using an electronic spreadsheet makes the successive approximations as simple as loading a revised price into a personal computer and touching the *recompute* key (in most spreadsheet programs, even the *recompute* command is automatic).

SUMMARY

Decision signals generated by discounted cash-flow models are extremely sensitive to differences in the discount rates employed. A minor shift in the rate can alter the rankings of investment alternatives. For this reason, choosing a discount rate is a vital element in the usefulness of an analytical model.

One approach, now largely abandoned, to deriving a discount rate is the summation technique. This involves choosing a risk-free rate, a risk premium and rates to compensate for illiquidity and for the burden of investment management. The sum of these separate rates is held to be the appropriate discount rate. Difficulty in determining the rates for each of these elements renders the summation technique more a historical curiosity than a helpful tool for analysis.

Many analysts do employ a risk-adjusted discount rate, usually derived from observation of rates available in the marketplace. Conceptually, the rate is the sum of a risk-free rate and a risk premium. The most commonly used proxy for a risk-free rate is the yield on short-term government securities. To this must be added a premium that will vary depending upon the amount of risk perception associated with a particular investment venture.

Marginal cost of capital is the cost of procuring one more unit. Many analysts believe this to be the appropriate rate to employ when considering the advisability of an investment venture. Since cash-flow forecasting generally yields a forecast of the cash flow to the equity investor, the marginal cost of equity capital is the most appropriate measure. Opportunity cost—the benefit forgone by not accepting the best available alternative investment proposition—is frequently taken as the best estimate of the marginal cost of equity capital.

Investment-decision rules that employ discounted cash-flow analysis must be adjusted to accommodate varying circumstances facing an investor or an analyst. When projects require different amounts of initial equity cash expenditure, the present value can be expressed as a profitability index. This measure indicates the present value per dollar of equity investment.

When comparing mutually exclusive projects, choose the one with the largest net present value (present value minus equity cash expenditure). When evaluating mutually dependent projects, group them into sets of mutually dependent alternatives. Evaluate each set as if it were a single investment venture.

Investment value is the most an investor is justified in paying for an asset, given the anticipated after-tax cash flows the asset will generate and the investor's minimum acceptable rate of return. To estimate investment value, add the available mortgage loan to the present value of anticipated after-tax cash flows to the equity position.

NOTES

1. See, for example, J. Fred Weston and Eugene F. Brigham, *Managerial Finance,* 9th ed. (Ft. Worth, TX: The Dryden Press, 1992).

2. Harold Bierman, Jr., and Seymour Smidt, *The Capital Budgeting Decision,* 8th ed. (Upper Saddle River, NJ: Prentice Hall, 1996).

RECOMMENDED READINGS

Brigham, Eugene F. *Fundamentals of Financial Management.* 7th ed. (Ft. Worth, TX: The Dryden Press, 1994).

REVIEW QUESTIONS

1. What is the significance of the discount rate chosen when evaluating investment opportunities?
2. What is the basis for the summation technique? What is assumed to be the appropriate rate of return in this technique?
3. What is a risk-free rate of return?
4. When is the opportunity cost of capital an appropriate discount rate?
5. How is the profitability index calculated, and when is it most useful?
6. Describe mutually dependent investment decisions. How should mutually dependent investments be treated?
7. What are mutually exclusive investment opportunities? Give some examples. When is a choice between mutually exclusive alternatives likely to occur?
8. What role does investment value play in the investment strategies of a buyer and seller?
9. What effect do the amount and cost of mortgage financing have on the present value and investment value of a property? How might this relationship be used in the negotiation process?

10. Bill Smith, the junior partner in the firm of Jones, Brown and Smith, has been offered, for $2.15 million, an apartment complex that is expected to generate after-tax cash flows from operations as indicated in the following chart. The forecast incorporates a first mortgage loan of $1.5 million. Smith expects to sell the property after seven years, and the best estimate of after-tax cash flow from disposal is $740,000.

Year	Expected After-Tax Cash Flow from Operations
1	$ 60,000
2	70,000
3	80,000
4	87,000
5	93,000
6	99,000
7	105,000

Required: Using a 10 percent discount rate, compute:
a. Net present value
b. Profitability index
c. Approximate investment value

11. What is the expected internal rate of return on the project in question 10?

DISCUSSION QUESTIONS

1. Since the opportunity cost of equity capital changes over time, should long-term and short-term commitments be evaluated using different opportunity costs?

2. When discounting long-term cash-flow forecasts using the opportunity cost of capital, should the rate employed reflect costs at the time the commitment is to be made, or should it reflect anticipated average capital costs over the forecast period?

PART FIVE: Case Problem

1. Byron Bigfee is a commercial real estate broker who also has a keen eye for personal investment opportunities. He has an opportunity to buy Academic Arms, an apartment building that caters to students. He estimates that he can acquire the asset for $1.3 million and that the seller will take back a $1.2 million first mortgage note in part payment. Credit terms include interest at nine percent and level amortization over 25 years, but with a seven-year call. Bigfee plans to sell the project when the loan balance falls due at the end of the seventh year.

   Bigfee has researched Academic Arms and has generated the following schedules, in which he has considerable confidence.

Academic Arms Apartments Projected After-Tax Cash Flows from Operations

	Year 1	Year 2	Year 3	Year 4	Year 5	Year 6	Year 7
Effective Gross Income	$286,442	$295,035	$303,887	$313,004	$322,393	$332,067	$342,029
Less: Operating Expenses	157,543	162,269	167,138	172,152	177,316	182,637	188,116
Net Operating Income	$128,899	$132,766	$136,749	$140,852	$145,077	$149,430	$153,913
Less: Debt Service	126,370	126,370	126,370	126,370	126,370	126,370	126,370
Before-Tax Cash Flow	$ 2,529	$ 6,396	$ 10,379	$ 14,482	$ 18,707	$ 23,060	$ 27,543
Less: Depreciation	36,967	38,575	38,575	38,575	38,575	38,575	36,967
Plus: Principal Paid	6,671	7,369	8,141	8,993	9,935	10,975	12,124
Taxable Income (Loss)*	$(27,767)	$(24,810)	$(20,055)	$(15,100)	$(9,933)	$(4,540)	$ 2,700
Times: Tax Rate	.28	.28	.28	.28	.28	.28	.28
Tax (Tax Saving)	$(7,775)	$(6,947)	$(5,615)	$(4,228)	$(2,781)	$(1,271)	$ 756
Before-Tax Cash Flow	$ 2,529	$ 6,396	$ 10,379	$ 14,482	$ 18,707	$ 23,060	$ 27,543
Less: Tax (*Plus:* Savings)	(7,775)	(6,947)	(5,615)	(4,228)	(2,781)	(1,271)	756
After-Tax Cash Flow	$ 10,304	$ 13,343	$ 15,994	$ 18,710	$ 21,488	$ 24,331	$ 26,787

*Bigfee has adequate passive income to offset these losses.

Academic Arms Apartments Anticipated Income Tax Consequences of Disposal *(at the end of seventh year of ownership)*	
Sales Price	$1,700,000
Less: Adjusted Tax Basis before Sale	1,195,191
Taxable Gain	$ 504,809
Times: Marginal Income Tax Rate	.28
Income Tax on Sale	$ 141,347

Academic Arms Apartments Anticipated After-Tax Cash Flow from Disposal *(at end of seventh year of ownership)*		
Sales Price		$1,700,000
Less:		
Income Taxes	$ 141,347	
Transaction Costs (.08 × $1,700,000)	136,000	
Mortgage Balance	1,135,792	1,413,139
After-Tax Cash Flow		$ 286,861

Required:
a. Using the first-year operating forecast, compute:
  • Gross income multiplier (using effective gross income)
  • Net income multiplier
  • Operating ratio
  • Break even, or default, ratio
  • Debt coverage ratio
  • Overall capitalization rate
  • Equity dividend rate
  • Cash-on-cash return
b. Using a 12 percent rate, discount the expected after-tax cash flows from this investment and determine:
  • Present value
  • Net present value
  • Profitability index
  • Investment value
c. Determine the project's anticipated internal rate of return.

2. Please refer to the case problem for Part Four. Assignments one and two of that case required you to develop projections of after-tax cash flows from operations and from disposal of The Sated Satyr apartments. If you have not completed that assignment, please do so now. Using your after-tax projections, compute:
a. The present value of the opportunity, discounting at 14 percent
b. The investment value, discounting at 14 percent
c. The internal rate of return.

PART SIX

The Risk Element

Traditional real estate investment literature has fallen behind related fields such as corporate capital budgeting and portfolio analysis by not systematically incorporating risk considerations into the investment equation. We now shift focus to address this critical element.

The intention of Part Six is to demonstrate that specific investment objectives can be related to probabilistic estimates of possible investment outcomes. Investors can compare expected outcomes with the probability that a particular venture will produce a yield equal to or greater than some predetermined minimum acceptable outcome. Faced with quantified risk and return trade-offs, investors will be well positioned to make rational investment decisions.

Chapter 16 discusses risk in general terms, with the objective of acquainting readers with the issues involved in comparing risk-return combinations of alternative investment opportunities. Chapter 17 reviews traditional approaches to dealing with the problem. Chapter 18 then introduces contemporary alternatives and demonstrates their application to real estate. Chapter 19 concludes the section by introducing risk management in a portfolio context.

CHAPTER 16

Risk in Real Estate Investment

Earlier chapters discuss investment evaluation based on a single best estimate of net cash flows over the projection period. The illusion of precision in these point estimates is seductive, but failing to appreciate the significance of possible forecasting errors can cause grievous investment miscalculations. All forecasts are probabilistic in nature, and the implication of precision found in statements with values rounded to the nearest whole dollar should be rejected.

This chapter introduces risk as an investment analysis issue. It distinguishes among major risk elements and discusses methods for controlling risk. It considers the relationship among risk, risk-taker and profit expectations. The chapter concludes with an introduction to problems in measuring risk and incorporating risk perception into the investment decision.

MAJOR RISK ELEMENTS

Risk elements can be usefully characterized according to their origins. The risk inherent in the use of borrowed funds, and thus determined by choice of financial arrangements, is called *financial risk*. Risk of loss from natural hazards (fire, flood, storm and so forth) can be transferred to insurance companies and so is characterized as *insurable risk*. Risk stemming from the possibility of making inappropriate business decisions or of misjudging the economic consequences of one's actions is labeled *business risk*.

Financial Risk

We saw in Part Three that financial leverage (using borrowed funds) increases the yield on an equity investment (and is therefore considered positive, or favorable) so long as the cost of borrowed funds is less than the yield on assets. Unfavorable leverage, in contrast, decreases the yield on an investor's equity funds. Financial leverage also amplifies the variability of possible returns to equity investors. Increased variability represents additional risk due to the financing decision and so is part of the financial risk associated with the investment.

Consider a property with an expected net operating income of $125,000 and a market value of $1 million. Assume the range of possible net operating income is $100,000 to $150,000. If an investor purchases this asset without using borrowed funds, the expected current yield (before income taxes) is $125,000 divided by $1,000,000, or 12.5 percent. Possible annual pretax yields (cash-on-cash) range from $100,000 divided by $1,000,000, or 10 percent, through $150,000 divided by $1,000,000, or 15 percent.

Suppose our investor finances $700,000 of the purchase price via a mortgage loan that requires equal monthly payments over 25 years with interest at 9 percent. The payments will be approximately $5,874 per month and the annual debt service obligation will be 12 times this amount, or approximately $70,488. Before-tax cash flow to the equity investor is, of course, reduced by the amount of the annual debt service obligation. With the loan, the range of possible before-tax cash flows is $100,000 minus $70,488, or $29,512 at the low end, and $150,000 minus $70,488, or $79,512 at the high end. The expected before-tax cash flow becomes $125,000 minus $70,488, or $54,512. These computations are presented in Table 16.1.

Of course, the mortgage loan also reduces the size of the required equity investment from $1 million to only $300,000. The expected annual pretax yield therefore becomes the expected before-tax cash flow of $54,512 divided by the

Table 16.1	Range of Possible Outcomes with Financial Leverage		
	Lower Bound	*Expected*	*Upper Bound*
Net Operating Income	$100,000	$125,000	$150,000
Less: Debt Service	70,488	70,488	70,488
Pretax Cash Flow	$ 29,512	$ 54,512	$ 79,512
Current Yield*	9.8%	18.2%	26.5%

*Current Yield = $\dfrac{\text{Pretax Cash Flow}}{\text{Equity Investment}}$:

Lower Bound = $\dfrac{\$29,512}{\$300,000}$ = .098, or 9.8%

Expected = $\dfrac{\$54,512}{\$300,000}$ = .182, or 18.2%

Upper Bound = $\dfrac{\$79,512}{\$300,000}$ = .265, or 26.5%

$300,000 equity investment, or 18.2 percent. The range of possible annual pre-tax yields with the mortgage loan is from 9.8 percent to 26.5 percent, as shown in Table 16.1.

Alterations in the range of possible outcomes due to financial leverage are illustrated in Figure 16.1. Leverage raises the expected annual pre-tax yield (depicted by the small vertical bars) from 12.5 percent to 18.2 percent, but it also increases the range of possible annual yields rather impressively. As depicted by the horizontal bars in Figure 16.1, annual yields with leverage can fall significantly below the range of possible yields without leverage. The graph also illustrates that the upper end of the range of possible yields is greatly increased by the leverage. This possibility is sometimes referred to as *upside risk* and is a much desired consequence. Whether the enhanced yield expectation and the greater upside risk justify the amplified downside risk attendant to financial leverage depends upon investor risk preferences, as discussed later in this chapter.

Since mortgage lenders have a prior claim on net operating income, with investors' before-tax cash flow being a residual, increasing the amount of borrowed funds (and thus the debt service obligation) also increases the probability that net operating income will be insufficient to meet the debt service obligation. This is an additional dimension of financial risk.

To illustrate, consider a 28-unit apartment project expected to generate $10,000 per unit of gross income. Assume the units require annual expenditures of approximately $5,000 per unit for variable operating expenses. An expected $5,000 per unit remains to cover fixed expenditures—including debt service—and to provide a return to the investor. If all the units are rented for the entire year at the expected rental rate, annual cash flow will be $140,000 before debt service and other fixed costs. Further assume that fixed charges other than debt

Figure 16.1   Most Likely Current Yield and Range of Possible Variation

Current (Pretax) Yield

service (these are comprised of insurance and property taxes) total $20,000. Expected rental revenues net of variable costs, at various occupancy levels, are depicted in Figure 16.2.

Occupancy levels are measured on the horizontal axis of Figure 16.2. Fixed costs are by definition the same regardless of occupancy level. Revenue varies directly with occupancy. Since, as we have seen, each unit generates $5,000 above its variable costs of operation, 100 percent occupancy will generate $140,000 to cover fixed costs and profit. Of this amount, $20,000 is applied to cover fixed costs, with the balance accruing to the investor. Therefore, with 100 percent occupancy the investor will earn before-tax cash flow of $140,000 minus $20,000, or $120,000.

Reductions in occupancy levels diminish revenue available for fixed costs and profit without affecting the fixed cost element. The entire reduction,

Figure 16.2   Break-even Occupancy Levels with and Without Financial Leverage

therefore, is reflected in reduced profits. At a 14 percent occupancy level (four of the 28 units rented for the entire year) revenue minus variable costs exactly equals the $20,000 of fixed costs; pretax profits are zero. The before-tax break-even occupancy level with no debt financing is therefore 14 percent.

Now see what happens when debt financing is used. Assume our investor borrows $750,000 at 12 percent interest, with the debt to be paid in equal monthly installments of principal and interest over 25 years. The monthly payment will be approximately $7,900 and the annual debt service obligation will be 12 times this amount, or $94,800. As with other fixed costs, the debt service obligation remains invariant regardless of occupancy levels.

Figure 16.2 also illustrates this revised financial picture. As before, when fully occupied the project will generate $140,000 above variable costs. Every vacant unit (if it remains vacant for a full year) will reduce this amount by $5,000. Since fixed costs and debt service are prior obligations, the entire reduction in revenue represents diminished before-tax cash flow to the investor. A full year's revenue from 23 units is required to meet fixed costs plus debt service. This represents an 82 percent occupancy level just to break even on the project (before taxes). Financial leverage has increased the occupancy level necessary to maintain solvency from 14 percent to 82 percent and has thereby greatly increased the probability (that is, the risk) of insolvency.

Figure 16.3 illustrates the same point but assumes rents are varied to maintain a target occupancy level. This alternative presentation places per-unit rental rates on the horizontal axis.

Insurable Risk

Accurate prediction of losses due to fire, flood and other natural hazards is virtually impossible for any particular building or property. It is possible, of course, to calculate the odds of such a loss, based on statistical sampling techniques. But to an investor who has just been wiped out by fire or flood, how significant is the fact that the likelihood of the occurrence was, say, one in 10,000?

Predictability based on statistical averages is the foundation of the insurance industry. Because their dollar losses are relatively predictable, insurers can develop fee schedules that compensate for all projected losses plus a premium for expenses and profits and a reserve for the unexpected. For large firms, the degree of uncertainty involved in the insurance function is very small. Investors can transfer many risk elements to insurance firms that specialize in bearing statistically predictable risk.

Fire and extended-coverage insurance shifts the risk of property damage by fire, smoke, wind, hail, lightning and so on, from the property owner to an insurance company. Liability insurance protects against claims resulting from injuries sustained on the property. Damage to plate glass can be covered, as can damage due to malfunctions in sprinkler systems. Other types of insurance that property owners frequently obtain include protection against loss or damage to building contents and coverage on mechanical equipment such as boilers, hot water heaters and air-conditioning units. If building owners have

Figure 16.3   **Break-even Rental Rates with and Without Financial Leverage**

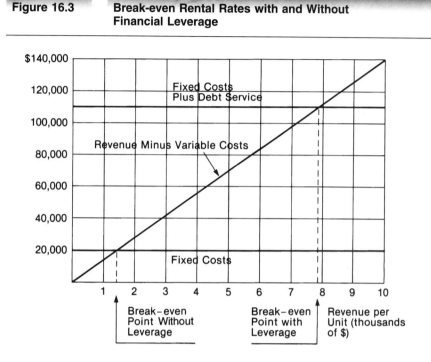

employees working on the premises, workers' compensation insurance may also be necessary.

Business Risk

Even the most precisely calibrated operating projections are subject to gross errors. The likelihood that actual operating results will vary from expectations is sometimes called *business risk*.

Business risk stems both from factors internal to the investment equation and from circumstances attributable to the economic environment surrounding a project. Management inefficiencies may cause operating expenses to exceed expectations, for example, or may result in an inordinately high vacancy rate. Sloppy credit investigation and lax rent collection practices may spawn unexpectedly high credit losses. Any of these events, all internal to the investment equation, will cause net operating income to fall below the forecast.

The economic environment may be less propitious than anticipated, and cause an unexpectedly low level of demand for real estate services. This means either a higher-than-expected vacancy rate or reduced rental rates. In either event, an unfortunate by-product will be gross rental revenue below that anticipated at the time an investment commitment was made. This in turn means that net operating income will fall below expectations.

CONTROLLING RISK

Risk analysis, after years of virtual neglect, has become a popular topic in real estate literature. Chapter 19 synthesizes much of current writing on the subject and consolidates generally accepted contemporary techniques into a comprehensive approach. These sophisticated techniques, however, are inappropriate when the additional cost of analysis more than offsets the benefit from avoiding selection error. For relatively inexpensive projects, or where outcomes are highly predictable, less complex analysis might be in order. Moreover, risk can often be greatly reduced with relatively simple risk management procedures.

Reducing Risk through Judicious Investment Selection

One way to decrease risk is simply to invest in less risky projects. Accepting only those opportunities whose outcomes are fairly well ascertainable reduces default risk essentially to zero and virtually eliminates uncertainty associated with the outcome of the investment itself (though not the uncertainty and risk of purchasing power loss through an inflation rate that exceeds the rate of return on the investment).

An unfortunate by-product of this strategy is that opportunities for extraordinary profits are also eliminated. The tendency for expected return to increase or decrease along with associated risk is an inescapable characteristic of free markets. Should opportunities for anticipated gains unaccompanied by commensurate risk appear, investors will quickly enter the market and drive expected returns down to a level approximating those available in other investment opportunities of the same general risk category.

There is, of course, a whole spectrum of risky investment opportunities in the economy. Financial markets allow investors to interact in competitive bidding so that an appropriate level of return is assigned by the market to each opportunity, commensurate with the level of risk perceived by market participants. Figure 16.4 depicts the trade-off between risk and expected return necessary to attract a potential investor into a project or projects. As risk increases, the investor requires a higher expected return to compensate for the additional risk exposure. Keep in mind that this diagram reflects investor *expectations* only. Expected profits may never materialize—the investor may in fact suffer substantial losses. But for the investor to accept a project in the first place, potential reward must be sufficiently high to justify bearing the perceived risk.

Whereas Figure 16.4 depicts expectations of an individual market participant, actual outcomes are more likely to be as illustrated in Figure 16.5. The dots in the diagram depict actual outcomes of market ventures as they relate to expectations of participants (depicted by the solid line *rr*). If the market is efficient, then actual outcomes will vary randomly about expected outcomes reflected by the market line (market efficiency is discussed in Chapter 2). Unusually high or low gains relative to expectations will occur randomly and will tend to cancel each other out. Since all participants in an efficient market have approximately

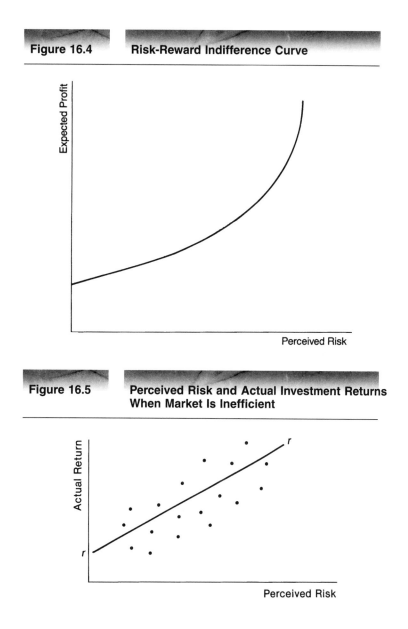

Figure 16.4   **Risk-Reward Indifference Curve**

Figure 16.5   **Perceived Risk and Actual Investment Returns When Market Is Inefficient**

the same information and draw approximately the same conclusions from that information, outcomes for individual participants will also vary randomly in approximately the same proportion as do outcomes for the entire market.

The significance of all this is that in an efficient market the only way to reduce risk associated with single investment ventures is to choose a venture with a lower expected return. We noted in Chapter 2, however, that real estate markets tend to be somewhat less efficient than are organized securities markets. As a consequence, real estate investors who exploit market inefficiencies are able to reap extraordinary profits without shouldering commensurately greater risk. To do this, they must consistently identify opportunities whose outcomes lie to the left of line *rr* in Figure 16.5. They might accomplish this by attaining a monopoly position within certain locations or with respect to significant market information.

Diversification as a Risk Management Tool

Investors can further control risk exposure by considering the relationship between assets already held and potential new acquisitions. Since factors influencing profitability and market value do not uniformly impact all properties, holders of diversified portfolios can expect a more stable (and predictable) pattern of earnings than would result from concentrating all wealth in a single project. Diversification does not ensure risk reduction, however, unless properties are chosen to avoid high correlation between investment performance among the various assets.

Portfolio diversification is a relatively simple proposition for multimillion dollar real estate investment corporations. They can diversify geographically to reduce the impact of regional shifts in economic activity. Likewise, they can easily acquire any desired mix of apartment complexes, office towers, suburban office parks and so on. Chapter 20 addresses this concept more extensively.

But most investors face budget constraints that complicate diversification efforts. If it means sacrificing economies of scale by investing in smaller properties, diversification may entail forgoing some expected return.

One solution is to pool equity funds with other investors facing the same dilemma. This rather popular approach to the problem is often called *syndication.* A frequent arrangement involves a promoter who organizes the syndicate and manages the venture for a fee plus a percentage ownership, while passive investors contribute all or most of the equity funds. Most syndicates are organized as limited partnerships. Syndications are discussed in greater detail in Chapter 25. Another alternative is to buy shares in equity Real Estate Investment Trusts (REITs). Since major income tax legislation in 1986 radically altered the tax shelter benefits from real estate limited partnerships, equity REITs have become relatively more significant as an investment vehicle. REITs are discussed in greater detail in Chapter 24.

Market Research as a Risk Control Tool

Real estate investors make assumptions about a venture's ability to generate income over an extended period. Risk can usefully be viewed as the possibility of variance between assumptions and actual outcomes. One of the best methods of reducing that variance is to make more accurate assumptions.

Part Two of this text discusses techniques for generating better information upon which to base assumptions. Meticulous study of market data permits better estimates of current operating results and more reliable forecasts.

Property Management To Control Risk

Professional property managers are uniquely positioned to enhance the accuracy of cash-flow projections. Their access to market data and their knowledge and experience regarding the economics of property operations are valuable forecasting ingredients. Competent management also plays a vital role in making outcomes conform to assumptions. Resident managers are a critical element, for they control day-to-day operations. They may be able to enhance revenue by controlling vacancy and rent losses and reducing tenant turnover. They can hold expenses down by monitoring all operations and through astute preventative maintenance.

Shifting Risk to Tenants

Lease agreements often permit landlords to shift some risk to tenants. *Expense stops* commit tenants to pay specified operating expenses above some contractual level. *Triple net leases* make tenants responsible for all expenses.

An additional strategy frequently employed with long-term leases pegs rental rates to changes in a price-level index such as the consumer price index or the wholesale price index. This effectively shifts purchasing power risk (the risk that future receipts will have less purchasing power due to general price inflation) to tenants.

Hedging To Control Risk

Hedging, a common practice in securities and commodities markets, may also reduce risk for real estate investors. *Purchase options* are a common form of hedging used in real estate. When contemplating a development project, for example, a developer might purchase an option to buy a selected site. This provides time to plan, to obtain required governmental approvals and to secure needed financing. Soil and engineering studies may also be completed while property is under option. Purchase options thus provide time to eliminate some of the uncertainty associated with the development process.

Interim or "standby" financing commitments are another hedging mechanism used by investor-developers. To avoid being committed to an unfavorably high interest rate, a developer who believes rates will decline during the construction period may purchase a loan commitment that is binding on the lender but is an option to the developer. The commitment is exercised only if better terms cannot be obtained.

RISK PREFERENCES AND PROFIT EXPECTATIONS

After all viable risk control techniques are exploited, a core of unavoidable risk remains. Attitudes toward this residual risk will vary with the personalities of investors and with their capacities to absorb financial reverses, as well as with personal investment objectives.

Typical investor attitudes toward risk are illustrated in Figure 16.6. Rational investors prefer a higher to a lower return for a given level of risk; for a specified level of return they prefer less risk to more risk. They accept additional risk only if accompanied by additional expected investment rewards.

Figure 16.6 also demonstrates increasing risk aversion as total risk exposure increases. To induce the investor whose attitude is depicted in Figure 16.6 to accept an increase in risk exposure from r_1 to r_2, there must be the expectation that returns will increase from P_1 to P_2. To persuade the same investor to accept another increment of risk (from r_2 to r_3), expected rewards must be increased by a substantially larger amount. The investor becomes so risk-averse when total risk exposure reaches r_4 that no amount of expected additional reward can induce further movement into the realm of risk. Because the investor will be equally satisfied by all risk-reward combinations depicted by the line in Figure 16.6, it is sometimes called a *risk-reward indifference curve.*

Recall the earlier observation that rational investors prefer less risk for a given level of expected return. This behavioral trait is depicted in Figure 16.6 by the arrow extending to the left from the risk-reward indifference curve, indicating that the investor will prefer any combination of risk and return that can be plotted on the figure in that direction. Since rational investors also prefer a greater return with a given level of risk, the arrow extending upward from the curve indicates a direction in which risk and reward combinations will leave our

Figure 16.6	Attitudes Toward Risk Differ

investor feeling better off than will any combination found on the curve. In fact, a whole set of indifference curves could be plotted, filling the entire plane upon which values from the two axes of Figure 16.6 intersect. Any curve above that shown in Figure 16.6 will represent a series of risk-reward combinations that will leave the investor more satisfied than the combinations on the illustrated curve. Since we have posited that the depicted curve illustrates minimum acceptable risk-reward combinations, it follows that all combinations above the one illustrated are even more acceptable. For this reason the area above the curve in Figure 16.6 is labeled "acceptable risk-reward combinations."

Similarly, it can be demonstrated that the investor will be less satisfied with more risk for a given level of return (depicted by the right-facing arrow in Figure 16.6) or less expected return for a given level of risk (depicted in Figure 16.6 by the arrow extending downward from the curve). No combination of risk and expected return below the curve depicting minimum acceptable combinations will satisfy the investor whose attitude is reflected in Figure 16.6. The area below the minimum acceptable set of combinations is therefore labeled "unacceptable risk-reward combinations."

Degrees of Risk Aversion

Of course the precise configuration of risk-reward indifference curves will depend upon the individual investor's personal attitude toward risk. Functions depicting various investors' attitudes will not necessarily have the same shape. The more risk-averse the individual, the more steeply sloped the indifference curve showing that person's preferences. The indifference curve of an investor who is completely indifferent toward risk would have no curvature at all; some investors may even be willing to trade expected return for the opportunity to bear greater risk and will therefore have a downward-sloping risk-reward indifference curve.

Rational Risk Taking

Rational risk taking is epitomized by successful insurance firms. This industry turns a handsome and highly predictable profit by allowing insured parties to substitute the certainty of a small loss (the insurance premium) for the uncertainty of a larger loss from catastrophes. Insurance companies can do this through astute risk management. They calculate the odds and charge a premium sufficient to compensate for the chance of loss.

Insurance firms might be characterized as risk takers by design. So might rational and knowledgeable real estate investors. Before committing substantial resources, such investors will do the following:

- Specify investment objectives concerning return on investment, timing of return and acceptable risk levels.
- Identify major risks involved and quantify them as completely as possible.
- Eliminate some risks, transfer others via insurance or other techniques and constrain remaining risks to acceptable levels.

- Make decisions to accept or reject specific investments, based on whether expected returns justify bearing the remaining risks in view of the contribution the venture makes toward overall investment objectives.

MEASURING RISK

Instead of quantifying risk perceptions, real estate analysts and investors have traditionally developed subjective impressions and attached a return premium in addition to that required in the absence of "above normal" risk. Traditional approaches to incorporating the risk premium have included shorter payback periods, higher required rates of return or downward adjustments to projected cash flows. All these techniques result in smaller investment values—the amount an investor is willing to pay for a project.

Traditional risk-adjustment techniques share a serious shortcoming: they do not permit quantification of the risk element. This makes inter-project comparisons difficult even for the analyst doing the risk estimating; it renders completely impossible the task of communicating risk perception to a second party. When analysts are working with client investors, the dilemma becomes more acute. Of what avail is an analyst's excellent grasp of the risk element if it cannot be communicated to the client?

Techniques are available for communicating risk assessment without incorporating the analyst's personal risk-bearing proclivities. Such techniques are discussed in Chapter 18. They are offered as alternatives to the traditional methods that are explored in Chapter 17.

SUMMARY

Risk is a ubiquitous problem in real estate investment analysis. Some risks can be shifted to other parties or minimized through investment-management techniques. But risk avoidance has a price. Many investors purposely shoulder risk because the expected rewards for so doing outweigh potential costs.

Risk must be made amenable to measurement and quantification before it can be properly incorporated into the analysis. Only then can trained analysts communicate their perceptions to clients, enabling the latter to make informed decisions.

Traditional means of adjusting for risk inextricably intertwine the analyst's risk perception and personal risk preference. These techniques are appropriate only on the rare occasions when analysts and clients share a common attitude toward risk. Because risk preference is influenced not only by wealth and pre-existing risk exposure, but also by subtle psychological factors, common attitudes toward risk are about as likely as identical fingerprint patterns.

RECOMMENDED READINGS

Brigham, Eugene F. *Fundamentals of Financial Management.* 7th ed. (Ft. Worth, TX: The Dryden Press, 1994).

REVIEW QUESTIONS

1. What is the effect of financial leverage on the pretax yield of a property? What is its effect on the level of risk associated with the venture?
2. What is insurable risk?
3. What is business risk, and how can it be reduced for the investor?
4. Are real estate markets efficient?
5. How is diversification used as a risk management tool?
6. How do landlords shift risk to tenants?
7. What steps are involved in rational risk taking?
8. List some of the traditional risk-adjustment techniques and their common shortcomings.

DISCUSSION QUESTIONS

1. Risk can be characterized as diversifiable or nondiversifiable, depending upon whether it is possible to eliminate the risk by holding a sufficiently diversified portfolio. Insurable risk is diversifiable. Why, then, don't real estate investors simply eliminate such risks by diversifying rather than paying an insurance company to handle the risk?
2. Since diversification, appropriately pursued, reduces risk, should investors extend their diversification until all diversifiable risk has been eliminated?
3. Diversification has been described as "not putting all of one's eggs in one basket," with the connotation that this is a good policy. Mark Twain's response was, "Put all of your eggs in one basket and watch that basket." Comment on this.
4. How might risk be:
   a. shifted by the wording of tenant leases?
   b. avoided by choice of organizational entity?

CHAPTER 17

Traditional Risk-Adjustment Methods

This chapter reviews traditional risk-adjustment and analysis practices with a view toward demonstrating their major strengths and shortcomings. Adjustments to the payback period, adjustments to the discount rate and adjustments to projected cash flow are discussed. In each case, both theoretical and practical objections to the techniques are presented. Partitioning and sensitivity analysis are then introduced as useful tools of analysis that have more recently found their way into common practice.

THE PAYBACK-PERIOD APPROACH

Recall from Chapter 13 that the payback period is the time required for cash inflows from an investment to equal the original cash outlay. If, for example, an investment requires a down payment of $16,000 and is expected to yield $2,000 per annum, the payback period is eight years. This is determined by dividing the down payment by the annual net cash inflow:

$$\frac{\$16,000}{\$2,000} = 8$$

Proponents of this technique adjust for risk by varying the minimum acceptable payback period. Risky investments are expected to have a shorter payback period than those that embody less risk. The precise amount of the adjustment is necessarily subjective, since risk itself is generally not measured. Analysts simply state how much shorter a particular investment's payback period is required to be, based on a subjective impression of risk.

Payback-period analysis is an inadequate method of evaluation even in the absence of risk, and adding risk renders it even less useful. Desirability of real estate opportunities often depends heavily upon expected gain from disposal. Risk, in those cases, is primarily a function of the certainty associated with the anticipated sales price. But if the disposal point extends beyond the payback period, neither anticipated benefit nor attendant risk will be included in the analysis.

Consider Example 17.1. A four-year payback period is virtually certain. But how can the required payback period be adjusted for the uncertainty associated with anticipated cash flow from sale of the property five years hence?

Example 17.1

A warehouse, available for $800,000, is almost certain to yield a net annual cash flow of $200,000 for the next five years, after which it is expected to have a market value such that the net cash flow from disposal will be $1,000,000. The annual cash flow during the holding period is secured by a tenant with an impeccable credit rating, who has five years remaining on her lease. The expected selling price after five years is predicated upon the tenant renewing the lease—an eventuality that is far from certain. If the tenant does not renew, then the selling price will depend on the investor's ability to find a comparable tenant at the same rental rate.

RISK-ADJUSTED DISCOUNT RATE

Discounted cash-flow analysis techniques are discussed in Chapter 14 and explained in Appendix A. Given the appropriate rate, discounting anticipated cash flows to arrive at an opportunity's present value is a mere arithmetical exercise. Left unanswered is the question of what discount rate is appropriate. The answer depends on how the risk-adjustment problem is handled.

Traditionally, the discounted cash-flow model has incorporated a risk-adjusted discount rate. A risk-free rate is proposed to represent the pure time value of money. To this a premium is added to compensate for risk. The risk-free rate is (presumably) the same regardless of the nature of the proposal under consideration, changing only to reflect variation in the disutility of waiting. Risk premiums, in contrast, vary with each proposal. The amount of the premium depends on attendant risk and the investor's attitude toward the risk.

The Risk-Free Discount Rate

Choosing an appropriate risk-free rate is more a theoretical than a practical problem. Most analysts simply select a risk-adjusted rate without bothering to stipulate values separately for the risk-free rate and the risk premium.

Analysts who wish to demonstrate the derivation of their risk adjustments do, of course, have this problem. Most adopt the expedient of using the rate available on short-term federal securities. Because they are short-term and highly secure, interest rates on Treasury bills are nearly devoid of premiums for default risk or interest rate risk.

The Risk Premium

Adjustments for perceived risk should be based on an investor's risk-return trade-off function, as discussed in Chapter 16. In practice, real estate analysts who use this approach have generally chosen a risk premium that embodies their perceptions of the risk and their personal risk-return trade-off functions. But since trade-off functions reflect individual attitudes toward risk, this will be appropriate only if the analyst's attitude corresponds exactly to that of the client-investor. Because attitude is determined by factors such as total wealth, pre-existing risk exposure and personal psychological preferences, there is no reason to suppose that an analyst's attitude will ever exactly match a client's. Indeed, even the analyst's attitude will likely differ when applied to an investment analyzed for a client rather than where the analyst's own resources are at risk. Making this approach operational by determining the appropriate risk premium presents a seemingly insurmountable hurdle.

Practical and Theoretical Problems

In spite of its problems, the risk-adjusted discount rate is probably the most commonly used approach. It is, nevertheless, fraught with both theoretical and practical difficulties.[1]

When riskless and risk premium portions of the discount rate are considered separately, the risk-free rate accounts for the pure time-value of money. But when an additional discount factor is introduced for risk, it also incorporates an adjustment for time. As a consequence, future risk is discounted more heavily than near-term risk. Yet near-term risk may be greater than far-distant risk.

Consider, for example, a new apartment project. The probability of construction cost overruns and of an unexpectedly lengthy rent-up period is generally far higher than the probability of significantly misestimating subsequent operating results. Yet the risk premium during the latter period is greater than that of the former. Each subsequent year of operation is discounted more heavily than the preceding, in spite of the fact that as neighborhoods mature, operating outcomes generally become more predictable.

Example 17.2

A ten-year project is under consideration, for which the appropriate risk premium is estimated to be six percent and the risk-free discount rate is estimated to be five percent. The overall discount rate, the sum of the risk-free rate and the risk premium, is therefore 11 percent. Discounting involves dividing each year's cash-flow projection by a number derived by raising the discount-rate-plus-one to a power equaling the number of years before the cash is expected to be received.

Example 17.2 illustrates the problem. Discount factors for the first three years (discounting at 11 percent) are, respectively, 1.11, $(1.11)^2$ and $(1.11)^3$. Were there no risk involved, the discount rate would be simply one plus the riskless rate, or 1.05. The factors for the first three years then would be 1.05, $(1.05)^2$ and $(1.05)^3$. The factor by which anticipated cash flow for each year is divided to account for perceived risk is the differences between risk-free and the risk-adjusted factors. For the first three years, the risk adjustments are:

Year	Risk Adjusted Discount Factor	Riskless Discount Factor	Risk Adjustment Factor
1	1.1100	1.0500	0.0600
2	1.2321	1.1025	0.1296
3	1.3676	1.1576	0.2100

Since the risk adjustment factor grows through time, investment desirability is more greatly impaired the further into the future the anticipated risk lies. This holds true in spite of the fact that the riskless discount rate has already accounted for the time value of money. A problem of double accounting for time is clearly evident.

For some investment ventures, risk might appropriately be viewed as increasing with the length of time involved in the forecast. H.Y. Chen and others have shown that when risk is viewed as an increasing function of time, the risk-adjusted discount rate is theoretically sound.[2] But for projects where risk is not a function of time, the technique is seriously flawed.

A second shortcoming is the impracticality of expressing risk-adjusted discount rates as policy statements. A policy that specifies minimum risk-return combinations permits subordinates to screen out obviously unacceptable investment projects. Only those opportunities that meet minimum standards are passed for review by final decision-makers. Because risk premiums must be determined individually for each project, they are not well suited to a policy of delegating preliminary investment decisions.

THE CERTAINTY-EQUIVALENT TECHNIQUE

Double accounting for risk in the risk-adjusted discount rate can be eliminated by adjusting projected cash flows instead of discount rates. The risk-adjusted cash-flow projections are then discounted at the risk-free rate. This approach, called the *certainty-equivalent technique,* also neatly sidesteps the need to quantify risk perceptions. It does introduce other practical problems, however. These include the cost of determining appropriate certainty-equivalent adjustments and the increased risk of client alienation. When final decisions are made by a committee instead of by an individual, these new problems become insurmountable.

Deriving Certainty-Equivalent Factors

Instead of a "best estimate" of future cash flows, the certainty-equivalent cash-flow technique substitutes a lesser amount that leaves the investor indifferent between expected receipt of the best estimate (with associated risk of variation from expectations) and absolute certainty of receiving the lesser substitute. This substitute amount, or *certainty equivalent,* is discounted at the risk-free rate.

An early step in determining certainty equivalents is to explain carefully to the investor the expected future business environment. After being acquainted with major risk factors, the client is asked to indicate a preference for forecasted cash flows or specified riskless cash-flow alternatives. Various riskless alternatives are postulated until an amount is specified that leaves the investor indifferent between the risky and the riskless flows. This procedure might result in a set of certainty equivalents for a project such as those in Example 17.3.

Example 17.3

A project offers an anticipated net cash flow of $10,000 per annum for three years, followed at the end of the third year by an anticipated net cash receipt of $80,000 from sale of the project. Realization of the cash from disposal is contingent upon drastic alteration of currently prevailing economic conditions. If anticipated economic changes do not materialize, the sales proceeds will be much less. Perceived risk and the investor's attitude toward risk are reflected in the following certainty-equivalent cash-flow transformation:

	Cash Flow		Certainty-Equivalent Factor
Year	Expected	Equivalent Risk-Free Alternative	
1	$10,000	$ 9,600	0.960
2	10,000	9,600	0.960
3	10,000	9,600	0.960
3	80,000	68,800	0.860

The certainty-equivalent factors in Example 17.3 are derived by dividing the risk-free equivalent cash flow by the expected cash flow for each year. The risk-free, or certainty-equivalent, cash flow is the amount of money, receivable with certainty, that is just as satisfactory to the investor as the risky expectation of receiving the forecast cash flow for that year. Thus the investor in Example 17.3 is indifferent between 96 cents received for certain in years one through three and the risky expectation of receiving $1 from operations in each of those years.

The riskier an expected cash flow is perceived to be, the smaller the certainty-equivalent factor. In Example 17.3, expected sales proceeds at the end of the projection period are viewed as more problematic than the project's annual cash flows from operations. Hence a smaller certainty-equivalent factor is associated with the $80,000 expected cash flow from that source.

Implied in the preceding discussion is that the present value (*PV*) of an anticipated series of annual cash flows (*CF*₁) can be expressed as:

$$PV = \sum_{t=1}^{n} \frac{CF_t}{(1 + k)^t} = \sum_{t=1}^{n} \frac{\alpha \, CF_t}{(1 + i)^t}$$

where *k* is a risk-adjusted discount rate, *i* is the risk-free rate and α represents a certainty-equivalent factor such as illustrated in Example 17.3.

If, for example, the appropriate risk-free rate of return in Example 17.3 is 5.25 percent, then the present value of the certainty-equivalent cash flows is approximately $85,000. Likewise, expected cash flows have a present value of approximately $85,000 when discounted at 10 percent. This implies a risk premium in the risk-adjusted discount rate of approximately ten minus 5.25, or 4.75 percent. Here are the computations:

Year	Expected Cash Flow	Present Value at 10%	Certainty-Equivalent Cash Flow	Present Value at 5.25%
1	$10,000	$ 9,091	$ 9,600	$ 9,121
2	10,000	8,264	9,600	8,666
3	10,000	7,513	9,600	8,234
3	80,000	60,105	68,800	59,010
Totals		$84,973		$85,031

Problems with the Certainty-Equivalent Approach

Certainty equivalents, in effect, translate risk-preference functions such as discussed in Chapter 16 into risk-indifference functions. Determining numerical values for these certainty-equivalent factors is the principal difficulty associated with applying the approach. The values can be estimated by presenting an investor with a series of combinations of risky and risk-free cash flows and asking for a stated preference between each set. An extended series of such experiments will result in a preference map representing the investor's attitude toward risk. From this map, certainty-equivalent factors can be extracted.

Getting an investor to state preferences in this fashion, however, is difficult and time-consuming. The time and the attendant expense might cause the investor to rebel. Success depends on the analyst's powers of persuasion. These powers will be sorely taxed as the necessity of making ever finer distinctions between risky and risk-free cash flows becomes increasingly frustrating to a client who is both paying for the exercise and doing the bulk of the mental work.

Where preliminary investment decisions are delegated, this method is particularly unsatisfactory. Because a new preference map must be drawn for each investment opportunity (reflecting the risk elements peculiar to that venture) and for each decision maker (reflecting personal attitudes toward risk), the certainty-equivalent method cannot be grafted onto a policy statement without major modification in the way certainty-equivalent factors are generated.

One such modification, suggested by Steven E. Bolten,[3] is to first quantify the risk element by using standard deviation as a risk measure. Cash-flow estimates are then reduced by a number of standard deviations to ensure virtual certainty that actual cash flow will prove to equal or exceed the certainty equivalent cash flow. This eliminates the subjective attitude toward risk associated with an individual decision maker and permits discounting at the risk-free discount rate.

PARTITIONING PRESENT VALUES

We have seen that real estate is valued solely for the anticipated future stream of benefits that ownership bestows. Real estate investment, therefore, can be seen as the purchase of a set of assumptions about a property's ability to produce a benefit stream. The generally accepted measure of benefits is after-tax cash flow. Factors contributing to this flow include annual pre-tax cash flows, income tax consequences, loan amortization, changes in property value over the projected holding period and so forth.

In Part One, investment value was divided into present value of equity and present value of debt. Similarly, the present value of the equity position can be partitioned into its component parts. Expressing each component as a percentage of the total permits the relative importance of each to be assessed. Components that comprise major segments of the total present value of the equity position will merit extended analysis.

Example 17.4

Simon's Sylvan Setting, a luxury apartment complex, can be purchased for $2,300,000, inclusive of transaction costs. The venture requires an equity investment of $500,000, with the $1,800,000 balance of the purchase price to be financed via a fully amortizing, 30-year mortgage note. Interest on the borrowed funds will be at 12 percent per annum. Payments on the mortgage note will be made monthly. Depreciation allowances are based on a building value of $2,000,000, employing the straight-line method over 27.5 years. The property is expected to be worth

$2,900,000, net of transaction costs, at the end of an expected six-year holding period. The investor is in the 28 percent marginal income tax bracket and expects to remain in that bracket throughout the investment period. If the property is acquired, it is expected that the closing will occur early in the first month of the tax year and that the subsequent sale will close late in the last month of the sixth year of the investment period. This information is incorporated with estimates of rental revenue and operating expenses to generate the six-year cash-flow forecast presented in Table 17.1.

Consider the investment proposal in Example 17.4. Table 17.1 contains after-tax cash-flow projections based on the data in the example, using procedures discussed in Part Three. Table 17.2 details the after-tax cash-flow forecast from disposal at the end of the anticipated holding period. Tax due on sale is calculated as illustrated in Chapter 10.

Table 17.3 illustrates the technique of discounting to express expected after-tax cash flows in terms of present value equivalents. To estimate the importance of each element in the analysis in Table 17.3, discount each element separately. For example, note in Table 17.3 that the first year's expected after-tax cash flow of $13,237 has a present value equivalent of $12,034 when discounted at 10 percent and rounded to the nearest whole dollar. Reference to Table 17.1 reveals that the first year's after-tax cash-flow estimate is comprised of the following elements:

Effective Gross Income	$393,000
Less: Operating Expenses	177,000
Net Operating Income	$216,000
Less: Annual Debt Service	222,180
Before-Tax Cash Flow	$ (6,180)
Plus: Income Tax Savings	19,417
After-Tax Cash-Flow Forecast	$ 13,237

Discounting each of the above elements separately and summing the present value equivalents yields the same present value estimate (except for a $1 rounding error) shown in Table 17.3. The alternative computations are:

	Amount	×	Present Value Factor	=	Present Value
Gross Income	$ 393,000		.9091		$ 357,276
Less:					
Operating Expenses	(177,000)		.9091		(160,911)
Debt Service	(222,180)		.9091		(201,984)
Plus: Tax Savings	19,417		.9091		17,652
Present Value of After-Tax Cash Flow					$ 12,033

Table 17.1 **Simon's Sylvan Setting, Six-Year Cash-Flow Projection**

	Year					
	1	*2*	*3*	*4*	*5*	*6*
Effective Gross Income	$393,000	$405,000	$417,000	$429,000	$442,000	$455,000
Less: Operating Expense	177,000	194,000	200,000	205,000	212,000	220,000
Net Operating Income	$216,000	$211,000	$217,000	$224,000	$230,000	$235,000
Less: Debt Service	222,180	222,180	222,180	222,180	222,180	222,180
Before-Tax Cash Flow	$ (6,180)	$(11,180)	$ (5,180)	$ 1,820	$ 7,820	$ 12,820
Plus: Principal	6,532	7,360	8,294	9,346	10,531	11,866
Less: Depreciation	69,697	72,727	72,727	72,727	72,727	69,697
Taxable Gain (Loss)	$(69,345)	$(76,547)	$(69,613)	$(61,561)	$(54,376)	$(45,011)
Tax (Tax Saving)	$(19,417)	$(21,433)	$(19,492)	$(17,237)	$(15,225)	$(12,603)
Before-Tax Cash Flow	$ (6,180)	$(11,180)	$ (5,180)	$ 1,820	$ 7,820	$ 12,820
Tax Consequences	19,417	21,433	19,492	17,237	15,225	12,603
After-Tax Cash Flow	$ 13,237	$ 10,253	$ 14,312	$ 19,057	$ 23,045	$ 25,423

Table 17.2 **Simon's Sylvan Setting: After-Tax Cash Flow from Sale**

Sales Price (Net)		$2,900,000
Less:		
Mortgage Balance	$1,746,071	
Tax Due on Sale	288,484	2,034,555
After-Tax Cash from Sale		$ 865,445

Constituent parts of the after-tax cash-flow forecast for each year can be discounted separately in this manner. Table 17.4 shows present value equivalents in this fashion. Note that the final column of Table 17.4 is the same as the present value estimates computed in Table 17.3, except for a $4 difference due to cumulative rounding error.

The present value of each constituent part of the expected after-tax cash flow, as computed in Table 17.4, is presented in summary form in Table 17.5. The final column of Table 17.5 presents each element as a percent of the total present value estimate. These measures give the analyst valuable clues concerning the seriousness of errors in the forecast.

Note, for example, that the anticipated outcome is almost totally dependent upon cash flows from tax savings and appreciation during the holding period. Approximately 14 percent and 60 percent of the present value, respectively, is expected to be generated from these sources. Consequently, results will be disproportionately dependent upon appreciation, placing a premium upon accurate forecasting of increases in market value during the holding period.

Table 17.3   **Simon's Sylvan Setting: Measures of Investment Performance**

Year	After-Tax Cash Flow	Present Value Factor @ 10%	Discounted Cash Flow
1	$ 13,237	.9091	$ 12,034
2	10,253	.8264	8,473
3	14,312	.7513	10,753
4	19,057	.6830	13,016
5	23,045	.6209	14,309
6	25,423	.5645	14,351
Sales Proceeds	865,445	.5645	488,544
Present Value of Equity			$ 561,480
Available Financing			1,800,000
Investment Value			$2,361,480

Table 17.4   **Simon's Sylvan Setting, Present Value of Partitioned Cash Flows***

Year	Gross Rent $\times 1/(1 + i)^t$	−	Operating Expense $\times 1/(1 + i)^t$	−	Debt Service $\times 1/(1 + i)^t$	+	Tax Consequence $\times 1/(1 + i)^t$	=	After-Tax Cash Flow $\times 1/(1 + i)^t$
1	$ 357,276		$160,911		$201,984		$17,652		$12,033
2	334,692		160,322		183,610		17,712		8,472
3	313,292		150,260		166,924		14,644		10,752
4	293,007		140,015		151,749		11,773		13,016
5	274,438		131,631		137,952		9,453		14,308
6	256,848		124,190		125,421		7,114		14,351
Totals	$1,829,553		$867,329		$967,640		$78,348		$72,932

Add Present Value of Cash Flow from Disposal:

Loan Amortization $\times 1/(1 + i)^n$ = $53,929 $\times$ .5645*	=	$ 30,443	
Appreciation $\times 1/(1 + i)^n$ = $600,000 $\times$ .5645	=	338,700	
Taxes $\times 1/(1 + i)^n$ = $(288,484) $\times$ .5645	=	(162,849)	
Capital Recovery[2] $\times 1/(1 + i)^n$ = $500,000[†] $\times$ .5645	=	282,250	488,544
Present Value of Equity Position			$561,476

*Present value factors at 10 percent.
[†]Original equity investment (down payment).

SENSITIVITY ANALYSIS

Sensitivity analysis is a logical extension of partitioning to determine what portions of the forecast merit further refinement. Whereas partitioning emphasizes the relative importance of various sources of cash flow, sensitivity analysis reveals how forecasting errors will affect the present value of actual after-tax cash flows. The technique consists of altering components of the forecast one at

Table 17.5	Simon's Sylvan Setting: Sources of Present Value	

Source of Present Value	Amount of Present Value	Percent of Total
Effective Gross Income	$1,829,553	325.8
Operating Expenses	(867,329)	(154.5)
Debt Service	(967,640)	(172.3) } (1.0)
Tax Consequences of Operations	78,348	14.0
Loan Amortization	30,443	5.4
Increase in Market Value	338,700	60.3
Tax Liability on Sale	(162,849)	(29.0)
Capital Recovery on Sale	282,250	50.3
Totals	$ 561,476	100.0

a time and studying their impact on investment value or present value of the equity position.

To see how sensitivity analysis works, consider again the venture in Example 17.4. Suppose we wanted to appraise the impact of a plus-or-minus 10 percent error in the forecasted selling price. The after-tax cash flow under each of these alternatives is computed in Table 17.6. Substituting these alternative after-tax cash proceeds into Table 17.3 alters the expected present value and the investment value of the venture rather significantly:

Change in Selling Price	Present Value of Equity	Investment Value
No Change (See Table 17.3)	$561,480	$2,361,480
10% Decrease	443,612	2,243,612
10% Increase	679,347	2,479,347

There is, of course, an alternative expected present value and investment value for every possible assumption about the rate of appreciation (and thus the sales price) of the property. Figure 17.1 illustrates the relationship between per-

Table 17.6	Simon's Sylvan Setting: Impact of +/– 10% Variation in Sales Price on After-Tax Cash Flow from Disposal		

	After-Tax Cash Flow from Disposal		
	With – 10% Variation	Expected	With + 10% Variation
Sales Price	$2,610,000	$2,900,000	$3,190,000
Less:			
Loan Balance	1,746,071	1,746,071	1,746,071
Tax on Sale	207,284	288,484	369,684
After-Tax Cash Flow	$ 656,645	$ 865,445	$1,074,245

Figure 17.1	**Relationship Between Changes in Forecast Variables and Changes in Investment Value**

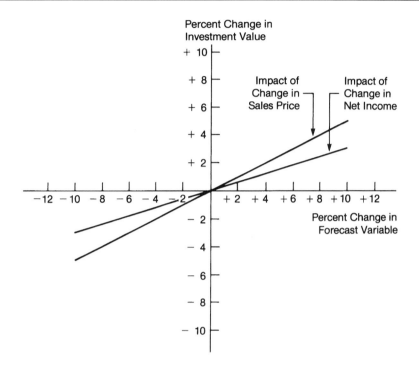

centage changes in the sales price and percentage changes in the investment value. A 10 percent change in expected selling price, either plus or minus, produces a corresponding 5 percent change in the venture's investment value.

Now suppose the appreciation rate had been forecasted correctly, but the annual net operating income had been overstated by 10 percent. What impact will this have on investment value?

Since the taxpayer in our example is assumed to be in the 28 percent marginal income tax bracket, after-tax cash flow will be changed by 72 percent of the amount of the change in taxable income. Discounting yields the dollar change in present value that results from this forecasting error. These calculations are shown in Table 17.7. The present value and investment value of the venture after incorporating this change are shown below:

Change in Gross Revenue	*Change in Value of ATCF*	*Present Value*	*Investment Value*
No Change (See Table 17.3)	$ 0	$561,480	$2,361,480
10% Decrease (from Table 17.7)	−$69,272	492,201	2,292,201
10% Increase (from Table 17.7)	+$69,272	630,759	2,430,759

| Table 17.7 | | Simon's Sylvan Setting: Impact of a +/– 10% Variation in Net Operating Income on Present Value of Future Cash Flows | | |

Year	Change in Annual After-Tax Cash Flow*	×	Present Value Interest Factor	=	Present Value of Change
1	$15,552		.9091		$14,138
2	15,192		.8264		12,555
3	15,624		.7513		11,738
4	16,128		.6830		11,015
5	16,560		.6209		10,282
6	16,920		.5645		9,551
Total					$69,279

*Ten percent of net operating income from Table 17.1, adjusted by the investor's 28 percent marginal income tax bracket.

The relationship between percentage changes in annual net operating income and percentage changes in investment value is also illustrated in Figure 17.1. That the investment outcome is less sensitive to errors in the operating income forecast than in the appreciation forecast is reflected in the steeper slope of the line depicting the latter relationship. A similar graph could be constructed to show the relative impact of error in each segment of the forecast.

In general, the steeper the graph of the relationship, the more significant the error in the forecast; therefore, the greater the amount of time and expense the analyst is justified in expending to refine the forecast. If anticipated cash flows prove sensitive to variations in the vacancy allowance, for example, the analyst might wish to generate a more refined analysis of marketability; if results are sensitive to variations in the operating expense ratio, one might experiment with lease clauses that shift any upward variations to the tenants.

SUMMARY

Traditional techniques employed to adjust for perceived risk associated with real estate investment have proven inadequate. They fail to produce a risk measure separate from the analyst's personal attitude toward risk and thus are not amenable to precise communication of risk perception. In addition, they cannot readily be incorporated into a policy statement enabling delegation of preliminary decision-making tasks.

The payback-period method of analysis is not, strictly speaking, a risk-adjustment technique. But risk perception, interfaced with attitude toward risk, can be expressed in terms of the maximum acceptable payback period for a particular venture.

A technique that does explicitly consider risk, and is widely employed within the industry, is the risk-adjusted discount rate. Users add to the risk-free rates of return premiums based on their perceptions of attendant risk. Thus the appropriate discount rate increases directly with perceived risk. The technique fails, however, to divorce risk perception from the analyst's personal attitude toward risk. It also contains a technical flaw in that it discounts risk more heavily the further into the future the risk lies.

Risk-adjusted discount rates adjust for increased risk by increasing the size of the divisor in the discounting equation. The certainty-equivalent technique accomplishes the same goal by decreasing the size of the dividend. Both approaches result in a lower present value for a given expected future cash flow as perceived risk increases.

The certainty-equivalent technique avoids some of the objections associated with the risk-adjusted discount rate but introduces new problems. Principal among these are difficulty in determining the appropriate adjustment factor and need to remake the determination for each project and each decision maker. Time and expense make this approach generally impractical as a continuing risk-adjustment technique.

Partitioning and sensitivity analysis, although not methods of adjusting for risk, are useful means of sharpening risk perception. They do this by illustrating how varying degrees of error in different elements of a forecast result in discrepancies between estimated and actual cash flows.

Partitioning reveals the relative significance of each source of after-tax cash flow. Sensitivity analysis takes a speculative approach by postulating variance at different points in the analysis and recomputing outcomes with revised estimates.

NOTES

1. For an extended discussion of these difficulties, see A.A. Robichek and S.C. Myers, "Conceptual Problems in the Use of Risk-Adjusted Discount Rates," *Journal of Finance,* vol. 21 (December 1966) pp. 727–730.

2. H.Y. Chen, "Valuation under Uncertainty," *Journal of Financial and Quantitative Analysis,* vol. 2 (September 1967) pp. 313–326.

3. Steven E. Bolton, *Managerial Finance,* 2nd ed. (Boston: Houghton Mifflin, 1981).

RECOMMENDED READING

Brigham, Eugene F. *Fundamentals of Financial Management.* 7th ed. (Ft. Worth, TX: The Dryden Press, 1994).

REVIEW QUESTIONS

1. How do users of the payback-period approach adjust for risk? Why is the payback-period approach inadequate for evaluating real estate opportunities?
2. What does the "risk-free" rate mean? Is it really risk free?
3. What problems does the risk-adjusted discount rate have?
4. Outline the relative advantages and disadvantages of the certainty equivalent technique.
5. What is meant by partitioning the present value of the equity position?
6. Describe how sensitivity analysis works and how it is used in evaluating a real estate investment opportunity.

DISCUSSION QUESTIONS

1. Partitioning the present value of the equity position is described as a risk evaluation measure. Discuss the probable role of electronic spreadsheets in the growth of this procedure. Will dedicated computer programs that do not include this procedure nevertheless lend themselves to using partitioning?
2. How do partitioning and sensitivity analysis complement each other as risk measurement tools?

CHAPTER 18

Contemporary Risk Measures

Cash-flow forecasting techniques, discussed in Part Three, generate point estimates of revenue and expenditures that are, in effect, single best estimates of most probable outcomes. They are, nevertheless, only estimates; actual outcomes will almost certainly differ from the forecasts. Risk associated with cash-flow forecasting can conveniently be defined as the probability of variation between actual and expected outcomes. More formally, risk is the measurable likelihood of variance from the most probable outcome.

This operational definition forms the takeoff point for modern risk analysis. It permits risk estimates to be expressed quantitatively and enables analysts to rank investment opportunities in terms of investor risk-return preferences.

Probabilistic risk estimates are commonplace in corporate finance and capital budgeting literature. Real estate analysts have adopted the techniques somewhat more cautiously.

Defenders of the traditional risk measures discussed in Chapter 17 object that modern quantification is simply not practical in real estate analysis. They argue that inefficient localized markets, spotty statistical data and high information costs make real estate a special case in which generally accepted capital budgeting and risk analysis techniques are inappropriate.

These objections miss the point. Data are even more sparse and less reliable in corporate capital budgeting situations than in real estate. Yet modern risk analysis is an integral part of the capital budgeting process in most corporations. Techniques employed there are directly applicable to real estate investment decisions.

Real estate analysts do develop some subjective "feel" for the risk inherent in investment opportunities. This is the basis for the traditional adjustments described in Chapter 17. All that is needed to accommodate modern risk analysis is a language that permits analysts to express their perceptions in numeric form and articulate a set of decision criteria against which to weigh the outcomes.

This chapter provides these additional tools. After distinguishing between risk and uncertainty, the chapter reviews basic probability concepts and demonstrates how point estimates of possible outcomes might be converted into probability distributions. It then applies traditional statistical decision rules in a real estate investment context.

PROBABILITY AS A RISK MEASURE

Probability is the chance of occurrence associated with any possible outcome. If, for example, a six-sided die is tossed onto a flat surface, there is an equal chance that any side might face up when the die comes to rest. The probability of any given side facing up is, therefore, one in six, or one-sixth, or .1667.

Probabilities associated with any possible occurrence range from zero to one. If the probability of occurrence equals zero, the event certainly will not occur. A probability of one indicates certainty of occurrence. In our die-tossing example, one of the six sides must certainly face up. The sum of all associated probabilities must therefore equal one.

Formally, this is expressed as:

$$\sum_{i=1}^{n} P_{xi} = 1$$

where P_{xi} is the probability of occurrences of outcome x, and the summation of the values for i includes all possibilities. When all possible outcomes are arrayed over their associated probabilities, the result is a probability distribution.

Risk Differs from Uncertainty

Decision situations are conveniently divisible into *certainty, risk* and *uncertainty.* With certainty there can be only one possible outcome, and decisions are based solely on the decision maker's preference among the certain alternatives. Few decision makers, however, face such clear-cut choices. More typically, they must choose among alternatives whose outcomes incorporate elements of risk, elements of uncertainty or both.

Uncertainty implies an unknown number of possible outcomes, with no significant information about their relative chances of occurrence. Since it is by definition unmeasurable, there is no way to communicate degrees of uncertainty. Under such conditions, almost anything can happen.

Risky events also have a number of possible outcomes, but the analyst is able to generate information upon which to estimate the probability of occurrence of each. Some risk elements are susceptible to more or less precise measure, based on sampling techniques and statistical inference. Others are subject only to educated guesses about the range of possible outcomes from one extreme possibility to the other. Formal risk analysis shapes these measures, estimates and guesses into a concrete, standardized format, incorporating probability as the measure of risk.

The distinction between risk and uncertainty is that with uncertainty, probabilities are neither known nor estimable, whereas with risk, the probabilities associated with various possible outcomes are either known or estimable. Authorities differ regarding the importance of this distinction.[1] For our purpose it is valuable, because decision-makers exercise some control over the category into which certain elements fall. Uncertainty can sometimes be resolved with additional research or the passage of time. As better information becomes available, many uncertain elements can be converted to risk factors by incorporating into the analysis their associated probability distributions.

✳ Estimating Probabilities

When the influence of all factors bearing on an outcome can be held relatively constant, past experience provides a reliable indication of future events. In such circumstances, experimentation or observation of sample data permits inferences about future outcomes.

This is illustrated by the earlier example of a (presumed fair) six-sided die. The intuitive deduction that each side has an equal chance of facing up can be verified by observing the outcome of repeated tosses. Various sides may face up with unequal frequency during early tosses, but (if the die is fair) these are mere chance variations. The greater the number of tosses, the smaller is the role played by chance and so the greater the tendency for each side to be equally represented.

Weight one side of the die or shave a corner, and the probability of each side facing up will no longer be equal. A new set of probabilities can be estimated quickly, however, by recording the outcome of repeated tosses. A sizable sample of such tosses yields a highly reliable indication of the average outcome of any future series of tosses, so long as major determinants of the outcome (such as the playing surface and the degree to which the die is weighted or shaved) remain constant. Varying any factor produces a whole new set of probabilities.

Investment analysts are not blessed with such reliable probability estimating techniques. Estimating future cash flows from real estate ventures might best be described as part art and part science. It involves studying all factors that significantly influence outcomes, making estimates of or assumptions about the level of each factor and relating these to a specific investment forecast and its associated probability.

Point estimates of cash flow, such as those discussed in Part Three, necessarily assume some specific economic environment. Were the analyst to anticipate a different environment, a revised forecast would be required. A series of such revisions will generate a whole spectrum of net cash-flow forecasts, each reflecting a slightly modified set of assumptions about economic and social conditions during the projection period.

There is, of course, no way to determine precisely what the future portends. Yet we can develop informed estimates, which enable us to say with relative confidence that various possible outcomes will materialize. In some instances estimates can be derived objectively by applying statistical techniques to accumulated data. In other instances lack of objective data might force reliance on the distilled wisdom of an analyst's experience as a basis for estimating which of the alternative economic environments is most likely.

Regardless of how estimates are generated, relative confidence in various potential outcomes can be expressed by coupling each with a probability estimate. This procedure produces a probability distribution of possible cash flows. If estimates are derived objectively with statistical techniques, risk is said to be measured by *objective probability distributions.*

When statistical measuring techniques cannot be applied, estimates will represent a quantification of the analyst's subjective impression of the risky nature of anticipated cash flows. Such risk estimates are expressed as *subjective probability distributions.* They represent the quantified perception of a trained analyst and are only as reliable as the judgment of the person whose opinion they incorporate. Subjective probability measures do not simplify the analyst's task in any way; they do add precision to the communication of conclusions.

Opinions expressed in precise, readily understandable terms permit investment decisions consistent with the analyst's assessment, yet reflecting the decision maker's personal investment philosophy and risk preference. This is the special virtue of using subjective probability distributions to communicate risk. The adjective *subjective* is appended to indicate that the probability estimates are statements of opinion or beliefs held by an individual analyst.

Example 18.1

A shopping center analyst develops estimates of annual net cash flow from percentage leases under economic conditions ranging from good to poor, both with and without the existence of a competing center. The analyst's estimates are as follows:

Competing Center Built?	Cash Flow Under General Business Conditions		
	Good	Fair	Poor
No	$250,000	$200,000	$150,000
Yes	225,000	175,000	125,000

Consider Example 18.1. Multiple cash-flow projections in the example reflect an analyst's estimate of the influence of general business conditions and of the presence or absence of a competing shopping center. Regardless of general business conditions, construction of a competing center will have an adverse impact on cash flows and thus on the investment's profitability. The better the general economic environment during the lease period, the more cash a lease will generate, whether or not the competing center is built.

Example 18.1 could be extended to incorporate as many additional possibilities as circumstances warrant. A different set of cash-flow possibilities could be developed to reflect the expected impact of labor strife or major change in the general level of employment. Additional sets of possibilities might be shown, depending upon what happens to tax laws, whether a proposed highway interchange is actually built and so on. Expansion possibilities are virtually endless. The analyst's task is to identify those possible events that have a significant likelihood of actually transpiring and that will have a measurable impact on investment outcome. Separate forecasts are then made to reflect possible outcomes for all particularly crucial eventualities.

Conventional Probability Rules

By convention, the probability assigned to the likelihood of an event's occurrence must be a positive number between zero and one, where zero represents impossibility of occurrence and one represents absolute certainty. If events are mutually exclusive (only one of them *can* occur) and exhaustive (one of them *must* occur), then the sum of the probabilities associated with events in the set must equal one.

To illustrate, on any given day it will either rain or not rain. Therefore, the sum of the probabilities associated with these two possibilities must be one. If the probability of rain is 0.4, then the probability that it will not rain must be 1.0 minus 0.4, or 0.6.

Application of Joint Probabilities

A very important probability rule is sometimes called the *multiplicative law of probability.* It is used to express the probability of occurrence of an event whose outcome depends in turn on the outcome of some prior event. If we call these events A and B, then the probability of event B is the product of the probability of event A times the probability of occurrence event B, given that event A occurs. This is an example of *joint probabilities.*

To apply the concept to real estate investment, consider again the illustration in Example 18.1. The analyst assigns subjective probabilities to the likelihood of each specific event. (Accept, for the present, the convenient fiction that these are the only possible outcomes.)

Assessing the economic environment, the analyst arrives at the probabilistic estimates of most likely general economic conditions during the forecast period, as indicated in Table 18.1.

Table 18.1	Probabilistic Forecast of Various Economic States	

Economic Environment	*Associated Probability*
Good	.20
Fair	.60
Poor	.20
Total	1.00

Table 18.2 expands Example 18.1 by relating various economic environments and the probability that a competing shopping center will be constructed. Note that the probabilities in Table 18.2 are *conditional:* they depend on various economic conditions. For each possible set of economic conditions a competitive center either will or will not be built. Therefore, the sum of the mutually exclusive probabilities under each set of possible conditions must equal one.

Combining probabilistic estimates from Tables 18.1 and 18.2 generates joint probabilities concerning various possible economic environments and competitive conditions. For example, Table 18.1 indicates a probability of 0.20 that economic conditions will be good, and Table 18.2 reflects a probability of 0.80 that a competitive center will be built if economic conditions are good. The probability that economic conditions will be good *and* that a competitive center will be built is the product of these two underlying probabilities: 0.20 *times* 0.80, or 0.16. This, and all other joint probabilities generated from Tables 18.1 and 18.2, are shown in Table 18.3.

Since Table 18.3 exhausts all possible combinations of general economic conditions and competitive environments, the sum of the probabilities in the table must equal one. Moreover, the probability of various general economic conditions can be determined by summing the factors in the table vertically. Comparing the footings from Table 18.3 with the probabilities in Table 18.1 confirms that the probability of good economic conditions is 0.20; of fair conditions, 0.60; and of poor conditions, 0.20. Summing Table 18.3 horizontally gives the probability of competition. Finally, since there either will or will not be competition, and some general economic condition must prevail, both vertical sums and horizontal crossfootings in Table 18.3 must sum to one.

Table 18.2	Probability That Competing Shopping Center Will Be Built, under Various Economic Conditions		

Probability That Competing Center Will	*Economic Environment*		
	Good	*Fair*	*Poor*
Be Built	.80	.50	.20
Not Be Built	.20	.50	.80
Total	1.00	1.00	1.00

Table 18.3	**Probability Estimates of Economic Conditions and Related Competitive Environments**

| *Competing* | *Economic Conditions* | | | |
Center Built?	*Good*	*Fair*	*Poor*	*Σ*
Yes	0.16	0.30	0.04	0.50
No	0.04	0.30	0.16	0.50
	0.20 +	0.60 +	0.20 =	1.00

INTERPRETING RISK MEASURES

Probabilistic estimates of possible outcomes provide valuable intelligence about relative risk. Projections can be made even more useful with additional manipulation of data to provide estimates of most likely outcomes and associated probability distributions of all possible alternatives.

Probability Distributions

An array of all possible outcomes and their related probabilities of occurrence is called a *probability distribution.* The probability distribution of possible net cash flows from the venture described in Example 18.1 is presented in Table 18.4. The possible net cash flows from Example 18.1 are multiplied by their related probabilities as generated in Table 18.3. The products are summed in column four of Table 18.4 to generate an expected (that is, most probable) cash flow from the shopping center project.

Table 18.4	**Expected Annual Cash Flow from Proposed Shopping Center Project**

(1)	*(2)*	*(3)*	*(4)*
	Related Cash-	*Probability of*	*Weighted*
Possible Economic	*Flow Forecast*	*Occurrence*	*Average*
Environment	*(from Example 18.1)*	*(from Table 18.3)*	*(2) × (3)*
Competing Center Built, and Economic Environment Is:			
Poor	$125,000	0.04	$ 5,000
Fair	175,000	0.30	52,500
Good	225,000	0.16	36,000
No Competing Center, and Economic Environment Is:			
Poor	150,000	0.16	24,000
Fair	200,000	0.30	60,000
Good	250,000	0.04	10,000
	Total =	1.00	CF = $187,500

Distributions such as that shown in Table 18.4 are called *discrete* probability distributions, to reflect the assumption that possible outcomes are limited to specific point estimates presented in the computation. The bar graph in Figure 18.1 shows the same data.

Table 18.4 incorporates an assumption that the six cash-flow alternatives from Example 18.1 exhaust all possibilities associated with the venture. This is, of course, merely a convenient fiction. Since net cash flow from percentage leases is a function of leaseholders' sales revenue, the actual distribution must encompass all intermediate values as well. This is descriptive of a continuous probability distribution.

The discrete probability distribution of Figure 18.1 can be converted to a *continuous* distribution by explicit recognition of values between and beyond the point estimates of Table 18.4 as being in the realm of probabilities. This is illustrated in Figure 18.1 by the solid line tracing the outer range of the discrete estimates of possible outcomes.

Expected Value

The *expected value* of a probability distribution of possible cash flows is the weighted average of the possible cash flows making up the distribution, with each value weighted by its attendant probability of occurrence. The relationship can be expressed as:

$$\overline{CF} = \sum_{i=1}^{n} CF_1 P_1$$

Figure 18.1   Probability Distribution of Cash Flows

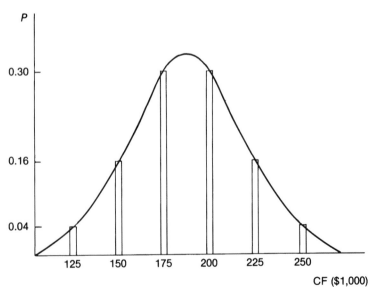

where $\overline{CF}$ is the expected value of the cash-flow distribution, CF_i is the value associated with the ith probability and P_i is the probability associated with that value.

Table 18.4 applies this formulation to compute the expected value of the cash-flow projections from Example 18.1. Column two of the table gives the various possible values of the CF_i, and column three expresses the values of the P_i. The product of CF_iP_i is shown in column four. The summation of column four, and the solution to the above equation, is the expected cash flow from Example 18.1: $187,500.

Measuring Dispersion

Recall that risk is defined as the possibility of variation of actual outcomes from expectations. Expressing the expected outcome as a probability-weighted average permits using variance or standard deviation as a measure of risk.

Variance. *Variance* is the weighted average of the squared differences between each possible outcome and the expected outcome. Expressed algebraically, this relationship is:

$$V = \sum_{i=1}^{n} (CF_i - \overline{CF})^2\, P_i$$

where V is the variance, CF_i is the value of the ith possible outcome, $\overline{CF}$ is the expected value and P_i is the related probability. Applying this formula to the possible nth-year cash flow in Example 18.1 and combining the previously calculated expected value of $187,500 with probability measures from Table 18.4 yields a variance estimate of $856,250,000. Computations are shown in Table 18.5.

Standard Deviation. Because variance employs squared differences between observed values and the mean of a distribution, the relationship is nonlinear. The

---

Table 18.5   **Variance of the Probability Distribution of Possible Cash Flows from Shopping Center in Example 18.1**

Possible Cash Flow	Expected Cash Flow	$CF_i - \overline{CF}$	Probability (P_i)	$(CF_i - \overline{CF})^2 P_1$
$125,000	$187,500	(62,500)	0.04	$156,250,000
150,000	187,500	(37,500)	0.16	225,000,000
175,000	187,500	(12,500)	0.30	46,875,000
200,000	187,500	12,500	0.30	46,875,000
225,000	187,500	37,500	0.16	225,000,000
250,000	187,500	62,500	0.04	156,250,000
		$\Sigma =$ 1.00		$V =$ $856,250,000

square root of the variance, called *standard deviation,* provides a much more usable measure of dispersion, particularly when it is used to compare alternative investment opportunities with significantly different expected values. This eliminates the distorting effect of squaring differences that vary greatly in magnitude.

The formula for the standard deviation is:

$$\sigma = \sqrt{\sum_{i=1}^{n} (CF_i - \overline{CF})^2 P_i}$$

where σ is the standard deviation, the CF_i are the various possible values of the cash flows, $\overline{CF}$ is the mean of the distribution of possible cash flows and P_i is the probability of occurrence of each possible value.

Standard deviation has mathematical properties that make it particularly useful as a measure of risk. So long as the underlying probabilities are symmetrically distributed about the mean of the distribution, approximately 68.3 percent of all possible values will lie within one standard deviation of the expected value. Two standard deviations encompass approximately 95 percent of all possible outcomes, and three standard deviations to either side of the expected values include virtually all possible outcomes. Figure 18.2 illustrates this relationship.

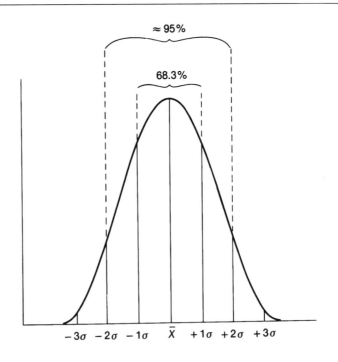

Figure 18.2   **Percent of Area Under Normal Curve Encompassed by *X* Standard Deviations from the Mean**

Once the mean and the standard deviation are established, the probability of occurrence of values over any desired interval within the distribution can be determined by reference to a table of standardized values expressing the relationship. Such a table, sometimes called a table of *Z-values,* is given in Appendix D. It shows the portion of the area under the normal distribution lying to the left or right of various specified values. The Z-value from the table is simply the number of standard deviations from the mean to the value in question. The relationship is frequently expressed algebraically as:

$$Z = \frac{X - \overline{X}}{\sigma_x}$$

where X is some specified value under a symmetric distribution (often called a *normal curve*), $\overline{X}$ is the midpoint of the distribution (the expected value) and σ_X is the value of one standard deviation.

Having earlier determined the variance of the distribution of possible net cash flows in Example 18.1 to be $856,250,000 (see Table 18.5), the standard deviation can be computed by simply deriving the square root of this amount: approximately $29,262. The expected value (that is, the midpoint) of the distribution was previously determined to be $187,500 (see Table 18.4). These two parameters, the expected value and the standard deviation, effectively determine the entire distribution of any normally distributed variable. Standard deviation serves well as the sole measure of risk only when the probability distribution is relatively symmetrical. If it is significantly skewed to either side, a measure of skewness may need to be incorporated into the model. This is possible, but it vastly complicates the mathematics. Our analysis considers only the symmetric distribution.[2]

Figure 18.3 illustrates the relationship calculated for Example 18.1. The expected value of $187,500 is the midpoint of the distribution. One standard deviation is plus-or-minus $29,262, which we can determine (using the table of Z-values in Appendix D) encompasses approximately 68.3 percent of all possible values. The probability of the actual value falling within any range corresponds to the percent of the total area under the curve that falls within that range. Therefore, the probability is approximately .683 that the actual cash flow will prove to be within plus-or-minus $29,262 of $187,500, which is to say between $158,238 and $216,762.

To determine this by reference to the table in Appendix D, first calculate the percent of the total area *not* falling within one standard deviation of the midpoint (the unshaded area in Figure 18.3). Since this is a symmetric distribution (that is, the sides of the probability distribution of possible cash flows are mirror images of each other, with 50 percent of the area under the curve lying on either side of the mean), we need to solve the problem for only one side of the curve. The same value will also apply to the other side. Refer to the table of Z-values in Appendix D to find the percent of the total area under the curve to the left of point X. The area is 0.1587, or 15.87 percent. Now, since 50 percent of the total area under the curve lies to the left of the midpoint, it follows that the area from point X to the midpoint must be 50 percent minus 15.87 percent, or 34.13 per-

Figure 18.3   **Probability That Present Value Will Fall Within Plus-or-Minus One Standard Deviation from the Mean**

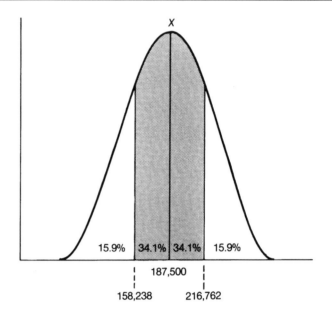

cent. The total portion of the area under the curve that lies between one standard deviation and the midpoint, therefore, is two times 34.13 percent, or approximately 68.3 percent.

As an exercise, use the table of Z-values to determine the probability that cash flow in Example 18.1 will equal or exceed $170,000. The first step is to determine how many standard deviations this variable, CF_i, lies from the mean, $\overline{CF}$:

$$Z = \frac{CF_i - \overline{CF}}{\sigma_{CF}} = \frac{\$170,000 - \$187,500}{\$29,262} = -0.60$$

From the table in Appendix D, determine that approximately 0.2743 of the total area lies to the left of the point associated with −0.60 standard deviations. Since 0.50 *minus* 0.2743 equals 0.2257, we can be 22.57 percent confident that the cash flow will actually be between $170,000 and $187,500, provided we have correctly specified the parameters of the problem. Moreover, we know that 50 percent of the possible outcomes are above $187,500. It follows that the probability of cash flow equal to or more than $170,000 is .50 *plus* .2257, or about .73.

Coefficient of Variation.   Standard deviation serves admirably as a comparative measure of risk when evaluating alternatives involving approximately the same level of annual cash flow. When dissimilar cash flows must be compared, it is sometimes useful to go one step further and to calculate the *coefficient of variation,* which is the standard deviation of the cash flow divided by the expected cash flow. For the project in Example 18.1 the coefficient of variation is:

$$\frac{\text{Standard Deviation}}{\text{Expected Cash Flow}} = \frac{\$29,262}{\$187,500} = 0.156$$

When alternatives are being compared with respect to expected outcomes and relative riskiness, rather than for derivation of a bid price, the coefficient of variation offers the advantage of permitting direct comparisons when the mean values of the cash-flow distributions vary.

STANDARD DEVIATION AND THE DISCOUNTED CASH-FLOW MODEL

Several methods of incorporating risk into the investment decision have been utilized, the most appropriate being in part determined by the nature of the analysis. A second major factor is the pattern of the anticipated stream of investor benefits and the relationship between year-to-year forecasts.

Mean/Standard Deviation Approach

Perhaps the most useful approach to incorporating risk into an investment decision is to use the *mean/standard deviation* model. It involves developing both an expected cash flow and a standard deviation measure for each year of the projection period. The technique is best illustrated by using a single-period cash flow forecast. This avoids complications introduced when annual cash flows are influenced by outcomes from previous years. After demonstrating the principle with this simplifying assumption concerning cash-flow patterns, we will examine more complex situations.

Example 18.2

A proposal requires an initial equity investment of $25,000. After three years it is expected that the investment position will be liquidated with a net cash inflow of $50,000. The standard deviation of the cash flow in the third year is estimated to be $7,000, and the range of possible cash flows are assumed to be distributed symmetrically about the expected amount. Cash flow during the first two years is virtually certain to be zero. The investor's opportunity cost of equity capital (the appropriate discount rate) is 10 percent.

Consider Example 18.2. Though the forecast includes a point estimate of cash flow for the third year, there is in fact a whole spectrum of possible cash flows for that year. This is evidenced by the estimated $7,000 standard deviation of the cash flows. The standard deviation estimate, you will recall, is derived by comparing the range of possible outcomes with the expected outcome.

There is a present value associated with each possible cash-flow outcome in Example 18.2. Were it possible to discount every possible outcome, a probability distribution of possible present values would result. This distribution of present values also, of course, will have an expected value (the midpoint of the distribution) and a standard deviation.

Since the distribution of possible cash flows in Example 18.2 is assumed to be distributed symmetrically about its mean, the distribution of present values also will be symmetrically distributed. Moreover, the midpoint of the distribution of present values will be the discounted value of the midpoint of the distribution of cash flows. This expected present value is $37,566, calculated as follows:

$$\overline{PV} = \frac{\overline{CF}}{(1+i)^3} = \frac{\$50,000}{1.10^3} = \$37,566$$

Where there is only one anticipated future cash flow (rather than a series of forecasted outcomes), computing the standard deviation of the present value distribution is equally uncomplicated. Simply discount the standard deviation of the cash-flow distribution at the same discount rate employed in determining the midpoint of the distribution of possible present values. For Example 18.2, the computation is;

$$\sigma_{PV} = \frac{\sigma_{CF}}{(1+i)^3} = \frac{\$7,000}{1.10^3} = \$5,259$$

Recall that when the rate of return equals the discount rate, the present value of future cash flows will equal the amount of the initial cash outlay. Should the actual cash flow from the project in Example 18.2 be such that its present value (discounting at 10 percent) proves to be $25,000 or more, it follows that the actual rate of return on the project will have been 10 percent or better. The probability that this will occur equals the percent of the total area under the probability distribution of possible present values lying to the right of the point where the actual outcome is $25,000.

Figure 18.4 depicts the probability distribution of possible present values of the cash flows from Example 18.2. The probability that the actual present value will be $25,000 or better (and thus, the rate of return will be 10 percent or more) is represented by the unshaded area under the curve. We can determine what percent of the total area this represents by using the equation discussed earlier in the chapter:

$$Z = \frac{(PV_x - \overline{PV})}{\sigma_{PV}}$$

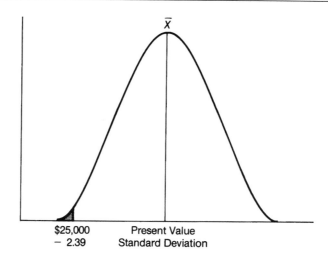

Figure 18.4   **Probability of Acceptance Error (Probability That Actual Present Value Will Be Less Than Minimum Acceptable)**

$\overline{X}$

$25,000   Present Value
− 2.39   Standard Deviation

where:

Z = the standardized value from Appendix D

PV_x = minimum acceptable present value

$\overline{PV}$ = the expected present value (that is, the arithmetic mean)

σ_{PV} = the standard deviation of the present value

Substituting values from Example 18.2 into the equation yields:

$$Z = \frac{\$25,000 - \$37,566}{\$5,259} = -2.39$$

Reference to the table of Z-values in Appendix D reveals that the area to the left of PV = $25,000 is just slightly more than 0.8 percent of the total area under the distribution. The probability that this project will generate at least a ten percent rate of return, therefore, is estimated to be more than 0.99. Expressed another way, the investor can be more than 99 percent confident of earning a rate of return equal to or more than the opportunity cost of capital.

Establishing Acceptable Risk Profiles

The probability that a venture will generate less than the minimum acceptable rate of return and thus that its acceptance will prove to have been a mistake is called the *probability of acceptance error.* Having specified an absolute maximum probability of acceptance error beyond which no investment opportunity will be undertaken, there remains the problem of discriminating between acceptable and unacceptable risk-reward combinations that lay within the range of provisional acceptability. Within that range there are gradients of risk. Investors expect compensation for all incremental risk assumed.

To facilitate choosing among risky opportunities, and to ensure consistency over time, investors may specify the maximum acceptable probability of acceptance error associated with various levels of present values per dollar of invested cash or with various expected rates of return. This permits a more refined preliminary screening by subordinates, further reducing the time spent by final decision makers on projects destined for ultimate rejection.

Before risk profiles can be constructed, expected outcomes must be expressed in terms that permit interproject comparisons of cost and benefit. Profitability indices (discussed in Chapter 15) have this characteristic, inasmuch as they represent the ratio of present value to initial cash outlay. They convert absolute present value estimates to measures of relative present value per dollar of required initial cash expenditure. To illustrate, consider again the investment in Example 18.2. The midpoint of the distribution of possible outcomes, expressed in present value terms, is $37,566, and the initial cash outlay is $25,000. The expected value of the probability distribution of possible profitability indices, $\overline{PI}$, is:

$$\overline{PI} = \frac{\$37,566}{\$25,000} = 1.50$$

Recall from Chapter 15 that when present value just equals the initial cash outlay, the profitability index is exactly one and the net present value is zero. Also, recall that this means the internal rate of return exactly equals the discount rate used to determine present value. Present value, net present value and the profitability index, therefore, all measure the same relationship. An advantage of the profitability index is that it permits comparisons among projects of different magnitudes.

Figure 18.5 replicates Figure 18.4, with a second scale measured in terms of the profitability index. Note that at the point where the present value of future net cash flows equals the initial cash outlay of $25,000, the profitability index is one, indicating that this corresponds to an internal rate of return just equal to the 10 percent minimum acceptable rate.

Specifying maximum levels of risk for various values of profitability indices (expected benefits) permits project evaluation by reference to a risk profile that does not depend upon the magnitude of the commitment. If the dispersion of possible outcomes indicates the project is too risky for the benefit it is expected to generate per dollar invested, the proposal is automatically rejected. If not, it is passed to the investor for a final decision. All projects passing this preliminary filtering process are considered, and final decisions are made according to portfolio risk-return considerations, with available cash acting as a constraint.

A tabulation of acceptable combinations of risk and expected benefits will reflect a positive relationship between expected profitability and dispersion of possible returns (risk). The exact trade-off depends upon the investor's attitude toward risk. This permits interface of the investor's risk preferences with the analyst's informed opinion regarding the risk implicit in a particular project.

Figure 18.5	**Probability of Acceptance Error (Probability That Actual Profitability Index Will Be Less Than Minimum Acceptable**

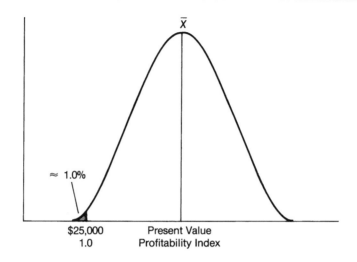

Risk profiles for two investors are presented in Table 18.6 and illustrated in Figure 18.6. The table presumes that anticipated after-tax cash flows have been discounted at a rate representing the minimum acceptable yield on the investor's equity investment. If the actual yield falls below this minimum rate, the profitability index will be less than one (that is, the present value of the cash flows will be less than $1 for each $1 of equity investment). Should this occur, the investment venture will prove to have been a mistake.

Table 18.6	**Risk-Return Profiles for Two Investors Who Express Risk in Terms of Probability of Earning Less Than a Specified Minimum Acceptable Rate of Return**

Expected Profitability Index	*Minimum Acceptable Probability That Profitability Index Will Be Equal to or Less Than One*	
	Investor A	*Investor B*
0.0	0.0000	0.0000
1.2	0.0150	0.0150
1.4	0.0230	0.0260
1.6	0.0290	0.0345
1.8	0.0330	0.0430
2.0	0.0350	0.0460
2.2	0.0350	0.0490
2.4	0.0350	0.0500

If the expected profitability index is greater than one, indicating an expected rate of return in excess of the minimum acceptable rate, the investor is willing to accept some risk (measured as probability) that the actual rate of return will fall below the minimum acceptable level. Thus, with an expected profitability index of 1.2 ($1.20 of present value for each $1 of equity cash invested), investor A in Table 18.6 will accept a probability of as much as 0.0150 that the actual profitability index will be one or less and therefore that the rate of return will be equal to or less than the minimum acceptable rate. The higher the expected profitability index (and thus the expected rate or return), the greater the acceptable risk (probability) that the actual rate of return will fall below acceptable levels and the venture will prove to be a mistake.

Figure 18.6 graphically portrays the relationship between expected present value per dollar invested (profitability indices) and acceptable levels of risk for the investors whose risk-return preferences are charted in Table 18.6. For each investor the area below the lines in Figure 18.6 represents acceptable combinations of risk and expected profitability indices; the area above the lines represents unacceptable combinations.

DEALING WITH MORE COMPLEX CASH-FLOW PATTERNS

To avoid premature complications, our discussion thus far has assumed a single period cash-flow pattern. This simplifies the dialogue but, for most real estate ventures, is highly unrealistic. Cash flows (both positive and negative) usually occur periodically over a number of years. It becomes necessary, therefore, to estimate the mean and standard deviation of the cash flows for each year in the projection period, including the cash flow from disposing of the project at the end of the holding period.

Figure 18.6   Risk-Return Profiles Expressed in Terms of Profitability Index

With multiple-year patterns, cash flow in subsequent periods will depend at least in part upon what happens in earlier periods. If projections prove overly optimistic in early years, chances are that the same will hold for the entire life of the project. Likewise, if cash flows in early years are greater than anticipated, favorable deviations are likely to occur in future years as well, so long as the same causal influences are present. The extent to which causal factors influence cash flows over two or more periods is called *serial correlation.* It is measured by the *coefficient of correlation,* which can range from zero to plus-or-minus one. When the correlation coefficient equals zero, serial cash flows are completely independent of each other. A coefficient of plus-or-minus one indicates perfect correlation of the cash flows.

Serial correlation (or its absence) does not affect the expected present value of a series of cash-flow projections. It will, however, drastically alter the standard deviation of the probability distribution of possible present values. In general, the greater the degree of serial correlation of annual cash flows, the wider the dispersion of possible outcomes about the mean and the greater the standard deviation of the probability distribution of possible present values.

Perfectly Correlated Cash Flows

When serial cash flows are perfectly correlated, deviation from the expected outcome in one period will result in deviations in all future periods. If actual cash flows in one period are exactly, say, one-half standard deviation to the right or left of the mean value of the probability distribution of possible cash flows for the period, then actual cash flows for all future periods will be exactly one-half standard deviation to the right or left of the probability distributions of all possible cash flows.

The standard deviation of the present value of a perfectly correlated stream of cash flows is:

$$\sigma_{PV} = \sum_{t=1}^{n} \sigma_{CF_t}/(1 + i)^t$$

where σ_{PV} is the standard deviation of the present value distribution, σ_{CF} is the standard deviation of the cash-flow distribution for time period t, and i is the discount rate used to derive the expected present value. For perfectly serially correlated cash flows, therefore, simply discount the standard deviation of the cash-flow distributions to derive the standard deviation of the present value distribution.

To see how the degree of serial correlation affects the standard deviation of the probability distribution of present values, consider the series of cash-flow projections in Example 18.3.

Recall that the expected value (the *mean*) of the probability distribution of possible present values associated with a symmetrically distributed cash-flow distribution is simply the present value of the mean of the cash-flow distribution.

Example 18.3

A real estate project requires an initial equity outlay of $50,000. An analyst develops the following estimate of the midpoints and standard deviations for annual cash flows over the projected life of the investment venture:

Year	Mean of Cash-Flow Distribution	Standard Deviation
1	$15,000	$5,400
2	15,000	4,500
3	40,000	9,000

The probability distributions of annual cash flows are assumed to be symmetrical about the means, and the serial correlation coefficients are all assumed to be +1. The investor's minimum acceptable rate of return (and therefore the appropriate discount rate) is 12 percent.

Discounting the means from Example 18.3 and summing the present values yields the mean of the probability distribution of possible present values of all cash flows from the venture. These computations are shown in Table 18.7.

Recall also that the standard deviation of the probability distribution of possible present values for perfectly serially correlated cash flows is derived by simply discounting the standard deviations of the cash-flow distributions. These computations are also illustrated in Table 18.7.

Table 18.7   Mean and Standard Deviation of Probability Distribution of Present Values from Example 18.3

Year	Expected Cash Flow	×	Present Value Factor at 12%	=	Mean of Present Value
1	$15,000		.8929		$13,394
2	15,000		.7972		11,958
3	40,000		.7118		28,472
					$53,824

Year	Standard Deviation of Cash Flow	×	Present Value Factor at 12%	=	Standard Deviation of Present Value
1	$ 5,400		.8929		$ 4,822
2	4,500		.7972		3,587
3	9,000		.7118		6,406
					$14,815

Uncorrelated Cash Flows

Expected present value does not change when the possibility of serially indepen-dent (uncorrelated) cash flows is introduced, but the standard deviation of the pres-ent value distribution may be greatly altered. In general, the greater the degree of serial correlation of the annual cash flows, the greater will be the dispersion—and thus the greater the standard deviation—of the probability distribution of possible present values.

To see this relationship, consider again the cash-flow projections in Exam-ple 18.3, but recompute the standard deviation of the present value under the revised assumption that the actual cash flow for each year is considered to be completely independent of that for other years. The formula for computing the standard deviation of the present value is:

$$\sigma_{PV} = \sqrt{\sum_{t=1}^{n} \frac{\sigma_{CF_t^2}}{(1+i)^{2t}}}$$

where σ_{PV} is the standard deviation of the present value, σ_{CF} is the standard deviation of the cash flow for year t and i is the discount rate used to derive the present value of the cash flows. Substituting the standard deviation of the cash flows and the discount rate from Example 18.3 yields a standard deviation of the present value of $8,784. Here is the calculation:

$$\sigma_{PV} = \sqrt{\frac{(\$5,400)^2}{(1.12)^2} + \frac{(\$4,500)^2}{(1.12)^4} + \frac{(\$9,000)^2}{(1.12)^6}} = \$8,784$$

Comparing this with the standard deviation of the present value under the assumption of perfect serial correlation, as derived in Table 18.7, makes clear the consequence of serial correlation; moving from perfect to zero serial correla-tion reduced the standard deviation of the present value by $6,031, or almost 41 percent.

Partially Correlated Cash Flows

Shifting from an assumption of serial independence to one of perfect serial correlation changes the computation of standard deviation and thus the disper-sion of the probability distribution of possible outcomes from an investment, but does not seriously complicate the arithmetic. Problems do arise, however, where there is *partial* serial correlation.

In situations involving less-than-perfect serial correlation, some of the expected cash flows may be highly correlated over time, while others may be more nearly independent. This is illustrative of most real world circumstances. When this occurs, the standard deviation problem becomes complex.

To deal with the issue, Frederick S. Hillier has developed a model that is particularly applicable to real estate investment situations.[3] His model groups annual cash flows on the basis of whether they are more nearly independent or serially correlated over time. The two groups are then treated as if they were *completely independent* and *perfectly correlated,* respectively.

The present value of the segmented income streams is unaffected by the treatment afforded in Hillier's model. The formula for the revised standard deviation of the present value, however, becomes:

$$\sigma_{PV} = \sqrt{\left[\sum_{t=1}^{n} \sigma_{CF_t} \bigg/ (1 + i)^t\right]^2 + \left[\sum_{t=1}^{n} \sigma_{CF_t^2} \bigg/ (1 + i)^{2t}\right]}$$

where the first bracketed term under the radical applies to the standard deviation for the cash flows assumed to be perfectly correlated and the second bracketed term applies to the standard deviation for the stream of net cash flows assumed to be serially independent (Uncorrelated).

To illustrate the use of Hillier's model, consider the data in Example 18.4, which represent a breakdown of supporting data from Example 18.3.

Example 18.4

Attempting a better grip on the risk element associated with the investment in Example 18.3, the analyst separates net cash flow projections into receipt and expenditure components. Separate standard deviation estimates are developed for each component.

Because rental revenues are so dependent on locational factors, the revenue stream is considered to be highly correlated over time. If the location is less desirable than anticipated, less-than-expected revenues will occur in each of the forecast years. The same factor will affect the selling price of the property at the end of the holding period, which is included in the expected cash flow for that year.

Operating expenses, on the other hand, are largely independent of locational influences. They are considered to be serially independent and are expected to vary from projected values only as a result of random factors.

Annual projections of revenue and expenditures, and associated standard deviation estimates, are determined to be as follows:

	Revenue Projections		Expenditure Projections	
Year	Projected Revenue	Standard Deviation	Projected Expenditures	Standard Deviation
1	$27,000	$3,780	$12,000	$1,620
2	27,000	3,500	12,000	1,000
3	52,000	6,000	12,000	2,700

The expected present value of the venture in Example 18.4 remains unchanged (except for rounding differences) from that of Example 18.3:

$$PV = \frac{\$27,000 - \$12,000}{1.12} + \frac{\$27,000 - \$12,000}{1.12^2} + \frac{\$52,000 - \$12,000}{1.12^3}$$

$$= \$53,822$$

The standard deviation of the expected present value, however, is drastically altered by the assumption of serial correlation of gross reve–nues. Substituting standard deviation measures from Example 18.4 in the formula developed by Hillier gives:

$$\sigma_{PV} = \sqrt{\left[\frac{\$3,780}{1.12} + \frac{\$3,500}{(1.12)^2} + \frac{\$6,000}{(1.12)^3}\right]^2 + \left[\frac{(\$1,620)^2}{(1.12)^2} + \frac{(\$1,000)^2}{(1.12)^4} + \frac{(\$2,700)^2}{(1.12)^6}\right]}$$

$$= \$10,739$$

SUMMARY

Modern risk-analysis techniques developed in the fields of corporate finance and capital budgeting can be applied to real estate investment analysis. The techniques allow risk to be expressed in terms of probability of variance from expectations. Because data are not available for statistical sampling of the type employed in the physical and biological sciences, probabilities in real estate investment analysis are frequently subjective, reflecting the informed opinion of an analyst rather than being generated from objective information sources.

Techniques for expressing risk in probabilistic terms involve developing probability distributions of possible outcomes and estimating related standard deviations. This in turn permits expression of likely investment consequences as ranges of possible outcomes and accompanying levels of confidence. Probability distributions of possible outcomes may be expressed as present values, net present values, profitability indices or any number of other measures as desired by an analyst or client.

NOTES

1. For contrasting approaches, compare the distinction made by Steven E. Bolten, *Managerial Finance,* 2nd ed. (Boston: Houghton Mifflin, 1981) with that of J. Fred Weston and Eugene F. Brigham, *Managerial Finance,* 9th ed. (Ft. Worth, TX: The Dryden Press, 1992). For a more detailed treatment of the distinction, see R. Duncan Luce and Howard Raiffa, *Games and Decisions* (New York: John Wiley, 1957).

2. For a discussion of probability estimation involving asymmetrical distributions, see John G. Kemeny et al., *Finite Mathematical Structures* (Englewood Cliffs, NJ: Prentice-Hall, 1959) pp. 172–78.

3. See Frederick S. Hillier, "The Derivation of Probabilistic Information for the Evaluation of Risky Investments," *Management Science* volume 9 (April 1963) pp. 443–457.

RECOMMENDED READING

Brigham, Eugene F. *Fundamentals of Financial Management.* 7th ed. (Ft. Worth, TX: The Dryden Press, 1994).

REVIEW QUESTIONS

1. What objections to modern techniques do users of traditional risk measures have? Why are their objections off target?
2. Describe the difference between risk and uncertainty.
3. How might one estimate probabilities related to real estate investments? What role do subjective probability measures play in the analysis?
4. Explain *discrete* and *continuous* probability distributions.
5. Explain the usefulness of variance and standard deviation in risk measurement.
6. Describe the calculation for the coefficient of variation and explain its purpose in the analysis.
7. How are profitability indices used in development of risk profiles?

DISCUSSION QUESTIONS

1. Do you think the probability distribution approach to risk measurement discussed in this chapter is more likely to be adopted as computer literacy becomes increasingly widespread?
2. If probabilities cannot be measured using sample data, but must be expressed as subjective probabilities, is there any benefit in expressing them in quantitative terms?
3. What are some examples of events or contract provisions that could skew or attenuate the probability distribution of possible cash flows from a real estate development?

CHAPTER 19

Risk Management in a Portfolio Context

Earlier chapters explore the relationship between expected return and risk, and define risk as expected variance. To treat equally both positive and negative variance from expectations, without the distorting effect of simply squaring the variance, we used the square root of the sum of the squared variances—standard deviation. When more than one asset is included in a portfolio, a third dimension must be incorporated in the risk-return equation: covariance of returns.

Covariance measures the way the total variance is altered when additional assets are added to a portfolio. It is a function of the correlation between the returns on portfolio assets. The lower the covariance, the smaller the risk in the portfolio. This lumping together within the portfolio of assets that exhibit low covariance is the cornerstone of diversification to reduce aggregate risk.

MODERN PORTFOLIO THEORY AND RISK MANAGEMENT

Modern portfolio theory, fathered by Harry Markowitz, was born at midcentury. Most authorities mark its beginning in 1952 with the publication of Markowitz' seminal article, "Portfolio Selection."[1] The literature expanded exponentially during the 1960s and 1970s, and the proliferation continues little abated.

The essence of modern portfolio theory is that among the universe of possible investment portfolios there is a subset that represents optimal combinations of expected return and risk, and that the precise choice from among this subset depends upon an investor's attitude toward risk. Contemporary literature on real estate portfolio management indicates that modern portfolio theory is the dominant influence that molds institutional portfolio managers' strategy.

Systematic and Unsystematic Risk

It is impossible to eliminate all risk through diversification: Some risk is inherent in the market itself. This *market risk* is inherent in the market system, and for that reason is often called *systematic risk*. It exists without regard to selection of specific assets.

In contrast, risk associated with a specific asset (or a specific industry or geographic locale) can be eliminated in a portfolio by matching the asset with others that exhibit low or negative covariance. Because this risk element is asset-specific and not inherent in the system, it is sometimes called *unsystematic risk*.

The relationship between systematic and unsystematic risk, and the reduction in unsystematic risk through diversification, is illustrated in Figure 19.1. It is widely accepted that unsystematic risk accounts for roughly half the total risk in the stock market. We lack data to support a generalization of this type regarding real estate markets, but the localized nature of real estate assets suggests that unsystematic risk probably accounts for a larger portion of total risk.[2] Variation in rent levels and vacancy rates due to market-wide changes in supply and demand variables are examples of systematic risk associated with real estate assets. Site-specific factors such as building defects, and micro-market variables that affect rents and vacancy rates are unsystematic risks that can be eliminated by diversification without reducing expected returns.

Market prices, to the extent the market is efficient, reflect systematic but not unsystematic risk. This implies that investors are compensated by higher expected returns for bearing systematic risk but are not compensated for bearing unsystematic risk, and that holding a poorly diversified portfolio is more costly for real estate investors than for stock or bond investors. Stated another way, real estate investors stand to gain more in terms of risk reduction by diversifying their portfolios than do other investors.

| Figure 19.1 | Eliminating Nonsystematic Risk through Diversification |

The Efficient Frontier

Figure 19.2 portrays various portfolios, measured in terms of their expected return and risk. If every possible portfolio of risky assets—every attainable combination of risk and return—were included in the figure it would of course have more dots, but there is no reason to expect that it would differ in configuration. Of particular interest are the attainable combinations along the top border of the universe of attainable combinations. These embody the maximum returns obtainable with given levels of risk or the minimum risk possible for given levels of return. All portfolios located elsewhere in the universe of attainable combinations are suboptimal, since it is possible to gain higher expected returns without shouldering more risk or to reduce risk without sacrificing expected returns, by altering the portfolio.

Modern Portfolio Theory identifies the sets of attainable combinations along the upper border as *efficient portfolios,* because no others offer higher expected returns for the same or lower levels of risk, or lower risk with the same or higher levels of expected return. In the aggregate, these efficient portfolios represent the *efficient frontier.* The idea is to select from among the efficient portfolios that single alternative that maximizes investor satisfaction, given the investor's objectives, capital constraints and attitude risk.

An important observation is that the set of attainable combinations contains not just real estate investments, but the entire universe of risky investments. The optimal efficient portfolio will almost certainly include some real estate assets and some other risky assets as well.

Moreover, modern portfolio theory posits that the efficient frontier changes when borrowing and lending opportunities are introduced. Investors can choose assets that have no default risk and that are so short term as to virtually eliminate interest rate risk. When these assets, called *risk-free assets,* are added to the portfolio, the efficient frontier becomes a straight line below point *C* on Figure 19.3.

Figure 19.2   **The Efficient Frontier**

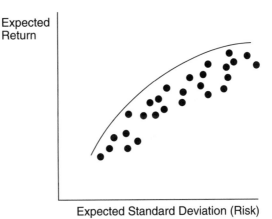

Expected Standard Deviation (Risk)

Figure 19.3   **The Efficient Frontier with a Risk-Free Asset**

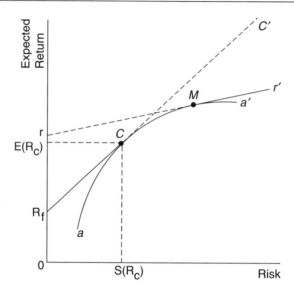

A highly risk-averse investor might choose to hold only the risk-free asset, in which case the risk would be zero and the expected return R_f. Alternatively, the risk-averse investor could chose to hold the portfolio indicated by point *M,* or any other portfolio along the efficiency frontier above point *C.*

If the investor could borrow as well as lend at the risk-free rate, the set of efficient portfolios would extend beyond point *C* in Figure 19.3, along the broken line. Portfolios between R_f and *C* are combinations of risky and the risk-free asset. Portfolio *C* is comprised wholly of risky assets. After committing all available funds to portfolio *C,* the investor could borrow at rate R_f to increase the size of the investment in portfolio *C.* This would move the portfolio out into the risk-return plane along the broken line *CC'* in Figure 19.3.

It is highly unlikely, however, that an investor could borrow at the risk-free rate. When borrowing costs are higher than risk-free lending rates, the only part of the line $R_f CC'$ which will be included in the set of attainable combinations is the segment $R_f C$. If the investor's borrowing rate is given by the point *r* on the vertical axis of Figure 19.3, then the risk-return combinations available through borrowing to increase the size of the portfolio is given by the segment *Mr'* of the line *rMr'.*[3]

Under these conditions the set of attainable combinations in the efficient portfolio is given by the line $R_f CMr'$ in Figure 19.3. This line is reproduced in Figure 19.4 without the broken segments. The efficient portfolio is comprised of a combination of the risk-free assets and portfolio *C* in varying proportions to the point where the expected return is $E(R_c)$, at which point the portfolio con-

Figure 19.4	The Efficient Frontier with Borrowing and Lending

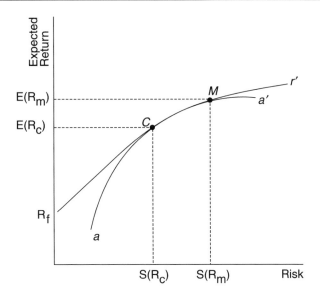

tains none of the risk-free asset. Beyond this point expected returns can be increased by altering the portfolio of risky assets as indicated by the efficiency frontier from point *C* to point *M*. Upon reaching the combination of risky assets represented by point M in Figure 19.4, the expected return is $E(R_m)$ and the perceived risk is $S(R_m)$. Higher levels of expected return with minimum risk can be obtained by borrowing at interest rate *r* and purchasing an ever larger quantity of the invariant portfolio of risky assets represented by point *M*. This moves the investor out into the risk-return plan along the line segment *Mr′*. The length of the line segment is determined by the amount of financial leverage the investor can undertake without increasing the cost of borrowing.

REAL ESTATE'S ROLE IN THE EFFICIENT PORTFOLIO

Remember that, given the assumptions underlying Modern Portfolio Theory, any portfolio of risky assets other than those between points *C* and *r* in Figure 19.4 represent inefficient combinations. Investors holding other combinations can increase return without shouldering more risk, or reduce risk without sacrificing return by altering their portfolio until it represents a point along this line segment. Several research studies have indicated that real estate will represent a significant proportion of these efficient portfolios.[4]

Nobody knows exactly where the efficient frontier lies, of course, or exactly what assets it will encompass. Even if sufficient data were available, performing the mathematical computations to identify the frontier would be a prodigious task. Sanders, Pagliari and Webb note, for example, that to create an optimal portfolio of common stocks from the Wilshire 5000 Index would require estimating approximately 12.5 million paired correlation coefficients.[5] When real estate is added to the universe of possible investments, the problems of data availability and reliability are magnified several times over. The result has been described as a "fuzzy" efficient frontier.[6] This implies that instead of a single efficient portfolio occupying each point on the efficient frontier, representing a discrete return-risk expectation, numerous dissimilarly weighted portfolios offer the same expected risk-return combination.

Given these observations, it is not surprising to find widespread disagreement regarding the proper role of real estate in institutional portfolios. With only a few exceptions, studies suggesting particular portfolio allocations to real estate conclude that 10 to 20 percent is optimal. Yet research into actual real estate holdings among pension funds revealed an average of only 4.37 percent of assets committed to real estate equities in 1991 (the study was limited to funds that exceed $100 million in assets).[7] The commitment ranged from zero to 17 percent of assets.

REAL ESTATE DIVERSIFICATION STRATEGIES

Real estate's positive impact on portfolio performance has been well documented. There is widespread disagreement about how much real estate should be included in a diversified portfolio, but little dissension concerning the merit of its inclusion. Moreover, modern portfolio theory and its subsequent spinoffs argue uniformly for diversification to eliminate nonsystematic risk. There remains the question of how diversification should be pursued—geographically, across asset categories and through time.

Joseph L. Pagliari, Jr., suggests categorizing product alternatives by the defining characteristics of geography, product type, and stage in product life-cycle.[8] He illustrates the alternatives using a diagram similar to Figure 19.5, and observes that each cell in the array has risk and expected return characteristics that are at least partially unique.

Geographic Diversification

Risk reduction by geographic diversification presupposes geographic locals where levels of economic activity are not highly correlated. Nothing is accomplished by acquiring widely separated assets that behave economically as if they were side by side. Owning property on the east and west coast will not reduce

| Figure 19.5 | **The Range of Diversification Alternatives** |

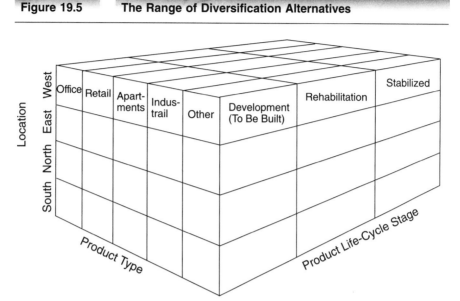

SOURCE: Adapted from "Real Estate In 3-D: See It Now!" by Joseph L. Pagliari, Jr., *Real Estate Issues,* vol. 15, no. 2 (Fall/Winter 1990).

the volatility of one's portfolio, for example, if the coastal cities are subject to roughly similar economic forces.

SUMMARY

When assets are considered in a portfolio context rather than individually, the focus shifts to risk and expected return for the portfolio. Risk associated with an individual asset is less important than the effect the asset has on total portfolio risk. An asset that, taken individually, is more risky than the total risk for the portfolio to which it is being added can actually reduce the aggregate riskiness of the portfolio.

Most portfolio managers address their task from the perspective of modern portfolio theory, which emphasizes identification of the subset of portfolios that generate the maximum return for a given level of aggregate risk, and selecting the specific subset that matches the profile of the investor in terms of return objectives and attitude toward risk.

Investigators generally agree that real estate is an essential component of efficient portfolios. They do not agree concerning the percentage of the portfolio that should be devoted to real estate. Portfolio managers appear skeptical of recommendations from academic researchers about how much real estate should be included in their portfolios.

NOTES

1. Harry Markowitz, "Portfolio Selection," *Journal of Finance,* March 1952, pp. 77–91.

2. See Anthony B. Sanders, Joseph L. Pagliari, Jr., and James R. Webb, "Portfolio Management Concepts and Their Application to Real Estate," *The Handbook of Real Estate Portfolio Management,* Chicago: Richard D. Irwin, Inc., 1995, p. 131.

3. Nicholas W. Schrock, "Asset Choice under Uncertainty with Borrowing Introduced," *Western Economic Journal,* March 1967, pp. 201–210.

4. See Vickie L. Bajtelsmit and Elaine M. Worzala, "Real Estate Allocation in Pension Fund Portfolios," *The Journal of Real Estate Portfolio Management,* vol. 1, no. 1, 1995, pp. 25–38. The authors summarized 11 studies published between 1984 and 1991, that recommended substantial commitments to real estate in institutional portfolios.

5. Anthony B. Sanders, Joseph L. Pagliari, Jr., and James R. Webb, *op. cit.,* p. 139.

6. Richard B. Gold, "Why the Efficient Frontier for Real Estate Is 'Fuzzy'," *The Journal of Real Estate Portfolio Management,* vol. 1, no. 1, 1995, pp. 59–66.

7. Bajtelsmit and Worzala, *op. cit.*

8. Joseph L. Pagliari, Jr., "Real Estate in 3-D: See It Now!" *Real Estate Issues,* Fall–Winter, 1990, pp. 16–19.

RECOMMENDED READINGS

Pagliari, Joseph L. Jr., editor. *The Handbook of Real Estate Portfolio Management.* Chicago: Richard D. Irwin, Inc., 1995.

Pagliari, Joseph L., Jr., James R. Webb and Joseph J. Del Casino. "Applying MPT to Institutional Real Estate Portfolios: The Good, the Bad and the Uncertain." *The Journal of Real Estate Portfolio Management,* vol. 1, no. 1, 1995. pp. 67–88.

REVIEW QUESTIONS

1. Describe the relationship between variance and covariance.
2. What is the relationship between covariance and portfolio riskiness?
3. In modern portfolio theory, how do portfolios on the efficient frontier differ from others in the universe of possible portfolios?
4. Distinguish between systematic and unsystematic risk.
5. How does the inclusion of a risk-free asset change the configuration of the efficient frontier?
6. What portion of an efficient portfolio do academic researchers generally conclude should be comprised of real estate equities?

7. Why is it unlikely that actual portfolios will in fact always lay along the efficient frontier?
8. Under what circumstances would geographic diversification not necessarily reduce portfolio risk?
9. In what sense is the efficient frontier "fuzzy"?

DISCUSSION QUESTIONS

1. Would the shape of the efficient frontier likely be different for a taxable and an nontaxable institutional investor? How might income taxes alter the configuration of the efficient frontier?
2. If you conclude that income taxes do alter the shape of the efficient frontier for some institutions and not for others, is this likely to affect investment decisions in a way that is beneficial to society at large, or is the effect likely to be harmful? Will the effect be neutral?

PART SIX: Case Problem

Refer again to the Academic Arms Apartments case problem at the end of Part Five.

1. Discounting at 12 percent, what will be the present value of the project if the investor's marginal income tax rate is increased to 33 percent for the third and all subsequent years of the investment period (including the tax levied on the gain on disposal)? Will this reduce the equity yield below the investor's 12 percent minimum acceptable expected rate of return?
2. Suppose the income tax rate does not change, but actual net operating income and selling price are five percent below expectations? How will this affect the desirability of the investment outcome?
3. Suppose NOI and selling price are 5 percent above the expected level.
4. Would it be helpful to know something about the degree of confidence the forecaster has in the cash-flow forecast?

PART SEVEN

The Investment Analysis Process Illustrated

Readers have by now been exposed to the entire real estate investment analysis process. The road has been long and involved, however, and our final objective has at times been obscured by emphasis on detail. This section is designed to bring together procedures from the preceding sections by applying the discounted cash-flow model to solve actual investment analysis problems. To demonstrate the basic model's flexibility and universal applicability, a variety of problems are introduced. Each example illustrates a separate aspect of the analysis process, and none should be omitted from the serious student's reading program.

CHAPTER 20

Investment Feasibility Analysis

We have seen that real estate investors, whether they take a debt or an equity position (that is, whether they are mortgage lenders or equity investors), place funds at risk in anticipation of receiving a future stream of cash receipts. They are in effect buying a set of assumptions about the project's ability to generate the anticipated revenue streams. Feasibility analysis addresses the likelihood that the specific course of action will be successful.

Simply stated, a proposal is feasible if there is a reasonable probability of achieving individual or organizational goals. Feasibility analysts seek to answer the question, "Will it work?" In an investment analysis context, this involves estimating the amount and timing of required cash expenditures and expected cash inflows and assessing the degree of confidence that attaches to the estimates. More precisely:

> A real estate project is "feasible" when the real estate analyst determines that there is a reasonable likelihood of satisfying explicit objectives when a selected course of action is tested for fit to a context of specific constraints and limited resources.[1]

This definition implies a careful and explicit statement of objectives against which expected outcomes can be measured. It implies also that a proposed action fits the constraints imposed by the physical, financial and social environment in which the program will be carried out.

Rather than a single specific course of action, several alternatives may have been identified. Feasibility analysis seeks to determine whether all, none or some of the alternatives offer an acceptable probability of achieving minimum investor objectives.

THE NATURE OF THE FEASIBILITY QUESTION

A *financial feasibility study,* whether formal or informal, addresses the question of whether the project's operating income will be adequate to service a proposed mortgage indebtedness or whether a proposed offering price will result in a minimum acceptable investment outcome. For a proposed development or redevelopment, the study addresses the question of whether the relationship between development costs and market acceptance will enable the developer to meet minimum acceptable investment targets.

Relationship to Investment Analysis

That a proposed course of action is feasible does not imply that it is appropriate. There may be feasible alternatives that are more attractive. Feasibility analysis provides the investment analyst with only a point of departure. It answers the question of what an investor *can do* but not what an investor *should do.*

One widely employed book explains the distinction this way: "Feasibility analysis is more reportorial than valuative or action-oriented. . . . Investment analysis, on the other hand . . . is concerned with *selection* from among alternative courses of action to achieve the 'best' results in terms of the client/investor's objectives."[2]

Feasibility Analysis and Valuation Analysis

Valuation analysis (appraisal) addresses the question of value. It seeks answers to the question, *what is the asset worth?* When the value being estimated is market value, the appraisal must incorporate the assumption that the asset will be employed in its *highest and best use,* the use that generates the greatest value.[3]

Valuation analysts (appraisers) start with no preconceived notion of the use to which an asset will be put. Rather, they identify a set of alternatives thought to be nominally feasible: uses that offer a reasonable probability of meeting prevailing financial performance standards. From this set of feasible alternatives, the analyst seeks to identify one specific use that supports the greatest value indication for the property.

This implies that even though valuation analysis and feasibility analysis differ in terms of the question they seek to answer, they employ much of the same analytical data. In both cases the analyst estimates the stream of net revenue a property is likely to generate. Therefore, both require careful study and analysis of market data.

Dimensions of the Feasibility Question

Feasibility analysts are likely to approach their craft with a bias flavored by their professional backgrounds. Thus, engineers are likely to concentrate on physical characteristics of the site and the structure, while a land planner might be especially concerned with land use regulations and an overall land use plan. In like manner, investment analysts are inclined to approach feasibility questions from a financial perspective.

Yet for a proposal to be feasible, it must be physically possible, given the constraints of the site; legally feasible, given the constraints of laws, regulations and land use restrictions; and financially feasible.

Figure 20.1 illustrates the point. There is likely to be a broad range of physically feasible uses and a broad range of legally feasible uses. Similarly, there will be a significant set of alternatives that, if they were legally and physically feasible, would offer a reasonable probability of achieving the investor's financial objectives. Within each set, most of the alternatives are ruled out because they are not also in the other two sets. Only those alternatives in the shaded area in Figure 20.1 are simultaneously physically, legally and financially feasible.

The Primacy of the Objective

Before feasibility analysts can address the question of individual or enterprise objectives and the likely outcome of a proposed course of action, the objectives themselves must be delineated. Expressed differently, the feasibility problem must be defined. James Graaskamp has argued that real estate feasibility analysis divides conveniently into three problems:

1. *With a Predetermined Site, Investigate Alternative Uses.* The enterprise has identified a specific site and is searching among alternative possible uses for one that offers the best probability of meeting enterprise objectives. The physical and legal characteristics of the site and its location with reference to its economic environment become the takeoff point for the analysis.
2. *With a Predetermined Use, Investigate Alternative Sites.* The enterprise has a specific activity in mind and is searching for the most appropriate site or set

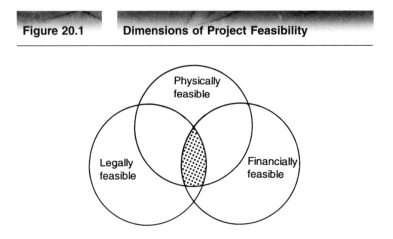

Figure 20.1   Dimensions of Project Feasibility

of existing improvements. The needs of the specific use and the economics of its locational needs are the takeoff point for feasibility analysis under these circumstances.

3. *With Predetermined Funds, Investigate Alternative Investment Opportunities.* The enterprise wishes to identify the subset of available opportunities that fit its investment objectives so that it can choose the most promising alternative.

The Significance of Limitations

All economic activity is undertaken with the handicap of limited resources, and these constitute a constraint on the range of feasible alternatives. Values, goals and objectives also place limitations, as do attitudes toward bearing risk.

Physical characteristics of sites limit the range of improvements they will support or the nature of activity they will tolerate. Society, through ordinances (zoning codes, building codes, fire codes, housing codes and so forth) and regulatory oversight, places limits by stating what must be done and what may not be done at specific sites. Limitations should be identified and defined explicitly early in the feasibility analysis process.

STEPS IN THE FEASIBILITY ANALYSIS PROCESS

Whether undertaken on a formal or an informal basis, feasibility analysis proceeds through distinctly identifiable steps. The general steps in the process are listed here as if they take place in sequence. However, the process is iterative and continuous through the period of development or acquisition.

1. Assess physical and legal aspects of the site. Appropriate specialists are employed as required to ascertain the adequacy or physical capability of the site in terms of zoning, sewer, water, subsoil, drainage, freedom from contaminants and so forth.
2. Estimate demand for the proposed real estate services. Determine required amenities and users' basic space requirements. Depending on the type of improvements, determine the need for transportation, accessibility, services, taxes and so forth.
3. Analyze competitive space. Consider present and future competitive sites to estimate the degree of pressure on rents and likely vacancy rates.
4. Estimate the cost of construction, alteration, rehabilitation or fix-up, as proposed in the initial concept, and the cost of facility operations. If several alternative proposals are involved, estimate the costs associated with each.
5. Estimate the cost of financing for various possible combinations of equity and debt financing packages. This includes an estimate of likely mortgage loan ratios, amortization periods, interest rates, front-end fees and income tax consequences.
6. Estimate the rate at which units will be rented or sold *(absorbed)*.

7. Develop a schedule of cash inflows and outflows. This involves projecting the cost and timing of development or redevelopment expenditures, the cash receipts from financing and from rental operations and the cost of operations and debt service. The output from this process is a multiple-year operating cash flow projection such as that illustrated in earlier chapters.

8. Evaluate the anticipated cash flows for adequacy, given the investor's minimum acceptable rate of return and the degree of risk the investor is prepared to accept.

PRELIMINARY FINANCIAL FEASIBILITY

A full-scale feasibility study is time-consuming and expensive. Investors therefore need a simplified process for identifying projects that can be eliminated early in the analysis. Consequently, feasibility analysis should be viewed as a continuous process that becomes progressively more involved as the investor approaches the final decision.

Recall that a project is feasible if it has a reasonable probability of achieving the goals of participating individuals and organizations. If the venture is a new development or a redevelopment, this includes regulatory authorities who must approve the project. For both new and existing projects, it will include an investor or group of investors who will take an equity position and a separate investor or group of investors who will take a debt position.

Regulatory Authorities

Real estate is highly regulated. The public sector is a partner in every development or redevelopment project, whether the private developer likes it or not. Just as the private investor approaches the development or redevelopment project with a set of explicit goals, so does the public sector. Approval for a project—rezoning or zoning variances, building permits and occupancy permits—will not be forthcoming unless the regulatory authorities believe it has a reasonable expectation of meeting the public sector's goals.

Lender Objectives

Simply stated, lender objectives are that the project generate sufficient cash flow to permit repayment of interest and principal on the mortgage loan and that the project's most probable selling price will be sufficient, in the event of default and foreclosure, to generate through a forced sale the cash necessary to retire the mortgage loan. Two common measures of this ability are the debt coverage ratio and the loan-to-value ratio, both of which were introduced in Chapter 7.

The debt coverage ratio is the relationship between a project's expected net operating income and the annual debt service obligation. Lenders specify a minimum acceptable ratio that varies with the degree of confidence they have in the project and with the availability of funds. Minimum debt coverage ratios of 1.10 to 1.30 are common.

The loan-to-value ratio is the relationship between a project's estimated market value and the amount of the mortgage loan. Lenders specify maximum acceptable loan-to-value ratios, and these often range between .70 and 1.0, depending on the nature of the project, the availability of borrowed money and the borrower's personal credit rating.

Equity Investors' Objectives

Equity investors' objectives are often stated in terms of minimum acceptable rates of return on equity funds. They often also specify a minimum acceptable curent yield: the relationship between current-year cash flow to the equity investors and the amount of equity funds invested.

Front-Door Approach

Preliminary financial feasibility deals with threshold questions concerning a proposed venture: will initial operating results satisfy the threshold criteria of both debt and equity investors? This type of investigation has been characterized as solvency testing. It enables a quick look at the impact of alternative revenue sources for a project and of alternative financing structures. Two common approaches to preliminary solvency testing have been called front-door and back-door approaches.[4]

When project cost is given or assumed, the front-door approach involves estimating the minimum gross rent that will be required to meet investors' threshold criteria. To see how the approach is applied when there are both equity and debt investors, both of whom have specified minimum threshold criteria, consider Example 20.1.

Example 20.1

A small office building (27,200 square feet of net leasable area) is available for $2,880,000. A one-year operating forecast for the property has yielded the following operating estimates:

Market rent, per square foot	$23.50
Vacancy and uncollectible rent (as a percent of potential gross)	8%
Operating expenses, per square foot	$ 9.20

A check with likely mortgage lenders reveals that the best available loan terms are interest at 11.5 percent per annum on a fully amortizing 20-year loan whose rate will be subject to renegotiation after seven years. Moreover, the investor is unlikely to be able to borrow more than 75 percent of the purchase price, and the minimum acceptable debt coverage ratio appears to be 1.20.

The prospective equity investors are a small group of partners in a professional practice, and they have agreed that their minimum acceptable pre-tax current yield is six percent. The maximum acceptable default ratio (the occupancy level at which the net operating income is just sufficient to cover the debt service) is 85 percent.

Information from Example 20.1 is incorporated into Figure 20.2, which illustrates the approach. Consider first the lender's criteria. Since the lender has specified a maximum loan-to-value ratio of .75, the maximum mortgage loan is 75 percent of the project's cost, or $2,160,000 (cost in this case serves as a proxy for market value—the two are not necessarily the same). The lender has also cited loan terms: a fully amortizing 20-year loan with interest at 11.5 percent per annum, with a seven-year call. The loan constant associated with these terms is .12797, and this implies maximum annual debt service of $276,415. Here are the calculations in summary:

Project cost	$2,880,000
Times: Loan-to-value ratio	.75
Maximum mortgage loan	$2,160,000
Times: Annual debt service constant	.12797
Maximum annual debt service	$ 276,415

Equity funds are required to bridge the gap between project cost and the available mortgage loan. Since the lender will provide no more than 75 percent of project cost, equity investors must provide the remaining 25 percent: $720,000. The equity investors who will be involved in this project require a 6 percent annual yield on equity funds. This implies a minimum annual cash flow to the equity investors of $43,200:

Project cost	$2,880,000
Times: One minus loan-to-value ratio	.25
Equity funds required	$ 720,000
Times: Minimum annual yield	.06
Minimum annual cash flow to equity investors	$ 43,200

Debt service and before-tax cash flow to equity investors necessarily come from net operating income (unless, as is sometimes the case, the investment starts with cash reserves to make up the annual shortfall). The first year's net operating income, therefore, must be equal to these two amounts: $276,415 + $43,200 = $319,615.

Figure 20.2   **Preliminary Feasibility Analysis**
Front-Door Approach

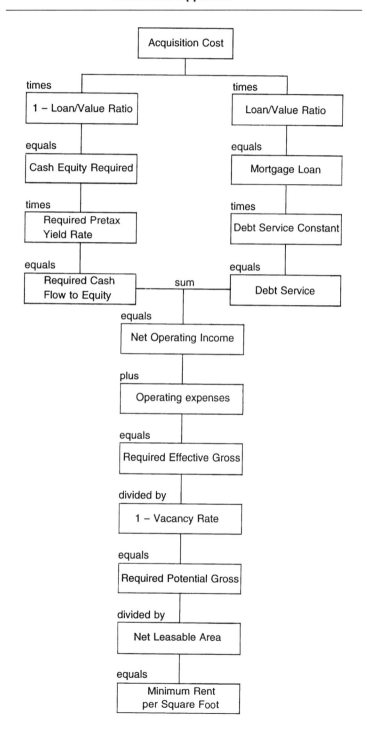

Effective gross income must cover operating expenses (including reserves for repairs and replacements if any are planned) and net operating income requirements. The first year's effective gross, therefore, must be $569,855:

Net operating income	$319,615
Plus: Operating expenses ($9.20 × 27,200 sq. ft.)	250,240
Effective gross income	$569,855

Since Example 20.1 indicates an estimated vacancy and bad debt loss equaling 8 percent of potential gross income, it follows that effective gross income will be (1 – .08), or .92 times the potential gross. The minimum potential gross, therefore, is (effective gross /.92): $569,855/.92 = $619,408. Dividing the minimum potential gross revenue by the 27,200 square feet of net leasable space yields a minimum acceptable rent of $22.77 per square foot. This compares favorably with the market rent of $23.50 per square foot cited in Example 20.1, a number that would have been generated with reference to the rate in comparable units in the market area.

The front-door preliminary analysis can be extended to determine the default ratio, the occupancy level below which net operating income will be insufficient to cover operating expenses and debt service, and the debt coverage ratio. Both of these ratios are dimensions of risk analysis.

The default ratio, or break-even occupancy level, is determined by adding the operating expense to the debt service and dividing by the gross potential revenue. For the project in Example 20.1, the ratio is 85 percent, just barely low enough to satisfy the equity investors. Here is the computation:

$$\text{Default ratio} = \frac{\text{Operating Expenses} + \text{Debt Service}}{\text{Gross Potential Revenue}} = \frac{\$250,240 + \$276,415}{\$619,408}$$
$$= .85, \text{ or } 85 \text{ percent}$$

The debt coverage ratio is 1.16, too low to satisfy lender requirements:

$$\text{Debt coverage ratio} = \frac{\text{Net Operating Income}}{\text{Debt Service}} = \frac{\$319,615}{\$276,415} = 1.16$$

Since the front-door approach to preliminary feasibility satisfies the equity investors but not the lenders, we need to look at the project from the lender's perspective. This involves a back-door approach.

Back-Door Approach

As presented in Example 20.1, a survey of comparable projects in the market area has generated an estimate of possible gross rents and operating expenses that can be employed to estimate the maximum supportable mortgage loan. From this we can back into the maximum amount the equity investors can com-

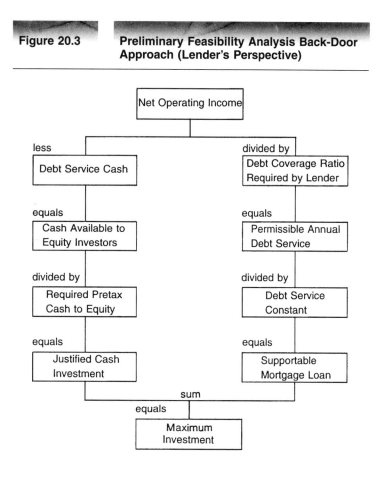

Figure 20.3 **Preliminary Feasibility Analysis Back-Door Approach (Lender's Perspective)**

mit to the project, given their minimum acceptable current yield. Figure 20.3 illustrates relationships involved in the back-door approach.

If the space is leased at the average rate in the market area for comparable properties ($23.50 per square foot, as shown in Example 20.1), the cash flow available to service the debt and provide cash (dividends) to the equity investors will be $333,824. Here are the numbers:

Potential Gross (27,200 sq. ft. @ $23.50)	$639,200
Less: Vacancy Loss @ 8%	51,136
Effective Gross Income	$588,064
Less: Operating Expenses (27,200 sq. ft. @ $9.20)	250,240
Net Operating Income	$337,824

Since lenders have indicated that they will insist on a debt coverage ratio of at least 1.20 ($1.20 of net operating income for every $1.00 of annual debt service), the maximum supportable debt service is $337,824/1.20, or $281,520. For the loan terms given in Example 20.1, this implies a mortgage loan of no more than $2,199,925 (say $2.2 million), determined as follows:

Net Operating Income	$ 337,824
Divided by: Minimum Debt Coverage Ratio	1.20
Maximum Supportable Debt Service	$ 281,520
Divided by: Debt Service Constant, 11.5%, 20 years	.127968
Maximum Mortgage Loan	$2,199,925

A mortgage loan of this amount, consuming $281,520 of the annual net operating income, will leave just $56,304 available for the equity investors. Earning a current yield of six percent implies an equity investment of no more than $938,400 and a total cost of no more than $3,138,325, calculated as follows.

Net Operating Income	$ 337,824
Less: Annual Debt Service	281,520
Cash Flow to Equity Investors	$ 56,304
Divided by: Equity Yield Rate	.06
Maximum Equity Investment	$ 938,400
Plus: Available Mortgage	2,199,925
Maximum Project Cost	$3,138,325

Remembering that the lenders will accept a loan-to-value ratio of no more than 75 percent, we note the relationship between the mortgage loan and the maximum project cost in the preceding calculations: $2,199,925/ $3,138,325 = .70, or 70 percent; the loan-to-value criterion is satisfied. Note also that this formulation meets the equity investors' insistence that the default ratio not exceed 85 percent:

$$\text{Default Ratio} = \frac{\text{Operating Expenses} + \text{Debt Service}}{\text{Potential Gross}} = \frac{\$250,240 + \$281,520}{\$639,200}$$
$$= .83, \text{ or } 83 \text{ percent}$$

Rational equity investors will also have an after-tax rate of return target for the entire anticipated investment cycle. We have seen in prior chapters, however, that developing such an estimate involves an extensive and somewhat involved forecasting and discounting operation. Committing time and money to accomplish the more detailed and complete analysis will be justified only if the investment proposal meets the preliminary screening criteria just investigated. Those that meet the preliminary criteria are subjected to a long-term forecast and analyzed on an after-tax cash-flow basis.

FORMAT FOR A FEASIBILITY REPORT

The report's organization should reflect its purpose and facilitate its use, not merely meet some predetermined criteria for appropriateness. Thus the format suggested here is not in any way definitive. Figure 20.4 presents the suggested format in summary form. Here is a description of each element:

- *Title Page.* In addition to being laid out attractively, the title page should identify the nature of the report and the property involved, as well as the analyst who has prepared the report. It may also identify the party for whom the report is prepared and the date of preparation.
- *Table of Contents.* The table of contents is designed to facilitate finding material in the report. A very short report might have no table at all. Longer reports must have a table of contents that, as a minimum, tells the page number on which each major report section begins. The extent of detail in the table—the levels of subheadings for which page numbers are provided—will depend on the report's length and complexity. The issue is easily resolved if you keep in mind the purpose of preparing the table: to facilitate finding specific information in the report.
- *Lists of Tables and Exhibits.* Most feasibility reports are liberally sprinkled with tables, maps and—in many cases—photographs. This is as it should be; well-designed tables and exhibits communicate masses of information economically. For tables and exhibits to be useful, however, the reader must be able to find them. This is best assured by separate lists of tables and exhibits immediately following the table of contents.
- *Executive Summary.* Executive summaries are of two basic types: narrative and outline. Both should be brief and succinct. They should give their reader key information including the analyst's findings and conclusions, devoid of all explanatory or substantiating detail. Readers who want further detail will look to the body of the report.
- *Scope and Limitations.* Cost or time considerations often impose limits on feasibility analysts. Clients may prefer that the analyst simply accept that certain assumptions are correct, for example, or may wish that data collected for some alternative use be incorporated without having the earlier research

Figure 20.4   **Format for a Feasibility Report**

- Title page
- Table of Contents
- Lists of Tables and Exhibits
- Executive Summary
- Scope and Limitations
- Regional and City Analysis
- Location and Site Analysis
- Market Analysis
- Financial Analysis and Cash-Flow Projections
- Conclusions and Recommendations

replicated. This section tells what the analyst did and did not do. It specifies the extent of the investigation and clearly and unequivocally describes any unsubstantiated premises or assumptions such as the physical nature of the soil, the legal character of property title or any other pertinent item that the analyst did not personally verify.

- *Regional and City Analysis.* Only information about the region and city that bears directly on the feasibility analysis is reported. Analysts are often tempted to include everything that they know or can find, whether or not it has any direct bearing on the project's feasibility. Resist this temptation by forcing yourself to observe the discipline of directly relating each piece of information to the feasibility analysis and showing its pertinence in the report. Then, after completing a semifinal draft of the report, go over this section and see how much you can edit out without reducing the report's usefulness. The principal types of information included in regional and city analysis are growth trends and economic base analysis.

- *Location and Site Analysis.* Include physical characteristics that bear on the feasibility of the proposed site use. Examples include width and depth, typography, drainage, soil composition, utilities and so forth. Also include relevant legal characteristics: easements, zoning, setback requirements and other restrictions that might limit the feasible uses of the site. Do not include irrelevant information.

- *Market Analysis.* This section should explain the overall market conditions for the type of property being considered and the direction and strength of market trends. Supply and demand analysis, an integral part of the market analysis, will include an extensive analysis of supply considerations: the current supply of competing space, developments now in progress and the prospects for future development. Demand will also be analyzed: current vacancy rates, the absorption rate under current market conditions and the prospects for future absorption rates. From these supply and demand projections should flow a forecast of future rental rates and/or prices for competing space.

- *Financial Analysis and Cash-Flow Projections.* Market analysis provides the input for projecting cash flow from the proposed development or acquisition. The cash-flow section requires consideration of financing arrangements, cost and operating expenses. The cash-flow model should include estimates of income tax consequences of ownership and operation (and of disposal, if applicable) and anticipated equity buildup through paying down the balance of mortgage indebtedness and of appreciation. This section of the report will include computation of appropriate investment indices such as operating ratios, break even cash throw-off ratio, payback period ratio and debt service coverage ratio. Investment risk should be evaluated in terms of possible market changes, investment rate movements, legal exposure, changes in the political environment and natural hazards.

- *Conclusions and Recommendations.* This section may include a set of recommendations. It should summarize the findings in such key areas as security and risk, current cash-flow prospects, future cash flow and appreciation, investment liquidity, inflationary hedge, tax consequences and nonpecuniary objectives if applicable.

SUMMARY

Feasibility analysis addresses the question of whether a planned course of action is likely to achieve individual or enterprise objectives, given the available resources and specific constraints. Key issues are the legal, physical and financial feasibility of a project proposal. Feasibility typically addresses the issue of the most appropriate use for a particular site, the most appropriate site for a predetermined use or the most appropriate outlet for investment funds.

Feasibility analysis is iterative and continuous. It involves the following eight steps:

1. Assessing the physical and legal aspects of the site
2. Estimating demand for the space
3. Analyzing competitive space
4. Estimating costs of acquisition, construction or rehabilitation
5. Estimating the cost and availability of borrowed funds
6. Estimating absorption rates
7. Developing cash-flow schedules
8. Evaluating the estimated cash flows in terms of acceptability of the expected outcome

Financial feasibility presumes that both equity investors' and lenders' financial objectives will be met if the project goes forward. Before undertaking a full-scale financial feasibility analysis, it is prudent to use a screening technique to identify with minimum cost projects that obviously are not feasible. The preliminary analysis should proceed from both the equity investors' and the lenders' points of view.

NOTES

1. James A. Graaskamp, *A Guide to Feasibility Analysis* (Chicago: Society of Real Estate Appraisers, 1970), p. 4.

2. Stephen D. Messner, Byrl N. Boyce, Harold G. Trimble and Robert L. Ward, *Analyzing Real Estate Opportunities: Market and Feasibility Studies* (Chicago: National Association of Realtors®, 1977) p. 86.

3. On page 171, *The Dictionary of Real Estate Appraisal,* 3rd ed. (Chicago: Appraisal Institute, 1993) defines highest and best use as the reasonably probable and legal use that results in the highest value.

4. James A. Graaskamp, *Fundamentals of Real Estate Development, ULI Development Component Series* (Washington, DC: ULI—The Urban Land Institute, 1981) pp. 13–23.

RECOMMENDED READINGS

Derbes, Max J. "Feasibility Income Deficiency." *The Appraisal Journal* 57(1): 88–98 (January 1989).

Graaskamp, James A. *Fundamentals of Real Estate Development, ULI Development Component Series.* Washington, DC: ULI—The Urban Land Institute, 1981.

Miles, Mike E., Richard L. Haney, Jr., and Gayle Berens. *Real Estate Development, Principles and Process.* 2nd ed. Washington, DC: ULI—The Urban Land Institute, 1996, Chapter 16.

REVIEW QUESTIONS

1. What question does feasibility analysis address?
2. What are the key dimensions of the feasibility question?
3. What are the steps in feasibility analysis?
4. How does a preliminary feasibility inquiry differ from a full-scale feasibility analysis? Why bother with a preliminary investigation?
5. How do equity investors' and lenders' objectives with respect to a project differ?
6. Describe the front-door approach to preliminary financial feasibility analysis.
7. Describe the back-door approach to preliminary financial feasibility analysis.
8. The following data, objectives and constraints have been provided with respect to a proposed investment venture:

Cost (including transactions costs)	$3,200,000
Net leasable area (square feet)	29,000
Financing specifications:	
a. Mortgage loan terms: 12 percent interest; 25-year amortization schedule; renegotiable after ten years.	
b. Minimum acceptable current yield on equity funds: six percent.	
Operating forecast for first year:	
Market rent per square foot (based on analysis of comparable properties)	$23.50
Vacancy rate (percent)	10
Operating expenses, per sq. ft. of leasable area	$9.50

Required: If the maximum available loan-to-value ratio is .75 and the minimum acceptable debt coverage ratio is 1.15, what is the minimum gross annual rental revenue that would make this project financially feasible?

9. If the minimum acceptable debt coverage ratio is 1.20 and the maximum loan-to-value ratio is .70, what is the maximum total investment (combined debt and equity funds) that will make the proposal in question 8 financially feasible?

DISCUSSION QUESTIONS

1. How does feasibility analysis differ from investment analysis?
2. So long as the present loan-to-value ratio is sufficient to assure adequate current collateral for a mortgage loan, should the lender be concerned about future cash flows or the trend of values for property of the type being financed? Discuss.

CHAPTER 21

Analyzing Subdivision Proposals

Subdivision, in the generally accepted sense, consists of purchasing large tracts of land and selling off smaller parcels. From an analytical perspective, subdividing vacant land, converting large buildings into condominium or cooperative units and converting buildings into time-share units all have a great deal in common. These latter activities might profitably be thought of as vertical subdivision. All require initial cash outlays for property purchase and improvement, and all are expected to produce cash inflows as individual units are sold. Subdivision is considered an ongoing business activity, and profits are generally taxed as ordinary income from operating a business.

Proliferating land-use controls and increasingly complex regulatory provisions have transformed land development operations, commonly called *subdivision.* What was once a simple process of "buying by the acre and selling by the square foot" has become a sophisticated business operation requiring skilled legal, financial and marketing talent combined with adept community planning ability. Business operations vary in scale from part-time subdividers who control only a few acres to multimillion-dollar corporations that subdivide land tracts extending over several square miles.

OVERVIEW OF THE SUBDIVISION PROCESS

Subdivision ventures grow out of a developer's perception of unsatisfied demand for certain types of buildable sites. If the contemplated use conforms to current zoning laws and governmental land-use plans, the developer may order a feasibility study to determine the probability that subdivision operations will be successful.

345

Where development objectives require extensive governmental approvals, the subdivider may acquire an option to purchase the land. With a secure option, the subdivider might analyze the feasibility of the project and create a detailed plan. If the intended use appears feasible and all necessary governmental permits prove obtainable, the option is exercised and the development plan is put into operation.

Title acquisition and land planning are followed by a land survey. Street locations are laid out, boundaries of individual lots are plotted and utility easements are delineated in the survey.

Physical improvements follow completion of the surveying process. Major land grading, streetbeds and utilities installation usually come first. Curbs, sidewalks and street surfacing follow. These latter improvements are often accomplished concurrently with building construction. Many subdividers are reluctant to finish streets and add curbs and sidewalks while heavy construction equipment is active in the subdivision.

Sales, the final step in subdivision development, may begin upon completion of the land plan and run concurrently with all other activities. Prospective residents, builders and investors may be willing to purchase sites prior to completion of land improvements. They may receive some discount for purchasing at this stage and will have their pick from among the choicest sites. In times of high demand, subdividers may be able to sell their entire inventory before land improvements are completed.

Subdivision is not limited to creating residential building sites. Whereas some subdividers specialize in residential projects, others create industrial parks and office parks. Apartment building sites, shopping centers, recreational parks, hospitals, cemeteries and many other projects are created through the initiative of real estate subdividers.

Significance of Location Decisions

Subdivision location decisions must be responsive to needs of ultimate users. Residential subdivisions require convenient access to schools, shopping facilities and transportation. Industrial subdivisions benefit from convenient access to materials sources and to markets. Availability of truck and rail transportation facilities, therefore, frequently plays an important role in industrial site location decisions.

Subdividers also need to consider current and potential uses of abutting sites. Large-scale subdividers frequently seek to control sufficiently large tracts of land so that they can successfully buffer their improvements from incompatible abutting uses.

Coping with Regulatory Requirements

Governmental land-use control is exercised through zoning laws and master land-use plans. Governmental agencies also exercise control through enforcement of building codes and environmental protection statutes. Many small-scale subdividers limit their land acquisition to appropriately zoned tracts. This strategy minimizes necessary interaction between developer and public agencies. Large-scale subdividers, in contrast, frequently develop plans requiring extensive rezoning and myriad government approvals. Such plans are presented for consideration by appropriate agencies and may require substantial revision before final approval.

Municipalities often seek to influence the level of subdivision activity through their control over public utilities. Subdivision may be encouraged if sewer and water are readily available. In many cases, additional capacity must be developed if these services are to be provided to a new subdivision. Some municipalities pay all costs to provide such services. Others require developers to pay all or a substantial portion. Municipalities sometimes seek, by levying special assessments, to pass these costs to ultimate purchasers.

Creating the Subdivision Plan

Contents of land plans vary with the size of developments. Large-scale plans typically divide the area by specialized use categories, provide detailed street layouts, plot individual sites and provide a utility distribution plan with appropriate easements. At the other extreme, a modest subdivision plan might entail nothing more than plotting individual sites and making provision for utility easements. In all cases, however, the plan should be detailed enough so that working drawings for streets and utilities may be developed and so that individual lots and streets may be surveyed.

Financing the Project

Subdividers generally use land acquisition and development loans to raise capital for their projects. These loans provide funds to purchase unimproved land as well as to improve it prior to resale. Lenders usually disburse loan proceeds on a piecemeal basis as improvements are completed. They regularly inspect projects to verify the existence and quality of improvements. Before disbursing any funds, lenders often require subcontractors to waive their rights to file liens against the project.

Most lenders view subdivision loans as riskier than construction loans. Lenders know that subdividers depend upon proceeds from land sales for funds to repay loans. Lenders, therefore, are vitally concerned with project marketability. For the same reason, lenders should be more interested in the subdivider's record of past successes than in his or her current net worth. Good market research and thorough investigation of subdivider credentials are essential to intelligent underwriting decisions.

INDUSTRIAL SUBDIVISION: A CASE STUDY

Subdivision encompasses a variety of projects. Some subdividers specialize in creating residential building sites; others create industrial, commercial or office sites. Apartment building sites, shopping centers, industrial parks, recreational parks, cemeteries and hospitals are all prospective uses for developable land.

Subdividers must choose the most appropriate project from the spectrum of alternatives that may appear economically and legally feasible.

To illustrate major land development issues, the balance of the chapter is devoted to analyzing an industrial subdivision proposal. Property to be developed is currently owned by a railroad and was previously used as a rail switching yard. Having recently abandoned local switching operations, the railroad considers the land surplus and has offered it for sale.

Site Characteristics

Site dimensions are approximately 3,733 feet by 3,733 feet, comprising 320 acres. The property is currently zoned for heavy industrial use, and surrounding uses are primarily manufacturing. Consequently, few governmental approvals are needed for the proposed project. Desirable features of the location include good railroad and truck access. Moreover, proximity of reliable public transportation allows area businesses to draw on the surrounding labor pool.

Prior to declaring this property surplus, the railroad itself launched an industrial subdivision project. Before corporate financial difficulties led it to abandon its development plans, it had completed a site plan. The railroad also procured written assurances from appropriate sources that the site can be provided with combination sewers, water, natural gas and electricity in capacities adequate to support industrial usage. It conducted traffic studies that indicate existing public streets are adequate to handle vehicular traffic to and from buildings to be located on the site. As a consequence of predevelopment activity already completed by the railroad, a would-be developer need only purchase the property, complete necessary improvements and sell off the subdivided parcels.

Of the total 320 acres, 64 acres will be needed for streets, rail spurs, storm water retention and so forth. The remaining 256 acres will be incorporated into subdivided parcels. The site plan provides a street pattern that allows maximum flexibility regarding size of individual sites. This allows the developer to meet the needs of a wide variety of prospective industrial users.

The railroad has agreed to remove all existing improvements, which consist primarily of rail and a few small buildings. Further site preparation will be the responsibility of the purchaser or developer. A detailed survey will be required to locate streets and identify boundaries of individual parcels. Installation of underground utilities, curbs, gutters, streets and street lighting will complete site preparation activities. As a part of its own development plans, the railroad has prepared a detailed schedule, based on local contractors' estimates, of all subdivision costs. The projections include legal and survey expenses but exclude financing costs. Total estimated development costs are $3,840,000, or an average of $15,000 for each of the 256 salable acres.

Market Research

The railroad's real estate department did an excellent job of preparing the site plan and estimating development costs but undertook no research to estimate marketability of the industrial sites. To generate this essential information, the prospective purchasers hired a real estate consulting firm to estimate market demand and probable absorption rates for this project. (*Absorption rates* refers to the rate at which units of a product are purchased in the marketplace. The relationship between anticipated absorption rates and rates at which competitors will place new units on the market indicates the degree of balance between quantities demanded and quantities supplied.)

Interviews with local industrial brokers indicate major competition from two other large industrial parks in the area. Investigation reveals that one of these projects, the Swampy Knolls Industrial Park, has recently sold its last available parcel. The other, Tri-City Industrial Park, has an estimated five-year supply of sites. Some brokers expect sales in the Tri-City project to increase now that Swampy Knolls is sold out.

Sales information regarding the competing parks, gleaned from a search of the county recorder's files, is presented in Table 21.1. Note that 43 sales, ranging in size from 2.8 to 25 acres, occurred between 1986 and 1996 in the Swampy Knolls project. Forty-five sales ranging in size from 3 to 35 acres occurred in the Tri-City park between 1988 and 1996. Data from Table 21.1 are summarized in Table 21.2, which indicates that an average of 35.89 acres were sold each year in Swampy Knolls and that the Tri-City project had average annual sales of 64.57 acres. Thus, combined sales of comparable industrial land in the market

Table 21.1   Historic Absorption Rates: Industrial Park Properties

	Parcels Sold					
Year	Swampy Knolls Individual Sales (Acres)			Tri-City Individual Sales (Acres)		
1986	14.00	15.60	11.10	No Sales		
	4.60	5.40				
1987	14.30	7.60	10.17	No Sales		
1988	15.04	16.30	10.05	18.70	20.00	15.30
				7.60	10.50	
1989	7.50	9.30	4.60	14.80	15.30	18.90
	15.60	4.70	5.40	7.03		
1990	16.30	8.30		18.20	15.30	10.01
1991	5.60	4.30	6.10	5.40	8.30	6.20
	5.24			3.03	3.00	
1992	12.50	8.40	5.30	30.00	25.00	9.50
	7.70			3.07	5.00	
1993	16.03	5.80	4.30	8.50	4.50	9.30
	4.60	5.40		8.20	6.40	9.40
				8.32	8.00	
1994	18.00	10.10	5.00	15.80	18.67	
1995	25.00	5.90	8.70	35.00	15.70	10.30
	3.20	7.20		11.06		
1996	14.30	7.50	2.80	25.00	17.50	14.60
				27.00	34.20	5.40
				3.20	8.50	6.53

Table 21.2	Sales Records of Industrial Park Properties	

	Total Sales (Acres)	
Year	*Swampy Knolls*	*Tri-City*
1986	50.70	0
1987	32.07	0
1988	41.39	72.10
1989	47.10	56.03
1990	24.60	43.51
1991	21.24	25.93
1992	33.90	75.57
1993	36.13	62.62
1994	33.10	34.47
1995	50.00	72.06
1996	24.60	141.83
Totals	394.83	581.12

area between 1988 and 1996 have totaled 893.18 acres, representing average annual absorption of 99.24 acres.

Interviews with management in local industrial firms indicate that the proposed industrial park will enjoy substantial locational advantages over major competitors. The Tri-City park appears the second most desirable and Swampy Knolls the least desirable of the three. Local industrial brokers generally agree with these conclusions. They report that parcels in Swampy Knolls have been somewhat less attractive to potential purchasers than those in the Tri-City park. They also point out, however, that Tri-City has attracted users of larger sites.

Sales prices in Swampy Knolls and Tri-City for the last two years are also examined. It is noted that land in both projects has sold at an average price of $2.50 per square foot during this period. Given the competitive nature of the local industrial land market, and noting that Swampy Knolls has completely sold out, the consulting firm concludes that $2.50 per square foot will make the proposed project competitive. At that price the firm estimates the proposed project can capture 40 percent of the market currently shared by Swampy Knolls and Tri-City. Therefore, it projects average annual sales for the new industrial park at 40 acres per year.

Investment Analysis

A group of ten real estate practitioners is considering purchase and subdivision of this property. They plan to use a general partnership, with each partner holding an equal interest in the project. Since subdivision is an ongoing business enterprise, all profits will be taxed as ordinary income.

The industrial broker who originally presented this property to the investors is willing to supervise all phases of the subdivision project for a fee of $75,000 per year. Financial projections are based on anticipated sales of 40 acres per year for six years and sale of the remaining 16 acres in the seventh year of the marketing program.

The railroad is asking $8 million for the property. A lender is willing to provide a mortgage loan for 80 percent of the purchase price, or $6,400,000, and an additional $3,840,000 to cover the cost of planned improvements. Borrowers will be required to pay interest at 9.0 percent per annum on the outstanding loan balance and to repay $40,000 of principal for each acre of land sold. Table 21.3 shows a repayment schedule based on the assumption that 40 acres will be sold during each of the first six years of the project, with the remaining 16 acres sold in the seventh year.

As land is sold, total annual real estate taxes are expected to decrease. Taxes need not be paid on the 64 acres dedicated to streets, rail, etc. Tax liability will accrue on the 256 acres owned during year one, the 216 acres owned during year two and so forth. Tax rates for vacant land in this area produce a liability of about ten cents per square foot. Multiplying the number of square feet owned by ten cents produces an estimate of the partners' annual property tax liability. These computations are illustrated in Table 21.4.

Annual gross revenue projections are derived by simply multiplying the expected sales price per acre by anticipated sales volume for each year. Annual expenditures for brokerage commissions are expected to total five percent of gross sales. Administrative expenses of $75,000 per year will be incurred in years one through six. The agreement with the managing broker provides that this expense will decline to $25,000 in the seventh year. Advertising expenses are expected to be $50,000 the first year, $25,000 in years two through six and $8,250 in year seven. Advertising expenses for the first year include the cost of maps, brochures and signs, which do not represent recurring expenditures. Insurance expenses are based on a quotation obtained from a local insurance broker. Table 21.5 consolidates income, expense and mortgage loan information to produce estimates of annual before-tax cash flows for each year of the project.

Table 21.6 illustrates the calculation of annual taxable income. Cost of land sold is subtracted from total sales revenue to derive gross profit. Deducting operating expenses and financing costs from this amount yields taxable income.

Cost of land sold includes the original purchase price and all expenditures to prepare the land for sale. It also includes the purchase price and site preparation costs of land dedicated for public utilities and thoroughfares. Although many of these expenditures are incurred during the first year of operations, they

Table 21.3	Loan Repayment Schedule: Industrial Subdivision			
Year	*Beginning Balance*	*Principal Repaid*	*Interest Paid*	*Ending Balance*
1	$10,240,000	$1,600,000	$921,600	$8,640,000
2	8,640,000	1,600,000	777,600	7,040,000
3	7,040,000	1,600,000	633,600	5,440,000
4	5,440,000	1,600,000	489,600	3,840,000
5	3,840,000	1,600,000	345,600	2,240,000
6	2,240,000	1,600,000	201,600	640,000
7	640,000	640,000	57,600	0

Table 21.4   Calculation of Real Estate Taxes: Industrial Subdivision

	Year 1	Year 2	Year 3	Year 4	Year 5	Year 6	Year 7
Sq. Ft. Owned*	11,151,360	9,408,960	7,666,560	5,924,160	4,181,760	2,439,360	696,960
Times: Property Tax per sq. ft.	$0.10	$0.10	$0.10	$0.10	$0.10	$0.10	$0.10
Estimated Property Taxes	$1,115,136	$940,896	$766,656	$592,416	$418,176	$243,936	$69,696

*Acres in inventory times square feet per acre

Table 21.5   Calculation of Before-Tax Cash Flows: Industrial Subdivision

	Year 1	Year 2	Year 3	Year 4	Year 5	Year 6	Year 7
Gross Sales Revenue	$4,356,000	$4,356,000	$4,356,000	$4,356,000	$4,356,000	$4,356,000	$1,742,400
Less: Brokerage Fees	217,800	217,800	217,800	217,800	217,800	217,800	87,120
Net Sales Revenue	$4,138,200	$4,138,200	$4,138,200	$4,138,200	$4,138,200	$4,138,200	$1,655,280
Less:							
Administrative Expenses	75,000	75,000	75,000	75,000	75,000	75,000	25,000
Advertising Expenses	50,000	25,000	25,000	25,000	25,000	25,000	8,250
Insurance Expenses	2,000	2,000	2,000	1,000	1,000	1,000	1,000
Real Estate Taxes	1,115,136	940,896	766,656	592,416	418,176	243,936	69,696
Net Operating Income	$2,896,064	$3,095,304	$3,269,544	$3,444,784	$3,619,024	$3,793,264	$1,551,334
Less:							
Interest	921,600	777,600	633,600	489,600	345,600	201,600	57,600
Loan Repayment	1,600,000	1,600,000	1,600,000	1,600,000	1,600,000	1,600,000	640,000
Before-Tax Cash Flow	$ 374,464	$ 717,704	$1,035,944	$1,355,184	$1,673,424	$1,991,664	$ 853,734

Table 21.6   Annual Taxable Income: Industrial Subdivision

	Year 1	Year 2	Year 3	Year 4	Year 5	Year 6	Year 7
Income	$4,356,000	$4,356,000	$4,356,000	$4,356,000	$4,356,000	$4,356,000	$1,742,400
Less: Cost of Land Sold							
Purchase Price	1,000,000	1,000,000	1,000,000	1,000,000	1,000,000	1,000,000	400,000
Improvements	600,000	600,000	600,000	600,000	600,000	600,000	240,000
Dedicated Land Costs	250,000	250,000	250,000	250,000	250,000	250,000	100,000
Gross Profit	$2,506,000	$2,506,000	$2,506,000	$2,506,000	$2,506,000	$2,506,000	$1,002,400
Less: Operating Expenses							
Brokerage Commissions	217,800	217,800	217,800	217,800	217,800	217,800	87,120
Administrative	75,000	75,000	75,000	75,000	75,000	75,000	25,000
Advertising	50,000	25,000	25,000	25,000	25,000	25,000	8,250
Insurance	2,000	2,000	2,000	1,000	1,000	1,000	1,000
Real Estate Taxes	1,115,136	940,896	766,656	592,416	418,176	243,936	69,696
Interest	921,600	777,600	633,600	489,600	345,600	201,600	57,600
Taxable Income	$ 124,464	$ 467,704	$ 785,944	$1,105,184	$1,423,424	$1,741,664	$ 753,734

Table 21.7   Calculation of After-Tax Cash Flows: Industrial Subdivision

	Year 1	Year 2	Year 3	Year 4	Year 5	Year 6	Year 7
Taxable Income	$124,464	$467,704	$ 785,944	$1,105,184	$1,423,424	$1,741,664	$753,734
Times: Tax Rate	.28	.28	.28	.28	.28	.28	.28
Tax Liability	$ 34,850	$130,957	$ 220,064	$ 309,452	$ 398,559	$ 487,666	$211,046
Before-Tax Cash Flow	$374,464	$717,704	$1,035,944	$1,355,184	$1,673,424	$1,991,664	$853,734
Less: Income Tax	34,850	130,957	220,064	309,452	398,559	487,666	211,046
After-Tax Cash Flow	$339,614	$586,747	$ 815,880	$1,045,732	$1,274,865	$1,503,998	$642,688

must be allocated to the inventory of salable land and are not deductible for tax purposes until the land is sold.

Investors are all assumed to be in the 28 percent marginal income tax bracket both before and after considering the consequence of this investment. (Our demonstration ignores state and local income taxes and sales taxes, which vary in different localities. An actual analysis would incorporate any such tax consequences.) It is also assumed that their federal income tax position will allow them to use any losses produced by this venture. Table 21.7 shows anticipated after-tax cash flow from the project. Annual taxable income (or tax-deductible loss) is simply multiplied by the investors' presumed 28 percent marginal tax rate. Before-tax cash flows are then adjusted for tax consequences to produce annual after-tax cash-flow forecasts.

After-tax cash-flow estimates are discounted at a rate of 20 percent and summed, producing a $2,862,324 present value of the equity position. Required equity equals land cost of $8,000,000 less available financing of $6,400,000, or $1,600,000. Net present value is equal to present value of the equity minus required equity, or $1,262,324. Positive net present value indicates a profitable venture if income and expenses occur as expected.

Investment value can also be calculated. Table 21.8 illustrates this computation. Since available financing includes the cost of subdivision improvements, funds intended for this purpose must be subtracted to isolate financing available for land. To this is added the present value of the equity position. Investment value of $9,262,324 is greater than the asking price of $8,000,000, indicating a desirable project.

Table 21.8   Cash-Flow Analysis: Industrial Subdivision

Year	After-Tax Cash Flow	20% Discount Factor	Discounted Cash Flow
1	$ 339,614	0.833333	$ 283,012
2	586,747	0.694444	407,463
3	815,880	0.578704	472,153
4	1,045,732	0.482253	504,307
5	1,274,865	0.401878	512,340
6	1,503,998	0.334898	503,686
7	642,688	0.279082	179,363

Present Value of Equity	$ 2,862,324
Less: Initial Equity Investment	1,600,000
Net Present Value	$ 1,262,324
Available Financing	$10,240,000
Less: Cost of Improvements	3,840,000
Financing for Land	$ 6,400,000
Plus: Present Value of Equity	2,862,324
Investment Value of Land	$ 9,262,324

Table 21.9   Allocation of Before-Tax Cash Flows: Industrial Subdivision

Year	Before-Tax Cash Flow	Individual Partner's Share
1	$ 374,464	$ 37,446
2	717,704	71,770
3	1,035,944	103,594
4	1,355,184	135,518
5	1,673,424	167,342
6	1,991,664	199,166
7	853,734	85,373

Table 21.10   Allocation of Taxable Income: Industrial Subdivision

Year	Taxable Income	Individual Partner's Share
1	$ 124,464	$ 12,446
2	467,704	46,770
3	785,944	78,594
4	1,105,184	110,518
5	1,423,424	142,342
6	1,741,664	174,166
7	753,734	75,373

From these data each partner's individual interest can be analyzed. Tables 21.9 and 21.10 split before-tax cash flows and taxable income into an individual partner's share. This involves dividing before-tax cash flows and taxable income, shown in Tables 21.6 and 21.7 respectively, by the number of partners. Since partners have equal interests, simply divide by ten. If individual partners had unequal interests, the total would be allocated in accordance with the partnership agreement.

SUMMARY

Subdivision is a term applied to the land development process. It consists of purchasing raw land, adding necessary improvements and selling the property in piecemeal fashion. The scale of subdivision projects may range from individuals dividing small parcels into a few building sites to large organizations dividing large tracts into areas devoted to multiple uses. Acquisition and development loans are used to finance subdivision.

RECOMMENDED READINGS

Barren, G. Vincent, and John P. Blair. *How To Conduct and Analyze Real Estate Market and Feasibility Studies* 2nd ed. New York: Van Nostrand Reinhold Company, 1988, pp. 71–133.

Rabinowitz, Alan. *The Real Estate Gamble: Lessons from 50 Years of Boom and Bust.* NY: Amacom, 1980, pp. 235–259.

REVIEW QUESTIONS

1. Explain the concept of subdivision and some of the major concerns of the subdivider.
2. Describe the process used to determine the best selling price for the subdivision of the proposed industrial park and to determine the projected annual sales.
3. Explain the considerations incorporated in the development of the revenue and expense projections over the selling period.
4. Table 21.8 illustrates the calculation of the net present value and the investment value of the project. Do both values indicate the same investment decision?
5. What does the analysis of the individual partner's shares show? Is this project worthwhile from an individual standpoint?
6. What would be the effect of the use of a lower discount factor on the cash-flow analysis shown in Table 21.8?

DISCUSSION QUESTIONS

1. In what ways are residential subdivision and condominium developments similar from the perspective of the developer, and in what important ways might they differ?
2. If you were offering individual investors an opportunity to invest in a subdivision project under your direction, would you provide them with detailed worksheets showing the reasoning behind your cash-flow projections? Why or why not?

CHAPTER 22

Development and Rehabilitation

We saw in Chapter 21 that subdivision consists of improving and shaping land into usable parcels by grading, paving, installing utilities and so forth. In contrast, development involves placing improvements—usually buildings—on the land. Rehabilitation is the renovation and, in some cases, remodeling of existing structures.

Many developers, most particularly residential homebuilders, construct buildings primarily for resale. Others complete construction projects not for resale, but as additions to their own property portfolios. Regardless of their specific strategies, creative developers are often able to satisfy an as yet unmet demand and thereby reap the economic benefits of short-term monopoly. As other developers produce competing projects, the innovative pioneer usually moves on to exploit other unfilled market niches.

This chapter provides an overview of the development process. Concepts are illustrated with a case study of a small shopping center development project. Because rehabilitation of existing structures is a development opportunity of growing importance, this topic is also considered. The chapter concludes with a case study analyzing a proposal to rehabilitate a building that qualifies for an investment tax credit as a historic commercial structure.

OVERVIEW OF DEVELOPMENT

Real estate development projects range in size and complexity from single-family residences completed according to stock plans to entire new cities carved from decaying segments of older urban areas or from agricultural acreage or wasteland. At the lower end of the size spectrum, a developer might acquire a single-building lot and construct a house on a speculative basis. Proceeds from sale of the first house often provide necessary capital for the next single-residence venture. At the other end of the scale, developers may collaborate with major institutional leaders and with local, state or federal government agencies to complete grandiose construction schemes designed to overcome urban blight or to provide badly needed new living or working environments.

Ventures often originate with a concept for finished urban space and a perception of unmet demand. This situation has been described as "an idea in search of a site." The developer who identifies an entrepreneurial opportunity seeks out a site upon which the demand can be satisfied. In most situations, the site will be controlled through an option agreement until all details of the development can be worked out.

An equally likely impetus for a new development project is a developer or an investor seeking an appropriate use for a previously acquired site. This has been appropriately described as "a site in search of an idea." Whether development originates with a site to be exploited or a vision to be fulfilled, the common denominator is a need for the particular blending of talent and organizational skill that characterizes successful real estate developers.

Feasibility Analysis

Once a development proposal has been matched with a prospective site, a detailed feasibility study may be commissioned. Results of the market research phase of this study are relayed to the developer's architect for incorporation into a physical design. Architects and engineers provide cost estimates that are incorporated into the financial phase of the feasibility analysis. (Large-scale developments may require a master plan, as described in the subdivision discussion. Planning efforts will be closely coordinated with the work of feasibility analysts, architects and engineers.)

Feasibility studies are generally divided into two major sections. The first consists of market research and attempts to determine the physical and locational characteristics that will have the greatest consumer appeal, as well as to determine what pricing structure the market will bear. The second section analyzes the economics of a proposed project. Construction costs are measured against project value to determine whether the proposed development is financially or economically viable.

Market research will vary with the situation. If a developer has a specific site in mind, researchers will seek to determine the type of improvements demanded at that location as well as the prices consumers are willing to pay. Consideration should be given to area demographics, to local trends and to competitive supply. Researchers might go a step further and use survey techniques to measure consumer desires for specific amenities. If a developer is not tied to a specific site, the researchers may also analyze the area in search of some unmet space demand.

Project cost is always a major feasibility consideration. Architects are frequently commissioned to provide cost estimates. Alternatively, estimates might be derived from a firm that specializes in providing such information. Many developers generate their own cost estimates based on a combination of data from these sources and from their own past experiences.

Value estimates also require detailed information. Sales price or rental rates for competitive properties are collected and analyzed. Income-producing properties require a detailed estimate of operating expenses. If projections are being made over longer time horizons, trend data will also be studied.

Economic estimates are always based on assumptions derived from market research and can be no better than the research or the assumptions they incorporate. Adequate research should result in reliable estimates, which then form the foundation for sound development decisions.

Financing Real Estate Development

In most large-scale developments, the site will be controlled through an option agreement rather than an outright purchase. After determining that a planned use is feasible, and after receiving all necessary municipal approvals, the developer is ready to exercise the option to purchase a site. At this stage, financial arrangements become a major consideration. The scarcity and cost of financing are hurdles that trip up many grandiose development schemes.

Developers generally look to construction lenders for the bulk of their development capital. Responsive lenders shoulder a substantial burden of risk. Builders may be unable to complete projects or may fall far behind schedule. Construction costs are difficult to estimate, and projects often run considerably over budget. This forces construction lenders to advance additional funds and thereby increase their risk exposure.

Lender risk can be reduced considerably by insisting that developers acquire end-loan commitments. These are agreements from other lenders to provide long-term financing upon project completion. An end-loan commitment ensures that funds with which to repay the construction loan upon completion of the project will be available.

If a developer cannot obtain an end-loan commitment prior to arranging a construction loan, standby or gap financing may be used. Under this arrangement, a lender agrees to provide funds for the gap between the time a project is completed and the time an end loan is secured. In most cases the end loan is secured before any funds are actually drawn in connection with a standby loan commitment.

The Construction Phase

Construction is one of the most important industries in our economy. It is the largest single contributor to the gross national product, it employs more people than any other industry and it uses more capital than most other industries. Construction, like other economic activity in a capitalistic economy, depends upon the relationship between supply and demand as discussed in Chapter 2.

Construction projects are carried out on either a custom or a speculative basis. Custom building takes place on land owned by the ultimate purchaser, and the structure is built to the purchaser-user's exact specifications. Speculative construction is limited primarily (but not exclusively) to single-family residences. In this situation, a developer-builder sees a demand for certain types of homes in a particular location. The builder will start construction before any homes are sold. Upon completion, the homes are sold to users.

The nature of the construction process makes the industry unique among manufacturers. Construction takes place on site—that is, where the product will be used—imposing a special set of managerial and technological problems. A successful construction company is able to expand and contract its size in response to economic conditions and differences in the scale of construction projects.

General contractors are the prime operatives on most construction projects. They look to subcontractors for excavating, cement work, brick work, plumbing, heating, electrical work, roofing and so forth. A user might enter into a contract with a general contractor for construction of a building. The general contractor then enters into agreements with subcontractors for the necessary labor and materials. General contractors coordinate the work of subcontractors and oversee construction progress.

Construction work is often put out for bid, with the job awarded to the lowest bidder. Many people, however, are more comfortable working with contractors who have proven track records, regardless of their fees. They may choose a contractor who charges for all labor and material and adds a predetermined fee to cover overhead and profit. The alternative of a fixed-price contract is much riskier for the builder. New union agreements may cause labor costs to increase, or building material prices may rise unexpectedly. The larger the job and the longer the time necessary to complete it, the greater the risk associated with a fixed-price contract.

Building contractors' modes of operation vary greatly. A small-scale homebuilder may employ only a few carpenters and own no equipment other than a small truck. On the other hand, an excavating contractor may have an enormous capital investment in such equipment as cranes, tractors and a fleet of trucks. Large-scale developers may employ artisans from all building trades and own the equipment necessary to complete massive construction projects.

Construction, unlike most other industries, is not dominated by large firms. Given the wide variety of functions involved in building construction, and the fact that general contractors and subcontractors typically do not form lasting relationships, it is unlikely that substantial economies of scale can be achieved. This implies that large firms do not gain a competitive advantage by size alone.

A DEVELOPMENT CASE STUDY

A developer recently purchased a commercially zoned site upon which to build a 75,000-square-foot neighborhood shopping center. The anchor tenant will be a food store, with the remainder of the space devoted to smaller specialty shops.

(Shopping centers are designated as community, regional or superregional, according to the sizes of their market areas. Anchor tenants are major stores whose customer drawing power is expected to generate shopper traffic that will benefit other merchants in the center. These and other shopping center concepts are discussed in Chapter 23.) The anchor tenant has already signed a lease, and approximately 20,000 square feet of the specialty shop space has been taken. An investment group has agreed to purchase the shopping center upon completion and lease-up. The developer expects to deliver a fully occupied shopping center within 16 months.

An architectural firm has drawn plans and specifications for the building, and several general contractors submitted construction bids. The general contractor selected did not present the lowest bid but did have the most experience in shopping center construction. It is the developer's opinion that the contractor selected should be able to complete the project on time and within the budget constraints set by estimated building costs, as illustrated in Table 22.1.

Table 22.1	Estimated Building Costs for Shopping Center Project	
Excavating		$111,000
Cement Work		240,000
Masonry		279,000
Steel and Bar Joists		142,000
Metal Door Frames		23,000
Carpentry Work		172,385
Roofing		88,000
Plumbing and Sewer Work		116,000
Electrical Work		169,000
Heating and Air-Conditioning		368,320
Insulation		2,400
Drywall		80,000
Acoustical Ceiling		42,965
Hardware		8,200
Cabinets and Mirrors		2,050
Painting		12,200
Electrical Fixtures		61,015
Tile and Carpet		50,850
Paving		150,850
Parking Lot Striping		3,500
Outdoor Lighting		8,500
Sprinkler System		110,000
Roof Paneling		30,500
Plate Glass		68,315
Gyp Roof Material		83,350
Weather Stripping		2,000
Architect Fees		93,525
Permits		40,665
Surveys		2,000
Contractor's Overhead and Profit		285,000
Estimated Total Cost		$2,846,590

Financing Arrangements

Total project costs include $1,500,000 for land purchase and $2,846,590 for construction, for a total of $4,346,590. A lender is willing to advance funds for the construction phase but requires the developer to acquire the land from equity resources. Construction funds will be advanced in three installments (draws) as work progresses. For financial planning purposes it is assumed that three equal draws of $948,863.33 will be made. The first draw will be outstanding for 12 months, the second for eight months and the third for four months, as indicated in Table 22.2. Interest on construction loan funds will accrue at a rate of 9 percent per annum on the outstanding balance. Total interest on the construction loan is expected to be $170,795.

Project Cost Estimates

Table 22.3 summarizes total estimated project costs. Building costs were estimated at $2,846,590, as illustrated in Table 22.1. Total land cost equals $1,500,000, and financing costs were estimated at $170,795. The total of these items, or total project cost, is estimated at $4,517,385.

Estimated Net Operating Income

Results of a survey of rental rates in similar shopping centers are summarized in Table 22.4. After considering this information, the developer has entered into lease agreements with a food store, which will serve as the center's anchor

Table 22.2	Financing Costs for Shopping Center Project
First Draw	
$948,863.33 at 9% for 12 months	$ 85,398
Second Draw	
$948,863.33 at 9% for eight months	56,931
Third Draw	
$948,863.33 at 9% for four months	28,466
Estimated Total Financing Costs	$170,795

Table 22.3	Total Project Costs for Shopping Center
Building Construction	$2,846,590
Land Cost	1,500,000
Financing Costs	170,795
Total Construction Costs	$4,517,385

	Table 22.4		Competitive Rental Survey for Shopping Center Project

Shopping Center	Anchor Tenants' Rental Rates (per sq. ft.)	Other Tenants' Rental Rates (per sq. ft.)
Marshy Valley	$6.50	$7.00–13.00
Lakemoor Commons	6.25	6.50–13.00
Floating Bogs	6.50	7.00–13.00
Swampy Basins	6.00	6.00–13.00

tenant and occupy 40,000 square feet. Approximately 20,000 of the remaining 35,000 square feet have been rented to smaller tenants.

Rental rates will be $6.50 per square foot occupied per year for the food store and $10.00 per square foot for the smaller tenants. Rentals are on a net basis, with the tenants paying all expenses, including repairs, maintenance, insurance and real estate taxes. Tenants will also pay a pro rata share of any common-area maintenance costs, such as parking lot repairs.

Net operating income estimates are shown in Table 22.5. Effective gross income is estimated by multiplying the amount of space devoted to a particular use by the rental rate for that type of space. The food store lease contains a clause calling for increased rentals based on sales (percentage leases), but the tenant is not expected to reach this sales volume within the next three years. The prospective purchaser has decided to ignore the possibility of percentage rentals and will have the property managed by a firm that charges seven percent of gross income. Based on these considerations, net operating income is estimated at $567,300.

Sales Price

Data from recent shopping center property transactions, gathered by the prospective purchaser of this project, are summarized in Table 22.6. The intended buyer notes that sales one and five in the table involved newly constructed centers and that sale number four was an almost new center. Dividing net operating

	Table 22.5		Pro Forma Income and Expense Statement for Shopping Center Project

Food Store	
40,000 sq. ft. at $6.50/sq. ft.	$260,000
Other Space	
35,000 sq. ft. at $10.00/sq. ft.	350,000
Estimated Effective Gross Income	$610,000
Less: Management Fee, at (rounded) 7%	42,700
Estimated Net Operating Income	$567,300

Table 22.6			Recent Neighborhood Shopping Center Sales	
Sale	Age (Years)	Sales Price	Net Operating Income	Indicated Capitalization Rate
1	New	$8,525,000	$852,500	10.00%
2	2	5,650,000	621,500	11.00
3	3	3,888,000	486,000	12.50
4	.5	6,069,000	606,900	10.00
5	New	6,060,500	606,050	10.00
6	2	4,065,000	396,338	9.75

income by the sales prices of these properties indicated that they were all purchased on the basis of a 10 percent overall rate of return.

Based on this information, the buyer agrees to purchase this shopping center at an overall rate of 10 percent. Dividing the projected net operating income of $567,300 by 0.10 yields an expected sales price of approximately $5,673,000.

Developer's Profit

Table 22.7 illustrates calculation of the developer's total expected profit. Estimated total construction costs are subtracted from expected sales price, producing a before-tax net profit estimate of $1,155,615. Income tax consequences are estimated by multiplying expected profit by the developer's marginal tax rate. Adjusting expected pretax profit for tax consequences produces a developer's profit estimate of $832,043.

Developer's profit is frequently expressed (on a before-tax basis) as a percentage of the initial equity investment (in this case, the cost of the land). For the project under analysis, this measure is expected to be $1,155,615/$1,500,000, or 74.4 percent (rounded).

Net present value of expected cash flow can also be calculated. The developer must expend $1,500,000 of equity cash resources to purchase the land. Positive cash flows consisting of return of invested funds plus after-tax profit occur at the end of construction. If the project takes 16 months to complete, and the developer uses a 15 percent discount rate, net present value is calculated as shown in Table 22.8.

Table 22.7	Estimated After-Tax Profits	
Sales Price		$5,673,000
Less: Total Construction Costs (Table 22.3)		4,517,385
Before-Tax Profits		$1,155,615
Less: Taxes (28% Marginal Bracket)		323,572
After-Tax Profits		$ 832,043

Table 22.8	Net Present Value Estimate for Shopping Center Project	
Sales Price of Shopping Center		$5,673,000
Less: Loan Balance (Table 22.2):		
Principal Amount	$2,846,590	
Interest	170,795	3,017,385
Cash Flow Before Income Taxes		$2,655,615
Less: Income Tax Consequences (Table 22.7)		323,572
After-Tax Cash Flow		$2,332,043
Times: Discount Factor at 15%		0.828157
Present Value of Future Cash Flows		$1,931,298
Less: Initial Investment		1,500,000
Net Present Value		$ 431,298

REHABILITATION

Unlike new construction, where developers begin with vacant sites and create buildings, rehabilitation begins with existing structures in need of renovation. The rehabilitator takes a deteriorated or functionally obsolete (that is, inappropriately designed) building and improves its physical condition or brings it up to modem design standards. Many rehabilitation projects involve both of these changes.

Gentrification, or the reclamation of residential areas containing physically deteriorated buildings, has provided much of the impetus for recent rehabilitation activity. Structurally sound buildings of interesting architectural styles are prime targets for rehabilitation. Such buildings can often be acquired at bargain prices due to their deteriorated condition or the nature of the surrounding area. As rehabilitation efforts develop in a neighborhood, property values and rental rates often soar.

Prime areas for rehabilitation seem to be older inner-city neighborhoods with convenient transportation links to places of employment. These areas should have buildings with unique or unusual architecture and should contain single-family or two- to three-unit buildings. Smaller buildings allow entry by the first wave of rehabilitators: the urban pioneers. These individuals are willing to take the risk of purchasing in older areas. They are also willing to perform many of the rehabilitation tasks themselves. As they and others build "sweat equity" in their properties, the neighborhood often gains a reputation for economic resurgence. This reputation eventually attracts professional profit-oriented rehabilitators.

Incentives for Rehabilitation

Various incentives induce people to undertake real estate rehabilitation efforts. Urban pioneers can often acquire property inexpensively. They are also able to build equity by performing many of the rehabilitation tasks themselves. The risks they bear as pioneers are often rewarded with high returns.

Real estate is a unique commodity in that it allows builders and rehabilitators the opportunity to create lasting monuments to their entrepreneurial abilities. Just as a developer might claim "that building is there because I put it there," the rehabilitator might claim "that building escaped the wrecking ball through my efforts." A rehabilitator may also enjoy the satisfaction of making a great impact on the destiny of an area or a neighborhood.

Profit expectations are, of course, among the more compelling motives for undertaking rehabilitation projects. The Congress has enhanced these expectations by enacting tax legislation to reward qualifying rehabilitation efforts. Investment tax credit (discussed in detail in Chapter 12) may be earned for rehabilitating older structures or structures that have been designated historically significant. Since anticipated credits generate reductions in quarterly tax payments, they are usually treated for analytical purposes as a reduction in initial cost outlays.

Judging Feasibility of Rehabilitation Proposals

Intelligent analysis of rehabilitation proposals begins with consideration of the value or expected selling price of the completed project. Once expected value of the completed project has been estimated, rehabilitation costs must be considered. Subtracting all costs and expected profit from estimated value as completed leaves the amount available for purchase of the property. If the property can be purchased for less, the project is feasible; if the cost is greater, the project is not feasible.

Consider the two projects illustrated in Example 22.1. Estimated value after rehabilitation for both projects is $200,000. Subtracting construction costs and expected profit leaves $80,000 available for purchase. Since the asking price for project *A* is $60,000, this project is feasible. Project *B* has similar completed value and costs. However, the asking price of $100,000 is greater than the amount the rehabber can afford to pay. If $100,000 is paid, the rehabber's expected profits are reduced to zero.

Example 22.1

	Project A	Project B
Completed Value	$200,000	$200,000
Less:		
Construction Costs	100,000	100,000
Expected Profit	20,000	20,000
Available for Purchase	$ 80,000	$ 80,000
Asking Price	$ 60,000	$100,000

COMMERCIAL REHABILITATION: A CASE STUDY

Dr. R. E. Habam's office is located on a busy commercial street next to a 60-year-old frame residence. This 60-year-old structure has been vacant for two years, is in need of extensive repair and is currently available for $30,000. An architect has inspected the building and determined that it can be rehabilitated in about three months at a cost of $130,000. Two general contractors have submitted bids for the rehabilitation work; both bids were for $130,000.

Dr. Habam is aware that a ten percent investment tax credit is available if this building is rehabilitated as a commercial structure. Ten percent of estimated rehabilitation costs of $130,000 equals a credit of $13,000. Since a local financial institution is willing to make a loan covering total rehabilitation costs (see the following discussion of financing), the doctor figures his initial investment is reduced by the amount of the investment tax credit. Total equity investment (net of the investment tax credit) is therefore expected to be only $17,000. Here are the computations:

Acquisition Cost		$ 30,000
Rehabilitation Costs		130,000
Total Costs		$160,000
Less:		
Mortgage Loan	$130,000	
Tax Credit	13,000	143,000
Required Equity Investment		$ 17,000

While working with the architect, Dr. Habam has also been negotiating a lease with a medical laboratory for the 2,400 square feet of space his rehabilitation efforts will produce. A tentative rental agreement has been reached at $8.50 per square foot for three years and $9.50 per square foot for three additional years. The lease will be on a net basis; the tenant will pay all operating costs. These costs include utilities, repairs, maintenance, insurance, real estate taxes and so forth.

Financing

A real estate appraiser has estimated the value of the completed project at $185,000. Using a 70 percent loan-to-value ratio, a financial institution is willing to make a $130,000 loan on this project. Loan terms are 9 percent interest for 25 years, with payments to be made monthly. The lender has retained the right to renegotiate loan terms after five years. Table 22.9 splits annual payments into interest and principal components.

Cost Recovery (Depreciation) Allowances

The straight-line method of computing the cost recovery (depreciation) allowance must be used. The basis for the allowance equals rehabilitation expendi-

Table 22.9   **Loan Amortization Schedule for Commercial Rehabilitation Project**

Year	Annual Debt Service	Interest	Principal
1	$13,091	$11,641	$1,450
2	13,091	11,505	1,586
3	13,091	11,356	1,735
4	13,091	11,193	1,898
5	13,091	11,015	2,076

tures of $130,000 plus the $10,000 of the purchase price properly allocable to the building shell, minus the amount of tax credit. (Had this building been designated a historic structure, the rehabilitation tax credit would have totaled 20 percent of qualifying rehabilitation expenditures.) This amount, $127,000, will be recovered via the cost recovery allowance over a 39-year period.

The annual cost recovery allowance is $127,000 divided by 39, or $3,256. The first year's allowance is reduced, as the developer plans to spend the first two-and-a-half months completing rehabilitation work. First and last year's cost recovery allowances are also adjusted for the half-month convention and assuming the property is put into service during the third month of the investor's taxable year and sold during the final month. Table 22.10 illustrates the cost recovery allowance schedule.

Calculating Annual After-Tax Cash Flows

Table 22.11 shows the calculation of annual after-tax cash-flow projections. A five percent management fee is subtracted from estimated gross income to arrive at estimated net operating income. Subtracting annual debt service from net operating income yields before-tax cash-flow estimates. Principal payments are added to before-tax cash flows, and capital cost recovery allowances are subtracted, to generate estimates of annual taxable income. Tax consequences are then estimated by multiplying expected taxable income by the investor's 28 per-

Table 22.10   **Depreciation Allowances for Commercial Rehabilitation Project**

Year	Beginning Balance	Depreciation Allowance	Ending Balance
1	$127,000	$2,306	$124,694
2	124,694	3,256	121,438
3	121,438	3,256	118,182
4	118,182	3,256	114,926
5	114,926	3,120	111,806

Table 22.11	**Calculation of After-Tax Cash Flows for Commercial Rehabilitation Project**				
	Year 1	*Year 2*	*Year 3*	*Year 4*	*Year 5*
Gross Income	$15,300	$20,400	$20,400	$22,800	$22,800
Less: Management Fee (5%)	765	1,020	1,020	1,140	1,140
Net Operating Income	$14,535	$19,380	$19,380	$21,660	$21,660
Less: Interest	11,641	11,505	11,356	11,193	11,015
Depreciation	2,306	3,256	3,256	3,256	3,120
Taxable Income	$ 588	$ 4,619	$ 4,768	$ 7,211	$ 7,525
Times: Tax Rate	.28	.28	.28	.28	.28
Tax Liability	$ 165	$ 1,293	$ 1,335	$ 2,019	$ 2,107
Net Operating Income	$14,535	$19,380	$19,380	$21,660	$21,660
Less: Debt Service	13,091	13,091	13,091	13,091	13,091
Before-Tax Cash Flow	$ 1,444	$ 6,289	$ 6,289	$ 8,569	$ 8,569
Less: Income Tax	165	1,293	1,335	2,019	2,107
After-Tax Cash Flow	$ 1,279	$ 4,996	$ 4,954	$ 6,550	$ 6,462

cent marginal income tax bracket. After-tax cash flows are calculated by adjusting expected before-tax cash flows for tax consequences.

Estimating the Selling Price

Dr. Habam expects to sell the property after five years. Because the initial lease is for a period of ten years, Dr. Habam thinks a purchaser will be getting a good building with a good tenant. If it is assumed that the relationship between income and value remains constant, a gross income multiplier can be used to estimate selling price. The current gross income multiplier is calculated by dividing the first full year's gross income into the purchase price:

$$\frac{\$160,000}{\$20,400} = 7.84$$

A sales price can then be estimated by multiplying the sixth year's expected gross income by the calculated gross income multiplier. This yields a calculated sales price of $178,752:

$$\$22,800 \times 7.84 = \$178,752$$

Calculated selling price is rounded, producing an estimated selling price of $180,000.

Estimating Income Tax and Cash Proceeds from Sale

The first step in estimating tax consequences from selling the property is to estimate the gain on sale. This is simply the estimated sales price minus the adjusted basis at time of sale and minus selling costs incurred. The gain on sale is treated as ordinary income in the year in which it occurs. Multiplying the estimated taxable income by the investor's 28 percent marginal tax rate produces estimated taxes on sale: $13,494. Subtracting transaction costs, income taxes and the mortgage balance from the estimated sales price yields the expected after-tax cash flow from the sale. These computations are illustrated in Tables 22.12 and 22.13.

Evaluating Expected After-Tax Cash Flows

Investment value is calculated by adding the present value of the equity position to the present value of available financing. In a rehabilitation project, the investor receives an additional benefit from the investment tax credit; this must also be added to the present value of the after-tax cash flows. Table 22.14 illustrates analysis of expected after-tax cash flows for Dr. Habam's proposed project, given an appropriate discount rate (that is, target rate of return) of 15 percent.

As illustrated in Table 22.14, the present value of expected after-tax cash flows is $37,603. Adding the tax credit and available financing to this amount yields an investment value of $180,603.

Net present value can be obtained by subtracting the required equity investment from the present value of equity cash flows. Recall that the initial investment of $30,000 is reduced by a $13,000 investment tax credit to $17,000. This project is expected to produce positive net present value of $37,603 minus $17,000, or $20,603. If all assumptions hold, undertaking this project will increase Dr. Habam's net wealth by $20,603.

Table 22.12	Calculation of Tax on Sale for Commercial Rehabilitation Project		
Estimated Sales Price (Net)			$180,000
Less: Adjusted Basis			
Land (Cost)		$ 20,000	
Building		111,806	131,806
Gain on Sale			$ 48,194
Times: Marginal Tax Rate			.28
Tax on Sale			$ 13,494

Table 22.13	After-Tax Cash Flow from Disposal for Commercial Rehabilitation Project	
Sale Price		$180,000
Less:		
Loan Balance		121,255
Tax on Sale		13,494
After-Tax Cash Flow from Disposal		$ 45,251

| Table 22.14 | **Analysis of After-Tax Cash Flows Commercial Rehabilitation Project** |

Year	Expected After-Tax Cash Flow	Present Value Factor at 15%	Discounted Cash Flow
1	$ 1,279	0.8696	$ 1,112
2	4,996	0.7561	3,777
3	4,954	0.6575	3,257
4	6,550	0.5718	3,745
5	6,462	0.4972	3,213
(From Disposal)	45,251	0.4972	22,499

Present Value of Equity	$ 37,603
Plus:	
Tax Credit	13,000
Available Financing	130,000
Investment Value	$180,603
Present Value of Equity	$ 37,603
Less: Required Equity	17,000
Net Present Value	$ 20,603

SUMMARY

Development involves placing improvements—usually buildings—on the land. Rehabilitation is the renovation and, in some cases, remodeling of existing structures. Many developers engage in both development and rehabilitation activities.

Development projects range in size and complexity from single-family residences built one at a time to entire cities carved from agricultural land or from decaying segments of older cities. Ventures might originate from a developer with an idea who looks for an appropriate site, from an investor with funds looking for an investment outlet or from a site owner looking for an appropriate way to utilize a property. The project might be developed on a custom basis (designed to exact specifications of a purchaser/user) or on a speculative basis (built in the expectation that a purchaser can be found after the project is completed).

Rehabilitation projects spring from existing structures in need of extensive renovation. The rehabilitator starts with a building that is physically deteriorated or functionally obsolete and improves its physical condition or brings it up to modern design standards.

RECOMMENDED READINGS

Alenick, Jerome B. *Real Estate Development Manual*. Boston: Warren, Gorham and Lamont, 1990.

Beyard, Michael D. *Business and Industrial Park Development Handbook*. Washington, DC: ULI—The Urban Land Institute, 1988.

Casazza, John A., and Frank H. Spink, Jr. *Shopping Center Development Handbook, Second Edition.* Washington, DC: ULI—The Urban Land Institute, 1985.

Martin, Thomas J., et al. *Adaptive Use, Development Economics, Process, and Profiles.* Washington, DC: ULI—The Urban Land Institute, 1980.

Miles, Mike E., Emil E. Malizia, Marc A. Weiss, Gayle L. Berens and Ginger Travis. *Real Estate Development, Principles and Process.* Washington, DC: ULI—The Urban Land Institute, 1991.

O'Connor, Joseph W., "Real Estate Development: Investment Risks and Rewards." *Real Estate Issues,* vol. 11, no. 1 (Spring–Summer 1986) pp. 6–11.

O'Mara, Paul W. *Office Development Handbook.* Washington, DC: ULI—The Urban Land Institute, 1982.

Pederson, Rick "Downtown Development: Why and How?" *Real Estate Issues,* vol. 12, no. 2 (Fall–Winter 1987) pp. 49–51.

REVIEW QUESTIONS

1. How does the development concept of "an idea in search of a site" relate to "a site in search of an idea?"
2. How are feasibility studies used in the development process?
3. What types of financing are generally used in new development?
4. How do custom building and speculative construction differ?
5. Who bears the greatest risk in a fixed-price contract?
6. Describe an area that would be considered prime for rehabilitation.
7. Why are people willing to take on a rehabilitation project?
8. Outline the process of judging the feasibility of a rehabilitation proposal.

DISCUSSION QUESTIONS

1. In general, would you expect cost estimates to be more precise for new development projects or for rehabilitation projects?
2. Is there a minimum size for a project (measured in dollar terms) below which a feasibility study would not be warranted prior to undertaking development efforts?
3. How does a general contractor differ from a real estate developer?

CHAPTER 23

Industrial Property, Office Building and Shopping Center Analysis

This chapter demonstrates analysis of investment proposals involving industrial property, office buildings and small shopping centers. Examples of each are presented to illustrate differences as well as similarities. Demand factors and locational considerations are discussed for each property category. Brief case studies demonstrate differences in procedure dictated by variations in institutional arrangements or market characteristics. The industrial building case study, for example, involves a property leased on a net basis to a single tenant. The office building case study illustrates a multitenant operation with expenses paid by the property owner. Percentage leases are introduced in the shopping center case study.

INVESTING IN INDUSTRIAL BUILDINGS

Industrial buildings are perennial favorites among real estate investors. Reliable, creditworthy tenants, long-term leases and opportunities to shift many if not all operating expenses to tenants account for the popularity of these structures among investors. For their part, business operators frequently find themselves short of operating capital and prefer to channel available resources into business expansion rather than into real estate ownership. Investors and business tenants thus find in leased industrial buildings a symbiotic relationship.

Demand for Industrial Space

Demand for industrial space is largely a function of the demand for products produced by the industrial sector. Forces that increase demand for manufactured goods also increase demand for industrial space, and, conversely, any situation that causes a decrease in demand for manufactured goods will cause a decrease in demand for industrial space; economists refer to this as a *derived demand.* Of course, changes in demand for space are not as volatile as changes in demand for industrial goods. Manufacturers generally adjust their space needs based on long-term projections of product demand.

Periodic shifts in demand for industrial space of various types and in different locations reflect alterations in composition of the industrial sector. Growth in service and technology-based industries has in recent years sparked increased demand for light assembly and research facilities. Decrease in demand for the products of heavy industry has greatly reduced the demand for structures employed in these manufacturing processes.

Locational Factors

Processing industries have a wide degree of locational discretion. They may choose sites near their raw materials sources, near markets for their finished products, near their major sources of labor supply or at some intermediate point. Their choices are usually conditioned by the economics of moving people, materials or products between various sites. Industries that process heavy or bulky raw material into light or compact products may gain significant transportation economies by locating near their raw materials sources.

Location Near Fuel or Power Supply.   For some industries, raw materials can be moved less expensively than other factors of production. Examples include processors that consume large quantities of fuel or power. The nation's first steel-making centers were located near coal mines because of the large quantities of that fuel required in early steel-making processes. High electrical power requirements favor the location of aluminum and electrometallurgical processors near sources of relatively inexpensive hydroelectric power.

Location Near Markets.   Home building, commercial baking and beverage bottling are examples of industries where transportation costs increase as the product approaches the end of the production process. Accordingly, these products are generally fabricated near the location of their final use. This tendency to choose location in order to reduce the cost of transportation to the final marketplace is sometimes offset by a desire to concentrate manufacturing to gain economies of scale in production.

Location of Footloose Industries.   Many industrial location decisions defy all the preceding classifications. Because transportation is not a major item in their production costs, some manufacturers base location decisions on other criteria. They frequently choose locations remote from both raw materials and markets, thus incurring double transfer costs, in order to gain reductions in other processing costs. These have been described as *footloose industries.*

Labor is the most expensive productive factor for many footloose industries. Labor-intensive firms find it economical to seek sites that minimize labor-related costs. If they need predominantly unskilled or semiskilled labor, they are likely to choose locations where there is an abundant supply at comparatively low wage rates. If they require ready access to a pool of highly skilled workers, they will probably prefer a location near other employers who require similar skills or a locale that prospective employees will find particularly attractive.

Types of Industrial Buildings

There is no official classification system for industrial buildings. Yet a building can be characterized usefully according to the nature of its construction or the type of tenant it attracts. Approached from this perspective, most industrial structures can be classified as either heavy industrial, loft, modern single-story or incubator buildings.

Heavy Industrial Buildings.   Petroleum, steel and rubber processing facilities, as well as truck and auto manufacturing facilities, are all examples of heavy industrial buildings. Structures housing such industries are usually custom-designed to accommodate specific needs. These types of properties are typically owner-occupied and of little or no interest to investors.

Loft Buildings.   Loft buildings were one of the nation's earliest types of industrial building. They are multistory structures, usually with wood or concrete frames and masonry exterior walls. Loft buildings were designed to accommodate manufacturing processes as they existed in the early 1900s. Many loft buildings are located near central business districts, and many have been converted to uses other than manufacturing.

Modern One-Story Structures.   The most common industrial structure built today is the modern one-story facility, typically located in a suburban industrial park. These buildings are usually designed for occupancy by a single tenant and are frequently owner-occupied. Yet many are owned by investors and leased to manufacturing firms. Such buildings are attractive to institutional investors because tenants are often responsible for all upkeep and operating expenses.

Incubator Buildings.   Incubator buildings are smaller multitenant structures. New firms rent space in such buildings and, as business expands, they move to larger quarters. Incubator buildings are usually owned by investors, who collect rents and pay many operating expenses. Tenants are usually responsible for their own utility bills and may be required to compensate the owners for any operating expense increases during the period of the lease.

AN INDUSTRIAL BUILDING CASE STUDY

Single-story net-leased industrial buildings are among the simplest types of investment properties to analyze. Net leases require tenants to pay all or most of the expenses associated with operating the leased property; most of the responsibilities of real estate ownership are transferred to tenants. Investors merely collect rents and make debt service payments. This simple arrangement makes these types of buildings a favorite among institutional investors. In simplicity of operation, such investments resemble the purchase of bonds or long-term notes. Net-leased properties, however, provide income tax benefits not available with securities.

To illustrate the analytical procedures associated with net-leased industrial buildings, consider the case of an old but well-maintained one-story structure containing 35,000 square feet of rentable space. A developer recently signed a creditworthy tenant to a six-year lease calling for rentals of $3.50 per square foot annually for three years and $4 per square foot for the remaining three years of the lease. The tenant is to pay all operating expenses, including insurance and property taxes. The prospective purchaser of this net-leased property expects to sell after a five-year holding period.

Forecasting Income and Expenses

Net operating income is simple to forecast in this situation. Rental income will be $3.50 per square foot, or $122,500 ($3.50 times 35,000 square feet) annually for the first three years; thereafter it will be $4 times 35,000 square feet, or $140,000. Because the investor will acquire title subject to an existing lease, there will be no rental expense and no need to investigate market rental rates.

Financing

A loan of $700,000 (requiring monthly payments) is available. The interest rate will be 9 percent per annum. Table 23.1 presents a loan amortization schedule for the first five years of a 20-year amortization period. The remaining balance at the end of the anticipated five-year holding period will be approximately $620,949.

	Table 23.1	**Loan Amortization Schedule for One-Story Industrial Building**	
Year	*Annual Debt Service*	*Annual Interest*	*Principal*
1	$75,577	$62,468	$13,109
2	75,577	61,238	14,339
3	75,577	59,893	15,684
4	75,577	58,422	17,155
5	75,577	56,813	18,764

Annual Income Tax Consequences

For income tax computations the investor will use the straight-line cost recovery (depreciation) method over a 39-year period. (See Chapter 10 for details of depreciation rules and the income tax consequences of alternative tax strategies available to investors.) Twenty percent of the $875,000 anticipated purchase price is properly attributable to the land, with the remaining $700,000 attributable to the building. Annual depreciation allowances, therefore, are $700,000/ 39, or $17,949. Because of the half-month convention, the depreciation allowance in the first and last years of the holding period (assuming the property is acquired during the first month of the tax year and sold during the last month) is $17,201. Table 23.2 summarizes these computations.

Table 23.3 combines operating income, mortgage financing and cost recovery allowance data to estimate annual after-tax cash flows. Annual debt service is subtracted from net operating income to yield before-tax cash flow. Taxable income is derived by subtracting the depreciation allowance and interest expense from net operating income. Note that this property is expected to produce positive taxable income in each year of the holding period. The prospective investor expects to be in the 28 percent marginal tax bracket both before and after considering the impact of this investment opportunity. Thus, income tax consequences are calculated by multiplying taxable income by 28 percent. Adjusting expected before-tax cash flows for anticipated tax consequences produces annual after-tax cash-flow forecasts as shown at the bottom of Table 23.3.

Forecasting Sales Proceeds

The final cash flow to the supplier of equity in a real estate venture is the after-tax proceeds from disposal. Forecasting these proceeds starts with an estimate of the sales price. Expected income tax consequences of disposal are computed under the assumption that current income tax laws will still be in effect.

The relationship between a property's market value and anticipated net operating income for the forthcoming year can be expressed as a ratio called a *capitalization rate.* The relationship is:

$$R = I/V$$

Table 23.2	Depreciation Allowance Schedule for One-Story Industrial Building		
Year	*Beginning Balance*	*Depreciation Allowance**	*Ending Balance*
1	$700,000	$17,201	$682,799
2	682,799	17,949	664,850
3	664,850	17,949	646,901
4	646,901	17,949	628,952
5	628,952	17,201	611,751

*Assumes acquisition during first month of tax year, disposal during last month.

Table 23.3   **After-Tax Cash Flow Forecast for Single-Story Industrial Building**

	Year 1	Year 2	Year 3	Year 4	Year 5
Net Operating Income	$122,500	$122,500	$122,500	$140,000	$140,000
Less:					
Interest Expense	62,468	61,238	59,893	58,422	56,813
Depreciation Allowance	17,201	17,949	17,949	17,949	17,201
Taxable Income	$ 42,831	$ 43,313	$ 44,658	$ 63,629	$ 65,986
Times: Tax Rate	.28	.28	.28	.28	.28
Tax Liability	$ 11,993	$ 12,128	$ 12,504	$ 17,816	$ 18,476
Net Operating Income	$122,500	$122,500	$122,500	$140,000	$140,000
Less: Debt Service	75,577	75,577	75,577	75,577	75,577
Before-Tax Cash Flow	$ 46,923	$ 46,923	$ 46,923	$ 64,423	$ 64,423
Less: Income Tax	11,993	12,128	12,504	17,816	18,476
After-Tax Cash Flow	$ 34,930	$ 34,795	$ 34,419	$ 46,607	$ 45,947

where R is the capitalization rate, I is the net operating income, and V is the property value. Substituting the purchase price and the first year's forecast net operating income for the property under analysis yields a capitalization rate of 14 percent:

$$0.14 = \$122,500/\$875,000$$

Assuming that this relationship still prevails when the property is sold five years hence, the value at that time can be estimated by dividing the sixth year's anticipated net operating income (which is identical to that for year five) by the capitalization rate:

$$0.14 = \$140,000/V$$

Therefore:

$$V = \$140,000/.14$$
$$\$1,000,000$$

Subtracting the adjusted basis at time of sale from the expected sales price yields the anticipated gain on disposal. The property's adjusted basis immediately prior to the sale will be initial cost minus cumulative depreciation allowances. (Any additional capital expenditures during the holding period will have been added to the property's basis. Basis computations and adjustments are discussed at length in Chapter 10.) Multiplying the gain by the assumed 28 percent tax rate yields the expected income tax consequences of disposal. Detailed computations are shown in Table 23.4.

Subtracting the anticipated income tax liability and the remaining balance of the mortgage loan from the net sales proceeds generates an estimate of the

Table 23.4   **Tax on Sale of One-Story Industrial Building**

Sales Price		$1,000,000
Less: Adjusted Basis		
Land (Cost)	$175,000	
Building	611,751	786,751
Taxable Gain		$ 213,249
Times: Marginal Tax Rate		.28
Tax on Sale		$ 59,710

after-tax cash flow from disposal. As shown in Table 23.5, the expected after-tax cash flow from selling this property after five years is $319,341.

Evaluating After-Tax Cash Flows

The final step in the analysis is to estimate investment value and net present value of the equity position. Investment value is calculated by discounting expected annual after-tax cash flows and the anticipated after-tax proceeds of sale and adding the amount of the mortgage loan that was incorporated into the cash-flow forecast. Assuming the investor is seeking a 15 percent rate of return on equity funds, investment value is $987,585. Table 23.6 illustrates the computations. Since investment value is greater than the expected purchase price, equity funds expended for this project are expected to yield more than the investor's desired rate of return.

An alternative way to show expected investment consequences is to compute the net present value of the venture. Acquiring the property at the asking price involves an equity investment of $175,000. Net present value is simply the present value of expected after-tax cash flows minus the required equity investment. Since the net present value of $112,585 is greater than zero, the project is expected to yield a rate of return in excess of the 15 percent discount rate. This computation is also illustrated in Table 23.6.

Table 23.5   **After-Tax Equity Reversion for One-Story Industrial Building**

Sales Price		$1,000,000
Less:		
Tax on Sale	59,710	
Loan Balance	620,949	680,659
After-Tax Equity Reversion		$ 319,341

Table 23.6	Investment Value of One-Story Industrial Building		
Year	Annual After-Tax Cash Flow	Present Value Factor (15%)	Discounted Cash Flow
1	$ 34,930	0.8696	$ 30,375
2	34,795	0.7561	26,309
3	34,419	0.6575	22,630
4	46,607	0.5718	26,650
5	45,947	0.4972	22,845
(From Disposal)	319,341	0.4972	158,776
Present Value of Equity			$287,585
Available Financing			700,000
Investment Value			$987,585
Present Value of Equity			$287,585
Less: Required Equity			175,000
Net Present Value			$112,585

INVESTING IN OFFICE BUILDINGS

Dramatic growth in the service sector of the economy has greatly increased the demand for office space in recent years. Modern high-rise structures are rapidly replacing older, smaller buildings in central business districts. Many office centers have also sprung up in suburban locations. These are usually high-rise buildings or one- and two-story structures in office parks.

Demand for office space, like that for industrial space, is a derived demand. It is related to the demand for services supplied by occupants of office buildings. Increases in the number and size of service industries such as law firms, accounting firms and financial institutions are translated into expanded demand for space to house these activities. Moreover, total demand for office space has expanded due to the trend among employers to provide more working space per employee.

Owner-occupied office buildings are often designed to project the desired image of the owner-occupant. Investor-owned buildings, in contrast, tend to be somewhat more functional and less luxurious. High-rise buildings usually have multitenant floors located near the base and single-tenant floors near the top. This minimizes space utilization problems that might otherwise be created by the need to accommodate elevator core space. Full-floor occupants usually pay for all space on their floors, including washrooms and corridors.

Office building tenants typically enter into multiyear leases. Office building owners learned long ago that if they are unable to raise their rentals annually, increases in operating expenses will greatly erode their profits. As a result, they pioneered the process of passing increases in expenses on to their tenants. Leases often contain a clause stating that the landlord will pay operating expenses up to some specified amount per square foot. Any increases above this amount are passed to the tenant. This represents a significant decrease in the risk office building ownership would otherwise impose.

Tenants often take options to renew leases on occupied space. Such lease arrangements inevitably contain a formula for computing increased rental rates for the renewal period, based upon changes in the general price level. Such a provision spares the tenant the expense and bother of finding new quarters and spares the landlord the expense of locating a new tenant.

AN OFFICE BUILDING CASE STUDY

The property to be analyzed is a two-story, multitenant office building containing 10,000 square feet of rentable space. The building is situated on a 25,000-square-foot site that is partially landscaped and contains parking for about 35 automobiles. The property is being offered for $500,000. An investor who will remain in the 28 percent marginal tax bracket after the effects of purchase is considering acquisition.

Reconstructing the Income and Expense Statement

Multitenant office buildings are generally leased on a gross rental basis. In this case, the property owner pays all operating expenses with the exception of tenants' heat and electricity. The landlord supplies heat and electricity to common areas only. All leases also contain real estate tax stops, which require tenants to pay property taxes above a stipulated base amount.

Current income from the building is $10.51 per square foot of gross rentable area, for a total of $105,100 per annum before vacancy losses. Comparable buildings in the area are generating per-square-foot rentals of between $10.25 and $10.75 for similar space. Considering competition, current rentals seem appropriate. Office buildings in the area also experience a vacancy rate equal to about seven percent of gross income. Reducing gross income by a vacancy allowance of approximately 7 percent produces effective gross income of approximately $97,700.

Table 23.7 contains a reconstructed income and expense statement for the property. Expenses were estimated after studying the building's operating history and that of comparable buildings in the area. Estimates appear reasonable when compared with averages in the Building Owners and Managers Association International's current *Downtown and Suburban Office Building Experience Exchange Report* and with the Institute of Real Estate Management's current edition of *Income-Expense Analysis: Suburban Office Buildings.*[1]

Financing

A loan of $375,000 is available at 9 percent interest with a 20-year amortization schedule and monthly payments. The rate is renegotiable after five years, which

Table 23.7	Reconstructed Income and Expense Statement for 10,000-Square-Foot Office Building		

Potential Gross Income			$105,100
Less: Vacancy at 7%			7,400
Effective Gross Income			$ 97,700
Less: Operating Expenses			
Electricity		$2,000	
Water		400	
Sewer Fees		30	
Heating Fuel		3,600	
Payroll/Contract Cleaning		7,600	
Cleaning Supplies		700	
Janitorial Payroll		4,300	
Janitorial Supplies		400	
Heating/Air-Conditioning		2,100	
Electrical Repairs		400	
Plumbing Repairs		500	
Exterior Repairs		400	
Roof Repairs		400	
Parking Lot Repairs		200	
Decorating (Tenant)		1,800	
Decorating (Public)		400	
Miscellaneous Repairs		1,100	
Management Fees		4,500	
Other Administrative Fees		1,000	
Landscaping Maintenance		400	
Trash Removal		600	
Window Washing		200	
Snow Removal		2,200	
Miscellaneous Services		500	
Total Operating Expenses			35,730
Real Estate Taxes			15,800
Net Operating Income			$ 46,170

is beyond the investor's expected holding period. Table 23.8 presents an amortization schedule for this loan. Annual debt service payments are $40,488, and loan balance at the end of the expected holding period is $332,651.

Depreciation Allowance

The investor will use the straight-line depreciation computation method over a 39-year period. Expected purchase price of $500,000 is allocated 85 percent, or $425,000, to the building and 15 percent, or $75,000, to the land. This allocation is supported by the local tax assessor's records. Annual depreciation allowance

	Table 23.8		**Loan Amortization Schedule for 10,000-Square-Foot Office Building**	

Year	Annual Payment	Annual Interest	Principal
1	$40,488	$33,465	$ 7,023
2	40,488	32,806	7,682
3	40,488	32,086	8,402
4	40,488	31,298	9,190
5	40,488	30,436	10,052

deductions will be $425,000/39, or $10,897. Because of the half-month convention, the allowance for the first and last years of the holding period is $10,443, assuming the property is acquired during the first month of the taxable year and sold during the last month. Computations are summarized in Table 23.9.

Forecasting Annual After-Tax Cash Flows

Table 23.10 contains calculations of forecasted annual after-tax cash flows. Income and expense estimates come from the reconstructed income and expense statement contained in Table 23.7. Income and expenses are expected to grow at five percent per year. This rate appears justified after analysis of the local office market. Note that the tax stops cause real estate taxes to remain stable over the expected five year holding period.

Debt service is subtracted from net operating income to produce before tax cash flows. Taxable income or loss is multiplied by the investor's marginal tax rate to produce expected annual income tax consequences of ownership. Before-tax cash flows are adjusted for tax consequences to produce annual after-tax cash flows.

	Table 23.9		**Depreciation Schedule for 10,000-Square-Foot Office Building***	

Year	Beginning Balance	Depreciation Allowance	Ending Balance
1	$425,000	$10,443	$414,557
2	414,557	10,897	403,660
3	403,660	10,897	392,763
4	392,763	10,897	381,866
5	381,866	10,443	371,423

*Assumes purchase during first month of taxable year, sale during last month

Table 23.10	After-Tax Cash Flow Forecast: 10,000 Square Foot Office Building				
	Year 1	*Year 2*	*Year 3*	*Year 4*	*Year 5*
Potential Gross Rent	$105,100	$110,355	$115,873	$121,666	$127,750
Less: Vacancy	7,400	7,770	8,159	8,566	8,995
Effective Gross Income	$ 97,700	$102,585	$107,714	$113,100	$118,755
Less:					
Operating Expenses	35,730	37,516	39,392	41,362	43,430
Property Tax	15,800	15,800	15,800	15,800	15,800
Net Operating Income	$ 46,170	$ 49,269	$ 52,522	$ 55,938	$ 59,525
Less:					
Interest Expense	33,465	32,806	32,086	31,298	30,436
Depreciation Allowance	10,443	10,897	10,897	10,897	10,443
Taxable Income	$ 2,262	$ 5,566	$ 9,539	$ 13,743	$ 18,646
Times: Tax Rate	.28	.28	.28	.28	.28
Tax Liability	$ 633	$ 1,558	$ 2,671	$ 3,848	$ 5,221
Net Operating Income	$ 46,170	$ 49,269	$ 52,522	$ 55,938	$ 59,525
Less: Debt Service	40,488	40,488	40,488	40,488	40,488
Before-Tax Cash Flow	$ 5,682	$ 8,781	$ 12,034	$ 15,450	$ 19,037
Less: Income Tax	633	1,558	2,671	3,848	5,221
After-Tax Cash Flow	$ 5,049	$ 7,223	$ 9,363	$ 11,602	$ 13,816

Forecasting After-Tax Cash Flow from Disposal

A capitalization rate based on the current relationship between income and market value is computed and applied to expected income from the property five years from the current date. This comprises the basis for estimated market value five years hence. The current rate is:

$$\$46,170/\$500,000 = 0.09234$$

Sales price can then be estimated by dividing the sixth year's operating income forecast by the calculated capitalization rate:

$$\$63,291/0.09234 = \$685,413$$

This estimate is rounded to $685,000. Subtracting an estimated selling cost equaling 11.5 percent of the sales price yields an expected net sales price (rounded) of $606,300. The property's adjusted basis (initial cost minus cumulative depreciation allowances) is subtracted from the expected net sales price to derive expected gain on disposal. This expected gain will be taxed at the investor's 28 percent marginal income tax rate. There results an anticipated $44,766 income tax liability due to the sale. These computations are presented in Table 23.11.

Table 23.11	Tax Consequences of Sale of 10,000-Square-Foot Office Building		
Sales Price			$685,000
Less: Selling Expenses			78,700
Net Sales Price			$606,300
Less: Adjusted Basis			
Land (Cost)		$ 75,000	
Building		371,423	446,423
Gain on Sale			$159,877
Times: Tax Rate			.28
Tax Consequences of Sale			$ 44,766

Subtracting the expected income tax liability and the remaining mortgage balance from the anticipated net sales price of the property yields the $228,883 forecast of after-tax cash proceeds from disposal. Table 23.12 shows the details of this arithmetic.

Analyzing After-Tax Cash-Flow Forecasts

Anticipated after-tax cash flows are discounted at the investor's required rate of return on equity capital. Subtracting the required equity investment of $125,000 from the present value of expected future net cash flows generates net present value. Since the net present value is greater than zero, we conclude that the project offers an expected yield in excess of the investor's required rate of return. These computations are shown in Table 23.13.

Alternately, we sum the present value of the anticipated future cash flows and the mortgage loan that was incorporated into the cash-flow forecast. The resulting investment value is the most the investor is justified in paying for the property (assuming, of course, that actual financing is the same as that incorporated into the forecast). Because this amount exceeds the asking price for the property, the project offers the prospect of earning more than the required yield on equity funds. Table 23.13 also summarizes these calculations.

Table 23.12	After-Tax Cash Flow from Disposal of 10,000-Square-Foot Office Building		
Sales Price			$685,000
Less:			
Selling Costs		$ 78,700	
Loan Balance		332,651	
Tax on Sale		44,766	456,117
After-Tax Cash Flow			$228,883

Table 23.13   **Present Value Analysis for 10,000-Square-Foot Office Building**

Year	Annual After-Tax Cash Flows	Present Value Factor (10%)	Discounted Cash Flows
1	$ 5,049	0.9091	$ 4,590
2	7,223	0.8264	5,969
3	9,363	0.7513	7,034
4	11,602	0.6830	7,924
5	13,816	0.6209	8,578
(From Sale)	228,883	0.6209	142,113

Present Value of Equity	$176,208
Less: Required Equity	125,000
Net Present Value	$ 51,208
Present Value of Equity	$176,208
Add: Available Financing	375,000
Investment Value	$551,208

INVESTING IN SHOPPING CENTERS

Relationships between landlords and tenants in shopping centers differ from those in freestanding stores and other structures. Major stores in shopping centers, called *anchor tenants,* attract shoppers to the center and thereby create customers for smaller specialty shops. Investors and developers have long provided favorable lease terms to anchor tenants and achieved their greatest returns on rentals received from specialty tenants. More recently, developers have allowed major tenants to construct their own buildings on sites leased from the owners or have sold sites and portions of the parking lots to the anchors. This reduces the owners' investment and often increases their return because they no longer own space subject to rental rates favoring tenants.

Lease arrangements also differ in shopping centers. A shopping center owner sets a base rental rate and often increases the rental rate as the tenant's sales volume increases. This is known as a *percentage clause* in a lease. Percentage clauses have the effect of making the shopping center owner a partner in the business of the tenants. For this reason, tenant selection as well as tenant mix is very important.

Large shopping center tenants typically lease space on a net basis; that is, they pay all expenses associated with operation of their spaces. Smaller tenants often pay their own utility expenses, while the landlord pays other operating expenses. Because these leases often extend for a number of years, landlords pay operating expenses up to some specified amount, and the tenant pays any excess costs. Shopping center tenants also often pay a common area maintenance fee. This fee reimburses the owners for maintenance of common areas such as parking lots or mall space.

Shopping centers are usually classified according to the size of the trade area from which they draw customers and according to the types of merchandise sold by their major tenants. Categories include neighborhood centers, community centers, regional centers and superregional centers.

Neighborhood Shopping Centers

Neighborhood centers serve a relatively small trade area, roughly that from which customers can commute by automobile within five to ten minutes. As anchor tenants, neighborhood centers usually have a food store and drugstore, which may occupy a combined total area of 35,000 to 50,000 square feet. The food store is expected to generate customer traffic from which other tenants— mostly purveyors of convenience goods—will benefit. Total area within neighborhood shopping centers ranges between 50,000 and 100,000 square feet.

Community Shopping Centers

In addition to a major food store, most community centers feature a junior department store or a major discount department store as an anchor tenant. The department store, typically ranging in size from 50,000 to 100,000 square feet, is usually located at the opposite end of the center from the food store, with specialty shops in between. This layout maximizes customer traffic past the specialty shops and distributes customer automobiles more evenly throughout the parking area. Having two anchor tenants increases the range of a community center's trade area, which may extend from ten to 15 minutes in driving time from the center.

Regional Shopping Centers

Considerably larger than community centers, regional shopping centers may encompass 200,000 to 400,000 square feet of retail space. They are usually enclosed malls, and feature one or two major department stores as anchor tenants. They provide facilities to a variety of retailers ranging from convenience goods to shopping goods such as furniture and appliances. As in community centers, anchor tenants at regional centers are considered the major attractive force for customers and are usually located at opposite ends of the center. Regional shopping centers have a trade area extending from 15 to 30 minutes in driving time from the facility.

Superregional Malls

Superregional shopping malls are a by-product of the nation's high-speed, limited-access freeway system. Ease and speed of travel have greatly expanded the trade areas of centers with good freeway access, enabling them to support much larger concentrations for retail facilities. In contrast to their regional counterparts, superregional malls may feature as many as four major department stores as anchor tenants. They tend to be very large, often encompassing from 500,000 to 750,000 or more square feet of retail space.

A SHOPPING CENTER CASE STUDY

The property to be analyzed is a community shopping center containing a discount department store that occupies 105,000 square feet, a food store occupying 30,000 square feet and a savings and loan association occupying 3,000 square feet. A fast-food operation has leased 30,000 square feet of the center's 435,600-square-foot site and constructed a restaurant building. All leases in the center are on a net basis, with tenants paying a pro-rata share of any common area maintenance expenses.

A group of six real estate practitioners is contemplating purchase of this center for $3,800,000. They are intrigued by real property ownership and plan to hold the center for five years. They plan to purchase through a general partnership with each investor acquiring a one-sixth interest. The group will also incur an annual management fee representing five percent of base rentals.

Financing

Title will be transferred subject to an existing first mortgage loan, which has a remaining balance of $1,640,042 and requires no assumption fee. Annual payments of approximately $160,876 include interest on the outstanding balance at a rate of 7.5 percent per annum. Sellers will take back a promissory note (to be secured by a second mortgage) for $1,511,970, leaving a balance of $647,988 to be paid in cash at the closing. Terms of seller financing will be 10.5 percent interest, annual payments of approximately $167,116 (representing a 30-year amortization schedule), with the remaining balance of $1,484,167 due at the end of three years. Prospective purchasers believe that they will be able to refinance the outstanding balance of the second mortgage note when the balance becomes due. They anticipate refinancing terms to involve 13.5 percent interest with a 25-year amortization period. They realize that this new loan may have a variable interest rate or require a balloon payment, but they believe that they will have disposed of the property before any such provisions are reflected in annual cash flows.

Table 23.14 provides an amortization schedule for the existing first mortgage note, for the second mortgage note to be supplied by the sellers and for the anticipated refinancing after three years. Table 23.15 combines these amortization schedules into a consolidated debt service schedule.

Depreciation Schedule

For income tax purposes, the investment group will use straight-line depreciation over a 39-year period. The expected purchase price of $3,800,000 is properly allocable 80 percent to the building and 20 percent to the land. Therefore, the annual allowance will be $3,040,000/39, or $77,949. The first and last year's

| Table 23.14 | Loan Amortization Schedules for Community Shopping Center |

Existing Loan

Year	Annual Payment	Annual Interest	Principal	Balance
1	$160,876	$123,003	$37,873	$1,602,169
2	160,876	120,163	40,713	1,561,456
3	160,876	117,109	43,767	1,517,689
4	160,876	113,827	47,049	1,470,640
5	160,876	110,298	50,578	1,420,062

Seller Financing

Year	Annual Payment	Annual Interest	Principal	Balance
1	$167,116	$158,757	$ 8,359	$1,503,611
2	167,116	157,879	9,237	1,494,374
3	167,116	156,909	10,207	1,484,167

Refinancing of Seller Financing

Year	Annual Payment	Annual Interest	Principal	Balance
4	$209,186	$200,363	$ 8,823	$1,475,344
5	209,186	199,171	10,015	1,465,329

| Table 23.15 | Combined Loan Amortization Schedule for Community Shopping Center |

Year	Annual Payment	Annual Interest	Principal	Balance
1	$327,992	$281,760	$46,232	$3,105,780
2	327,992	278,042	49,950	3,055,830
3	327,992	274,018	53,974	3,001,856
4	370,062	314,190	55,872	2,945,984
5	370,062	309,469	60,593	2,885,391

allowance, assuming purchase during the first month of the taxable year and sale during the last month, will be $74,701, due to the half-month convention. Table 23.16 contains a depreciation schedule indicating an adjusted basis for the building of $2,656,751 at the projected time of sale.

Forecasting Income

If this property is acquired, title will be transferred subject to existing leases. Examination of these leases reveals that base rentals for the department store and the food store will be $183,750 and $50,000 respectively over the anticipated five-year holding period. Rental for the fast-food restaurant will be

Table 23.16 **Depreciation Schedule for Community Shopping Center**

Year	Beginning Balance	Depreciation	Ending Balance
1	$3,040,000	$74,701	$2,965,299
2	2,965,299	77,949	2,887,350
3	2,887,350	77,949	2,809,401
4	2,809,401	77,949	2,731,452
5	2,731,452	74,701	2,656,751

$30,000 annually in the first three years and $32,000 in years four and five. The savings and loan association will pay $50,000 per year.

Leases of the department and food stores also contain percentage clauses. These require the department store to pay percentage rental equal to 1.5 percent of the net sales to the extent this exceeds the $700,000 base sales. The food store must pay one percent of gross sales when the percentage exceeds its $50,000 base sales. Prospective purchasers have been supplied with audited sales figures for both stores for the past ten years. Year-to-year sales receipts have fluctuated rather widely, but both stores have experienced average annual sales growth rates of about five percent per year. Purchasers believe this rate will continue over the anticipated holding period. Table 23.17 shows projected percentage rentals based on these estimates.

Forecasting Annual Cash Flows and Taxable Income

Table 23.18 combines operating income, financing and cost recovery allowance data into an estimate of annual after-tax cash flows. Net operating income is

Table 23.17 **Percentage Rentals for Community Shopping Center**

Department Store	Year 1	Year 2	Year 3	Year 4	Year 5
Estimated Annual Sales	$2,200,000	$2,310,000	$2,425,500	$2,546,775	$2,674,113
Less: Base Sales	700,000	700,000	700,000	700,000	700,000
Percentage Sales	$1,500,000	$1,610,000	$1,725,500	$1,846,775	$1,974,113
Times: Percentage	.015	.015	.015	.015	.015
Percentage Rental	$ 22,500	$ 24,150	$ 25,882	$ 27,702	$ 29,612
Food Store					
Estimated Annual Sales	$6,050,000	$6,352,500	$6,670,125	$7,003,631	$7,353,813
Times: Percentage	.01	.01	.01	.01	.01
	$ 60,500	$ 63,525	$ 66,701	$ 70,036	$ 73,538
Less: Base Rent	50,000	50,000	50,000	50,000	50,000
Percentage Rental	$ 10,500	$ 13,525	$ 16,701	$ 20,036	$ 23,538

Table 23.18	Calculation of Annual After-Tax Cash Flows for Community Shopping Center				
	Year 1	*Year 2*	*Year 3*	*Year 4*	*Year 5*
Base Rentals					
Department Store	$183,750	$183,750	$183,750	$183,750	$183,750
Food Store	50,000	50,000	50,000	50,000	50,000
Savings and Loan	50,000	50,000	50,000	50,000	50,000
Out-Parcel	30,000	30,000	30,000	32,000	32,000
Total Base Rentals	$313,750	$313,750	$313,750	$315,750	$315,750
Percentage Rentals					
Department Store	22,500	24,150	25,882	27,702	27,612
Food Store	10,500	13,525	16,701	20,036	23,538
Total Rentals	$346,750	$351,425	$356,333	$363,488	$366,900
Less: Management Fee	15,687	15,687	15,687	20,036	20,036
Net Operating Income	$331,063	$335,738	$340,646	$343,452	$346,864
Less: Debt Service	327,992	327,992	327,992	370,062	370,062
Before-Tax Cash Flow	$ 3,071	$ 7,746	$ 12,654	$ (26,610)	$ (23,198)
Plus: Principal	46,232	49,950	53,974	55,872	60,593
Less: Depreciation	74,701	77,949	77,949	77,949	74,701
Taxable Income (Loss)	$ (25,398)	$ (20,253)	$ (11,321)	$ (48,687)	$ (37,306)

simply anticipated rental revenue minus the management fee. Subtracting annual debt service from this amount yields before-tax cash flows. Adding back the principal portion for the debt service (the nondeductible part) and subtracting annual cost recovery allowances results in forecast of taxable income or tax-deductible losses for each year of the anticipated holding period.

Estimating Taxable Income and Cash Proceeds from Sale

As in previous examples, computing a capitalization rate facilitates estimating the market value of the property as of the anticipated sales date. The implied capitalization rate at the time of purchase is calculated by dividing the first year's net operating income by the purchase price:

$$\$331,063/\$3,800,000 = .087122$$

Market value at the anticipated selling date is estimated by dividing the sixth year's net operating income (which is expected to be approximately the same as that for year five) by the capitalization rate calculated for year one. Estimated sales price is:

$$\$351,113/.087122 = \$4,030,130$$

Estimated sales price, rounded to $4,030,000, is reduced by estimated selling expense of $220,180. Net sales price is then gross selling price of $4,030,000, minus $220,180, producing $3,809,820.

Table 23.19	Taxable Gain on Sale of Community Shopping Center	
Estimated Sales Price		$4,030,000
Less: Selling Costs		220,180
Net Sales Price		$3,809,820
Less: Adjusted Basis		
Land Cost	$ 760,000	
Building*	2,656,751	3,416,751
Gain on Sale		$ 393,069

*Cost minus accumulated cost recovery allowances.

Table 23.19 illustrates calculation of the taxable gain on sale of the property. Adjusted basis is subtracted from net sales price, producing the gain on sale. The gain on sale is $393,069. Subtracting the outstanding loan balance at the sale date from the net sales price yields the expected before-tax cash proceeds from disposal. Table 23.20 illustrates this calculation, which produces a before-tax cash-flow estimate of $924,429. Tax consequences for partners are discussed later.

Evaluating After-Tax Cash Flows

One partner is assumed to be in the 28 percent marginal tax bracket during the first four years of the investment period. Taxable income generated from selling the property will also be taxed at the 28 percent marginal rate. Table 23.21 shows the distribution of expected before-tax cash flows and income or loss from the investment for this partner. Since the partners have not arrived at a contrary agreement, all items are distributed evenly. Table 23.22 illustrates adjustments for income tax consequences to yield after-tax cash-flow estimates for the partner.

Table 23.23 shows estimation of after-tax proceeds from sale for this partner, Table 23.24 illustrates computation of present value of the partner's equity position, with a ten percent target rate of return. Since the present value of expected after-tax cash flows is less than the individual partner's share of the required equity investment ($86,850 present value versus equity investment of $107,977.88), the partner cannot expect this project to generate a yield in excess

Table 23.20	Before-Tax Cash Flow from Disposal of Community Shopping Center	
Estimated Sales Price		$4,030,000
Less:		
Selling Costs	$ 220,180	
Mortgage Balance	2,885,391	3,105,571
Before-Tax Cash Flow Estimate		$ 924,429

Table 23.21   **Partner's Share of Cash Flows and Income or Loss on Community Shopping Center**

Year	Total Before-Tax Cash Flow (Table 23.18)	Individual Partner's Share
1	$ 3,071	$ 512
2	7,746	1,291
3	12,654	2,109
4	(26,610)	(4,435)
5	(23,198)	(3,866)

	Taxable Income (Loss) (Table 23.18)	Partner's Share
1	$ (25,398)	$ (4,233)
2	(20,253)	(3,376)
3	(11,321)	(1,887)
4	(48,687)	(8,115)
5	(37,306)	(6,218)

	Before-Tax Cash Proceeds from Sale (Table 23.20)	Patner's Share
5	$924,429	$154,072

	Taxable Gain on Sale (Table 23.19)	Partner's Share
5	$393,069	$ 65,512

Table 23.22   **Annual After-Tax Cash Flows to Partner in 28 Percent Bracket on Community Shopping Center**

	Year 1	Year 2	Year 3	Year 4	Year 5
Partner's Taxable Income (Loss) (Table 23.21)	$(4,233)	$(3,376)	$(1,887)	$(8,115)	$(6,218)
Times: Tax Rate	.28	.28	.28	.28	.28
Tax (Savings)	$(1,185)	$ (945)	$ (528)	$(2,272)	$(1,741)
Partner's Before-Tax Cash Flow (Table 23.21)	$ 512	$ 1,291	$ 2,109	$(4,435)	$(3,866)
Tax Consequences	1,185	945	528	2,272	1,741
Partner's After-Tax Cash Flow	$ 1,697	$ 2,236	$ 2,637	$(2,163)	$(2,125)

of the discount rate. Remember, however, that the cash-flow projections and present value computations presuppose a specific purchase price and set of financing arrangements. The project can be made more attractive by lowering the price or offering more favorable mortgage terms. Financing terms can be

Table 23.23	Partner's After-Tax Cash Flow from Disposal of Shopping Center

Partner's Share of Sale Proceeds (Table 23.21)		$154,072
Less: Taxes		
Partner's Share of Gain (Table 23.21)	$65,512	
Times: Partner's Marginal Tax Rate	.28	18,343
Partner's After-Tax Cash Flow		$135,729

Table 23.24	Present Value of Partner's After-Tax Cash Flow on Shopping Center Project

Year	Partner's After-Tax Cash Flow	Present Value Factor (10%)	Present Value of Cash Flows
1	$ 1,697	0.9091	$ 1,543
2	2,236	0.8264	1,848
3	2,637	0.7513	1,981
4	(2,163)	0.6830	(1,477)
5	(2,125)	0.6209	(1,319)
(From Disposal)	135,729	0.6209	84,274
Present Value			$86,850

enhanced by lowering the interest rate, lengthening the repayment period or reducing the size of the down payment.

SUMMARY

Investment analytical procedures can be applied in a similar fashion to evaluate different types of real property. This has been demonstrated by applying the discounted cash-flow model to analyze an industrial building, an office building and a shopping center. In each case the procedure begins with demand analysis and proceeds to an after-tax cash-flow forecast. The anticipated cash flows, including the forecast after-tax cash flow from disposal at the end of the anticipated holding period, are discounted at the appropriate discount rate to generate a present value of the anticipated future flow of benefits.

NOTES

1. The *Downtown and Suburban Office Building Experience Exchange Report* (Washington, DC: Building Owners and Managers Association International) is published annually, as are editions of *Income-Expense Analysis: Suburban Office Buildings* (Chicago: Institute of Real Estate Management).

RECOMMENDED READINGS

Kinnard, William N., Jr., Stephen D. Messner, and Byrl N. Boyce. *Industrial Real Estate.* 3d ed. Washington, DC: Society of Industrial Realtors, 1979.

McMahon, John. *Property Development: Effective Decision Making in Uncertain Times.* NY: McGraw-Hill, 1976, pp. 153–202.

Urban Land Institute. *Real Estate Development Principles and Process.* 2nd ed. Washington DC: The Urban Land Institute, 1996.

REVIEW QUESTIONS

1. Why are investors attracted to industrial buildings as investment vehicles?
2. How do locational factors influence the choice of an industrial building site?
3. Consider the cash-flow projections of the industrial property illustrated in Table 23.3. In year four, the owner will have to pay taxes on income from operations. Does this mean there is no longer a tax shelter associated with the property?
4. What is the major determining factor in the demand for office space?
5. Describe the structure of most office building leases.
6. A capitalization rate was used to estimate the sales price of the office building in the case study. What other method might have been used to estimate the probable selling price?
7. Outline the lease arrangements commonly found in shopping center properties.
8. Describe the various types of shopping centers.
9. Is the community shopping center analyzed in this chapter a good investment for all the partners?

DISCUSSION QUESTIONS

1. If demand in your marketing area were about the same for rental apartments and industrial space, would you generally prefer to develop apartments or industrial buildings? What are some key factors that would affect your choice?
2. If demand factors were about equal, what would be some other considerations determining your preference for developing and owning single-tenant industrial buildings or incubator-type buildings?
3. Compare and contrast management functions in major shopping centers with those in large office buildings.
4. If demand were about equal, what are some factors that would affect your choice between developing a major regional shopping center and committing an equal amount of funds to developing a string of neighborhood or community shopping centers?

PART SEVEN: Case Problem

Gary Goldblest asks your advice concerning a perplexing situation. Having recently read a book about how someone turned $1,000 into $2 million in real estate in his spare time, Goldblest is anxious to participate in this bonanza. His job as an executive assistant in a major commodities brokerage firm is secure but offers no opportunity for advancement. Goldblest feels, therefore, that real estate investment is his best chance to build a personal fortune.

Goldblest talked with three real estate brokers, each of whom presented him with a different investment opportunity. Because his funds are limited to $500,000 recently presented to him by a relative, he cannot accept all of these alternatives. He therefore discussed all three ventures with each broker and became extremely confused. Although using the same financial data and operating projections, the brokers drew conflicting conclusions about probable rates of return on the investments.

THE INVESTOR

Further questioning reveals that Goldblest is employed by his father under a long-term contract at a salary that puts him solidly in the 28 percent marginal income tax bracket (his state does not have an income tax). His employment contract (which requires him to stay away from his father's place of business, to avoid public identification with the firm and to remain unmarried throughout the contract period) provides for no salary increases, so Goldblest expects that his income from sources other than real estate will remain essentially unchanged for the next ten years.

Goldblest tells you he is interested in tax shelter, cash flow, capital appreciation and security of principal. He asks you to study data concerning the three investment opportunities. He would like you to reconcile conflicting yield expectations reported by different brokers and to make a definitive recommendation concerning his best course of action.

THE PROPERTIES

Industrial Building

The first broker offered a three-year-old, 35,000-square-foot industrial building for which the owner is asking $35 per square foot, or $1,225,000. The broker feels the property can be acquired for $1 million, or $30 per square foot. The building is under lease to a Class A tenant for $3.50 per square foot, or $122,500 per year, on a netlease basis. Based partly on the tenant's financial standing, a lender will provide a mortgage loan for 80 percent of the purchase price. The loan will be interest only (at 8.5 percent), payable monthly, with the principal amount due in ten years.

Seven years remain on a ten-year lease. The tenant has an option to buy the property for $1,200,000 when the lease expires, and is expected to do so. The building accounts for 75 percent of total property value.

Apartment Building

Broker number two recommended a 55-unit apartment building that currently generates a gross income of $297,000. The property is listed at $25,000 per unit, for a total price of $1,375,000. The owners are desperate, however, and the broker reports the property can almost certainly be acquired for $1,200,000. Of this amount, $960,000 is attributable to the improvements.

Operating expenses and vacancy losses are currently running about 50 percent of gross income. Both gross income and expenses are expected to remain constant over the (anticipated) seven-year holding period. At the end of the seventh year, the property is expected to have a market value of $1,200,000.

A 25-year, 8 percent mortgage loan is available for 75 percent of the purchase price. There will be no origination fee or prepayment penalty. Level payments will be made monthly.

Office Building

The final alternative is a 20,000-square-foot office building that is advertised for sale at $60 per square foot ($1,200,000 total) but can probably be bought for $1,100,000. Buildings and other improvements account for 80 percent of the property's total value.

During the first year of the prospective holding period, this property should yield gross rent of $10 per square foot and incur operating expenses of about $4 per square foot. Both gross revenue and operating expenses are expected to increase thereafter at a compound annual rate of five percent. If the building is acquired, Goldblest will probably hold it for seven years. At that time he should be able to sell it for about $1,250,000.

A lender has indicated that she will make a 25-year, 8 percent mortgage loan for 75 percent of Goldblest's purchase price (with a ten-year call provision). There will be no origination fee and no prepayment penalty. Payments must be made monthly.

THE ANALYSIS

For each investment opportunity, develop an after-tax cash-flow projection for the anticipated seven-year holding period. Project after-tax cash proceeds from disposal at the end of the holding period. Which of these propositions, if any, seems appropriate for Goldblest? What will you advise? (In your analysis, assume that expected purchase prices include transaction costs and that expected sales prices are net of transaction costs.)

PART EIGHT

Real Estate as a Security

Real estate analysts who must evaluate specific investment proposals or choose among alternative real estate ventures will find the analytical model developed in Parts One through Seven universally applicable. Many people, however, have neither the time nor the inclination to undertake extensive analysis of specific ventures. Others have inadequate equity funds to exploit the intelligence such analysis generates. Share ownership in real estate limited partnerships or real estate investment trusts represents a possible alternative for such investors. Fulfilling these investor needs enables syndicators and trusts to marshal large amounts of investor funds and thereby generate both unusual market strength and economies of scale in investment operations.

Real estate limited partnership syndications are discussed in Chapter 24. Publicly offered syndications have become a major intermediary for channeling funds from individual investors into real estate equities. The syndicates provide some of the tax-advantaged investment opportunities available to those who make direct investment in real estate ventures, plus the additional advantages of strictly limited personal financial liability and freedom from management responsibilities.

Chapter 25 explores the operation of real estate investment trusts, commonly called REITs (pronounced "reets"). Readers with long memories may have considered REITs to be yesterday's news. Yet REITs have emerged as a convenient and popular way to incorporate real estate into securities portfolios.

CHAPTER 24

Real Estate Syndication

Real estate syndicators generally use the limited partnership form of ownership to combine funds from passive investors with the real estate expertise of promoters who function as general partners. Estimates vary, but it is generally agreed that syndicators funneled approximately $1 billion of equity funds into real estate between 1970 and 1979. In 1980 alone, they equaled the prior ten years' performance by attracting another $1 billion to real estate. This record was dwarfed by their performance during 1981, when, by most estimates, they placed over $3 billion of capital into real estate ventures. In 1984, 1985 and 1986, public real estate syndications attracted $5.6 billion, $8 billion and $8.3 billion respectively. The Tax Reform Act of 1986 greatly reduced income tax benefits, and the allure of limited partnerships dimmed considerably; in 1994 net capital inflow was only $340 million.

CHARACTERISTICS OF LIMITED PARTNERSHIPS

All limited partnerships have at least one general partner and one or more limited partners. General partners have operational control and bear unlimited liability for partnership obligations. Limited partners, in contrast, have no voice in partnership management and bear no personal liability unless they specifically agree to do so. Limited partners receive all investment benefits that typically accrue to real estate investors and may reap additional advantages from choosing this form of participation.

Investor Benefits

Potential benefits from investing in real property have been discussed at length throughout the text. These include tax shelter, equity buildup through repayment of mortgage loans, appreciation in property values, cash flows from operations and from the net proceeds of refinancing and so forth. These advantages are potentially available to anyone willing to commit funds to real estate. Limited partnerships make them available to individuals with limited capital resources and little or no real estate experience. Limited partnerships offer investors a number of benefits that would be difficult to obtain through direct real estate ownership. These include limited liability for obligations spawned by the venture and economies of scale combined with small initial equity investments. Other advantages include risk reduction through investment diversification and professional property selection and management.

Many investors rank limited liability among the premier advantages associated with real estate limited partnerships. Limited partners are at risk only to the extent of their capital contributions plus their ownership interests in undistributed profits. Liability is extended in some partnerships due to partner agreements for subsequent assessments or as a consequence of delinquent taxes or outstanding liabilities arising from premature partnership liquidation.

Investment units in limited partnership ventures sold to the general public are often priced as low as $500 each, with a minimum subscription of as few as five units. Since 1982, many partnership promoters have made shares available in units requiring an initial investment of only $2,000, where the shares are purchased by an individual retirement account. Public limited partnership offerings thus make real estate investment available to individuals with relatively small amounts of investable funds.

Investment units made available only to selected investors (private offerings) generally require larger investments due to government restrictions on the number of people to whom such units can be sold. Minimum initial investments in these ventures typically range between $10,000 and $150,000.

Investing in a limited partnership that acquires a heterogeneous real estate portfolio can accomplish diversification objectives that for individual owners might require hundreds of thousands, or even millions, of dollars. We saw in Part Six that diversification—spreading funds over a number of ventures or investing in geographically dispersed assets—has important risk-management implications. Participating as a limited partner in a real estate venture enables investors with limited financial resources to gain the same risk-reduction benefits from diversification that might otherwise be available only to the very wealthy.

Property search and negotiating skills are crucial elements in consistently favorable investment performance. Large-scale promoters of limited partnership ventures usually employ a staff of specialists who quickly gain experience and may be particularly adept at finding properties and structuring transactions on favorable terms. Of course, mere volume of transactions or size of financial resources at one's disposal does not assure that performance will be superior or even average. Large organizations do have resources, however, with which individual market participants will be hard-pressed to compete. In any event, participating as a limited partner frees the harried business or professional person from the time-consuming task of looking for good properties and arranging the myriad acquisition details.

Investment in real estate limited partnerships also provides individuals with access to professional property managers. Most large-scale promoters have their own property management divisions. Since investment performance is related directly to the quality of property management, such firms are motivated to provide the best possible service. While limited partners indirectly pay for this service, they need not spend time arranging for and monitoring management performance, as must those who invest as individual owners.

Disadvantages of Participating as Limited Partners

Offsetting the very real advantages of the limited partnership form of real estate investment are several potential difficulties. Expected income tax benefits associated with real estate ownership might not materialize for the limited partner. Limited liability, a major consideration for many investors, may prove to be illusory. Investors who find themselves facing an unexpected need for cash resources may find it impossible or prohibitively expensive to liquidate their limited partnership interests. Not least important, it is frequently difficult or impossible to assess the investment merits of limited partnership ventures.

Investment decisions based primarily on anticipated income tax advantages are always risky. Subsequent legislation may well deprive the investor of part or all of the anticipated tax benefits. In addition, tax law changes may reduce the attractiveness of the property to other investors and so undermine its marketability or market value.

Actions taken by general partners, over which limited partners have absolutely no control, may deprive all the partners of expected favorable income tax treatment:

- Net losses that might otherwise be tax deductible are characterized as passive activity losses when incurred by limited partnerships. The losses cannot be offset against taxable income from other sources.
- The partnership may be deemed a taxable entity rather than a tax conduit.
- On audit, some profits and losses may be reallocated between the partners, or some losses may be completely disallowed.
- Disposition of a limited partnership interest, or dissolution of the partnership itself, may trigger unanticipated income tax liability—perhaps exceeding the pre-tax cash distribution from the disposition or dissolution.

These and other income tax issues associated with real estate partnership interests are discussed in detail in Chapter 11.

Limited partners wishing to dispose of their interests before the partnership itself is dissolved face dismal prospects. The secondary market for most limited partnership shares is narrow. Unless the general partners are willing to buy back the limited partner's interest, liquidation may entail a substantial capital loss.

Limited partnership investment also entails shouldering some unique economic risks. Many ventures in which the public is invited to participate (called *public offerings*) involve raising large pools of equity that are subsequently invested in a diverse menu of properties. At the time of their commitment, investors have only a general idea of the type of properties involved. They therefore have no opportunity to evaluate the investment merits of the assets upon which investment performance depends. Investors are forced to rely on the sponsor's past performance record as their sole indication of likely investment outcome.

Investors also face the risk that the limited partnership shares may not be fully subscribed. Should this occur, invested funds may be returned with only nominal interest, or the partnership may proceed on a scaled-down basis. Either of these eventualities may result in investment yields far below those anticipated at the time of the initial commitment.

REGULATION

Real estate limited partnerships are subject to regulation at both the state and the federal level. In states where it has been adopted, the Uniform Limited Partnership Act governs relations between general and limited partners and specifies the rights and responsibilities of each. If the partnership is to escape the burden of federal income taxation, it is subject to a number of Internal Revenue Service regulations. Limited partnership shares are securities and are therefore subject to both federal and state securities regulations. This plethora of regulations and regulators renders compliance difficult and costly.

The Uniform Limited Partnership Act

The Uniform Limited Partnership Act has been adopted in every state except Louisiana, albeit in some cases in highly modified form. It specifies rights and responsibilities of general and limited partners and defines their legal relationship with third parties. Limited partners have the right to inspect the partnership's books (courts have generally interpreted this as the right to receive audited financial statements) and to seek dissolution of the partnership. They also have the right to share in financial benefits and losses of the partnership.

A certificate of limited partnership must be filed with the appropriate state agency to create a limited partnership. If this certificate is not filed, all partners will be treated as general partners, and all become jointly and severally liable for all partnership obligations. If the certificate is filed in appropriate form, the limited partners will have no personal liability for partnership obligations.

Exercising any functions reserved for general partners by the Uniform Limited Partnership Act may cause a limited partner to lose limited liability. Section 7 of the act says, "A limited partner shall not become liable as a general partner unless in addition to the exercise of his rights as a limited partner, he takes part in control of the business." The act does not define *control,* but courts have held a limited partner liable to a third party when the limited partner's actions led the person to believe the limited partner was a general partner. In deciding whether the limited liability "shield" has been pierced, courts have also considered the ability of limited partners to initiate and determine partnership actions. In some cases potential rather than actual ability was considered when making this determination.

Some states have adopted a new Modified Uniform Limited Partnership Act. This new act removes many of the questions regarding actions that can be undertaken by limited partners without endangering their limited liability. Limited partners' powers or rights under this new act include the right to vote on dissolution of the partnership, to approve changes in partnership business, to approve amendments to partnership agreements, to remove general partners, to approve changes in partnership financing and to approve sale of partnership assets. Under this modified law, limited partners may also be employed by the partnership, and they may discuss partnership business with the general partner.

Limited Partnership Syndications and the Internal Revenue Service

Limited partnerships owe their popularity in large part to their special status under the Internal Revenue Code. Unlike corporations, partnerships are not taxable entities. Whereas corporate earnings may be taxable income to the corporation when earned, and again to shareholders when distributed, partnership income or losses are reported directly by individual partners. For this reason, partnerships (prior to 1986) became the favored ownership entity for investments that generated tax-deductible losses during the early years of operations. Such losses passed through the partnership conduit and were reported by partners in accordance with their individual ownership interests in the partnership. After a five-year phase-in starting in 1986, losses became passive activity losses and their deductibility was strictly circumscribed. Prospective tax benefits and pitfalls associated with limited partnerships are discussed in Chapter 11.

Limited Partnerships and the Securities and Exchange Commission

Limited partnership shares are considered securities just as are corporate stocks and bonds. As securities, they are potentially subject to both federal and state securities laws. If required to register their offerings with the Securities and Exchange Commission (SEC), syndicators must file a preliminary prospectus (known as a *red herring*) prior to any advertising. A final, approved and definitive prospectus must be provided before any shares are actually offered for sale. Sales of registered limited partnership shares may be made only through registered securities dealers.

Real estate limited partnerships may claim exemption from registration on two bases. If their partnership constitutes a private placement or an intrastate offering, they may save the time and expense associated with registration. Because exemptions are risky, securities lawyers usually advise claiming both so that a fallback position is available should one basis for exemption be denied. It should be noted that exemption from registration does not relieve the syndicator from compliance with state and federal securities laws.

Private Placement Exemption.   To qualify for a private placement exemption, promoters must refrain from general solicitation or advertising. All purchasers must acquire securities solely for their personal investment portfolios rather than for resale. SEC Rule 506 specifies sufficient compliance.

Rule 506 classifies investors as either accredited or nonaccredited purchasers. Private placements may be offered to no more than 35 nonaccredited purchasers but may also be offered to an unlimited number of accredited purchasers. Nonaccredited purchasers are those who do not qualify as accredited purchasers but who are sufficiently sophisticated to understand the risks and potential rewards associated with a securities offering.

Accredited purchasers, as defined by Rule 506, include most institutional investors and all individual investors who meet at least one of three specified criteria. An individual must either:

- Purchase at least $150,000 of the offered securities and be sufficiently wealthy that the purchase does not exceed 20 percent of his or her net worth;
- Have a net worth in excess of $1 million (including the net worth of his or her spouse); or
- Have income in excess of $200,000 for each of the last two years and expect that his or her income will exceed $200,000 in the current year.

Intrastate Offering Exemption.   SEC Rule 147 clarifies the nature of an intrastate offering and thereby reduces the risk of inadvertent noncompliance. Rule 147 requires the general partner to be a resident of the state in which the offering is made. It also limits offers to sell partnership interests to residents of the same state and places responsibility for determining residency solely upon the offerer. There can be no out-of-state resales within nine months of completion of the offering. The rule also specifies that at least 80 percent of partnership assets must be within the state, and 80 percent of the revenues must originate there.

State Securities Regulation

Escaping registration at the federal level does not always ensure that an offering will not have to be registered with a state securities commission. Most states consider the size of the offering, the number of offerees, the methods of advertising and the size of fees to be received by the offeror and his or her representatives when determining whether or not to require registration.

State securities laws vary widely yet have a number of elements in common. State registration typically requires filing a preliminary prospectus prior to any advertising. Regulatory approval of this preliminary filing is required before any securities are sold. Most states also require that sales of registered securities be made through registered securities dealers. Many real estate salespeople have a special securities license that allows them to sell public real estate limited partnership shares.

Many states also have "blue sky" laws that allow state regulators to evaluate the investment quality of securities offerings. These states may refuse registration for an offering that is considered too risky. They may also refuse registration if promoter's fees are too large or if the distribution of profits and losses between sponsor and limited partners is deemed inequitable.

Documentation

Securities regulations require that a potential investor be supplied with a prospectus that fully discloses the nature of the offering. In addition to the prospectus, potential investors are usually given a copy of the partnership agreement. Investors also sign a subscription agreement that spells out the nature of the relationship between limited partners and the sponsoring general partner. Private placements or intrastate offerings may also require potential investors to fill out a questionnaire designed to assess their ability to qualify as limited partners.

Prospectuses or offering memoranda are designed to satisfy full disclosure requirements, which stipulate that they must contain information sufficient for investors to intelligently evaluate the offering. A summary of the contents is usually provided in the introductory section. The body of the document must include disclosure of any sponsor conflicts of interest and must specify the relationship between the general partners and any of their subsidiaries that do business with the partnership.

If the sponsors have arranged to acquire specific properties on behalf of the partnership, the prospectus or offering memorandum will contain a section providing detailed information about investment properties. Otherwise there will be a section outlining partnership investment objectives. A catalog of risks associated with the venture is also included. Accounting information such as a partnership balance sheet and a statement of sources and uses of partnership funds is typically included. A description of the general partner and the underwriters and a brief summary of the partnership agreement are also included. Other information may be included, depending on the nature of the venture.

The partnership agreement defines the relationship between limited and general partners as well as the rights and responsibilities of each. This agreement also specifies the nature of the partnership's business. Partnership agreements also often contain sections limiting transferability of partnership interests, circumstances under which the partnership may be dissolved and conditions under which limited partners may need to make additional cash contributions.

APPROACHES TO LIMITED PARTNERSHIP FORMATION

Limited partnership promoters, commonly called *syndicators,* may first acquire a property interest and seek investors. Just as frequently they start with a pool of investors and seek an appropriate property. In the first instance, called a *specific asset syndication,* the syndicator may control a property through a purchase option or outright ownership and will assemble a group of investors. In the second situation, called *blind pool syndication,* the promoter assembles a group of investors with the purpose of acquiring an undesignated asset of a specific type. Specific asset syndications were once the more popular approach. As syndicators have developed favorable reputations and as syndication has gained greater investor acceptance, blind pool offerings have become more common.

Blind Pool Syndications

Registered blind pool offerings, called *nonspecified properties programs* by the Midwest Securities Commissioners Association, are subject to a number of restrictions. In states that have adopted the commissioners' recommendations, the minimum net proceeds from blind pool offerings, net of all marketing and organizational expenses, must be $1 million. Such offerings may not extend for more than one year, and within two years all funds must be either invested or refunded. Sponsors of blind pool syndications must have had at least five years of real estate experience in an executive capacity. The commissioners also require two years of experience in management and acquisition of the type of property the prospectus indicates the pool will acquire. Finally, detailed quarterly and annual reports must be sent to all investors. It should also be pointed out that the Securities and Exchange Commission does not permit cash-flow projections in offering circulars of registered blind pool syndications.

While investors in specified asset syndications have an opportunity to evaluate the property or properties as well as the promoter, those who put funds into a blind pool have only the promoter's track record to guide them in making their investment decisions. For this reason, blind pool syndications might well be called "blind faith" ventures. Some states prohibit blind pool syndications.

REWARDS OF SPONSORSHIP

Prospective sources of financial benefits from sponsoring real estate limited partnership ventures are too numerous to catalog here. The most common sources, however, include organizational fees, property acquisition fees and reimbursement of expenses. Other sources include promotional fees, property management fees, leasing commissions, brokerage commissions and insurance commissions.

The North American Securities Administrators Association (NASAA) limits initial sponsor compensation to the greater of an amount that (a) does not exceed 80 percent of equity capital contributions reduced by .1625 percent for each one percent of borrowed capital or (b) results in not less than 67 percent of capital contributions being invested in partnership assets.

Consider a partnership that raises $10,000,000 in equity capital. If there are no borrowed funds, 80 percent or $8,000,000 must be invested, with the remaining $2,000,000 available for sponsor expenses and compensation. Subtracting the sponsor's $2,000,000 leaves 80 percent of capital contributions for investment in partnership assets; criteria (a) and (b) have both been met.

Now consider a partnership that raises $10,000,000 in equity capital and plans to finance 80 percent of asset costs with borrowed funds. NASAA specifies in criterion (a) that sponsor's fees must not exceed 80 percent of equity capital contributions reduced by .1625 percent for each one percent of borrowed funds. This limits sponsor compensation to $3,300,000. Here is the computation:

Percent of Investment To Be Financed by Borrowing	80%
Less: Percent Reduction due to borrowing	
(80% of 0.1625)	13
Percent of Equity Capital That Must Be Invested	67%
Total Equity Capital Raised	$10,000,000
Times: Portion That Must Be Invested	.67
Amount That Must Be Invested in Partnership	$ 6,700,000
Total Equity Capital Raised	$10,000,000
Less: Amount That Must Be Invested	6,700,000
Maximum Sponsor Compensation	$ 3,300,000

Since these computations result in 67 percent of equity capital being invested in partnership assets, NASAA's criterion (b) is also satisfied. With 80 percent of the purchase price of partnership assets being financed with borrowed funds, the $6,700,000 of equity remaining after maximum sponsor compensation translates to $33,500,000 in assets. Sponsor compensation will have been $3,300,000/$33,500,000, which equals 9.85 percent of the total value of partnership property acquired.

Sponsors are also permitted by NASAA to charge a promotional fee consisting of a percentage of annual cash flow, a percentage of proceeds of any refinancing or a percentage of proceeds of sale. They are allowed to retain as much as 25 percent of the cash generated from any of these sources after the limited partners have recouped their equity investments plus six percent cumulative interest.

Sponsors may also receive a brokerage commission for selling partnership realty. This fee is limited to the lesser of a competitive rate or six percent of the sales price of the property.

Property management fees also are allowed. For residential properties, the maximum management fee (including any rental or leasing fees) is five percent of gross income. For properties subject to long-term leases, sponsors may collect management fees of no more than three percent of gross income the first year and one percent per year thereafter. Maximum management fees for commercial and industrial properties are six percent of gross income if the sponsor is also the leasing agent; if the sponsor is not the leasing agent, the maximum management fee is three percent of gross income.

Sponsors may also charge for securing insurance. Cost of insurance plus all related fees must be less than the lowest quote from one of two outside insurance agents. Sponsors who collect insurance fees must be in the insurance business, however. Being "in the business" implies collecting at least 75 percent of total insurance revenue from noncaptive purchasers.

MASTER LIMITED PARTNERSHIPS

Master limited partnerships are much like other limited partnerships, except that their shares are designed to be readily transferable and are traded as are shares of stock. The intention is that investors will enjoy the special tax benefits associated with limited partnership status yet benefit from the liquidity created by an active secondary market for the shares.

Master limited partnerships quickly became popular with promoters and investors but not with the Internal Revenue Service. A special provision (Section 7704) was added to the Internal Revenue Code that makes most new master limited partnerships (those created after December 17, 1987) taxable as corporations and will make most of those that existed prior to that date taxable as corporations after December 31, 1997.

SUMMARY

Real estate limited partnerships match passive investor equity funds with sponsors who function as general partners. Real estate limited partnership sponsors have emerged as important intermediaries in channeling investors' funds into real estate equities.

Investors receive the benefit of limited liability for real estate ownership. Individuals are able to commit small amounts of capital to a variety of projects while taking advantage of expert acquisition and management skills. Investors also receive numerous tax-shelter benefits.

Limited partnership syndications are not without risk. Expected tax-shelter benefits and projected cash flows may never materialize. Limited partnership shares are difficult to dispose of, as no secondary market exists. Early disposal may trigger tax liability in excess of cash received.

Real estate limited partnerships are formed in one of two ways. In a specific asset offering, a sponsor gains control of a property and then finds investors. Blind pool offerings involve sponsors who raise capital before acquiring the properties.

Limited partnership offerings are regulated from a number of sources. The Uniform Limited Partnership Act specifies the legal relationship among all parties and the responsibilities and rights of each. The Internal Revenue Service sets a number of requirements that must be met to achieve expected tax conduit treatment. Limited partnership shares are securities and as such are subject to regulation by state and federal securities officials.

RECOMMENDED READING

Kapplin, Steven D., and Arthur L. Schwartz, Jr. "An Analysis of Recent Rates of Return and of the Secondary Market for Public Real Estate Limited Partnerships." *The Journal of Real Estate Research,* vol. 1, no. 1 (Fall 1986) pp. 33–44.

REVIEW QUESTIONS

1. List major differences between the positions of general and limited partners.
2. Describe the advantages of investing in a public limited partnership as opposed to direct ownership of real estate.
3. List several activities that may cause limited partners to lose their limited liability status.
4. Explain the private placement exemption.
5. What is necessary to qualify a public real estate offering for the intrastate exemption?
6. How do "blue sky" laws differ from federal securities regulations?
7. How do blind pool and specific asset real estate offerings differ?
8. Describe the relationship between the amount of financing used and the amount of front-end fees a real estate limited partnership sponsor may collect.

DISCUSSION QUESTIONS

1. What are some of the factors you would consider when choosing between investing (as a limited partner) in a *public offering* and investing in a *private placement?*
2. From an investor's perspective, does it really make any difference whether a limited partnership venture is organized as a *specific asset* or a *blind pool* offering?

CHAPTER 25

Real Estate Investment Trusts

Real estate investment trusts (REITs) channel funds from passive investor-shareholders into real estate. Section 856 of the Internal Revenue Code provides tax-free status to qualifying REITs. This permits shareholders to enjoy many of the benefits associated with direct real estate investment, while also exploiting the limited liability and enhanced liquidity of publically owned corporate stock.

REITS have become more attractive relative to real estate limited partnerships since passive income and loss rules were incorporated into the Internal Revenue Code in 1986 (see Chapter 11); REITS are treated for tax purposes as portfolio assets rather than passive assets. In recent years REITS have become a popular way for pension trusts to include real estate in their portfolios.

REIT REGULATION

Organized as corporations or trusts, REITs are chartered in the state in which they are headquartered and are subject to the regulations and statutes of that state. They are also subject to federal law: Internal Revenue Code provisions specify minimum conditions under which they will be granted the special income tax status to which they owe their popularity with investors; Securities and Exchange Commission rules govern their relationship with the investing public.

Tax-Exempt Status

To qualify for tax-exempt status, REITS must conform to a staggering array of conditions, the most significant of which are:

- Shares must be held by at least 100 persons, and five or fewer shareholders cannot own 50 percent or more of the shares during the last half of any tax year. Since 1993, a pension fund trust is not considered a single individual for purposes of applying the "five or fewer" rule. Code Section 856(h) provides that pension trust beneficiaries are considered to be holding the REIT shares in proportion to their interest in the pension trust.
- At least 75 percent of assets must consist of real estate, mortgage notes, cash, cash items or government securities. Income from stocks and bonds purchased with the proceeds of new capital may qualify as part of this 75 percent during the first year after raising the funds.
- At least 95 percent of ordinary income (as distinguished from capital gains) must be distributed to shareholders within one year after the end of each fiscal year. This requirement is eased for certain types of noncash income.
- No more than 30 percent of gross annual income can represent gains from the sale of securities held for less than a year or real estate held less than four years.

Shareholder Rights

REIT shareholders have approximately the same rights as stockholders in any other corporation. They elect the trustees or directors. They also have the right to vote on proposed changes in the charter, declaration of trust or bylaws, as well as on major decisions such a new stock issues, voluntary changes in tax status or changes in investment policy.

Trustees and Directors

Shareholders elect trustees or directors who are responsible for conducting REIT investment and business activities. Guidelines enforced by the Securities and Exchange Commission dictate that the majority of trustees or directors be independent of the business activities and affiliates of the trust. Mortgage REITs usually draw trustees from the real estate lending industry; equity REITs draw from the general real estate community.

REIT MANAGEMENT

Trustees or directors hire managers to conduct the general affairs of the REIT. Some REITs have internal managers, while others use external managers, called *advisors*. The managers or advisors are responsible for property acquisition and disposition, financing arrangements, property management or loan servicing and all other functions associated with day-to-day operations.

Most REITs elect to engage outside advisors to handle day-to-day operations. Advisory companies may be owned by financial conglomerates or by individual business people. In almost all cases, the advisory company is a subsidiary of the individual or firm that originally sponsored the REIT.

Advisor Responsibilities

In addition to overseeing day-to-day operations, advisors frequently provide investment counsel. For this service, they may engage outside professionals such as investment bankers or securities underwriters, lawyers, real estate brokers, accountants or mortgage companies to supplement their own abilities and efforts. Advisors also select property managers to oversee operation of rental property owned by the trust. Trust advisors handle property purchases and dispositions and may supervise loan origination operations or mortgage portfolio purchases and sales (in the case of REITs engaged in mortgage lending). They may also service loans on behalf of their REIT client and administer mortgage loan foreclosure or "workouts" of problem loans. REIT advisors also perform clerical functions and prepare quarterly and annual financial reports for REIT shareholders.

Advisor Compensation

The North American Securities Administrators Association's guidelines for setting advisory fees specify that independent trustees shall determine at least annually that fees paid are "reasonable" for the nature and quality of services performed. Some advisory firms are paid on a fee-for-service basis, whereby compensation depends entirely on the volume of services performed. This approach became prevalent in the mid-1970s amid widespread financial disarray among REITs. In addition to fee-for-service and expense reimbursement, some advisors receive an annual fee computed as a percent of REIT assets. Compensation might also be a fixed fee, a percent of net income or a percent of cash flow.

REIT ASSETS

Total REIT assets were approximately $88 billion at the end of 1994. Approximately 27 percent was invested in long-term, mortgage-secured loans; slightly less than half of this represented fractional interests in mortgage pools. Real estate equities (based on cost less accumulated depreciation) accounted for about 63 percent of the total; the balance was in cash or miscellaneous other assets. Detailed asset and liability data for selected years are presented in Table 25.1.

REITs are classified as equity, mortgage or hybrid, according to the type of investments they favor. *Equity REITs* take equity positions in real estate projects. Some *mortgage REITs* make primarily long-term loans; others specialize in short-term loans to finance real estate construction. *Hybrid REITs* do not fit neatly into either category. They are active as both equity investors and mortgage lenders.

Equities accounted for slightly more than 50 percent of total REIT assets in the late 1960s. This percentage decreased steadily during subsequent years (although equities continued to grow in absolute terms), while REITS concen-

Table 25.1	Aggregate Balance Sheet Data for REITs ($ billions, year-end data)				
	1976	*1981*	*1986*	*1991*	*1994*
Assets					
Land, Development and Construction Loans	$ 1.97	$ 0.71	$ 1.41	$ 5.58	$ 0.97
Other Loans	2.67	1.93	12.23	23.29	23.67
Property Owned*	5.08	3.89	8.74	18.64	55.70
Loss Reserves	(0.64)	(0.05)	(0.13)	(0.41)	(0.20)
Other Assets	0.62	0.59	1.46	1.06	8.03
Total Assets	$ 9.70	$ 7.07	$23.71	$46.04	$88.17
Liabilities					
Bank Borrowings and Commercial Paper	$ 3.96	$ 1.11	$ 2.07	$ 5.24	$ 6.05
Mortgages	2.00	1.93	2.79	4.79	18.73
Mortgage-Backed Bonds	—	—	6.68	14.85	8.95
Other Liabilities	1.10	0.94	2.56	4.44	21.12
Total Liabilities	$ 7.06	$ 3.98	$14.10	$29.32	$54.85
Shareholders' Equity	2.64	3.09	9.61	16.72	33.32
Total Liabilities and Shareholders' Equity	$ 9.70	$ 7.07	$23.71	$46.04	$88.17

SOURCE: For years prior to 1991, *REIT Fact Book 1988.*
For 1991 and 1994, National Association of Real Estate Investment Trusts, Research Department.
*Net of accumulated depreciation

trated on mortgage lending as their primary vehicle for growth. After reaching a nadir of 16 percent of total assets in 1974, equities began growing in their importance to REIT portfolios. By 1977 they again comprised more than half of total REIT assets, but declined once more—to about 40 percent of the total by 1992—before reversing direction once more and reaching the level shown in Table 25.1. Equity investments run the gamut of imaginable ventures, from residential rental projects through massive office towers and shopping centers to special-purpose properties.

REITS AS INVESTMENT VEHICLES

REITs are a beguiling alternative to direct investment in real estate assets. Actively traded REIT shares are highly liquid, virtually eliminating one of the most serious objections to real estates investment. They are also a predictable, reliable generator of cash dividends.

REIT shareholders are in a position somewhat analogous to that of the limited partners in real estate limited partnerships. Shareholders may incur income tax liability as a consequence of cash distributions, but they avoid the double taxation to which distributed corporate earnings are generally subject. They thereby benefit from such corporate attributes as limited liability, centralized management, continuity of life and free transferability of interests, without incurring associated tax disadvantages.

Shareholders benefit from REITs' investments in real estate equities in much the same manner as they would from taking a position directly in real estate assets. They receive the annual cash flows, and equity buildup from retirement of mortgage debt, as well as growth in property value. Because they are required to distribute the majority of their income each year, REITs provide a steady source of cash dividends. This makes REITs particularly attractive to investors who desire substantial current cash flow coupled with the inflation protection afforded by assets that have appreciation potential. Figure 25.1 shows why: equity REITs' dividends have been more than twice those of stocks included in the Standard and Poor's 500-stock index.

Income Tax Consequences

Since they are not taxable entities, REITs themselves do not benefit from tax shelter benefits frequently associated with real estate equity investment. Instead, REIT shareholders report their distributive shares of REIT taxable income on

Figure 25.1   **Yield Comparison of Equity REITs with S&P 500**

SOURCE: REIT data: NAREIT Research Department
    S&P Data: *Standard and Poors Security Price Index Record*

their personal income tax returns. A portion of the cash distributed to share-holders, therefore, is sheltered from income tax liability by deductions for cost recovery or depreciation allowances. Net losses, however, are not passed through to shareholders as they are in real estate limited partnerships.

REIT ownership subjects investors to the investment interest limitation rules explained in Chapter 11. Interest incurred to acquire or carry portfolio assets, including REIT shares, can be offset only against income from portfolio assets. If portfolio interest expense exceeds portfolio income, the excess is carried forward to be offset in future years.

Diversification and Liquidity

REIT ownership enables investors of limited means to acquire indirect interests in large-scale real estate ventures. They thereby benefit from economies of scale that may not be available from smaller operations. Because REITS spread their investments over a large number of assets, investment risk is reduced through diversification.

REIT shares are generally more liquid than shares in real estate limited partnerships or direct ownership of real estate assets. Most REIT shares are traded on organized stock exchanges or in the over-the-counter market and are traded reasonably actively. Their market prices are thus readily ascertainable, and they can be sold without incurring prohibitive transaction costs. In contrast, real estate limited partnership shares may not be marketable at all.

Professional Guidance

Individual investors may lack the time or the knowledge necessary to search out properties, negotiate purchases, secure financing, oversee management and supervise disposition. Investment in REIT shares provides indirect access to professionals who perform these services. REIT advisors or managers (discussed earlier) engage professional property managers and monitor their performance. They also arrange financing and supervise property disposition. Investors indirectly pay for these services, but the cost per REIT share is generally modest. The same services might be prohibitively expensive for individuals committing a small amount of capital to direct ownership.

Investment Risk

REIT shareholders face the same risks as owners of any other common stock. Dividend distributions may vary from year to year, reflecting fluctuations in the performance of REIT assets. Share resale values are affected by general market conditions and by changes in performance of REIT asset portfolios.

Equity REITs' dividends and share values may decline due to decreasing occupancy levels or unforeseen operating expense increases in their real estate portfolio. Operating performance and asset values may also be adversely affected by ill-chosen or poorly timed investments.

Mortgage REITs face all the risks generally associated with real estate mortgage lending. Borrowers may default on loan payments, reducing trust income, which in turn reduces ability to pay dividends. Foreclosures may result in loan losses, depressing both cash distributions and net asset value of REIT shares. Any events adversely affecting REIT revenue or net worth will ultimately be reflected in the value of shares.

An Additional Layer of Risk

The volatility associated with an individual REIT's shares can be diversified away. There remains the nondiversifiable, or systematic risk that can be reduced only by accepting a lower rate of expected return. A comparison of returns and return variation between equity REITs and unsecuritized real estate showed that swings in REIT returns (primarily due to changes in market value) were more highly correlated with changes in the stock market than with changes in the market for unsecuritized real estate.[1] Because the stock market responds quickly (and, some would argue, exaggeratedly) to daily events, REIT returns—dividend yields plus-or-minus changes in share prices—swing widely from year to year. Table 25.2 illustrates this by showing the annual returns generated by a broad cross-section of equity REITs for the years 1990 through 1994. The Index, compiled by the National Association of Real Estate Investment Trusts (NAREIT) includes 175 equity REITS with an aggregate market capitalization in excess of $46 billion. Though the average annualized rate of return for the five years is 10.2 percent, year-to-year returns ranged from a 15.35 percent loss in 1990 to a 35.7 percent gain in 1991. Dividends tend to be fairly stable from year to year, so most of the return volatility is due to price swings.

Relative returns to REITs and other assets reflect ephemeral investor interests and concerns, and fluctuate wildly. This is evident on Table 25.3, which shows average annual returns to a cross-section of equity REITs for various time periods and compares them with selected alternatives. The return to equity REITs in 1994 was only 3.17 percent, yet the five-year and ten-year average returns were almost identical at slightly more than 10 percent. Longer term, the yields to equity REITs were very similar to those for the S&P 500 stock index.

Table 25.2	Total Returns (Dividend Yield Plus-or-Minus Price Changes) of Equity REITs Tracked by the National Association of Real Estate Investment Trusts

Year	*Return*
1994	3.17%
1993	19.65
1992	14.59
1991	35.70
1990	−15.35
Five-year average	10.20

SOURCE: NAREIT

Table 25.3	Comparative Performance Measures				
	Total Returns for Periods Ending December 31, 1994				
	1 Year	*5 Years*	*10 Years*	*15 Years*	*20 Years*
Equity REITs	3.17	10.20	10.62	13.80	16.83
Mortgage REITs	−24.30	−1.0	−1.99	4.40	8.42
Hybride REITs	4.00	7.98	3.45	10.43	14.24
S&P 500 Index	1.29	8.68	14.39	14.52	14.68

SOURCE: NAREIT

As noted earlier, share values do not necessarily reflect current operations of the underlying property portfolio. There is superimposed on that relationship a layer of investor interpretations of future industry prospects, and the market value of REIT shares will fluctuate with the level of investor optimism or pessimism. After analyzing the performance of securitized and unsecuritized real estate portfolios, Steven Kaplan and Arthur Schwartz concluded, ". . . once real estate is securitized, risk/return performance becomes more dependent upon the behavior of securities' markets and less a function of the underlying assets in the securitized investment portfolio."[2]

REIT MUTUAL FUNDS

A simple and relatively inexpensive way to gain portfolio diversification on a limited budget is to purchase shares in a *mutual fund.* Like REITs, mutual funds avoid income taxes by distributing the bulk of their earnings to their shareholders each year. Whereas REITs invest in real estate or mortgage-secured debt, mutual funds invest in bonds or the stock of other companies. *Open-ended mutual funds* buy or sell their own shares upon demand, with the price determined daily by the value of the mutual fund's portfolio at the close of business on the previous day (closed-end funds operate more like REITs: their shares are traded on the secondary market and are not routinely bought or sold by the fund itself).

Several open-ended mutual funds hold portfolios comprised almost entirely of REIT shares. Some specialize in equity REITs, others in mortgage REITs, and some hold both in a blended portfolio. Most have diversified holdings in many states and a few are diversified internationally. By buying shares in a REIT mutual fund, investors acquire fractional ownership in a more diversified portfolio with a smaller total financial commitment than they could by investing directly in the REITs. They also get the benefit of specialized, and presumably informed, portfolio selection and management. REITs are highly specialized and relatively complex. The cost is an annual management fee expressed as a percentage of portfolio value.

SOURCES OF REIT INFORMATION

Because REITs are relatively new phenomena and comprise a small slice of the total securities market, sources of reliable REIT information have been slow to develop. Here are five sources that provide up-to-date information:

- *REIT Handbook* (Washington, DC: National Association of Real Estate Investment Trusts). Published annually, the handbook contains industry statistics and data on approximately 300 REITs.
- *Lehman Brothers Equity REIT Index.* Published by Shearson Lehman Brothers (American Express Tower, World Financial Center, New York, NY 10285–1400), this index tracks the performance of the REIT industry and of individual industry segments.
- *SNL REIT Weekly.* This newsletter, published by SNL Securities, L.P. (410 East Main Street, Charlottesville, VA 22902), tracks the performance of approximately 225 REITs and reports industry happenings.
- *Value Line Investment Survey.* Value Line (220 East 42nd Street, New York, NY 10017) includes 18 REITs in the list of securities covered on a regular basis.
- *REIT Score Property Directory.* This quarterly publication reports on more than 100 REITs, including property acquisitions and property holdings by metropolitan area. It is published by National Real Estate Index, 2200 Powell Street, Suite 700, Emeryville, CA 94608.

SUMMARY

REITs use the corporate form of ownership to channel funds from passive investor shareholders into real estate. They issue common stock, commercial paper and debt securities, and invest the proceeds in real estate debt or equities. They were one of the first intermediaries to tap the stock, bond and commercial paper markets for funds to invest in real estate.

REITs are often characterized by the type real estate assets in which they specialize, and are called mortgage, equity or hybrid trusts. Mortgage trusts make real estate loans and equity trusts purchase properties outright. Hybrids do both.

By distributing most of their earnings to shareholders each year, REITs can avoid income tax liability. REIT shareholders thus avoid the double taxation that characterizes investment in corporate shares, yet benefit from the limited liability, centralized management, free transferability of interest and other characteristics that make corporate stock attractive. Investors often gain some degree of diversification, as REITS frequently invest in a number of projects. Further diversification can be achieved with a limited budget by investing in REIT mutual funds.

REITs give investors access to economies of scale in real estate management and the expertise of real estate professionals that is generally unaffordable by small-scale investment directly in real estate equities. REIT ownership though, exposes investors to fluctuations in the market price of stock as well as the possibility of variations in annual dividend distributions.

REITs are organized much like corporations. Shareholder owners elect trustees or directors. Trustees or directors appoint managers or use outside managers known as advisors. Managers or advisors oversee the day-to-day operations of the trust.

NOTES

1. Neil F.C. Myer and James R. Webb, "Return Properties of Equity REITS, Common Stocks, and Commercial Real Estate: A Comparison," *The Journal of Real Estate Research,* vol. 8, no. 1, Winter 1993, pp. 87–106.

2. Steven D. Kapplin and Arthur L. Schwartz, Jr., "Recent Performance of U.S. Real Estate Securities," Arthur L. Schwartz, Jr., and Steven D. Kapplin, Ed., *Alternative Ideas In Real Estate Investments* (Boston: Kluwer Publishers, 1995) page 17.

RECOMMENDED READINGS

Chen, K. C., and Daniel D. Tzang. "Interest-Rate Sensitivity of Real Estate Investment Trusts." *The Journal of Real Estate Research,* vol. 3, no. 3 (Fall 1988) pp. 13–22.

Gilbert, Michael S. "Equity Real Estate Investment Trusts and Real Estate Returns." *The Journal of Real Estate Research,* vol. 5, no. 2 (Summer 1990) pp. 259–64.

Kuhle, James L., Carl H. Walther and Charles H. Wurtzebach. "The Financial Performance of Real Estate Investment Trusts." *The Journal of Real Estate Research,* vol. 1, no. I (Fall 1986) pp. 67–76.

Myer, F.C. Neil, and James R. Webb, "Return Properties of Equity REITS, Common Stocks, and Commercial Real Estate: A Comparison," *The Journal of Real Estate Research,* vol. 8, no. 1, Winter, 1993, pp. 87–106.

Webb, James R., and Willard McIntosh, "Real Estate Investment Acquisition Rules for REITS: A Survey." *The Journal of Real Estate Research,* vol. 1, no. 1 (Fall 1986) pp. 77–98.

REVIEW QUESTIONS

1. What is a real estate investment trust?
2. What are the major differences among mortgage, equity and hybrid real estate investment trusts?
3. Describe the advantages of investing in real estate investment trusts rather than limited partnerships.
4. How do investor tax benefits in a real estate investment trust differ from those of a partner in a real estate partnership?

5. Describe the functions of real estate investment trust advisors.
6. Describe the conditions that must be met for a real estate investment trust to retain its trust status under the Internal Revenue Code.
7. Describe the sources from which real estate investment trusts draw funds for investment.
8. Explain the reasons why a group of investors might want to gain control of a real estate investment trust through common stock acquisition.

DISCUSSION QUESTIONS

1. From an individual investor's perspective, contrast a publicly offered REIT with a publicly offered limited partnership in terms of
   a. regulatory supervision
   b. liquidity
   c. income tax treatment
2. From an individual investor's perspective, consider the relative merits of mortgage REITs, equity REITs and hybrids.
3. Since buying a REIT mutual fund subjects investors to an additional layer of management fees, wouldn't it make more financial sense to invest directly in a variety of REITs, thus gaining the advantages of diversification without incurring the additional expense?

PART EIGHT: Case Problem

Several friends are debating the pros and cons of various approaches to real estate investment:

Terry Talkalot (40 years old) is a vocational education specialist who teaches woodworking and blueprint reading at a local high school. Talkalot's school does not offer summer classes, so he is employed for only nine months each year. Talkalot is married and has three children, all of whom are in secondary school. The Talkalot family's annual income averages about $42,000, and their net worth is about $100,000.

Sharon Shortsell (age 40) is a stockbroker. She earns more than $160,000 annually and works about 60 hours each week. She has a portfolio of common stocks worth more than $1 million and thinks real estate is an ideal way to diversify her portfolio. Shortsell is unmarried and has no dependents.

Gary Gladson (age 60) recently inherited $3 million from his father, whereupon he resigned his job as a clerk at the local library. Though he has little education beyond high school, Gladson intends to invest his inheritance and manage his own portfolio.

Formelda Hyde is a 34-year-old physician who works about 50 hours weekly and earns about $120,000 per year. Hyde is the sole source of support for three dependent children, whose ages range from three to 12. Her assets have a net value of about $200,000.

Required: These friends are arguing over the relative merits of REITS, limited partnership shares, general partnership interests, shares of stock in real estate corporations and direct investment as a sole owner of rental property.

1. To what extent might differences of opinion be attributable to personal circumstances?

2. To what extent might differences of opinion be attributable to personal education and background or professional experience?
3. To what extent might differences of opinion stem from varying attitudes toward risk?
4. Making the necessary assumptions where information is lacking, suggest possible avenues for real estate investment by each of these friends.

Appendix A

Mathematics of Compounding and Discounting

Since real estate decisions generate benefits and costs that are spread differentially through time, it is necessary to adjust for timing differences to make them directly comparable. This appendix explains how such adjustments are made under a variety of circumstances.

Economic rationale for time adjustments is the first topic. The appendix then addresses how to measure growth of money through the compounding of interest income. Present value of a future sum is closely related to how a present amount grows and is logically the next topic of exploration. The text then moves a step further in complexity by considering the present value of a series of future amounts. Since payments to retire a loan are reciprocal to the present value of a series of future receipts, these topics are presented back to back. A final topic addressed is techniques for extending the usefulness of compound interest and discount tables.

CONCEPTUAL BASIS FOR COMPOUNDING AND DISCOUNTING

Compound interest and *discount* are based upon two fundamental propositions: More is better than less, and sooner is better than later. From these propositions it follows that people will insist upon being compensated for waiting and that there will be a trade-off between the amount received and timeliness of receipt.

That more of a good thing is better than less is not a matter for serious dispute. Economists have considered this a self-evident proposition since the dawn of their discipline. If one bottle of champagne is gratifying, two will be even more so; three are even more desirable than two; and so forth. Fundamental to this concept (and certainly to our example) is that one need not consume the greater quantity if one does not wish to do so. Increased gratification stems from certain knowledge that more is readily available if desired. Two bottles thus provide the same option as one, plus the intoxicating choice of still more refreshment.

A preference for present over future receipt is only a small step further into abstraction. Who would not (other things being equal) prefer $500 today to the certain promise of $500 next month? Choosing the promise of future receipt reduces one's option for present consumption without offering anything in return. Current receipt, in contrast, provides the option of consumption now, next month or at any time in the distant future. Clearly, the want-satisfying power of a good is generally enhanced by current receipt.

The more intense the desire for immediate gratification, the greater will be the rate of trade-off, as illustrated in Figure A.1. This relationship is sometimes called *time preference for money,* or the *time value of money.* The topmost line in Figure A.1 represent an individual who has a very high time preference. The individual's strong preference for immediate receipt indicates that he or she will insist upon handsome compensation for waiting. The lower line in the figure represents the trade-off function of someone who has relatively low time preference and can therefore be induced to wait with very little compensation. The middle line represents the trade-off function of one with only a moderate time preference.

Growth in the amount available for consumption, as a consequence of waiting, is called *compound interest.* Reducing the amount available, as a consequence of opting for more immediate receipt, is called *discounting.* The greater the rate of compound interest or discount, the steeper will be the slope of the trade-off functions in Figure A.1.

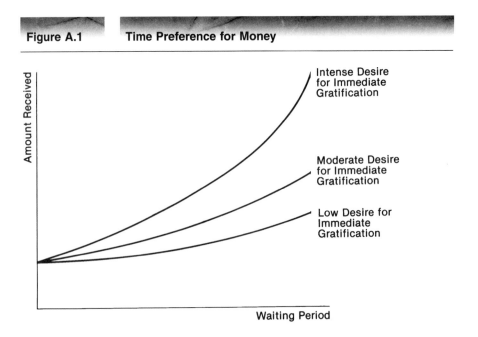

Figure A.1   **Time Preference for Money**

HOW MONEY PLACED ON DEPOSIT WILL GROW

If $1,000 placed on deposit for one year earns seven percent interest, the amount of interest will be .07 times $1,000, or $70. The amount on deposit at the end of the year (assuming no withdrawals of either principal or interest) will be $1,000 plus $70, or $1,070. This simple example incorporates all the elements of compound interest. The general relationship can be expressed as:

Final Amount = Original Amount + Interest Earned

Since annual interest is usually expressed as a rate or percentage of the amount on deposit (the *principal*), the same relationship can be expressed as:

Final Amount = Original Amount + (Original Amount × Interest Rate)

Rearranging terms on the right-hand side of the equation yields:

Final Amount = Original Amount × (1 + *i*)

where *i* is the interest rate. In the illustration of $1,000 placed on deposit for one year at seven percent interest, this becomes:

$$\$1,070 = \$1,000 \times 1.07$$

Suppose now that the $1,000 principal amount is left on deposit for three years, with interest at seven percent per year compounding annually. Annual compounding means that accumulated interest itself earns interest in all subsequent periods. Table A.1 illustrates how compound interest accumulates so that the final amount after three years (hereafter called the *compound value*) totals $1,225.04. Expressed in terms of the preceding equation, the compound value at the end of three years is:

After 1 year: $1,000 × 1.07
After 2 years: ($1,000 × 1.07) (1.07)
After 3 years: ($1,000 × 1.07) (1.07) (1.07)
$$= (\$1,000) (1.07)^3$$
$$= \$1,000 \times 1.22504$$
$$= \$1,225.04$$

Table A.1   **How a Debt Accumulates at Compound Interest**

Year	Amount Owed at Start of Current Year	Plus Interest at 7%	Amount Owed at Year End
1	$1,000.00	0.07 × $1,000.00	$1,070.00
2	$1,070.00	0.07 × $1,070.00	$1,144.90
3	$1,144.90	0.07 × $1,144.90	$1,225.04

This relationship among principal, compound interest and time is summarized in more general fashion as:

$$V_n = PV(1 + i)^n$$

where V_n is the compound value, PV is the initial amount deposited (or borrowed), i is the interest rate and n is the number of time periods involved.

The only laborious arithmetic in the formula is raising $(1 + i)$ to the nth power. For the problem illustrated, there are only three periods over which to calculate the compound value. But suppose there had been 75 periods! In the absence of a good calculator or a set of tables, the calculation of $(1 + i)^n$ would be tedious in the extreme.

Fortunately, inexpensive financial calculators will quickly handle the computational chores. Also, tables are readily available that give solutions to $(1 + i)^n$ for various values of both i and n. An excerpt from such a table, showing representative values of i and n, is reproduced here as Table A.2. A more complete table appears in Appendix C as Table C.2. Time periods in the table are expressed as years, but they could just as well be days, months, quarters or any other period appropriate to the problems being considered.

The solution shown above can be derived quickly by referring to Table A.2. Simply extract the value for $(1 + i)^n$ by reading down the column in Table A.2 under the seven percent rate and across the row indicating value after three years. That factor (1.2250) is the compound amount of $1 left on deposit for three years at seven percent. Multiplying this factor by the $1,000 initial payment yields the value for V.

Now consider a real estate application of compound interest. Suppose a vacant residential building lot, currently worth $5,000, is expected to increase in value at a compound annual rate of ten percent for at least the next six years. The lot's expected value after six years is expressed by the equation:

Table A.2   **Compound Value of $1 Left on Deposit [$(1 + i)^n$]**

Year	6%	7%	8%	9%	10%	12%	14%
1	1.0600	1.0700	1.0800	1.0900	1.1000	1.1200	1.1400
2	1.1236	1.1449	1.1664	1.1881	1.2100	1.2544	1.2996
3	1.1910	1.2250	1.2597	1.2950	1.3310	1.4049	1.4815
4	1.2625	1.3108	1.3605	1.4116	1.4641	1.5735	1.6890
5	1.3382	1.4026	1.4693	1.5386	1.6105	1.7623	1.9254
6	1.4185	1.5007	1.5869	1.6771	1.7716	1.9738	2.1950
7	1.5036	1.6058	1.7138	1.8280	1.9487	2.2107	2.5023
8	1.5938	1.7182	1.8509	1.9926	2.1436	2.4760	2.8526
9	1.6895	1.8385	1.9990	2.1719	2.3579	2.7731	3.2519
10	1.7908	1.9672	2.1589	2.3674	2.5937	3.1058	3.7072
15	2.3966	2.7590	3.1722	3.6425	4.1772	5.4736	7.1379
20	3.2071	3.8697	4.6610	5.6044	6.7275	9.6463	13.7435
25	4.2919	5.4274	6.8485	8.6231	10.8347	17.0001	26.4619

$$V_6 = PV \times (1.10)^6$$
$$= \$5,000 \times 1.7716$$
$$= \$8,858$$

where V_6 is the expected value at the end of the sixth year. The factor (1.7716) can be derived by solving for $(1.10)^6$, or it can be taken from a table such as Table A.2. Multiplying the factor by the initial \$5,000 market value of the property gives its expected value of \$8,858.

PRESENT VALUE OF A FUTURE AMOUNT

The equation for the future value of an initial amount can easily be altered to solve for the present value of a known future amount. The restructured equation is:

$$PV = V_n/(1 + i)^n$$

where the symbols have the same meaning as before, but the initial amount PV is the unknown. In this form, the equation is used to solve problems involving the present value of known or estimated future amounts or the interest (discount) rate required to equate known present values with known or estimated future amounts.

Example A.1

A parcel of land is expected to be worth \$1,500 per acre when water mains are extended five years hence. How much can an investor pay for the land today and still expect to earn 12 percent per annum on his investment before considering transaction costs and income taxes, assuming carrying costs (the cost to maintain the land) exactly equal rental revenue from the property?

Example A.1 illustrates. To solve the problem, first express it as:

$$PV = V_n/(1 + i)^n$$
$$= \$1,500/(1.12)^5$$
$$= \$1,500/1.7623$$
$$= \$851$$

With simple algebraic sleight of hand we can reconfigure $PV = V_n/(1 + i)^n$ to read $PV = V_n \times 1/(1 + i)^n$. Note that performing the multiplication in our restructured equation (that is, multiplying V_n by 1) takes us right back to the original formulation. With this restructured format we are able to consistently multiply by factors in compound interest or discount tables. Table C.1 in Appendix C provides values for $1/(1 + i)^n$, which we use when solving for present values of single sums due in the future. Table A.3 is an excerpt from Table C.1.

To employ Table A.3 to answer the question posed in Example A.1, we restate the equation as:

$$PV = V_5 \times [1/(1 + i)^n]$$

The value of $1/(1 + i)^n$ can be solved with a calculator or taken from a table such as Table A.3. To use the table, read down the 12 percent column and across the five-year row. The factor at the intersection of the column and row is 0.5674. Multiplying this factor by the $1,500 expected future value of the land gives the present value per acre (rounded to the nearest dollar) of $851 when the future value is discounted at 12 percent.

Note the distinction between Tables A.2 and A.3. The first gives values for $(1 + i)^n$, while the latter gives values for $1/(1 + i)^n$. Because these are reciprocals of each other, separate tables are not really needed. All the values for either table can be derived by dividing the corresponding values from the other table into 1. This reciprocal relationship is illustrated in Figure A.2, with reference to Example A.1. The future value of the land ($1,500) is the compound amount of $851 growing at 12 percent per annum for five years. Conversely, the value to the investor ($851) is the present value of $1,500 to be received in five years, when discounted at 12 percent per annum.

A by-product of the convenience of separate tables for present and future values is the problem of determining which to use. One way to keep this straight is to remember that the solution to factors on the future-value table is always greater than that for the present value at the same interest rate (so long as the rate is greater than zero). This reflects the basic idea that an amount received in the present is always more valuable than the promise of receiving the same amount at a future date. The future amount must be larger to induce one to wait.

| Table A.3 | | | Present Value of $1 Due at a Future Date [$1/(1 + i)^n$] | | | | |

				Annual Discount Rate			
Year	*6%*	*7%*	*8%*	*9%*	*10%*	*12%*	*14%*
1	0.9434	0.9346	0.9259	0.9174	0.9091	0.8929	0.8772
2	0.8900	0.8734	0.8573	0.8417	0.8264	0.7972	0.7695
3	0.8396	0.8163	0.7938	0.7722	0.7513	0.7118	0.6750
4	0.7921	0.7629	0.7350	0.7084	0.6830	0.6355	0.5921
5	0.7473	0.7130	0.6806	0.6499	0.6209	0.5674	0.5194
6	0.7050	0.6663	0.6302	0.5963	0.5645	0.5066	0.4556
7	0.6651	0.6227	0.5835	0.5470	0.5132	0.4523	0.3996
8	0.6274	0.5820	0.5403	0.5019	0.4665	0.4039	0.3506
9	0.5919	0.5439	0.5002	0.4604	0.4241	0.3606	0.3075
10	0.5584	0.5083	0.4632	0.4224	0.3855	0.3220	0.2697
15	0.4173	0.3624	0.3152	0.2745	0.2394	0.1827	0.1401
20	0.3118	0.2584	0.2145	0.1784	0.1486	0.1037	0.0728
25	0.2330	0.1842	0.1460	0.1160	0.0923	0.0588	0.0378

Figure A.2   **Relationship Between Present Value and Future Value When Compounding and Discounting at 12 Percent**

HOW A SERIES OF DEPOSITS WILL GROW

Our discussion so far has focused on the present and the future value of a single sum: how a deposit grows or the present value of a single amount due in the future. But suppose a series of amounts is to be left on deposit or the present value of a series of payments or receipts must be determined.

Consider first the case of a series of fixed payments left on deposit. Any series of equal periodic amounts is called an *annuity*. Conventionally, annuity payments are assumed to be made at the end of each period, though this is not a necessary assumption. Tables can be designed with any desired assumption about the timing of periodic cash flows. As a matter of convention, however, most annuity tables are designed with the assumption that all cash flow occurs instantaneously at the end of each period. For example, payments of $500 per annum made at the end of each year for five years constitute a five-year annuity. If these payments were deposited into an account paying seven percent per annum, how much would be in the account at the time the last payment is made?

The first payment draws interest for four years, the second for three years, the third for two years, the fourth for one year and the final payment draws no interest at all. If the compound values of all these payments are summed, the total is the compound value of the annuity. The problem is expressed algebraically as:

$$S = R_1 (1 + i)^{n-1} + R_2 (1 + i)^{n-2} + R_3 (1 + i)^{n-3} + \ldots +$$
$$R_{n-1} (1 + i) + R_n$$
$$= R_k [(1 + i)^{n-1} + (1 + i)^{n-2} + (1 + i)^{n-3} + \ldots +$$
$$(1 + i) + 1]$$

where S is the compound value of the series of payments, R is the amount of the level annual payment, i is the compound annual interest rate and n is the number of payments to be made. For convenience, the above expression is frequently condensed as follows:

$$S = R_k \left[\sum_{t=1}^{n-1} (1 + i)^t + 1 \right]$$

where $\sum_{t=1}^{n-1}$ simply means add together the values of $(1 + i)^t$ for n minus one periods, and t indicates the time periods from one through n minus one.

Substituting $500 for R_k, seven percent for i, and five years for n, we solve for the compound value of $100 per year for five years:

$$S = \$500 \left[\sum_{t=1}^{4} (1.07)^t + 1 \right]$$
$$= \$500 [(1.07) + (1.07)^2 + (1.07)^3 + (1.07)^4 + 1]$$
$$= \$500 \times 5.75074$$
$$= \$2,875.37$$

The solution can be reached much more conveniently by referring to tables that give the value of the bracketed term in the preceding equation. Values for the bracketed term can be derived with a financial calculator or extracted from a table such as Table C.5 of Appendix C and in the excerpt from that table presented here as Table A.4. Read across the top of the table to the seven percent column and down the left margin to the five-year row. The value found at the intersection of the column and row is 5.75074. Substituting this value for the bracketed term in the preceding equation, we determine the compound amount to be $500 × 5.75074 = $2,875.37. This solution is diagramed in Figure A.3.

PRESENT VALUE OF AN ANNUITY

We have seen that any series of periodic payments received or paid at regular intervals may be called an annuity. Examples include pension checks from a retirement fund or payments on a fully amortized installment note. While all such regular periodic streams of cash technically qualify as annuities, not all are popularly known as such. The present value of an annuity is best thought of as the amount that, if invested today at a given interest rate, will provide the known periodic payments for the prescribed period.

Table A.4   **How \$1 Deposited at the End of Each Year Will Grow:** $\left[\sum_{t=1}^{n-1}(1+i)^t + 1\right]$

				Annual Interest Rate			
Year	*6%*	*7%*	*8%*	*9%*	*10%*	*12%*	*14%*
1	1.00000	1.00000	1.00000	1.00000	1.00000	1.00000	1.00000
2	2.06000	2.07000	2.08000	2.09000	2.10000	2.12000	2.14000
3	3.18360	3.21490	3.24640	3.27810	3.31000	3.37440	3.43960
4	4.37462	4.43994	4.50611	4.57313	4.64100	4.77933	4.92114
5	5.63709	5.75074	5.86660	5.98471	6.10510	6.35285	6.61010
6	6.97532	7.15329	7.33593	7.52333	7.71561	8.11519	8.53552
7	8.39384	8.65402	8.92280	9.20043	9.48717	10.08901	10.73049
8	9.89747	10.25980	10.63663	11.02847	11.43589	12.29969	13.23276
9	11.49132	11.97799	12.48756	13.02104	13.57948	14.77566	16.08535
10	13.18079	13.81645	14.48656	15.19293	15.93742	17.54874	19.33730
15	23.27597	25.12902	27.15211	29.36092	31.77248	37.27971	43.84241
20	36.78559	40.99549	45.76196	51.16012	57.27500	72.05244	91.02493
25	54.86451	63.24904	73.10594	84.70090	98.34706	133.33387	181.87083

Figure A.3   **How \$500 Deposited at the End of Each Year for Five Years Will Grow**

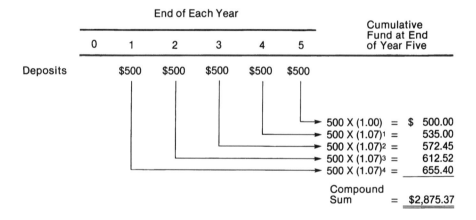

To illustrate, suppose funds are to be placed on deposit with interest at six percent per annum, sufficient to permit withdrawals in \$1,000 increments at the end of each year for three years. To determine the amount of the required initial deposit (assuming there is to be a balance of exactly zero after the third annual withdrawal), the problem might be broken into three separate subquestions:

- *Subquestion 1:* How much must be deposited today to accumulate \$1,000 in one year? To solve this question, first restructure the basic equation to solve for the present value of a single future amount:

$$PV = R_1 \times 1/(1 + i)$$

where R_1 is the first periodic withdrawal, i is the interest rate and there is just one compounding period. The $1/(1 + i)$ is taken from Table A.3 or derived with a calculator. Substituting the appropriate numerical values into the equation, we have:

$$PV = \$1,000 \times 1/(1.06)$$
$$= \$1,000 \times .9434$$

- *Subquestion 2:* How much must be deposited today to accumulate $1,000 in two years? Again, substituting the appropriate numbers into the basic equation, we have:

$$PV = \$1,000 \times .1/(1.06)^2$$
$$= \$1,000 \times .8900$$

- *Subquestion 3:* How much must be deposited today to provide $1,000 in three years? Numerical substitution results in the following equation:

$$PV = \$1,000 \times 1/(1.06)^3$$
$$= \$1,000 \times .8396$$

The total amount to be deposited to provide for the three annual withdrawals is the sum of the three values just calculated. Therefore, the total present value PV, the amount to be placed on deposit, is:

$$PV = [\$1,000 \times 1/(1.06)] + [\$1,000 \times 1/(1.06)^2] + [\$1,000 \times 1/(1.06)^3]$$
$$= \$1,000 [1/(1.06) + 1/(1.06)^2 + 1/(1.06)^3]$$

Values for $(1/1.06)^t$, where t ranges from one through three, were derived in subquestions one through three. Summing these three values, we get:

$$PV = \$1,000 \times (0.9434 + 0.8900 + 0.8396)$$
$$= \$1,000 \times 2.6730$$
$$= \$2,673$$

The general form of the preceding computation can be expressed as:

$$PV = R_k \times [1/(1 + i) + 1/(1 + i)^2 + \ldots + 1/(1 + i)^n]$$

where R_k is the amount of a level periodic receipt, PV is the initial deposit and i is the discount (interest) rate.

Alternatively, the same concept can be expressed as:

$$PV = R_k \left[\sum_{t=1}^{n} 1/(1 + i)^t \right]$$

The practical problem in solving these calculations is the time required to do the computations when the number of compounding periods and thus the number of values to be summed is very large. Precomputed tables for the cumulative values simplify the problem, as does the availability of a financial calculator (procedures using a financial calculator are explained in Appendix B).

Table A.5	Present Value of an Annuity of $1 Per Year $\sum_{t=1}^{n} 1/(1+i)^t$						

			Annual Discount Rate				
Year	*6%*	*7%*	*8%*	*9%*	*10%*	*12%*	*14%*
1	0.9434	0.9346	0.9259	0.9174	0.9091	0.8929	0.8772
2	1.8334	1.8080	1.7833	1.7591	1.7355	1.6901	1.6467
3	2.6730	2.6243	2.5771	2.5313	2.4869	2.4018	2.3216
4	3.4651	3.3872	3.3121	3.2397	3.1699	3.0373	2.9137
5	4.2124	4.1002	3.9927	3.8897	3.7908	3.6048	3.4331
6	4.9173	4.7665	4.6229	4.4859	4.3553	4.1114	3.8887
7	5.5824	5.3893	5.2064	5.0330	4.8684	4.5638	4.2883
8	6.2098	5.9713	5.7466	5.5348	5.3349	4.9676	4.6389
9	6.8017	6.5152	6.2469	5.9952	5.7590	5.3282	4.9464
10	7.3601	7.0236	6.7101	6.4177	6.1446	5.6502	5.2161
15	9.7122	9.1079	8.5595	8.0607	7.6061	6.8109	6.1422
20	11.4699	10.5940	9.8181	9.1285	8.5136	7.4694	6.6231
25	12.7834	11.6536	10.6748	9.8226	9.0770	7.8431	6.8729
30	13.7648	12.4090	11.2578	10.2737	9.4269	8.0552	7.0027

These cumulative values are presented in Table C.3 in Appendix C. An excerpt is presented here as Table A.5.

Returning to the problem of a three-year annuity of $1,000 per year with a six percent per annum discount (interest) rate, determining the present value (that is, the required initial deposit) involves finding the annuity factor in Table A.5, which lies at the intersection of the six percent column and the three-year row. This factor (2.6730) multiplied by the $1,000 annual annuity payment equals the amount of the initial deposit ($2,673):

$$PV = R_k \times \sum_{t=1}^{3} \frac{1}{(1.06)^t}$$
$$= \$1,000 \times 2.6730$$
$$= \$2,673$$

PRESENT VALUE OF A PERPETUAL ANNUITY

A *perpetuity* is a never-ending stream of payments or receipts. For such a cash flow pattern to exist, it must necessarily be the case that each installment represents only accrued interest. If some principal were retired with each payment, then the principal would eventually be exhausted and the stream would end; there would not be a perpetual flow. This being the case, it follows that each payment is simply the interest rate per period multiplied by the principal amount of the annuity:

$$R_k = PV \times i$$

where R_k is the periodic payment or receipt, P is the present value (principal amount) of the annuity and i is the rate of interest per period. To solve for the present value, simply transpose the symbols in the equation:

$$PV = R_k/i$$

To illustrate, consider a perpetual annuity of $10,000 per annum, with interest at eight percent per annum. The present value of the perpetuity is:

$$\begin{aligned} PV &= R_k/i \\ &= \$10,000/.08 \\ &= \$125,000 \end{aligned}$$

Suppose the appropriate discount rate associated with the above annuity moves to, say, ten percent per annum. This reduces the present value of the perpetuity to $100,000:

$$\begin{aligned} PV &= R_k/i \\ &= \$10,000/.10 \\ &= \$100,000 \end{aligned}$$

This result leads to the generalized observation that there is an inverse relationship between the discount rate and the present value of any future series of payments or receipts.

PAYMENTS TO AMORTIZE A LOAN

Suppose you were to receive a lump-sum educational grant of $10,000 to be spent during four years of university study. How much could you withdraw at the end of each year, in four equal installments, to exactly exhaust the fund with the last annual withdrawal if the balance in the fund draws interest at six percent? This is an annuity problem not unlike those investigated earlier. Recall the general expression for a level annuity, which is:

$$PV = R_k \left[\sum_{t=1}^{n} 1/(1 + i)^t \right]$$

The essential difference here is that the initial payment PV is known and the periodic receipt R_k is the unknown quantity. The problem can be solved with a calculator or by using factors from Table A.5. To use the table, find the value for the summation of $1/(1 + i)^t$, where the interest rate, i, is six percent, and the time periods range from one through four years. The factor is 3.4651. The problem can thus be expressed as:

$$\begin{aligned} PV &= R_k \times \sum_{t=1}^{4} 1/(1.06)^t \\ &= R_k \times 3.4651 \end{aligned}$$

and, since the value of *PV* is known to be $10,000:

$$\$10,000 = R_k \times 3.4651$$

Solving for R_k yields:

$$R_k = \$10,000/3.4651$$
$$= \$2,885.92$$

Note that the final solution involves dividing by an annuity factor. Recall that division is the same as multiplying by a reciprocal (that is, a/b = a × 1/b). Tables can easily be generated that incorporate reciprocals of values from an annuity table. Such a table (incorporating monthly, rather than annual, payments) is included here as Table A.6. A more complete table appears as Table C.4 in Appendix C.

The factors in Table A.6 are often called *loan-amortization factors,* or *debt constants.* The table itself is then referred to as an *amortization table.* It gives the equal periodic payment necessary to repay a $1 loan, with interest, over a specified number of payment periods. (A table showing the distribution of a specific payment schedule between principal and interest is frequently called an *amortization schedule.*) Because Table A.6 gives repayment factors based on monthly payments, it is not reciprocal to Table A.5. A table of annual payments, however, would be.

To see how an amortization table works, consider a $100,000 loan that calls for interest at eight percent per annum on the unpaid balance. If the loan is to be repaid in equal monthly installments (including both interest and principal) over, say, five years, monthly payment obligations can be determined by multiplying the $100,000 face amount by the amortization factor from Table A.6, which lies at the intersection of the eight percent column and the five-year row.

Table A.6   **Monthly Payment to Amortize a $1 Debt**

				Annual Interest Rate			
Year	6%	7%	8%	9%	10%	12%	14%
1	0.086066	0.086527	0.086988	0.087451	0.087916	0.088849	0.089787
2	0.044321	0.044773	0.045227	0.045685	0.046145	0.047073	0.048013
3	0.030422	0.030877	0.031336	0.031800	0.032267	0.033214	0.034178
4	0.023485	0.023946	0.024413	0.024885	0.025363	0.026334	0.027326
5	0.019333	0.019801	0.020276	0.020758	0.021247	0.022244	0.023268
6	0.016573	0.017049	0.017533	0.018026	0.018526	0.019550	0.020606
7	0.014609	0.015093	0.015586	0.016089	0.016601	0.017653	0.018740
8	0.013141	0.013634	0.014137	0.014650	0.015174	0.016253	0.017372
9	0.012006	0.012506	0.013019	0.013543	0.014079	0.015184	0.016334
10	0.011102	0.011611	0.012133	0.012668	0.013215	0.014347	0.015527
15	0.008439	0.008988	0.009557	0.010143	0.010746	0.012002	0.013317
20	0.007164	0.007753	0.008364	0.008997	0.009650	0.011011	0.012435
25	0.006443	0.007068	0.007718	0.008392	0.009087	0.010532	0.012038
30	0.005996	0.006653	0.007338	0.008046	0.008776	0.010286	0.011849

The product, $2,027.60, is the amount the lender must receive each month for five years to recover the initial $100,000 outlay and receive eight percent per annum interest on the outstanding balance of the loan.

Had the $100,000 loan in the preceding example called for annual payments, Table A.6 would not have been usable. No table of annual amortization payments is given, because loans seldom provide for this repayment pattern. But an amortization factor can be derived easily by calculating the reciprocal of the factor for an eight percent, five-year annuity. Divide the annuity factor, 3.9927, from Table A.5, into one. The quotient, 0.25046, is the annual payment to retire a five-year, eight percent loan of $1, with annual payments. Multiplying this factor by a $100,000 loan amount gives the annual payment necessary to retire the loan in five years: $25,046. The problem also can be solved without reference to tables. With annual payments, the equation is:

$$\text{Payment} = \text{Loan Amount} \times \left[i/(1 - [1/(1 + i)^n]) \right]$$

If payments are made monthly, the equation is revised accordingly:

$$\text{Payment} = \text{Loan Amount} \times \left[(i/12)/(1 - [1/(1 + i/12)^{12 \times n}]) \right]$$

Note that an annual payment is somewhat more than the sum of 12 monthly payments on a loan of the same size with the same amortization period and interest rate ($25,046 vs. $24,331.20 in the preceding example). This is because interest on the outstanding balance is greater for the annual payment note as a result of the balance not having been "paid down" at monthly intervals during the year. In general, the more frequently payments are made, the less the total interest obligation will be and thus the less the total debt service payment.

EXTENDING THE USEFULNESS OF FINANCIAL TABLES

Even though they are rapidly being rendered superfluous by inexpensive financial calculators, tables can be used to solve a wide variety of real estate investment and financial problems. Several applications are illustrated here to provide additional exercise in using the tables, as well as to demonstrate their versatility. These extended uses are by no means exhaustive. They are intended rather to demonstrate the flexibility of compound interest and discount concepts, the total usefulness of which is limited only by imagination and inventiveness.

Finding Values Not in the Tables

Interest and discount tables give factors for values at intervals over a wide range. Sometimes, however, the rate under consideration falls at an intermediate point between those in a table. When this happens, estimate the actual value by *interpolating* between table values most nearly approximating the rate being sought.

Interpolation involves assuming a linear relationship between tabular values. This introduces a degree of error, since the actual relationship is quadratic rather than linear. The convenient assumption greatly simplifies calculations, however, and the error will generally be insignificant if interpolation is between those tabular values closest to the unknown factor.

The problem is illustrated in Figure A.4. The curved line shows the relationship between values from Table A.5 for discount rates of seven and eight percent and for all intermediate discount rates. Interpolation results in estimates of values not in the table, as indicated by the straight line in the illustration. Distance between the curved (actual) function and the straight (estimated) line represents error introduced by interpolation. Obviously, the wider apart the known values from which an unknown factor is estimated, the greater the error introduced by the assumption of linearity.

Figure A.4 depicts the consequence of using straight-line interpolation to estimate the appropriate present value factor for a five-year annuity when the discount rate is 7.25 percent. Table A.5 gives annuity present value factors for discount rates of seven and eight percent but for no intermediate rates. Since 7.25 percent falls one-fourth of the way between these given factors, approximate an appropriate factor by moving one-fourth of the distance between the factor for seven percent and that for eight percent. The seven percent factor is 4.1002, and that for eight percent is 3.9927. Multiply the difference by 0.25 and subtract this amount from the factor for seven percent. The result is a factor of 4.0733, determined as follows:

$$4.1002 - 0.25 \ (4.1002 - 3.9927) = 4.0733$$

Figure A.5 diagrams the preceding calculations. The total number of percentage points between seven and eight percent is eight minus seven, or one point. The distance between discount rates of seven and 7.25 percent is 7.25 minus seven, or 0.25 point. Since 0.25 point is 25 percent of one point, the "target" discount rate lies 25 percent of the distance between the known values.

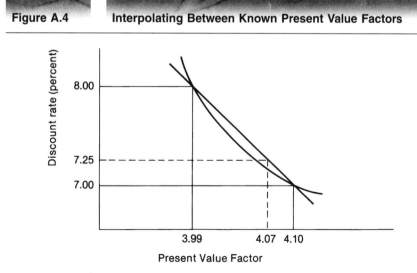

Figure A.4   **Interpolating Between Known Present Value Factors**

Figure A.5	Interpolating to Find Values Not on the Tables

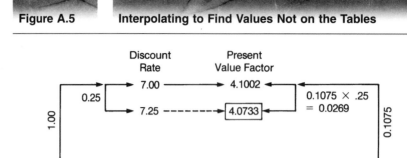

Assume a linear relationship and estimate the discount factor for the 7.25 percent rate by moving 25 percent of the distance between the discount factor for seven percent and that for eight percent.

The total distance between the factor for seven percent, 4.1002, and that for eight percent, 3.9927, is 0.1075. Twenty-five percent of this distance is 0.25 × 0.1075, or 0.0269. Moving this far from the 4.1002 value associated with the seven percent discount rate results in an estimate of 4.0733 for the factor associated with a discount rate of 7.25 percent.

Remaining Balance of a Note

Understanding the reciprocity of annuity tables and amortization tables (with the same time period between payments) sets the stage for easily determining the remaining balance on a fully amortizing note. The face amount of a note can be thought of as the present value of an annuity whose periodic receipts are the debt service payments. But amortization tables are used because the present value is known and the future payments are unknown, whereas with conventional annuity problems the known factors are the future payments, and the present value is unknown.

To see this relationship clearly, consider a $100,000 loan calling for level monthly payments to fully amortize the loan over 25 years, with interest at nine percent. Referring to the amortization table (Table A.6), multiply the factor found at the intersection of the nine percent column and the 25-year row by the $100,000 face amount of the loan. The monthly payment is found to be $839.20. The same answer results from solving the equation, as discussed earlier, or using a financial calculator.

Now, remembering the reciprocal relationship between annuity and amortization factors, treat the remaining payments as a level monthly annuity and discount (the annuity period will be the number of monthly payments remaining, and the discount rate will be one-twelfth the contract rate of interest). You can also use the amortization table to determine the present value of a monthly annuity of $839.20 that extends for 25 years, when discounted at nine percent.

To derive the present value factor for the monthly annuity using the table, go back to the intersection of the nine percent column and 25-year row of the amortization table and divide the factor into one. The result ($1/.008392 = 119.16$), when multiplied by the monthly payment, yields the remaining balance of $100,000. We, of course, already knew this to be the present value, since that is the amount of the original loan. The approach, however, can be used to determine the remaining balance at any future date by simply substituting the remaining number of payments for the period.

Present Value of a Deferred Annuity

To find the present value of an annuity that does not start until some time in the future, find the value of the annuity at the beginning of the first year of payments or receipts and then discount this amount to the present as a single sum. Alternatively, solve for an annuity that extends over both the annuity payment period and the period of the deferral and subtract the present value of the annuity for the period of the deferral; the remainder is the present value of the deferred annuity.

Example A.2

Determine the present value, when discounting at six percent per annum, of a five-year annuity of $1,000 per annum (paid at the end of each year), with the first annuity payment due four years hence.

Example A.2 illustrates the problem. The first annuity payment or receipt is due in four years. Since payments are made at the end of each year, the annuity period actually starts at the beginning of the year in which the first payment is made. There is, therefore, a three-year lapse before the annuity period starts.

Solution Alternative A.   The first step is to solve for the value of the annuity at the beginning of the annuity period (three years hence). At that point there is a straightforward five-year annuity of $1,000 per annum. The value at that point (which we will call V_3) is $4,212.40, determined as follows:

$$V_3 = R_k \times \sum_{t=1}^{5} 1/(1.06)^t$$
$$= \$1,000 \times 4.2124$$
$$= \$4,212.40$$

The second step is to discount V_3 as a single sum due three years hence. The present value is $3,537. Here is the calculation:

$$PV = V_3 \times 1/(1.06)^3$$
$$= \$4,212.40 \times .8396$$
$$= \$3,536.73$$

These two steps can, of course, be combined into a single mathematical operation, with the same results. Here is the combined computation:

$$PV = R_k \left[\sum_{t=1}^{5} 1/(1.06)^t \right] \times [1/(1.06)^3]$$

$$= \$1,000 \ (4.2124 \times .8396)$$
$$= \$1,000 \times 3.53673$$
$$= \$3,536.73$$

Solution Alternative B.   Determine what the present value would be if the annuity extended over both the deferral period and the payment period (three years + five years = eight years). From this value subtract the value of the annuity for the first three years (the period of the deferral). The remainder is the present value of the annuity for the period in which it is actually to be received.

For the annuity in Example A.2., the present value would be $6,209.80 if payments extended over the entire eight-year period:

$$PV = R_k \times \sum_{t=1}^{8} 1/(1.06)^t$$

$$= \$1,000 \times 6.2098$$
$$= \$6,209.80$$

From this amount subtract the value of the annuity for the period of the deferrral. This is three years, and the value to be subtracted is $2,673, determined as follows:

$$PV = R_k \times \sum_{t=1}^{3} 1/(1.06)^t$$

$$= \$1,000 \times 2.6730$$
$$= \$2,673$$

The present value of the five-year annuity that will be received, starting after three years, is simply the present value of the last five years of the eight-year annuity. To find this amount, subtract the present value of the three-year annuity (the portion of the eight-year annuity that will not be received) from the present value of the eight-year annuity. The computation yields the same solution as before, except for a small rounding error. Here are the numbers:

$$PV = \$6,209.80 - \$2,673$$
$$= \$3,536.80$$

These computations can also be consolidated into a single equation, with the same results:

$$PV = R_k \left[\sum_{t=1}^{8} 1/(1.06)^t \right] - \left[\sum_{t=1}^{3} 1/(1.06)^t \right]$$
$$= \$1,000 \ (6.2098 - 2.6730)$$
$$= \$1,000 \times 3.5368$$
$$= \$3,536.80$$

Annuities in Advance

Our earlier statement that annuity payments or receipts are treated as if the transaction occurred at the end of each period needs further elaboration. This is not a necessary assumption for using discounting and compounding; it is merely a convention adopted when constructing annuity tables. A table incorporating the assumption that cash flow occurs at the beginning of each period, or at any intermediate point within the periods, could easily be developed.

Such tables are not frequently available. Existing tables must therefore be modified when working with cash flows that occur at the beginning of each period. Annuities with this sort of schedule are conventionally called *annuities in advance.*

To find the present value of annuities in advance, simply multiply the annual amount by

$$\sum_{t=1}^{n-1} 1/(1 + i)^t$$

and add one more payment. Example A.3 illustrates.

Example A.3

Determine the present value of an annuity of $1,000 per annum for five years when the appropriate discount rate is six percent per annum and when the annuity payment is made at the beginning of each year. Round all values to the nearest whole dollar.

$$PV = [R_k \times \sum_{t=1}^{4} 1/(1.06)^t] + R$$
$$= (\$1,000 \times 3.4651) + \$1,000$$
$$= \$3,465 + \$1,000$$
$$= \$4,465$$

To find the compound value of an annuity when payments are made at the beginning rather than the end of each period, multiply the amount of the annual annuity payment by

$$\left[\sum_{t=1}^{n+1} 1/(1 + i)^t \right]$$

where *n* is the actual number of payments, and subtract the amount of one payment. Example A.4 demonstrates these calculations.

Example A.4

Determine the compound (future) value of an annuity of $1,000 per annum for five years when the compound interest rate is six percent per annum and when payments are made at the beginning of each year. Round all amounts to the nearest whole dollar.

$$S = R_k \left[\sum_{t=1}^{6} 1/(1.06)^t \right] - R$$

$$= \$1,000 \ (6.9753) - \$1,000$$

$$= \$6,975 - \$1,000$$

$$= \$5,975$$

Appendix B

Compounding and Discounting with Financial Calculators

Financial tables such as those discussed in Appendix A and presented in Appendix C have for many years been a major labor-saving device for analysts by greatly simplifying computational chores. The tables themselves are well on their way to being outmoded, however, by the ready availability of low-cost electronic calculators programmed to do financial computations. Many of these calculators are not much larger than a standard business card (some are even incorporated into wristwatches), and many of them cost less than a book of financial tables.

This appendix is intended to demonstrate the use of financial calculators to solve problems such as those explained in Appendix A. To show comparability of calculator solutions with those derived from tables, each example demonstrates how table values themselves may be derived by using calculators. Illustrations then show how calculators can be utilized to find other values that are not found in the tables.

FUTURE VALUE OF A DOLLAR

The future value interest factor (Table C.2 of Appendix C) is used to calculate how a sum left on deposit at a compound rate of interest will grow. The compound interest formula is:

$$FV = PV \, (1 + i)^n$$

where:

FV = Future Value
PV = Present Value (amount invested today)
i = Rate
n = Number of Periods

445

Example B.1

The future value interest factor for three years at eight percent (shown in Table C.2 in Appendix C) is calculated as follows:

$$FV = (1 + .08)^3$$
$$= 1.2597$$

The future value interest factor in Example B.1 can be determined by using a calculator with the keys $\boxed{n}$, $\boxed{i}$, $\boxed{PV}$, $\boxed{PMT}$ and $\boxed{FV}$ by entering $\boxed{n}$ = 3, $\boxed{i}$ = 8, $\boxed{PV}$ = 1 and solving for $\boxed{FV}$. To calculate the factors for Example B.1 and all following examples in this appendix, use the following substitutions:

1. *Monthly Factors*

   n = Number of Months
   i = Annual Rate/12

2. *Quarterly Factors*

   n = Number of Quarters
   i = Annual Rate/4

3. *Semiannual Factors*

   n = Number of Half Years
   i = Annual Rate/2

Example B.2

1. *FV* of one for three years at eight percent per annum, compounded monthly.

   $$FV = (1 + .006667)^{36}$$
   $$= 1.27025$$

   Calculator solution:

   $\boxed{n}$ = 36 $\boxed{i}$ = 8/12
   $\boxed{PV}$ = 1 $\boxed{FV}$ = ?

2. *FV* of one for three years at eight percent, compounded quarterly.

   $$FV = (1 + .02)^{12}$$
   $$= 1.26824$$

   Calculator solution:

   $\boxed{n}$ = 12 $\boxed{i}$ = 8/4
   $\boxed{PV}$ = 1 $\boxed{FV}$ = ?

3. *FV* of one for three years at eight percent, compounded semiannually.

$$FV = (1 + .04)^6$$
$$= 1.26532$$

Calculator solution:

$\boxed{n} = 6$ $\boxed{i} = 8/2$
$\boxed{PV} = 1$ $\boxed{FV} = ?$

COMPOUND VALUE OF AN ANNUITY

The compound value of an annuity equation is used to calculate how much an amount invested periodically will be worth at some future date if it earns interest at a compound rate. The compound value formula is:

$$FV = PMT \times \left([(1 + i)^n - 1]/i\right)$$

where:

FV = Future Value
PMT = Payment (amount invested periodically)
i = Rate
n = Number of Periods

Example B.3

The future worth of an annuity factor for three years at eight percent is calculated as follows:

$$FV = \left([(1 + .08)^3 - 1]/.08\right)$$
$$= 3.2464$$

The factor in Example B.3 can be determined with a financial calculator by entering $\boxed{n} = 3$, $\boxed{i} = 8$, $\boxed{PMT} = 1$ and solving for $\boxed{FV}$.

Example B.4

1. *FV* of $1 per month for three years at eight percent per annum, compounded monthly.

$$FV = \$1 \times \left([(1 + .00667)^{36} - 1]/.00667\right)$$
$$= \$40.54$$

Calculator solution:

$\boxed{n} = 36 \quad \boxed{i} = 8/12$
$\boxed{PMT} = 1 \quad \boxed{FV} = ?$

2. *FV* of $1 per quarter for three years at eight percent per annum, compounded quarterly.

$$FV = \$1 \times \left([(1 + .02)^{12} - 1]/.02 \right)$$
$$= \$13.41$$

Calculator solution:

$\boxed{n} = 12 \quad \boxed{i} = 8/4$
$\boxed{PMT} = 1 \quad \boxed{FV} = ?$

3. *FV* of $1 semiannually for three years at eight percent per annum, compounded semiannually.

$$FV = \$1 \times \left([(1 + .04)^6 - 1]/.04 \right)$$
$$= \$6.63$$

Calculator solution:

$\boxed{n} = 6 \quad \boxed{i} = 8/2$
$\boxed{PMT} = 1 \quad \boxed{FV} = ?$

PRESENT VALUE OF A DOLLAR

The present value of a dollar formula is used to calculate how much some amount to be received in the future is worth today considering compound interest. The formula is:

$$PV = FV \times 1/(1 + i)^n$$

where:

PV = Present Value
FV = Future Value
i = Rate
n = Number of Periods

Example B.5

The present value interest factor for three years at eight percent (found in Table C.1 in Appendix C) is calculated as follows:

$$PV = 1/(1 + .08)^3$$
$$PV = .7938$$

The present value interest factor in Example B.5 can be determined using a calculator by entering $\boxed{n}$ = 3, $\boxed{i}$ = 8, $\boxed{FV}$ = 1 and solving for $\boxed{PV}$.

Example B.6

1. *PV* of $1 at the end of three years at eight percent per annum, compounded monthly.

$$PV = 1/(1 + .00667)^{36}$$
$$= .7873$$

Calculator solution:

$\boxed{n}$ = 36 $\boxed{i}$ = 8/12
$\boxed{FV}$ = 1 $\boxed{PV}$ = ?

2. *PV* of $1 at the end of three years at eight percent per annum, compounded quarterly.

$$PV = 1/(1 + .02)^{12}$$
$$= .7885$$

Calculator solution:

$\boxed{n}$ = 12 $\boxed{i}$ = 8/4
$\boxed{FV}$ = 1 $\boxed{PV}$ = ?

3. *PV* of $1 at the end of three years at eight percent per annum, compounded semiannually.

$$PV = 1/(1 + .04)^{6}$$
$$= .7903$$

Calculator solution:

$\boxed{n}$ = 6 $\boxed{i}$ = 8/2
$\boxed{FV}$ = 1 $\boxed{PV}$ = ?

PRESENT VALUE OF A LEVEL ANNUITY

The present value annuity formula is used to calculate how much an amount to be received periodically in the future is worth today, for a given rate of interest or discount. The formula is:

$$PV = PMT \times \left[\left(1 - [1/(1 + i)^n]\right)/i\right]$$

where:

PV = Present Value
PMT = Payment per Period
i = Rate
n = Number of Periods

Example B.7

The present value interest factor of an annuity for three years at eight percent (found in Table C.3 in Appendix C) is calculated as follows:

$$PV = \left[\left(1 - [1/(1 + .08)^3]\right)/.08\right]$$
$$= 2.5771$$

Example B.7 can be solved using a calculator by entering $\boxed{n}$ = 3, $\boxed{i}$ = 8, $\boxed{PMT}$ = 1 and solving for $\boxed{PV}$.

Example B.8

1. *PV* of $1 per month for three years at eight percent per annum.

$$PV = 1 \times \left[\left(1 - [1/(1 + .0066667)^{36}]\right)/.0066667\right]$$
$$= 31.9118$$

Calculator solution:

$\boxed{n}$ = 36 $\boxed{i}$ = 8/12
$\boxed{PMT}$ = 1 $\boxed{PV}$ = ?

2. *PV* of $1 per quarter for three years at eight percent per annum.

$$PV = 1 \times \left[\left(1 - [1/(1 + .02)^{12}]\right)/.02\right]$$
$$= 10.5753$$

Calculator solution:

$\boxed{n}$ = 12 $\boxed{i}$ = 8/4
$\boxed{PMT}$ = 1 $\boxed{PV}$ = ?

3. *PV* of $1 per period semiannually for three years at eight percent per annum.

$$PV = 1 \times \left[\left(1 - [1/(1 + .04)^6]\right)/.04\right]$$
$$= 5.2421$$

Calculator solution:

$\boxed{n}$ = 6 $\boxed{i}$ = 8/2
$\boxed{\text{PMT}}$ = 1 $\boxed{\text{PV}}$ = ?

AMOUNT TO AMORTIZE $1 (MORTGAGE CONSTANT)

The *mortgage constant* is used to calculate the payment on a fully amortizing loan. It is the percentage of the original loan that must be paid periodically in order to fully repay principal and interest over the term of the loan. The formula is:

$$MC = i/\left(1 - [1/(1 + i)^n]\right)$$

where:

MC = Mortgage Constant
i = Rate
n = Number of Periods

Example B.9

The mortgage constant for a three-year loan at eight percent interest, with annual payments, is calculated as follows:

$$MC = (.08)/\left(1 - [1/(1 + .08)^3]\right)$$
$$= .3880$$

The constant in Example B.9 can be derived using a financial calculator by entering $\boxed{n}$ = 3, $\boxed{i}$ = 8, $\boxed{\text{PV}}$ = 1 and solving for $\boxed{\text{PMT}}$.

Example B.10

1. Payment *(PMT)* per period to amortize $1 over three years at eight percent per annum, with monthly payments.

$$PMT = .006667/\left(1 - [1/(1 + .006667)^{36}]\right)$$
$$= .0313$$

Calculator solution:

$\boxed{n}$ = 36 $\boxed{i}$ = 8/12
$\boxed{\text{PV}}$ = 1 $\boxed{\text{PMT}}$ = ?

2. Payment *(PMT)* per period to amortize $1 over three years at eight percent per annum, with quarterly payments.

$$PMT = .02/\left(1 - [1/(1 + .02)^{12}]\right)$$
$$= .0946$$

Calculator solution:

$\boxed{n} = 12$ $\boxed{i} = 8/4$

$\boxed{PV} = 1$ $\boxed{PMT} = ?$

3. Payment *(PMT)* per period to amortize $1 over three years at eight percent per annum, with semiannual payments.

$$PMT = .04/\left(1 - [1/(1 + .04)^{6}]\right)$$
$$= .1908$$

Calculator solution:

$\boxed{n} = 6$ $\boxed{i} = 8/2$

$\boxed{PV} = 1$ $\boxed{PMT} = ?$

Appendix C

Financial Tables

Table C.1   **Present Value of $1**

PVIF $(r,n) = (1 + r)^{-n}$

Period	1%	2%	3%	4%	5%	6%	7%	8%	9%	10%
1	.9901	.9804	.9709	.9615	.9524	.9434	.9346	.9259	.9174	.9091
2	.9803	.9612	.9426	.9246	.9070	.8900	.8734	.8573	.8417	.8264
3	.9706	.9423	.9151	.8890	.8638	.8396	.8163	.7938	.7722	.7513
4	.9610	.9238	.8885	.8548	.8227	.7921	.7629	.7350	.7084	.6830
5	.9515	.9057	.8626	.8219	.7835	.7473	.7130	.6806	.6499	.6209
6	.9420	.8880	.8375	.7903	.7462	.7050	.6663	.6302	.5963	.5645
7	.9327	.8706	.8131	.7599	.7107	.6651	.6227	.5835	.5470	.5132
8	.9235	.8535	.7894	.7307	.6768	.6274	.5820	.5403	.5019	.4665
9	.9143	.8368	.7664	.7026	.6446	.5919	.5439	.5002	.4604	.4241
10	.9053	.8203	.7441	.6756	.6139	.5584	.5083	.4632	.4224	.3855
11	.8963	.8043	.7224	.6496	.5847	.5268	.4751	.4289	.3875	.3505
12	.8874	.7885	.7014	.6246	.5568	.4970	.4440	.3971	.3555	.3186
13	.8787	.7730	.6810	.6006	.5303	.4688	.4150	.3677	.3262	.2897
14	.8700	.7579	.6611	.5775	.5051	.4423	.3878	.3405	.2992	.2633
15	.8613	.7430	.6419	.5553	.4810	.4173	.3624	.3152	.2745	.2394
16	.8528	.7284	.6232	.5339	.4581	.3936	.3387	.2919	.2519	.2176
17	.8444	.7142	.6050	.5134	.4363	.3714	.3166	.2703	.2311	.1978
18	.8360	.7002	.5874	.4936	.4155	.3503	.2959	.2502	.2120	.1799
19	.8277	.6864	.5703	.4746	.3957	.3305	.2765	.2317	.1945	.1635
20	.8195	.6730	.5537	.4564	.3769	.3118	.2584	.2145	.1784	.1486
25	.7798	.6095	.4776	.3751	.2953	.2330	.1842	.1460	.1160	.0923
30	.7419	.5521	.4120	.3083	.2314	.1741	.1314	.0994	.0754	.0573
40	.6717	.4529	.3066	.2083	.1420	.0972	.0668	.0460	.0318	.0221
50	.6080	.3715	.2281	.1407	.0872	.0543	.0339	.0213	.0134	.0085
60	.5504	.3048	.1697	.0951	.0535	.0303	.0173	.0099	.0057	.0033

*The factor is zero to four decimal places.

12%	14%	15%	16%	18%	20%	24%	28%	32%	36%
.8929	.8772	.8696	.8621	.8475	.8333	.8065	.7813	.7576	.7353
.7972	.7695	.7561	.7432	.7182	.6944	.6504	.6104	.5739	.5407
.7118	.6750	.6575	.6407	.6086	.5787	.5245	.4768	.4348	.3975
.6355	.5921	.5718	.5523	.5158	.4823	.4230	.3725	.3294	.2923
.5674	.5194	.4972	.4761	.4371	.4019	.3411	.2910	.2495	.2149
.5066	.4556	.4323	.4104	.3704	.3349	.2751	.2274	.1890	.1580
.4523	.3996	.3759	.3538	.3139	.2791	.2218	.1776	.1432	.1162
.4039	.3506	.3269	.3050	.2660	.2326	.1789	.1388	.1085	.0854
.3606	.3075	.2843	.2630	.2255	.1938	.1443	.1084	.0822	.0628
.3220	.2697	.2472	.2267	.1911	.1615	.1164	.0847	.0623	.0462
.2875	.2366	.2149	.1954	.1619	.1346	.0938	.0662	.0472	.0340
.2567	.2076	.1869	.1685	.1372	.1122	.0757	.0517	.0357	.0250
.2292	.1821	.1625	.1452	.1163	.0935	.0610	.0404	.0271	.0184
.2046	.1597	.1413	.1252	.0985	.0779	.0492	.0316	.0205	.0135
.1827	.1401	.1229	.1079	.0835	.0649	.0397	.0247	.0155	.0099
.1631	.1229	.1069	.0930	.0708	.0541	.0320	.0193	.0118	.0073
.1456	.1078	.0929	.0802	.0600	.0451	.0258	.0150	.0089	.0054
.1300	.0946	.0808	.0691	.0508	.0376	.0208	.0118	.0068	.0039
.1161	.0829	.0703	.0596	.0431	.0313	.0168	.0092	.0051	.0029
.1037	.0728	.0611	.0514	.0365	.0261	.0135	.0072	.0039	.0021
.0588	.0378	.0304	.0245	.0160	.0105	.0046	.0021	.0010	.0005
.0334	.0196	.0151	.0116	.0070	.0042	.0016	.0006	.0002	.0001
.0107	.0053	.0037	.0026	.0013	.0007	.0002	.0001	*	*
.0035	.0014	.0009	.0006	.0003	.0001	*	*	*	*
.0011	.0004	.0002	.0001	*	*	*	*	*	*

Table C.2   Future Value of $1 at the End of n Periods

$FVIF^{k,n} = (1 + k)^n$

Period	1%	2%	3%	4%	5%	6%	7%	8%	9%	10%
1	1.0100	1.0200	1.0300	1.0400	1.0500	1.0600	1.0700	1.0800	1.0900	1.1000
2	1.0201	1.0404	1.0609	1.0816	1.1025	1.1236	1.1449	1.1664	1.1881	1.2100
3	1.0303	1.0612	1.0927	1.1249	1.1576	1.1910	1.2250	1.2597	1.2950	1.3310
4	1.0406	1.0824	1.1255	1.1699	1.2155	1.2625	1.3108	1.3605	1.4116	1.4641
5	1.0510	1.1041	1.1593	1.2167	1.2763	1.3382	1.4026	1.4693	1.5386	1.6105
6	1.0615	1.1262	1.1941	1.2653	1.3401	1.4185	1.5007	1.5869	1.6771	1.7716
7	1.0721	1.1487	1.2299	1.3159	1.4071	1.5036	1.6058	1.7138	1.8280	1.9487
8	1.0829	1.1717	1.2668	1.3686	1.4775	1.5938	1.7182	1.8509	1.9926	2.1436
9	1.0937	1.1951	1.3048	1.4233	1.5513	1.6895	1.8385	1.9990	2.1719	2.3579
10	1.1046	1.2190	1.3439	1.4802	1.6289	1.7908	1.9672	2.1589	2.3674	2.5937
11	1.1157	1.2434	1.3842	1.5395	1.7103	1.8983	2.1049	2.3316	2.5804	2.8531
12	1.1268	1.2682	1.4258	1.6010	1.7959	2.0122	2.2522	2.5182	2.8127	3.1384
13	1.1381	1.2936	1.4685	1.6651	1.8856	2.1329	2.4098	2.7196	3.0658	3.4523
14	1.1495	1.3195	1.5126	1.7317	1.9799	2.2609	2.5785	2.9372	3.3417	3.7975
15	1.1610	1.3459	1.5580	1.8009	2.0789	2.3966	2.7590	3.1722	3.6425	4.1772
16	1.1726	1.3728	1.6047	1.8730	2.1829	2.5404	2.9522	3.4259	3.9703	4.5950
17	1.1843	1.4002	1.6528	1.9479	2.2920	2.6928	3.1588	3.7000	4.3276	5.0545
18	1.1961	1.4282	1.7024	2.0258	2.4066	2.8543	3.3799	3.9960	4.7171	5.5599
19	1.2081	1.4568	1.7535	2.1068	2.5270	3.0256	3.6165	4.3157	5.1417	6.1159
20	1.2202	1.4859	1.8061	2.1911	2.6533	3.2071	3.8697	4.6610	5.6044	6.7275
21	1.2324	1.5157	1.8603	2.2788	2.7860	3.3996	4.1406	5.0338	6.1088	7.4002
22	1.2447	1.5460	1.9161	2.3699	2.9253	3.6035	4.4304	5.4365	6.6586	8.1403
23	1.2572	1.5769	1.9736	2.4647	3.0715	3.8197	4.7405	5.8715	7.2579	8.9543
24	1.2697	1.6084	2.0328	2.5633	3.2251	4.0489	5.0724	6.3412	7.9111	9.8497
25	1.2824	1.6406	2.0938	2.6658	3.3864	4.2919	5.4274	6.8485	8.6231	10.835
26	1.2953	1.6734	2.1566	2.7725	3.5557	4.5494	5.8074	7.3964	9.3992	11.918
27	1.3082	1.7069	2.2213	2.8834	3.7335	4.8223	6.2139	7.9881	10.245	13.110
28	1.3213	1.7410	2.2879	2.9987	3.9201	5.1117	6.6488	8.6271	11.167	14.421
29	1.3345	1.7758	2.3566	3.1187	4.1161	5.4184	7.1143	9.3173	12.172	15.863
30	1.3478	1.8114	2.4273	3.2434	4.3219	5.7435	7.6123	10.063	13.268	17.449
40	1.4889	2.2080	3.2620	4.8010	7.0400	10.286	14.975	21.725	31.409	45.259
50	1.6446	2.6916	4.3839	7.1067	11.467	18.420	29.457	46.902	74.358	117.39
60	1.8167	3.2810	5.8916	10.5196	18.679	32.988	57.946	101.26	176.03	304.48

*FVIF > 99,999

12%	14%	15%	16%	18%	20%	24%	28%	32%	36%
1.1200	1.1400	1.1500	1.1600	1.1800	1.2000	1.2400	1.2800	1.3200	1.3600
1.2544	1.2996	1.3225	1.3456	1.3924	1.4400	1.5376	1.6384	1.7424	1.8496
1.4049	1.4815	1.5209	1.5609	1.6430	1.7280	1.9066	2.0972	2.3000	2.5155
1.5735	1.6890	1.7490	1.8106	1.9388	2.0736	2.3642	2.6844	3.0360	3.4210
1.7623	1.9254	2.0114	2.1003	2.2878	2.4883	2.9316	3.4360	4.0075	4.6526
1.9738	2.1950	2.3131	2.4364	2.6996	2.9860	3.6352	4.3980	5.2899	6.3275
2.2107	2.5023	2.6600	2.8262	3.1855	3.5832	4.5077	5.6295	6.9826	8.6054
2.4760	2.8526	3.0590	3.2784	3.7589	4.2998	5.5895	7.2058	9.2170	11.703
2.7731	3.2519	3.5179	3.8030	4.4355	5.1598	6.9310	9.2234	12.166	15.917
3.1058	3.7072	4.0456	4.4114	5.2338	6.1917	8.5944	11.806	16.060	21.647
3.4785	4.2262	4.6524	5.1173	6.1759	7.4301	10.657	15.112	21.199	29.439
3.8960	4.8179	5.3503	5.9360	7.2876	8.9161	13.215	19.343	27.983	40.037
4.3635	5.4924	6.1528	6.8858	8.5994	10.699	16.386	24.759	36.937	54.451
4.8871	6.2613	7.0757	7.9875	10.147	12.839	20.319	31.691	48.757	74.053
5.4736	7.1379	8.1371	9.2655	11.974	15.407	25.196	40.565	64.359	100.71
6.1304	8.1372	9.3576	10.748	14.129	18.488	31.243	51.923	84.954	136.97
6.8660	9.2765	10.761	12.468	16.672	22.186	38.741	66.461	112.14	186.28
7.6900	10.575	12.375	14.463	19.673	26.623	48.039	85.071	148.02	253.34
8.6128	12.056	14.232	16.777	23.214	31.948	59.568	108.89	195.39	344.54
9.6463	13.743	16.367	19.461	27.393	38.338	73.864	139.38	257.92	468.57
10.804	15.668	18.822	22.574	32.324	46.005	91.592	178.41	340.45	637.26
12.100	17.861	21.645	26.186	38.142	55.206	113.57	228.36	449.39	866.67
13.552	20.362	24.891	30.376	45.008	66.247	140.83	292.30	594.20	1178.7
15.179	23.212	28.625	35.236	53.109	79.497	174.63	374.14	783.02	1603.0
17.000	26.462	32.919	40.874	62.669	95.396	216.54	478.90	1033.6	2180.1
19.040	30.167	37.857	47.414	73.949	114.48	268.51	613.00	1364.3	2964.9
21.325	34.390	43.535	55.000	87.260	137.37	332.95	784.64	1800.9	4032.3
23.884	39.204	50.066	63.800	102.97	164.84	412.86	1004.3	2377.2	5483.9
26.750	44.693	57.575	74.009	121.50	197.81	511.95	1285.6	3137.9	7458.1
29.960	50.950	66.212	85.850	143.37	237.38	634.82	1645.5	4142.1	10143.
93.051	188.88	267.86	378.72	750.38	1469.8	5455.9	19427.	66521.	*
289.00	700.23	1083.7	1670.7	3927.4	9100.4	46890.	*	*	*
897.60	2595.9	4384.0	7370.2	20555.	56348.	*	*	*	*

Table C.3   **Present Value of an Annuity of $1 per Period for _n_ Periods**

$$PVIFa(r,t) = \sum_{i=1}^{n} \frac{1}{(1 + r)^t} = \frac{\left[1 - \dfrac{1}{(1 + r)^n}\right]}{r}$$

Number of payments	1%	2%	3%	4%	5%	6%	7%	8%	9%
1	0.9901	0.9804	0.9709	0.9615	0.9524	0.9434	0.9346	0.9259	0.9174
2	1.9704	1.9416	1.9135	1.8861	1.8594	1.8334	1.8080	1.7833	1.7591
3	2.9410	2.8839	2.8286	2.7751	2.7232	2.6730	2.6243	2.5771	2.5313
4	3.9020	3.8077	3.7171	3.6299	3.5460	3.4651	3.3872	3.3121	3.2397
5	4.8534	4.7135	4.5797	4.4518	4.3295	4.2124	4.1002	3.9927	3.8897
6	5.7955	5.6014	5.4172	5.2421	5.0757	4.9173	4.7665	4.6229	4.4859
7	6.7282	6.4720	6.2303	6.0021	5.7864	5.5824	5.3893	5.2064	5.0330
8	7.6517	7.3255	7.0197	6.7327	6.4632	6.2098	5.9713	5.7466	5.5348
9	8.5660	8.1622	7.7861	7.4353	7.1078	6.8017	6.5152	6.2469	5.9952
10	9.4713	8.9826	8.5302	8.1109	7.7217	7.3601	7.0236	6.7101	6.4177
11	10.3676	9.7868	9.2526	8.7605	8.3064	7.8869	7.4987	7.1390	6.8052
12	11.2551	10.5753	9.9540	9.3851	8.8633	8.3838	7.9427	7.5361	7.1607
13	12.1337	11.3484	10.6350	9.9856	9.3936	8.8527	8.3577	7.9038	7.4869
14	13.0037	12.1062	11.2961	10.5631	9.8986	9.2950	8.7455	8.2442	7.7862
15	13.8651	12.8493	11.9379	11.1184	10.3797	9.7122	9.1079	8.5595	8.0607
16	14.7179	13.5777	12.5611	11.6523	10.8378	10.1059	9.4466	8.8514	8.3126
17	15.5623	14.2919	13.1661	12.1657	11.2741	10.4773	9.7632	9.1216	8.5436
18	16.3983	14.9920	13.7535	12.6593	11.6896	10.8276	10.0591	9.3719	8.7556
19	17.2260	15.6785	14.3238	13.1339	12.0853	11.1581	10.3356	9.6036	8.9501
20	18.0456	16.3514	14.8775	13.5903	12.4622	11.4699	10.5940	9.8181	9.1285
25	22.0232	19.5235	17.4131	15.6221	14.0393	12.7834	11.6536	10.6748	9.8226
30	25.8077	22.3965	19.6004	17.2920	15.3725	13.7648	12.4090	11.2578	10.2737
40	32.8347	27.3555	23.1148	19.7928	17.1591	15.0463	13.3317	11.9246	10.7574
50	39.1961	31.4236	25.7298	21.4822	18.2559	15.7619	13.8007	12.2335	10.9617
60	44.9550	34.7609	27.6756	22.6235	18.9293	16.1614	14.0392	12.3766	11.0480

10%	12%	14%	15%	16%	18%	20%	24%	28%	32%
0.9091	0.8929	0.8772	0.8696	0.8621	0.8475	0.8333	0.8065	0.7813	0.7576
1.7355	1.6901	1.6467	1.6257	1.6052	1.5656	1.5278	1.4568	1.3916	1.3315
2.4869	2.4018	2.3216	2.2832	2.2459	2.1743	2.1065	1.9813	1.8684	1.7663
3.1699	3.0373	2.9137	2.8550	2.7982	2.6901	2.5887	2.4043	2.2410	2.0957
3.7908	3.6048	3.4331	3.3522	3.2743	3.1272	2.9906	2.7454	2.5320	2.3452
4.3553	4.1114	3.8887	3.7845	3.6847	3.4976	3.3255	3.0205	2.7594	2.5342
4.8684	4.5638	4.2883	4.1604	4.0386	3.8115	3.6046	3.2423	2.9370	2.6775
5.3349	4.9676	4.6389	4.4873	4.3436	4.0776	3.8372	3.4212	3.0758	2.7860
5.7590	5.3282	4.9464	4.7716	4.6065	4.3030	4.0310	3.5655	3.1842	2.8681
6.1446	5.6502	5.2161	5.0188	4.8332	4.4941	4.1925	3.6819	3.2689	2.9304
6.4951	5.9377	5.4527	5.2337	5.0286	4.6560	4.3271	3.7757	3.3351	2.9776
6.8137	6.1944	5.6603	5.4206	5.1971	4.7932	4.4392	3.8514	3.3868	3.0133
7.1034	6.4235	5.8424	5.5831	5.3423	4.9095	4.5327	3.9124	3.4272	3.0404
7.3667	6.6282	6.0021	5.7245	5.4675	5.0081	4.6106	3.9616	3.4587	3.0609
7.6061	6.8109	6.1422	5.8474	5.5755	5.0916	4.6755	4.0013	3.4834	3.0764
7.8237	6.9740	6.2651	5.9542	5.6685	5.1624	4.7296	4.0333	3.5026	3.0882
8.0216	7.1196	6.3729	6.0472	5.7487	5.2223	4.7746	4.0591	3.5177	3.0971
8.2014	7.2497	6.4674	6.1280	5.8178	5.2732	4.8122	4.0799	3.5294	3.1039
8.3649	7.3658	6.5504	6.1982	5.8775	5.3162	4.8435	4.0967	3.5386	3.1090
8.5136	7.4694	6.6231	6.2593	5.9288	5.3527	4.8696	4.1103	3.5458	3.1129
9.0770	7.8431	6.8729	6.4641	6.0971	5.4669	4.9476	4.1474	3.5640	3.1220
9.4269	8.0552	7.0027	6.5660	6.1772	5.5168	4.9789	4.1601	3.5693	3.1242
9.7791	8.2438	7.1050	6.6418	6.2335	5.5482	4.9966	4.1659	3.5712	3.1250
9.9148	8.3045	7.1327	6.6605	6.2463	5.5541	4.9995	4.1666	3.5714	3.1250
9.9672	8.3240	7.1401	6.6651	6.2492	5.5553	4.9999	4.1667	3.5714	3.1250

Table C.4   Monthly Installment to Amortize a $1 Loan

$$PMT = \cfrac{\cfrac{i}{12}}{1 - \left[\left\{\cfrac{1}{\left(1 + \cfrac{i}{12}\right)}\right\}12n\right]}$$

Years	6.0%	6.5%	7.0%	7.5%	8.0%	8.5%	9.0%	9.5%	10.0%
1	.086066	.086296	.086527	.086757	.086988	.087220	.087451	.087684	.087916
2	.044321	.044546	.044773	.045000	.045227	.045456	.045685	.045914	.046145
3	.030422	.030649	.030887	.031106	.031336	.031568	.031800	.032033	.032267
4	.023485	.023715	.023946	.024179	.024413	.024648	.024885	.025123	.025363
5	.019333	.019566	.019801	.020038	.020276	.020517	.020758	.021002	.021247
6	.016573	.016810	.017049	.017290	.017533	.017778	.018026	.018275	.018526
7	.014609	.014849	.015093	.015338	.015586	.015836	.016089	.016344	.016601
8	.013141	.013386	.013634	.013884	.014137	.014392	.014650	.014911	.015174
9	.012006	.012255	.012506	.012761	.013019	.013279	.013543	.013809	.014079
10	.011102	.011355	.011611	.011870	.012133	.012399	.012668	.012940	.013215
11	.010367	.010624	.010884	.011148	.011415	.011686	.011961	.012239	.012520
12	.009759	.010019	.010284	.010552	.010825	.011101	.011380	.011644	.011951
13	.009247	.009512	.009781	.010054	.010331	.010612	.010897	.011186	.011478
14	.008812	.009081	.009354	.009631	.009913	.010199	.010489	.010784	.011082
15	.008439	.008711	.008988	.009270	.009557	.009847	.010143	.010442	.010746
16	.008114	.008391	.008672	.008958	.009249	.009545	.009845	.010150	.010459
17	.007831	.008111	.008397	.008687	.008983	.009283	.009588	.009898	.010212
18	.007582	.007866	.008155	.008450	.008750	.009055	.009364	.009679	.009998
19	.007361	.007649	.007942	.008241	.008545	.008854	.009169	.009488	.009813
20	.007164	.007456	.007753	.008056	.008364	.008678	.008997	.009321	.009650
21	.006989	.007284	.007585	.007892	.008204	.008522	.008846	.009174	.009508
22	.006831	.007129	.007434	.007745	.008062	.008384	.008712	.009045	.009382
23	.006688	.006991	.007299	.007614	.007935	.008261	.008593	.008930	.009272
24	.006560	.006865	.007178	.007496	.007821	.008151	.008487	.008828	.009174
25	.006443	.006752	.007068	.007390	.007718	.008052	.008392	.008737	.009087
26	.006337	.006649	.006968	.007294	.007626	.007964	.008307	.008656	.009010
27	.006240	.006556	.006878	.007207	.007543	.007884	.008231	.008584	.008941
28	.006151	.006470	.006796	.007129	.007468	.007812	.008163	.008519	.008880
29	.006070	.006392	.006721	.007057	.007399	.007748	.008102	.008461	.008825
30	.005996	.006321	.006653	.006992	.007338	.007689	.008046	.008409	.008776

10.5%	11.0%	11.5%	12.0%	13.0%	14.0%	15.0%	16.0%	17.0%
.088149	.088382	.088615	.088849	.089317	.089787	.090258	.090731	.091205
.046376	.046608	.046840	.047073	.047542	.048013	.048487	.048963	.049442
.032502	.032739	.032976	.033214	.033694	.034178	.034665	.035157	.035653
.025603	.025846	.026089	.026334	.026827	.027326	.027831	.028340	.028855
.021494	.021742	.021993	.022244	.022753	.023268	.023790	.024318	.024853
.018779	.019034	.019291	.019550	.020074	.020606	.021145	.021692	.022246
.016861	.017122	.017386	.017653	.018192	.018740	.019297	.019862	.020436
.015440	.015708	.015979	.016253	.016807	.017372	.017945	.018529	.019121
.014351	.014626	.014904	.015184	.015754	.016334	.016924	.017525	.018136
.013494	.013775	.014060	.014347	.014931	.015527	.016133	.016751	.017380
.012804	.013092	.013384	.013678	.014276	.014887	.015509	.016143	.016788
.012241	.012536	.012833	.013134	.013746	.014371	.015009	.015658	.016319
.011775	.012075	.012379	.012687	.013312	.013951	.014603	.015267	.015943
.011384	.011691	.012001	.012314	.012953	.013605	.014270	.014948	.015638
.011054	.011366	.011682	.012002	.012652	.013317	.013996	.014687	.015390
.010772	.011090	.011412	.011737	.012400	.013077	.013768	.014471	.015186
.010531	.010854	.011181	.011512	.012186	.012875	.013577	.014292	.015018
.010322	.010650	.010983	.011320	.012004	.012704	.013417	.014142	.014879
.010141	.010475	.010812	.011154	.011849	.012559	.013282	.014017	.014764
.009984	.010322	.010664	.011011	.011716	.012435	.013168	.013913	.014668
.009846	.010189	.010536	.010887	.011601	.012330	.013071	.013824	.014588
.009725	.010072	.010424	.010779	.011502	.012239	.012989	.013750	.014521
.009619	.009970	.010326	.010686	.011417	.012162	.012919	.013687	.014465
.009525	.009880	.010240	.010604	.011343	.012095	.012859	.013634	.014418
.009442	.009801	.010165	.010532	.011278	.012038	.012808	.013589	.014378
.009368	.009731	.010098	.010470	.011222	.011988	.012765	.013551	.014345
.009303	.009670	.010040	.010414	.011174	.011945	.012727	.013518	.014317
.009245	.009615	.009989	.010366	.011131	.011908	.012695	.013491	.014293
.009193	.009566	.009943	.010324	.011094	.011876	.012668	.013467	.014273
.009147	.009523	.009903	.010286	.011062	.011849	.012644	.013448	.014257

Table C.5   How $1 Deposited at the End of Each Year Will Grow (CFIFa)

$$CFIFa = \frac{(1 + i)^n - 1}{i}$$

Years	1%	2%	3%	4%	5%	6%	7%	8%	9%
1	1.00000	1.00000	1.00000	1.00000	1.00000	1.00000	1.00000	1.00000	1.00000
2	2.01000	2.02000	2.03000	2.04000	2.05000	2.06000	2.07000	2.08000	2.09000
3	3.03010	3.06040	3.09090	3.12160	3.15250	3.18360	3.21490	3.24640	3.27810
4	4.06040	4.12161	4.18363	4.24646	4.31013	4.37462	4.43994	4.50611	4.57313
5	5.10101	5.20404	5.30914	5.41632	5.52563	5.63709	5.75074	5.86660	5.98471
6	6.15202	6.30812	6.46841	6.63298	6.80191	6.97532	7.15329	7.33593	7.52334
7	7.21354	7.43428	7.66246	7.89829	8.14201	8.39384	8.65402	8.92280	9.20044
8	8.28567	8.58297	8.89234	9.21423	9.54911	9.89747	10.25980	10.63663	11.02847
9	9.36853	9.75463	10.15911	10.58280	11.02656	11.49132	11.97799	12.48756	13.02104
10	10.46221	10.94972	11.46388	12.00611	12.57789	13.18079	13.81645	14.48656	15.19293
11	11.56683	12.16872	12.80780	13.48635	14.20679	14.97164	15.78360	16.64549	17.56029
12	12.68250	13.41209	14.19203	15.02581	15.91713	16.86994	17.88845	18.97713	20.14072
13	13.80933	14.68033	15.61779	16.62684	17.71298	18.88214	20.14064	21.49530	22.95338
14	14.94742	15.97394	17.08632	18.29191	19.59863	21.01507	22.55049	24.21492	26.01919
15	16.09690	17.29342	18.59891	20.02359	21.57856	23.27597	25.12902	27.15211	29.36092
16	17.25786	18.63929	20.15688	21.82453	23.65749	25.67253	27.88805	30.32428	33.00340
17	18.43044	20.01207	21.76159	23.69751	25.84037	28.21288	30.84022	33.75023	36.97370
18	19.61475	21.41231	23.41444	25.64541	28.13238	30.90565	33.99903	37.45024	41.30134
19	20.81090	22.84056	25.11687	27.67123	30.53900	33.75999	37.37896	41.44626	46.01846
20	22.01900	24.29737	26.87037	29.77808	33.06595	36.78559	40.99549	45.76196	51.16012
21	23.23919	25.78332	28.67649	31.96920	35.71925	39.99273	44.86518	50.42292	56.76453
22	24.47159	27.29898	30.53678	34.24797	38.50521	43.39229	49.00574	55.45676	62.87334
23	25.71630	28.84496	32.45288	36.61789	41.43048	46.99583	53.43614	60.89330	69.53194
24	26.97346	30.42186	34.42647	39.08260	44.50200	50.81558	58.17667	66.76476	76.78981
25	28.24320	32.03030	36.45926	41.64591	47.72710	54.86451	63.24904	73.10594	84.70090
26	29.52563	33.67091	38.55304	44.31174	51.11345	59.15638	68.67647	79.95442	93.32398
27	30.82089	35.34432	40.70963	47.08421	54.66913	63.70577	74.48382	87.35077	102.72310
28	32.12910	37.05121	42.93092	49.96758	58.40258	68.52811	80.69769	95.33883	112.96820
29	33.45039	38.79223	45.21885	52.96629	62.32271	73.63980	87.34653	103.96590	124.13540
30	34.78489	40.56808	47.57542	56.08494	66.43885	79.05819	94.46079	113.28320	136.30750

10%	12%	14%	16%	18%	20%	22%	24%	26%
1.00000	1.00000	1.00000	1.00000	1.00000	1.00000	1.00000	1.00000	1.00000
2.10000	2.12000	2.14000	2.16000	2.18000	2.20000	2.22000	2.24000	2.26000
3.31000	3.37440	3.43960	3.50560	3.57240	3.64000	3.70840	3.77760	3.84760
4.64100	4.77933	4.92114	5.06650	5.21543	5.36800	5.52425	5.68422	5.84798
6.10510	6.35285	6.61010	6.87714	7.15421	7.44160	7.73958	8.04844	8.36845
7.71561	8.11519	8.53552	8.97748	9.44197	9.92992	10.44229	10.98006	11.54425
9.48717	10.08901	10.73049	11.41387	12.14152	12.91590	13.73959	14.61528	15.54575
11.43589	12.29969	13.23276	14.24009	15.32700	16.49908	17.76231	19.12294	20.58765
13.57948	14.77566	16.08535	17.51851	19.08585	20.79890	22.67001	24.71245	26.94043
15.93742	17.54874	19.33730	21.32147	23.52131	25.95868	28.65742	31.64344	34.94495
18.53117	20.65458	23.04452	25.73290	28.75514	32.15042	35.96205	40.23787	45.03063
21.38428	24.13313	27.27075	30.85017	34.93107	39.58050	44.87370	50.89495	57.73860
24.52271	28.02911	32.08865	36.78620	42.21866	48.49660	55.74591	64.10974	73.75063
27.97498	32.39260	37.58107	43.67199	50.81802	59.19592	69.01001	80.49608	93.92580
31.77248	37.27971	43.84241	51.65951	60.96527	72.03511	85.19221	100.81510	119.34650
35.94973	42.75328	50.98035	60.92503	72.93901	87.44213	104.93450	126.01080	151.37660
40.54470	48.88367	59.11760	71.67303	87.06804	105.93060	129.02010	157.25340	191.73450
45.59917	55.74971	68.39407	84.14072	103.74030	128.11670	158.40450	195.99420	242.58550
51.15909	63.43968	78.96923	98.60323	123.41350	154.74000	194.25350	244.03280	306.65770
57.27500	72.05244	91.02493	115.37970	146.62800	186.68800	237.98930	303.60060	387.38870
64.00250	81.69874	104.76840	134.84050	174.02100	225.02560	291.34690	377.46480	489.10980
71.40275	92.50258	120.43600	157.41500	206.34480	271.03070	356.44320	469.05630	617.27830
79.54302	104.60290	138.29700	183.60140	244.48680	326.23690	435.86070	582.62980	778.77070
88.49733	118.15520	158.65860	213.97760	289.49450	392.48420	532.75010	723.46100	982.25110
98.34706	133.33390	181.87080	249.21400	342.60350	471.98110	650.95510	898.09160	1238.63600
109.18180	150.33390	208.33270	290.08830	405.27210	567.37730	795.16530	1114.63400	1561.68200
121.09990	169.37400	238.49930	337.50240	479.22110	681.85280	971.10160	1383.14600	1968.71900
134.20990	190.69890	272.88920	392.50280	566.48090	819.22330	1185.74400	1716.10100	2481.58600
148.63090	214.58280	312.09370	456.30320	669.44750	984.06800	1447.60800	2128.96500	3127.79800
164.49400	241.33270	356.78680	530.31170	790.94800	1181.88200	1767.08100	2640.91600	3942.02600

Appendix D

Normal Distribution Table

Area of Normal Distribution that Is X Standard Deviations to the Left or Right of the Mean

Number of Standard Deviations	Area to the Left or Right	Number of Standard Deviations	Area to the Left or Right
0.00	0.5000	1.55	0.0606
0.05	0.4801	1.60	0.0548
0.10	0.4602	1.65	0.0495
0.15	0.4404	1.70	0.0446
0.20	0.4207	1.75	0.0401
0.25	0.4013	1.80	0.0359
0.30	0.3821	1.85	0.0322
0.35	0.3632	1.90	0.0287
0.40	0.3446	1.95	0.0256
0.45	0.3264	2.00	0.0228
0.50	0.3085	2.05	0.0202
0.55	0.2912	2.10	0.0179
0.60	0.2743	2.15	0.0158
0.65	0.2578	2.20	0.0139
0.70	0.2420	2.25	0.0122
0.75	0.2264	2.30	0.0107
0.80	0.2119	2.35	0.0094
0.85	0.1977	2.40	0.0082
0.90	0.1841	2.45	0.0071
0.95	0.1711	2.50	0.0062
1.00	0.1587	2.55	0.0054
1.05	0.1469	2.60	0.0047
1.10	0.1357	2.65	0.0040
1.15	0.1251	2.70	0.0035
1.20	0.1151	2.75	0.0030
1.25	0.1056	2.80	0.0026
1.30	0.0968	2.85	0.0022
1.35	0.0885	2.90	0.0019
1.40	0.0808	2.95	0.0016
1.45	0.0735	3.00	0.0013
1.50	0.0668		

Appendix E

Key Formulas and Frequently Used Symbols

SUMMARY OF KEY FORMULAS

Compound Interest and Discount

1. Future value (compound amount):

$$FV = PV(1 + i)^n$$

2. Present value:

$$PV = FV/(1 + i)^n$$

3. Future (compound) value of an annuity:

$$FV = PMT \times \left([(1 + i)^n - 1]/i \right)$$

4. Present value of an annuity:

$$PV = PMT \times \left[\left(1 - [1/(1 + i)^n] \right)/i \right]$$

Investment Analysis Relationships

1. Net present value:

$$NPV = \sum_{t=1}^{n} ATCF_t/(1 + i)^t - \text{Initial equity investment}$$

2. Internal rate of return (IRR):

$$\sum_{t=1}^{n} ATCF_t/(1 + IRR)^t - \text{Initial equity investment} = 0$$

3. Profitability index:

$$PI = PV \text{ of benefits/Initial equity investment}$$

Standard Deviation of the Present Value Distribution

1. With perfect serial correlation:

$$\sigma_{pv} = \sigma_\alpha/(1 + i)^t$$

2. With zero serial correlation:

$$\sigma_{pv} = \sqrt{\sigma_\alpha^2/(1 + i)^{2t}}$$

3. Hillier's model:

$$\sigma_{pv} = \sqrt{\sigma_{yt}^2/(1 + i)^{2t} + [\sigma_{xt}/(1 + i)^t]^2}$$

FREQUENTLY USED SYMBOLS

ATCF	After-tax cash flow
CF_t	Cash flow in year t
$\overline{CF}$	Mean of a probability distribution of possible cash flows
CV	Covariance
FV	Future value
IRR	Internal rate of return
i	Interest rate
k	Discount or capitalization factor; the cost of capital
PV	Present value
Q	Quantity produced, purchased or sold
PMT	Periodic payment or receipt
R_f	Risk-free interest rate
S_n	Compound sum
σ	Standard deviation
σ^2	Variance
t	Time period
Z	Number of standard deviations from the mean

Glossary

absolute monopoly. A market that has only one supplier of a good or service for which there are no reasonably acceptable substitutes.

absorption rates. Rates at which the market will "absorb" a product; the rate at which units will be purchased.

abstract and opinion. A summary of the chain of past title transfers for real property and an attorney's written opinion that the title contains no defects.

abstract of title. A brief summary of each recorded document pertaining to title to a specified parcel of land.

accelerated method. A method of computing depreciation or cost recovery allowances whereby large annual allowances are claimed in the early years of ownership, offset by smaller allowances in later years.

acceleration clause. A clause that permits the mortgagee to declare the full amount of a debt due and payable if the mortgagor defaults on any of the agreed-upon terms.

acceptance. The act of a party to whom a thing is offered by another, whereby he or she receives the thing with the intention of retaining it.

accredited purchasers. Investors who either (1) are sufficiently wealthy so that a contemplated securities purchase (of $150,000 or more) will not exceed 20 percent of their net worth, (2) have a net worth in excess of $1 million or (3) have a two-year earnings record of more than $200,000 per annum and expect their current earnings to exceed $200,000.

accretion. A gradual increase in land area adjacent to a body of water because of soil deposited by wave and current action.

accrued depreciation. A loss in value due to physical deterioration, functional obsolescence and economic or locational disadvantages.

acknowledgment. Certification by a notary public or other appropriate public official that the grantor has stated before the official that he or she executed the acknowledged document.

ad valorem. A Latin term used to describe the taxing of property according to value.

adjusted basis. The amount paid for property, plus all subsequent capital expenditures made to improve it, minus all tax deductions for depreciation or cost recovery allowances.

adjusted gross income. Gross taxable income minus a set of specific deductions spelled out in the Internal Revenue Code.

adjusted rate of return. Modified version of the internal rate of return, designed to eliminate problems associated with negative cash flows.

adverse possession. Wrongful occupancy of real estate in a manner and for a time period described in state statutes. Title then vests in the adverse possessor by operation of law and is independent of any previously recorded title to the property.

affirmative covenant. A mutual promise between neighbors that a property will be used in some specified manner.

after-tax cash flow. Cash flow generated from a property after accounting for all operating expenses, all debt service obligations and all income tax consequences for the current period.

agglomeration economies. An amorphous term referring to cost reductions ascribed to proximity.

all-inclusive mortgage. See wraparound mortgage.

alternative minimum tax. A provision that specifies the minimum amount of federal income tax for which all taxpayers are liable. After computing tax liability the regular way, taxpayers must perform the alternative computation. They are required to pay the greater of the regular or the alternative minimum tax.

alternative minimum taxable income. The income upon which liability for the alternative minimum tax is computed.

amortization table. A schedule of equal periodic payments necessary to repay a $1 loan, with interest, over a specified number of payment periods.

amortize. To claim an expenditure, which is incurred at the beginning of the period, as an annual expense or income tax deduction over an extended period of years.

anchor tenants. Tenants who are expected to attract customers to a shopping center and thereby generate business for other merchants in the center.

annual compounding. Accumulated interest that in and of itself earns interest in all subsequent periods.

annual mortgage constant. The percent of the original principal amount that must be paid annually in order to fully repay interest and principal over the term of the loan.

annuity. Any series of periodic payments received or paid at regular intervals.

annuity table. A schedule providing factors used to calculate the present value of a compound level annuity.

articles of agreement. See installment sales contract.

asset liquidity. See liquidity.

assignment. Transfer of contractual rights from one contracting party (the assignor) to another person (the assignee) who is not a party to the contract.

assumption clause. A clause whereby mortgagors agree not to sell mortgaged property subject to the mortgage or to have a buyer assume an existing mortgage without prior approval of the mortgagee.

assumption fee. A fee charged by a lender as a condition for permitting assumption of mortgage indebtedness by a party other than the original mortgagor. This permits mortgagees to adjust their rates of return to the current market when interest rates have risen.

atomistic markets. A market in which no one person or group can measurably affect market prices. Market participants are simply price takers, in that they have a choice of accepting prevailing prices or of not participating in the market at all.

avulsion. A sudden and perceptible shift in land boundaries due to floods or sudden alterations in the course of rivers or streams.

back-door approach. A type of preliminary financial feasibility study that involves estimating the maximum amount of equity financing that investors can commit to a project, given their minimum acceptable current yield.

band of investment technique. A technique used to calculate the weighted average cost of capital for a property. The cost of each source of funds is weighted by a factor equal to the proportion of total funds that will be derived from that source.

base lines. A set of imaginary lines running east and west employed by surveyors for reference in locating and describing land under the government survey method of property description.

basic rate. The sum of the weighted average cost of capital and the equity buildup factor used in order to determine the appropriate overall capitalization rate.

bid-rent curve. A functional relationship that depicts the absolute maximum rent a firm with a specific profit profile can pay and still find remaining in business a worthwhile endeavor.

blanket mortgage. The pledge of two or more parcels of property as security for a single loan.

blind pool syndication. A form of limited partnership in which the promoter assembles a group of investors with the purpose of acquiring an undesignated asset of a specific type.

book value. The value at which assets are recorded on a firm's books of account (that is, its accounting records); usually cost minus accumulated depreciation or cost recovery allowances.

boot. (See also like-kind exchange) Assets received as consideration in what would otherwise be an exchange of entirely like-kind assets. Receipt of boot may trigger tax liability in what would otherwise be a tax-deferred transaction.

breakeven ratio. The relationship between cash expenditure requirements and gross revenue from an investment project. Sometimes called a *default ratio.*

broker's rate of return. A rate-of-return measure that adjusts the cash-on-cash return to include equity buildup from debt amortization and thereby shows a slightly more favorable return than does the cash-on-cash measure.

building codes. The set of laws that establishes minimum standards for constructing new buildings or altering existing structures. Building codes are intended to ensure minimum protection against fire damage and to safeguard against faulty design in construction.

business risk. Risk stemming from the possibility of making inappropriate business decisions or of misjudging the economic consequences of actions.

capital assets. All assets held by a taxpayer (whether or not connected with the person's trade or business) except those specifically enumerated by the Commissioner of Internal Revenue. Generally, assets of a fixed or permanent nature or those employed in carrying on a business or trade.

capital expenditure. An expenditure of funds that extends the useful life of a capital asset or adds to its value.

capital formation. The raising of debt or equity funds for real estate projects.

capital goods. Products destined to be employed in the production of other goods or services.

capitalization rate. The relationship between net income from a real estate investment and the value of the investment. This relationship is usually expressed as a percentage.

capitalize. To add an amount to the tax basis of a property.

capital recovery. The portion of an overall capitalization rate comprised of recovery of the owner's capital outlay.

cash-on-cash rate of return. The first year's expected after-tax cash flow, divided by the initial cash outlay required to acquire the investment.

central business district. The focal point of urban places where goods and services are exchanged.

central place theory. The postulate that if the surrounding countryside were a flat, undifferentiated plane, central places would be located so as to minimize the distance from all points in the tributary area. It states further that the larger the city, the larger its tributary area must be.

certainty equivalents. Substitute cash flows determined by the certainty-equivalent technique.

certainty-equivalent technique. A procedure that seeks to establish substitute cash flows that leave an investor indifferent between absolutely certain receipt of the substitute amounts and the expectation of receiving the point estimates, along with attendant risk.

certificate of limited partnership. A document that must be filed with the appropriate state agency to create a limited partnership.

certified historic structure. (See also registered historic district) Any structure that is either listed in the National Registry of Historic Places or located in a registered historic district and certified as being of historic significance to the district.

ceteris paribus. A Latin term used by economists to mean that demand schedules are applicable only so long as all factors other than price that influence buyer behavior do not change.

city planning. A procedure for formulating land-use schemes, employed by municipalities in their efforts to reach specified goals in the utilization of land within the municipality.

coefficient of correlation. A measure of the extent to which the values of variables in a sample or a population are interdependent.

coefficient of determination. A measure of the percent of variation in the dependent variable associated with variation in the value of the independent variable. In regression analysis, designated by the term *r-square* (r^2).

coefficient of multiple correlation. A measure of the percentage of variance in the dependent variable that is "explained" by variation in the independent variables.

coefficient of serial correlation. A measure of the degree to which outcomes in subsequent periods are related. Possible coefficients range from zero to plus-or-minus one.

coefficient of variation. Standard deviation of the distribution of possible outcomes, divided by the expected outcome.

collective goods. See public goods.

commitment letter. A letter to a prospective borrower, wherein a lender states terms and conditions under which it will provide the requested funds. A precise period is usually specified during which the commitment remains effective. Commitment letters generally state conditions under which the lender may revoke the commitment and set forth any further provisions upon which the commitment is contingent.

community shopping center. A shopping center that typically draws most of its customers from

an area extending from ten to 15 minutes in driving time. Community shopping centers usually feature a food store and a junior department store or a discount store as anchor tenants. Size may range from 50,000 to 100,000 square feet of retail space.

comparative advantage. An economic principle developed by the economist David Ricardo that provides an explanation of why some areas tend to concentrate on producing a limited number of goods and seek much of what they consume from other areas.

comparative sales approach. An appraisal procedure that analyzes recent sales data from similar properties and draws inferences about the value of the property being appraised.

comparative unit method. A valuation approach that estimates costs by comparison with similar buildings whose construction costs are known. To render buildings of slightly different size more directly comparable, costs are expressed on the basis of some standardized unit of measure, such as per square foot or per cubic foot.

complements. Goods or services whose consumption occurs in tandem with that of the item in question. A change in the price of one good or service can cause a shift in the demand curves for its complements.

compound amount. The summation of principal and compounded interest over a specified holding period.

compound interest. Interest income attributable to previously accrued interest that has been left on deposit.

concentric zone model. An urban economic model developed by Earnest W. Burgess in the 1920s. The concentric zone model was designed to explain urban development through the use of transitional zones.

concessions. See rent concessions.

condemnation proceeding. The consequence of a property owner's refusal to voluntarily convey title at a price offered by a governmental agency seeking to convert the property to public use.

condominium. An ownership arrangement whereby title to specified portions of a property vests in individual users, and title to common area vests in all users jointly.

condominium association. An association, composed of all those owning interest in a condominium, which serves as a governing and managing body, usually through an elected board of directors.

condominium declaration. The enabling document that creates a condominium. The declaration describes both individual and common areas of the premises and provides for assessment of owners for costs of maintaining and insuring common areas.

conduit. See tax conduit.

consideration. Under contract law, the impelling reason to enter into a contract. Something of value given in exchange for a promise.

constructive notice. A legal doctrine under which notice may be attributed even though a party may be completely ignorant of the facts. Recording statutes provide that recording a document in the public record constitutes constructive notice to the world.

consumer good. The end product of the production process.

consumer price index. An index of changes in the price of a representative "market basket" of consumer goods, relating the current price to that in a designated base year.

contract for deed. See installment sales contract.

contract price. Total selling price minus any pre-existing mortgage to which a property will remain subject when sold under conditions permitting the transaction to be reported for tax computation purposes under the installment sales method. If the pre-existing mortgage exceeds the seller's adjusted basis in the property, the excess of the mortgage over the seller's basis must be added back to the contract price.

cooperative. An apartment the tenant purchases by buying stock in the corporation that owns the building rather than simply buying the apartment.

corporations. Artificial entities, created under state laws, that are empowered to own property and transact business in their own names. They may buy, sell and otherwise enter into contracts. As legal entities, corporations have an identity separate and distinct from that of their owners.

cost approach. An appraisal technique whereby an estimate of land value is added to the estimated cost of reproducing existing improvements on the land (net of accrued depreciation) to derive a value estimate for the entire property.

cost recovery allowance. An income tax rule that provides for recovery of capital expenditures on property having a finite useful life, acquired on or after January 1, 1981, and used in a trade or business or for production of income.

cost recovery assets. Assets on which tax-deductible cost recovery allowances may be claimed.

cotenancy. Real property title held in the name of two or more owners.

counseling. Providing competent, unbiased advice on diversified problems in the broad field of real estate involving any or all segments of the business, such as merchandising, leasing, management, planning, financing, appraising, court testimony and other similar services.

covenant against removal. A restriction imposed by the mortgagee prohibiting the mortgagor from removing or demolishing any part of the building without the lender's consent.

covenant against waste. A restriction imposed by a mortgagee prohibiting the mortgagor from allowing the building to deteriorate during the period of the mortgage.

covenant of insurance. A mortgage clause in which the mortgagor promises to maintain adequate insurance coverage against fire and other specified hazards.

covenant of seizin. (See also seizin) A mortgage clause whereby the mortgagor warrants that he or she is the lawful owner of the property being mortgaged.

covenant of title. A promise or assurance made by the grantor in connection with title transfer.

covenants. Promises that property will, or will not, be used in some specified manner.

covenant to pay taxes. A common mortgage clause in which the mortgagor promises to pay all property taxes and assessments levied against the property during the period of the mortgage.

cross-sectional surveys. Surveys involving one-time sampling from a population of research interest. All elements are measured at a single point in time. Cross-sectional surveys provide a "snapshot" of the variables under observation as of the time of the survey.

curtesy. A husband's interest in his wife's property.

custom construction. A construction project that takes place on land owned by the ultimate purchaser, involving a structure built to the exact specifications of the purchaser-user.

dealer. In real estate, one who is in the business of buying and selling property interests for one's own account. Gains on dealers' sales are reported as ordinary income rather than as capital gains.

debentures. Bonds secured by the borrower's income stream.

debt amortization. The process of gradually extinguishing a debt by a series of periodic payments to the creditor.

debt constant. The percentage of the original principal amount that must be paid annually in order to fully repay interest and principal over the term of the loan. The constant can be expressed as an annual percentage or monthly percentage. Sometimes called a *debt service constant*.

debt coverage ratio. The relationship between a project's annual net operating income and the obligation to make principal and interest payments on borrowed funds. Debt coverage ratios are often employed to evaluate a lender's margin of safety regarding mortgage loans.

debt service. Payments to a lender. Debt service obligations may involve payment of interest only or both principal and interest so as to fully or partially amortize a debt over a specified term.

debt service constant. See debt constant.

debt-to-equity ratio. The ratio between borrowed funds and equity funds.

decision model. A systematic process for identifying opportunities that show promise of contributing adequately to predetermined investment goals.

declining balance method. A method of computing annual depreciation or cost recovery allowances that provides the greatest allowance in the first year of ownership and progressively smaller allowances for each successive year.

decree. The judgment of a court of equity, ordering execution of the provisions of that judgment.

deed. A legal document that conveys title in real property from one party to another. The document must be signed, witnessed, delivered and accepted.

deed of trust. A deed passing title to property from an owner to a trustee, who holds that property as collateral for a mortgage loan advanced by another. Also called a *trust deed* or *trust indenture*.

default. A mortgagor's failure to fulfill any of the agreed-upon terms in a security agreement.

default ratio. See breakeven ratio.

defeasance clause. Mortgage provisions intended to render nominal conveyance void upon satisfaction of the mortgagor's obligation.

deficiency judgment. A judgment against a debtor's personal assets beyond those assets owned on a defaulted debt instrument.

delivery. The legal act of transferring ownership of real estate.

demand. An economic term that refers to the entire range of relationships between price and quantity.

demand curve. A graphic illustration of the relationship between price and the quantity of a good or service buyers will take off the market. Also called a *demand function.*

demand function. See demand curve.

demand schedule. A table that relates quantity demanded to a good's or service's price, at all relevant prices.

demand to purchase. Desired increase in a market participant's inventory of a product, at a specific price.

dependency exemption. An amount of adjusted gross income that taxpayers may exempt from taxable income for each person dependent upon them for financial support.

dependent variable. In regression or correlation analysis, a variable whose value is thought to be affected by the value of other variables (independent variables) included in the analysis.

deposit insurance. An insurance program that protects depositors from loss due to bank failures.

depreciable asset. See depreciable property.

depreciable property. Property upon which a tax-deductible depreciation allowance may be claimed.

depreciation. Decline in an asset's value or useful life, due to wear, tear, action of the elements or obsolescence.

depreciation allowance. A tax-deductible allowance to account for the decline in value or useful life of an asset due to wear, tear, obsolescence or action of the elements.

derived demand. Demand for a good or service that stems from the use of that good or service in the production of something else.

descriptive statistics. A statistical application that employs quantitative expressions to describe characteristics of a sample or an underlying population.

development. A real estate activity that involves adding improvements such as buildings.

differentiated product. Products that are sufficiently different from competitive products to reduce the degree of substitutability. Producers of differentiated products have some degree of control over price.

diminishing marginal utility. The economic principle that as additional units of a good are possessed or consumed per unit of time, the additional (marginal) utility of each successive unit is less than that of the preceding unit.

discounted cash-flow approach. An investment evaluation technique that incorporates adjustments for both volume and timing of anticipated future cash flows and is generally accepted as the most desirable approach to evaluating opportunities.

discounting. Expressing anticipated future cash flows as present-worth equivalents.

discount points. A reduction in net loan proceeds to make the effective interest rate equal the current market rate.

discount rate. A rate that measures return on investment after the recovery of invested capital.

discrete probability distribution. A probability distribution in which possible outcomes are limited in number.

disintermediation. The situation where people, seeking better yields, withdraw their savings from major institutional lenders and participate directly in financial markets.

diversification. The reduction in total risk through holding a variety of property types and spreading ownership over a wide geographic area.

dominant tenement. Land that reaps the benefit of an easement.

dower. A wife's interest in her husband's property.

dram shop insurance. Insurance against liability arising from incidents related to liquor consumption.

due process. Proceedings in accordance with legal precedent, statutes and constitutional provisions, designed to protect the rights of all parties to a dispute.

earnest money. Money paid as evidence of good faith or actual intent to complete a transaction, usually forfeited by willful failure to complete the transaction.

earnest money deposit. A good faith deposit into an escrow account (or into a broker's trust account), typically accompanied by a purchase offer.

easement. Nonpossessory interest that permits limited use of someone else's land. Conveys only a right to use the land.

easement appurtenant. An easement created on one parcel of land (the servient tenement) for the benefit of an adjacent parcel (the dominant tenement).

easement by expressed grant. Easement created by a specific agreement between the affected parties.

easement by implication. An easement created as a consequence of a landowner selling property to which access requires crossing other property that the landowner also owns. Easements by implication are created when reasonably necessary, when the need is apparent at the time property is conveyed and when the need appears to be permanent in nature.

easement by prescription. An easement acquired through the open, continuous, adverse use of real property for a specified period of time.

easement in gross. An easement that constitutes personal property, independent of any related land interest.

economic base analysis. A study that divides economic activity into domestic and export sectors and seeks to determine the degree to which activity in the domestic sector is dependent upon the level of activity in the export sector.

economic base theory. An explanation of urban growth that postulates that total economic activity in an urban area is a function of the level of activity in its export sector.

economic obsolescence. Loss in value due to inappropriate location.

Economic Recovery Tax Act of 1981. A major revision of the Internal Revenue Code, enacted into law in 1981.

economic rent. Profit generated by a good or service in excess of the profit necessary to induce firms to produce the good or service. Sometimes referred to as *pure profit.*

effective gross income. Potential gross rental revenue, minus losses for vacancies and uncollectible accounts, plus income from related sources.

effective interest rates. Rates actually paid for the use of borrowed funds. Effective rates are a function of the amount borrowed and the amount and timing of the required repayment.

efficient markets. Markets in which all relevant information is immediately and fully reflected in market prices. Participants in efficient markets are unable to consistently achieve above-average market yields. The hypothesis that a market is completely efficient is referred to as the strong form of the efficiency hypothesis.

eminent domain. Authority vested in both federal and state governments allowing them to take private property for public use without the owner's consent.

encumbrances. A lien, charge or claim against real property that diminishes the value of the property but does not prevent the passing of title.

end loan. A loan secured by a mortgage on a completed building, terminating a chain of loans to finance land acquisition and construction. Also called a *permanent loan* or a *takeout loan.*

end-loan commitment. An agreement by a lender to provide an end loan upon satisfaction of all contingencies specified by the lender.

equilibrium. In economics, a stable, balanced or unchanging system. A situation in which there is no tendency for anything to change.

equilibrium price. The price at which there will be sufficient quantity of a product to satisfy the desires of all consumers at that price but with no surplus remaining on the market; the market clearing price.

equitable right of redemption. The legal right of a borrower, or the borrower's heirs or assigns, to redeem mortgaged property for a limited period of time after default. Also called *equity of redemption.*

equity. The concept of fairness and justice applied to the portion of common law relating to the rights and duties of individuals. Also the money value of what is owned, arrived at by subtracting all that is owed from the value of the ownership to arrive at a net ownership value figure.

equity buildup. The accumulation and growth of the money value of what is owned. That is, an increase in the net financial interest in a specific property.

equity dividend rate. Before-tax cash flow expressed as a percentage of the required initial equity cash outlay.

equity of redemption. See equitable right of redemption.

equity REIT. A type of real estate investment trust that concentrates its resources on equity interests in real property.

equity yield rate. Interest earned on recovered capital.

escalator clause. Lease clause that requires tenants to pay all operating expenses above amounts specified in the lease.

escheat. The legal principle that property title reverts to the state when an intestate owner (one with no will) dies with no heirs.

escrow. The holding by a third party of something of value that is the subject of a contract between two other parties until the contract has been consummated.

escrow agent. A disinterested third party who acts as agent for parties to an escrow agreement.

escrow agreement. A contract between parties to a transaction and a third party who functions as an escrow agent. The agreement contains written escrow instructions, which govern the agent's action in performance of his or her escrow duties.

estate for years. A leasehold interest that extends for an exactly specified period, after which the interest automatically expires.

estate subject to a condition precedent. An estate created (rather than terminated) upon the happening of some specified contingency.

excess accumulated earnings tax. A penalty tax levied on corporations that accumulate earnings in excess of corporate needs.

excess cost recovery allowance. Cost recovery allowance actually claimed, minus what would have been claimed had the taxpayer used the straight-line cost recovery method from the beginning.

executory. A contract that lacks some necessary performance by one of its parties and is therefore not yet completed.

expected value. The midpoint of a symmetric probability distribution; the most likely outcome.

explicit transfer costs. (See also implicit transfer costs) Costs measurable in dollars; specifically, cost per mile of chosen transportation mode, plus the dollar value of the time spent en route.

external costs. (See also external diseconomies) Costs incurred by the public from the act or nonact of a private party.

external diseconomies. External costs where benefits accrue to the decision maker while costs are borne by others.

external economies. (See also externality) A good side effect of production or consumption, for which no payment is received or made.

externality. A good or bad side effect of production or consumption, for which no payment is received or made.

facilities management. Overseeing the physical upkeep of properties as well as keeping records of income and expenses associated with their operation.

factor of production. Goods or services that are themselves intended to be utilized in producing other goods or service.

feasibility analysis. An analysis of the likelihood of success of a specific proposed course of action.

feasibility study. A study of the costs and benefits of a proposed course of action, to determine the likelihood of achieving project goals within the context of specified constraints and available resources. A proposal that has a reasonable probability of satisfying explicit objectives is considered feasible. A financial feasibility study addresses the question whether the proposed course of action will meet financial objectives.

Federal Deposit Insurance Corporation (FDIC). An independent federal agency that insures deposits up to a certain amount in all national banks and in all state banks that have been accepted as FDIC members.

fee simple absolute. The greatest real property interest recognized by law. This term expresses the idea that the interest is held with no preconditions or qualifications.

fee simple defeasible. A qualified fee estate that may be subject to a condition subsequent or determinable, depending upon the nature of the qualification. Some states also permit creation of fees subject to conditions precedent.

fee simple estate. Any real property interest.

fee splitting. Analogous to life estates and remainders whereby title passes to or reverts upon the occurrence of some event.

fee subject to a condition subsequent. A fee that extends only until the happening of some specified act or event.

fee tail. A carryover from the feudal system, requiring that title pass to lineal descendants of the property owner.

fiduciary. One who is in a position of trust or confidence with respect to another person.

financial assets. Assets such as promissory notes, bonds and commercial paper that represent financial claims rather than ownership of physical assets.

financial intermediaries. Institutions such as commercial banks, savings and loan associations, credit unions and so on that act as go-between from savers to user-borrowers.

financial leverage. The impact of borrowed money on investment return. That is, the use of borrowed money to amplify consequences to equity investors.

financial management rate of return. A modification of the internal rate of return, designed to eliminate problems encountered when negative cash flows are included in the forecast.

financial risk. Risk that cash flow from a project will be insufficient to meet the investor's debt service obligation.

fiscal policy. Exercise of influence on the economy by controlling government spending and taxation.

footloose industries. Industries in which firms are not restricted geographically by transportation cost considerations. Such firms frequently seek locations with a ready supply of labor or minimal labor costs.

forecasting. Predicting a future value from known, related data.

foreclosure by sale. Sale of mortgaged property at public auction as a consequence of default by the mortgagor. Foreclosure by sale extinguishes the equitable right of redemption.

foreclosure decree. A court order specifying an exact time period (a period determined by state laws) during which the equity of redemption will exist.

free and clear rate of return. See overall capitalization rate.

freehold. An estate in real property that, unless assigned or otherwise conveyed, remains in perpetuity, or for life.

front-door approach. A type of preliminary financial feasibility study that involves estimating the minimum gross rent required to meet investors' threshold investment acceptability criteria.

fully amortized. The ultimate retirement of a mortgage debt through installment payments that include both interest and principal over the term of the loan.

functional efficiency. A measure of how well a property performs its intended function.

functional obsolescence. The loss of functional efficiency due to defective or dated design. This reduces a building's competitive position relative to more functionally efficient structures and may eventually lead to abandonment or succession of use.

fundamental analysis. An investment analysis technique that emphasizes investigation of the underlying business activity being undertaken by the firm whose securities are being considered.

gap financing. See standby financing.

general contractor. A contractor who takes full responsibility for construction of a project by formal agreement with the owner or developer and hires others as subcontractors to perform specific tasks.

general partner. See limited partnership.

general partnership. An entity in which all partners have equal rights to management and conduct of the firm; each partner is, in effect, an agent for the partnership.

gentrification. Reclamation of residential areas containing physically deteriorated buildings and restoration of a deteriorated neighborhood for the use of predominantly middle-class residents.

goods or services. (See also product) Items offered for sale in the marketplace.

graduated-payment mortgage (GPM). A mortgage that allows a borrower, in effect, to borrow additional money during the early years of the mortgage to reduce the monthly mortgage payment obligation during those early years. This additional loan is added to the mortgage and is repaid by increased debt service obligations in the later years.

grantee. A person to whom a grant is made; the purchaser.

grantor. A person who conveys real estate by deed; the seller.

gross income. For income tax computation purposes, all revenue generated from any source, unless specifically excluded by provisions of the Internal Revenue Code.

gross income multiplier. (See also income multiplier analysis and net income multiplier) Evaluation technique that describes the relationship between most probable sales price and gross revenue. Sometimes called a *gross rent multiplier.*

gross rent multiplier. See gross income multiplier.

health and safety codes. Rules and regulations designed to promote public health and safety in the construction and/or demolition of improvements to real property.

hedging. Taking an investment position that will pay off if the investor's primary investment does not. Hedging reduces aggregate investor risk.

historic structure. See certified historic structure.

holdover tenant. A tenant who remains in possession of real estate after the expiration of the lease.

housing codes. Laws specifying minimum building standards, with the objective of promoting public health, safety or welfare.

hurdle rate. The minimum acceptable yield on investment funds. Projects that are not expected to yield at least the investor's hurdle rate are rejected.

hybrid REIT. A real estate investment trust that mixes mortgage and equity instruments in its portfolio.

implicit transfer costs. (See also explicit transfer costs) Indirect costs of moving goods or people between linked sites. Although they are often more difficult to identify than are explicit transfer costs, they may also be larger.

income. For purposes of determining federal income tax liability, all revenue generated from any source unless specifically excluded by provisions of the Internal Revenue Code.

income multiplier analysis. (See also gross income multiplier and net income multiplier) A technique for expressing the relationship between price and either gross or net income.

incubator buildings. Relatively small, multi-tenant structures in which new or small but growing firms rent space on an interim basis until growth generates a need for larger quarters.

independent variable. In regression or correlation analysis, a variable whose value is thought to be determined by factors other than those under analysis, but which is thought to affect the value of one or more other variables (the dependent variables) in the analysis.

indifference curve. A graphic presentation of combinations of values for two variables, representing the preferences of an individual who will be indifferent among the various combinations.

inferential statistics. The drawing of conclusions from evidence contained in statistical data.

inferior goods. Consumer goods for which demand decreases as purchasing power rises.

information search costs. The cost of generating relevant market information. High information search costs tend to reduce market efficiency.

initial tax basis. The tax basis of a property at the time of acquisition. Usually, cost plus any additional outlays required to assure good and defensible title.

installment method gain. The difference between gain on disposal of an asset that qualifies for installment method reporting and the recapture of accumulated depreciation or cost recovery allowances. Only this portion of the gain may be reported using the installment method. The remainder must be recognized in the taxable year of the transaction.

installment sales contract. Contract that sets forth terms and conditions under which a seller is obligated to render deeds of conveyance to the buyer at some future date. Also called a *land contract, contract for deed,* or *articles of agreement.*

installment sales method. A method for reporting sales to the Internal Revenue Service whereby a portion of the resulting income tax liability may be deferred when some of the proceeds from the sale are not collected during the current taxable year.

insurable risk. Risk of loss from natural hazards such as fire, flood, storm and so forth, which can be transferred to an insurance company.

interim financing. Financing used during the construction phase, to be superseded by takeout financing after construction is completed.

intermediate goods. A good combined with other goods to create consumer products.

internal rate of return. A financial analysis technique that involves setting net present value at zero and finding a discount rate to satisfy the equality condition; that is, the discount rate that makes present value exactly equal to required initial cash outlay.

Internal Revenue Code. Public Law 591—Chapter 736. This law (as subsequently revised) constitutes the statutory authority for income, employment, estate and gift taxes levied by the Internal Revenue Service. Generally referred to by tax practitioners more simply as *the Code.*

interpolation. A procedure for estimating values that fall between tabular amounts.

intrastate offering. A security issue offered for sale solely within one state by an issuer resident in or a corporation incorporated and doing business in that state. A qualifying intrastate offering is exempt from requirements for federal registration.

investment. Commitment of money or other assets in expectation of financial gain.

investment income. See portfolio income.

investment interest limitation. Provision of the Internal Revenue Code that places a dollar limit on the amount of investment interest that can be deducted in any one taxable year on loans used to finance investments.

investment tax credit. A credit against income tax liability, earned as a consequence of investing in qualifying assets.

investment value. The summation of the present value of the equity position plus the present value of the debt position. The present value of the equity position is calculated on an after-tax basis and considers the tax consequences to a specific investor.

investor. Any person or entity who takes an equity position in real estate for use in a trade or business or for production of income.

itemized deductions. Taxpayer expenditures, listed in Sections 161 through 195 of the Internal Revenue Code, that may be deducted from adjusted gross income to arrive at taxable income.

joint probabilities. The probability of joint occurrence of two or more events. The probability that both event A and event B will occur equals the probability that A will occur times the probability that B will occur, given that A occurs.

This relationship is sometimes referred to as the *multiplicative law of probability.*

joint tenancy. (See also right of survivorship) An estate held jointly by two or more persons under the same title in which each has the same degree of interest and the same right of possession. Joint tenancy usually entails the right of the surviving tenant(s) to take title to a decedent's interest (right of survivorship).

joint tenants. Parties who hold equal and undivided interests under joint tenancy.

judgment samples. A sampling technique that regards individual observations, with respect to certain characteristics, as typical of the underlying universe.

judicial partition. A court proceeding to terminate a cotenancy arrangement when the co-owners are unable to agree upon terms for sale or physical division of jointly owned real estate.

junior mortgage. A mortgage that is legally subordinate to another (senior) mortgage.

land contract. See installment sales contract.

land development. The business activity of acquiring large tracts of land, subdividing and selling off individual smaller tracts. Also frequently called *subdivision.*

land-use controls. Publicly imposed controls on land usage aimed at assuring orderly development.

lease. Legal document conveying limited right to use a property. Document generally specifies all terms of lease as well as permitted use.

leasehold. Right of a tenant in leased property.

leasehold estate. Estate of a tenant in a leased property.

leasehold interest. Interest of a tenant in a leased property.

lessee. A property owner who transfers certain rights for a limited period to a tenant. Generally referred to as a *landlord.*

lessor. The holder of a leasehold interest in a property. Generally referred to as a *tenant.*

license. Privilege to enter onto the land of a licenser in order to do certain things that would otherwise be considered trespassing.

lien. Claim against a property that allows the proceeds from a forced sale of the property to be used to satisfy the debt.

life estate. Grants a life tenant full property rights for the remainder of his or her life.

life tenant. Individual possessing full property rights in a specific property for the remainder of his or her life.

like-kind exchange. Exchanges of assets deemed under Internal Revenue Code Section 1031 to be of like kind. Gains or losses on exchanges that involve only like-kind assets must be deferred until the newly acquired (substitute) asset is disposed of. Transactions that are only partially like-kind may result in total or partial recognition of gains or losses. Also frequently called *tax-free exchanges* or *Section 1031 exchanges.*

limited partner. See limited partnership.

limited partnership. An ownership arrangement involving one or more general partners and one or more limited partners. General partners assume full liability for debts of the partnership and exercise control over operations, while a limited partner's liability is limited to the extent of actual capital contribution to the partnership or additional liability voluntarily assumed.

linkages. Relationships requiring the movement of goods or people from one location to another.

linked sites. Sites that are interrelated by linkages; that is, related by the need to move goods or people from one site to the other.

liquidation damages. Monetary award specified in a contract to be awarded to the damaged party in the event of a breach by either party.

liquidity. Ability to convert an asset to cash without incurring loss.

loanable funds. Monies held by financial intermediaries in excess of required reserves; monies available to borrowers.

loan broker. Individual who places loans with primary lenders for a fee.

loan commitment. Obligation of a lender to provide specific funds at some future date. Terms may be specified, or they may be those prevailing on the date funds are advanced.

loan origination fee. A charge by a lender, assessed at the time a loan commitment is made or at the time funds are advanced.

loan proceeds. The face amount of a loan minus amounts deducted by the lender for items such as loan origination fees or discount points.

loan-to-value ratio. Relationship of debt funds to total project value, stated as a percentage.

locational advantages. Advantages, garnered by an occupant, due solely to the locational desirability of a site.

locational benefits. The benefits derived from the use of real estate that are properly attributable to the desirability of the site location.

longitudinal studies. Studies of relationships among variables, measuring changes in the variables through time. They involve repeated measures of the same phenomena to record any variation through time. Also called *time series studies.*

long run. Economic term used to describe the length of time necessary for the operation of market forces to produce equilibrium.

long-term capital gains. Term used in tax accounting to refer to gains realized on disposal of assets held for more than six months.

marginal benefits. Economic term used to describe the benefits derived from an additional unit of production. In a financial sense, it might be used to describe the financial rewards of additional investment.

marginal cost. Economic term used to describe the cost associated with production of each additional unit of a good or service.

marginal cost of capital. The cost of an additional dollar of new capital funds.

marginal cost of production. The cost of adding one more unit per period to one's rate of production.

marginal revenue. Economic term used to describe revenue derived from an additional unit of a good or service sold.

marginal utility. Satisfaction derived from the consumption of an additional unit of some economic good or service.

market. Institutional arrangement that facilitates the exchange of goods and/or services.

market data approach. One of the three traditional appraisal approaches. Produces an indication of value through the analysis of recent sales of similar properties.

market demand curve. Curve showing the amount of an economic good or service that will be demanded at various price levels. Demand curves are typically downward sloping, indicating that as price increases, demand decreases.

market price. See transaction price.

market rent. The rent a property would command on the open market if it were currently vacant and available.

market research. Activity undertaken to determine consumer attitudes; attempts to determine what consumers want, where they want it and how much they are willing to pay for it.

market simulation. An attempt to replicate the actions of buyers and sellers in the marketplace. In real estate, it would be an attempt to estimate the outcome of a transaction involving real property by simulating the actions of "most probable" buyers and sellers.

market value. The price at which a property can be acquired on the open market in an arm's-length transaction under all conditions requisite to a fair sale. The generally accepted definition presumes that both buyer and seller act prudently and knowledgeably and that the price is not affected by undue stimulus experienced by either party.

materialmen. Suppliers of materials in connection with construction or improvements of real property.

materialman's lien. Claim arising from having supplied materials in connection with construction or improvement of real property.

mean. In statistics, the arithmetic average.

mechanic's lien. Lien securing a claim that stems from having provided services in connection with construction or improvement of a property.

metes and bounds. A method of delineating real property boundaries by reference to enduring landmarks.

microeconomic theory. Theory of small economic units. Generally referred to as the *theory of the firm.*

modified internal rate of return. A variant of the internal rate of return, intended to eliminate the multiple root problem by discounting all negative cash flows back to the time an investment commitment must be made and by compounding all positive cash flows forward to the end of the final year of the investment holding period. The modified internal rate of return is the discount rate that equates the present value of all negative cash flows with the future value of all positive cash flows.

modified pass-throughs. Government National Mortgage Association security backed by a pool of insured mortgage loans. A pro-rata share of the repayment of interest and principal is "passed through" to holders of the pass-through securities.

Modified Uniform Limited Partnership Act. A modified version of the Uniform Limited Partnership Act, which carefully specifies actions limited partners can take without endangering their limited liability.

monetary policy. Use of control over the money supply to stimulate or dampen economic growth.

monopolistic competition. A market arrangement where any number of competitors sell goods or services sufficiently differentiated that buyers will not be entirely indifferent among them, so that selection will be affected by elements other than price alone.

monopoly elements. A characteristic of a good or service that differentiates it from other goods or services and thereby makes the others less acceptable as substitutes.

monthly constant. The monthly debt service obligation expressed as a percentage of the amount borrowed.

mortgage. A document that pledges real estate as collateral for a loan.

mortgage-backed securities. Securities backed by real estate mortgages as collateral.

mortgage bankers. Individuals or firms that originate real estate loans. They may either hold such loans in their own investment portfolios or sell them in the secondary market.

mortgage commitment. Obligation on the part of a lender to provide funds at some future date. Loan terms may be either fixed or those that prevail at the time the funds are to be advanced.

mortgage correspondents. Individual mortgage bankers or brokers representing an institutional lender in a specified geographic location.

mortgagee. Party to whom real estate is pledged under the terms of a mortgage. Typically the lender in a real estate transaction.

mortgage participation certificates. A bond backed by real estate as collateral. Bondholders participate in the proceeds of a group of mortgages that back the certificates.

mortgage REIT. A real estate investment trust that invests primarily in real estate loans secured by first mortgages.

mortgage warehousing. The process of inventorying real estate loans. Mortgage bankers or brokers sometimes inventory loans while assembling pools of loans for subsequent transfer to larger institutional real estate lenders.

mortgagor. Party pledging real estate under the terms of a mortgage. Borrower who pledges real estate as collateral for a loan.

most fitting use. Real estate use that optimally reconciles all public and private interests.

most probable selling price. A probabilistic estimate of the price at which a future property transaction will occur; a prediction of the transaction price that will emerge if a property is offered for sale under current market conditions for a reasonable length of time at terms of sale currently predominant for such properties.

most probable use. Use to which a property is most likely to be put. Recognizes that use is not certain. Most probable use is that use having the highest probability of occurrence. Recognizes the possibility of other uses while assigning lower probabilities to them.

multiple nuclei. The theory that once a metropolitan area's major central business district is completely developed, a series of miniature central business districts will spring up throughout the metropolitan area.

multiple regression. Statistical technique used to measure the association between a dependent variable and multiple independent variables.

multiplicative law of probability. See joint probabilities.

natural price. Adam Smith's concept of long-run, market-determined price. Smith held that the price of all goods and services will, over the long run, equal the cost of production.

neighborhood. Sometimes referred to as a grouping of similar buildings, residents or business enterprises.

neighborhood influences. Factors influencing the desirability of a neighborhood. These include physical, economic and locational characteristics.

neighborhood shopping centers. Shopping centers that serve a trade area from which customers can commute by automobile within roughly five to ten minutes. Anchor tenants are usually food stores and drugstores, which may occupy a combined total area between 35,000 and 50,000 square feet.

net cash flow. Net monetary benefits an individual or group of individuals receive as a reward for committing funds to an enterprise. Net cash flow before taxes ignores the tax effect of investments, and net cash flow after taxes accounts for the tax effects of investment.

net income multiplier. (See also gross income multiplier and income multiplier analysis) Property market value expressed as a multiple of its net operating income.

net lease. Lease arrangement under which tenants are required to pay all property operating costs.

net operating expenses. Total expenses associated with the operations of a real estate project.

net operating income. Effective gross revenue minus operating expenses.

net present value. Current capital value of all the benefits of an investment, minus the required initial cash outlay.

nominal interest rates. Quoted cost of borrowing. Actual or effective interest rates may be substantially higher due to charges such as loan origination fees and the cost of maintaining required compensating balances.

normalized expenses. An appraisal term for the operating expenses of a property as they would occur in a typical year.

normalized net operating income. The net income figure that would result when a typical year's operating expenses were subtracted from a typical year's effective gross income.

obligee. Individual who makes a promise to pay a specified sum under the terms of a promissory note. Typically a borrower.

obligor. Individual to whom a promise is made to pay a specified sum under the terms of a promissory note. Typically a lender.

offering memorandum. A document intended to fully disclose the nature of a private offering of a security.

oligopoly. A market arrangement characterized by few producers, into which entry by new producers is extremely difficult.

operating expense ratio. Operating expenses expressed as a percentage of effective gross income.

operating expenses. Cash expenditures required to maintain property in sufficient condition to generate effective gross revenue.

operating ratio. See operating expense ratio.

operative words of conveyance. Words used to indicate the intention to transfer title to real property.

opportunity cost of capital. Forgone opportunity to earn interest on funds committed to other investments.

option agreement. An agreement giving one party the right to buy or sell an asset within a specified time period at a fixed or determinable price.

overall capitalization rate. Net operating income divided by a property's market value. Also called the *free and clear rate of return.*

partial release. A mortgage clause providing for segments of a property to be released after specified lump-sum payments on the loan. Typically used in subdivision and development financing.

partnership. An association of two or more people who join together to carry on a business for profit.

partnership agreement. Document that specifies the rights and responsibilities of individuals who join together to carry on a business for profit. May be oral, but is usually written.

party wall. An exterior wall common to two contiguous structures, each under different ownership.

passive activity. Any trade or business is a passive activity for a taxpayer who is not actively involved in operations on a "regular, continuous, and substantial (year-round) basis."

passive activity income. (See also passive activity) Income from passive trade or business activities. Income from passive activities can be used to offset losses from other passive activities. Any passive activity income not offset by losses is merged with taxable income from other sources.

passive activity losses. (See also passive activity) Losses from passive trade or business activities. Passive activity losses can generally be offset against only passive activity income. Any remaining passive activity losses, with certain important exceptions, must be carried over and applied against future years' passive activity income, even though a taxpayer may have substantial taxable income from nonpassive sources during the year of the loss.

pass-through certificates. Certificates backed by a pool of insured mortgages. Interest and principal collected is used to pay interest on the certificates as well as retire them.

payback period. The amount of time required for an investor to recover the capital committed to a venture.

payee. Individual to whom a promise has been made to repay a specified sum at some future date under the provisions of a promissory note.

percentage clause. Lease provision that specifies rental based on some base rate, plus a percentage of the tenant's gross sales.

percentage lease. Lease that provides for rental payments based upon the tenant's gross sales.

permanent loan. See end loan.

perpetuity. A never-ending stream of payments or receipts.

personal consumption expenditures. Economic term used to describe individual spending on such items as food, shelter and clothing.

personal property. Ownership interests in all properties other than real property. Examples include securities, partnership interest in a business and ownership of an automobile. Also called *personalty.*

personalty. See personal property.

physical deterioration. Term used by appraisers to describe any loss in value due to physical wear.

physical durability. Ability of a building to withstand physical wear and tear.

plat. Diagram of a proposed subdivision, showing the location of all streets, sites and easements.

police power. Power of a municipality to enforce laws designed to promote health, safety, morals and general welfare. Building codes, planning objectives and zoning ordinances are all enforced through the exercise of police power.

population. In statistics, the entire universe of data from which samples are drawn.

portfolio income. Income from interest, dividends, rents, royalties, gain from disposition of investment property, passive activity income that is treated as portfolio income under the phase-in rules of the Tax Reform Act of 1986 and income from a trade or business in which the taxpayer does not materially participate (unless the activity is a "passive activity" under the passive loss rules).

portfolio risk. Overall risk associated with ownership of a group of assets. Risks associated with one investment may decline when combined with another investment having offsetting risk patterns.

possibility of a reverter. Residual interest in a property that becomes effective when a life estate terminates.

potential gross income. The maximum amount of revenue a property would produce if fully rented at market rates.

potential gross rent. The amount of rental revenue a property would generate if there were no vacancies.

preliminary prospectus. Memorandum providing full disclosure of all items pertinent to a public security offering. A preliminary prospectus must be submitted to and approved by the Securities and Exchange Commission prior to any advertising of the offering.

prepaid interest. Interest paid prior to the date on which it is due. In real estate loans, prepaid interest is often deducted from the loan amount when funds are advanced.

prepayment clause. Typically a clause in a mortgage specifying penalties to be paid by the borrower in the event a loan is prepaid.

present value. The value today of anticipated future receipts or disbursements.

present value approach. Technique used to express anticipated future cash flows in terms of their current worth by adjusting for the opportunity cost of capital.

present value of an annuity. Present worth of a series of level payments received at even intervals. Current value reflects the compounded opportunity cost of capital.

price elasticity. A measure of the responsiveness of supply (price elasticity of supply) or demand (price elasticity of demand) to changes in price of a product or service.

price inelastic. (See also price elasticity) A market condition in which price reductions cause a decline in total revenue and price increases result in increased total revenue.

price makers. Economic units operating on a large enough scale to have some control over the price of their goods or services in the marketplace.

price searchers. Economic units that recognize that they cannot completely control the price at which goods are exchanged, but also understand that they do affect market prices. Price searchers must be constantly aware of the impact their pricing decisions will have on the decisions of competitors.

price takers. Economic units operating on such a small scale that they have no control over the price of their goods or services in the marketplace.

primary data. Data gathered by researchers specifically for the problem with which they are currently grappling.

primary mortgage markets. Markets in which real estate loans originate.

principal. In finance, the amount upon which interest liability is computed.

principal meridians. Imaginary lines extending north and south between the Earth's poles, used as reference lines in property surveys.

principle of substitution. Valuation principle stating that a person is not justified in paying more for a property than the cost to construct or acquire a substitute property.

private goods. Economic goods where consumption by one individual reduces the amount available for consumption by others.

private grants. Voluntary transfer of title to real property. These include transfer for consideration, gifts and bequests.

private offering. See private placement.

private placement. Sale of a securities offering to a small group as opposed to a public offering, where sale is advertised to the general public. Sometimes called a *private offering.*

private placement memorandum. Prospectus for a private placement. Does not have to be submitted for SEC approval, but must provide full disclosure.

probability. A measure of the chance of occurrence associated with any possible outcome.

probability distribution. An array of all possible outcomes and their related probabilities of occurrence.

probability of acceptance error. The probability that accepting a proposed investment will prove to have been a mistake.

processing costs. The cost of converting unfinished goods to finished goods.

product. (See also goods and services) The end result of the production process.

productivity. The ability of a property to generate utility, or want-satisfying power. A property's ability to command rent is a measure of its productivity.

profitability index. Measure of present value per dollar of cash outlay, calculated by dividing the present value of expected future cash flows by the initial cash outlay.

promissory note. Agreement containing promise to pay a specified sum at some specific future date.

property management. Overseeing the operations of real property for others. Includes renting space, collecting rentals, supervising maintenance, budgeting, etc.

prospectus. A document that fully discloses the nature of a securities offering.

public goods. Economic goods or services for which consumption by one individual does not reduce the amount available for consumption by others. Also called *collective goods.*

public infrastructure. In real estate, the systems used to deliver public services to a site. Includes streets, sidewalks, sewer pipes, water pipes, etc.

public issue. Securities issue offered for sale to the general public. Such an issue requires registration of a prospectus with the Securities and Exchange Commission. Also referred to as a *public offering.*

public offering. See public issue.

purchase-money mortgage. Mortgage given by a buyer to a seller to secure part payment of the purchase price. A purchase-money mortgage is

typically recorded when deed is passed, establishing its precedence over all other claims.

purchase option. The right to purchase a property within a specified time and at a predetermined price.

pure profit. See economic rent.

quantity demanded. Amount of an economic good or service purchasers will buy per period of time at a specific price.

quantity survey method. A technique used to estimate the cost of new real property improvements. Costs are estimated in the same way an architect or builder figures construction costs.

quarter sections. Squares resulting from the intersection of guide meridians and standard parallels are divided into 36 sections, each containing 640 acres. Sections are then divisible into four quarter sections containing 160 acres each.

quiet title suit. Suit filed by an adverse possessor to gain title to property by adverse possession.

quitclaim deed. A deed that purports to convey only those rights in a property that are possessed by the person making the conveyance, with no warrants that any such rights in fact exist.

radial/axial development. Theory of urban development based on the idea that businesses locate along major arterial streets, creating a radial or axial pattern of growth outward from the central business district.

real assets. Physical things with economic value, such as land, buildings, machinery, gold, antiques and so forth. In contrast with financial assets such as promissory notes, bonds and commercial paper, real assets tend to hold their value during periods of price inflation.

real estate investment. Acquiring an ownership or a leasehold interest in real property, with a profit motive.

real estate investment trusts (REITs). Untaxed corporate entities organized to pool the resources of individual investors for investment in real estate. Some REITs invest in mortgages while others take ownership positions.

real estate service. Benefits of use of real property. Real estate provides shelter and location for users.

Real Property Administrator (RPA). Professional designation conferred on property managers by the Building Owners and Managers Association International. Designation is a sign of professional achievement for those who completely fulfill prescribed educational and experiential requirements.

recording statutes. Statutory provisions for permanent records of all transactions involving real property.

recovery property. Property subject to the cost recovery allowance provisions first introduced into the tax system by the 1981 revision of the Internal Revenue Code.

rectangular survey system. Use of a grid-type arrangement to identify land in a branch area by reference to a single geographic point.

redevelopment. Process of clearing older structures in an area and replacing them with new buildings.

red herring. Term sometimes used for a preliminary securities prospectus, which must be submitted to and approved by the Securities and Exchange Commission before any advertising is undertaken for a public issue.

redlining. Term used to describe the unwillingness of certain financial institutions to provide real property financing in certain areas; derived from the practice of delineating areas with red lines on city maps.

regional planning. Setting standards for the overall development of large geographical areas. Standards apply to land use, transportation systems, infrastructure, etc.

regional shopping center. A shopping center that draws the majority of its customers from a trade area extending from 15 to 30 minutes in

driving time from the center. It may encompass 200,000 to 400,000 square feet of retail space and usually features one or two major department stores as anchor tenants.

registered historic district. Any area listed in the National Registry of Historic Places. Also includes any area so designated by appropriate state or local statute, provided that the Secretary of the Interior certifies that the statute will substantially achieve its purpose of preservation and rehabilitation and that the district meets substantially all the requirements for listing in the National Registry.

regression analysis. Statistical technique used to measure the association among two or more variables.

Regulation B. Implementing regulation of the Federal Reserve to enforce provisions of the Equal Credit Opportunity Act enacted in 1974.

Regulation Z. Implementing regulation of the Federal Reserve to enforce provisions of the Truth-in-Lending Law enacted in 1969.

rehabilitation. Process of refurbishing older or physically deteriorated buildings for current use.

reliction. Recession of the water line of a lake or river resulting in the exposure of additional dry land.

remainderman. Individual possessing a remainder interest in real property. Remainder interest becomes operative upon expiration of a life estate.

remainders. (See also reversion) Residual interests that become effective when the life estate of another ends.

renegotiable rate mortgage. Mortgage with an interest rate subject to redetermination at fixed intervals, as specified in the body of the mortgage or the accompanying promissory note.

rent concessions. Agreements between landlord and tenant that reduce actual rental payments or receipts below those specified in a lease. A landlord might, for example, give one month's free occupancy, thereby reducing the effective rental rate over the entire occupancy period. Also simply called *concessions.*

rent escalator clauses. Lease provisions that require tenants to pay all operating expenses above amounts specified in their leases.

rent roll. A record of all tenants, showing the rent paid by each.

replacement cost. Appraisal term used to describe the cost of building a structure similar in utility to the one for which value is being estimated. Replacement cost assumes construction at current standards.

reproduction cost. Appraisal term used to describe the cost of building a structure identical to the one for which value is being estimated.

reservation. Clause used in a deed to withhold some portion of the grantor's property rights.

reserve for repairs and replacements. Appraisal adjustment used in the normalization of operating expenses to account for repairs or replacements that do not occur on an annual basis.

residential member (RM). Professional designation conferred by the American Institute of Real Estate Appraisers on individuals specializing in residential valuation. Designation signifies satisfaction of prescribed educational and experiential requirements.

residential specialists. Real estate brokers who concentrate on the sale of single-family detached dwellings, townhouses, condominiums or cooperatives.

residual capitalization. Appraisal technique that splits income between land and building. If building value is known, remaining income is capitalized to estimate land value, and if land value is known, remaining income is capitalized to estimate building value.

restrictive covenant. Promise to refrain from using land or buildings for purposes specified in the clause creating the covenant.

revenue bonds. Securities used to finance revenue-generating projects where the income produced by the undertaking will be used for interest payments and retirement of securities.

reversion. Term used to describe the interest of one who will receive title if a conditional fee is extinguished.

right of survivorship. (See also joint tenancy) A right unique to joint tenancy. Should one joint tenant die, his or her interest passes to the remaining joint tenants.

right to rescind. Right of an individual to terminate an agreement, returning all parties to the legal position or relationship existing prior to the agreement.

riparian lands. Lands abutting waterways or lakes. Title may extend to the water's edge or to the center of the water, depending on whether the waterway is navigable.

risk. Measurable likelihood of variance from an expected outcome. Risk is generally measured as variance or standard deviation.

risk-adjusted discount rate. A discount rate that includes the minimum acceptable yield on a riskless investment, plus a premium to compensate the investor for perceived risk associated with the venture under consideration.

risk averters. Refers to the economic concept that individuals prefer less risk to more at a given level of return. Most individuals avoid risk and will assume additional risk only if it is accompanied by expectations of additional return.

risk-free discount rate. Opportunity cost of capital based on riskless alternative investments.

risk premium. Incremental return necessary to induce investors to assume additional risk.

risk-reward indifference curve. A graphic representation of the relationship between perceived risk and acceptable rates of expected return where the investor will be equally satisfied by all risk-reward combinations.

r-square (r^2). See coefficient of determination.

S corporation. See tax option corporation.

sample. A group of observations drawn from a larger body of data (called a *population* or *universe*) and thought to be representative of the larger body.

secondary data. Data employed in a research project that were previously gathered for some other purpose.

secondary financial markets. Markets comprised of arrangements for buying and selling existing financial instruments.

secondary mortgage market. A market in which existing mortgage notes are traded.

Section 1031 exchange. See like-kind exchange.

sector theory. A theory developed by Homer Hoyt and based upon the observation that successive waves of residential development within a given socioeconomic class tend to continue outward from the urban center in a wedge-shaped pattern.

seizin. A covenant found in a warranty deed whereby the grantor warrants that he or she does in fact possess the rights or interest being transferred.

senior mortgage. A mortgage that takes priority over all other mortgages.

Senior Real Estate Analyst (SREA). A professional designation awarded by the Society of Real Estate Appraisers.

Senior Real Property Appraiser (SRPA). A professional designation awarded by the Society of Real Estate Appraisers. The SRPA designation is awarded to commercial and industrial appraisers.

Senior Residential Appraiser (SRA). A professional designation awarded by the Society of Real Estate Appraisers.

sensitivity analysis. Financial analysis in which all variables but one are held constant and the

result of a change in the remaining variable on the outcome is analyzed.

serial bonds. Secured debt instruments that are retired in the sequence of their individual serial numbers.

serial correlation. A measure of the extent to which causal factors influence outcomes over two or more time periods.

servient tenement. Land bearing the burden of an easement appurtenant.

shift in demand. The result of a shift in the relationship between price and quantity.

short-term capital gains. Taxable gains on the sale of capital assets that have been owned for six months or less.

simple linear regression. A statistical technique used to measure the association between two variables.

simulation. The construction of a model intended as a simplified representation of reality, within which the impact of various factors can be isolated and quantified.

sinking fund payments. Payments drawn from a fund set aside from the income of property that, with accrued interest, will eventually pay for replacement of the improvements.

sinking fund recapture technique. A recapture computation that involves computing the recapture rate such that the sum of recovered capital and compound interest thereon will, over the useful life of the wasting asset, accumulate an amount equal to its cost.

space-time. A four-dimensional concept combining the three dimensions of space with a fourth dimension of time. Real estate services are typically sold in space-time units.

special agent. One whose authority to act is limited to a particular job or a specific task. Typically, a real estate broker acts in the capacity of a special agent.

special assessment. A legal charge against real estate by a public authority in order to pay the cost of public improvements such as streetlights, sidewalks and other street improvements.

special warranty deed. A deed in which the grantor warrants or guarantees title only against defects arising during his or her ownership of the property and not against preexisting defects.

specific asset syndication. A type of syndication where the promoter gains control of a property and then assembles a group of investors.

speculation. Assumption of business risk in hope of gain; purchase or sale of assets in hope of benefiting from market fluctuations.

speculative construction. A business strategy where a developer/builder starts construction before any homes are sold, in anticipation of sufficient market demand to render the project profitable.

spread. The difference between interest earned on mortgage loans and interest paid to depositors by financial intermediaries.

standard deviation. A measure of dispersion about the mean of a probability distribution, frequently employed as an indication of risk associated with an investment venture. The square root of the variance.

standard error of the forecast. The degree of confidence to be placed in a forecast value for a dependent variable. Conceptually similar to the same measure as calculated in simple linear regression.

standard metropolitan statistical area. A federally designated geographically described urban area with cohesive patterns of trade, communication, employment and transportation.

standard parallels. Imaginary lines running parallel with base lines (east-west lines) at 24-mile intervals, used as reference points in surveys employing the rectangular survey method.

standby financing. An arrangement where a lender agrees to keep a certain amount of money available to a prospective borrower for a specified period of time.

standby forward commitment. An agreement for future purchase of mortgage notes at yield rates specified in advance. These commitments are sold by and binding upon the Federal National Mortgage Association but are optional for holders of the commitments.

standby loan commitment. A binding option sold for a nonreturnable standby fee by a lender to a borrower, providing that the lender will loan a specific amount on stated terms to a borrower at any time within a stated future period. The borrower may or may not exercise the option.

statistical induction. Drawing conclusions about an underlying population from data contained in a sample.

statistical inference. Drawing conclusions about the future from a measured record of the past.

statutory exemption. The portion of income that is exempt from the alternative minimum tax.

statutory right of redemption. A statutory right granting a defaulting mortgagor an additional opportunity to recover foreclosed property. Limited in time by state statute.

straight-line method. A method of computing depreciation or cost recovery allowances whereby the allowance is claimed in equal annual increments.

strict foreclosure. Foreclosure accomplished by transferring a defaulting mortgagor's title directly to the mortgagee.

strong form efficiency hypothesis. See efficient markets.

subagent. One appointed by an agent to perform some duty, in whole or in part relating to the agency.

subcontractor. A person who contracts to do work for someone who has a larger contract to do the job. For example, electrical work on a new house might be done on a subcontract for the contractor who has overall responsibility for building the house.

subdivider. One who buys undeveloped acreage wholesale, segments it into smaller parcels and sells it retail.

subdivision. See land development.

subdivision controls. Regulations imposed by various levels of government to regulate or control subdivision operations.

subjective value. The value of an asset to the present owner or to a prospective purchaser. Similar to the economic concept of value in use.

subordination agreement. A clause in a mortgage or lease stating that the right of the holder shall be secondary or subordinate to a subsequent encumbrance.

subscription agreement. A document that specifies the relationship between limited partners and the sponsoring general partner in a limited partnership arrangement.

substitute basis. The initial tax basis of property acquired in a like-kind exchange. The substitute basis reflects any deferred gain or loss on the property tendered in the exchange.

summation technique. A method used for developing capitalization rates, based upon the idea that investors must be compensated to induce them to invest their wealth and that additional compensation is required for risk bearing and for illiquidity.

superregional shopping center. A shopping center that draws customers from an extremely wide geographical area and supports very large concentrations of retail facilities. Superregional centers frequently feature as much as 500,000 to 750,000 square feet of retail space. They may have as many as four major department stores as anchor tenants.

supply. The relationship between price and the quantity of a product suppliers place on the market during a specified time period, for all possible prices.

supply to sell. Desired decrease in a market participant's inventory of a product, at a specific price.

symmetric probability distribution. A probability distribution in which each side is a mirror image of the other.

syndicate. A group of two or more people united for the purpose of making and operating an investment. A syndicate may operate as a corporation, a general partnership or a limited partnership.

table of residuals. A listing of differences between actual values for a variable and those values predicted by a regression equation.

takeout loan. See end loan.

tax auction. A procedure for selling tax-delinquent land or real property where verbal or written offers are taken and the property is sold to the highest bidder.

tax basis. See initial tax basis.

tax conduit. A partnership characteristic whereby tax-deductible losses "pass through" the partnership "conduit" and are reported by each partner in accordance with his or her individual ownership interest in the partnership.

tax credits. Direct offsets against a taxpayer's income tax liability, provided as tax incentives to induce actions thought to be in the best interests of the nation.

tax deductions. (See also itemized deductions) Reductions in taxable income.

tax deed. A deed to property taken by government for nonpayment of taxes and resold at auction pursuant to law.

tax-deferred exchange. See like-kind exchange.

tax-free exchange. See like-kind exchange.

tax lien. A lien placed on a taxpayer's property by government for nonpayment of taxes.

tax option corporation. A qualifying corporation whose shareholders have elected to be taxed directly for their shares of corporate income, rather than having the corporation itself incur income tax liability. Provisions are found in Subchapter S of the Internal Revenue Code. Sometimes called an S corporation.

tax preference item. Tax deductions or exemptions that are added back to adjusted gross income for purposes of computing the alternative minimum tax liability.

tax schedule income. The amount of taxable income used as a reference for computing income tax liability when employing tax rate schedules provided by the Internal Revenue Service.

tax stops. Lease provisions that require tenants to pay all property taxes beyond some specified level.

technical analysis. Attempting to estimate future changes in market values by investigating the past market behavior.

tenancy at sufferance. Wrongful occupancy, which can be terminated by a property owner at any time.

tenancy at will. A tenancy stating no fixed period and that either landlord or tenant may terminate at any time, or in the time specified by statute, usually 30 days.

tenancy by the entirety. A type of joint tenancy that can exist only between spouses, in which wife and husband take conveyance of the tenancy interest in common, with that interest being treated as a single, indivisible unit and with the survivor continuing to hold the tenancy as a matter of right.

tenancy from period to period. A tenancy by one who holds a leasehold interest for an unstated period and pays rent each period, each payment serving as renewal for an additional period. This often results from the holding over of a previous specified-term tenancy on which rental was paid each period.

tenancy in common. Tenancy by two or more parties holding an interest in the same property,

that interest being undivided, although not necessarily equal in each holder.

theorems. Fundamental mathematical rules from which various mathematical operations are derived.

time preference for money. Preference for more immediate rather than delayed receipt of funds, so that investment benefits are more valued the sooner they are received.

time series surveys. See longitudinal studies.

time value of money. See time preference for money.

title closing. The meeting of parties to a sales contract at a designated place and time for the purpose of executing the contract.

title defect. A possible legal difficulty that may limit the marketability of the title.

title insurance. Insurance against losses resulting from the passage of legally invalid title, issued by a title insurance company after a title search by that company has established that legally valid title exists in the seller, who then is able to pass that title to the insured.

title insurance policy. A contract wherein the title insurer agrees to indemnify the insured against losses resulting from imperfect title.

title search. A circumspect review of all documents and records in the recorder's office pertaining to a property to determine if the seller has good title to the property.

title transfer. To convey or relinquish title to another party.

Torrens system. A system of registering title to real property that accurately determines the ownership of land and every lien and claim upon it. Under this system, land title is registered in much the same way as is title to an automobile.

township. A six-mile-square area containing 36 sections, each one mile square, used in the rectangular survey system of land description.

trade area. The geographic area from which a store or shopping center draws the majority of its patronage.

transaction costs. Items such as brokerage fees, recording fees, transfer taxes and attorney fees, incurred in connection with a real estate transaction.

transaction price. The price at which a transaction actually occurred; the outcome of a bargaining process between buyer and seller. Sometimes called *market price.*

transaction range. The range of prices at which a transaction can occur between an owner and a prospective purchaser. The owner's subjective value determines the lower level of the transactions range; the prospective buyer's subjective value determines the upper level.

transactions balances. The quantity of money required to finance general business operations and satisfy day-to-day demands of householders.

transfer costs. (See also implicit transfer costs, explicit transfer costs) Costs of transportation between linked sites.

transport breakpoints. Points along major transportation routes where the mode of transport must change.

trust account. A bank account separate and apart and physically segregated from a broker's own funds, in which a broker is required by state law to deposit all monies collected for clients. Similar to an escrow or special account.

trust agreement. A document that sets forth terms of security arrangements and instructs the trustee in the event of default.

trust deed. See deed of trust.

trustee. The person in a trust relationship who holds property for the benefit of another person (the beneficiary).

trust indenture. See deed of trust.

Truth-in-Lending Law. One of a series of modern consumer protection acts, requiring lenders to fully disclose the rates of interest, other charges and all terms and conditions of each loan, in writing and clearly stated.

uncertainty. An environment holding an unknown number of possible outcomes, where there is no significant information about the relative chance of occurrence of each.

unfavorable financial leverage. Use of borrowed funds when their cost exceeds the rate of return on assets being financed.

Uniform Limited Partnership Act. A model law to govern creation and operation of limited partnership entities that has been enacted (in some cases, in substantially revised form) by every state except Louisiana.

unit-in-place method. A means of assessing replacement costs, in which an appraiser estimates the cost of building components separately, developing a unit cost for each component, and including overhead and profit allocation estimates as well as direct labor and materials cost, and then adds all costs together to reach total cost and thereby replacement cost.

universal agents. Agents who are empowered to perform all legal acts for their principals.

universe. In statistics, the entire population of data from which samples are drawn.

urban growth. An increase in the intensity of use of land resources. This may or may not entail an increase in population of an urban land area. It usually includes higher capital investment per unit of land employed and increased productivity associated with urban economic processes.

useful life. The period over which a property will benefit the owner's trade or business.

utility. An economic term for the want-satisfying power embodied in a good or service.

value in exchange. The value an asset can command in the marketplace.

value in use. The value of an asset to its owner or to a prospective owner.

variable-rate mortgage. A financing instrument that permits the lender to alter the interest rate, with a certain period of advanced notice, based on a specific base index.

variance. A measure of dispersion of possible values about the midpoint of a probability distribution of possible outcomes, frequently employed as a measure of risk. The square of the standard deviation.

vendee. The purchaser of real estate under articles of agreement or a contract for deed.

vendor. The seller of real estate under articles of agreement or a contract for deed.

void. To have no force or effect; that which is unenforceable.

voidable. That which is capable of being adjudged void but is not void unless action is taken to make it so.

voluntary conveyance. Voluntary transfer by a defaulting mortgagor of the mortgaged property to the mortgagee, to avoid a foreclosure suit and a possible deficiency judgment.

warranty deed. A deed that contains a clause warranting that title to real property is clear and the property is unencumbered.

weighted average cost of capital. Capital cost computed by weighting the cost of each component in accordance with the proportion of total capital it comprises.

wholesale price index. An index of changes in the wholesale price of a representative "basket" of goods, referenced to a specified base period.

worker's compensation insurance. Insurance against claims for injuries sustained by employees.

wraparound lender. (See also wraparound mortgage) Assumes responsibility for meeting debt service obligations on the mortgage note that has been "wrapped."

wraparound mortgage. A mortgage subordinate to, but still including, the balance due on a pre-existing mortgage note, in addition to any amount to be disbursed on the new note. Also called an *all-inclusive mortgage.*

zoning ordinance. The fixing by government of geographic areas in which specified kinds of buildings and businesses may be developed.

zoning regulations. See zoning ordinance.

Index

A

Absolute monopoly, 33
Absorption rates, 350
Acceleration clause, 128
Acquisition
  cost, 160
  credit, 212–13
Active investors, 4–5
Active participation, 216
Adjustable rate mortgage (ARM), 131
Adjusted rate of return, 243–44
After-tax cash flow (ATCF), 166–67, 185
  for commercial rehabilitation, 368–71
  forecast, 257
  for industrial building, 379–80
  for industrial subdivision, 353
  for office building, 383–85
  for shopping center, 392–94
Agriculture census, 79
All-inclusive mortgage, 134–36
Alternative minimum tax, 214, 217
Amortization, 117–18
  alternatives, 130–31
  factor, 142–43
  monthly payment on one-dollar debt,
    142
  schedule, 152, 437
  table, 437, 440–41
Anchor tenants, 386
Annuity
  in advance, 443–44
  deferred, 441–42
  payments, 431–32
  perpetual, 435–36
  present value of, 432–35
  tables, 440
Apartment building
  after-tax cash flow, 167, 185
  capitalization rates, 104
  debt amortization schedule, 151–52
  depreciation schedule, 164–65
  initial tax basis, 160
  operating statement example, 88–92
  property sales cash flow, 183–84
  selling and tax consequences, 184
Appraisal, 161, 331
Appraisal Journal, 3
Appreciation, 114–16
Articles of agreement, 132–33
Asset
  liquidity, 168
  performance data, 9
Atomistic market, 32–33, 39
  market equilibrium, 35–36
  market research and, 50

At-risk rule, 171–72
Axial development pattern, 44, 45

B

Back-door feasibility approach, 338–40
Balance sheet, 414
Balloon payment, 130, 241
BankAmerica Corp., 212
Barrett, G. Vincent, 58
Beck, Kenneth, 65
Before-tax cash flow, 151, 336, 352, 355
Benefit stream, 13–15
Berkshire Hathaway, Inc., 212
Bid-rent curve, 44–50
Blair, John P., 58
Blanket mortgages, 129, 137
Blind pool syndication, 407
Blue sky laws, 406
Bolten, Steven E., 286
Boot, 191–93, 203–4
Borrowed money, 105
Break-even
  occupancy level, 269–70, 338
  ratio, 226
  rental rates, 271
Brigham, Eugene F., 241
Brokerage commissions, 408
Broker's rate of return, 229
Brueggeman, William, 9
Building cost estimate, 361
Building Owners and Managers
    Association (BOMA), 79, 381
Buildings, 5
Bullet loan, 130–31
Burgess, Ernest W., 43, 44
Business. *See also* Corporation; Limited
    partnership; Partnership
  location decisions, 44
  risk, 266, 271
Buyer
  position summary, 253
  transaction range, 254

C

Cambon, Barbara, 9
Canadian rollover loan, 131
Capital
  cost of, 249–50
  cost recovery allowances, 368–69. *See
    also* Cost recovery
  expenditures, 166
  gains/losses, 182–83
Capitalization rate (k), 103–4, 227
  for industrial building, 377–79
  for office building, 384

for shopping center, 391
Capital recovery schedule, 383
Cash flow (CF), 58
  after-tax, 166–67, 185
    for commercial rehabilitation, 368–71
    forecast, 257
    for industrial building, 379–80
    for industrial subdivision, 353
    for office building, 383–85
    for shopping center, 392–94
  analysis for industrial subdivision, 354
  before tax, 151, 336
    for industrial subdivision, 352, 355
  discounted
    model, 307–12
    technique, 254–59
  distribution and value relationships,
    14–15
  expected annual, 301
  financial alternatives and, 113–15, 119
  forecasting, 295, 390–91
  partially correlated, 315–17
  patterns, 312–17
  perfectly correlated, 313–14
  probability distribution of, 302
  projections, 288, 342
  property sales and, 183–84
  uncorrelated, 315
Cash-on-cash rate of return, 228–29
Cash proceeds, 369–70
Census Bureau, 68, 72
Center for Strategic and International
    Studies, 8
Central business district, 44
Centralized management, 173
Certainty, 296
Certainty-equivalent, 283–86, 293
Certified historic structure, 210
CFIFa, 462–63
Chen, A.H., 9
Chen, H.Y., 283
Churchill, Jr., Gilbert A., 59, 62
City analysis, 342
Coefficient
  of correlation, 313
  of variation, 306–7
Coldwell Banker, 7
Commerce Department, 68
Commercial banks, 121–22
Commercial Mortgage Alert, 123
Commercial mortgage-backed securities
    (CMBS), 123
Commercial rehabilitation, 367–71
Commingled real estate fund (CREF), 9
Communication, 69
Community shopping centers, 387

Comparable properties, 89–90
Competitive analysis, 66
Complexity, 60
Compound interest, 223, 425, 426–29, 467
Compound value, 427–29, 447–48
Computerization
  data processing, 24
  financial calculator, 445–52
  modeling, 4
Concentric ring model, 43
Concession, 88
Conditional probabilities, 300
Condominium expense data, 79
Conduit lending sources, 123
Consideration, 180
Construction, 208, 359–61
Consumer price index, 275
Consumer profile, 69
Continuity of life, 173
Continuous distribution, 302
Contractors, 360
Contract price, 186–87
Contract rate, 140
Control, 404
Corporation, 169, 177
Cost
  of borrowing, 120–21
  of land, 351, 354
  profits to operate and, 25–26
Cost recovery, 114
  allowable periods, 162
  for commercial rehabilitation, 367–68
  computing allowance, 162–63
  depreciation schedule for, 164–65
  recapture, 181–82
Cost-benefit trade-off, 61
Cotenancy arrangement, 168–69
Covariance (CV), 319
Credit
  government-sponsored, 136–37
  instruments, 127–30
  terms, 130–32
Cross-sectional data, 70
Current yield, 114–15, 268
Custom building, 360

D

Data collection/analysis
  complexity and, 60
  cost-benefit trade-off, 61
  cross-sectional, 70
  for descriptive research, 69–71
  geographic information systems, 71–74
  market conditions and, 60
  for market research, 62–64
  peer-group property comparisons, 83–86
  processing, 24
  sources, 67–69, 78–80
  for subject property, 82–83
  time series, 70
Dealer property, 182
Debt, 4, 5
  accumulation, compound interest and, 427
  amortization schedule, 151–52
  constants, 437
  investor, 5
  position, 13, 14

Debt coverage ratio, 226–27
  constraints, 149–50
  financial leverage and, 116–18
  lender objectives, 334–35, 338
Debt service, 336, 383
Debt service constant, 114
Debt-to-equity ratio, 116
Decision model, 12–13
Deeds of trust, 129–30
Default
  provisions, 128
  ratio, 338, 340
Deferred annuity, 441–42
Deferred interest loans, 131
Demand, 22, 60, 95–96, 106
  analysis, 66
  closed market system, 30
  curve, 22, 23
  derived, 374
  determinants, 23–24
  function, 22
  for industrial space, 373–74
  for office space, 380
  shifters, 22–26
Depreciation, 114. *See also* Cost recovery
  allowance, 162–65, 255
  for commercial rehabilitation, 367–68
  for office building, 382–83
  recapture of, 181–82
  shopping center schedule, 388–89, 390
Descriptive research, 69–71, 75
Development, 357–58, 371
  construction phase of, 359–60
  developer profit, 364
  feasibility analysis, 358–59
  financing, 359
  patterns, 43–44
  shopping center case study for, 360–65
Directors, 412
Discount (k), 223, 425, 426
  formulas, 467
  points, 140–41, 145
  rate, 247–50, 281–83, 293
Discounted cash flow
  analysis, 281
  model, standard deviation, 307–12
  technique, 254–59
Discrete probability distributions, 302
Distribution
  geographic, 324–25
  normal, 465
  objective probability, 298
  probability, 301–2
  subjective probability, 298
Diversification, 320, 401
  real estate investment trusts and, 416
  real estate strategies for, 324–25
  risk management tool for, 274
Dividends, 417
Documentation, of securities, 406
Dollars and Cents of Shopping Centers, 79
Downtown and Suburban Office Building Experience Exchange Report, 79, 281

E

Economic states, forecast of, 300–301
Effective gross income, 88–90, 92–93, 338

Effective interest rate, 140–49, 152
Efficient frontier, 321–23
Efficient market, 273–74
Efficient portfolio, 321, 323–24
Employee Retirement Income Security Act (ERISA), 6
End-loan commitment, 359
Equilibrium, 35, 36, 60
Equilibrium price, 26
Equity, 4, 5
  dividend rate, 227–28
  funds, 335–36
  investor, 5, 335, 338–40
  kickers, 132
  liquidating, 208
  participation, 132, 137
  position, 13, 14
  real estate investment trust, 412, 413–14, 416, 418
  reversion, after tax, 379
  valuation. 4
Estate settlement, 169
Estate taxes, 202
Excess accumulated earnings tax, 169
Exchange rates, 7
Exchanges, 200–201
Executive summary, 66, 341
Executory contracts, 132
Expected value, 302–3
Expense Analysis: Condominiums, Cooperatives and PUDs, 79
Expense stops, 275
Explicit transfer costs, 45

F

Feasibility analysis, 330, 343
  development, 358–59
  financial, 331–33
  preliminary, 334–40
  purpose of, 331–33
  rehabilitation proposal, 366
  report format, 341–42
  steps in, 333–34
Federal Reserve Banks, 68
Financial analysis, 342
Financial calculators, 445–52
Financial leverage, 123
  amount of, 117–21
  break-even occupancy levels, 269
  break-even rental rates, 271
  cost of borrowing, 120–21
  gain amplification, 114–16
  measurement of, 116–17
  popularity of, 112–16
  range of outcomes, 267–68
  risk and, 118–19, 267
  spread and, 113–14
  taxation and, 114, 207–8
Financial management rate of return, 244
Financial ratios, 226–27
Financial risk, 266, 267–70
Financial tables, 437–44
Financing
  alternative arrangements, 132–36, 146–49
  for commercial rehabilitation, 367
  for development, 359
  for industrial building, 376

for office building, 381–82
for shopping center, 362, 388
for subdivision, 347
Findley, M. Chapman, 244
Fire and extended coverage insurance, 270
Footloose industries, 374–75
Forecasting
after-tax cash flow, 166–67, 357–58, 383–85
discounted cash flow, 255–56
first-year operating, 256
four-quadrant matrix, 64–65
gross income, 95–99
industrial building income and expenses, 376
net operating income, 100–103
operating expenses, 99–100
reconstruction and, 92
rental revenue, 66
revenue, 105
sales proceeds, 377–79
shopping center cash flow, 389–92
Foreign exchange rates, 7
Foreign Investment Real Property Tax Act (FIRPTA), 216–17
Foreign investors, 7–8. 216–17, 218
Free-and-clear rate of return, 227
Free transferability of interests, 173, 174
Front door feasibility approach, 335–38
Fully amortizing loans, 130
Functional efficiency, 86–87, 96
Functional obsolescence, 87, 96
Future value (FV)
of annuity, 447–48, 467
of dollar, 445–47, 456–57
formulas, 467
relationship to present value, 431
Fuzzy efficient frontier, 324

G

Gains, 203–4
capital, 182
financial leverage and, 114–16
installment method, 186
as ordinary income, 181–82
realized, 180–81
recognized, 184–85, 187–88
on sales, 183–84
Gap financing, 130–31
General partnership, 170
Gentrification, 365
Geographic distribution, 324–25
Geographic information systems (GIS), 71–74, 75
Gift
of property, 201–3
taxes, 201, 202
Giliberto, Michael, 9
Government census, 79
Graaskamp, James, 332
Graduated payment mortgages, 131
Gross income
effective, 88–90, 92–93, 338
estimated, 91
forecasting, 95–99
for industrial subdivisions, 351
multipliers, 225–26, 369
Gross profit ratio, 188

Gross rent, 92
multiplier, 256
basis, 381

H

Heavy industrial buildings, 375
Hedging, 275
Hillier, Frederick S., 315–16
Hillier's model, 468
Historic structures, 210
Hotel census, 80
Housing census, 78
Housing and Urban Development (HUD), Department of, 68, 136, 210–11
Hurdle rate, 241, 249
Hybrid REITs, 413, 418

I

Ibbotson Associates bond index, 9
Implicit transfer costs, 46
Improvements, 164
Imputed interest, 188
Income
multipliers, 225–26
shopping center forecast, 389–90
Income-Expense Analysis: Conventional Apartments, 79–80, 102
Income-Expense Analysis: Office Buildings, 80
Income-Expense Analysis: Shopping Centers, 80
Income-Expense Analysis: Suburban Office Buildings, 381
Income and expense statement
for office building, 381, 382
for shopping center project, 3
Income tax
commercial rehabilitation estimate, 369–70
consequences, 184, 257, 377
considerations, 157–58
credits, 208–10
law, 114
real estate investment trusts, 415–16
tax basis and, 159–62
Incubator buildings, 375
Indebtedness, 190
Industrial buildings
case study, 375–80
investing in, 373–75
location decisions, 46–47
types of, 375
Industrial subdivision case study, 347–55
Inefficient market, 273
Inferential analysis, 70–71, 75
Information
difficulty in obtaining, 35
prompt receipt of, 37–38
Innovation, 37
Installment method gain, 186
Installment sales
contracts, 132–33, 137
reporting, 185–88
Institute of Real Estate Management, 79–80, 102, 381
Institutional investors, 6–7
Insurable risk, 266, 270–71
Insurance companies, 122–23, 146

Insurance fees, 409
Insurance risk, 270–71
Interest, 152
construction-period, 208
deductibility, 208, 218
expense, 123, 140–46
Interest-only loans, 130
Interest rate (i)
alternative provisions, 131–32
effective, 140–49, 152
foreign investors and, 7–8
Interim financing, 275
Intermediary, 200
Internal rate of return (IRR), 236–44, 467
Internal Revenue Code (IRC), 105, 157–58, 169, 182
on installment sales, 185, 188
on limited partnerships, 404
on loss limits, 214–15
on master limited partnerships, 409
on real estate investment trusts, 411
on tax-exempt bonds, 136
Internal Revenue Service (IRS), 157, 173, 212
Interpolation, 437–44
Intrastate offering exemption, 405
Investment
analysis
feasibility relationship to, 331
of industrial subdivision, 350–55
performance, 8–9
state of the art, 3–4
decision, 12–13, 250–52
income taxation of, 105
performance measurement, 289
real estate as, 4–5
returns, 273. *See also* Profitability
risk, 416–17
selection, 272–74
strategy, 208, 252–54
tax credit, 366
value, 10, 18, 21, 370
estimation of, 12–17, 258–59, 260
and forecast variable changes, 291
for one-story industrial building, 380
strategy and, 252–54
transaction range and, 254
Investor
benefits, 401–2
expectations, 272, 273
identification of, 6–8
Isolated State, The, 43

J

Jaffe, Austin, 237
Japanese investors, 8
Joint probabilities, 299–301
Joint tenancy, 168, 169
Junior (liens) mortgages, 133–34, 241

K

Kaplan, Steven, 418
Kerr, H.S., 244
Kinnard, William, 31

L

Labor Department, 68
Labor-intensive firms, 374–75

Land, 5
  availability, 98
  contracts, 132–33
  planning, 346
  use, 41–44, 346–47
Laventhol and Horwath, CPAs, 80
Legacy, 203
Lehman Brothers Equity REIT Index, 419
Lender, 121–23, 334–35
Level annuity, 449–51, 458–59
Leverage, 123
  amount of, 117–21
  break-even occupancy levels, 269
  break-even rental rates, 271
  cost of borrowing and, 120–21
  gain amplification, 114–16
  measurement of, 116–17
  popularity of, 112–16
  range of outcomes, 267–68
  risk and, 118–19, 267
  spread and, 113–14
  taxation and, 114, 207–8
Liability insurance, 270
Lifetime gifts, 201
Like-kind exchanges, 188–201
  between related parties, 200–201
  nonsimultaneous, 200
  property's purpose, 190
  sale and purchase vs., 189–90
  Section 1031 and, 197–98
  substitute basis, 199–200
  taxation of, 190–97
Like-kind property, 190
Limited liability, 173, 401, 402
Limited liability companies, 176
Limited partnership, 170–76
  characteristics of, 400–403
  formation of, 407
  passive status of, 214–15
  regulation of, 403–6
  sponsorship rewards, 407–9
Linkages, 105, 106
  analysis of, 97
  location decisions and, 46–47
  market area, 83
  transfer costs and, 44–46
Liquidity, 168, 169, 416
Loan amortization
  alternatives, 130–31
  factors, 437
  payments, 436–38
Loan amortization schedule, 256
  commercial rehabilitation project, 368
  office building, 383
  one-story industrial building, 376
  shopping center, 389
Loan amount, anticipated, 150
Loan balance, 440–41
Loan origination fee, 140–41, 145, 147, 148
Loan proceeds, 141
Loan repayment schedule, 351
Loan-to-value ratio, 116, 118, 149, 150, 335
Location, 42–43
  analysis, 342
  characteristics/factors, 96–97, 374–75
  decisions, 44, 48, 346
Lodging industry census, 80

Loft buildings, 375
Longitudinal studies, 70
Losses
  capital rules, 182
  limits on, 214–15
  realized, 180–81
  recognition of, 184–85
  and Section 1031 exchanges, 197–98
Low-income housing, 210–13, 218

M

McMahan, John, 84–85
Maintenance, 166
Manufacturers census, 78
Marginal cost, 35, 36, 249, 259
Marginal income tax rate, 166–67
Marginal revenue, 35
Market
  adjustment of, 37, 49–50
  analysis
    feasibility report format, 342
    report outline, 66
    sequential components of, 63
  area
    establishment of, 83–84
    estimation of, 85
    office boundaries, 85–86
    peer property identification, 86–87
  clearing price, 34–35
  conditions, research and, 60
  definition of, 31
  efficiency, 21, 29–35, 37, 38
  inefficiency, 34–35, 273
  location, 374
  real estate assets, 27–29
  rental space, 48–50
  risk, 320
  share, 95–96
  structure
    absolute monopoly, 33
    atomistic, 32–33
    reactions to, 34
    residential, 84
    retail trade, 84–85
Market research, 50–51, 75
  amount of, 59–62
  complexity, 60
  data collection/analysis, 62–64
  data sources, 67–69
  descriptive, 69–71
  development, 358
  four-quadrant forecasting matrix, 64–65
  geographic information systems, 71–74
  importance of, 57
  industrial subdivision, 348–50
  need for, 58–59
  market conditions and, 60
  for portfolio decisions, 58–59
  property management, 59
  report preparation, 65–66
  risk management tool, 274
Market value, 10, 114
  estimation of future, 103–4
  relative, 199–200
  shopping center, 391
Markowitz, Harry, 319
Master limited partnerships, 409
Material participation, 214

Maximum debt service, 150
Mean, 304, 305, 313, 314, 465
Mean/standard deviation model, 307–9
Messner, Stephen D., 244
Midwest Securities Commissioners
    Association, 407
Mineral industries census, 78–79
Modern portfolio theory, 319–26
Modified internal rate of return, 242–43
Modified Uniform Limited Partnership
    Act, 404
Monopolies, 38
  absolute, 33
  competition, 33
Mortgage
  amortization, 130–31. *See also* Loan
    amortization schedule
  conduits, 123
  constant, 451–52, 460–61
  giving property subject to, 201–2, 204
  indebtedness, 192, 255–56
  interest rates, 131–32, 149
  notes, 127–28
  REITs, 412, 413, 417, 418
  sources of, 121–23
  types of, 128–29
Mortgage-backed promissory notes, 5
Most probable selling price, 10, 21
Multiplicative law of probability,
    299–301
Mutual funds, 418
Mutually dependent opportunities, 252
Mutually exclusive opportunities, 251–52
Myers, Dowel, 65

N

National Association of Real Estate
    Investment Trusts (NAREIT), 6,
    417, 419
National Real Estate Index, 419
National Registry of Historic Places, 210
Near money, 33
Neighborhood, 31, 32, 38
  environmental factors, 98
  influences, 83–84, 105, 106
  shopping centers, 364, 387
Net capital gains/losses, 183
Net debt relief, 192–93
Net income multipliers, 226
Net lease, 133, 375–76
Net operating income (NOI), 103, 114,
    376, 383
  forecast, 100–103
  less than expected, 119
  rental property, 82
  shopping center development estimates,
    362–63
  variation in, 292
Net present value, 235–36, 370, 467
  of expected cash flow, 364–65
  project comparisons and, 251–52, 260
Net Section 1231 gains or losses, 183
Nodal office development, 85–86
Nominal interest rates, 140–46, 148–49
Nonamortizing loans, 130–31
Nonsimultaneous exchanges, 200
Nonspecified properties programs, 407
Normal curve, 305–6

North American Securities Administration
 Association (NASAA), 408, 413

O

Objective probability distributions, 298
Obligee, 127
Obligor, 127
Observation, 69
Occupancy levels, 269–70
Offering memorandum, 406
Office building
 case study, 381–86
 investments, 380–81
Office market area boundaries, 85–86
Oligopoly, 33
100 percent location, 42–43, 46–47, 48,
 49
150 percent declining-balance
 depreciation, 164
Open-ended mortgages, 129, 137
Open-ended mutual funds, 418
Operating expense, 82
 averages for, 99–100
 changes in levels, 24
 estimation of, 87
 forecasting, 99–100
 ratio, 102, 103
 reconstruction of current, 90–91
Operating forecast
 borrowing into, 149–52
 first year, 101, 256
 six-year, 102
Operating ratio, 226
Operating statement, 81–82, 92
 apartment building example, 88–92
 revising, 91–92
Opportunity cost of capital, 249–50
Option agreement, 359
Option to purchase, 346
Ordinances, 333
Ordinary income, 181–82, 186
Outlet malls, 85
Outstanding indebtedness, 188
Overall capitalization rate, 227
Ownership interest, 28–29, 167–76

P

Pagliari, Jr., Joseph L., 324
Partially amortizing loans, 130
Partial release clause, 129
Partial serial correlation, 315
Partitioning, 286–89, 293
Partnership, 170–77
Passive activities, 214–16
 losses, 215–16
 rules, 175–76
Passive asset loss rules, 214
Passive investors, 4–5
Passive loss limitation, 173
Payback period, 230–31, 280–81
Payee, 127
Pebble Beach Golf Club, 8
Peer-group properties, 83–86, 99
Peer property identification, 86–87
Pension funds, 6, 7, 9, 122–23
Perceived risk, 273
Percentage lease, 386, 373, 390
Perfect competition, 32–33

Perpetual annuity, present value of, 435–36
Personalty, 169
Physical characteristics, 96, 105, 333
Physical durability, 87, 96
Physical improvements, 346
Planned unit developments (PUDs), 79
Planning, descriptive research, 69–70
Pooling-of-equity arrangement, 168
Population census, 78
Portfolio
 decisions, 58–59
 diversification, 274
Potential gross rent, 82
Predetermined funds, 333
Predetermined site, 332
Predetermined use, 332–33
Preliminary prospectus, 404
Prepaid interest, 207–8
Prepayment
 penalty, 147, 148
 terms, 128
Present value (PV), 13–14, 234–35,
  241–42, 253–54, 259–60
 annual cash flows, 285
 annuity, 432–35, 449–51, 458–59, 467
 annuity in advance, 443–44
 anticipated after-tax cash flows, 258
 calculations, 429–31
 cash flows, 308–9
 deferred annuity, 441–42
 dollar, 448–49, 454–55
 formulas, 467
 Hillier model, 316
 interpolation between factors, 439
 loan amortization and, 436–38
 net, 235–36
 net operating income variation, 292
 office building, 386
 partially correlated cash flow, 315–17
 partitioning, 286–89, 293
 perfectly correlated cash flow, 313–14
 perpetual annuity, 435–36
 shopping center after-tax cash flow, 394
 sources of, 290
 standard deviation of distribution, 468
 uncorrelated cash flow, 315
Price
 as consensus, 26
 -level adjustments, 145–46
 most probable selling, 10, 21
 supply-demand relationship to, 28–29
Price searchers, 50–51
 definition of, 33
 market efficiency and, 33–34
Price takers, 32–33, 50
Primary data, 68–69, 75
Primary trade area, 84–85
Private placement exemption, 405
Private source (activity) bonds, 136–37
Probability, 3, 296–301
 of acceptance error, 309–12
 conventional rules of, 299
 distributions, 301–2
 estimation of, 297–99
 joint, 299–301
Problem formulation, 62
Product differentiation, 35, 98–99
Profitability, 25–26
 developer's after-tax, 364

index, 227–31, 250–51, 310–12, 467
 opportunities for, 29–35
 potential, 21
Project costs, 359, 362
Promissory notes, 127–28, 137, 152
Promotional fee, 408
Property
 desirability of, 95–99
 disposal of, 176, 180–81. *See also* Sale
 highly appreciated, 202–3
 receipt of, 191–92
 rehabilitation of, 208–10
 tax basis, 194–97
Property management
 fees, 409
 market research and, 59
 risk management control and, 275
Property managers, 402, 416
Prospectus, 406
Public offerings, 403
Public utilities, 347
Purchase money mortgages, 129, 137
Purchase options, 275
Purchasing power risk, 275
Pure competition, 32–33

Q

Quality, 231
Quantity (Q), 231
Quantity demanded, 23, 24

R

Radial development pattern, 44, 45
Ratcliff, Richard U., 3
Ratio analysis, 224–32
Rational risk taking, 277–78
Real Estate Capital Markets Report, 123
Real estate investment trust (REIT), 6, 9,
  133–34, 411–19
 assets, 413–14
 information sources for, 419
 investment vehicles for, 414–18
 management of, 412–13
 mutual fund and, 418
 regulation of, 411–12
Real interest rates, 145–46
Realized gains, 181–84
Realty, 169
Recapture rules, 208–10
Recognized gain, 184–85, 187–88
Reconstruction, 88–92
Redevelopment bonds, 137
Red herring, 404
Refinancing, 143
Regional analysis, 342
Regional shopping centers, 387
Registered historic district, 210
Regulation
 of limited partnerships, 403–6
 of real estate investment trusts, 411–12
 subdivision and, 346–47
Regulatory authorities, 334
Rehabilitation, 208–10, 365–66, 371
 commercial case study, 367–71
 credit, 212
 incentives, 365–66
Reinvestment rate, 238–40
REIT Handbook, 419

REIT Score Property Directory, 419
Relative market value, 199–200
Relative scarcity, 26
Rent
  ability to command estimation, 82–87
  differentials, 47
  income from, 66, 215
  shopping center project survey, 363
  terms of, 69
Rental property
  annual net operating income, 82
  market for, 48–50
  portfolio of, 28
  supply-demand relationship for, 29
  value of, 41
Rental rates, 23–24, 27–29, 35
  break-even, 271
  comparable properties, 89–90
Repairs, 166
Resales, 182
Resident profile, 69
Residential market area, 84
Retail location
  decisions, 48–49
  trade census, 78
  trade market area, 84–85
Returns, 8–9, 18
Revenue forecasting, 105
Reverse annuity mortgages, 131
Risk, 123, 296
  adjustment, 9, 272–75, 278
    certainty-equivalent technique,
      283–86, 293
    discount rate, 281–83, 293
    payback-period approach, 280–81,
      292
    present value partitioning, 286–89,
      293
    sensitivity analysis, 289–92, 293
  analysis, 12–13, 317
  attitudes toward, 15, 17, 18, 275–78
  cash flow forecasting and, 295
  cost of borrowing, 120–21
  financial leverage and, 118–19
  investor objectives and, 15–17
  major elements of, 266–71
  management, 319–23
  measurement, 278, 301–7
  premium, 248, 249, 282
  probability as measure, 296–301
  REITs, 417–18
  return relationship, 16, 17, 273, 276,
    312
Risk-adjusted discount rate, 248–49, 259,
  281–83
Risk-free assets, 321–22
Risk-free discount rate, 249, 281–82
Risk-return profiles, 312
Risk-reward indifference curve, 273, 276
Rockefeller Center, 8
Rollover loan, 131
Roulac Group, 7
Renegotiable rate mortgages (RRMs), 131

S

Sale, 346
  cash proceeds from shopping center,
    391–92
    records, 350
    tax consequences of, 379, 385
Sale and leaseback arrangements, 133
Sales price
  commercial rehabilitation estimate, 369
  shopping center development, 363–64
  variation in, 290
Sanders, Anthony B., 324
Schwab, Bernhard, 3
Schwartz, Arthur, 418
S corporations, 169, 170
Secondary data, 67–68, 75
Section 1031, 189–90, 191–92
Section 1031 exchanges, 197–200
Section 1231 assets, 182–83
Securities, 190, 403–406
Securities and Exchange Commission
    (SEC)
  blind pool syndications and, 407
  limited partnerships and, 404–5
  real estate investment trusts, 412
  Rule 147, intrastate offering exemption,
    405
  Rule 506, private placements exemption,
    405
Security instruments, 127–30
Seller
  position summary, 254
  summary of position, 254
  transaction range, 254
Selling price, commercial rehabilitation
    estimate, 369
Senate Finance Committee, 216
Sensitivity analysis, 289–92
Serial correlation, 313–14, 315–16, 468
Service industries census, 78
Shared appreciation mortgage (SAM), 132
Shared equity participation (SEP)
    mortgage, 132
Shareholder
  liability, limited, 169
  rights, 412
Shaw, George Bernard, 62
Shearson Lehman Brothers, 419
Shopping center
  case study, 360–65, 388–94
  census, 79, 80
  investment, 386–88
Site
  analysis, 342
  characteristics, 348
  linked, 45
Small-scale operators, passive activity
    losses and, 215–16
SNL REIT Weekly, 419
SNL Securities, L.P., 419
Spatial modeling, 71, 72
Special assessments, 347
Specialization of function, 42
Specific asset syndication, 407
Specific funds, 333
Specific site, 332
Specific use, 332–33
Speculative building, 360
Spread, 113–14
Standard deviation, 303–6, 314
  discounted cash-flow model, 307–12
  expected present value, 317
  normal distributions, 465
    present value distribution, 468
Standard & Poor's 500 index, 9, 415, 417,
    418
Standby financing, 275, 359
State laws, limited partnership offerings
    and, 405–6
Statistics, 70–71
Statute of frauds, 128
Straight-term loans, 130
Subdivision
  definition of, 345, 355
  industrial case study, 347–55
  plan, 347
  process, 345–47
Subjective probability distributions, 298
Submarket, 31, 32, 66
Substantial assets, 173
Substitute basis, 199–200
Summation technique, 248, 259
Superregional shopping malls, 387–88
Supply, 22, 60, 95–96, 106
  analysis, 27–29, 35, 66, 98–99
  closed market system, 30
  curve, 27, 35
  element, 26–27
  factor, 98–99
  time and, 30
Support facilities, 98
Sweat equity, 365, 366
Symbols, 468
Syndication, 274, 400–410
Syndicators, 407
Systematic risk, 320

T

Take-back mortgage, 129
Tax assessor, 161
Taxation
  financial leverage and, 207–8
  of foreign investors, 216–17
  industrial subdivision and, 352, 353,
    355
  of like-kind exchanges, 190–97
  ownership form and, 167–76
  property sales and, 176
  realized gains/losses, 181–83
  of shopping center income, 391–92
Tax basis
  of acquired property, 194–97
  adjustments to, 162–65, 166
  allocating, 160–62, 199–200
  initial, 159–60
  losses and, 197–98
  and partnership, 172
  and property received as gift, 202
Tax conduit treatment, 173, 175, 176
Tax credit, 209, 218
  acquisition, 212–13
  aggregate, 211
  annual limit on, 213–14
  for low-income housing, 210–13
  minimum compliance period, 213
Tax-exempt bonds, 136–37
Tax-exempt real estate investment trusts,
    411–12
Tax-free exchanges. *See* Like-kind
    exchanges
Tax guides, 158

Tax-option corporations, 169, 170
Tax Reform Act of 1986, 210
Tax shelter, 114
Technology, changes in and demand, 24
Tenancy in common, 168
Tenant
  landlord risk shifting to, 275
  profile, 69
  variation in the number of, 23–24
Theorems, 70
Thibodeau, T.G., 9
TIGER, 72
Time (t)
  -adjusted return measures, 231–32
  element, in supply analysis, 26–27
  series data, 70, 72
  supply and, 30
Time value of (preference for) money, 3,
    282, 426
Timing, 231
Title, 177
  acquisition, 346
  vested in corporation, 169
  vested in individuals, 168–69
Topologically Integrated Geographically
    Encoded Reference (TIGER), 72
Total return, on assets, 119
Total yield, 113
Transaction costs, 35, 166, 183, 193
Transaction range, 10–11, 254
Transfer costs, 51
  alteration of, 97–98
  commercial location decision and, 48
  linkages and, 44–46
  market area, 83–84
Transportation
  census, 79

costs, 43
  importance of, 44–48
Treasury bills, 249
Treasury Department, 157, 216
Treasury notes, 149
Treasury regulations, 173–75
Trend, 100
Trends in the Hotel Industry, 80
Triple net leases, 275
Trust advisors, 413
Trust agreement, 129–30
Trust deed, 129–30
Trustees, 412

U

Uncertainty, 296
Unified and graduated gift and estate tax,
    201
Unified tax rate schedule, 202
Uniform Limited Partnership Act, 173,
    403–4, 410
U.S. Lodging Industry, 80
Unsystematic risk, 320
Upside risk, 268
Urban Land Institute, 79, 84–85
Utility function, 3

V

Vacancy rates, 89–92
Valachi, Donald, 243
Valuation analysis
  benefit stream, 13–15
  feasibility analysis, 331
  investment, 10
Value Line, 419
Value Line Investment Survey, 419

Value relationships
  buyer's perspective, 10, 11
  cash-flow distribution and, 14
  seller's perspective, 10, 11
  transaction range, 10, 12
Variable rate mortgages (VRMs), 131
Variance, 303
Vendees, 132
Vendors, 132
Vernor, James D., 62
Volatility, 417–18
Von Thunen, Johann Heinrich, 43, 44

W

Webb, James R., 324
Wholesale price index, 275
Wholesale trade census, 78
Wilshire 5000 Index, 324
Workers' compensation insurance, 271
Wraparound mortgages, 134–36, 137

Y

Yield, 58
  available in other assets, 24
  data, 8–9, 18
  rate, 135–36
  REITs and S&P 500, 415, 417, 418
Young, Michael, 244

Z

Zerbst, Robert H., 9
Zero serial correlation, 468
ZIP codes, 72
Zoning, 98, 346–47
Z-values, 305, 308–9